INTERNATIONAL LAW AND GOVERNANCE OF NATURAL RESOURCES IN CONFLICT AND POST-CONFLICT SITUATIONS

Natural resource wealth is conducive to a country's development. Nevertheless, the last few decades have shown a harsher reality, where natural resources have also triggered, financed or fuelled a number of internal armed conflicts. Examples include the armed conflicts in Cambodia, Sierra Leone, Liberia and the Democratic Republic of the Congo, which have been financed by the exploitation of a variety of valuable natural resources, including diamonds, gold, timber, oil and cocoa. The aim of this book is to assess the contribution of international law in ensuring that natural resources are used to promote development and to achieve sustainable peace instead of financing armed conflict. For this purpose, the author discusses the international legal framework for the governance of natural resources in States in general, in situations of armed conflict and as part of conflict resolution and post-conflict peacebuilding efforts.

DANIËLLA DAM-DE JONG is an assistant professor at the Department of Public International Law and the Grotius Centre for International Legal Studies at Leiden University, the Netherlands. Her research interests include international humanitarian law, international human rights law, international environmental law and the law on the use of force.

CAMBRIDGE STUDIES IN INTERNATIONAL AND COMPARATIVE LAW

Established in 1946, this series produces high quality scholarship in the fields of public and private international law and comparative law. Although these are distinct legal sub-disciplines, developments since 1946 confirm their interrelations.

Comparative law is increasingly used as a tool in the making of law at national, regional and international levels. Private international law is now often affected by international conventions, and the issues faced by classical conflicts rules are frequently dealt with by substantive harmonisation of law under international auspices. Mixed international arbitrations, especially those involving state economic activity, raise mixed questions of public and private international law, while in many fields (such as the protection of human rights and democratic standards, investment guarantees and international criminal law) international and national systems interact. National constitutional arrangements relating to 'foreign affairs', and to the implementation of international norms, are a focus of attention.

The series welcomes works of a theoretical or interdisciplinary character, and those focusing on the new approaches to international or comparative law or conflicts of law. Studies of particular institutions or problems are equally welcome, as are translations of the best work published in other languages.

A list of books in the series can be found at the end of this volume.

INTERNATIONAL LAW AND GOVERNANCE OF NATURAL RESOURCES IN CONFLICT AND POST-CONFLICT SITUATIONS

DANIËLLA DAM-DE JONG

CAMBRIDGE
UNIVERSITY PRESS

CAMBRIDGE
UNIVERSITY PRESS

University Printing House, Cambridge CB2 8BS, United Kingdom

Cambridge University Press is part of the University of Cambridge.

It furthers the University's mission by disseminating knowledge in the pursuit of education, learning and research at the highest international levels of excellence.

www.cambridge.org
Information on this title: www.cambridge.org/9781107093836

First published 2015

A catalogue record for this publication is available from the British Library

Library of Congress Cataloguing in Publication data
Dam-de Jong, Daniëlla, 1978– author.
International law and governance of natural resources in conflict and post-conflict situations / Daniëlla Dam-de Jong.
pages cm. – (Cambridge studies in international and comparative law ; 121)
Includes bibliographical references and index.
ISBN 978-1-107-09383-6 (hardback)
1. International law. 2. Natural resources – Law and legislation. 3. War (International law) I. Title.
KZ3410.D34 2015
346.04′4 – dc23 2015003498

ISBN 978-1-107-09383-6 Hardback

To my father, Pieter-Jan de Jong,
and my grandmother, Fokje Bakker-Geertsma,
in loving memory

'Natural resources are neither a curse nor a blessing; they are simply a source of opportunity. They can be used for tremendous good or they can be wasted.'

(Former Secretary-General Kofi Annan, addressing the UN Security Council, 19 June 2013)

CONTENTS

ACKNOWLEDGEMENTS

I could not have written this book without the support of a number of people, who are special to me in different ways. First of all, I would like to thank my former Ph.D. supervisors, Professor Nico Schrijver and Professor Larissa van den Herik, for their invaluable advice and guidance throughout the process of writing this book. I am most grateful to Professor Schrijver for teaching me most of what I know of international law today. From the moment he gave me the opportunity to assist him when I was still a student, he has been a source of inspiration to me. This book has greatly benefitted from his perceptive comments and profound knowledge of international law. I would like to thank Professor van den Herik for her thought-provoking ideas, which have helped me to critically reassess some of my own ideas on several issues of relevance to this book.

This book has also benefitted from the many discussions I had with my other colleagues at Leiden University over the past years. I would like to thank in particular Vid Prislan, Erik Koppe, Robert Heinsch and Professor Niels Blokker. Special thanks further go to my two successive roommates, Otto Spijkers and Emilie Kuijt, who both supported me in different phases of my research. I have immensely enjoyed the many conversations – some serious, some less serious – I have had with them. I would also like to thank Professor Eyal Benvenisti of Tel Aviv University for his useful comments on an earlier version of this manuscript. In addition, this book has benefitted from the skilful editing work done by Tony Langham, Plym Peters and William Stoddard. Furthermore, I would like to thank the Netherlands Organisation for Scientific Research (NWO) for their financial support.

Last but not least, I would like to thank my family for their continuous support throughout my research. I would like to thank my mother, Joukje de Jong-Bakker, and my brother, David de Jong, for showing an active interest in my work. Most of all, I would like to thank Peter-Paul Dam for his love and continuous support, as well as our two sons, Alexander and Noam, who are an infinite source of joy to me.

This book was completed on 1 October 2014.

TABLE OF TREATIES

1899 Convention (II) with Respect to the Laws and Customs of War on Land and its annex: Regulations Concerning the Laws and Customs of War on Land, The Hague, 29 July 1899 (entry into force: 4 September 1900), 246

1907 Hague Regulations, annexed to Convention (IV) Respecting the Laws and Customs of War on Land, The Hague, 18 October 1907 (entry into force: 26 January 1910), 209

1930 ILO Convention No. 29 Concerning Forced or Compulsory Labour, Geneva, 28 June 1930 (entry into force: 1 May 1932), *39 UNTS 55*, 398

1933 Convention on the Rights and Duties of States, Montevideo, 26 December 1933 (entry into force: 26 December 1934), *165 LNTS 19*, 50

1945 Charter of the United Nations, San Francisco, 26 June 1945 (entry into force: 24 October 1945), *1 UNTS xvi*, 37, 62, 69

1946 Convention for the Regulation of Whaling, Washington, DC, 2 December 1946 (entry into force: 10 November 1948), *161 UNTS 72*, 120

1948 Charter of the Organization of American States, Bogotá, 30 April 1948 (last amended on 10 June 1993), *119 UNTS 3*, 55

1949 Convention (IV) Relative to the Protection of Civilian Persons in Time of War, Geneva, 12 August 1949 (entry into force: 21 October 1950), *75 UNTS 973*, 202, 218, 221, 223, 228, 247

1954 Convention for the Protection of Cultural Property in the Event of Armed Conflict, The Hague, 14 May 1954 (entry into force: 7 August 1956), *249 UNTS 240*. 140, 141

1958 Convention on Fishing and the Conservation of the Living Resources of the High Seas, Geneva, 29 April 1958 (entry into force: 20 March 1966), *559 UNTS 285*. 114

1966 International Covenant on Economic, Social and Cultural Rights (ICESCR), New York, annex to UNGA Resolution 2200 (XXI) of 16 December 1966 (entry into force: 3 January 1976), *993 UNTS 3*. 47, 49, 71, 77–8, 83, 86, 89, 90, 92, 93, 100, 168–71, 427

1966 International Covenant on Civil and Political Rights (ICCPR), New York, annex 2 to UNGA Resolution 2200 (XXI) of 16 December 1966 (entry into force: 23 March 1976), *999 UNTS 171*. 49, 61, 71, 77, 88–9, 100, 104, 165, 168–72, 197–9, 232, 427

TABLE OF CASES

International Court of Justice

Corfu Channel (*United Kingdom* v. *Albania*), Merits, Judgment of 9 April 1949, *I.C.J. Reports 1949*, p. 22, 123

Barcelona Traction, Light and Power Company, Limited (*Belgium* v. *Spain*), Judgment of 5 February 1970, Second phase, *I.C.J. Reports 1970*, p. 3, 80

Legal Consequences for States of the Continued Presence of South African Namibia (South West Africa) notwithstanding Security Council Resolution 276 (1970), Advisory Opinion of 21 June 1971, *I.C.J. Reports 1971*, p. 16, 74, 270

Fisheries Jurisdiction (*United Kingdom* v. *Iceland*; *Federal Republic of Germany* v. *Iceland*), Order of 2 February 1973, *I.C.J. Reports 1973*, p. 302 and 313, 185

Fisheries Jurisdiction (*United Kingdom* v. *Iceland*; *Federal Republic of Germany* v. *Iceland*), Judgment of 25 July 1974, *I.C.J. Reports 1974*, p. 3 and 175, 116

Western Sahara, Advisory Opinion of 16 October 1975, *I.C.J. Reports 1975*, p. 12, 73, 74

Military and Paramilitary Activities in and against Nicaragua (*Nicaragua* v. *United States of America*), Judgment of 27 June 1986, *I.C.J. Reports 1986*, p. 14, 15, 80, 206, 210, 211

East Timor (*Portugal* v. *Australia*), Judgment of 30 June 1995, *I.C.J. Reports 1995*, p. 90, 74, 80, 81

Advisory Opinion on the Legality of the Threat or Use of Nuclear Weapons, 8 July 1996, *I.C.J. Reports 1996*, p. 226, 25, 41, 120, 124, 164–6, 169–70, 172–4, 178, 241, 246

Gabčíkovo–Nagymaros Project (*Hungary* v. *Slovakia*), Judgment of 25 September 1997, *I.C.J. Reports 1997*, p. 7, 116, 124, 125, 133, 183, 185, 187, 190

Oil Platforms (*Islamic Republic of Iran* v. *United States of America*), Judgment of 6 November 2003, *I.C.J. Reports 2003*, p. 161, 162, 216, 217

Legal Consequences of the Construction of a Wall in the Occupied Palestinian Territory, Advisory Opinion of 9 July 2004, *I.C.J. Reports 2004*, p. 136, 165–6, 169, 218

Armed Activities on the Territory of the Congo (*Democratic Republic of the Congo* v. *Uganda*), Judgment of 19 December 2005, *I.C.J. Reports 2005*, p. 168, 15, 127, 166, 193–4, 209, 220, 232–3

Armed Activities on the Territory of the Congo (New Application: 2002) (*Democratic Republic of the Congo* v. *Rwanda*), Judgment of 3 February 2006, *I.C.J. Reports 2006*, p. 6, 11, 209

International criminal tribunals

Permanent Court of Arbitration

WTO Dispute Settlement Mechanism

Human rights courts and monitoring bodies

Inter-American Court of Human Rights, Case of *Bámaca-Velasquez* v. *Guatemala*, Judgment of 25 November 2000, 167

African Commission on Human and Peoples' Rights, Decision Regarding Communication 155/96, Social and Economic Rights Action Center, *Center for Economic and Social Rights* v. *Nigeria*, 30st session, Banjul, October 2001, 85

African Commission on Human and Peoples' Rights, *Centre for Minority Rights Development (Kenya) and Minority Rights Group International on behalf of Endorois Welfare Council* v. *Kenya*, 276/2003, 102

European Court of Human Rights, *Khashiyev and Akayeva* v. *Russia*, Applications nos. 57942/00 and 57945/00, Judgment of 24 February 2005, 167

European Court of Human Rights, *Isayeva* v. *Russia*, Application no. 57950/00, Judgment of 24 February 2005, 167

European Court of Human Rights, *Estamirov and Others* v. *Russia*, Application no. 60272/00, Judgment of 12 October 2006, 167

Inter-American Court of Human Rights, *Case of the Saramaka People* v. *Surinam*, Judgment of 28 November 2007, 86

Commission on Human and Peoples' Rights v. *Great Socialist People's Libyan Arab Jamahiria*, Application No. 004/2011, Order for provisional measures, 25 March 2011, 167

European Court for Human Rights, *Al-Skeini and Others* v. *the UK*, Application No. 55721/07, Judgment of 7 July 2011, 167

Inter-American Court of Human Rights, *The Kichwa People of Sarayaku* v. *Ecuador*, Judgment of 26 July 2012, 86

International Tribunal for the Law of the Sea

Southern Bluefin Tuna Cases (*New Zealand* v. *Japan*; *Australia* v. *Japan*), Requests for Provisional Measures, Order of 27 August 1999, 117, 135–6

Mox Plant Case (*Ireland* v. *United Kingdom*), Request for Provisional Measures, Order of 3 December 2001, 135–6, 147

Case Concerning Land Reclamation by Singapore in and around the Straits of Johor (*Malaysia* v. *Singapore*), Order of 8 October 2003, 128, 135–6, 147

Responsibilities and Obligations of States Sponsoring Persons and Entities with Respect to Activities in the Area, Advisory Opinion of 1 February 2011, 135

Other courts

Trail Smelter Arbitration (*United States* v. *Canada*), Judgment of 11 March 1941, *Reports of International Arbitral Awards* Vol. III, United Nations (2006), pp. 1905–1982, 41, 123

1

Introduction

An abundance of natural resources in a country is conducive to its development. It is precisely this assumption that constitutes the basis for traditional development thinking.[1] The basic premise of this study is that natural resources undoubtedly can and do play an important role in kick-starting the economy of a country. Nevertheless, the last few decades have shown a harsher reality, where natural resources have triggered, financed or fuelled a number of internal armed conflicts. Examples include armed conflicts in Cambodia, Angola, Sierra Leone, Liberia, Côte d'Ivoire and the Democratic Republic of the Congo (DR Congo), which have been financed by the exploitation of a variety of valuable natural resources, including diamonds, gold, timber, oil and cocoa.[2]

Some of these internal armed conflicts were internationalised with the involvement of foreign States looking for a share in the natural resource wealth of the countries where the conflict was taking place. For example, access to the natural resources of the DR Congo proved to be an important motivation for Uganda and Rwanda to continue their military presence in the DR Congo.[3] Similarly, the involvement of the Liberian president Charles Taylor in the internal armed conflict in neighbouring Sierra Leone

[1] See, e.g., the UNCTAD Integrated Programme for Commodities, *UNCTAD Resolution 93(IV)* (1976), as well as documents that are related to the NIEO, in particular the Declaration on the Establishment of a New International Economic Order, *UNGA Resolution 3201 (S-VI)* of 1 May 1974.

[2] Another example is Colombia, where coca and opium play a major role in sustaining the armed conflict between the government and the FARC. However, the current study deals only with those natural resources that can be traded on legitimate markets, because of their significance for promoting sustainable development.

[3] See the reports of the UN Panel of Experts on the Illegal Exploitation of Natural Resources and Other Forms of Wealth of the Democratic Republic of the Congo, in particular the Final Report of 16 October 2002, *UN Doc. S/2002/1146*, which describes in great detail the involvement of Uganda, Burundi and Rwanda in the illegal exploitation of Congolese natural resources.

was in part motivated by his desire to gain access to high-quality diamonds from that country.[4]

These resource-related armed conflicts have had devastating effects on the civilian populations of the afflicted countries. Serious human rights violations have been committed in resource-related armed conflicts, many of which have been extensively documented in reports from UN Panels of Experts and from nongovernmental organisations (NGOs).[5] Some of these are directly related to the exploitation of natural resources, while other violations have taken place as part of general conflict situations. Examples include the burning and plundering of villages, the use of forced labour by armed groups for the extraction of natural resources, sexual violence, and the maiming of civilians as part of campaigns of terror. All these violations are in some way linked to natural resources, either because they are committed to gain access to or to retain control over the natural resources or because the natural resources serve as the means of financing the armed conflicts in which the atrocities are committed.[6]

In addition, unsustainable patterns of resource exploitation by belligerents have had a severe impact on the natural environment in most of these armed conflicts. In many cases natural resources have been extracted by

[4] See Special Court for Sierra Leone, Trial Chamber, Judgment of 18 May 2012 in the Case against Charles Taylor, *Case No. SCSL-03-01-T*, in particular paras. 5843–6149 on diamonds.

[5] On Angola, see, e.g., Global Witness, *A Rough Trade: The Role of Companies and Governments in the Angolan Conflict* (1998). On Sierra Leone, see, e.g., Human Rights Watch, *Sierra Leone: Sowing Terror: Atrocities against Civilians in Sierra Leone* (1998). On the DR Congo, see, e.g., the Final Report of the Group of Experts on the Democratic Republic of the Congo, Prepared in Accordance with Paragraph 8 of Security Council Resolution 1857 (2008), *UN Doc. S/2009/603*; and the Report of the Mapping Exercise Documenting the Most Serious Violations of Human Rights and International Humanitarian Law Committed within the Territory of the Democratic Republic of the Congo Between March 1993 and June 2003 (hereafter Mapping Report), Office of the High Commissioner for Human Rights (2010).

[6] In this respect, see the Mapping Report, p. 350. This report, which was drawn up by a team of human rights officers documenting human rights abuses during the conflict in the DR Congo, identifies three different types of links between natural resources exploitation and human rights abuses. These relate to (1) violations of human rights and IHL committed within the context of the struggle by parties to an armed conflict to gain access to and control over the areas of the country rich in natural resources; (2) human rights abuses committed by parties to an armed conflict as part of a regime of terror and coercion established in resource-rich areas under their control; and (3) the role of natural resources in funding armed conflicts, which are themselves a source and cause of violations of human rights and IHL. Although the findings of the mapping team are based on the situation in the DR Congo alone, the links identified in the report exist for other resource-related conflicts as well.

armed groups with little regard for the protection of the environment. For example, extensive logging by all parties to the armed conflict in Cambodia significantly diminished the country's forest cover.[7] Similarly, highly organised and systematic exploitation activities within and around UNESCO World Heritage sites in the DR Congo, including ivory poaching, logging and mining, have posed a significant threat to the integrity of these biodiversity reserves.[8] Another example is the land degradation that occurred in Sierra Leone as a result of substantial diamond mining during the conflict. Exhausted mining sites were not restored, resulting in severe environmental degradation.[9] The environmental damage caused by the unsustainable extraction of resources during armed conflict seriously hinders the prospects for the economic reconstruction of conflict-afflicted States.

Some of the conflicts dealt with in this book have come to an end. The Cambodian Khmer Rouge movement was put to a halt in the late 1990s. The armed conflict in Sierra Leone ended in 2002 and members of the Revolutionary United Front (RUF), as well as the former Liberian president Charles Taylor, recently went on trial before the Special Court for Sierra Leone for crimes committed during this civil war. Furthermore, Liberia has implemented significant institutional reforms under the leadership of President Ellen Johnson-Sirleaf.

However, peace is fragile. The leading economist Paul Collier showed that even a decade after an armed conflict has ended, there is an almost 15 per cent chance that a country will relapse.[10] Armed conflicts that involve natural resources are actually twice as likely to reignite as those that do not involve natural resources.[11]

Some of the armed conflicts discussed in this book have not yet been resolved. The armed conflict in the DR Congo is a salient example. The growing demand for raw materials on the world market, in particular for rare metals and oil, underscores the need to find lasting solutions to the problems associated with resource-related armed conflict. Disregarding

[7] For more details on the links between logging and the armed conflict in Cambodia, see Le Billon and Springer, 'Between War and Peace', pp. 17–36.

[8] Interim Report of the Panel of Experts on the Illegal Exploitation of Natural Resources and Other Forms of Wealth of the Democratic Republic of the Congo, *UN Doc. S/2002/565*, paras. 50 and 52.

[9] See UNEP, Sierra Leone: Environment, Conflict and Peacebuilding Assessment, February 2010, p. 45.

[10] Collier, Hoeffler and Rohner, 'Beyond Greed and Grievance', p. 16.

[11] Beevers, 'Forest Resources and Peacebuilding', p. 368.

the role played by natural resources in these conflicts will only prolong them and increase the risk of relapse after the conflict has ended. Conversely, integrating the adequate management of natural resources and the environment into strategies for conflict resolution and post-conflict peacebuilding is imperative for creating the conditions for a sustainable peace.[12]

1.1 Relationships between natural resource wealth and armed conflict

In order to devise strategies for the prevention and resolution of resource-related armed conflicts, it is first of all necessary to have a proper understanding of the relationships between natural resource wealth and armed conflict. There is a large body of academic literature, in particular in the economic and political sciences, that has studied the so-called 'political economy of armed conflict' or the economic dimensions of civil war.[13] The sudden increase in 'self-financing'[14] internal armed conflicts during the 1990s highlighted the relationships between natural resource wealth and armed conflict.

Early academic research into the self-financing nature of armed conflicts drew attention to the role of natural resources in providing the *means* to finance an armed conflict as an alternative to other sources of funding. The armed conflicts in Cambodia and Angola, for example, were originally funded with external sponsorship. When this funding dried up as a result of the end of the Cold War, the parties to the conflict turned to

[12] Ibid., p. 368; UNEP, From Conflict to Peacebuilding: The Role of Natural Resources and the Environment (2009), p. 19. This was also recognised in a Presidential Statement of the UN Security Council, which stressed that 'in countries emerging from conflict lawful, transparent and sustainable management . . . and exploitation of natural resources is a critical factor in maintaining stability and in preventing a relapse into armed conflict'. See the Statement by the President of the Security Council made in connection with the Council's consideration of the item entitled Maintenance of International Peace and Security, *UN Doc. S/PRST/2007/22*, 25 June 2007.

[13] See, e.g., Ballentine and Nitzschke (eds.), *Profiting from Peace*; Ballentine and Sherman (eds.), *The Political Economy of Armed Conflict*; Bannon and Collier (eds.), *Natural Resources and Violent Conflict*; Collier, *The Bottom Billion*; Collier and Hoeffler, 'Resource Rents, Governance, and Conflict', pp. 625–33; Collier and Hoeffler, 'Greed and Grievance in Civil War', pp. 563–95; Collier and Hoeffler, 'On Economic Causes of Civil War', pp. 563–73; Collier, Hoeffler and Rohner, 'Beyond Greed and Grievance'; Le Billon, *Wars of Plunder*; Le Billon, *Fuelling War*; Renner, The Anatomy of Resource Wars; and Ross, 'What Do We Know about Natural Resources and Civil War?' pp. 337–56.

[14] Ballentine and Sherman (eds.), *The Political Economy of Armed Conflict*, pp. 1–3.

natural resources to fund their armed struggle. In Cambodia, the Khmer Rouge movement exploited timber and gemstones to finance its rebellion. In Angola, the rebel movement UNITA turned to diamonds, while the government used oil revenues to suppress the rebellion.

In addition, belligerents' access to natural resource wealth also proved to be an important factor in *prolonging* internal armed conflicts. Natural resources give parties to an armed conflict access to weapons and to political support. In addition, the profits obtained from resource exploitation can prove to be a disincentive for armed groups to sit down at the negotiating table.[15] Exact data are not available, but it is estimated that the RUF made at least 25 million dollars a year from the trade in diamonds. This is relatively little compared to the revenue generated by the Khmer Rouge from logging, estimated at 120 million dollars a year at least.[16]

Furthermore, more fundamental relationships between natural resource wealth and armed conflict can also be identified. In particular, natural resources have been linked to the *outbreak* of armed conflict.[17] These theories focus on the institutional effects of resource wealth, on the role of natural resources as the motivation for the outbreak of armed conflict and on the role of natural resources in providing opportunities to start an armed conflict.

According to the 'resource curse thesis' described by the economist Richard Auty, resource wealth can lead to economic stagnation and underperformance. Large rents for resources may make governments less accountable, because these rents replace tax revenues for which governments must account to the population. This in turn may lead to the weakening of governmental institutions, making a country vulnerable to the outbreak of an armed conflict.[18]

15 See, e.g., Bannon and Collier (eds.), *Natural Resources and Violent Conflict*, pp. 217–18. A 2013 Report of the Secretary General in relation to the DR Congo indicates that, for armed groups operating in the Eastern part of the DR Congo, 'the benefits derived from the illegal exploitation of [natural] resources not only finance their acquisition of illicit weapons, but have also become an end in themselves'. See UN Secretary General, Special Report on the Democratic Republic of the Congo and the Great Lakes Region, *UN Doc. S/2013/119 (2013)*, para. 48.

16 For these and other estimates, see Renner, The Anatomy of Resource Wars, p. 7.

17 On this subject, see Le Billon, *Wars of Plunder*, p. 17.

18 See Auty, *Sustaining Development in Mineral Economies*. In this sense, the concept is related to notions such as the 'Paradox of Plenty' and the 'Dutch disease'. Since then, several studies, both in economics and in political science, have confirmed the hypothesis of the resource curse. See, e.g., Ross, 'The Political Economy of the Resource Curse', pp. 297–322; and Sachs and Warner, 'The Curse of Natural Resources', pp. 827–38.

Grievances and greed theories focus on the role of natural resources in provoking the outbreak of armed conflicts. According to the grievances theory, perceived injustices relating to the use of natural resources may be a cause for the outbreak of armed conflict. These perceived injustices may relate to the effects of the exploitation of natural resources on the living environments of particular ethnic or social groups, or they may relate to the (unequal) distribution of the benefits obtained from the exploitation of natural resources.[19] According to the greed theory, the likelihood of armed conflict breaking out is increased if rebel groups try to obtain rent from natural resources. The prospect of gaining access to large deposits of natural resources which these groups can exploit for their personal gain may be an incentive for them to start an armed conflict.[20]

Unlike grievances and greed theories, which focus on the role of natural resources in provoking armed conflict, the feasibility thesis focuses on the opportunities for starting an armed conflict created by natural resource wealth. This theory assumes that a rebellion will occur if it is militarily and financially feasible. According to this theory, an armed conflict is therefore more likely to occur in a country where large quantities of easily accessible natural resources are available to rebels.[21]

A fourth theory about the relationship between natural resource wealth and armed conflict focuses on the opportunities created by the outbreak of an armed conflict for third parties to engage in the looting of natural resources. Recent incidents of elephant poaching in the Central African Republic where conflict broke out after a coup d'état on 24 March 2013 are an example of this. Poachers were reported to have killed a large number of elephants in the Dzanga-Ndoki national park, a UNESCO World Heritage Site.[22] Part of the poaching in the Central African region is directly linked to the financing of armed groups,[23] prompting the Security Council in 2014 to impose targeted sanctions on individuals and entities supporting armed groups and criminal networks involved in the illegal trade in wildlife in the Central African Republic.[24] However, the poaching in itself

[19] See, e.g., Klare, *Resource Wars*, p. 208; and Ross, 'How Do Natural Resources Influence Civil War?' p. 41.

[20] Collier and Hoeffler, 'Greed and Grievance in Civil War', pp. 563–95.

[21] Ross, 'What Do We Know about Natural Resources and Civil War?' pp. 337–56.

[22] See 'Elephant Poaching on Rise in Chaos-Hit Central African Republic', 26 April 2013, www.reuters.com.

[23] See the Statement by the President of the Security Council on the Central African Region, *UN Doc. S/PRST/2013/6*, 29 May 2013, para. 10.

[24] UNSC Resolution 2134 (2014), para. 37(d).

constitutes a broader problem related to weaknesses in law enforcement.[25] The outbreak of an armed conflict is merely a factor that exacerbates these types of situations, in the sense that the chaos and instability created by the outbreak of an armed conflict increases the opportunities for individuals or groups to engage in the looting of natural resources. As the relationship between natural resources and armed conflict is less direct in these situations, it is not of immediate interest to the current study.

In conclusion, natural resources can provide the *means* to finance an armed conflict; they can *prolong* existing armed conflicts; and they can play a role in the *outbreak* of an armed conflict. In addition, the outbreak of an armed conflict may create opportunities for third parties to loot natural resources for their personal gain. Of course, natural resources can also play many different roles in armed conflicts. In Sierra Leone, for example, the Truth and Reconciliation Commission established after the armed conflict concluded that diamonds had provided the RUF with the means to finance – and maybe even prolong – their rebellion.[26] At the same time, the Commission considered that the economic mismanagement of the natural resource wealth in that country – which involved not only diamonds, but also bauxite, coffee and cocoa – and the resulting failure of successive governments to use the proceeds from these exports to enhance the standard of living of the population, were important factors in the outbreak of the armed conflict in 1991.[27]

1.2 The actors involved in resource-related armed conflicts

Strategies for the prevention and resolution of resource-related armed conflicts require a proper understanding of the roles and the legal positions of the different actors involved in the exploitation of natural resources in situations of armed conflict. Resource-related armed conflicts involve a range of different actors. Most of the armed conflicts discussed in this book are internal armed conflicts involving a State and/or one or more armed groups engaged in the exploitation of the State's natural

[25] See Report of the Secretary-General on the Activities of the United Nations Regional Office for Central Africa and on the Lord's Resistance Army-Affected Areas, *UN Doc. S/2013/297*, 20 May 2013, paras. 7–9.

[26] See *'Witness to Truth', the Final Report of the Sierra Leonean Truth and Reconciliation Commission*, Vol. Three B, Chap. One.

[27] Ibid., Vol. Three A, Chap. Two.

resources.[28] These armed groups either exploit the natural resources themselves or levy taxes from companies by granting them concessions.

However, in some of the armed conflicts discussed in this book, foreign States are also involved in the exploitation of a State's natural resources. In some cases, it is carried out directly by these States, either by their national armies or by companies that are offered access to exploitation sites in territory under the control of these States. In other cases, the involvement of foreign States is limited to assisting the armed groups engaged in the exploitation. For example, this assistance can consist of offering smuggling routes to these armed groups or of trading natural resources with them.

From a legal perspective, the range of actors involved in resource-related armed conflicts entails many challenges, not least with regard to determining the applicable rules. There are relevant rules in several fields of international law, in particular in international economic, environmental, human rights and humanitarian law.[29] However, as discussed in more detail in Part II of this book, the applicable legal framework varies depending on the actors involved and, in addition, depends on the typology of the armed conflict.

The following subsections briefly touch upon some of the issues that are of particular relevance for understanding the legal positions of the different actors involved, as well as their roles in resource-related armed conflicts. To illustrate these issues, reference is made as much as possible to existing conflict situations.

1.2.1 Domestic governments

International law accords a right to States and peoples to exercise sovereignty over their natural resources. This right, including the right to exploit the State's natural resources, is exercised by the government, subject to a number of conditions derived principally from international human rights and environmental law. The role of the government is therefore crucial to the proper functioning of the legal framework. Moreover, several of the armed conflicts that are at the heart of this book show that a strong political will to address the links between natural resources and armed conflict at the national level is essential for achieving a sustainable

[28] On the typology of armed conflicts, see Chapter 6 of this study.

[29] Chapter 5 discusses the general presumption that the outbreak of hostilities does not *ipso facto* affect the operation of treaties.

peace. However, at the same time, it is possible to identify several challenges relating to the role of the government.

The first challenge that is relevant to the current study concerns the legitimacy of the government. International law accords the right to exploit domestic resources to the State and its people; it does not accord this right to the government. The latter can exercise this right only on behalf of the State and its people. The question therefore arises whether a government that does not or can no longer be considered to represent the State and its people is entitled to exercise sovereignty over the State's natural resources. For example, in the armed conflict that raged in Angola for decades between 1975 and 2002, both the ruling MPLA and the opposing UNITA claimed to be the legitimate government of Angola. Another example concerns the civil conflict in Libya in 2011, when the Gaddafi government lost its legitimacy during the course of the armed conflict. This issue is discussed in more detail in Part I of this book.

Furthermore, the way in which governments exercise authority over the State's natural resources can also present a challenge. The failure of governments to exercise authority over the State's natural resources in the proper manner underlies many of the armed conflicts examined in this book. The armed conflict in Sierra Leone referred to above is a relevant example. Economic mismanagement and the resulting failure of successive governments to use the proceeds from the exports of the country's natural resources to raise the standard of living of the population have been identified as root causes for the outbreak of armed conflict in 1991.[30]

Similar patterns can be recognised in the DR Congo, where political elites have used the natural resource wealth of the country for their personal enrichment, leaving the population with very little to survive on. The DRC Mapping Report, drafted by independent experts under the auspices of the Office of the High Commissioner for Human Rights, concluded, for example, that

> During Mobutu's rule, natural resource exploitation in Zaire was characterised by widespread corruption, fraud, pillaging, bad management and a lack of accountability. The regime's political/military elites put systems in place that enabled them to control and exploit the country's mineral resources, thereby amassing great personal wealth but contributing nothing to the country's sustainable development... The two Congolese wars of 1996 and 1998 represented a further major setback to development,

[30] See '*Witness to Truth*', Vol. Three A, Chap. Two.

> causing the destruction of a great deal of infrastructure and propagating the practice of resource pillaging inherited from Mobutu's kleptocratic regime, under the pretext of funding the war effort.[31]

In addition, economic mismanagement can be a factor in sustaining armed conflicts. Opaque systems of public administration have allowed the governments of Liberia and Côte d'Ivoire, for example, to procure weapons in contravention of UN Security Council sanctions. In Liberia, the Taylor government largely excluded revenues from the timber and rubber sectors from the public administration. The evidence suggests that these revenues were used both for President Taylor's personal expenditure and for the procurement of weapons in contravention of UN Security Council sanctions.[32] In Côte d'Ivoire, the procurement of weapons was financed with the proceeds from the cocoa and oil industries.[33] In both countries, the natural resources industries were to a large extent controlled by the government.

These examples clearly show the significance of properly functioning institutions for the prevention and resolution of armed conflicts. This issue is examined in more detail in Section 1.3 of this introductory chapter.

1.2.2 Foreign States

Foreign States have played a role in several of the armed conflicts examined in this book. In the DR Congo, for example, Uganda and Rwanda have been both directly and indirectly involved in the ongoing armed conflict. Between 1998 and 2003 both countries engaged in the exploitation of the DR Congo's natural resources, while controlling parts of the territory of the DR Congo.[34] The Panel of Experts, set up by the UN Security Council to investigate the illegal exploitation of natural resources and other forms of wealth of the DR Congo, concluded that the exploitation of natural

[31] Office of the High Commissioner for Human Rights, Mapping Report (2010), p. 351.

[32] Report of the Panel of Experts Pursuant to Security Council Resolution 1343 (2001), Paragraph 19, Concerning Liberia, *UN Doc. S/2001/1015*, paras. 309–50.

[33] See, e.g., Midterm Report of the Group of Experts on Côte d'Ivoire Submitted in Accordance with Paragraph 11 of Security Council Resolution 1842 (2008), *UN Doc. S/2009/188*, paras. 59–72; Final Report of the Group of Experts on Côte d'Ivoire, Prepared in Accordance with Paragraph 14 of Security Council Resolution 1980 (2011), *UN Doc. S/2012/196*, para. 113.

[34] See the Final Report of the Panel of Experts on the Illegal Exploitation of Natural Resources and Other Forms of Wealth of the Democratic Republic of the Congo, *UN Doc. S/2002/1146*, paras. 65–131.

resources constituted one of the principal reasons for the continued presence of these countries in the DR Congo.[35]

In 2002, the DR Congo initiated proceedings against both countries before the International Court of Justice, but the Court could only exercise jurisdiction in relation to the DR Congo's case against Uganda.[36] With respect to Uganda, the Court found evidence of the involvement of senior officers of the Ugandan army, as well as of individual soldiers, in the exploitation of the DR Congo's natural resources.[37] It also found that high-ranking officers of the Ugandan army facilitated the illegal trafficking of natural resources by commercial entities from territories occupied by the Ugandan army. The Court attributed responsibility for the conduct of members of the Ugandan army to the Ugandan State and found that the failure of the Ugandan authorities to take adequate measures to prevent such acts from being committed constituted a breach of Uganda's international obligations.[38]

Although both Uganda and Rwanda have officially left the territory of the DR Congo, there is evidence to suggest that they still play a major role behind the scenes. The 2012 final report of the Group of Experts on the DR Congo, which replaced the Panel of Experts on the Illegal Exploitation of Natural Resources and Other Forms of Wealth of the Democratic Republic of the Congo, points to the role of Uganda and Rwanda in providing direct military support to the rebel movement M23. There are even strong indications to suggest that these countries sent in troops in July 2012 to help M23 gain control over Congolese territory.[39]

Another example of a State providing support to armed groups in a foreign country was the support provided by Liberia under President Charles Taylor to rebel groups operating in Sierra Leone, in particular to the RUF, between 1997 and 2002. A report of the Panel of Experts on Sierra Leone, published in 2000, already pointed to the active involvement of President Taylor in fuelling the armed conflict in Sierra Leone. The

[35] Ibid.

[36] See International Court of Justice, Armed Activities on the Territory of the Congo (*Democratic Republic of the Congo* v. *Uganda*), Judgment of 19 December 2005, *I.C.J. Reports 2005*. For the judgment of the Court with respect to the determination of jurisdiction in relation to Rwanda, see International Court of Justice, Armed Activities on the Territory of the Congo (*Democratic Republic of the Congo* v. *Rwanda*), Jurisdiction and Admissibility, Judgment of 3 February 2006, *I.C.J. Reports 2006*, p. 6.

[37] Ibid., para. 242. [38] Ibid., para. 243.

[39] See the Final Report of the Group of Experts on the DR Congo, Prepared in Pursuance of Paragraph 4 of Security Council Resolution 2021 (2011), *UN Doc. S/2012/843*, 15 November 2012.

report indicated that Taylor and his inner circle were 'in control of a covert sanctions-busting apparatus that include[d] international criminal activity and the arming of the RUF in Sierra Leone'.[40] The report also noted that this sanctions-busting was 'fed by the smuggling of diamonds and the extraction of natural resources in both Liberia and areas under rebel control in Sierra Leone'.[41] A subsequent report published by the Panel of Experts on Liberia confirmed these conclusions.[42] The issue of Taylor's involvement in the exploitation of diamonds by the RUF in Sierra Leone was also examined in the trial against Charles Taylor before the Special Court for Sierra Leone. The Court held, *inter alia*, that it had been proved beyond reasonable doubt that diamonds were delivered to Taylor in exchange for weapons and ammunition.[43]

These examples show that the involvement of foreign States in the exploitation of natural resources in situations of armed conflict can take many forms. A State can be involved because it is trading with armed groups (Taylor-RUF), but it can also be directly involved in the exploitation of the natural resources (Uganda in the DR Congo). From a legal perspective, a further distinction must be made between a State that exploits natural resources in another State without exercising control over part of that State's territory and a State that exploits natural resources in territory where it is exercising *de facto* authority as an occupying power. Different rules apply to these two different situations. Therefore, it is very important to determine the precise role played by a State in an armed conflict. This issue is discussed in more detail in Part II of this book.

1.2.3 Armed groups

Armed groups have been involved in most of the armed conflicts examined in this book. Examples include the Khmer Rouge in Cambodia; the National Union for the Total Independence of Angola (UNITA); the RUF and the Armed Forces Revolutionary Council (AFRC) in Sierra Leone;

40 Report of the Panel of Experts Appointed Pursuant to Security Council Resolution 1306 (2000), Paragraph 19, in Relation to Sierra Leone, *UN Doc. S/2000/1195*, December 2000, para. 212.

41 Ibid.

42 Report of the Panel of Experts Pursuant to Security Council Resolution 1343 (2001), Paragraph 19, Concerning Liberia, *UN Doc. S/2001/1015*, 26 October 2001, paras. 112–124.

43 Special Court for Sierra Leone, *Prosecutor* v. *Charles Ghankay Taylor, Case No. SCSL-03-01-T*, Trial Chamber II, Judgment of 18 May 2012, paras. 5948 and 6057.

the Forces Nouvelles in Côte d'Ivoire; and the Patriotic Forces for the Liberation of Congo (FPLC) and the Mai Mai groups in the DR Congo. These armed groups have all financed their armed struggles by means of the trade in natural resources.

As regards the legal rules that apply to these armed groups, a distinction must first of all be made between armed groups, such as UNITA and the Forces Nouvelles, that were able to control large areas of State territory over a long period of time and other groups, such as the Mai Mai, that are loosely organised militia groups with no control over territory. While the activities of all armed groups are subject to the basic obligations formulated in Article 3 of the 1949 Geneva Conventions, the activities of highly organised armed groups such as UNITA and the Forces Nouvelles that exercise control over a part of State territory may fall under the scope of Additional Protocol II to the 1949 Geneva Conventions. However, two additional criteria must be met before Additional Protocol II actually applies to an internal armed conflict. The first relates to its material scope of application. Additional Protocol II applies only to armed conflicts to which the government is a party. The second relates to the Protocol's formal applicability. While the 1949 Geneva Conventions have been ratified by all States, the Additional Protocol II enjoys wide yet not universal ratification. Angola, for example, is not a party to Additional Protocol II, while the DR Congo only ratified the protocol in 2002.[44]

The issue of ratification of Additional Protocol II by the State draws attention to another issue that has raised quite a lot of debate in the academic literature, i.e., the legal basis for imposing direct obligations on armed groups without allowing these groups to formally accede to the relevant treaties.[45] The Geneva Conventions are concluded between the 'plenipotentiaries of the Governments represented at the Diplomatic Conference', also referred to as the 'High Contracting Parties', while Additional Protocol II is only open for signature by the Parties to the Geneva Conventions.[46] At the same time, common Article 3 of the Geneva Conventions and the provisions of Additional Protocol II address armed groups directly. Common Article 3 determines that 'each Party to the conflict shall be bound to apply' certain minimum humanitarian standards, while Article 1(1) of Additional Protocol II states that it 'develops and supplements Article 3 common to the Geneva Conventions'.

[44] See www.icrc.org for information regarding ratification of the protocol.

[45] See Zegveld, *Accountability of Armed Opposition Groups in International Law*, p. 14.

[46] Ibid.

It is not sufficient to assume that, by ratifying a legal instrument, a government binds not only itself, but also the population it represents, including armed groups.[47] As Liesbeth Zegveld argues, this sort of 'hierarchical' view of the relationship between the government and non-State armed groups is undermined by the mere fact that non-State armed groups often 'seek to exercise public authority, and in doing so they question the authority of the established government, including the government's laws'.[48] Therefore, if the obligations of armed groups cannot be based on the consent of the State to be bound by relevant instruments, what would then constitute the legal basis for imposing obligations upon these groups? As Lindsay Moir argues, an alternative, more plausible argument would be to consider the obligations of non-State armed groups to be based directly on international rather than domestic law. In his view, non-State armed groups are bound by international humanitarian law (IHL) not as members of the population of a State but as 'individuals under international law', upon whom international law directly confers rights and obligations.[49]

In international practice the inability of armed groups to participate in the process of international law-making is not considered to constitute an impediment to imposing direct obligations upon these groups. In several of its cases, the International Court of Justice has confirmed that armed groups are bound by IHL. In its judgment of 27 June 1986 in the *Case Concerning Military and Paramilitary Activities in and against*

[47] See the following note, prepared by Claude Pilloud, staff lawyer of the ICRC, for the 1947 preparatory meeting for the 1949 Diplomatic Conference, reported in Kalshoven, 'The Undertaking to Respect and to Ensure Respect in All Circumstances', p. 12, note 28: 'La formule adoptée par les experts au sujet de la guerre civile ne semble pas donner satisfaction, car elle implique le principe de réciprocité que la Division juridique voudrait, dans toute la mesure du possible, éliminer. C'est pourquoi la Division juridique désirerait mettre sur pied une disposition qui prévoit que les Gouvernements, en signant la Convention, s'engagent non seulement en tant que Gouvernements, mais engagent aussi l'ensemble de la population dont ils sont les représentants. On pourrait alors en déduire que toutes les parties de la population d'un Etat qui entreprend une action en guerre civile est liée ipso facto par la Convention.' Also see Momtaz, 'Le droit international humanitaire applicable aux conflits armés non internationaux', *Recueil des cours*, p. 72. Also see the Report of the Secretary-General on Respect for Human Rights in Armed Conflicts, *UN Doc. A/7720* of 20 November 1969, para. 171.

[48] Zegveld, *Accountability of Armed Opposition Groups in International Law*, p. 16. Unfortunately, Zegveld does not provide an alternative theory. Rather, she emphasises that there is actually a problem and examines how this problem is dealt with in practice by international bodies.

[49] Moir, *The Law of Internal Armed Conflict*, p. 56.

Nicaragua, the International Court of Justice expressly noted that the acts of the *contras* towards the Nicaraguan Government were governed by the law applicable to noninternational armed conflicts.[50] Furthermore, in its judgment of 19 December 2005 in the *Case Concerning Armed Activities on the Territory of the Congo*, the Court noted that Uganda should have prevented 'violations of... international humanitarian law by other actors present in the occupied territory, including rebel groups *acting on their own account*'.[51] Despite the fact that the particular circumstances of the case induced the Court to attribute responsibility for the acts of the armed groups to Uganda, the case suggests that armed groups 'acting on their own account' can commit violations under IHL.

Where there are sufficient indications for the direct applicability of IHL to armed groups, another question that arises is whether armed groups are bound by other fields of international law as well, in particular by international human rights and environmental law. Unlike IHL, which directly confers obligations on non-State armed groups, international human rights and environmental law almost exclusively formulate obligations for States. Only a few international human rights and environmental conventions directly confer obligations on private parties. For non-State armed groups, reference can be made to the Optional Protocol to the Convention on the Rights of the Child on the involvement of children in armed conflict. This Protocol prohibits armed groups to 'recruit or use in hostilities persons under the age of 18 years'.[52] International environmental law, on the other hand, does not formulate any direct obligations for armed groups.

As both international human rights and environmental law primarily formulate obligations for States, most of the obligations for armed groups contained in these fields of international law must be implemented by

[50] International Court of Justice, Military and Paramilitary Activities in and against Nicaragua (*Nicaragua* v. *United States of America*), Judgment of 27 June 1986, *I.C.J. Reports 1986*, para. 219; Zegveld, *Accountability of Armed Opposition Groups in International Law*, p. 10.

[51] International Court of Justice, Armed Activities on the Territory of the Congo (*Democratic Republic of the Congo* v. *Uganda*), Judgment of 19 December 2005, *I.C.J. Reports 2005*, para. 179. Author's emphasis added.

[52] Optional Protocol to the Convention on the Rights of the Child on the Involvement of Children in Armed Conflict, Adopted on 25 May 2000, *U.N. Doc. A/54/49 (2000)*, Article 4. It should be noted that the Convention formulates a soft obligation: armed groups '*should* not, under any circumstances, recruit or use in hostilities persons under the age of 18 years'. Author's emphasis added. In addition, see Ryngaert, 'Human Rights Obligations of Armed Groups', p. 364.

means of domestic law. Both fields of international law formulate 'due diligence' obligations for States, which means that the State must ensure that private actors respect the relevant obligations. Problems arise in situations where States cannot exercise control over the activities of private actors, in particular the activities of armed groups. It can be difficult or even impossible for States to ensure compliance with international human rights and environmental standards in territories that are under the control of armed groups.

The question is therefore whether armed groups that are in control of parts of the State territory can be considered to be directly bound by international human rights and environmental law, especially when they exercise functions of governmental authority.[53] This is an extremely difficult question to answer *in abstracto*. There are relatively few examples of armed groups that behave like *de facto* authorities, even though they may be highly organised. Mention can be made, for example, of the Forces Nouvelles in Côte d'Ivoire. Although this opposition force was in full control of the north of Côte d'Ivoire and established a well-organised administration there,[54] it did not truly function as a local authority. The Group of Experts established by the UN Security Council to investigate violations of the arms and diamond embargoes concluded in its 2009 final report that, notwithstanding the formal reintroduction of local government in the north of Côte d'Ivoire, '[t]he political situation in northern Côte d'Ivoire currently bears more resemblance to a warlord economy than to a functioning government administration'.[55]

A closer look at international practice does not provide direct support for the thesis that armed groups are bound by international human rights or environmental law. However, it does provide some support for the thesis that there is, in the words of Cédric Ryngaert, a 'legitimate expectation of the international community' that armed groups will comply with international human rights law, not as a legal but as a moral

[53] With respect to human rights, see, e.g., Clapham, 'Human Rights Obligations of Non-State Actors in Conflict Situations', pp. 491–523; and Ryngaert, 'Human Rights Obligations of Armed Groups', pp. 355–81.

[54] See, e.g., the Report of the Group of Experts Submitted in Accordance with Paragraph 7(e) of Security Council Resolution 1727 (2006) of 14 June 2007, *UN Doc. S/2007/349*, para. 89, on the organisation of the economic and financial management in the rebel-controlled part of the country.

[55] Final Report of the Group of Experts Submitted in Accordance with Paragraph 11 of Security Council Resolution 1842 (2008) of 9 October 2009, *UN Doc. S/2009/521*, para. 36.

obligation.[56] In several of its resolutions, the UN Security Council has called upon parties to an internal armed conflict to respect international human rights law. Examples include Resolution 1231 of 11 March 1999 on the situation in Sierra Leone, in which the Council 'calls upon all parties to the conflict in Sierra Leone fully to respect human rights and international humanitarian law'; and Resolution 1291 of 24 February 2000 on the situation in the DR Congo, in which the Security Council calls on all parties to the conflict in the DR Congo 'to protect human rights and respect international humanitarian law and the Convention on the Prevention and Punishment of the Crime of Genocide of 1948'.[57]

All in all, current practice does not indicate that the proposition that armed groups are bound by human rights law is accepted, and there is no evidence at all for the proposition that armed groups are bound by international environmental law. Of course, armed groups can always choose to assent to human rights or environmental obligations, either through agreements with the government or through unilateral declarations. In fact, there are several examples of peace agreements between governments and armed groups, where armed groups agree to respect human rights as well as other international legal obligations.[58]

A final issue that deserves consideration is the question whether non-State armed groups are bound by customary international law. In this respect, Yoram Dinstein argues that '[t]he inability of individuals, either singly or as insurgent groups, to participate in custom-formation does not affect the fundamental principle that – once formed... – customary international law is binding on all human beings without exception'.[59] This is a rather bold statement which needs to be put into perspective.

The better view would be that non-State actors can be directly bound by customary international law in the same way that they are directly bound by treaties. In other words, non-State armed groups can be directly bound

[56] For the notion of 'legitimate expectations' of the international community as a more realistic alternative to legally binding obligations, see Ryngaert, 'Human Rights Obligations of Armed Groups', pp. 355–81.

[57] See UNSC Resolution 1231 (1999), para. 4; and S/RES/1291 (2000), para. 15.

[58] See, e.g., Article 3(3) of the Global and All Inclusive Agreement on the Transition in the Democratic Republic of the Congo concluded between the Congolese government and five armed opposition groups, in which the parties 'reaffirm their support for the Universal Declaration of Human Rights, the International Pact on Civil and Political Rights of 1966, the International Pact on Economic and Socio-Cultural Rights of 1966, the African Charter on Human Rights and the Rights of Peoples of 1981, and duly ratified international conventions'.

[59] Dinstein, 'The Interaction between Customary International Law and Treaties', p. 2344.

by customary norms that address these groups, either directly or as parties to an armed conflict. By way of example, reference can be made to the rules embodied in common Article 3 of the 1949 Geneva Conventions, which are considered to apply to all internal armed conflicts, both as a matter of treaty law and as customary international law. According to the International Court of Justice in the *Nicaragua case*, common Article 3 reflects 'elementary considerations of humanity'.[60] Other customary international norms that apply to internal armed conflicts, and which therefore can be assumed to bind armed groups directly, include the core principles of IHL, in particular the principles of humanity, distinction, necessity and proportionality.

In contrast, armed groups cannot be directly bound by customary norms that are exclusively addressed to States. This means, for example, that armed groups are not directly bound by the international environmental principles of sustainable use and prevention. As explained in Chapter 4 of this book, these principles are addressed to States and must be made effective for other actors through implementation in national law.

As a general rule, it can thus be argued that armed groups can only be directly bound by rules of customary international law that address these groups, while they are not directly bound by rules that exclusively address States. There appears to be one exception to this general rule. Reference can be made to the Martens clause, as inserted, *inter alia,* in the preamble to Additional Protocol II applicable to internal armed conflicts. This clause, which is discussed in more detail in Chaper 6 of this book, aims to ensure that human beings remain protected in situations of armed conflict, even in the absence of specific treaty rules. It is argued that this clause enables the application to armed groups of some customary international law rules that normally address States only, in particular customary international law rules relating to the protection of human rights. However, it is relevant to note that these customary norms do not then apply to armed groups as a matter of customary international law but rather as a matter of treaty law, namely, through the Martens clause.

1.2.4 Companies

Because of their involvement at every stage of the production and distribution process related to natural resources, companies play a key role

[60] International Court of Justice, Case Concerning Military and Paramilitary Activities in and against Nicaragua, Judgment of 27 June 1986, *I.C.J. Reports 1986*, p. 14, para. 218.

in resource-related armed conflicts. They are able to make an important contribution to solving these armed conflicts, but they can also exacerbate the situation with their practices. To illustrate the negative impact of companies on resource-related armed conflicts, reference can be made to the reports of various panels of experts established by the UN Security Council in relation to the conflicts in Angola, Sierra Leone, Liberia and the DR Congo. These reports show the involvement of companies in such diverse practices as the extraction of natural resources controlled by rebel groups, the smuggling of natural resources, and breaking weapons embargoes introduced by the UN Security Council.[61]

The Dutchman Guus Kouwenhoven is a well-known example of a businessman who was directly involved in illegal practices related to an armed conflict. He was the director of the Oriental Timber Company, the largest timber company operating in Liberia during the presidency of Charles Taylor. Kouwenhoven is suspected of being involved in the delivery of arms to Taylor in Liberia and the RUF in Sierra Leone, in contravention of the embargo imposed by the UN Security Council,[62] a crime for which he is currently standing trial before the Dutch Appeals Court.[63] In addition, the Panel of Experts on Liberia found evidence to suggest that Kouwenhoven's Oriental Timber Company, as well as other timber companies, helped Taylor to divert revenues from the timber industry for extra-budgetary activities.[64]

Furthermore, several panels of experts have reported on companies that had direct business dealings with armed groups. The report of the Panel of Experts on Angola, also known as the Fowler Commission after its chairman, indicated that before the imposition of the diamond sanctions

[61] See, e.g., the Final Report of the Monitoring Group on Angola, *UN Doc. S/2000/1225*, in particular paras. 154–61, and the Report of the Panel of Experts Appointed Pursuant to Security Council Resolution 1306 (2000), Paragraph 19, in Relation to Sierra Leone, *UN Doc. S/2000/1195*, December 2000.

[62] See the Report of the Panel of Experts Appointed Pursuant to Security Council Resolution 1306 (2000), Paragraph 19, in Relation to Sierra Leone, *UN Doc. S/2000/1195*, December 2000, para. 215.

[63] The trial has been on the roll for several years now. In 2006, Guus Kouwenhoven was convicted by the Dutch district court for the delivery of weapons to Taylor. In appeal, Kouwenhoven was acquitted. The Dutch Supreme Court has finally referred the case back to the Court of Appeal, which is bound to make a decision very soon. For a discussion of this case and the difficulties of exercising extra-territorial jurisdiction, see Herik, 'The Difficulties of Exercising Extraterritorial Criminal Jurisdiction', pp. 211–26.

[64] Report of the Panel of Experts Pursuant to Security Council Resolution 1343 (2001), Paragraph 19, Concerning Liberia, *UN Doc. S/2001/1015*, 26 October 2001, paras. 321–50.

on Angola, UNITA had auctioned off mining permits to foreign companies for the exploitation of mines within UNITA-controlled territory. In addition, the Panel found that UNITA had granted various diamond buyers a licence to operate within the areas under its control in exchange for a commission.[65]

In addition to these examples of direct company involvement in resource-related armed conflicts, there are also many examples of companies that are or have been indirectly involved in resource-related armed conflicts. This is partly due to the character of these conflicts. Natural resources that are used to finance armed conflict clearly have an economic value, which makes them valuable to companies further up the supply chain as well. Companies that produce consumer goods such as jewellery and electronic devices buy their raw materials – such as diamonds, gold and coltan – from other companies. Because of these purchases, these companies can also be indirectly involved in the financing of armed conflicts. Several reports of panels of experts have demonstrated the relative ease with which diamonds from countries like Angola, Sierra Leone, Liberia and Côte d'Ivoire were able to enter the legitimate diamond market. The Fowler report specifically pointed to the diamond market's lax controls and regulations to explain the relative ease with which illegal diamonds could find their way onto the market.[66]

While these examples show the negative impact that companies can have on resource-related armed conflicts, they also show the possibilities that exist for companies to make a positive contribution to ending them. In fact, several initiatives have been launched in recent years to end corporate complicity in the trade in resources from countries engaged in conflicts. Important initiatives include the Kimberley Process for the Certification of Rough Diamonds (KPCS) and the OECD Due Diligence Guidance for Responsible Supply Chains of Minerals from Conflict-Affected and High-Risk Areas. In addition, initiatives have been launched to address the role of companies in fostering corruption, in particular the Extractive Industries Transparency Initiative (EITI). These initiatives are discussed in more detail in Part III of this book.

It is also important to note that all of these initiatives have a voluntary character. Their effectiveness depends on the willingness of companies to

65 See the Report of the Panel of Experts on Violations of Security Council Sanctions against UNITA, *UN Doc. S/2000/203*, 10 March 2000, paras. 78 and 79.

66 Report of the Panel of Experts on Violations of Security Council Sanctions against UNITA, 10 March 2000, *UN Doc. S/2000/203*, paras. 87–93.

implement these instruments. In addition, as discussed in more detail in Part III of this book, these instruments all respond to the particular needs of the State where the natural resources are located. The question therefore arises of whether international law could also impose binding obligations on companies. In this respect, reference can be made to the 1969 International Convention on Civil Liability for Oil Pollution Damage, which directly confers responsibility for damage caused by oil pollution on private shipowners.[67] Furthermore, the 1982 UN Convention on the Law of the Sea (UNCLOS) prohibits natural or legal persons from appropriating parts of the deep seabed and its resources.[68] However, these are among the few examples of international legal instruments that directly impose binding obligations on companies. For the most part, the legal position of companies is regulated by national law, both of the home and of the host State. Companies must respect these national laws in their business practices.

1.3 Implications for strategies to address resource-related armed conflicts

The preceding sections showed that there are several links between natural resources and armed conflict. Natural resources can provide the means to finance an armed conflict, they can be associated with the outbreak of an armed conflict and they can prolong armed conflicts. Moreover, a wide range of actors are involved in these armed conflicts, whose activities are subject to different legal regimes. These factors require a multifaceted and comprehensive approach to the prevention, containment and resolution of resource-related armed conflicts.

Two main challenges can be identified in this respect. The first concerns stopping natural resources from financing or fuelling armed conflicts. This implies, first of all, the adoption of strategies that address the trade in natural resources as well as other forms of financing related to natural resources, such as the issuing of mining and timber concessions by armed groups and foreign States, as well as illegal taxes on natural resources. It also implies adopting strategies aimed at returning the control over the State's natural resources to the government.

[67] International Convention on Civil Liability for Oil Pollution Damage, adopted on 29 November 1969, *973 UNTS 3*.

[68] United Nations Convention on the Law of the Sea, adopted on 10 December 1982, *1833 UNTS 3*, Article 137.

The second challenge is to improve governance over natural resources within States in order to resolve existing armed conflicts and to prevent a relapse into armed conflict. Strategies focusing on the financial aspects of natural resources exploitation address only some of the problems associated with resource-related armed conflicts. They do not provide solutions for grievances related to environmental degradation or the misuse or improper distribution of profits obtained from natural resources. Nor do they provide solutions for institutional failures related to the resource curse. These problems require a more structural approach aimed at resolving resource-related armed conflicts and preventing the outbreak of new conflicts.

A key aspect of this sort of structural approach is to address failures in the governance of States with regard to natural resources. For the purposes of the present book, the term 'governance' seeks to denote the broader framework for the exercise of political authority with respect to the management of natural resources within States.[69] Although it is the government of a State that is entrusted with the task of managing the State's natural resources, it does so within a broader social and political framework. First of all, the government exercises authority over the State's natural resources on behalf of the State and its people. Therefore it has to take into account the interests of groups and individuals within society. In addition, international actors can also be involved in the governance of natural resources. For example, the Security Council can use its powers under Chapter VII of the UN Charter to assist a government to implement reforms in its natural resources policies. Therefore the term 'governance' should primarily be understood to refer to this broader participatory framework, or in other words, to the process of governing.

Furthermore, the term 'governance' is often associated with the quality of governance, and reference is made to 'good governance'. Although there is no common definition of the concept of good governance, it is possible to identify certain common elements. These include abiding by the rule of law, public participation, transparency, accountability, control of corruption and government effectiveness.[70] All these elements can be found in the definition of good governance as incorporated into Article

[69] On the concept of governance and related concepts, see Weiss, 'Governance, Good Governance and Global Governance', pp. 795–814; Knight, 'Democracy and Good Governance', pp. 620–33; Brown-Weiss and Sornarajah, 'Good Governance', pp. 516–28; and Ladeur, 'Governance, Theory of', pp. 541–53.

[70] See Brown-Weiss and Sornarajah, 'Good Governance', pp. 516–28.

9(3) of the 2000 Cotonou Convention concluded between the European Union and its member States on the one hand, and the members of the African, Caribbean and Pacific Group of States on the other. The Cotonou Convention defines good governance as

> the transparent and accountable management of human, natural, economic and financial resources for the purposes of equitable and sustainable development. It entails clear decision-making procedures at the level of public authorities, transparent and accountable institutions, the primacy of law in the management and distribution of resources and capacity building for elaborating and implementing measures aimed in particular at preventing and combating corruption.[71]

As a comprehensive definition, the Cotonou definition can serve as a benchmark for understanding the concept of good governance and its implications. Furthermore, it provides a very useful point of reference for the present study, which focuses on good governance in relation to natural resources management. For the purposes of the present study, good governance refers to

> the sustainable, transparent and accountable management of natural resources for the purposes of equitable and sustainable development. It entails clear and participatory decision-making procedures at the level of public authorities, transparent and accountable institutions and the primacy of law in the management and distribution of natural resources and their revenues, as well as capacity building for elaborating and implementing measures aimed in particular at preventing and combating corruption in the public administration of revenues from natural resources.

Taking the Cotonou definition as a point of reference, this definition focuses on some of the particular challenges associated with the governance of natural resources, while adding the elements of participation and sustainability to the definition. This book argues that for the management of natural resources good governance requires the active involvement of citizens in decision-making processes as well as due regard for environmental protection, which is reflected in the concept of sustainability. Furthermore, good governance is considered an essential prerequisite for achieving sustainable development. This was recently confirmed in the

[71] Partnership Agreement between the Members of the African, Caribbean and Pacific Group of States of the One Part, and the European Community and Its Member States, of the Other Part, 23 June 2000 (last revised: 2010).

Rio+20 Declaration, 'The Future We Want.'[72] Arguably, good governance constitutes the basis of natural resource governance to prevent and resolve armed conflicts. One of the objectives of this book is to assess whether and to what extent these requirements for good governance are reflected in international law, as well as in current approaches to addressing the links between natural resources and armed conflict.

1.4 Definition of terms used in this book

Some terms are used throughout this book without further clarification. One of these is 'natural resources'. Natural resources can be defined as 'those materials or substances of a place which can be used to sustain life or for economic exploitation'[73] or as 'any material from nature having potential economic value or providing for the sustenance of life'.[74] These definitions first of all emphasise the economic function of natural resources. In this sense, natural resources constitute primary commodities, i.e., 'raw or unprocessed material[s] that [are] extracted or harvested and also require very little processing before consumption'.[75] Indeed, for the purposes of this book, their economic value as raw materials is a defining characteristic of natural resources. It is for this reason that natural resources constitute an important source of funding for armed conflicts. Natural resources can often be relatively easily obtained by parties to an armed conflict and can be sold without further processing. The primary focus of this book is therefore on those natural resources that are relatively easy to obtain but are highly profitable, such as timber, minerals and rare metals.

[72] The relevant section of the Rio+20 Outcome Document reads, 'We acknowledge that democracy, good governance and the rule of law, at the national and international levels, as well as an enabling environment, are essential for sustainable development, including sustained and inclusive economic growth, social development, environmental protection and the eradication of poverty and hunger. We reaffirm that to achieve our sustainable development goals we need institutions at all levels that are effective, transparent, accountable and democratic.' See UNGA Resolution 66/288 of 11 September 2012, para. 13.

[73] Oxford English Dictionary Online, Oxford: Oxford University Press (2007).

[74] *Black's Law Dictionary*, 8th edn. (2004), p. 1056.

[75] Ibid. UNCTAD distinguishes the following groups of primary commodities: foods and tropical beverages (includes basic foods, coffee, cocoa and tea); vegetable oilseeds and oil; agricultural raw materials (includes timber and rubber); and minerals, ores and metals (includes copper, tin, tungsten, gold and crude petroleum). See UNCTAD, *Handbook of Statistics* (2012).

Nevertheless, natural resources are not only economic goods. They also form an integral part of the environment, and may perform an important ecological function as well. For example, trees not only provide timber, but also help to reduce climate change. In addition, forests are the habitat for numerous different species. This is also expressed in the definitions given above. As elements of the environment, natural resources can be necessary to 'sustain life'. In this respect, reference can be made to Principle 2 of the 1972 Stockholm Declaration, which refers to 'the natural resources of the earth, including the air, water, land, flora and fauna and especially representative samples of natural ecosystems'.[76]

The environment, which is another term used throughout this book, can then be defined in relation to natural resources. The environment comprises the air, water, land, flora and fauna, which interact as part of different ecosystems. It can be argued that the environment needs protection for two distinct but interrelated reasons. First, the environment needs protection for the inherent values it represents. Furthermore, human beings are dependent upon the environment. In its Advisory Opinion on the *Legality of the Threat or Use of Nuclear Weapons,* the International Court of Justice stated, 'the environment is not an abstraction but represents the living space, the quality of life and the very health of human beings, including generations unborn'.[77]

In relation to natural resources, reference is often made to the term 'exploitation'. The Panel of Experts on the Illegal Exploitation of Natural Resources and Other Forms of Wealth of the Democratic Republic of the Congo opted for a very broad definition of this term, to include the extraction, production, commercialisation and export of natural resources, and other services such as transport and financial transactions.[78] The present book largely follows this definition, although 'other services' are not covered by the term 'exploitation'. Where this book refers to the exploitation of natural resources, it generally refers to extraction, production and trade in natural resources, unless a further distinction is required.

In some cases this book refers to the 'illicit' or 'illegal' exploitation of natural resources to designate exploitation activities that are conducted

[76] Declaration of the United Nations Conference on the Human Environment, Stockholm, 16 June 1972, *11 I.L.M. 1416 (1972).*

[77] International Court of Justice, Advisory Opinion on the Legality of the Threat or Use of Nuclear Weapons, 8 July 1996, *I.C.J. Reports 1996*, p. 226.

[78] Report of the Panel of Experts on the Illegal Exploitation of Natural Resources and Other Forms of Wealth of the Democratic Republic of the Congo, *UN Doc. S/2001/357*, para. 16.

in violation of rules of international law. It is important to note that the term 'illegal', as used in legal documents, often fails to distinguish between resource exploitation that is contrary to international law and resource exploitation that is contrary to national law. Mining without an official permit under domestic law constitutes 'illegal exploitation' from the domestic perspective, even if it does not necessarily violate any rule of international law. This is reflected in the definition of the Protocol against the Illegal Exploitation of Natural Resources, adopted by the International Conference on the Great Lakes Region, which defines illegal exploitation as 'any exploration, development, acquisition, and disposition of natural resources that is contrary to law, custom, practice, or principle of permanent sovereignty over natural resources, as well as the provisions of this Protocol'.[79] References to 'illegal exploitation' in this book, however, primarily designate activities that are contrary to international law.

Another term that is sometimes used in this book is 'conflict resources'. There is as yet no legal definition of the term. The only official document that uses a related term is the KPCS, a voluntary agreement between State, civil society and the diamond sector to combat the trade in 'conflict diamonds'. The definition of 'conflict diamonds' adopted in the Scheme focuses exclusively on the role of rebel movements. According to the Scheme, conflict diamonds are 'rough diamonds used by rebel movements or their allies to finance conflict aimed at undermining legitimate governments'.[80]

The NGO Global Witness proposed adopting the following alternative definition of conflict resources: 'conflict resources are natural resources whose systematic exploitation and trade in a context of conflict contribute to, benefit from, or result in the commission of serious violations of human rights, violations of international humanitarian law or violations amounting to crimes under international law'.[81] The advantage of this definition is that it does not distinguish between natural resources exploited by rebel groups and those exploited by the government, which makes it more neutral. However, in another sense the definition is too narrow. In order to designate natural resources as conflict resources under this definition, it is necessary to establish that the natural resources have

[79] Protocol against the Illegal Exploitation of Natural Resources, adopted by the International Conference on the Great Lakes Region on 30 November 2006, Article 1.

[80] Kimberley Process Certification Scheme, Section I.

[81] Global Witness, *The Sinews of War: Eliminating the Trade in Conflict Resources*, p. 10.

contributed to violations of international law. This is problematic in the sense that not all natural resources that contribute to armed conflicts necessarily contribute to, benefit from, or result in violations of international law. This book therefore prefers to define conflict resources as natural resources whose systematic exploitation and trade finance or fuel armed conflicts.

1.5 Aim of the book

This book addresses the problem of resource-related armed conflicts from an international law perspective. More specifically, it aims to identify and assess the role of international law in ensuring that natural resources are used to promote development as well as sustainable peace in countries that are experiencing or that have experienced armed conflicts which are either caused, financed or fuelled by natural resources. Since the issue of resource-related armed conflicts is relatively new, it has not yet been addressed in a systematic way in formal law-making processes. To determine the applicable rules, it is therefore first of all necessary to rely on the existing rules of international law that pertain to the governance of natural resources within States in general, as well as on the rights and obligations of parties to an armed conflict. Furthermore, relevant standards can be derived from ad hoc processes, in particular from Security Council resolutions and from political agreements and codes of conduct adopted to address the issue of resource-related armed conflicts.

For this purpose, this book assesses first of all the general legal framework for the governance of natural resources within States. The principal question to be answered here is to what extent current international law provides rules to ensure that natural resources are exploited for the purpose of achieving sustainable development. In this respect, the first role of international law is that it establishes legal rights and obligations with regard to the exploitation of natural resources in States, including legal entitlements to the benefits derived from their exploitation. This book aims to identify these legal rights and obligations deriving from international economic, environmental and human rights law, as the legal framework relevant to the exploitation of natural resources in situations of armed conflict, as well as to the governance of natural resources as part of a strategy for conflict resolution and post-conflict peacebuilding.

Furthermore, this book aims to establish whether and to what extent the general legal framework for the governance of natural resources continues to apply in times of armed conflict. In addition, it aims to assess the extent to which rules from the law of armed conflict address the illicit exploitation, looting and plundering of natural resources by parties to an armed conflict, including the resulting environmental damage. Does international law provide adequate rules to prohibit these practices and to address the related environmental damage?

Finally, the book aims to identify standards for the governance of natural resources in States recovering from armed conflict. Most of these standards have been developed by ad hoc approaches, in particular UN Security Council resolutions and informal multi-stakeholder processes. This book assesses the contribution of both types of mechanisms to the legal framework for the governance of natural resources. The principal question addressed in this part is whether and to what extent norms and standards developed with ad hoc mechanisms contribute to improving governance over natural resources in States that are recovering from armed conflict.

1.6 Structure of the book

This book consists of three parts. Part I deals with the international legal framework for the governance of natural resources within States. The underlying hypothesis is that the rights and obligations identified in this part not only are relevant to the governance of natural resources by governments in situations of peace, but also are relevant in situations of armed conflict. It comprises three chapters. Chapter 2 discusses the principle of permanent sovereignty over natural resources as the basis for the governance of natural resources within States. The principle of permanent sovereignty formulates a right for States and peoples to freely exploit their natural resources for the purposes of development. The main conclusion of this chapter is that the principle of permanent sovereignty over natural resources entails a right for governments to exploit the State's natural resources on behalf of the State and its people on condition that it does so for national development and the well-being of the people of the State. Chapter 3 discusses these conditions in greater detail through the lens of collective or 'peoples'' rights. It identifies groups that are eligible to exercise peoples' rights and examines the implications of peoples' rights for the governance of natural resources within States. Finally, Chapter 4 discusses the protection of natural resources under international environmental law. It assesses the obligations imposed by international environmental law on States with regard to the protection of the environment, as well as the implications of these obligations for the governance of natural resources within States.

Part II of this book discusses the international legal framework regulating the protection and management of natural resources during armed conflict. Chapter 5 examines the question of whether and to what extent norms of international human rights and environmental law continue to apply in situations of armed conflict. For this purpose, the chapter looks at how armed conflict affects treaties, a topic which has been the object of a recent study by the International Law Commission (ILC), resulting in the adoption of a set of articles. The chapter discusses the work of the ILC in this respect. It also looks at the broader issue of how treaties operate during armed conflict. In addition to treaty law, this chapter also analyses the role of customary international law in situations of armed conflict. Even if a particular treaty is considered not to apply in times of armed conflict, specific obligations contained in its provisions may continue to be valid because of their customary international law status. Chapter 6 assesses the protection afforded to natural resources and the environment by IHL. This field of law is of particular relevance, as it is the only field of international law that contains obligations directly binding non-State armed groups. In addition, it is the principal source of rights and obligations for States with a military presence on the territory of a foreign State. This chapter argues that IHL contains only a few rules that were specifically developed to regulate the use of natural resources by parties to an armed conflict. Therefore, for the most part, recourse must be made to more general rules of this body of law relating to the protection of property and civilian objects. In order to address the specific challenges posed by resource-related armed conflicts, these more general rules of IHL are interpreted in light of the more specific rules of international environmental and human rights law relating to natural resources.

Part III of this book discusses the international legal and political framework regulating the governance of natural resources as part of conflict resolution and post-conflict peacebuilding strategies. Chapter 7 discusses the approach of the Security Council to the role of natural resources in financing armed conflict. In many cases the UN Security Council has resorted to imposing sanctions to address the links between natural resources and armed conflict. The objective of Chapter 7 is to assess whether and to what extent the Security Council resolutions have, in addition, developed standards for the governance of natural resources. For this purpose, Chapter 7 discusses a range of sanction regimes imposed by the Security Council in order to address resource-related armed conflicts. In addition, it assesses the extent to which peacekeeping operations, as well as the Peacebuilding Commission, implement and consolidate the measures imposed by the Council. Furthermore, Chapter 8 discusses informal political instruments that have been developed in response to resource-related armed conflicts. In addition to States, the business community and civil society have been involved in the design of these instruments and have been given a stake in their implementation. These instruments are part of a growing trend in international politics towards drafting 'guidelines', 'codes of conduct' or other nonbinding instruments rather than negotiating formal treaties. Nevertheless, these informal instruments do formulate standards for the management of natural resources in States emerging from armed conflict. This chapter examines these standards in more detail and assesses the extent to which informal instruments can be regarded to provide credible alternatives to formal treaties.

The concluding Chapter 9 summarises the general conclusions of this book. It assesses the adequacy of the overall international legal framework for the governance of natural resources within States and contains recommendations for how international law can be better equipped to prevent, contain and resolve resource-related armed conflicts.

PART I

The legal framework for the governance of natural resources in States

Introductory remarks to Part I

The objective of this part of the book is to examine the international legal framework for the governance of natural resources within States. In an independent State, it is obviously the government that first and foremost has the right to exercise political authority in relation to the exploitation of natural resources. This is explored in more detail in Chapter 2, which discusses permanent sovereignty over natural resources as the organising principle for the governance of natural resources within States and their economic jurisdictions. However, the right of the government to exploit the State's natural resources is qualified by obligations arising from international human rights and environmental law. Furthermore, this chapter discusses the legal position of the government itself. Chapter 3 discusses the obligations of governments under human rights law, while Chapter 4 examines obligations for governments resulting from international environmental law.

2

Defining the right of peoples and States to freely exploit their natural resources

Permanent sovereignty over natural resources

2.1 Introductory remarks

International law establishes a right of States and peoples to freely exploit their natural resources. This right originates in UN General Assembly Resolution 523 (IV) of 12 January 1952, which formulates a right of 'under-developed countries' to freely determine the use of their natural resources. Soon after the adoption of this resolution, the right developed along two different but interrelated tracks. First, it was asserted in terms of the principle of permanent sovereignty over natural resources.[1] In addition, as Chile proposed, the right of peoples to freely dispose of their natural resources was inserted into the two human rights covenants of 1966 as inherent in their right to self-determination.[2]

Today, the right of States and peoples to freely dispose of their natural resources is firmly established in the principle of permanent sovereignty over natural resources, which incorporates this right. The principle of permanent sovereignty over natural resources constitutes the very foundation on which the protection and management of natural resources in modern international law is based. Its relevance to the protection and management of natural resources has been confirmed in many international legal instruments, as well as in resolutions of the UN Security Council and

[1] It should be noted that the concept of permanent sovereignty over natural resources itself was for a long time asserted as a right before it received recognition as a legal principle. For example, compare the landmark 1962 Declaration on Permanent Sovereignty over Natural Resources, which designates permanent sovereignty over natural resources as a right accruing to both peoples and nations. See UNGA Resolution 1803 (XVII) on Permanent Sovereignty over Natural Resources, 14 December 1962.

[2] The original proposal for Article 1(2) introduced by Chile in 1952 provided in relevant part that 'the right of the peoples to self-determination shall also include permanent sovereignty over their natural wealth and resources'. For a discussion of the Chilean proposal, see Schrijver, *Sovereignty over Natural Resources*, pp. 49–56.

the UN General Assembly. In addition, the International Court of Justice has recognised its importance and considers it to constitute a principle of customary international law.[3]

This chapter aims first to determine the content of the right of States and peoples to freely dispose of their natural resources. For this purpose, it examines the evolution, the nature, and the legal status of the principle of permanent sovereignty over natural resources. Furthermore, the principle of permanent sovereignty identifies States and peoples as holders of the right to freely dispose of 'their' natural resources. This chapter examines the implications of this dual ownership in relation to the right to freely dispose of natural resources. It argues that the dual ownership construction has two implications. First, it emphasises that the right to exercise permanent sovereignty over natural resources is an essential component of State sovereignty, which other States must respect in their international relations. Second, the recognition of peoples in addition to States as being subjects of the principle of permanent sovereignty over natural resources must be interpreted as qualifying the right of the government of a State to dispose of the State's natural resources. The government exercises this right on behalf of the people of the State.

2.2 Evolution of the principle of permanent sovereignty over natural resources

This section outlines the evolution of the principle of permanent sovereignty over natural resources. It demonstrates that this is a dynamic principle, which has adapted to changing circumstances. For this reason, the principle not only has remained relevant over time, but in fact has become the governing principle for the management and protection of natural resources.

2.2.1 Early recognition: permanent sovereignty and the right to self-determination

The principle of permanent sovereignty over natural resources originates in resolutions of the UN General Assembly. It emerged in the 1950s following the decolonisation movement and was advanced by newly independent and developing countries as a means of protecting their ownership rights over the natural wealth and resources situated within

[3] International Court of Justice, Case Concerning Armed Activities in the Territory of the Congo (*Democratic Republic of the Congo* v. *Uganda*), Judgment of 19 December 2005, *I.C.J. Reports 2005*, para. 244.

their territories.[4] At the time, the main idea behind (what was then still called) the *right* to permanent sovereignty over natural resources was to provide these countries with the legal tools to regain control over their natural resources and to exploit them for their own benefit. Therefore, initially the principle was primarily associated with such controversial issues as the right of States to regulate foreign investment, and in particular with the right to nationalise natural resources. In this respect, Resolution 626 (VII) was the first resolution to make an express link between the right of peoples to freely exploit their natural resources, on one hand, and the exercise of sovereignty, on the other.[5]

A few years later, Resolution 837 (IX) determined that the right to permanent sovereignty over natural resources was an inherent part of the right of self-determination and requested the Commission on Human Rights to make recommendations concerning the right of peoples and nations to self-determination, 'including recommendations concerning their permanent sovereignty over their natural wealth and resources'.[6] This resolution marked the beginning of a process aimed at the clarification of the concept of permanent sovereignty over natural resources, leading up to the 1962 Declaration on Permanent Sovereignty over Natural Resources.[7]

2.2.2 The 1962 Declaration and the following years: regulating foreign investment

The Declaration on Permanent Sovereignty over Natural Resources, adopted by the General Assembly on 14 December 1962 by 87 votes to 2, with 12 abstentions, lays down eight basic principles concerning the

[4] For a detailed examination of the principle of permanent sovereignty over natural resources, see Schrijver, *Sovereignty over Natural Resources*; Rosenberg, *Le Principe de Souveraineté des Etats sur Leurs Ressources Naturelles*; Elian, *The Principle of Sovereignty over Natural Resources.*

[5] UNGA Resolution 626 (VII) of 21 December 1952 on the right to exploit freely natural wealth and resources determines that 'the right of people fully and freely to use and exploit their natural wealth and resources is inherent in their sovereignty'. This resolution is quite controversial, because of its political context. Although references to a right to nationalise natural resources ultimately were not inserted into the text, the resolution became known as the 'nationalisation resolution'. See Schrijver, *Sovereignty over Natural Resources*, pp. 41–9.

[6] UNGA Resolution 837 (IX) of 14 December 1954 on recommendations concerning international respect for the right of peoples and nations to self-determination.

[7] Instrumental in this development has been the Commission on Permanent Sovereignty over Natural Resources, set up by the UN General Assembly in Resolution 1314 (XIII) of 12 December 1958 'to conduct a full survey of [permanent sovereignty over natural wealth and resources as a] basic constituent of the right to self-determination'.

exercise of permanent sovereignty over natural resources.[8] The focus of the Declaration is on the regulation of foreign investment in the natural resources sector. In this respect, the Declaration aims to strike a balance between the interests of States exporting capital in protecting their investments and the interests of States importing capital in retaining control over their natural resources.[9]

Furthermore, the Declaration attempts to clarify the nature and scope of the concept of permanent sovereignty over natural resources. In this respect, paragraph 1 of the Declaration asserts a right to permanent sovereignty over 'natural wealth and resources', i.e., over every part of the environment.[10] It attributes this right to 'peoples and nations' and specifies that it must be exercised 'in the interest of their national development and of the well-being of the people of the State concerned'.

Arguably this obligation is also incumbent upon States when they nationalise, expropriate or requisition natural wealth and resources. According to paragraph 4 of the Declaration, the nationalisation, expropriation or requisitioning of natural wealth and resources is permitted only on 'grounds or reasons of public utility, security or the national interest which are recognized as overriding purely individual or private interests, both domestic and foreign'. Although the primary objective of this paragraph is the protection of foreign investment, it can also be read as emphasising the obligation to exercise permanent sovereignty in the interest of national development and the well-being of the population of the State.

The final provision that is of interest is paragraph 7 of the Declaration, which determines that 'violation of the rights of peoples and nations to sovereignty over their natural wealth and resources is contrary to the spirit and principles of the Charter of the United Nations'. Although the objective of this provision was originally to protect developing States

[8] See Schrijver, 'Natural Resources, Permanent Sovereignty over', in Wolfrum (ed.), *Max Planck Encyclopedia of Public International Law* (2012), para. 10. For the voting records, see *Yearbook of the United Nations* (1962), pp. 502–3. The negative votes were cast by France and South Africa.

[9] The principal question that was before the Committee discussing the draft resolution was the 'achievement of a formula which would safeguard and reconcile two essential principles, namely, respect for the national sovereignty of developing countries in need of foreign capital for the development of their natural resources, and provision of adequate guarantees for potential investors'. *Yearbook of the United Nations* (1962), p. 500.

[10] See Schrijver, *Sovereignty over Natural Resources*, p. 16, who notes that the 'concept of natural wealth may come close to what is commonly called "the environment" as a description of a physical matter, being the air, the sea, the land, flora and fauna and the rest of the natural heritage'.

against foreign investors exploiting their natural resources on unequal terms, it is arguably also relevant to situations in which foreign States plunder a State's natural resources, which happened (and is still happening to some extent) in the DR Congo. In these cases, States are therefore committing internationally wrongful acts, activating the law on State responsibility.[11]

Subsequent General Assembly resolutions focus mainly on the implementation of the principle of permanent sovereignty over natural resources and place it in a more prominent developmental context. In addition, these resolutions increasingly point to States rather than peoples as the subjects of the principle of permanent sovereignty. Resolution 2158 (XXI) of 6 December 1966, for example, 'reaffirms the inalienable right of all *countries*', while Resolution 2692 (XXV) of 11 December 1970 is entitled 'Permanent Sovereignty over Natural Resources of Developing *Countries*' and Resolution 3171 (XXVIII) of 17 December 1973 '[s]trongly reaffirms the inalienable rights of *States* to permanent sovereignty over all their natural resources'.[12]

At the same time, these resolutions emphasise that States must exercise the right to permanent sovereignty in order to promote development. For example, Resolution 2158 (XXI) determines that countries exercise permanent sovereignty 'in the interest of their national development'. Similarly, Resolution 2692 (XXV) reaffirms that permanent sovereignty 'must be exercised in the interest of their national development and of the well-being of the people of the State concerned'.

The political situation changed dramatically as a result of the economic crisis that broke out in the early 1970s. Discontented with the existing international economic order, developing countries advocated

[11] Nevertheless, in the Congo–Uganda case, the Court of Justice dismissed the relevance of the principle of permanent sovereignty over natural resources to the particular situation of looting and plundering of the DR Congo's natural resources by soldiers of the Ugandan army. See International Court of Justice, Case Concerning Armed Activities in the Territory of the Congo (*Democratic Republic of the Congo* v. *Uganda*), Judgment of 19 December 2005, *I.C.J. Reports 2005*. These aspects of the case are discussed in more detail in Chapter 5 of this study.

[12] UNGA Resolution 2158 (XXI) on Permanent Sovereignty over Natural Resources, adopted on 6 December 1966; UNGA Resolution 2692 (XXV) on Permanent Sovereignty over Natural Resources of Developing Countries and Expansion of Domestic Sources of Accumulation for Economic Development, adopted on 11 December 1970; UNGA Resolution 3171 (XXVIII) on Permanent Sovereignty over Natural Resources, adopted on 17 December 1973. Author's emphasis added. It should be noted that contrary to what its title suggests, Resolution 2692 (XXV) reaffirms the right to permanent sovereignty of both nations and peoples, especially in para. 2.

the establishment of a New International Economic Order (NIEO), which was aimed at addressing inequities in the economic system. Among the founding principles of this new economic order, permanent sovereignty over natural resources figured prominently, and this was to extend to 'all economic activities'.[13] Therefore, the NIEO Declaration significantly extended the scope of the principle of permanent sovereignty over natural resources. This is one of the principal reasons for which the NIEO Declaration has continued to be controversial.[14]

Another interesting feature of the NIEO Declaration is that the principle of permanent sovereignty is considered to accrue exclusively to States and that it is no longer explicitly subject to the obligation to use this right in the interest of national development. At the same time, the Declaration expresses 'the need for developing countries to concentrate all their resources for the cause of development'.[15] This is considered one of the founding principles of the NIEO.

The NIEO Declaration is accompanied by a programme of action which stipulates the measures that need to be taken for it to become fully effective. One of the measures referred to in the programme of action is the adoption of a Charter of Economic Rights and Duties of States as 'an effective instrument towards the establishment of a new system of international economic relations based on equity, sovereign equality, and interdependence of the interests of developed and developing countries'.[16]

The purpose of the Charter of Economic Rights and Duties of States, which was adopted later that year by a majority of the UN General Assembly,[17] was to promote 'the new international economic order, based on equity, sovereign equality, interdependence, common interest and co-operation among all States'.[18] With regard to natural resources, the Charter proclaims the right for 'every State' to 'freely exercise full permanent

[13] See the Declaration on the Establishment of a New International Economic Order, UNGA Resolution 3201 (S-VI) of 1 May 1974, para. 4(e).

[14] See Schrijver, *Sovereignty over Natural Resources: Balancing Rights and Duties*, pp. 96–100.

[15] Ibid., para. 4(r).

[16] Programme of Action for the Establishment of a New International Economic Order, UNGA Resolution 3202 (S-VI) of 1 May 1974, under VI.

[17] The Charter was adopted by 120 votes to 6, with 10 abstentions. It met with considerable opposition from developed States. See Schrijver, *Development without Destruction*, pp. 50–54.

[18] UNGA Resolution 3281 (XXIX) of 12 December 1974 on a Charter of Economic Rights and Duties of States.

sovereignty, including possession, use and disposal, over all its wealth, natural resources and economic activities'.[19]

From these resolutions it may be inferred that, in the context of the debate in the UN General Assembly during the 1960s and early 1970s, the principle of permanent sovereignty over natural resources gradually shifted from a right accruing to peoples and nations, as in the 1962 Declaration, to a right accruing to States, as in the 1974 NIEO Declaration and Charter of Economic Rights and Duties of States. In addition, during this same period, the scope covered by the principle was extended from 'natural wealth and resources' in the 1962 Declaration to 'natural resources and all economic activities' in the NIEO Declaration, and finally to 'all its wealth, natural resources and economic activities' in the Charter of Economic Rights and Duties of States. However, the last continued to be controversial.

2.2.3 From resource rights to duties: permanent sovereignty and sustainable development

Whereas the main focus of the debates in the UN General Assembly during the first two stages of the evolution of the principle was on establishing rights, the principle was increasingly incorporated into declarations and treaties as a duty-based concept in the following decades. As a result of the evolution of international environmental law during the 1970s and 1980s, the exercise of permanent sovereignty over natural resources by States gradually became qualified by obligations pertaining to the protection and management of natural wealth and resources.[20] These obligations relate both to the extraterritorial effects resulting from the use of natural resources by States and to the protection of parts of the environment within State boundaries that represent a value to the international community as a whole.

The first obligation relates to the responsibility of States 'to ensure that activities within their jurisdiction or control do not cause damage to the environment of other States or of areas beyond the limits of national jurisdiction'. According to the International Court of Justice, this obligation has become part of 'the corpus of international law relating to

[19] The text was adopted in spite of criticism by the developed States. See Schrijver, *Sovereignty over Natural Resources*, pp. 102–3.

[20] For a detailed analysis of the impact of international environmental law on the notion of permanent sovereignty over natural resources, see Schrijver, *Sovereignty over Natural Resources*, Chaps. 8 and 10.

the environment'.[21] The obligation not to cause extraterritorial damage to the environment, which was first expressed in the 1941 *Trail Smelter case*,[22] was formulated in Principle 21 of the 1972 Stockholm Declaration on the Human Environment and in Principle 2 of the 1992 Rio Declaration on Environment and Development as a corollary of the sovereign right of States 'to exploit their own resources pursuant to their own environmental and – in the Rio Declaration – developmental policies'.[23]

In addition, the sovereign right of States to exploit their natural resources and the corresponding responsibility not to cause transboundary environmental harm has been incorporated into several international environmental conventions, including the 1985 Vienna Convention for the Protection of the Ozone Layer, the 1992 Convention on Biological Diversity (CBD), the 1992 UN Framework Convention on Climate Change (UNFCCC) and the 1994 Convention to Combat Desertification in Those Countries Experiencing Serious Drought and/or Desertification, Particularly in Africa.[24]

Moreover, some of these conventions formulate more precise obligations aimed at the prevention of extraterritorial damage to the 'global commons'.[25] For example, the 1985 Vienna Convention for the Protection of the Ozone Layer obliges parties to 'take appropriate measures . . . to protect human health and the environment against

[21] According to the Court, 'the existence of a general obligation of States to ensure that activities within their jurisdiction and control respect the environment of other States or of areas beyond national control is now part of the corpus of international law relating to the environment'. Advisory Opinion on the Legality of the Threat or Use of Nuclear Weapons, *I.C.J. Reports 1996*, p. 66, para. 29.

[22] In the Trail Smelter Arbitration, the arbitral tribunal held that 'under the principles of international law [. . .] no State has the right to use or permit the use of its territory in such a manner as to cause injury by fumes in or to the territory of another or the properties or persons therein, when the case is of serious consequence and the injury is established by clear and convincing evidence', Trail Smelter Arbitration (*United States* v. *Canada*) 16 April 1938, *3 RIAA 1907 (1941)*.

[23] Declaration of the United Nations Conference on the Human Environment, Stockholm, 16 June 1972, *11 I.L.M. 1416 (1972)*; Declaration of the United Nations Conference on Environment and Development, Rio de Janeiro, 13 June 1992, *31 I.L.M. 874 (1992)*.

[24] See the second paragraph of the preamble of the Convention for the Protection of the Ozone Layer, Vienna, 22 March 1985, *1513 UNTS 323*; Article 3 of the Convention on Biological Diversity, Rio de Janeiro, 5 May 1992, *1760 U.N.T.S. 79*; paragraph 8 of the preamble of the UN Framework Convention on Climate Change, Rio de Janeiro, 9 May 1992, *1771 U.N.T.S. 107*; and paragraph 15 of the preamble of the United Nations Convention to Combat Desertification in Countries Experiencing Serious Drought and/or Desertification, Particularly in Africa, New York, 17 June 1994, *1954 U.N.T.S. 3*.

[25] The term 'global commons' refers to what the Stockholm and Rio Declarations call the areas beyond national jurisdiction. For an examination of the concept of 'global commons', see Schrijver and Prislan, 'From Mare Liberum to the Global Commons', pp. 168–206.

adverse effects resulting or likely to result from human activities which modify or are likely to modify the ozone layer'.[26] Similarly, the 1992 UNFCCC formulates as a general principle that the parties should 'protect the climate system for the benefit of present and future generations' and to that end must, inter alia, 'promote sustainable management' of sinks and reservoirs.[27]

While the prohibition against causing extraterritorial damage to the environment relates to the protection of the environment of third States and of areas beyond national jurisdiction, international environmental law also contains obligations for States with regard to the protection of their own natural wealth and resources. These obligations flow from the general obligation to conserve and use natural wealth and resources in a sustainable way for the benefit of current and future generations, which is discussed in more detail in Chapter 4 of this book.[28]

While affirming the sovereignty of States over their natural resources, the 1972 Stockholm Declaration already placed great emphasis on the responsibility of humanity to protect the environment and the earth's natural resources.[29] The obligation to conserve and use natural wealth and resources in a sustainable way is also inherent in the notion of sustainable development, which is commonly described as 'development that meets the needs of the present without compromising the ability of future generations to meet their own needs'.[30]

Several international environmental treaties take the sovereignty of States over their natural resources as their starting point, but simultaneously contain obligations which qualify the exercise of this

[26] Article 1 of the Vienna Convention for the Protection of the Ozone Layer, Vienna, 22 March 1985, *1513 U.N.T.S. 323*, while paragraph 2 of the preamble recalls that States have 'the sovereign right to exploit their own resources pursuant to their own environmental policies'.

[27] Articles 3(1) and 4(1)(d) of the UNFCCC, while paragraph 8 of the preamble recalls that States have 'the sovereign right to exploit their own resources pursuant to their own environmental and developmental policies'.

[28] For an examination of the notions of sustainable use, intergenerational equity and other notions related to the concept of sustainable development, see Schrijver, 'The Evolution of Sustainable Development in International Law', Chap. 5.

[29] In this respect, Principle 1 of the Stockholm Declaration States that '[m]an . . . bears a solemn responsibility to protect and improve the environment for present and future generations'. In addition, Principle 2 determines that 'the natural resources of the earth . . . must be safeguarded for the benefit of present and future generations through careful planning or management'.

[30] Brundtland Commission, *Our Common Future*, Report of the World Commission on Environment and Development (1987).

sovereignty for the benefit of the international community as a whole. Examples include the 1972 UNESCO Convention for the Protection of the World Cultural and Natural Heritage, which obliges parties to identify, protect, conserve, present, and transmit to future generations sites that have been designated as 'natural heritage', i.e., natural features, geological and physiographical formations and natural sites 'for whose protection it is the duty of the international community as a whole to co-operate',[31] and the 1992 Convention on Biological Diversity, which obliges parties to cooperate with other States 'for the conservation and sustainable use of biological diversity', i.e., 'the variability among living organisms from all sources . . . and the ecosystems and ecological complexes of which they are a part', the conservation of which is designated by the convention as a 'common concern of humankind'.[32] In addition, the 1982 UN Convention on the Law of the Sea (UNCLOS) contains a mixed obligation, referring to parts of the sea both within and outside the jurisdiction of States. UNCLOS's Article 193, one of the convention's environmental provisions, asserts the sovereign right of States to exploit their own natural resources and links this right to the duty to protect and preserve the marine environment.[33]

It can therefore be stated that international environmental law has both expressed and qualified the sovereign right of States to exploit their own natural resources. International environmental law prescribes that States must take due account of the environment when they exercise the rights flowing from the principle of permanent sovereignty, both outside and inside their national jurisdiction.[34]

2.2.4 *Other duties: towards a people-oriented concept of permanent sovereignty*

During the 1990s and the first decade of this century, international legal and political instruments increasingly emphasised that sovereignty over

[31] Articles 4 and 6 of the Convention Concerning the Protection of the World Cultural and Natural Heritage, Paris, 23 November 1972, *1037 U.N.T.S. 151*. Article 6 also states that the parties to the Convention fully respect 'the sovereignty of the States on whose territory the . . . natural heritage . . . is situated'.

[32] Article 5, Article 2 and the third paragraph of the preamble of the Convention on Biological Diversity. Article 3 formulates the principle that States have 'the sovereign right to exploit their own resources pursuant to their own environmental policies'.

[33] United Nations Convention on the Law of the Sea, New York, 10 December 1982, *1833 UNTS 3*, Article 193.

[34] These obligations are discussed in more detail in Chapter 4 of this study.

natural resources should be exercised in the interests of the country and its people. In a way, this development can be regarded as a return to the foundations of the principle of permanent sovereignty. As mentioned previously, early resolutions related to permanent sovereignty over natural resources were based on the premise that States and people had the right to freely dispose of their natural resources on condition that the natural resources were exploited for national development and the well-being of the people. The very first principle of the 1962 Declaration on Permanent Sovereignty over Natural Resources proclaims that '[t]he right of peoples and nations to permanent sovereignty over their natural wealth and resources must be exercised in the interest of their national development and of the well-being of the people of the State concerned'.[35]

As noted by Nico Schrijver, this condition gradually disappeared from the permanent-sovereignty-related resolutions.[36] The condition reemerged in the context of resource-related armed conflicts. It was first referred to in legal and political instruments adopted to address resource-related armed conflicts. In a resolution entitled 'Strengthening Transparency in Industries', adopted in 2008, the UN General Assembly reaffirmed that 'every State has and shall freely exercise full permanent sovereignty over all its wealth, natural resources and economic activities' and in this respect recalled 'its resolution 1803 (XVII) of 14 December 1962, in which it declared that the right of peoples and nations to permanent sovereignty over their natural wealth and resources must be exercised in the interest of their national development and of the well-being of the people of the State concerned'.[37] In addition, Article VII of the Lomé Peace Agreement for Sierra Leone provides that 'the Government shall exercise full control over the exploitation of gold, diamonds and other resources, for the benefit of the people of Sierra Leone'.[38]

These legal and political instruments illustrate a new tendency to qualify the principle of permanent sovereignty over natural resources for the purpose of promoting development. Article 3 of the Protocol of the International Conference of the Great Lakes Region against the Illegal

[35] Declaration on Permanent Sovereignty over Natural Resources, *UNGA Resolution 1803 (XVII)* of 14 December 1962.

[36] See Schrijver, *Sovereignty over Natural Resources*, pp. 308–9.

[37] UNGA Resolution 62/274 on Strengthening Transparency in Industries, adopted on 26 September 2008, paras. 4 and 5.

[38] Peace Agreement between the Government of Sierra Leone and the Revolutionary United Front of Sierra Leone, 7 July 1999.

Exploitation of Natural Resources, a regional treaty adopted by the members of the International Conference on the Great Lakes Region to address the illegal exploitation of natural resources in the Great Lakes Region of Africa, provides first of all that 'Member States shall freely dispose of their natural resources' and adds that this right 'shall be exercised in the exclusive interest of the people'. It then specifies that 'in no case, the populations of a State shall be deprived of it'.[39] In addition, the Protocol determines that '[m]ember States shall develop and implement a participatory and transparent mechanism for the exploitation of natural resources, according to their respective economic and social systems'.[40]

It is interesting to note that Article 3 of the Protocol to a certain extent reproduces Article 21 of the African Charter on Human and Peoples' Rights, which provides that 'All peoples shall freely dispose of their wealth and natural resources. This right shall be exercised in the exclusive interest of the people. In no case shall a people be deprived of it'. However, there are some important textual differences between the Protocol and the African Charter. The Protocol vests the right to dispose freely of natural resources in States and not in peoples. In addition, it determines that 'populations' rather than 'peoples' may not be deprived of their right. By distinguishing so clearly between States on one hand and peoples and populations on the other, the Protocol emphasises the obligation of States to exploit their natural resources for national development and the well-being of the population.

A similar trend to qualify the principle of permanent sovereignty over natural resources can be recognised in resolutions of the Security Council. For example, in Resolution 1457 (2003) on the DR Congo the Security Council reaffirms the sovereignty of the DR Congo over its natural resources and emphasises that these should be exploited 'transparently, legally and on a fair commercial basis, to benefit the country and its people'.[41] In the same resolution, the Security Council encourages the Congolese government to reform the natural resources sector 'so that the riches of the Democratic Republic of the Congo can benefit the Congolese people'.[42] Another example is provided by Resolution 1521 (2003) on the situation in Liberia, in which the Security Council emphasises that

[39] Article 3(1) of the Protocol against the Illegal Exploitation of Natural Resources, adopted by the members of the International Conference on the Great Lakes Region of 30 November 2006.

[40] Ibid., Article 3(4).

[41] UNSC Resolution 1457 (2003); in particular, para. 4.

[42] Ibid., para. 7.

government revenues from the Liberian timber industry must be used 'for legitimate purposes for the benefit of the Liberian people, including development'.[43] It also encourages the Liberian government to 'establish transparent accounting and auditing mechanisms' for this purpose.[44]

These instruments reveal a trend towards the adoption of a people-oriented interpretation of the principle of permanent sovereignty over natural resources.[45] This people-oriented interpretation strengthens an interpretation of the principle of permanent sovereignty which concentrates on the obligations of governments vis-à-vis the people of the State. Thus, arguably, while the principle of permanent sovereignty has always given rise to horizontal rights and – at a later stage – obligations, a contemporary interpretation of the principle increasingly adds a vertical dimension to the right to exercise permanent sovereignty.[46]

2.3 The nature and legal status of the principle of permanent sovereignty over natural resources

The principle of permanent sovereignty over natural resources has acquired a strong status in international law. While it originated in resolutions of the UN General Assembly, the principle has received recognition in various binding legal instruments as well. First, several international environmental conventions take the sovereign right of States to exploit their natural resources as their starting point. Examples include the 1985 Vienna Convention for the Protection of the Ozone Layer, the 1992 UNFCCC, and the 1994 Convention to Combat Desertification in Those Countries Experiencing Serious Drought and/or Desertification, Particularly in Africa, which all refer to the principle in their preambles. In addition, the 1972 UNESCO Convention for the Protection of the World Cultural and Natural Heritage and the 1992 Convention on Biological Diversity contain references to the principle.

The principle of permanent sovereignty is also reflected in human rights law as a component of the right to self-determination. The 1966 Human Rights Covenants formulate a right for peoples to dispose freely

[43] UNSC Resolution 1521 (2003); in particular, para. 11. [44] Ibid., para. 13.

[45] Compare Duruigbo, 'Permanent Sovereignty and Peoples' Ownership of Natural Resources in International Law', pp. 33–100, for a thorough analysis of a people-centred construction of permanent sovereignty and its implications for the management of natural resources in a State.

[46] Also see Chapter 3 of this study.

of their natural resources,[47] while a similar provision has been inserted into the African Charter on Human and Peoples' Rights.[48] In addition, the principle has been included in the preamble and the provisions of the Protocol against the Illegal Exploitation of Natural Resources, referred to in the preceding section.[49]

Furthermore, the principle has found recognition in the practice of the UN Security Council in relation to the maintenance of international peace and security. In its Presidential Statement of 25 June 2007 on natural resources and conflict, the Security Council 'reaffirms that every state has the full and inherent sovereign right to control and exploit its own natural resources in accordance with the Charter and the principles of international law'.[50] The Security Council has also occasionally referred to the principle, e.g., in Resolution 330 (1973) on 'Strengthening of International Peace and Security in Latin America' and in Resolution 1457 (2003) on 'The Situation Concerning the Democratic Republic of the Congo', referred to in the preceding section.[51]

It can be concluded that the principle of permanent sovereignty over natural resources has found widespread recognition in legal and political documents. While not all of the treaties that refer to the principle of permanent sovereignty do so in their provisions, the principle of permanent sovereignty is consistently included as a basic principle for international regulations relating to natural resources found within national jurisdiction. Therefore, it can be argued that the principle of permanent

[47] See the identical Articles 1(2) of the International Covenant on Economic, Social and Cultural Rights (ICESCR), New York, Annex to UNGA Resolution 2200 (XXI) of 16 December 1966, *993 UNTS 3*; and of the International Covenant on Civil and Political Rights (ICCPR), New York, Annex 2 to UNGA Resolution 2200 (XXI) of 16 December 1966, *999 UNTS 171*.

[48] See Article 21 of the African Charter on Human and Peoples' Rights, Banjul, 27 June 1981, *21 I.L.M. 58 (1982)*.

[49] Protocol against the Illegal Exploitation of Natural Resources, adopted by the members of the International Conference on the Great Lakes Region of 30 November 2006, Article 3.

[50] Presidential Statement on 'Maintenance of International Peace and Security: Natural Resources and Conflict', *UN Doc. S/PRST/2007/22* of 25 June 2007, para. 2.

[51] In Resolution 330 on 'Strengthening of International Peace and Security in Latin America', adopted on 21 March 1973, the Security Council recalls several General Assembly resolutions and notes 'with deep concern the existence and use of coercive measures which affect the free exercise of permanent sovereignty over the natural resources of Latin American countries'. In Resolution 1457 on 'The Situation Concerning the Democratic Republic of the Congo', adopted on 24 January 2003, para. 2 of the preamble, the Security Council reaffirmed 'the sovereignty of the Democratic Republic of the Congo over its natural resources'.

sovereignty over natural resources is one of the organising principles of international law relating to natural resources.

It can also be argued that the principle of permanent sovereignty is part of customary international law. The status of the principle of permanent sovereignty over natural resources as a principle of customary international law was also expressly recognised by the International Court of Justice in the *DR Congo–Uganda case*.[52] However, the Court did not elaborate on its findings. Instead, it simply recalled that the principle of permanent sovereignty is expressed in the Declaration on Permanent Sovereignty over Natural Resources and is elaborated in greater detail in the NIEO Declaration and the Charter of Economic Rights and Duties of States.

The references of the Court to these three UN General Assembly resolutions raise some important questions. The first concerns the legal basis for the customary international law status of the principle of permanent sovereignty over natural resources. Did the Court imply that the principle of permanent sovereignty derives its status as a principle of customary international law from these UN General Assembly resolutions? This does not seem likely, given their legal status, as well as the controversies regarding the resolutions. Rather, it could be argued that the Court referred to these declarations because they comprehensively set out the principle of permanent sovereignty.

The second question concerns what is covered by the customary international law principle of permanent sovereignty. As discussed above, the NIEO Declaration, as well as the Charter of Economic Rights and Duties of States, significantly widened the scope of the principle of permanent sovereignty from 'natural wealth and resources' in the 1962 Declaration to 'all its wealth, natural resources and economic activities' in the Charter of Economic Rights and Duties. In line with international practice, it is argued here that as a legal principle, the principle of permanent sovereignty applies only to natural wealth and resources.

The final question concerns the rights and obligations related to the principle of permanent sovereignty. Does the customary international law status of the principle extend to all rights and obligations ensuing from the principle? In particular, does it include an obligation to exploit natural resources for national development and the well-being of the people, as formulated in the 1962 Declaration? In his Declaration on

[52] Armed Activities on the Territory of the Congo (*Democratic Republic of the Congo* v. *Uganda*), Judgment of 19 December 2005, *I.C.J. Reports 2005*, para. 244.

the judgment, Judge Koroma argues in favour of such an interpretation. Moreover, he argues that the obligation to exploit natural resources for national development and the well-being of the people, and the basic right to exploit natural resources, 'remain in effect at all times, including *during armed conflict and during occupation*.'[53]

2.4 Legal subjects of the principle of permanent sovereignty over natural resources

The principle of permanent sovereignty over natural resources accrues to States as well as peoples. For States, the principle of permanent sovereignty over natural resources must be regarded as an attribute of State sovereignty. This is how the principle appears in international environmental instruments. Principle 21 of the 1972 Stockholm Declaration, Principle 2 of the 1992 Rio Declaration and Article 3 of the 1992 Convention on Biological Diversity all proclaim that 'States have, in accordance with the Charter of the United Nations and the principles of international law, the sovereign right to exploit their own resources'. Similarly, Article 6 of the 1972 World Heritage Convention expresses its full respect for 'the sovereignty of the States on whose territory the cultural and natural heritage . . . is situated'.

Furthermore, the principle of permanent sovereignty has developed as part of the right to self-determination of peoples and has been inserted into the identical Articles 1(2) of the ICESCR and the ICCPR as a right for peoples to freely dispose over their natural resources. In this respect, it should be noted that peoples are referred to both as legal subjects and as beneficiaries of the principle of permanent sovereignty. This is particularly clear from the authoritative 1962 Declaration on the Principle of Permanent Sovereignty over Natural Resources, which declares that 'the right of *peoples* and nations to permanent sovereignty over their natural resources must be exercised in the interest of their national development and of the well-being of the *people* of the State concerned'.[54]

The dual character of peoples as subjects and beneficiaries of the principle of permanent sovereignty has two important implications. First, it

[53] Declaration of Judge Koroma to the Judgment of the International Court of Justice of 19 December 2005 in the Case Concerning Armed Activities on the Territory of the Congo (*Democratic Republic of the Congo* v. *Uganda*), *I.C.J. Reports 2005*, para. 11. Emphasis in original.

[54] See UNGA Resolution 1803 (XVII) on Permanent Sovereignty over Natural Resources, 14 December 1962, especially para. 1. Author's emphasis added.

implies that natural resources must be exploited for the benefit of the people of a State. Second, as legal subjects of the principle of permanent sovereignty, peoples can also assert rights over the State's natural resources. These issues are discussed in more detail in the following chapter, dealing with peoples' rights. That chapter will also deal with the preliminary question of defining the groups that qualify as 'peoples' under international law.

2.5 The position of governments under international law

International law designates States and peoples as subjects of the principle of permanent sovereignty, and there is an implicit assumption that States and peoples have institutions that exercise the relevant rights and obligations on their behalf. The existence of such institutions even constitutes one of the defining features of a State, as demonstrated by the definition of a State in the 1933 Montevideo Convention on the Rights and Duties of States. This definition, which is generally considered to be part of customary international law, determines that a State should possess the following qualifications: a permanent population; a defined territory; a government; and the capacity to enter into relations with other States.[55]

In most cases, States do have a government that represents the State and its people. In these cases, the government is also the appropriate body to exercise control over the State's natural resources. Nevertheless, there are also situations where the government of a State does not represent or no longer represents the people of the State. Examples include the illegal white minority regime that ruled Southern Rhodesia between 1964 and 1978 and the Gaddafi regime that lost its legitimacy as a result of its actions against the Libyan population during the armed conflict in 2011.

Furthermore, in most internal armed conflicts, the legitimacy of the government is contested by opposition forces. In some cases, there are even parallel government authorities that enjoy a certain measure of recognition by foreign States. One of the most prominent examples of this was the Angolan opposition group UNITA, which – until it lost the democratic elections in 1992 – enjoyed some support from Western States, notably from the United States and South Africa. During this period, UNITA was in control of part of the territory of Angola, where

[55] Article 1 of the Montevideo Convention on the Rights and Duties of States, 26 December 1933, *165 LNTS 19.*

it exploited diamonds and even issued concessions to companies to mine diamonds.

The question that arises is whether international law contains rules to determine whether particular entities in a State are entitled to exercise permanent sovereignty over natural resources. For the most part, international law remains silent on these matters.[56] Formally, international law deals with the recognition of States, and not of governments. It generally presumes that a government represents the State, even when the government has been installed as a result of an internal revolution.[57] Furthermore, international law presumes that the *de jure* government continues to represent the State as a whole, as long as an internal power struggle continues.[58]

The question that arises is whether these long-standing rules of customary international law have retained their relevance over time. An examination of modern State practice in relation to recent changes in government demonstrates the continuing relevance of these rules, but it also demonstrates the importance attached by the international community to the existence of a representative government in a State. This can be illustrated with reference to the response of the international community to the coups d'état in Haiti and Sierra Leone on the one hand, and to the revolutions in Libya and Syria on the other.

First, the response of the international community to the coups in Haiti in 1991 and Sierra Leone in 1997 underlines the importance it attaches to upholding democratic governance.[59] In both cases the international community condemned the coup d'état and proceeded to take further action, including military intervention, to restore the democratically elected government.

[56] For a thorough analysis of issues regarding the recognition of governments in international law, see, in particular Talmon, *Recognition of Governments in International Law*; and Roth, *Governmental Illegitimacy in International Law*. An older example is Lauterpacht, *Recognition in International Law*.

[57] See Lauterpacht, *Recognition in International Law* (paperback edn., 2012), pp. 91–3.

[58] Ibid., p. 93. For the distinction between *de jure* and *de facto* governments, see Talmon, *Recognition of Governments in International Law*, in particular pp. 226–31. Talmon defines a *de facto* government as 'an authority which has gained effective control of the State by overthrowing the constitutional government in a coup d'état or a revolution but [which] has not (yet) been recognized as legally qualified to represent the State on the international plane'. *De facto* governments should be distinguished from occupation governments, although the latter are also regarded as exercising *de facto* authority. However, in contrast to *de facto* governments, the legal position of occupants is regulated through international law. For more details, see Chapter 6 of this study.

[59] See also Manusama, *The United Nations Security Council in the Post-Cold War Era*, pp. 153–4.

In response to the coup d'état in Haiti in 1991, which brought down the democratically elected President Jean Bertrand Aristide, the UN General Assembly immediately adopted a resolution in which it strongly condemned 'the attempted illegal replacement of the constitutional President', considering 'as unacceptable any entity resulting from that illegal situation'. It also demanded 'the immediate restoration of the legitimate Government'.[60] Two years later, in its Resolution 841 (1993), the UN Security Council deplored the fact that 'despite the efforts of the international community, the legitimate government of Jean Bertrand Aristide has not been reinstated'. It went on to emphasise the 'unique and exceptional circumstances' of the situation, notably the requests by the Permanent Representative of Haiti and the Organization of American States to adopt sanctions, as well as the general humanitarian situation in Haiti, as the basis for further Security Council action.[61]

Reference can also be made to the coup d'état which took place in Sierra Leone in 1997. As a result of this coup, a military junta was established by the opposition group AFRC (and later joined by the RUF) which lasted over a year. The Security Council immediately condemned the coup. In particular, it demanded that the military junta 'take immediate steps to relinquish power in Sierra Leone and make way for the restoration of the democratically elected Government and a return to constitutional order'.[62]

While the cases of Haiti and Sierra Leone serve as examples of the attitude of the international community with regard to coups d'état against democratically elected governments, the recent revolutions in the Arab region, including the revolution in Libya in 2011 and the current revolution in Syria, are examples of the attitude of the international community to popular revolutions against authoritarian regimes.

The response of the international community to the situation in Libya is most telling in this respect.[63] It is relevant to note that during the armed conflict in Libya, neither the UN Security Council nor individual States made any explicit pronouncements about the illegality of the existing *de jure* government. For example, in the resolutions adopted by the UN Security Council in response to the events during the civil war in Libya in

[60] UNGA Resolution 46/7 of 11 October 1991, paras. 1 and 2.

[61] UNSC Resolution 841 (1993), preamble.

[62] See the Security Council's Presidential Statements of 27 May 1997 (S/PRST/1997/29), 11 July 1997 (S/PRST/1997/36) and 6 August 1997 (S/PRST/1997/42), as well as Resolution 1132 (1997), especially para. 1.

[63] For more details on the Libyan conflict, see Chapter 7.

2011, it refrained from making any pronouncements about the legal status of the Gaddafi regime. Even though it imposed economic and diplomatic sanctions against the regime, the Security Council continued to address the Gaddafi government in the role of the official authority representing the Libyan State in its resolutions. The UN Security Council did not pronounce on the status of the National Transitional Council (NTC), the main opposition group in Libya.

However, individual States started to express their recognition of the NTC during the course of the armed conflict, although these States did not recognise the NTC as the official government of Libya, but rather as the representative of the Libyan people.[64] In other words, the recognition by States of the NTC as the representative of the Libyan people did not affect the legal position of the Gaddafi regime as the official *de jure* government of Libya. The official position of States changed only after the defeat of the Gaddafi regime. In Resolution 2009 (2011), the Security Council implicitly recognised the NTC, formed by the opposition forces, as the new Libyan authorities.

Similar responses can be observed in relation to the ongoing conflict in Syria. In 2011, protests broke out in Syria, demanding democratic reforms. After these protests were violently repressed by the Syrian President Assad, an armed conflict broke out in the country. The opposition forces, organised in the National Coalition for Syrian Revolutionary and Opposition Forces (NCS), have gained control over parts of the country. However, the international community has so far been divided on the issue, and consequently the UN Security Council has not been able to adopt any concrete measures. Both the Council and the UN General Assembly have adopted several resolutions regarding Syria, calling on the Syrian authorities and the armed groups to put an end to violations of international humanitarian and human rights law, while both organs have requested the parties to the armed conflict to uphold their commitments under the peace process.[65] However, while the General Assembly stressed its support 'for the aspirations of the Syrian people for a peaceful,

[64] See Talmon, 'Recognition of the Libyan National Transitional Council'.

[65] See, e.g., UNSC Resolutions 2165 and 2139 (2014); UNGA Resolutions 66/176 of 19 December 2011, 66/253 of 16 February 2012, 67/183 of 20 December 2012 and 68/182 of 30 January 2014. There are important differences between the resolutions of the two organs in relation to the question of responsibility for the violations of international law, reflecting the political divergences within the Security Council. While the Council's resolutions consistently point to the Syrian government and the opposition alike, the General Assembly's resolutions take a firmer stance towards the responsibility of the government.

democratic and pluralistic society'[66] in several of its resolutions, it has not pronounced on the illegality of the Assad government.

Furthermore, while individual States have expressed their support for the opposition, recognising the NCS as the sole representative of the Syrian people, none of these States – except Libya – has recognised the NCS as the new government of Syria.[67] Nevertheless, as was the case in the Libyan conflict, third States have provided the NCS with active support. For example, in a 2013 decision, the European Union decided to ease its embargo on oil from Syria and to allow exports of oil from rebel-held territory in Syria in order to 'support and help the opposition'.[68] In addition, both the European Union and the United States expressed their intention to permit the supply of weapons to the Syrian opposition, if scheduled peace talks between the Syrian government and the opposition failed.[69]

These case studies lead to the conclusion that the international community makes a distinction between coups d'état against democratically elected governments and internal revolutions against authoritarian regimes. Whereas coups against democratically elected governments are unanimously condemned by the international community, regime changes that have been brought about through internal revolutions against authoritarian regimes are considered legitimate. This conclusion is supported by regional instruments that deal with the recognition of governments. It is relevant to note that the two regions that have suffered most from coup d'états in recent history, Africa and Latin America, have both adopted instruments that attach legal consequences to unconstitutional changes in government.

Article 7(g) of the 2002 Protocol Relating to the Establishment of the Peace and Security Council of the African Union provides that the African Peace and Security Council shall 'institute sanctions whenever an unconstitutional change of Government takes place in a Member State, as provided for in the Lomé Declaration'.[70] The Lomé Declaration

[66] See, e.g., UNGA Resolution 67/183 of 20 December 2012, para. 4.

[67] For the position of Libya, see 'Libya NTC Says [It] Recognises Syrian National Council', *Khaleey Times* of 11 October 2011.

[68] Council of the European Union, press release: Council Eases Sanctions against Syria to Support Opposition and Civilians, *EU Doc. 8611/13*, 22 April 2013.

[69] See, e.g., the Decision of the Council of the European Union of 27 May 2013 on Syria, available through www.consilium.europa.eu, in which the Council decided not to renew the existing weapons embargo. This decision has not been reviewed since.

[70] See Protocol Relating to the Establishment of the Peace and Security Council of the African Union, Adopted by the 1st Ordinary Session of the Assembly of the African Union, on 9 July 2002.

distinguishes between four situations of unconstitutional changes of government, including a military coup d'état against a democratically elected government, as happened in Sierra Leone in 1997, and the refusal by an incumbent government to relinquish power to the winning party after elections, as happened in Côte d'Ivoire in 2011.[71] Similarly, Article 9 of the Charter of the Organization of American States provides that the right to participate in the sessions of the principal organs of the organisation may be suspended for a member of the Organization whose democratically constituted government has been overthrown by force.[72]

An important conclusion that can be drawn from these regional instruments is that there is an indirect premise that the legitimacy of governments is based on a popular mandate. Although both instruments clearly show that neither of the regional systems recognises a government that has taken power by force, this applies only to the extent that this force is directed towards the overthrow of a democratically elected government. The instruments therefore leave open the possibility of recognising a government that has been established as a result of a coup d'état directed against an authoritarian regime.

Some cautious conclusions can be drawn from modern State practice in relation to regime change. The first conclusion is that regime change resulting from coups d'état against democratically elected governments is generally not accepted by the international community. In contrast, the international community does recognise governments that are established after a successful internal revolution against an authoritarian regime. This demonstrates the great importance attached by the international community to the representative character of governments. Another conclusion that can be drawn from modern State practice is that, even when States express their support to opposition forces, the status quo of a ruling *de jure* government is maintained until the conflict is over.

[71] The Lomé Declaration distinguishes the following situations as unconstitutional changes in government: i) military coup d'état against a democratically elected Government; ii) intervention by mercenaries to replace a democratically elected Government; iii) replacement of democratically elected Governments by armed dissident groups and rebel movements; iv) the refusal by an incumbent government to relinquish power to the winning party after free, fair and regular elections. See the Lomé Declaration of July 2000 on the framework for an OAU response to unconstitutional changes of government (AHG/Decl.5 (XXXVI).

[72] Charter of the Organization of American States, adopted on 30 April 1948 (last amended on 10 June 1993), *119 UNTS 3*.

There is still the question of the implications of modern State practice for the right of opposition groups to exploit natural resources and to issue mining concessions in situations where the legitimacy of the government is contested. The cases of Libya and Syria provide a partial answer to this question. Although official recognition of the opposition forces as the new government of the State has not occurred in either of these situations during the armed conflict, several States consider the opposition movements to be entitled to exploit the State's natural resources. This is clearly shown by the decision of the European Union referred to earlier, which lifted the EU embargo on oil from Syria for exports of oil from rebel-held territory.

How can this decision be explained? Arguably, the most logical explanation is to interpret the recognition granted to the opposition groups in Libya and Syria in light of the nineteenth-century theory of recognition of belligerency, discussed in Chapter 6 of this book. According to this theory, third States can recognise an armed group as an official belligerent, thus rendering the armed conflict international. This recognition has the effect of making armed groups that are in effective control of portions of the State territory subject to international occupation law, which grants occupants a qualified right to exploit the natural resources in occupied territory. Nevertheless, this does not absolve third States supporting these opposition movements from their responsibility under international law. The principal purpose of recognition of belligerency is to operationalise international neutrality law, which forbids third States to take sides in such conflicts.[73]

In conclusion, it can be stated that the right to exploit a State's natural resources pursuant to the principle of permanent sovereignty is normally vested in the government of a State. However, in cases where the legality of the government is contested, the right to exploit the State's natural resources can accrue to opposition groups as well, provided that these groups enjoy (implied) recognition by a sufficient number of third States as belligerents.[74] It can be inferred from the case studies and legal instruments referred to above that recognition is granted when the *de jure* government can no longer be considered to represent its people. It can

[73] See, e.g., Lauterpacht, *Recognition in International Law*, pp. 227–55.

[74] A distinction should, however, be made between a right of opposition movements to exploit natural resources in territories under their control and a right of third States to provide one-sided support to these movements by trading natural resources with them. The former is allowed, but the latter is not.

further be inferred from the case studies of Libya and Syria that this occurs when a government deliberately harms its people. This is what happened in Libya and Syria, where the *de jure* governments were accused of gross human rights violations against their own population.

2.6 Concluding remarks

The principle of permanent sovereignty is a typical product of the era of decolonisation. It was established to help newly independent and developing States regain control over their natural resources. It was intended to provide a shield for these countries to defend their interests against other countries and foreign companies, in particular against inequitable arrangements for the exploitation of their natural resources. Initially permanent sovereignty was therefore primarily a rights-based concept, applicable in inter-State relations.

Over the years, the principle of permanent sovereignty has proved to be a dynamic concept. It has become the organising principle for the governance of natural resources within States, entailing both rights and obligations for States. States have qualified their right to exercise permanent sovereignty over natural resources, amongst other things, to protect the environment. Moreover, the rights and obligations attached to the principle have increasingly been given a vertical as well as a horizontal dimension. Recent legal and political instruments emphasise the promotion of national development as the central objective of the exercise of permanent sovereignty over natural resources. In addition, these instruments assign a central position to peoples in this regard and stipulate that natural resources must be exploited for the benefit of the people.

The following chapters examine these issues in more detail. Chapter 3 discusses permanent sovereignty as an inherent part of the right to self-determination. In addition, it examines the closely related right to development. Subsequently, Chapter 4 discusses obligations arising from international environmental law and their impact on the principle of permanent sovereignty over natural resources.

3

A closer look at peoples as subjects and beneficiaries of the principle of permanent sovereignty over natural resources

3.1 Introductory remarks

The principle of permanent sovereignty accrues both to States and to peoples. For States, the right to freely dispose of their natural resources is an attribute of their sovereignty, while for peoples, the right to freely dispose of their natural resources is an inherent part of their right to self-determination. In both cases, it is the government of a State which has the primary responsibility for exercising the associated rights and for fulfilling the associated obligations on behalf of the State and its people. The responsibility of the government to exercise permanent sovereignty on behalf of the State and its people takes shape in an obligation to exercise the right to permanent sovereignty over natural resources for the purpose of promoting national development and ensuring the well-being of the people. This chapter aims to determine the implications of this obligation for the governance of natural resources within a sovereign State. What is meant by saying that natural resources must be exploited for national development and the well-being of the people? This chapter also examines the implications of considering peoples as subjects of the right to self-determination. What is meant by saying that peoples have the right to freely dispose over their natural resources?

These questions are examined from the perspective of the right to self-determination and the closely related right to development. Both rights have an external and an internal dimension. This chapter argues that the internal dimension of these rights must be interpreted first and foremost as entailing a corresponding obligation for governments to provide the possibility for peoples to participate in a State's decision-making processes. In addition, it is argued that the right to development entails a right for peoples as well as for individuals to enjoy the benefits deriving from development.

In order to fully understand the rights to self-determination and to development, as well as their implications for the governance of natural resources, it is essential to determine first which groups are eligible to exercise these rights. Therefore, Section 3.2 examines the notion of 'peoples'. Sections 3.3 and 3.4 discuss the evolution, content, nature and legal status of the right to self-determination and the right to development, as well as the implications of these rights for peoples living in sovereign States. Finally, Section 3.5 draws some final conclusions.

3.2 A more detailed definition of 'peoples'

International law does not contain a formal definition of the term 'peoples'. This section examines some of the definitions that have been elaborated to define 'peoples' in order to identify the groups eligible to exercise peoples' rights.

3.2.1 A definition of 'peoples'

International human rights law has granted peoples several rights, including the right to exist, the right to self-determination and the right to development. Over the years, several attempts have been made to identify the groups eligible to exercise the associated rights. Some of these definitions have focused on distinguishing peoples from minorities in order to determine which groups are entitled to exercise the right to external self-determination.[1] However, attempts have also been made to draft more general definitions which would apply to all 'third generation' rights.

Most definitions focus on a combination of common characteristics of group members on the one hand, and self-identification as a people on the other. For example, Yoram Dinstein argues that 'peoplehood must be seen as contingent on two separate elements, one objective and the other subjective'. In his opinion, 'the objective element is that there has to exist an ethnic group linked by common history', while the subjective basis for peoplehood consists of 'an ethos or state of mind'.[2]

[1] On the issue of minority rights, see Wheatley, *Democracy, Minorities and International Law*; Thio, *Managing Babel*; Dinstein and Tabory (eds.), *The Protection of Minorities and Human Rights*; Thornberry, *International Law and the Rights of Minorities*; Vukas, 'States, Peoples and Minorities', pp. 263–524.

[2] Dinstein, 'Collective Human Rights of Peoples and Minorities', p. 104. It should be noted that Dinstein primarily looked at the notion from the perspective of self-determination.

While Yoram Dinstein opts for a narrow interpretation of the term 'people' by confining its scope to ethnic groups, a broader definition emerged from an international meeting of experts convened by UNESCO in 1989 under the chairmanship of Justice Michael Kirby. The final report of the group of experts describes a 'people' as a group of individuals who enjoy certain common features, such as a common historical tradition, racial or ethnic identity, cultural homogeneity, linguistic unity, religious or ideological affinity, territorial connection and a common economic life. In addition, the group must have a size that exceeds a mere association of individuals within a State, it must either have the will to be identified as a people or the consciousness of being a people and the group must be able to express its common characteristics and will for identity in the form of institutions or by other means.[3]

The first drawback of this definition is that it does not properly recognise that the term 'people' refers to more than a 'group of individuals'. A people is an entity in itself, which – as a community – can have interests that do not coincide with the interests of each individual member of the group. There may even be a conflict between the interests of the group as a whole and the interests of some individuals in that group.

This is illustrated by a case brought before the Human Rights Committee relating to the traditional right of an indigenous people to engage in reindeer husbandry. This case has not been chosen to discuss the status of indigenous peoples as 'peoples' under international law,[4] but rather to illustrate the general point that communities have an identity that is distinct from that of their individual members.

In the case of *Kitok* v. *Sweden*, Swedish law restricted the right to engage in reindeer husbandry to members of Sami villages in order to protect the culture of the Sami community. There were important reasons for restricting the number of reindeer herders, above all to ensure the survival of the Sami community as a whole. Swedish legislation left it to the Sami community to determine who was a member of the community and who was not. The complainant was of Sami origin, but because his community did not accept him as a member of a particular Sami village, he could not engage in reindeer herding for a living. Therefore, there

[3] Final Report and Recommendations of the International Meeting of Experts on Further Study of the Concept of the Rights of Peoples, UNESCO, *Doc. SHS-89/CONF.602/7*, 22 February 1990, p. 8.

[4] It is relevant to note here that indigenous peoples do not constitute 'peoples' for the purpose of exercising a right to external self-determination. However, as this chapter will illustrate, indigenous peoples are eligible to assert particular peoples' rights.

was a clear conflict between the right of Mr. Kitok as a member of the Sami community to engage in an economic activity and the right of the Sami community as a whole to preserve its culture by refusing individual members the right to engage in this economic activity. In this case, the Human Rights Committee considered that the Swedish government had not violated Mr. Kitok's right to enjoy his culture. Specifically, the Committee considered that the method selected by the Swedish government to protect the interests of the Sami community as a whole was reasonable and consistent with Article 27 of the ICCPR.[5]

Despite the wording of Article 27 of the ICCPR, which proclaims a right for individuals belonging to particular minorities to enjoy their culture, it can therefore be concluded from the application of Article 27 in this case that a community is more than a group of individuals. It has a separate identity. This is not adequately recognised in the UNESCO definition of 'peoples'. Furthermore, as acknowledged by the UNESCO report itself, the practical relevance of the definition – or any definition for that matter – is limited. Not only are the elements that the definition identifies not sufficiently specific to distinguish peoples from other groups, but in addition the notion of peoples by its very nature is a dynamic concept, which may have different meanings in different contexts.[6] As Budislav Vukas noted, 'International practice does not even tend to provide and use one single definition and meaning of the expression "people". We witness an always more diversified use of this term simultaneously with the increased interest for the individual and different groups in international relations and in international law'.[7]

In fact, depending on the particular context in which it is used, the term "people" can refer to a variety of groups or entities, even within a single document. For example, as regards the UN Charter, there are slight variations in the use of the term throughout. The reference to 'We the peoples of the United Nations' in the opening words of the Charter –

[5] Human Rights Committee, *Ivan Kitok* v. *Sweden*, Communication No. 197/1985, *CCPR/C/33/D/197/1985* (1988).

[6] In this respect, the UNESCO report indicates that '[I]t is possible that, for different purposes of international law, different groups may be a "people". A key to understanding the meaning of "people" in the context of the rights of peoples may be the clarification of the function protected by particular rights. A further key may lie in distinguishing between claims to desirable objectives and rights which are capable of clear expression and acceptance as legal norms.' Final Report and Recommendations of the International Meeting of Experts on Further Study of the Concept of the Rights of Peoples, UNESCO, Doc. SHS-89/CONF.602/7, 22 February 1990, p. 8.

[7] Vukas, 'States, Peoples and Minorities', p. 318.

read together with the reference to 'our respective governments' in the closing paragraph of the preamble – may be said to refer to the peoples living in UN member States.[8] Articles 1(2) and 55 of the UN Charter – which indicate that friendly relations among nations should be based on respect for the principle of equal rights and self-determination of peoples – refer to peoples in a generic sense, including peoples living in UN member States as well as other peoples.[9] Finally, Article 73 of the UN Charter uses the term 'peoples' exclusively to designate the inhabitants of non-self-governing territories.

Another example is provided by the African Charter of Human and Peoples' Rights, which recognises, *inter alia,* the rights of peoples to existence (Article 20), to self-determination (Article 20), to free disposal of their wealth and natural resources (Article 21), to development (Article 22) and to an adequate environment (Article 24). A closer analysis of the use of the term 'peoples' in this legal instrument reveals that it refers to such groups as the populations of non-self-governing territories, to the State itself, to the entire population of a state and to indigenous peoples.[10] Therefore, it may be concluded that several groups are eligible to qualify as peoples for the purpose of exercising the rights associated with the term.

In conclusion, the term 'peoples' refers to a dynamic concept that can be applied to different groups, depending on the context and the particular right that is invoked. The term 'peoples' is used first and foremost to designate those groups that are eligible to exercise a right to external self-determination. In this sense, as explained in the following section, the term 'peoples' refers exclusively to colonial peoples and to peoples under external subjugation. Nevertheless, other groups are also eligible

[8] It is relevant to note that the reference to 'We the peoples' was inserted at the instigation of the United States delegation, which considered the reference as an expression of the democratic basis on which the new organisation was to be founded. However, as pointed out by the Netherlands, not all governments represented in San Francisco could be regarded as deriving their mandate directly from the people. This issue was resolved by establishing a connection between 'We the peoples' and 'our respective governments'. See Spijkers, *The United Nations, the Evolution of Global Values and International Law*, pp. 66–7.

[9] Indeed, the *travaux préparatoires* specify that 'peoples' should be understood to designate 'groups of human beings who may, or may not, comprise states or nations'. See Memorandum of the Secretary on a List of Certain Repetitive Words and Phrases in the Charter, Document WD381, CO/156, 18 June 1945, in *Documents of the United Nations Conference on International Organization* (UNCIO), Vol. 18, New York: United Nations (1954), p. 658.

[10] For a detailed analysis of the different meanings of the term 'peoples' in the African Charter on Human and Peoples Rights, see Kiwanuka, 'The Meaning of "people" in the African Charter on Human and Peoples' Rights', pp. 80–101.

to exercise peoples' rights. In particular, it is possible to identify two categories of peoples in the context of the sovereign State. These are the population of a State as a whole, as well as specific groups within a State, in particular, indigenous peoples and peoples that constitute a minority in independent States.[11]

All these groups benefit from the general protection provided by human rights law to the population of a State as a whole and to individuals within a society. Moreover, minorities and indigenous peoples have been assigned a special status in international law in order to protect their cultures. They are eligible to exercise peoples' rights only for this purpose. This section briefly discusses the position of indigenous peoples in international law, because these peoples have a special relationship with their lands and the natural resources situated on their lands.

3.2.2 'Peoples' in the sense of indigenous peoples

Indigenous peoples are communities in society that are descended from the traditional inhabitants of a country.[12] These communities have their own cultures and traditions that differ from the dominant culture in a given society. Examples include the Maori in New Zealand, the Sami in Finland and the San people in Southern Africa. More specifically, indigenous peoples can be defined as

> peoples in independent countries who are regarded as indigenous on account of their descent from the populations which inhabited the country, or a geographical region to which the country belongs, at the time of conquest or colonisation or the establishment of present state boundaries and who, irrespective of their legal status, retain some or all of their own social, economic, cultural and political institutions.[13]

[11] As regards minorities, a distinction can be made between four types of minorities, as recognised in the 1992 UN Declaration on the Rights of Persons Belonging to National or Ethnic, Religious and Linguistic Minorities. See UNGA Resolution 47/135, 18 December 1992. With the exception of national minorities, these groups enjoy the rights referred to in Article 27 of the ICCPR.

[12] For a more detailed analysis of the special position of indigenous peoples in international law, see Xanthaki, *Indigenous Rights and United Nations Standards*; and Schrijver, 'Unravelling State Sovereignty?' pp. 85–98. See also the final report of the Special Rapporteur of the Commission on Human Rights, Mrs. Erica Daes, on Indigenous Peoples' Permanent Sovereignty over Natural Resources, *UN Doc. E/CN.4/Sub.2/2004/30* of 13 July 2004, and its addendum, *UN Doc. E/CN.4/Sub.2/2004/30/Add.1* of 12 July 2004.

[13] Article 1(1)(b) of the ILO Convention 169 concerning Indigenous and Tribal Peoples in Independent Countries, Geneva, 27 June 1989 (entry into force: 5 September 1991), *28 ILM 1382 (1989).*

In many cases, indigenous peoples have a special relationship with the land they live on, which is an essential part of their culture. In order to protect their traditional way of life and their identity as a community, indigenous peoples have been granted a number of rights, including rights over land and natural resources.[14]

The principal binding legal instrument in which the rights of indigenous peoples were formulated is ILO Convention 169 concerning Indigenous and Tribal Peoples in Independent Countries.[15] However, this Convention has been ratified by only 22 States. The hesitancy of States to ratify the Convention is indicative of the controversies surrounding the recognition of indigenous rights. Key provisions of the Convention focus on the protection of the culture of indigenous peoples (Article 5), consultation with indigenous peoples regarding matters that directly affect them (Article 6) and the right of indigenous peoples to control their own development (Article 7).

Furthermore, in order to avoid any misunderstandings regarding the legal status of indigenous peoples under the Convention, Article 1(3) of ILO Convention 169 specifies that '[t]he use of the term "peoples" in this Convention shall not be construed as having any implications as regards the rights which may attach to the term under international law'. This provision should be interpreted as a safeguard to prevent indigenous peoples from claiming a right to secession.

In 2007, the General Assembly adopted a Declaration on the Rights of Indigenous Peoples.[16] This declaration does not define the term 'indigenous peoples', but it does indicate in Article 2 that 'indigenous peoples and individuals are free and equal to all other peoples and individuals'.[17]

The Declaration carefully defines and outlines the rights of indigenous peoples. Article 3 of the Declaration grants a right to self-determination to indigenous peoples, which, according to Article 4, concerns 'matters relating to their internal and local affairs'.[18] Other substantive rights

[14] For a general account of the position of indigenous peoples in international law, see Xanthaki, *Indigenous Rights and United Nations Standards.*

[15] ILO Convention 169 concerning Indigenous and Tribal Peoples in Independent Countries, Geneva, 27 June 1989 (entry into force: 5 September 1991), *28 ILM 1382 (1989).*

[16] United Nations Declaration on the Rights of Indigenous Peoples, Annex to *UNGA Resolution 61/295*, 2 October 2007.

[17] Author's emphasis added.

[18] In this regard, also see Article 46(1), which determines that nothing in the declaration may be construed as 'authorizing or encouraging any action which would dismember or impair, totally or in part, the territorial integrity or political unity of sovereign and

regulate specific matters relating to the special position of indigenous peoples, such as the right to practice their cultural and religious traditions, as formulated in Articles 11 and 12 of the Declaration.

The Declaration also contains detailed provisions regarding the protection of indigenous peoples' traditional lands. Article 26, for example, formulates a right for indigenous peoples 'to own, use, develop and control the lands, territories and resources that they possess'. In addition, Article 27 formulates an obligation for States to establish an impartial, open and transparent process 'to recognize and adjudicate the rights of indigenous peoples pertaining to their lands, territories and resources'. Finally, and of the utmost importance for the current book, Article 32 determines that States must

> consult and cooperate in good faith with the indigenous peoples concerned through their own representative institutions in order to obtain their free and informed consent prior to the approval of any project affecting their lands or territories and other resources, particularly in connection with the development, utilization or exploitation of mineral, water or other resources.

This provision constitutes the basis for the obligations of governments regarding the exploitation of natural resources on indigenous lands. This obligation was also recognised by the Human Rights Committee and the Committee on Economic, Social and Cultural Rights. The Guidelines of both Committees indicate that a proper implementation of the right to self-determination implies the recognition and protection of the rights of indigenous peoples to ownership of the lands and territories that they traditionally occupy or use for their livelihood. It also requires the establishment of procedures allowing indigenous and local communities to be duly consulted, as well as the adoption of decision-making processes which seek the prior informed consent of indigenous peoples and local communities regarding matters that affect their rights and interests under the Covenant.[19]

Of course, neither the Declaration on the Rights of Indigenous Peoples nor the Guidelines of these two authoritative human rights committees are

independent States'. This provision thus confirms that for indigenous peoples the right to self-determination does not entail a right to secession.

[19] Guidelines for the Treaty-Specific Document to be Submitted by States Parties under Article 40 of the International Covenant on Civil and Political Rights, *UN Doc. CCPR/C/2009/1* of 22 November 2010, under Article 1; Guidelines for the Treaty-Specific Documents to be Submitted by States Parties under Articles 16 and 17 of the International Covenant on Economic, Social and Cultural Rights, *UN Doc. E/C.12/2008/2* of 24 March 2009.

legally binding. Nevertheless, the obligation to consult indigenous peoples has also been recognised in the case law of the Human Rights Committee itself and in the case law of other human rights bodies, notably in relation to the protection of minority rights and the right to self-determination. This case law is discussed in Section 3.3 in relation to the right to self-determination.

3.2.3 Concluding remarks on the definition of 'peoples'

The notion of 'peoples' is a dynamic concept which can apply to different groups.[20] However, in the context of a sovereign State, the term 'peoples' refers in particular to all persons within a State as the sum of all the peoples living in the State, i.e., the population as a whole, and to distinct groups within a State possessing certain common characteristics – in particular, minorities and indigenous peoples.

This book focuses on the rights of peoples in relation to the exploitation of natural resources. In this respect, two rights are of particular importance. The first is the right to self-determination, because it is inextricably linked to the principle of permanent sovereignty over natural resources. The second is the right to development, which is both a logical extension of the right to self-determination and an expression of the obligation of States to exploit their natural resources for national development and the well-being of the people of the State concerned. The following sections examine both rights in turn and analyse their implications for peoples living in sovereign States.

3.3 The right to self-determination

The right to self-determination refers to a right of peoples to 'freely determine their political status and freely pursue their economic, social and cultural development'.[21] The most relevant aspect for this book is the fact that the right to self-determination, as enshrined in the 1966 Human Right Covenants, includes a right of peoples to freely dispose of their natural resources. This section examines the evolution, nature and legal

[20] For a study of the implementation of United Nations Resolutions regarding the right of colonial peoples to self-determination, see in particular H. Gros-Espiell, 'The Right to Self-Determination: Implementation of United Nations Resolutions – A Study', *UN Doc. E/CN.4/Sub.2/405/Rev.1 (1980).*

[21] The identical Articles 1 of the International Covenants on Economic, Social and Cultural Rights and on Civil and Political Rights.

status of the right to self-determination, with emphasis on its relation to the exploitation of natural resources. It also explores the implications of the right to self-determination for peoples living in independent States.

3.3.1 *Evolution of the right to self-determination*

Self-determination as a political postulate

The origins of the right to self-determination can be traced back to the birth of the nation-state, which was based on the idea that governmental authority should be derived from the consent of the governed. The 1581 Dutch Act of Abjuration was the first document to propose that the government is responsible for its population and that populations whose rights and freedoms are not respected have the right to choose another government.[22]

Thus, in its original form, self-determination refers to the right of a population of a State to choose its own government. This right has an internal and an external dimension. While the internal dimension of the right concerns the right of a population to choose its preferred form of government, the external dimension concerns a nation's right to determine its international status.[23]

These two dimensions of self-determination also form the basis of the 1776 American Declaration of Independence, which states that

[22] The Dutch Act of Abjuration (Plakkaat van Verlatinghe) states as follows: 'Whereas God did not create the people slaves to their prince, to obey his commands, whether right or wrong, but rather the prince for the sake of the subjects (without which he could be no prince), to govern them according to equity, to love and support them as a father his children or a shepherd his flock, and even at the hazard of life to defend and preserve them. And when he does not behave thus, but, on the contrary, oppresses them, seeking opportunities to infringe their ancient customs and privileges, exacting from them slavish compliance, then he is no longer a prince, but a tyrant... And particularly when this is done deliberately..., they may not only disallow his authority, but legally proceed to the choice of another prince for their defence.' English translation, available through www.let.rug.nl/~usa/D/1501-1600/plakkaat/plakkaaten.htm. The idea that governmental authority should be derived from the consent of the governed was not entirely new. Already, in 1215, English barons had forced King John of England, hated for his oppressive government, to sign a document in which their basic freedoms were recognised. However, this document, known as the *Magna Carta*, did not pronounce on the relationship between the government and the governed. It is rather a precursor to the idea that 'rule' should be according to 'law'. For the Magna Carta, see Holt, *Magna Carta*, pp. 441–73.

[23] See Raič, *Statehood and the Law of Self-Determination*, p. 205, who explains that external self-determination 'denotes the determination of the *international* status of a territory and a people', while internal self-determination 'refers to the relationship between the government of a State and the people of that State'.

> to secure [certain unalienable] rights, governments are instituted among men, deriving their just powers from the consent of the governed; that whenever any form of government becomes destructive of these ends, it is the right of the people to alter or to abolish it, and to institute new government, laying its foundation on such principles, and organizing its powers in such form, as to them shall seem most likely to effect their safety and happiness.[24]

In contrast, the 1789 French Declaration of the Rights of Man and of the Citizen focuses primarily on internal self-determination, when it determines that any form of governmental authority must be derived expressly from the people.[25] Of course, these differences can easily be explained from a historical perspective. While the American Declaration was a proclamation of independence from the British Empire, the French Declaration was drafted after an internal revolution.

In conclusion, it should be noted that these early expressions of the concept of self-determination give peoples a central place. Peoples have the right to choose the form of government that best represents their interests. Moreover, the declarations postulate that the government must be based on the consent of the governed. These ideas were further developed in later stages during the evolution of the concept of self-determination.

Self-determination as a legal principle

The notion of self-determination only became firmly rooted in international law well into the twentieth century.[26] While the concept of self-determination does not appear at all in the Covenant of the League of Nations, despite a proposal by the American President Wilson to insert a

[24] The American Declaration of Independence, text available through the Avalon Project, http://avalon.law.yale.edu/18th_century/declare.asp.

[25] *Déclaration des droits de l'Homme et du citoyen*, 26 August 1789, Article 3: 'Le principe de toute souveraineté réside essentiellement dans la Nation. Nul corps, nul individu ne peut exercer d'autorité qui n'en émane expressément', accessible through www.textes.justice.gouv.fr. In French, the word 'nation' is used in the sense of the Latin word 'natio' and designates the population of a state. The Larousse defines 'nation' as a 'grande communauté humaine, souvent installée sur un même territoire, qui possède une unité historique, linguistique et constitue une entité politique'. See the *Dictionnaire Larousse*, édition 2010.

[26] See generally on the right of self-determination, Cassese, *Self-Determination of Peoples*; Alston, 'Peoples' Rights: The State of the Art at the Beginning of the 21st Century', pp. 259–93; Thürer and Burri, 'Self-Determination'; Crawford, 'The Right of Self-Determination in International Law', pp. 7–67; Raič, *Statehood and the Law of Self-Determination.*

provision on self-determination into the Covenant,[27] and is only hinted at in the 1941 Atlantic Charter,[28] the notion finally appeared and was recognised as a legal principle in the UN Charter.[29]

Self-determination figures prominently as one of the main principles on which the new world order is based. Article 1(2) of the UN Charter determines that one of the purposes of the United Nations is to 'develop friendly relations among nations based on respect for the principle of equal rights and self-determination of peoples'. Furthermore, Article 55 of Chapter IX of the UN Charter on International Economic and Social Cooperation states that the creation of conditions of stability and well-being are necessary for peaceful and friendly relations among nations 'based on the principle of equal rights and self-determination of peoples'.

However, the Charter does not contain any further indications regarding the implications of the principle of self-determination for inter-State relations. In particular, it does not clarify whether the principle entails a right of secession for peoples. The discussions of the Committee drafting the relevant provision at San Francisco suggest that – at least as regards the opinion of some of the Committee members – the principle of self-determination was supposed to refer only to self-government.[30] In other words, the principle of self-determination was not supposed to entail a right of peoples to establish an independent State.

[27] Wilson's proposal stated, 'The Contracting Powers unite in guaranteeing to each other political independence and territorial integrity; but it is understood between them that such territorial readjustments, if any, as may in the future become necessary by reason of changes in present racial conditions and aspirations of present social and political relationships, pursuant to the principle of self-determination, and also such territorial readjustments as may in the judgment of three-fourths of the Delegates be demanded by the welfare and manifest interest of the peoples concerned, may be effected if agreeable to those peoples.' See Cassese, *Self-Determination of Peoples*, p. 23.

[28] The Atlantic Charter expresses the principle that territorial changes must accord 'with the freely expressed wishes of the peoples concerned' and proclaims a right of all peoples 'to choose the form of government under which they will live'. Atlantic Charter, *Yearbook of the United Nations* (1946–7), New York: United Nations (1947), p. 2.

[29] Or, as Cassese puts it, 'The adoption of the UN Charter marks an important turning-point: it signals the maturing of the political postulate of self-determination into a legal standard of behaviour'. Cassese, *Self-Determination of Peoples*, p. 43. On the debates at San Francisco, see Spijkers, *The United Nations, the Evolution of Global Values and International Law*, Chap. VII.

[30] The records note that 'the principle [of self-determination] conform[s] to the purposes of the Charter only insofar as it implie[s] the right of self-government of peoples and not the right of secession'. *Documents of the United Nations Conference on International Organization*, Sixth Meeting of Committee I, May 16, 1945, Vol. 6 (1945), p. 296.

However, a closer look at the UN Charter as a whole warrants a broader reading of the UN Charter principle of self-determination. This is illustrated by the text of Article 76 of the UN Charter regarding the international trusteeship system, which is aimed at 'progressive development towards self-government or independence' for trust territories. The reference to independence was inserted at the instigation of the USSR, which considered self-government alone, as proposed by the UK, to be an inadequate objective in the context of trustee territories.[31] Interestingly, the USSR stated that the reference in Article 76 to the purposes of the United Nations, including the principle of self-determination, implied that 'this principle could hardly be omitted from the trusteeship chapter', thus hinting at a broader definition of self-determination.

In any case, it can be concluded that the drafters of the UN Charter clearly wanted to exclude the possibility that in the UN Charter, self-determination would be interpreted as entailing a right to secession for colonial countries. In order to prevent any confusion on this matter, the term 'self-determination' is not mentioned at all in Article 73 of the UN Charter, the provision dealing with colonial countries. Article 73 refers only to 'self-government', without any general reference to the purposes of the United Nations as stated in Article 1 of the UN Charter.

Despite the general confusion about the scope of the principle of self-determination in the UN Charter, it is therefore clear that colonial peoples were not considered to have a right to independence. This can be regarded as one of the last manifestations of the era of colonialism. Since then, the political landscape has changed considerably as a result of the process of decolonisation. These changes have had a significant impact on the concept of self-determination as well. One of the most profound impacts is related to the recognition of self-determination as a human right, because the internal dimension of self-determination was strengthened as a result. Moreover, the range of subjects to which the principle applies was significantly extended.

Self-determination as a human right

Not long after being established as a legal principle, self-determination was also recognised as a human right.[32] At the instigation of the USSR,

[31] See *Documents of the United Nations Conference on International Organization*, Fourth Meeting of Committee II/4, May 14, 1945, Vol. 10 (1945), p. 441.

[32] Alston calls this development the second phase in the evolution of peoples' rights in international law. See Alston, 'Peoples' Rights: Their Rise and Fall', in P. Alston (ed.),

the right to self-determination was included in the identically formulated Articles 1 of the International Covenants on Economic, Social and Cultural Rights and on Civil and Political Rights.[33]

This Article consists of three components. Article 1(1) of the 1966 Covenants formulates a right of all peoples to 'freely determine their political status' and to 'freely pursue their economic, social and cultural development'. In order to pursue development, States must be in control of their economic means. This is recognised in Article 1(2) of the 1966 Covenants, which formulates a right of peoples to freely dispose of their natural resources and formulates a prohibition against depriving peoples of their means of subsistence. Finally, Article 1(3) formulates a positive obligation for States to promote the realisation of the right to self-determination and a negative obligation to respect the right.

The right to self-determination has civil and political, as well as economic and social dimensions. The inclusion of the right to self-determination in both human rights covenants emphasises the comprehensive nature of the right to self-determination.[34] This section first takes a closer look at the political dimension of self-determination and subsequently discusses the economic dimension. It should be noted that these two dimensions are mutually interdependent. The right to political self-determination cannot be achieved if the State does not control its own natural resources, while the right to economic self-determination cannot be achieved without proper structures for the governance of natural resources.

The right to political self-determination The concept of political self-determination, as it developed over time, has two basic tenets, giving rise to two separate yet interrelated rights. The right to external self-determination concerns the right of peoples to determine their international status, while the corresponding right to internal self-determination

Peoples' Rights, Academy of European Law, Oxford: Oxford University Press (2001), pp. 262–4.

33 International Covenant on Economic, Social and Cultural Rights (ICESCR), New York, Annex to UNGA Resolution 2200 (XXI) of 16 December 1966, *993 UNTS 3*; International Covenant on Civil and Political Rights (ICCPR), New York, Annex 2 to UNGA Resolution 2200 (XXI) of 16 December 1966, *999 UNTS 171*. For the proposal of the USSR to include a provision on self-determination, see the 1950 Yearbook of the United Nations, pp. 526–7.

34 See Crawford, 'The Right of Self-Determination in International Law', p. 27, who argues that '[i]ts inclusion in both Covenants suggests that self-determination is both a civil and political right and an economic, social and cultural right'.

concerns the right of peoples to choose a political system.[35] While the right to external self-determination is primarily important in inter-State relations, the right to internal self-determination determines the relationship between the government and the peoples living within a State. In the light of the aim of this book, which deals primarily with questions relating to the governance of natural resources within States, the emphasis of this section is therefore on internal rather than on external self-determination. The right to external self-determination is discussed mainly to provide the necessary context for a better understanding of the right to internal self-determination.

If the right to self-determination is interpreted as a right for peoples to determine their international status and/or a right to choose a political system, two questions immediately spring to mind. The first concerns the modalities for exercising the right to self-determination, while the second concerns the legal subjects of the right. Both questions were considered in some detail in two authoritative declarations of the UN General Assembly dealing with the issue of self-determination, the 1960 Declaration on the Granting of Independence to Colonial Countries and Peoples and the 1970 Declaration on Principles of International Law Concerning Friendly Relations and Co-operation among States in Accordance with the Charter of the United Nations, as well as in the case law of the International Court of Justice.

As regards the modalities for exercising the right to self-determination, the 1960 Declaration on the Granting of Independence to Colonial Countries and Peoples interprets the right to self-determination principally as a right for colonial peoples to gain independence. In particular, the Declaration refers to the need

> to transfer all powers to the peoples of [Trust and Non-self-governing Territories or all other territories which have not yet attained independence], without any conditions or reservations, in accordance with their freely expressed will and desire, without any distinction as to race, creed or colour, in order to enable them to enjoy complete independence and freedom.[36]

In addition, the 1970 Declaration on Principles of International Law Concerning Friendly Relations and Co-operation among States in Accordance

[35] See Higgins, *Problems and Process*, p. 120, who argues that the right of peoples to freely pursue their economic, social and cultural development implies their right to choose their government.

[36] Declaration on the Granting of Independence to Colonial Countries and Peoples, *UNGA Resolution 1514 (XV)*, 14 December 1960, paras. 2 and 5. In addition, see Dobelle, 'Article 1 Paragraphe 2', p. 341.

with the Charter of the United Nations – which treats self-determination alternatively as a principle and as a right – determines that the principle of equal rights and self-determination entails a right for all peoples to 'freely determine, without external interference, their political status and to pursue their economic, social and cultural development'.[37] Furthermore, the 1970 Declaration distinguishes between four modes of exercising the right to self-determination. The Declaration determines that

> The establishment of a sovereign and independent State, the free association or integration with an independent State or the emergence into any other political status freely determined by a people constitute modes of implementing the right of self-determination by that people.[38]

It is important to note that both declarations base the exercise of the right to self-determination on the free expression of the will of the peoples concerned. This interpretation of the right to self-determination as requiring a free and genuine expression of the will of the peoples concerned lies at the heart of the right to self-determination. This is also how the right to self-determination is interpreted by the International Court of Justice, which, in its *Advisory Opinion on the Western Sahara*, expressly provided that self-determination must be understood as 'the need to pay regard to the freely expressed will of peoples'.[39] This interpretation of the right to self-determination also explains the focus of United Nations practice on organising elections to determine the will of the people. In the context of decolonisation, the UN has provided assistance in the organisation of a number of plebiscites and elections for the purpose of determining the will of the people with regard to their political future.[40]

The right to self-determination is also invoked in relation to UN-supervised elections in States that have suffered from internal armed conflicts. Reference can be made in particular to UN Security Council resolutions in relation to the elections in Cambodia in 1993. In Resolution 745 (1992), the UN Security Council explicitly stated that it desired to ensure 'the right to self-determination of the Cambodian people through free and fair elections'.[41] Furthermore, in a subsequent resolution, the

[37] Declaration on Principles of International Law Concerning Friendly Relations and Co-operation among States in Accordance with the Charter of the United Nations, *UNGA Resolution 2625 (XXV)*, 24 October 1970, principle 5.

[38] Ibid., para. 4.

[39] International Court of Justice, *Western Sahara*, Advisory Opinion of 16 October 1975, *I.C.J. Reports* 1975, para. 59.

[40] For examples, see Cassese, *Self-Determination of Peoples*, pp. 76–8.

[41] UNSC Resolution 745 (1992), para. 4 of the preamble.

Council recalled that 'all Cambodians have . . . the right to determine their own political future through the free and fair election of a constituent assembly'.[42]

Therefore, it can be argued that in UN practice, elections generally serve as the principal means of ascertaining that a people has been able to freely exercise its right to self-determination. However, despite the importance of elections for ascertaining the will of peoples, they are only a way of achieving their right to self-determination. The essence of the modern right to political self-determination, which can be construed as a right to representative government, forms the basis for this. Self-determination in this sense is most clearly described in the 1970 Friendly Relations Declaration, which indicates that the UN Charter principle of equal rights and self-determination requires a government 'representing the whole people belonging to the territory without distinction as to race, creed or colour'.[43]

This paragraph is important for several reasons. First, it can be interpreted as a confirmation that the right to self-determination accrues to peoples living within independent States, which had been a matter of considerable controversy until the adoption of this Declaration.[44] Second, the paragraph emphasises the importance of a representative and nondiscriminatory government. This is also why the 1970 Declaration has often been quoted by advocates of the right to external self-determination for oppressed groups within a State. While the right to external self-determination is generally considered to accrue to colonial peoples and to peoples under alien subjugation,[45] some authors have argued in favour of extending the right to external self-determination to oppressed groups within States. These authors often point to the Friendly Relations Declaration and argue that the principle of equal rights and self-determination

[42] UNSC Resolution 792 (1992), para. 6 of the preamble.

[43] Declaration on Principles of International Law Concerning Friendly Relations and Co-operation among States in Accordance with the Charter of the United Nations, *UNGA Resolution 2625 (XXV)*, 24 October 1970, principle 5.

[44] See Rosenstock, 'The Declaration of Principles of International Law Concerning Friendly Relations', pp. 713–35, who argues on p. 732 that 'a close examination of its text will reward the reader with an affirmation of the applicability of the principle to peoples within existing states and the necessity for governments to represent the governed'.

[45] See International Court of Justice, Legal Consequences for States of the Continued Presence of South Africa in Namibia (South West Africa) notwithstanding Security Council Resolution 276 (1970), Advisory Opinion, *I.C.J. Reports 1971*, para. 52; International Court of Justice, Western Sahara, Advisory Opinion of 16 October 1975, *I.C.J. Reports 1975*, paras. 54–9; International Court of Justice, East Timor (*Portugal* v. *Australia*), Judgment, *I.C.J. Reports 1995*, p. 90.

does not preclude action that would break down or harm the territorial integrity or political unity of a State which is not 'possessed of a government representing the whole population'.[46]

The right of oppressed people within States to secede from those States is still an issue of considerable controversy.[47] In the *Advisory Opinion regarding Kosovo*, the International Court of Justice had an opportunity to pronounce on the matter. In a general sense, the Court considered

> Whether, outside the context of non-self-governing territories and peoples subject to alien subjugation, domination and exploitation, the international law of self-determination confers upon part of the population of an existing State a right to separate from that State is, however, a subject on which radically different views were expressed by those taking part in the proceedings and expressing a position on the question. Similar differences existed regarding whether international law provides for a right of 'remedial secession' and, if so, in what circumstances.[48]

Instead of taking a stand on the matter, the Court adhered to a strict reading of the question formulated by the General Assembly in its request for an Advisory Opinion. This question concerned the legality of the

[46] It should be noted that the relevant paragraph of the 1970 Declaration reads in full, 'Nothing in the foregoing paragraphs shall be construed as authorizing or encouraging any action which would dismember or impair, totally or in part, the territorial integrity or political unity of sovereign and independent States conducting themselves in compliance with the principle of equal rights and self-determination of peoples as described above and thus possessed of a government representing the whole people belonging to the territory without distinction as to race, creed or colour'. For proponents of an *a contrario* reading of this paragraph, see, e.g., Cassese, *Self-Determination of Peoples*, pp. 109–15; and Dobelle, 'Article 1 Paragraphe 2', p. 351, who argues that 'le droit à l'autodétermination externe est en principe exclu, à condition que le droit à l'autodétermination interne soit garanti. En revanche, la méconnaissance grave et persistante de ce dernier pourrait légitimement déboucher sur le droit à l'indépendance'. For a more cautious perspective, see Gross Espiell, *The Right to Self-Determination: Implementation of United Nations Resolutions*, UN Publication, Sales No. E/79.XIV.5, 1979, para. 60, who emphasises that if 'beneath the guise of ostensible national unity, colonial and alien domination in fact exist, whatever legal formula may be used in an attempt to conceal it, the right of the subject people concerned cannot be disregarded without international law being violated'. He further posits that the Declaration on Friendly Relations 'uses particularly apt language in spelling out this idea: it reaffirms the need to reserve the territorial integrity of sovereign and independent States, but ties this concept to the requirement that the States must be "possessed of a government representing the whole people belonging to the territory without distinction as to race, creed or colour".'

[47] For a more elaborate discussion of the right to remedial secession, see Van den Driest, *Remedial Secession*.

[48] International Court of Justice, Accordance with International Law of the Unilateral Declaration of Independence in Respect of Kosovo, Advisory Opinion of 22 July 2010, *I.C.J. Reports (2010)*, para. 82.

Declaration of Independence issued by the Provisional Institutions of Self-Government of Kosovo.[49] The Court concluded that international law does not in general prohibit the act of promulgating a declaration of independence.[50]

Although it concerns a national case, a previous judgment of the Supreme Court of Canada in the case of Quebec also illustrates this point. The Supreme Court was faced with the question of whether the population of Quebec, a linguistic minority living in Canada, had the right to secede from Canada. In this instance, the Supreme Court ruled as follows:

> Although much of the Quebec population certainly shares many of the characteristics of a people, it is not necessary to decide the "people" issue [in relation to the right of self-determination] because, whatever may be the correct determination of this issue in the context of Quebec, a right to secession only arises under the principle of self-determination of people at international law where 'a people' is governed as part of a colonial empire; where 'a people' is subject to alien subjugation, domination or exploitation; and possibly where 'a people' is denied any meaningful exercise of its right to self-determination within the state of which it forms a part. In other circumstances, peoples are expected to achieve self-determination within the framework of their existing state. A state whose government represents the whole of the people or peoples resident within its territory, on a basis of equality and without discrimination, and respects the principles of self-determination in its internal arrangements, is entitled to maintain its territorial integrity under international law and to have that territorial integrity recognised by other states.[51]

The Quebec case implies that the right to internal self-determination must first of all be achieved within the framework of the existing State. Whether a right to secession exists for peoples that are not represented through their government remains a matter of considerable controversy, as confirmed by the *Kosovo Advisory Opinion*. However, it can be argued that under current international law, questions about the representativeness of a government must primarily be resolved within the existing framework of the State. The following sections explain in greater detail how the right to self-determination can be achieved in an existing State.

[49] See International Court of Justice, Request for Advisory Opinion transmitted to the Court pursuant to General Assembly resolution A/RES/63/3 (A/63/L.2) of 8 October 2008, 'Accordance with International Law of the Unilateral Declaration of Independence by the Provisional Institutions of Self-Government of Kosovo'.

[50] International Court of Justice, Accordance with International Law of the Unilateral Declaration of Independence in Respect of Kosovo, Advisory Opinion of 22 July 2010, *I.C.J. Reports (2010)*, para. 79.

[51] Supreme Court of Canada, Reference re Secession of Quebec, [1998] 2 S.C.R. 217, Judgment of 20 August 1998.

The right to economic self-determination The right to freely pursue economic, social and cultural development as enshrined in Article 1(1) of the Covenants requires not only that peoples can choose the form of government to achieve this objective, but also that they have access to the economic means necessary to pursue development. Therefore, as a corollary of the political component of the right to self-determination, Article 1(2) of the Covenants contains a right for peoples to freely dispose of their natural wealth and resources.

This provision was inserted in 1955 on the initiative of Chile. It proclaims a right for all peoples to 'freely dispose of their natural wealth and resources without prejudice to any obligations arising out of international economic co-operation, based upon the principle of mutual benefit, and international law' . . . 'for their own ends'.[52] Therefore, the provision emphasises the freedom of peoples to control their natural resources, while at the same time it points to the need to respect their obligations under international law. In this way, the drafters of the Covenants have sought to create a careful balance between the interests of States endowed with natural resources, on one hand, and the interests of foreign investors, on the other.

Towards the end of the drafting of the Covenants, when the composition of the UN had changed considerably as a result of the process of decolonisation, a safeguard provision was inserted into both covenants. Article 25 of the ICESCR and Article 47 of the ICCPR, dealing with the implementation of the covenants, determine that nothing in the Covenants 'shall be interpreted as impairing the inherent right of all peoples to enjoy and utilize fully and freely their natural wealth and resources'. Some authors argue that Article 25 of the ICESCR and Article 47 of the ICCPR 'were aimed at "rectifying" Article 1(2) in order to meet new demands in the wake of the evolution of international politics and law that had taken place in the meantime'.[53]

However, a more convincing interpretation of Article 25 of the ICESCR and Article 47 of the ICCPR is that the provisions were meant to prevent the erosion of the right of peoples to freely dispose of their natural resources using the argument of 'obligations arising out of international

[52] For the original proposal made by Chile in 1952, see note 2 in Chapter 2.

[53] Cassese, *Self-Determination of Peoples*, p. 57. Similarly, Halperin, 'Human Rights and Natural Resources', pp. 770–87, who demonstrates that Article 25 of the ICESCR and Article 47 of the ICCPR have a strong anti-colonialist connotation, and Summers, *The Idea of the People*, p. 146, who argues that Articles 25 and 47 formulate an absolute right and 'can be seen . . . as an attempt to change the interpretation of the balance in article 1(2) without actually being an amendment to the paragraph'.

economic co-operation'. This is reflected in the wording of the provisions, which refer only to the Covenants themselves, and not to international law in general. Obligations arising from other legal instruments or from general international law cannot be set aside by Article 25 of the ICESCR or Article 47 of the ICCPR.[54]

In addition to formulating a right of peoples to freely dispose of their natural resources, Article 1(2) of the ICESCR and the ICCPR also contains a prohibition stipulating that '[i]n no case may a people be deprived of its own means of subsistence'. Although it was originally inserted with the aim of protecting newly independent States and developing countries from developed States and foreign investors, the prohibition is also a human right which can be invoked by peoples against their governments. In this sense, the prohibition establishes the ultimate limits for governments with respect to the use of the State's natural resources. It provides that the exercise of permanent sovereignty by the government may never result in peoples being deprived of their means of subsistence.

The provision can also be read as a prohibition of governments denying peoples the right of access to their means of subsistence. This right of access covers both physical and economic access.[55] For example, this means that local communities and indigenous peoples cannot be denied physical access to hunting grounds, rivers or forests, if this is necessary for their subsistence. In addition, the government is also precluded from denying peoples economic access to their means of subsistence. This means, for example, that governments cannot deny local communities access to mines if these communities are highly dependent on mining to earn a basic living. These issues, as well as their implications in

[54] This applies particularly for obligations arising out of the UN Charter. Article 103 of the UN charter determines that obligations under the UN Charter prevail over obligations under other international agreements. In this respect, Article 1(1) of the UN Charter determines that the purposes of the UN include the maintenance of international peace and security and that international disputes or situations which might lead to a breach of the peace must be adjusted or settled 'in conformity with the principles of justice and *international law*'. Author's emphasis added. It may be noted that in addition to the general rule contained in Article 103 of the UN Charter, both the ICESCR and the ICCPR contain explicit conflict clauses regulating the relation between the Covenants and the UN Charter. See Article 24 of the ICESCR and Article 46 of the ICCPR.

[55] For the distinction between physical and economic access in relation to the right to an adequate standard of living, and in particular to adequate food, protected under Article 11 of the ICESCR, see Committee on Economic, Social and Cultural Rights, General Comment No. 12, *UN Doc. E/C.12/1999/5* of 12 May 1999, para. 13.

situations of armed conflict, are examined in greater detail in Part II of this book.

The economic dimension of the right to self-determination was notably expressed in resolutions of the General Assembly relating to the principle of permanent sovereignty over natural resources, including the landmark 1962 Declaration on Permanent Sovereignty over Natural Resources and the 1974 Charter on Economic Rights and Duties of States.[56] An early reference can also be found in the 1960 Decolonisation Declaration, albeit in its preamble.[57] It is striking that the 1970 Declaration on Friendly Relations contains no reference whatsoever to economic self-determination. A proposal to insert a reference to natural resources was discussed in relation to the principle of sovereign equality, rather than in relation to the principle of equal rights and self-determination. It therefore seems that the Friendly Relations Declaration considered the economic component of self-determination to be an attribute of state sovereignty rather than a right of peoples.[58] The aim of the Friendly Relations Declaration, to clarify and further develop the principles of inter-State relations, as enshrined in the UN Charter, explains this perspective.

As regards treaty law, the right to economic self-determination was also expressed in Article 21 of the African Charter of Human and Peoples' Rights, which formulates a right comparable to Article 1(2) of the international covenants on economic, social and cultural rights and on civil and political rights. However, instead of formulating an obligation to 'respect obligations arising out of international economic co-operation', the provision formulates the much looser obligation to 'promote international economic cooperation'.

[56] UNGA Resolution 1803 (XVII) of 14 December 1962 on Permanent Sovereignty over Natural Resources; UNGA Resolution 3281 (XXIX) of 12 December 1974 on a Charter of Economic Rights and Duties of States. These resolutions are discussed in more detail in Chapter 2. For the relation between the right to self-determination and permanent sovereignty, see, *inter alia,* Gros Espiell, who argues that 'the economic content of the right of peoples to self-determination finds its expression in particular . . . in their right to permanent sovereignty over natural resources'. See Commission on Human Rights, 'The Right to Self-Determination: Implementation of United Nations Resolutions', study prepared by H. Gros Espiell (Uruguay), special rapporteur of the UN Sub-commission on Prevention of Discrimination and Protection of Minorities (1980), *UN Doc. E/CN.4/Sub.2/405/Rev.*1, para. 136.

[57] Declaration on the Granting of Independence to Colonial Countries and Peoples, *UNGA Resolution 1514 (XV)*, 14 December 1960, preamble, para. 8.

[58] For the drafting history of the Declaration on Friendly Relations, see Šahović, 'Codification des Principes du Droit International des Relations Amicales et de la Coopération entre les Etats', pp. 243–310.

Furthermore, this economic cooperation does not have to be based on 'mutual benefit and international law' as stipulated in the covenants, but must be based on 'mutual respect, equitable exchange and the principles of international law'.[59] It further provides that the right of peoples to freely dispose of their natural resources must be exercised 'by States parties' and 'in the exclusive interest of the people'. In addition, it provides for a right of lawful recovery and adequate compensation for peoples in case of the spoliation of their natural resources.

3.3.2 *The nature and legal status of the right to self-determination*

The concept of self-determination has attained a firm status in international law, both as a principle and as a human right. Since its inclusion in the UN Charter, self-determination has been incorporated into several binding legal instruments, including the 1966 Human Rights Covenants. In addition, several authoritative resolutions of the UN General Assembly refer to self-determination as well, including the authoritative 1960 Declaration on the Granting of Independence to Colonial Countries and Peoples and the 1970 Declaration on Principles of International Law Concerning Friendly Relations and Co-operation among States in Accordance with the Charter of the United Nations.[60] Moreover, in the *East Timor* case, the International Court of Justice confirmed that self-determination 'is one of the essential principles of contemporary international law' and that it 'has an *erga omnes* character'.[61]

[59] African Charter on Human and Peoples' Rights, Banjul, 27 June 1981, *21 I.L.M. 58 (1982)*. Author's emphasis added.

[60] Declaration on Principles of International Law Concerning Friendly Relations and Co-operation among States in Accordance with the Charter of the United Nations, *UNGA Resolution 2625 (XXV)*, 24 October 1970. Although the primary aim of the declaration was to elaborate upon the principles laid down in the UN Charter, the International Court of Justice treats the resolution as declaratory of customary international law. In the *Nicaragua* case, the Court determined that the effect of consent to the resolution might be considered as 'an acceptance of the validity of the rule or set of rules declared by the resolution by themselves'. Case Concerning Military and Paramilitary Activities in and against Nicaragua (*Nicaragua* v. *United States of America*), Merits, Judgment of 27 June 1986, *I.C.J. Reports 1986*, p. 14, para. 188.

[61] International Court of Justice, East Timor (*Portugal* v. *Australia*), Judgment of 30 June 1995, *I.C.J. Reports 1995*, p. 90, para. 29. In the *Barcelona Traction* case, the International Court of Justice determined that obligations *erga omnes* are 'by their very nature . . . the concern of all States'. International Court of Justice, Barcelona Traction, Light and Power Company, Limited (*Belgium* v. *Spain*), Judgment of 5 February 1970, Second phase, *I.C.J. Reports 1970*, p. 3, para. 33.

This case also implies that the principle of self-determination applies to the international community of States.[62] States have the obligation both to actively promote the right to self-determination – an obligation which is based on the UN Charter provisions regarding trust territories and, in subsequent State practice, non-self-governing territories – and the obligation not to interfere when a people rightfully exercises its right to self-determination, based, *inter alia,* on the Declaration on Friendly Relations.

When it comes to determining the nature of the concept of self-determination, a distinction must be made between its external and internal dimensions. As regards the external dimension, self-determination can first of all be interpreted as giving rise to a right of colonial peoples and of peoples under alien subjugation to establish an independent State, to associate with or integrate with another State, or to develop any other political status. In addition, the concept entails a right to exercise control over the natural resources found within the State territory.

Recently, the existence of the right to external self-determination for colonial peoples and peoples under alien subjugation was confirmed in the Advisory Opinion of the International Court of Justice regarding Kosovo. In the relevant part the Court stated, 'During the second half of the twentieth century, the international law of self-determination developed in such a way as to create a right to independence for the peoples of non-self-governing territories and peoples subject to alien subjugation, domination and exploitation'.[63] Whether such a right exists for oppressed groups within a State as well is a matter of considerable controversy, as explained in the preceding section. In international law, questions about the representativeness of a government must currently be primarily solved within the existing framework of the State.

Once a people has organised itself within an autonomous State, whether through secession, integration or association, it may be argued that the right to external self-determination, including economic

[62] As the International Court of Justice held that self-determination has an *erga omnes* character, it can be applied to the international community as a whole. East Timor (*Portugal* v. *Australia*), Judgment, *I.C.J. Reports 1995*, p. 90), para. 29. For a critical appraisal of this part of the judgment, see Thürer and Burri, 'Self-Determination', pp. 113–28, paras. 24–5. Thürer and Burri argue that the legal consequences of the *erga omnes* qualification are unclear.

[63] International Court of Justice, Accordance with International Law of the Unilateral Declaration of Independence in Respect of Kosovo, Advisory Opinion of 22 July 2010, *I.C.J. Reports (2010)*, para. 79.

self-determination, is mainly assimilated into the principle of State sovereignty and the related principles of territorial integrity and non-intervention, which must be respected by other States. What remains is a right of peoples within the State to internal self-determination.

In this context, the right to self-determination primarily concerns the right of the people of a State to freely choose the State's political and economic system, as well as the right for minorities to govern their local affairs.[64] As Rosalyn Higgins noted, 'Self-determination requires the ongoing choice of the people as to their governance, and, in turn, their economic, social and cultural development'.[65] In addition, the right to self-determination implies an obligation for the government to exploit the State's natural resources for the benefit of the people. As Antonio Cassese argued,

> Article 1(2) . . . provides that the right to control and benefit from a territory's natural resources lies with the inhabitants of that territory. This right, and the corresponding duty of the central government to use the resources in a manner which coincides with the interests of the people, is the natural consequence of the right to political self-determination.[66]

One of the main ways of achieving the right to internal self-determination is to establish proper procedures for decision making, which allow the participation of all the parties concerned. According to the Human Rights Committee, the relevant obligations in the identical Articles 1 of the Covenants include first of all the establishment of constitutional and political processes 'which in practice allow the exercise of th[e] right [to self-determination]'.[67] The Human Rights Committee's emphasis on 'practice' plays a central role in this. It requires States to put in place policies which effectively guarantee the exercise of the right to self-determination. These policies can be examined by the Human Rights Committee as part of its mandate to examine reports submitted by States under the general reporting obligations of the ICCPR.

[64] Or, as Cassese argues, '[i]nternal self-determination means the right to authentic self-government, that is, the right for a people really and freely to choose its own political and economic regime'. Cassese, *Self-Determination of Peoples*, p. 101.

[65] Higgins, *Problems and Process*, p. 120.

[66] Cassese, *Self-Determination of Peoples*, p. 55.

[67] See General Comment No. 12: The Right to Self-Determination of Peoples (Art. 1), adopted by the Human Rights Committee at its twenty-first session, 13 March 1984, Office of the High Commissioner for Human Rights, para. 3, and Guidelines for the Treaty-Specific Document to Be Submitted by States Parties under Article 40 of the International Covenant on Civil and Political Rights, *UN Doc. CCPR/C/2009/1* of 22 November 2010, under Article 1.

In addition, these policies can also arguably be judicially scrutinised before international human rights bodies.[68] More specifically, as indicated earlier, the Guidelines of the Human Rights Committee, as well as those of the Committee on Economic, Social and Cultural Rights, indicate that a proper implementation of the right to self-determination requires the establishment of procedures which allow indigenous and local communities to be duly consulted, as well as the adoption of decision-making processes aimed at obtaining the prior informed consent of indigenous peoples and local communities regarding matters which affect their rights and interests under the Covenant.[69]

However, the case law of these bodies relating to natural resources policies does not extend beyond the protection of minority rights. In general, human rights bodies do not accept claims regarding the protection of the public interest. For example, under the Optional Protocol of the ICCPR, individuals have to claim to be the 'victim' of violations of the ICCPR.[70] The Optional Protocol of the ICESCR that recently entered into force formulates a similar requirement.[71] This requirement forms an obstacle to challenging government decisions regarding the exploitation of natural resources, because it prevents persons who are not directly affected by a particular project from bringing a claim before a human rights body.

[68] It should be noted in this regard that the complaint mechanisms of the ICCPR and the ICESCR are open only to individuals, while the right to self-determination is a collective right. Therefore, the Human Rights Committee has consistently stated, both in its General Comments and in relevant cases, that it does not recognise claims by individuals of violations of Article 1 of the ICCPR. It does, however, accept claims under other provisions of the Charter that are relevant to the realisation of the right of self-determination, in particular Articles 25, 26 and 27 of the ICCPR. See, e.g., General Comment No. 23: The Rights of Minorities (Art. 27), *UN Doc. CCPR/C/21/Rev.1/Add.5*, 8 April 1994, para. 3.1, where the Committee explicitly states that '[s]elf-determination is not a right cognizable under the Optional Protocol. Article 27, on the other hand, relates to rights conferred on individuals as such . . . and is cognizable under the Optional Protocol'.

[69] Guidelines for the Treaty-Specific Document to be Submitted by States Parties under Article 40 of the International Covenant on Civil and Political Rights, *UN Doc. CCPR/C/2009/1* of 22 November 2010, under Article 1; Guidelines for the Treaty-Specific Documents to be Submitted by States Parties under Articles 16 and 17 of the International Covenant on Economic, Social and Cultural Rights, *UN Doc. E/C.12/2008/2* of 24 March 2009.

[70] Article 2 of the First Optional Protocol to the ICCPR, *999 U.N.T.S. 302*, states in the relevant part, 'individuals who claim that any of *their* rights enumerated in the Covenant have been violated . . . may submit a written communication to the Committee for consideration'. Author's emphasis added.

[71] Article 2 of the Optional Protocol to the International Covenant on Economic, Social and Cultural Rights, Annex to UNGA Resolution A/RES/63/117, of 10 December 2008.

3.3.3 *Implementation of the right to economic self-determination in the sovereign State*

The right to self-determination requires the establishment of constitutional and political processes 'which in practice allow the exercise of th[e] right'.[72] The question arises if and to what extent international law has recognised this obligation, specifically in relation to government decisions on the exploitation of natural resources, and, if so, whether international law offers possibilities for redress regarding such decisions that affect the population or distinct groups in society.

To answer these questions, it is necessary to look first at the growing body of concluding observations and case law of human rights bodies regarding violations of the rights of indigenous peoples resulting from natural resources projects conducted within their lands and initiated by governments. The Human Rights Committee has been very active in recent years in protecting the rights of indigenous peoples over their lands and resources, with the specific aim of preserving their cultures and traditional lifestyles. Although the Human Rights Committee can only assess claims regarding the violation of individual human rights under the Optional Protocol, the Committee has opened the door for indigenous peoples and (other) minorities to invoke the individual rights protected under the ICCPR as communities.

It did so with a broad interpretation of Article 27 of the ICCPR regarding the protection of the right of persons belonging to minorities to enjoy their own cultures, to profess and practise their own religions, or to use their own languages, in community with the other members of their group. In this respect, the Human Rights Committee linked the individual right embodied in Article 27 to the collective right embodied in Article 1 of the ICCPR.[73] The Human Rights Committee has consistently interpreted Article 27 as containing a right of indigenous peoples to participate in decisions that affect them, such as those regarding the use of their land, including the exploitation of the natural resources found there.[74]

[72] See General Comment No. 12: The Right to Self-Determination of Peoples (Art. 1), adopted by the Human Rights Committee at its twenty-first session, 13 March 1984, Office of the High Commissioner for Human Rights, para. 3 and Guidelines for the Treaty-Specific Document to Be Submitted by States Parties under Article 40 of the International Covenant on Civil and Political Rights, *UN Doc. CCPR/C/2009/1* of 22 November 2010, under Article 1.

[73] See also Schrijver, 'Unraveling State Sovereignty?' pp. 91–2.

[74] See, in particular, the landmark case of *Apirana Mahuika et al.* v. *New Zealand*, Communication No. 547/1993, 15 November 2000. Also see the concluding observations of

In addition, the rights of indigenous peoples over their lands were recognised to some extent by the Committee on Economic, Social and Cultural Rights, which, in its General Comment 7 on the right to adequate housing and on forced evictions, explicitly refers to the vulnerable position of indigenous peoples.[75] In its General Comment No. 20 on nondiscrimination in economic, social and cultural rights, the Committee also raises concerns about 'formal and substantive discrimination across a wide range of Covenant rights against indigenous peoples and ethnic minorities'.[76]

Furthermore, the African Commission on Human and Peoples' Rights decided in its landmark Ogoniland case that the right of a people to freely dispose of its natural resources, as protected under Article 21 of the African Charter on Human and Peoples' Rights, entails an obligation for the government to monitor and regulate the activities of private operators licensed to exploit the State's natural resources.[77] The complainants also referred to Article 21 of the African Charter and stated that 'in all their dealings with the Oil Consortiums, the government did not involve the Ogoni Communities in the decisions that affected the development of Ogoniland'. Although the African Commission did not specifically address this issue, it came to the general conclusion that the practice of the Nigerian government did not meet the minimum standard of conduct to be expected of a government, and that it therefore constituted a violation of Article 21 of the African Charter.[78]

Finally, the Inter-American Court of Human Rights has developed extensive case law regarding the rights of indigenous and tribal peoples over their communal lands. It has done so primarily based on the right to property, protected under Article 21 of the Inter-American Convention

the Human Rights Committee with regard to Surinam (UN Doc. CCPR/CO/80/SUR, 4 May 2004, para. 21); Sweden (UN Doc. CCPR/CO/74/SWE, 24 April 2002, para. 15); and Guyana (UN Doc. CCPR/C/79/Add.121, 25 April 2000, para. 21). Also see Anaya, 'The Human Rights of Indigenous Peoples', pp. 604–5.

[75] Committee on Economic, Social and Cultural Rights, General Comment 7 on the Right to Adequate Housing (Art. 11.1 of the Covenant): Forced Evictions, 20 May 1997, para. 10.

[76] Committee on Economic, Social and Cultural Rights, General Comment 20 on Non-discrimination in Economic, Social and Cultural Rights (Art. 2, para. 2, of the International Covenant on Economic, Social and Cultural Rights), *UN Doc. E/C.12/GC/20* of 2 July 2009, para. 18.

[77] Decision of the African Commission on Human and Peoples' Rights Regarding Communication 155/96, Social and Economic Rights Action Center, *Center for Economic and Social Rights* v. *Nigeria*, 30st session, Banjul, October 2001, paras. 55–8.

[78] Ibid.

on Human Rights. In this respect, the case of the *Saramaka People* v. *Surinam* is particularly relevant.[79] In that case, the Court determined first of all that Article 1 of the ICESCR and the ICCPR, to which Surinam was a party, grants a right to indigenous and tribal peoples to freely dispose of their natural wealth and resources in such a way as not to be deprived of their means of subsistence.[80] In the light of these provisions, the Court interpreted Article 21 of the Inter-American Convention relating to the protection of property to 'call for the right of members of indigenous and tribal communities to freely determine and enjoy their own social, cultural and economic development . . . grant[ing] to the members of the Saramaka community the right to enjoy property in accordance with their communal tradition'.[81]

Moreover, the Court determined that if the State wanted to impose restrictions on the property rights of the members of the Saramaka people by issuing concessions within their territory, the State must abide by the following three conditions: (1) the State must ensure the effective participation of the members of the Saramaka people in the project, including a duty to actively consult the community and to obtain their free, prior and informed consent; (2) the State must guarantee that the Saramakas will receive a reasonable benefit from any such project within their territory; and (3) the State must perform an environmental and social impact assessment prior to issuing concessions.[82]

In a recent case regarding the *Sarayaku People* v. *Ecuador*, the Inter-American Court elaborated on the duty to consult indigenous peoples. The most significant aspect of this is that the Court decided that the duty to consult constitutes a general principle of international law.[83] The Court also considered that the consultation process should entail a 'genuine dialogue as part of a participatory process in order to reach an agreement' and that the process must be construed as 'a true instrument of participation', carried out in 'good faith', with 'mutual trust' and with the goal of reaching a consensus.[84]

All of the case law of these international human rights bodies to some extent recognises the obligation of a State to engage people in decisions regarding the use of natural resources situated on their lands. This is a

[79] Inter-American Court of Human Rights, *Case of the Saramaka People* v. *Surinam*, Judgment of 28 November 2007.

[80] Ibid., para. 93. [81] Ibid., para. 95. [82] Ibid., para. 129, paras. 133–4.

[83] Inter-American Court of Human Rights, *The Kichwa people of Sarayaku* v. *Ecuador*, Judgment of 26 July 2012, para. 164.

[84] Ibid., paras. 167, 186 and 200. See also Brunner and Quintana, 'The Duty to Consult in the Inter-American System'.

strong argument for interpreting the right of peoples to freely dispose of their natural resources as a right to participate in government decision-making relating to the use of natural resources.

Such a right – or obligation – to public participation has been recognised in several instruments in relation to environmental matters. Principle 10 of the 1992 Rio Declaration, for example, proclaims that '[e]nvironmental issues are best handled with participation of all concerned citizens, at the relevant level'.[85] It also determines that individuals must have 'appropriate access to information concerning the environment that is held by public authorities . . . and the opportunity to participate in decision-making processes'.[86] This entails an obligation of the government to make information available and to provide access to justice for their citizens. Recently, the Rio+20 Declaration emphasised that 'broad public participation and access to information and judicial and administrative proceedings are essential to the promotion of sustainable development'.[87]

In terms of binding legal instruments, reference can be made to the Convention on Access to Information, Public Participation in Decision-Making and Access to Justice in Environmental Matters, concluded in Aarhus in 1998.[88] The Convention entered into force in 2009 and at present 46 parties, mainly European States, are parties to this convention. The Aarhus Convention is the most comprehensive multilateral treaty dealing with the right to public participation. Its objective is 'the protection of the right of every person of present and future generations to live in an environment adequate to his or her health and well-being'.[89] Therefore, parties to the Convention must 'guarantee the rights of access to information, public participation in decision-making, and access to justice in environmental matters'.[90] Relevant obligations for the government include an obligation to provide information to the general public under Article 4 of the Convention, an obligation to provide for the participation of the public concerned in decisions on specific activities, including an obligation to provide information and to be consulted under Article 6 of the Convention, and an obligation to provide access to justice to

[85] Rio Declaration on Environment and Development, Rio de Janeiro, 13 June 1992, *31 ILM 874* (1992).

[86] Ibid.

[87] Rio+20 Declaration: 'The Future We Want', UNGA Resolution 66/288, 11 September 2012, para. 43.

[88] Convention on Access to Information, Public Participation in Decision-Making and Access to Justice in Environmental Matters, 28 June 1998, *2161 UNTS 447*.

[89] Ibid., Article 1. [90] Ibid.

persons who have not received adequate information under Article 9 of the Convention.

Although the Convention is very ambitious and covers various kinds of industrial activities, including activities relating to the exploitation of natural resources, its geographical scope is limited. The Convention is open to all States, but has mainly been ratified by European States. The objective of the Convention is another limitation. It is not concerned with decisions on the exploitation of natural resources in general, but applies only to natural resource projects that may have an impact on the environment.

Furthermore, reference can be made to two international environmental treaties in terms of binding legal instruments, which include provisions on public participation. Article 14(1)(a) of the 1992 Convention on Biological Diversity provides that States must allow public participation in the EIA procedure. In addition, Article 3(a) of the Anti-desertification Convention provides that parties 'should ensure that decisions on the design and implementation of programmes to combat desertification and/or mitigate the effects of drought are taken with the participation of populations and local communities'.

Finally, the right to self-determination, interpreted as a right for peoples to participate in decision making, can also be implemented by means of individual rights protected under the Covenants. After all, the collective right to internal self-determination could be said to entail a right for all human beings living in a State to participate in the organisation of that State's political and economic system.[91] One of the key provisions in this respect is Article 25 of the ICCPR, which states,

> Every citizen shall have the right and the opportunity, without any of the distinctions mentioned in article 2 and without unreasonable restrictions:
> (a) To take part in the conduct of public affairs, directly or through freely chosen representatives;
> (b) To vote and to be elected at genuine periodic elections which shall be by universal and equal suffrage and shall be held by secret ballot, guaranteeing the free expression of the will of the electors;
> (c) To have access, on general terms of equality, to public service in his country.

[91] See, e.g., *The Study of the Historical and Current Development of the Right to Self-Determination*, prepared by A. Cristescu (Romania), Special Rapporteur of the UN Sub-commission on Prevention of Discrimination and Protection of Minorities, UN publication, Sales No. E.80.XIV.3 (1980).

Article 25 of the ICCPR formulates a right for all citizens, i.e., for all the nationals of a State, to participate in the State's decision-making process, a right which can be enforced against the will of the State itself. In its General Comment No. 25 on the right to participate in public affairs, voting rights and the right of equal access to public service, the Human Rights Committee explicitly stated that

> the rights under article 25 are related to . . . the right of peoples to self-determination. By virtue of the rights covered by article 1(1), peoples have the right to freely determine their political status and to enjoy the right to choose the form of their constitution or government. Article 25 deals with the right of individuals to participate in those processes which constitute the conduct of public affairs. Those rights, as individual rights, can give rise to claims under the first Optional Protocol.[92]

Furthermore, the effectiveness of the right is guaranteed by the requirement of genuine and periodic elections and by the implementation of other human rights, such as the right to freedom of expression formulated in Article 19 of the ICCPR and the right to freedom of association included in Article 22 of the ICCPR and Article 8 of the ICESCR.[93]

In addition, reference can be made to public participation in relation to the right of individuals to an adequate standard of living, as enshrined in Article 11 of the ICESCR. This provision contains an obligation for States to take measures, including specific programmes, which are needed

> To improve methods of production, conservation and distribution of food by making full use of technical and scientific knowledge, by disseminating knowledge of the principles of nutrition and by developing or reforming agrarian systems in such a way as to achieve the most efficient development and utilization of natural resources.

In its General Comment on the Right to Adequate Food, the International Committee on Economic, Social and Cultural Rights emphasised that the right to adequate food includes questions regarding the accessibility of natural resources.[94] Furthermore, the Committee provided that '[t]he formulation and implementation of national strategies for the

[92] Human Rights Committee, General Comment No. 25: The Right to Participate in Public Affairs, Voting Rights and the Right of Equal Access to Public Service (Art. 25), 12 July 1996, *UN Doc. CCPR/C/21/Rev.1/Add.7*, para. 2.

[93] Ibid., para. 25.

[94] International Committee on Economic, Social and Cultural Rights, General Comment No. 12: The Right to Adequate Food (Art. 11), *UN Doc. E/C.12/1999/5*, 12 May 1999, para. 13.

right to food requires full compliance with the principles of accountability, transparency, people's participation, decentralization, legislative capacity and the independence of the judiciary'.[95] In addition, the Committee determined that 'appropriate institutional mechanisms should be devised to secure a representative process towards the formulation of a strategy, drawing on all available domestic expertise relevant to food and nutrition'.[96]

Although Article 11 of the ICESCR approaches the issue of natural resources exploitation from the perspective of the right to have access to adequate food, the provision may also be relevant for broader issues relating to the use of natural resources. In particular, the provision can be linked to the prohibition on depriving a people of its means of subsistence, as enshrined in Article 1(2) of the ICESCR. In its General Comment relating to the Right to Adequate Food, the Committee on Economic, Social and Cultural Rights unambiguously emphasised the importance of involving citizens in the development of national strategies to promote the right to food, including access to natural resources.

It can be concluded that the right of a people to economic self-determination in the context of a sovereign State is primarily implemented through the modern right of communities, as well as of individual members of the population of a State, to take part in national and local decision-making processes. The State is obliged to establish proper procedures which allow these rights to be exercised in practice. Furthermore, international human rights bodies can, to a certain extent, assess whether States have met their obligation to provide for public participation.[97]

3.4 The right to development

The right to self-determination includes a right for peoples to 'freely pursue their economic, social and cultural development'. The right to development – as it appears in the Declaration on the Right to Development – constitutes one of the principal means to achieve the right to self-determination, because it formulates a right for peoples and individuals 'to participate in, contribute to, and enjoy economic, social, cultural

[95] Ibid., para. 23. [96] Ibid., para. 24.

[97] On the role of human rights monitoring mechanisms in achieving State compliance with treaty obligations, see Boerefijn, 'Establishing State Responsibility for Breaching Human Rights Treaty Obligations', pp. 167–205; and Zimmermann, 'Human Rights Treaty Bodies and the Jurisdiction of the International Court of Justice', pp. 5–29.

and political development, in which all human rights and fundamental freedoms can be fully realised'.[98]

Furthermore, the right to development 'implies the full realization of the right of peoples to self-determination', which includes sovereignty over natural wealth and resources.[99] In this sense, it can be regarded as a continuation of the right to self-determination for peoples who have organised themselves in independent States. This section traces the evolution, nature and legal status of the right to development and examines its implications for the governance of natural resources within a sovereign State.

3.4.1 Evolution of the right to development

The UN Charter provisions on economic and social cooperation

The right to development is rooted in the UN Charter provisions on international economic and social cooperation. Article 1(3) of the UN Charter states that the aims of the United Nations include achieving 'international co-operation in solving international problems of an economic, social, cultural, or humanitarian character and in promoting and encouraging respect for human rights and for fundamental freedoms for all without distinction as to race, sex, language, or religion'.[100] This rather broad aim was developed in Chapter IX of the UN Charter on international economic and social cooperation. In this respect, Article 55 specifies *inter alia* that the United Nations shall promote 'conditions of economic and social progress and development'. To achieve this aim, Article 56 provides that 'All Members pledge themselves to take joint and separate action in co-operation with the Organization'. Over the years, these provisions have

[98] Article 1(1) of the Declaration on the Right to Development, UNGA Resolution 41/128 of 4 December 1986. On the right to development, see in general, *inter alia*, Sengupta, 'On the Theory and Practice of the Right to Development', pp. 837–89; Abi-Saab, 'Droits de L'Homme et Développement', pp. 3–10; Bunn, 'The Right to Development', pp. 1425–67; Schrijver, 'The Evolution of Sustainable Development in International Law', pp. 269–74; L. Amede Obiora, 'Beyond the Rhetoric of a Right to Development', pp. 355–418; Pellet, *Le Droit International du Développement*; Donnelly, 'In Search of the Unicorn', pp. 473–509.

[99] Article 1(2) of the Declaration on the Right to Development, UNGA Resolution 41/128 of 4 December 1986.

[100] See De Frouville, 'Article 1 Paragraphe 3', p. 358. De Frouville calls Article 1(3) the second pillar of the positive dimension of peace, together with the principle of equal rights and self-determination of peoples.

become the legal foundation for a wide range of UN efforts in the field of international development cooperation.[101]

International Bill of Human Rights

In addition to the provisions of the UN Charter, the human rights instruments which were drawn up in the decades after the establishment of the UN also form the legal basis for the right to development. Although neither the Universal Declaration of Human Rights (UDHR) nor the International Covenants on Economic, Social and Cultural Rights (ICESCR) and on Civil and Political Rights (ICCPR) contain an express reference to a human right to development, constituent elements of such a right, as well as modalities for its realisation, can be found in all three instruments. Substantive elements of a right to development comprise first of all the right of peoples to 'freely pursue their economic, social and cultural development' and the right not to be deprived of their own means of subsistence, both of which are part of the right to self-determination included in the identical Articles 1 of the ICESCR and the ICCPR.

Furthermore, Article 25 of the UDHR and Article 11 of the ICESCR formulate a right for all human beings to an adequate standard of living, which includes a right to 'adequate food, clothing and housing, and to the continuous improvement of living conditions'. In addition, there is also the right to education incorporated in Article 26 of the UDHR and Article 13 of the ICESCR. In a general statement on the importance and relevance of the right to development, the Committee on Economic, Social and Cultural Rights emphasised the complementary character of the rights included in the Covenant and the right to development.[102]

As regards the modalities, Article 22 of the UDHR formulates a right for everyone to 'the realization, through national effort and international co-operation and in accordance with the organization and resources of each State, of the economic, social and cultural rights indispensable for his dignity and the free development of his personality'. In addition, Article

[101] See the Repertory of the Practice of United Nations Organs, in particular with regard to Article 55, available at www.un.org/law/repertory/. From the early beginnings of the world organisation, practice of UN organs relating to the promotion of development under Article 55 has covered a broad range of issues, including technical and financial assistance of developing countries, international trade and finance, natural resources and the protection of the environment. As Pellet noted, from the very start, the UN adopted an integrated approach to development issues. Pellet, 'Article 55, alinéas a et b', p. 1464.

[102] Committee on Economic, Social and Cultural Rights, Statement on the Importance and Relevance of the Right to Development, Adopted on the Occasion of the Twenty-Fifth Anniversary of the Declaration on the Right to Development, 12 July 2011, *UN Doc. E/C.12/2011/2*, para. 5.

28 of the UDHR formulates a right for everyone to a conducive social and international order.[103] Article 2(1) of the ICESCR also formulates an obligation for parties 'to take steps, individually and through international assistance and co-operation . . . with a view to achieving progressively the full realization of the rights recognised in the present Covenant by all appropriate means', including the above-mentioned right to an adequate standard of living.[104]

Towards the formulation of a right to development

In the years following the adoption of the 1966 Human Rights Covenants, the right to development started to materialise, notably through resolutions of the UN General Assembly and the work of the Commission on Human Rights. First, the UN General Assembly adopted a substantive Declaration on Social Progress and Development in 1969, which identified development as one of the 'common concerns of the international community'.[105] This reference to the notion of 'common concern' is significant. In international environmental law, the notion of 'common concern' has gained currency as a principle which forms the basis for imposing binding obligations for States in specific cases. These obligations concern not only affected States, but also the international community as a whole (*erga omnes* obligations). It is one of the guiding principles of the 1992 UN Framework Convention on Climate Change and the 1992 Convention on Biological Diversity.[106] Therefore, by referring to the notion of

[103] Universal Declaration of Human Rights, *UNGA Resolution 217 (III)* on an International Bill of Human Rights, adopted on 10 December 1948. In Alston's view, Article 28 of the UDHR must be seen as 'a fact of fundamental importance in establishing the principle that respect for human rights is not a narrowly focused obligation applying only within strict limits to relations between individuals and their States, but rather is an open-ended obligation applying to all societal relations whether at the local, national or international level'. Alston, 'The Shortcomings of a "Garfield the Cat" Approach to the Right to Development', p. 515.

[104] In this respect, the Committee on Economic, Social and Cultural Rights has issued a general comment in which it emphasised that 'in accordance with Articles 55 and 56 of the Charter of the United Nations, with well-established principles of international law, and with the provisions of the Covenant itself, international cooperation for development and thus for the realization of economic, social and cultural rights is an obligation of all States'. General Comment 3 of the Committee on Economic, Social and Cultural Rights on the Nature of States Parties Obligations (Art. 2, para. 1 of the Covenant), para. 14, Report of the Fifth Session, *UN Doc. E/1991/23*, 14 December 1990.

[105] Declaration on Social Progress and Development, *UNGA Resolution 2542 (XXIV)*, adopted on 11 December 1969, Article 9.

[106] For an analysis of the notion of 'common concern', see Shelton, 'Common Concern of Humanity', pp. 83–90; and Brunnée, 'Common Areas, Common Heritage and Common Concern', pp. 564–7.

'common concern', the Declaration not only emphasises the fundamental importance of development for the international community as a whole but also, arguably, lays the foundation for imposing binding obligations upon States.

The Declaration also incorporates some basic elements of a right to development. It formulates a right for all peoples and human beings to 'live in dignity and freedom and to enjoy the fruits of social progress'.[107] In addition, it includes a list of elements that are considered 'primary conditions of social progress and development', including permanent sovereignty over natural wealth and resources.[108]

The promotion of development is also the underlying rationale for the resolutions related to the call for a NIEO. One of the principal aims of the proposed new international economic order was to 'ensure steadily accelerating economic and social development . . . for present and future generations'.[109] The Charter of Economic Rights and Duties of States, adopted in the same year, lists '[i]nternational cooperation for development' among the fundamental principles of international economic relations.[110] In addition, Article 17 of the Charter formulates an obligation of States to cooperate for development, while Article 7 assigns the primary responsibility 'to promote the economic, social and cultural development of its people' to the national State.

Although these resolutions can be said to pave the way for the right to development, they approach development as an objective rather than as a right. In fact, development was not mentioned as a human right until 1977, when the Commission on Human Rights adopted a resolution in which it requested the UN Secretary-General to carry out a study on

> the international dimensions of the right to development as a human right in relation with other human rights based on international cooperation, including the right to peace, taking into account the requirements of the New International Economic Order and the fundamental human needs.[111]

[107] Declaration on Social Progress and Development, *UNGA Resolution 2542 (XXIV)*, adopted on 11 December 1969, Article 1.

[108] Ibid., Article 3.

[109] Declaration on the Establishment of a New International Economic Order, *UNGA Resolution 3201 (S-VI)*, adopted on 1 May 1974, third paragraph of the preamble.

[110] Charter of Economic Rights and Duties of States, *UNGA Resolution 3281 (XXIV)*, adopted on 12 December 1974, Chap. I, under (n).

[111] Resolution 4 (XXX-III) of the UN Commission on Human Rights, *UN Doc. E/CN.4/SR.1389 (1977)*, 21 February 1971. The report on the international dimensions of the right to development, published in 1979, was complemented with a report on the regional and national dimensions of the right to development as a human right in

This Resolution has served as a catalyst for successive efforts to determine the contents of the right to development as part of the so-called 'structural approach to human rights' which emerged in the late 1970s.[112] These efforts resulted in the 1986 Declaration on the Right to Development.

The 1986 Declaration on the Right to Development

The 1986 Declaration on the Right to Development, adopted with 146 votes in favour, eight abstentions and one negative vote from the United States, defines the human right to development as an 'inalienable human right' that entitles 'every human person and all peoples to participate in, contribute to, and enjoy economic, social and political development, in which all human rights and fundamental freedoms can be fully recognized'.[113] In this respect, 'development' is defined as a 'comprehensive economic, social, cultural and political process, which aims at the constant improvement of the well-being of the entire population and of all individuals on the basis of their active, free and meaningful participation in development and in the fair distribution of benefits resulting therefrom'.[114] Thus, the right to development may be defined as a collective and individual right to participate in the process of development and to enjoy the benefits resulting from it.

Article 1 also provides that the right to development 'implies the full realization of the right of peoples to self-determination, which includes, subject to the relevant provisions of both 1966 Human Rights Covenants, the exercise of their inalienable right to full sovereignty over all their natural wealth and resources'. Thus, the realisation of the right to self-determination is regarded as an essential precondition for exercising the right to development. After all, how can the right to development be

1981. However, neither of these reports, although both affirm the existence of a right to development, sheds any light on the contents of such a right. See Report of the Secretary-General on the International Dimensions of the Right to Development, *UN Doc. E/CN.4/1334 (1979)*; Report of the Secretary-General on the Regional and National Dimensions of the Right to Development, *UN Doc. E/CN.4/1421* (*Part I*) and *E/CN.4/1488 (PART II and III) (1981)*.

112 On the structural approach to human rights, see, e.g., Salomon, *Global Responsibility for Human Rights*.

113 Declaration on the Right to Development, *UNGA Resolution 41/128*, adopted on 4 December 1986, Article 1. For voting information, see the 1986 Yearbook of the United Nations, pp. 717–21. On the declaration, see Kiwanuka, 'Developing Rights', pp. 257–72. On the United States position towards the right to development, see Marks, 'The Human Right to Development', pp. 141–60.

114 Declaration on the Right to Development, preamble, second paragraph.

realised if people do not control their own economic means or have the political power to shape their own developmental policies?

Conversely, it could be argued that the right to self-determination can only be realised by exercising the right to development. It should be remembered that the right to self-determination is defined in the identical Articles 1(1) of the 1966 Covenants as a right for peoples to 'freely determine their political status and freely pursue their economic, social and cultural development'. To be able to freely pursue their economic, social and cultural development, peoples must have a right to shape their development process, and, both as individuals and communities, participate in this process and enjoy its benefits. This is precisely what the right to development seeks to achieve.[115] Therefore, the right to development and the right to self-determination must be regarded as being mutually reinforcing.

The Declaration also defines the subjects of the right to development. According to Article 1 of the Declaration, the right to development accrues to individuals and peoples. In this respect, Article 2(1) of the Declaration emphasises that the human person is both the 'central subject of development' and 'the active participant and beneficiary of the right to development'. As such, the human person is also responsible for the implementation of the right to development, both individually and collectively. However, primary responsibility for the implementation of the right to development is assigned to States. According to Article 3(1) of the Declaration, 'States have the primary responsibility for the creation of national and international conditions favourable to the realization of the right to development'.

At the international level, States have an obligation, *inter alia*, to take steps to formulate international development policies and must cooperate to promote, encourage and strengthen universal respect for and

[115] Declaration on the Right to Development, Article 1: 'The right to development is an inalienable human right by virtue of which every human person and all peoples are entitled *to participate in, contribute to, and enjoy* economic, social and political development', and Article 2(3): 'States have the right and the duty to formulate appropriate national development policies that aim at the constant improvement of the well-being of the entire population and of all individuals, *on the basis of their active, free and meaningful participation in development and the fair distribution of the benefits resulting therefrom*'. Author's emphasis added. Also see Bedjaoui, 'The Right to Development', p. 1188: 'There is little sense in recognizing self-determination as a superior and inviolable principle if one does not recognize at the same time a "right to development" for the peoples that have achieved self-determination. This right to development can only be an "inherent" and "built-in" right forming an inseparable part of the right to self-determination'.

observance of human rights.[116] At the national level, Article 8 of the Declaration provides that States should take all necessary measures for the realisation of the right to development and that they have an obligation to ensure, *inter alia,* equality of opportunity for all in their access to basic resources and the fair distribution of income. In addition, it provides that 'States should encourage public participation in all spheres as an important factor in development and in the full realization of all human rights'.

From the 1986 Declaration to the 1993 Vienna Declaration and beyond

The 1993 World Conference on Human Rights, which produced the Vienna Declaration and Programme of Action, was the next benchmark in the evolution of the right to development.[117] Like the Declaration on the Right to Development, the Vienna Declaration points to the human person as the central subject of development and assigns responsibility for the realisation of the right to States, both at the national and international level.[118]

The Declaration also designates the right to development 'as a universal and inalienable right and an integral part of fundamental human rights' and underlines the interrelationship between human rights and development by stipulating that 'while development facilitates the enjoyment of all human rights, the lack of development may not be invoked to justify the abridgement of internationally recognised human rights'.[119]

In addition, the Declaration establishes a direct link between the right to development, on one hand, and the protection of the environment, on the other. In this respect, paragraph 11 of the Vienna Declaration reiterates principle 3 of the 1992 Rio Declaration on Environment and Development, which states that '[t]he right to development should be

[116] Articles 4 and 6 of the Declaration.

[117] Vienna Declaration and Programme of Action, *UN Doc. A/CONF.157/23*, adopted on 12 July 1993.

[118] Paragraph 10 of the declaration determines that 'States should cooperate with each other in ensuring development and eliminating obstacles to development. The international community should promote an effective international cooperation for the realization of the right to development and the elimination of obstacles to development'. In addition, it stipulates that 'lasting progress towards the implementation of the right to development requires effective development policies at the national level, as well as equitable economic relations and a favourable economic environment at the international level'.

[119] Ibid.

fulfilled so as to meet equitably the developmental and environmental needs of present and future generations'.

In the years following the adoption of the Vienna Declaration, the right to development was confirmed in several important outcome documents, such as the Millennium Declaration, the Monterrey Consensus, the 2005 World Summit Outcome and the 2012 Outcome Document of the United Nations Conference on Sustainable Development.[120] Moreover, it served as a stimulus to the formulation of new development strategies, such as the Millennium Development Goals (MDGs), which are aimed at integrating all the aspects of the development process.[121] Nevertheless, it seems as though the idea of development as a human right has shifted to the background to some extent in favour of development as an all-encompassing objective.

3.4.2 *The nature and legal status of the right to development*

The right to development has evolved in particular in the resolutions of the UN General Assembly and other UN organs. The only legally binding instrument which formulates a right to development is the African Charter on Human and Peoples' Rights.[122] The lack of recognition of the right to development in legally binding instruments has led to a fierce debate in the legal literature on the status of the right to development as an autonomous legal right. As Nico Schrijver noted, advocates of the right to development have sometimes elevated it 'to lofty heights', while opponents regard it as 'a dangerous smokescreen'.[123] Moreover, some authors, such as Arjun Sengupta, try to avoid the issue altogether by making a

[120] See paragraph 11 of the Millennium Declaration, *UNGA Resolution 55/2 (2000)*, adopted on 18 September 2000; paragraph 11 of the Monterrey Consensus, Report of the International Conference on Financing for Development, *UN Doc. A/CONF.198/11*, adopted on 22 March 2002; paragraph 24(b) of the 2005 World Summit Outcome, *UNGA Resolution 60/1*, adopted on 24 October 2005; and paragraph 8 of the Outcome Document of the 2012 United Nations Conference on Sustainable Development, 'The Future We Want', *UNGA Resolution 66/288*, adopted on 11 September 2012.

[121] On the relationship between the MDGs and human rights, including the right to development, see Alston, 'Ships Passing in the Night', pp. 755–829.

[122] Article 22 of the African Charter determines that 'All peoples shall have the right to their economic, social and cultural development with due regard to their freedom and identity and in the equal enjoyment of the common heritage of mankind' and that 'States shall have the duty, individually or collectively, to ensure the exercise of the right to development'.

[123] Schrijver, 'The Evolution of Sustainable Development in International Law', 271. Proponents of a right to development include Alston, 'The Shortcomings of a "Garfield the Cat" Approach to the Right to Development', pp. 510–18; Sengupta, 'On the Theory and

distinction between human rights and legal rights. In Arjun Sengupta's opinion, it is perfectly possible for a right to be a human right without being a legal right.[124] However, in the present author's opinion, the significance of a moral right devoid of legal meaning is questionable.

Arguably it would be going too far to consider the right to development to be a full-fledged human right, but that is not to say that the right is without legal relevance. In Kiwanuka's words, '[e]ven if the Declaration [on the Right to Development] cannot be endowed with legal authority, in positivist terms, that would not necessarily mean that it is stripped of all relevance and utility in international law'.[125] On the contrary, in the present author's view, the right to development has two dimensions which add to the existing core of human rights and which give the right some legal significance.

First of all, at the very least, the right to development can be characterised as 'the sum of existing human rights', which include the right to life, to an adequate standard of living and to education.[126] By extension, the right to development may be defined as an umbrella right which integrates these individual economic, social and cultural rights, as well as some dimensions of civil and political rights, most notably empowerment rights such as the rights to freedom of opinion and association. The added value of the right to development would then primarily be its emphasis on the interrelated and indivisible qualities of these individual rights. In this sense, the right to development can first be characterised as a 'participatory right' aimed at the realisation of human rights pertaining to development.[127] At the national level, the right to development would then give rise to a right for all individuals to participate in the realisation of economic, social and cultural rights, as well as a corresponding obligation for the State to implement economic, social and cultural rights in such a way as to give due weight to the interests of all individuals in a State, and not only to a small segment of society.[128]

Practice of the Right to Development', pp. 1177–1203. Opponents include Ghai, 'Whose Human Right to Development?' and Donnelly, 'In Search of the Unicorn', pp. 473–509.

124 Sengupta, 'On the Theory and Practice of the Right to Development', pp. 859–60.

125 Kiwanuka, 'Developing Rights', p. 271. Bunn even argues that 'the prevailing view is that the right to development is, at the very least, on the threshold of acceptance as a principle of positive international law', but she does not sufficiently elaborate her argument. Bunn, 'The Right to Development', p. 1436.

126 Schrijver, 'The Evolution of Sustainable Development in International Law', p. 271.

127 For the idea of the right to development as a participatory right, see Orford, 'Globalization and the Right to Development', p. 138.

128 Compare Georges Abi-Saab, who argues that 'si la réalisation du droit collectif est une condition nécessaire pour garantir la pleine jouissance des droits individuels qui s'y

The legal basis for this obligation is found, in the first place, in Article 2 of the ICESCR concerning the obligations of States parties to the ICESCR and in Article 25 of the ICCPR concerning public participation in decision making.[129] At the international level, it can be argued that the right to development is reflected in the collective obligation of States to cooperate for the realisation of economic, social and cultural rights as incorporated in Article 2(1) and Article 23 of the ICESCR.

Furthermore, the right to development develops the principle of permanent sovereignty over natural resources, as well as the right to self-determination, in more detail. For the purposes of this book, one of the essential aspects is that the right to development not only entails a right to participate in the development process, but also entails a right to enjoy the fruits of development.[130] In this way, it extends the obligation of a government to exercise the right of permanent sovereignty over natural resources for national development and the well-being of the people, as well as the right to 'pursue economic, social and cultural development' as part of the right to self-determination. The principle of permanent sovereignty over natural resources and the right to self-determination

rattachent, elle n'en est pas une condition suffisante. Ainsi, la plupart des pays ayant accédé à l'indépendance après la seconde guerre mondiale, le respect des droits civils et politiques laisse beaucoup à désirer. Et le même danger guette le droit au développement, si les élites coercitives et exploitantes qui ont confisqué le pouvoir politique une fois l'indépendance acquise, réussissent à détourner à leur bénéfice exclusif les fruits du droit au développement ainsi conçu (c'est-à-dire les bienfaits d'un environnement économique plus favorable), plutôt que de les laisser se répandre à toutes les couches de la population'. Abi-Saab, 'Droits de L'Homme et Développement', pp. 6–7.

[129] In this respect, see General Comment No. 3 of the Committee on Economic, Social and Cultural Rights on the Nature of States Parties' Obligations (Art. 2, para. 1), Report of the Fifth Session, *UN Doc. E/1991/23*, para. 8: 'The Committee notes that the undertaking 'to take steps . . . by all appropriate means including particularly the adoption of legislative measures' neither requires nor precludes any particular form of government or economic system being used as the vehicle for the steps in question, *provided only that it is democratic and that all human rights are thereby respected*'. Author's emphasis added. Also see General Comment No. 20 on Non-discrimination in economic, social and cultural rights (Art. 2, para. 2), UN Doc. *E/C.12/GC/20*, 2 July 2009, which explains the different forms of and grounds for discrimination and which contains guidelines to assess the legitimacy of differential treatment.

[130] See the Declaration on the Right to Development. Article 1 of the Declaration formulates a right 'to participate in, contribute to, and *enjoy* economic, social, cultural and political development', while Article 2(3) formulates a duty for States 'to formulate appropriate national development policies that aim at the constant improvement of the well-being of the entire population and of all individuals, on the basis of their active, free and meaningful participation in development *and in the fair distribution of the benefits resulting therefrom*'. Author's emphasis added.

should then be interpreted as entailing a right for peoples to enjoy the fruits of development.

Therefore, it may be concluded that despite the present uncertainties regarding its precise content and legal implications, the right to development can play an important role in realising development. It can do so in four different ways. First, by means of its integrating function. As an umbrella right, the right to development can play an important role in connecting different human rights with the aim of realising economic, social and cultural development. Second, the collective dimension of the right to development emphasises the inclusive approach that is necessary to realise development. It clearly shows that the right to development can only be realised if all sectors of society are included in the development process. Third, the dual nature of the right to development as a collective as well as an individual right can be instrumental in facilitating interaction between collective and individual rights. Finally, the right to development can be instrumental in shaping the contents of other human rights related to development, such as the right to education. This was also recognised by the chairs of different UN treaty bodies, when they resolved in a joint statement 'to make a concerted effort to promote a development-informed and interdependence-based reading of all human rights treaties, so as to highlight and emphasize the relevance and importance of the right to development in interpreting and applying human rights treaty provisions'.[131]

3.4.3 The implementation of the right to development within the sovereign State

The right to development implies that States should implement procedures in their domestic legislation which permit individuals and communities to participate in the development process, while ensuring a fair distribution of the benefits of development in society. Nevertheless, there is rarely any practice or case law at the international level that develops these basic obligations.

As stated above, the African Charter on Human and Peoples' Rights is the only legally binding instrument that recognises a right to development. Some practice relating to the right to development can be found within the framework of this Convention. The most notable example is

[131] United Nations Office of the High Commissioner for Human Rights, *Joint Statement of Chairpersons of the UN Treaty Bodies*, 1 July 2011.

the case of the *Endorois People* v. *Kenya* before the African Commission on Human Rights. The Endorois people, an indigenous people living in Kenya, alleged that their right to development had been violated as a result of the State's creation of a Game Reserve in Endorois lands and its failure to adequately involve the Endorois in the development process. The African Commission stated that 'recognising the right to development requires fulfilling five main criteria: it must be equitable, non-discriminatory, participatory, accountable, and transparent, with equity and [freedom of] choice as important, over-arching themes in the right to development'.[132]

It also noted that consultation is an important element of the right to development. In this respect, consultation should be interpreted in terms of participation in government policies that concern those involved, rather than a mere right to be informed of such policies.[133] If a project carried out by a government on indigenous lands were to have a major impact on the territory, consultation should even be interpreted as implying a requirement to obtain the free, prior and informed consent of the indigenous people.[134]

The Commission also touched on the issue of sharing benefits, which it linked to the right of property and compensation for the loss of property, rather than directly to the right to development.[135] In relation to the right to development, the Commission merely stated that 'the right to development will be violated when the development in question decreases the well-being of the community'.[136] Although it is unfortunate that the Commission did not expressly state that the issue of sharing benefits is a constituent element of the right to development, the Commission's statement does have an interesting implication for the purposes of the present book. Arguably, it implies that a government that decreases the well-being of the population as a result of its governance of natural resources violates the right to development.

3.5 Appraisal

The current chapter has examined 'peoples' as subjects and beneficiaries of the principle of permanent sovereignty over natural resources. It addressed this issue from the perspective of peoples' rights, in particular

[132] *African Commission on Human and Peoples' Rights, Centre for Minority Rights Development (Kenya) and Minority Rights Group International on behalf of Endorois Welfare Council* v. *Kenya*, 276/2003, para. 277.

[133] Ibid., para. 281. [134] Ibid., para. 291. [135] Ibid., para. 294. [136] Ibid.

from the perspective of the right to self-determination, which incorporates the principle of permanent sovereignty over natural resources, and from the perspective of the closely related right to development.

In relations between States, the right to self-determination entails first of all a right for peoples to choose their political organisation, including – under exceptional circumstances – secession. In view of the major implications of this right, it accrues to very narrowly defined categories of peoples, mainly colonial peoples and peoples under foreign domination. In this sense, the right is addressed to 'other' States, in the sense that other States have to respect a people's right of self-determination. As soon as a people has organised itself in an independent State, the right to external self-determination becomes vested in the State. As such, it falls under State sovereignty and becomes subject to the principle of nonintervention. This sovereign dimension includes the State's right to freely dispose of its natural resources, excluding other States. The right to development is a logical continuation of the right to self-determination. Arguably, it entails an obligation for other States to assist each other with the development process. However, this right does not yet have a firm basis in international law.

Furthermore, this chapter has argued that the right to self-determination and the right to development have an internal dimension as well. In the context of the sovereign State, the right to self-determination refers first of all to the right of the population of a State, as the sum of the peoples of the State, to freely choose the State's political and economic system. It also includes the right of minorities and indigenous peoples to govern their local affairs.

In addition, the right to internal self-determination includes a right to freely pursue economic, social and cultural development. This right is expressed in the right to economic self-determination, which includes a right to have access to the economic means to achieve development. The right to freely pursue economic, social and cultural development can become effective based on the right to development, understood as a right of peoples and individuals to participate in, contribute to, and enjoy economic, social, cultural and political development.

As regards implementing the right to internal self-determination and the right to development, it is argued that the main way to give effect to these rights is by public participation in decision making. This implies, for example, that a government should consult local communities that may be affected by particular resource projects. However, it is striking that the relevant case law of human rights bodies on public participation focuses in particular on the protection of indigenous peoples. Those communities are given a right to participate in decision making with the specific aim of preserving their culture and traditional lifestyle.

One important drawback of most complaint mechanisms of human rights bodies is that they are open only to individuals who claim to be directly affected by government decisions. This requirement stands in the way of claims that serve a more general interest. For example, if concessions are issued in areas that are remote from human habitation, it is not possible to file a complaint before a human rights body, even if the concessions have a serious impact on the environment. Furthermore, on the same grounds, it is not possible to challenge a government's failure to provide for public participation regarding decisions on the expenditure of resource revenues.

The realisation of the right to self-determination and the right to development therefore depends largely on whether or not individual States implement the ensuing obligations in national law. According to the Human Rights Committee, the implementation of the right to self-determination requires States to put in place procedures that permit this right to be exercised in practice. The Human Rights Committee, as well as the Committee on Economic, Social and Cultural Rights, has the formal mandate to oversee the implementation of the identical Articles 1 of the 1966 Covenants. Both committees have devoted a great deal of attention to securing the right of indigenous peoples to self-determination through a combined reading of Article 1 of the ICESCR and the ICCPR and other provisions of the Covenants covering individual rights.

It would therefore be laudable if these – and other – human rights bodies were to adopt a more active approach to ensuring the proper implementation of the right to internal self-determination for other communities as well, most notably by emphasising the importance of public participation for the realisation of the right in their reports and comments. One possible avenue for these human rights bodies would be to interpret treaty provisions that have a bearing on participation of citizens in decisions affecting their well-being in the light of identical Articles 1 of the ICESCR and the ICCPR. Relevant provisions include the right to an adequate standard of living, enshrined in Article 11 of the ICESCR, and the right to participate in a State's decision-making processes, enshrined in Article 25 of the ICCPR.

4

Environmental law obligations relevant to the governance of natural resources

4.1 Introductory remarks

This chapter discusses the role of international environmental law in determining the right of States and peoples to freely dispose of their natural resources. It examines two principal ways in which international environmental law impacts this right. First of all, it examines principles formulated by international environmental law for the exploitation of natural resources and the protection of the environment. Relevant principles include the obligations to conserve and sustainably use natural wealth and resources, to safeguard natural resources for future generations, to prevent damage to the environments of other States, and to adopt a precautionary approach to the protection of the environment and natural resources.[1]

Second, international environmental law contains several 'common regimes' aimed at protecting natural resources or parts of the environment because of the importance they have for several States. The number of States with a stake in a common regime may vary from two, in the case of shared natural resources, to the entire community of States, in the case of world heritage. A general feature of these common regimes is that they impose obligations upon States to protect the interests of the larger community of States. The aim of this chapter is to assess how and to what extent all these obligations under international environmental law qualify the right of States to freely dispose of their natural resources.

One of the principal reasons for examining the principles and regimes discussed in this chapter is the hypothesis that they are relevant not

[1] For different categorisations of the principles of international law, see Atapattu, *Emerging Principles of International Environmental Law*; Birnie, Boyle and Redgwell, *International Law and the Environment*, 3rd edn.; Sands and Peel, *Principles of International Environmental Law*, 3rd edn.; Schrijver, *Sovereignty over Natural Resources*; and Schrijver, 'The Evolution of Sustainable Development in International Law', pp. 221–412.

only to the protection of natural resources and the environment in times of peace, but also relevant in situations of armed conflict. This is discussed in more detail in Chapter 6 of this book, while the current chapter focuses on the content of the obligations arising from these principles and common regimes and their implications for the principle of permanent sovereignty.

Section 4.2 discusses the origins and structure of international environmental law in order to provide the necessary context. Section 4.3 then discusses the relevant principles of international environmental law and their legal status. Section 4.4 discusses several common regimes and the obligations ensuing from them. Finally, Section 4.5 draws some final conclusions about the role of international environmental law and the limits it places on the right of States and peoples to freely dispose of their natural resources.

4.2 Origins and structure of international environmental law

This section briefly introduces international environmental law as a field of international law. International environmental law has some distinctive characteristics, and this section discusses some of them for a proper understanding of this field.

4.2.1 Origins of international environmental law

International environmental law has evolved relatively recently. Although early efforts aimed at the protection of particular ecosystems, such as rivers and forests, can be traced back to the nineteenth century, modern international environmental law originated particularly in the United Nations.[2] In this respect, the United Nations Conference on the Human Environment held in Stockholm in 1972 is usually seen as the catalyst for the development of a body of law pertaining to the protection of the environment.[3]

The principal objective of this modern international environmental law is to protect and conserve the environment for the benefit of present

[2] For a brief outline of the evolution of international environmental law, see Sand, 'The Evolution of International Environmental Law', pp. 29–43; and Sands and Peel, *Principles of International Environmental Law*, 3rd edn., Chap. 2.

[3] See Ragazzi, *The Concept of International Obligations Erga Omnes*, p. 154; and Sand, 'The Evolution of International Environmental Law', pp. 33–4, who emphasises that the Stockholm Conference was the 'culmination of an intense preparatory process'.

and future generations of humanity. The 1972 Stockholm Declaration of the United Nations Conference on the Human Environment rather poetically emphasised the importance of the environment for human life and development by stating that 'Man is both creature and moulder of his environment, which gives him physical sustenance and affords him the opportunity for intellectual, moral, social and spiritual growth', and it added that the environment is 'essential to his well-being and to the enjoyment of basic human rights – even the right to life itself'.[4]

Since the late 1980s, international environmental law has become integrated with international development law. These two fields of law have been connected by the principle of sustainable development, which was defined by the World Commission on Environment and Development, the Brundtland Commission, in its report *Our Common Future* as 'development that meets the needs of the present without compromising the ability of future generations to meet their own needs'.[5] The principle of sustainable development evolved to become one of the basic aims of international environmental law.[6] Conversely, environmental protection constitutes an integral part of sustainable development, which also embraces economic and social development.[7] This is especially clear from Principle 4 of the Rio Declaration, which proclaims that '[i]n order to achieve sustainable development, environmental protection shall constitute an integral part of the development process and cannot be considered in isolation from it'.[8]

[4] Declaration of the United Nations Conference on the Human Environment, Stockholm, 16 June 1972, *11 ILM 1416 (1972)*, para. 1 of the preamble.

[5] World Commission on Environment and Development, *Our Common Future*, Oxford: Oxford University Press 1987, p. 8.

[6] Bodansky, Brunnée and Hey even refer to it as 'the organizing principle for international environmental law'. See Bodansky, Brunnée and Hey, 'International Environmental Law: Mapping the Field', p. 15. Sustainable development has also been referred to as a 'meta-principle'. In this respect, see Lowe, 'Sustainable Development and Unsustainable Arguments', p. 31.

[7] In this respect, the Johannesburg Declaration has identified three 'interdependent and mutually reinforcing pillars of sustainable development': 'economic development, social development and environmental protection'. Johannesburg Declaration on Sustainable Development, Annex to the Report of the World Summit on Sustainable Development, A/CONF.199/20, 26 August–4 September 2002, para. 5. In addition, see Sands and Peel, *Principles of International Environmental Law*, 3rd edn., p. 10, who argue that sustainable development law is broader than international environmental law, in that it includes, apart from environmental issues, 'the social and economic dimension of development, the participatory role of major groups, and financial and other means of implementation'.

[8] Rio Declaration on Environment and Development, Rio de Janeiro, 13 June 1992, *31 ILM 874 (1992)*, Principle 4.

The need to strike a balance between economic development and the protection of the environment in order to preserve the long-term development potential of humanity is central to the principle of sustainable development. Arguably, this approach entails not only obligations for States regarding the use of natural resources which directly contribute to development, but also an obligation to conserve particular ecosystems or species because of the role they play in maintaining a balance in nature, which is essential to sustain human life in the long term.[9] This can be achieved by adopting an ecosystem approach to sustainable development. This approach is central to the 1992 Convention on Biological Diversity and can be described as 'a strategy for the integrated management of land, water and living resources that promotes conservation and sustainable use in an equitable way'.[10]

During the 1990s and early 2000s the principle of sustainable development was also promoted at a number of important international summits, including the 2000 Millennium World Summit, the 2002 Johannesburg Summit on Sustainable Development, the 2005 World Summit and, most recently, the 2012 Rio+20 Summit on Sustainable Development.[11] These summits have contributed to strengthening the legal status of the principle of sustainable development.

Reference should also be made to the New Delhi Declaration of Principles of International Law Relating to Sustainable Development, adopted by the International Law Association (ILA) in 2002.[12] Although this Declaration is not legally binding in any way, it can be considered to be an authoritative statement regarding the state of the law in relation to sustainable development, as it is based on an extensive study of State practice, judicial decisions and treaty law.[13]

This Declaration identifies seven principles that are considered 'instrumental in pursuing the objective of sustainable development in an effective way'. These are the duty of States to ensure the sustainable use of

[9] This is expressed through the concept of intergenerational equity. See Brown-Weiss, *In Fairness to Future Generations.*

[10] See www.cbd.int/ecosystem/ for more information on the ecosystem approach in relation to the Convention on Biological Diversity.

[11] See Schrijver, 'The Evolution of Sustainable Development in International Law', pp. 221–412. For the Rio+20 Summit, see the outcome document of the 2012 United Nations Conference on Sustainable Development, 'The Future We Want', annexed to UNGA Resolution 66/288 of 11 September 2012.

[12] ILA New Delhi Declaration of Principles of International Law Relating to Sustainable Development, adopted on 2 April 2002, *UN Doc. A/57/329* of 31 August 2002.

[13] See the fifth and final report of the ILA Committee on Legal Aspects of Sustainable Development (2002), the committee which prepared the New Delhi Declaration.

natural resources, the principle of equity and the eradication of poverty, the principle of common but differentiated responsibilities, the principle of the precautionary approach to human health, natural resources and ecosystems, the principle of public participation and access to information and justice, the principle of good governance and the principle of integration and interrelationship, in particular in relation to human rights and social, economic and environmental objectives. Some of these principles are examined in the current chapter, in particular the principle of sustainable use, the principle of equity and the precautionary principle, while others, in particular the principle of public participation and the principle of good governance, were discussed in previous chapters.

4.2.2 *Structure of international environmental law*

A proper understanding of international environmental law requires a brief introduction to its characteristics. One of the characteristics of international environmental law concerns its creation. In addition to the traditional sources of international law formulated in Article 38 of the ICJ Statute, the concept of 'soft law' is particularly important in international environmental law.[14] Soft law processes play a major role in the development of rules in the field of international environmental law.

The world conferences convened by the UN General Assembly and held in Stockholm in 1972 and in Rio de Janeiro in 1992 were particularly instrumental in this respect. These conferences produced important declarations that have had a great impact on the development of international environmental law. While the character of these declarations is partly declaratory in the sense that they formulate some well-established rules of customary international law, they have also had an important programming function.[15] Many of the principles expressed in the declarations subsequently found their way into international treaties or have crystallised as norms of customary international law.

[14] For discussions on the notion of soft law, see, e.g., Boyle and Chinkin, *The Making of International Law*; Shelton, 'International Law and "Relative Normality",' 141–71; Hillgenberg, 'A Fresh Look at Soft Law', 499–515; Kirton and Trebilcock, 'Hard Choices, Soft Law'; Ellis, 'Shades of Grey', 313–34; and Goldmann, 'We Need to Cut Off the Head of the King', 335–68. For a critical analysis of the notion of soft law, see Klabbers, 'The Redundancy of Soft Law', 167–82; and D'Aspremont, *Formalism and the Sources of International Law*.

[15] For a discussion of these terms and the impact of particular UN resolutions on the formation of international environmental law, see Dupuy, *Droit déclaratoire et droit programmatoire de la coutume sauvage a la 'soft law'*.

Other examples of soft law instruments that have stimulated the development of international environmental law include (nonbinding) decisions taken by the conferences of the parties (COP) in particular treaty regimes. Although COP decisions generally concern the implementation of obligations which are already binding under international treaties, some have also substantively and progressively developed the treaty obligations concerned.[16] In addition, reference can be made to the work of United Nations organs, such as the UN Environment Programme (UNEP), and NGOs such as the International Law Association (ILA), which have formulated important rules and guidelines for States.[17]

Another characteristic of international environmental law is directly related to the object it is protecting. Environmental problems often affect not only the interests of individual States, but also the interests of the larger international community of States. Examples include climate change, atmospheric pollution, pollution of the high seas and overfishing. This is why a relatively large number of environmental obligations either operate *erga omnes partes*, i.e., between the parties to a particular treaty regime, or sometimes even *erga omnes*, i.e., between all States whether or not they are party to a particular treaty.[18]

In other words, such international environmental obligations are characterised by their legal indivisibility, in the sense that they 'simultaneously [bind] each and every State concerned with respect to all the others', at least within the context of particular treaty regimes.[19] Thus with respect

[16] On the role of COP decisions in the development of international environmental law, see Gehring, 'Treaty-Making and Treaty Evolution', pp. 469–97.

[17] Compare the UNEP Draft Principles of Conduct in the Field of the Environment for the Guidance of States in the Conservation and Harmonious Utilization of Natural Resources Shared by Two or More States, *17 ILM 1097 (1978)*, discussed in Section 4.4.3, and the ILA New Delhi Declaration of Principles of International Law Relating to Sustainable Development, in *ILA Report of the Seventieth Conference*, New Delhi (2002).

[18] For the distinction between *erga omnes* and reciprocal obligations, see the Case Concerning the Barcelona Traction, Light and Power Company, Limited, Judgment of 5 February 1970, *I.C.J. Reports 1970*, p. 3, para. 33, where the Court stated that 'an essential distinction should be drawn between the obligations of a State towards the international community as a whole, and those arising vis-à-vis another State in the field of diplomatic protection. By their very nature the former are the concern of all States. In view of the importance of the rights involved, all States can be held to have a legal interest in their protection; they are obligations erga omnes'.

[19] See the definition of the concept of *erga omnes* obligation by Special Rapporteur Mr. Gaetano Arangio-Ruiz, Fourth Report on State Responsibility, *UN Doc A/CN.4/444 and Add. 1–3*, para. 92, in *Yearbook of the International Law Commission 1992*, Vol. II, Part One, p. 34. See also the commentary of the ILC on Article 48 of the Draft Articles on State Responsibility, which mentions obligations under environmental treaties as an example of obligations *erga omnes partes*. See the Report of the International Law Commission on the work of its fifty-third session, *UN Doc. A/56/10* (2001), p. 126. The concept of *erga*

to these obligations, several or even all States are deemed to have a legal interest in their observance.

This has important implications for the situation of armed conflict, because, arguably, the indivisibility of particular environmental obligations restricts the options for parties to an armed conflict to suspend their treaty obligations. For example, reference can be made to particular obligations for States under the Convention on Biological Diversity, which aims to protect the Earth's biological diversity in the interests of the international community. Article 8(c) of this Convention, for example, prescribes that States '[r]egulate or manage biological resources important for the conservation of biological diversity'.[20] It can be assumed that States are expected to continue to respect this obligation unless they are completely prevented from doing so.

A third characteristic of international environmental law is that environmental obligations can, to a certain extent, be invoked by entities other than States. The evolution of international law in the field of sustainable development has facilitated the interaction between international environmental law and international human rights law. Today international environmental law obligations of States are increasingly invoked by individuals and minority groups claiming a right to a decent, healthy or satisfactory environment, either directly or as part of their rights to life, private life, property or access to information and justice.[21]

Similarly, the emergence of the rights of future generations as part of the concept of sustainable development has also encouraged a human rights approach in international environmental law. The rights of future generations must expressly be taken into account by States as part of their environmental obligations. The fact that representatives of future generations cannot directly enforce their rights at the international level does not preclude the existence of these rights as such. Moreover, as discussed below, the rights of future generations have been expressly addressed by some national courts.

omnes and the resulting indivisibility are not to be confused with the concept of 'integral agreements' discussed in Chapter 6.

[20] However, it must be noted that Article 8 of the Biodiversity Convention formulates a conditional obligation which provides leniency to States that find themselves in a difficult situation. States are only to implement the obligations contained in the provision 'as far as possible and appropriate'.

[21] See, e.g., Birnie, Boyle and Redgwell, *International Law and the Environment*, 3rd edn., pp. 271–87; Sands and Peel, *Principles of International Environmental Law*, 3rd edn., pp. 775–89; Ebeku, 'Constitutional Right to a Healthy Environment and Human Rights Approaches to Environmental Protection in Nigeria', pp. 312–20; Fitzmaurice and Marshall, 'The Human Right to a Clean Environment – Phantom or Reality?' pp. 103–51.

4.3 Principles resulting from international environmental law

International environmental law formulates several principles, some of which lay down obligations for States with regard to the use of natural resources and the environment. This section reviews those principles of international environmental law that have special resonance for the situation of armed conflict. These are the obligations to conserve and sustainably use natural wealth and resources, to promote the equitable allocation of natural resources between generations, to adopt a precautionary approach to the protection of the environment and natural resources, a prohibition against causing extraterritorial damage; and an obligation to cooperate for the protection of the global environment.

4.3.1 The obligation to conserve and sustainably use natural wealth and resources

The obligation to conserve and sustainably use natural wealth and resources, or the principle of sustainable use, seeks to set limits on the ways in which States use the natural wealth and resources situated within their territory and beyond the limits of national jurisdiction, with the aim of safeguarding their capital for the benefit of present and future generations. The obligation is reflected in several of the principles of both the 1972 Stockholm and the 1992 Rio Declaration. Principle 2 of the Stockholm Declaration, for example, provides that '[t]he natural resources of the earth ... must be safeguarded for the benefit of present and future generations through careful planning or management, as appropriate'. In addition, Principle 7 of the Rio Declaration imposes an obligation on States to 'cooperate in a spirit of global partnership to conserve, protect and restore the health and integrity of the Earth's ecosystem'.

Arguably, the obligation to conserve and use natural wealth and resources in a sustainable way constitutes the core of the concept of sustainable development and of international environmental law in general.[22] This is reflected in the large number of international environmental and other resource-related treaties in which the obligation is enshrined. Some of these indicate specific measures required for the implementation of the obligation, or provide definitions of the terms 'conservation' or 'sustainable use'; others contain more general references to the obligation. For example, more general references are included in the 2006 International

[22] See French, *International Law and Policy of Sustainable Development*, p. 38.

Tropical Timber Agreement, which aims, *inter alia,* to encourage the members of the International Tropical Timber Organization to 'develop national policies aimed at sustainable utilization and conservation of timber producing forests'.[23]

The 1992 Convention on Biological Diversity is an example of a more explicit treaty. It defines the term 'sustainable use' as 'the use of components of biological diversity in a way and at a rate that does not lead to the long-term decline of biological diversity, thereby maintaining its potential to meet the needs and aspirations of present and future generations'.[24] In addition, Article 6 of the convention obliges parties to develop or adapt 'national strategies, plans or programmes for the conservation and sustainable use of biological diversity', as well as to 'integrate . . . the conservation and sustainable use of biological diversity into . . . plans, programmes and policies'. In Articles 8 and 9 it also outlines specific measures which parties need to adopt to conserve biological diversity and it contains in Article 10 a provision on the sustainable use of components of biological diversity.

The 1979 Convention on the Conservation of Migratory Species of Wild Animals, although focused mainly on conservation and not so much on sustainable use, also contains specific measures for the implementation of the obligation to conserve and sustainably use natural wealth and resources. Parties to the convention are required to take specific measures to conserve migratory species, especially those which are endangered (listed in Appendix I to the convention) or whose conservation status is unfavourable (listed in Appendix II to the convention).[25] In addition, the convention provides a definition of the term 'conservation status of a migratory species', thus also providing an indirect definition of the term 'conservation'. The conservation status of a migratory species is defined as 'the sum of the influences acting on the migratory species that may affect its long-term distribution and abundance'.[26]

The obligation to conserve and sustainably use natural wealth and resources takes different forms. In the 1971 Ramsar Convention on the Protection of Wetlands, it is expressed in the principle of the 'wise use'

[23] Article 1(m) of the International Tropical Timber Agreement, 27 January 2006.

[24] Article 2 of the Convention on Biological Diversity, Rio de Janeiro, 5 May 1992, *1760 U.N.T.S. 79.*

[25] The convention contains in Article 1(1)(d) and (e) express definitions of the terms 'unfavourable conservation status' and 'endangered'.

[26] Article 1(1)(b) of the Convention on the Conservation of Migratory Species of Wild Animals, 23 June 1979, *1651 UNTS 333.*

of wetlands and of migratory stocks of waterfowl.[27] The 1973 Convention on International Trade in Endangered Species of Wild Flora and Fauna (CITES) refers merely to the need to protect endangered species against 'overexploitation'.[28] International freshwater law uses the terms 'equitable and reasonable' as well as 'optimal and sustainable utilization'.[29] Furthermore, in international fisheries law as well as in the law of the sea, the principle of sustainable use takes the form of an obligation to preserve the 'maximum' or 'optimum sustainable yield'.[30]

Although these terms entail specific obligations in the fields in which they operate, they all imply the use of natural resources in such a way and at such a rate that the long-term survival and/or protection of the resources concerned is ensured. Moreover, in some cases, an evolution in the meaning of the terms can be detected. For example, this applies to the terms 'maximum' or 'optimum sustainable yield' in international fisheries law. While the 1958 Fisheries Convention used the term 'optimum sustainable yield' primarily in the context of guaranteeing a continuous and maximum supply of food,[31] the 1995 UN Straddling Fish Stocks Agreement refers to the 'long-term sustainability of straddling fish stocks and highly migratory fish stocks', as well as 'the objective

[27] Articles 3 and 2(6) of the Convention on Wetlands of International Importance Especially as Waterfowl Habitat, 2 February 1971, *996 UNTS 245.*

[28] Fourth paragraph of the preamble and Article II of CITES, 3 March 1973, *993 UNTS 243.*

[29] Articles 5(1) and 6(1)(f) of the UN Convention on the Law of the Non-navigational Uses of International Watercourses, 21 May 1997, *36 ILM 700 (1997).*

[30] See, e.g., the Convention on Fishing and the Conservation of the Living Resources of the High Seas, 29 April 1958, *559 UNTS 285*, Article 1(2) and 2; UN Convention on the Law of the Sea, 10 December 1982, *1833 UNTS 3*, Article 61; United Nations Agreement for the Implementation of the Provisions of the United Nations Convention on the Law of the Sea of 10 December 1982 relating to the Conservation and Management of Straddling Fish Stocks and Highly Migratory Fish Stocks, 4 August 1995, *2167 UNTS 88*, Article 5. For more on this topic, see Freestone, Barnes and Ong (eds.), *The Law of the Sea: Progress and Prospects*; Churchill and Lowe, *The Law of the Sea*, and Van der Burgt, *The Contribution of International Fisheries Law to Human Development*, pp. 147–56.

[31] Convention on Fishing and the Conservation of the Living Resources of the High Seas, 29 April 1958, *559 UNTS 285*, Article 1(2) and 2. Article 1(2) of this Convention contains a duty for States 'to adopt . . . such measures . . . as may be necessary for the conservation of the living resources of the high seas', while Article 2 defines the expression 'conservation of the living resources of the high seas' as 'the aggregate of the measures rendering possible the optimum sustainable yield from those resources so as to secure a maximum supply of food and other marine products. Conservation programmes should be formulated with a view to securing in the first place a supply of food for human consumption'.

of their optimum utilization' in relation to measures to protect marine ecosystems and the biodiversity of the sea.[32]

The obligation to conserve and to use natural resources in a sustainable way was also recognised in treaties which are not aimed at the protection of specific natural resources. Under the General Agreement on Tariffs in Trade (GATT), which has now become part of the 1994 WTO Agreement, parties can, for example, invoke environmental exceptions to the basic rules of the GATT regarding nondiscrimination between trading partners and between foreign and domestic products. These exceptions concern measures 'necessary to protect human, animal or plant life or health' and measures 'relating to the conservation of exhaustible natural resources'.[33]

The 1994 WTO Agreement also emphasises the relationship between sustainable resource use and global economic growth:

> relations in the field of trade and economic endeavour should be conducted with a view to raising standards of living, ensuring full employment and a large and steadily growing volume of real income and effective demand, and expanding the production of and trade in goods and services, *while allowing for the optimal use of the world's resources in accordance with the objective of sustainable development*, seeking both to protect and preserve the environment and to enhance the means for doing so in a manner consistent with their respective needs and concerns at different levels of economic development.[34]

Finally, the principle of sustainable use also to some extent forms the basis for the notion of 'usufruct' in the international law of armed conflict. The notion of usufruct is central to the exploitation of natural resources in situations of occupation. In this respect, Article 55 of the 1907 Hague Regulations provides that an occupier must, amongst other things, 'safeguard the capital' of forests and agricultural estates, and that he must 'administer them in accordance with the rules of usufruct'. However, it should be noted that this provision only reflects the principle of

[32] United Nations Agreement for the Implementation of the Provisions of the United Nations Convention on the Law of the Sea of 10 December 1982 relating to the Conservation and Management of Straddling Fish Stocks and Highly Migratory Fish Stocks, 4 August 1995, *2167 UNTS 88*, Article 5.

[33] See Article XX (b) and (g) of GATT, Annex 1A to the WTO Agreement, adopted on 15 April 1994, *1867 UNTS 187*.

[34] Agreement Establishing the World Trade Organization, adopted on 15 April 1994, *1867 UNTS 154*. Author's emphasis added.

sustainable use to a limited extent. In occupation law the rationale for protecting natural resources is not so much to protect the environment and its natural resources for the benefit of future generations, but rather to preserve the rights of the occupied State and its population to these resources. Therefore, the focus is on protecting property rights rather than on ensuring long-term sustainability.

The obligation to conserve and sustainably use natural wealth and resources has also been appealed to in the case law of international tribunals. Although these cases do not clarify the contents or the legal status of the principle of sustainable use in any more detail, they do confirm the existence of the principle itself. In the *Icelandic Fisheries case*, the International Court of Justice confirmed the existence of an obligation in international fisheries law to conserve the living resources of the sea. The Court considered that

> [i]t is one of the advances in maritime international law, resulting from the intensification of fishing, that the former *laissez-faire* treatment of the living resources of the sea in the high seas has been replaced by a recognition of a duty to have due regard to the rights of other States and the needs of conservation for the benefit of all.[35]

Furthermore, in the *Gabčíkovo–Nagymaros case*, the International Court of Justice pronounced on the need to take into account modern norms and standards related to sustainable development in a paragraph that is often quoted:

> Throughout the ages, mankind has, for economic and other reasons, constantly interfered with nature. In the past, this was often done without consideration of the effects upon the environment. Owing to new scientific insights and to a growing awareness of the risks for mankind – for present and future generations – of pursuit of such interventions at an unconsidered and unabated pace, new norms and standards have been developed, set forth in a great number of instruments during the last two decades. Such new norms have to be taken into consideration, and such new standards given proper weight, not only when States contemplate new activities but also when continuing with activities begun in the past. This need to reconcile economic development with protection of the environment is aptly expressed in the concept of sustainable development.[36]

[35] International Court of Justice, Fisheries Jurisdiction (*United Kingdom* v. *Iceland*), Judgment of 25 July 1974, *I.C.J. Reports 1974*, p. 3, para. 72.

[36] International Court of Justice, Gabčíkovo–Nagymaros Project (*Hungary* v. *Slovakia*), Judgment of 25 September 1997, *I.C.J. Reports 1997*, p. 7, para. 140.

In the *Pulp Mills on the River Uruguay case*, the International Court of Justice interpreted the implications of the obligation of optimum and rational utilisation in freshwater law. In this respect, the Court considered that

> the attainment of optimum and rational utilization requires a balance between the Parties' rights and needs to use the river for economic and commercial activities on the one hand, and the obligation to protect it from any damage to the environment that may be caused by such activities, on the other.[37]

The International Tribunal for the Law of the Sea (ITLOS) pronounced on the issue of sustainable use as well. In the *Southern Bluefin Tuna cases* concerning an experimental fishing programme started by Japan, the Tribunal noted that 'the conservation of the living resources of the sea is an element in the protection and preservation of the marine environment'. It also indicated that 'the parties should in the circumstances act with prudence and caution to ensure that effective conservation measures are taken to prevent serious harm to the stock of southern bluefin tuna' and that provisional measures were necessary in order to 'avert further deterioration of the southern bluefin tuna stock'.[38]

Therefore, in the light of this considerable and constantly growing body of case law and the numerous provisions in treaty law relating to the obligation to conserve and sustainably use natural wealth and resources, it is justified to conclude that States are required under international law to properly manage their own natural wealth and resources and to use with restraint the natural wealth and resources that belong to several or all States, such as the fish in the high seas.[39]

This has several implications for the rights of States relating to the exploitation of their natural resources, both directly regarding the exploitation activities themselves and regarding the effects of these activities on the environment. The principle of sustainable use requires States to use their natural resources in a way and at a rate that allows these natural resources to regenerate, or in the case of nonliving natural resources, to

[37] International Court of Justice, Case Concerning Pulp Mills on the River Uruguay (*Argentina* v. *Uruguay*), Judgment of 20 April 2010, *I.C.J. Reports 2010*, p. 14, para. 175.

[38] International Tribunal for the Law of the Sea, Southern Bluefin Tuna Cases (*New Zealand* v. *Japan*; *Australia* v. *Japan*), Requests for Provisional Measures, Order of 27 August 1999, paras. 70–85.

[39] Furthermore, as discussed in Section 4.3.5, States are under an obligation to cooperate for the conservation of these common resources.

safeguard these natural resources for long-term development. However, at the same time, the principle leaves States with a broad scope to decide what is sustainable and what is not. This is both a strength and a weakness of the principle.

4.3.2 *The obligation to safeguard natural resources for future generations*

The obligation to safeguard natural resources for future generations is expressed in the principle of equity. This principle, which is firmly established in general international law, has particular resonance in the context of international environmental law. The principle of equity as a principle of international environmental law places a dual responsibility on the present generation to ensure, on one hand, that all people living today have the opportunity to benefit from the natural resources that have been left behind by past generations, and on the other hand, to leave behind for future generations a healthy planet which they can use for their development.[40]

In other words, the principle of equity has two components. The intragenerational component formulates an obligation for the present generation to provide access to the legacy of past generations to its own members. This component of equity is reflected in particular in concepts such as 'optimum utilisation' in the international law of the sea, 'optimal use' and 'differential and more favourable treatment' in international economic law, and 'common but differentiated responsibilities' in international environmental law.

However, the intergenerational component of equity is the more relevant to the current book. It concerns the responsibility of the present generation to safeguard the opportunities of future generations to use natural wealth and resources for their needs and aspirations by protecting the diversity of natural resources, preserving the quality of the planet and maintaining access to the legacy of past generations.[41]

Intergenerational equity is one of the core principles of sustainable development. However, it is often presented as a philosophical or political

[40] On this principle, see, e.g., Brown-Weiss, *In Fairness to Future Generations*; D'Amato, 'Do We Owe a Duty to Future Generations to Preserve the Global Environment?' pp. 190–98; Schrijver, 'After Us, the Deluge?' pp. 59–78; Shelton, 'Equity', pp. 639–62; Fitzmaurice, 'International Protection of the Environment', pp. 186–201; Atapattu, *Emerging Principles of International Environmental Law*, pp. 113–19.

[41] See in particular Brown-Weiss, *In Fairness to Future Generations.*

concept rather than as a legal principle.[42] This may be due partly to some of the inherent difficulties of the principle, which relate to the beneficiaries and addressees of the associated rights and obligations.

The principle of intergenerational equity confers responsibilities on the present generation which may be demanded by future generations. With reference to Parfit's paradox and the chaos theory, it can be argued that the present generation cannot have a responsibility to an undefined group of people whose composition is unclear and may alter as a consequence of the actions taken by the present generation by fulfilling their obligations to future generations.[43] Although effectively refuted by Brown-Weiss, who emphasises that the rights of future generations are not individual rights but rather group rights or '*generational* rights, which must be conceived of in the temporal context of generations',[44] problems with regard to this idea do arise with respect to its implementation. It is for this reason that the principle of intergenerational equity cannot be regarded as a legal principle that formulates concrete obligations for States with regard to future generations. Rather, the principle of intergenerational equity formulates a general responsibility for States to take into account the long-term effects of their actions when they contemplate activities that could have negative effects on the environment or natural resources.

For the purposes of the present book, it is relevant to note the following observation of the Experts Group on Environmental Law of the World Commission on Environment and Development, which establishes an explicit connection between equity and the rights and obligations of parties to an armed conflict:

> the conservation or use of the environment and natural resources for the benefit of present and future generations also implies certain restraints for the parties to an international or non-international armed conflict in that they shall abstain from methods or means of warfare which are intended, or may be expected, to cause widespread, long-lasting or severe damage to the environment.[45]

[42] See, e.g., French, *Law and Policy of Sustainable Development*, p. 28, who distinguishes between equity 'as a recognized legal term', referring to the use of the term in jurisprudence, and its 'political meaning' within the context of the discussion on sustainable development. For philosophical views on the concept of intergenerational equity, see, *inter alia*, Rawls, *A Theory of Justice*.

[43] See, e.g., D'Amato, 'Do We Owe a Duty to Future Generations to Preserve the Global Environment?' pp. 190–98.

[44] Brown-Weiss, 'Our Rights and Obligations to Future Generations for the Environment', p. 205.

[45] Munro and Lammers, *Environmental Protection and Sustainable Development*, p. 45. This issue will be discussed in more detail in Part II of this book.

Although the accuracy of this statement can be questioned from a positivist perspective,[46] it can be argued in more general terms that parties to an armed conflict must take into account the effects of their actions on future generations. This corresponds to the general line of reasoning of the International Court of Justice in its Nuclear Weapons Advisory Opinion. As part of its assessment regarding the legality of the threat or use of nuclear weapons, the Court explicitly took into account the potential effects of nuclear weapons on future generations.[47] Thus the Court recognised that in their decisions and policies, States have to have due regard for the consequences of their actions on future generations. This includes the consequences for future generations resulting from their actions in armed conflict.

Intergenerational equity has been recognised as a guiding principle in several treaties. An early reference to future generations can be found in the 1946 Whaling Convention, which recognises in its preamble 'the interest of the nations of the world in safeguarding for future generations the great natural resources represented by the whale stocks'.[48] Other examples include the 1973 CITES Convention which recognises that 'wild fauna and flora in their many beautiful and varied forms are an irreplaceable part of the natural systems of the earth which must be protected for this and the generations to come', the 1992 UN Convention on Climate Change which states that '[t]he Parties should protect the climate system for the benefit of present and future generations of humankind', and the 1992 Biodiversity Convention, which states that parties are '[d]etermined to conserve and sustainably use biological diversity for the benefit of present and future generations'.[49]

[46] The statement uses the language of Articles 35(3) and 55 of Additional Protocol I relating to international armed conflicts, which does not have an equivalent in Additional Protocol II relating to noninternational armed conflicts. These provisions are discussed in more detail in Chapter 6 of this study.

[47] International Court of Justice, Advisory Opinion on the Legality of the Threat or Use of Nuclear Weapons, 8 July 1996, *I.C.J. Reports 1996*, p. 226, paras. 35 and 36.

[48] First paragraph of the preamble of the International Convention for the Regulation of Whaling, 2 December 1946, *161 UNTS 72.*

[49] See the first paragraph of the preamble of CITES, 3 March 1973, *993 UNTS 243*; Article 3(1) of the UN Framework Convention on Climate Change, 9 May 1992, *1771 U.N.T.S. 107*; and the last paragraph of the preamble of the 1992 Biodiversity Convention, 5 May 1992, *1760 U.N.T.S. 79.* For other references to future generations in treaty law, see the 1979 Convention on the Conservation of Migratory Species of Wild Animals which states in the second paragraph of the preamble that parties are '[a]ware that each generation of man holds the resources of the earth for future generations and has an obligation to ensure that this legacy is conserved and, where utilized, is used wisely'; the fifth paragraph of the preamble of the 1976 ENMOD Convention, which states that the parties realise 'that the

Reference can also be made to the 1972 World Heritage Convention, which aims to preserve parts of the cultural and natural heritage as part of the world heritage of mankind as a whole. Article 4 of this convention formulates an obligation for parties to ensure 'the identification, protection, conservation, presentation and transmission to future generations of the [world] cultural and natural heritage . . . situated on its territory'.[50] In addition to the references in treaty law, the 1972 Stockholm Declaration and the 1992 Rio Declaration also contain explicit references to responsibilities owed to present and future generations.[51]

While the references to intergenerational equity in these treaties serve to emphasise the general responsibility of States with regard to the rights of future generations, some national decisions have actually expressly recognised the rights of future generations. Furthermore, these decisions have identified corresponding obligations for national government authorities. In the often cited *Minors Oposa case*, the Philippine Supreme Court accorded legal standing to children, as well as unborn generations, to claim a constitutional right to a 'balanced and healthful ecology'. The Court explicitly recognised the obligation for the government to guarantee that right to future generations.[52] Reference can also be made to the national case of the *Fuel Retailers Association of Southern Africa* v.

use of environmental modification techniques for peaceful purposes could improve the interrelationship of man and nature and contribute to the preservation and improvement of the environment for the benefit of present and future generations'; Article 4 of the 1979 Agreement Governing the Activities of States on the Moon and Other Celestial Bodies, adopted on 18 December 1979, *1363 UNTS 21*, which states that in the exploration and use of the Moon and other celestial bodies '[d]ue regard shall be paid to the interests of present and future generations'; and the fifth paragraph of the preamble of the 1992 UN Convention on the Law of the Non-navigational Uses of International Watercourses, which expresses 'the conviction that a framework convention will ensure the utilisation, development, conservation, management and protection of international watercourses and the promotion of the optimal and sustainable utilisation thereof for present and future generations'.

50 It is further interesting to note that UNESCO's General Conference has adopted a Declaration on the Responsibilities of the Present Generations towards Future Generations in 1997, which outlines, *inter alia*, the environmental responsibilities of the present generation towards future generations. See UNESCO, *Records of the General Conference*, Twenty-Ninth Session, Paris, 21 October to 12 November 1997, Vol. 1, Resolutions, p. 69.

51 Principle 1 of the Stockholm Declaration provides that 'Man . . . bears a solemn responsibility to protect and improve the environment for present and future generations', while Principle 2 states that '[t]he natural resources of the earth . . . must be safeguarded for the benefit of present and future generations'; Principle 3 of the Rio Declaration states that '[t]he right to development must be fulfilled so as to equitably meet developmental and environmental needs of present and future generations'.

52 *Minors Oposa* v. *Secretary of the Department of Environmental and Natural Resources*, The Supreme Court of the Philippines, Judgment of July 1993.

the Director-General, in which the South African Constitutional Court considered that '[t]he present generation holds the earth in trust for the next generation. This trusteeship position carries with it the responsibility to look after the environment. It is the duty of the Court to ensure that this responsibility is carried out [by the responsible authorities]'.[53] Nevertheless, these cases continue to be exceptional.

The principle of intergenerational equity has therefore been recognised in international law to some extent, in particular in treaty law, where it appears as a guiding rather than a legal principle.[54] Although national judicial decisions show that the principle can entail concrete legal obligations for States as well, it is generally not considered to do so. However, the principle of intergenerational equity has also been expressed in other concepts. It is inextricably linked with and may be considered to be one of the principal rationales behind the obligation of conservation and sustainable use of natural wealth and resources.[55]

4.3.3 The obligation to prevent damage to the environment of other States

The obligation of States to prevent damage to the environment of other States and of areas beyond national jurisdiction can be regarded as one of the fundamental principles of international environmental law.[56] Based on the general rule referred to in the *Corfu Channel Case* that States have an obligation not to use their territory in a way contrary to the rights of other States, the obligation to prevent damage to the environment of other

[53] *Fuel Retailers Association of Southern Africa* v. *Director-General: Environmental Management Department of Agriculture, Conservation and Environment, Mpumalanga Province, and Others*, 2007 (6) SA 4 (CC), 2007, (10) BCLR 1059 (CC), para. 102, quoted in the third report of the International Committee on International Law on Sustainable Development of the International Law Association, *Report of the Seventy-Third Conference of the International Law Association*, Rio de Janeiro (2008), p. 904. See also the final report of the International Committee on International Law on Sustainable Development of the International Law Association, Sofia (2012), pp. 14–17.

[54] A recent report of the UN Secretary-General on 'Intergenerational Solidarity and the Needs of Future Generations' illustrates this. While the report examines the principle of intergenerational equity in depth, it does not refer to it as a legal principle. See Report of the Secretary-General, 'Intergenerational Solidarity and the Needs of Future Generations', *UN Doc. A/68/322*, 15 August 2013.

[55] In addition, see Schrijver, 'After Us, the Deluge?' pp. 59–78.

[56] See Bodansky, Brunnée and Hey, *The Oxford Handbook of International Environmental Law*, p. 9, who refer to the obligation as a 'cornerstone of international environmental law'. On this topic in more detail, see, e.g., Hanqin, *Transboundary Damage in International Law*; and Handl, 'Transboundary Impacts', pp. 531–49.

States and beyond national jurisdiction sets limits on the sovereignty of a State regarding the use of its territory in order to protect the sovereignty of other States.[57]

The obligation was formulated for the first time in the 1941 *Trail Smelter Arbitration case* concerning transboundary air pollution. In this case, the arbitral tribunal determined in its final judgment that

> under the principles of international law . . . no State has the right to use or permit the use of its territory in such a manner as to cause injury by fumes in or to the territory of another or the properties or persons therein, when the case is of serious consequence and the injury is established by clear and convincing evidence.[58]

Gradually the nature of the obligation shifted from being purely bilateral into having a more general application, extending not only to the territory of other States but also to areas beyond national jurisdiction.[59] It is in this form that the obligation was inserted in Principle 21 of the 1972 Stockholm Declaration, which formulates a responsibility for States 'to ensure that activities within their jurisdiction or control do not cause damage to the environment of other states *or of areas beyond the limits of national jurisdiction*'.[60]

This 'Principle 21 obligation', as it is often referred to in the literature, has since been recognised in several international conventions, including the conventions on climate change, biodiversity and desertification, and was restated in Principle 2 of the 1992 Rio Declaration.[61] In addition, the existence of the obligation was affirmed in the case law of several

[57] International Court of Justice, Corfu Channel (*United Kingdom* v. *Albania*), Merits, Judgment of 9 April 1949, *I.C.J. Reports 1949*, p. 22. See also Handl, 'Transboundary Impacts', p. 533.

[58] Trail Smelter Arbitration (*United States* v. *Canada*), Judgment of 11 March 1941, *Reports of International Arbitral Awards* Vol. III, United Nations (2006), p. 1965.

[59] See Birnie, Boyle and Redgwell, *International Law and the Environment*, 3rd edn., p. 145.

[60] Principle 21 of the Declaration of the United Nations Conference on the Human Environment, Stockholm, 16 June 1972, *11 ILM 1416 (1972)*. Author's emphasis added.

[61] See the preamble of the Convention on the Prevention of Marine Pollution by Dumping of Wastes and Other Matter, 29 December 1972, *1046 UNTS 120*; Article 194(2) of the United Nations Convention on the Law of the Sea, 10 December 1982, *1833 UNTS 3*; Article 3 of the Convention on Biological Diversity, 5 May 1992, *1760 U.N.T.S. 79*; paragraph 8 of the preamble of the UN Framework Convention on Climate Change, 9 May 1992, *1771 U.N.T.S. 107*; paragraph 15 of the preamble of the United Nations Convention to Combat Desertification in Countries Experiencing Serious Drought and/or Desertification, Particularly in Africa, 17 June 1994, *1954 U.N.T.S. 3*; Article 7 of the UN Convention on the Law of the Non-navigational Uses of International Watercourses, 21 May 1997, *36 ILM 700 (1997)*; Principle 2 of the Rio Declaration on Environment and Development, 13 June 1992, *31 ILM 874 (1992)*.

international tribunals, including the International Court of Justice and tribunals acting under the auspices of the Permanent Court of Arbitration (PCA).

In its *Advisory Opinion on the Legality of the Threat or Use of Nuclear Weapons*, the International Court of Justice expressly affirmed 'the existence of a general obligation of States to ensure that activities within their jurisdiction and control respect the environment of other States or of areas beyond national control' and stated that this obligation 'is now part of the corpus of international law relating to the environment'.[62] As Duncan French noted, the Court therefore confirmed the autonomous status of this rule in international environmental law.[63]

In two subsequent contentious cases – the 1997 *Gabčíkovo–Nagymaros case* and the 2010 *Pulp Mills on the River Uruguay case* – the Court took the opportunity to reaffirm its position.[64] In the *Iron Rhine Arbitration*, the arbitral tribunal operating under the auspices of the PCA also confirmed this obligation and added that it applies equally to activities undertaken by a State on the territory of another State in the exercise of rights guaranteed by treaty.[65]

As may be inferred from the text of Principle 21, which mentions environmental damage resulting from 'activities within [the] jurisdiction *or* control' of States,[66] the obligation to prevent extraterritorial damage applies both to extraterritorial damage caused by activities undertaken

[62] International Court of Justice, Advisory Opinion on the Legality of the Threat or Use of Nuclear Weapons, *I.C.J. Reports 1996*, p. 66, para. 29. For a more detailed analysis of the court's judgment in this respect, see the contributions of Weiss and Momtaz to Boisson de Chazournes and Sands, *International Law, the International Court of Justice and Nuclear Weapons*. It should be noted that there are some differences between the obligation as formulated by the court, on one hand, and Principle 21, on the other. These relate to the following points. On the one hand, the court constrains the obligation to activities which fall both within the jurisdiction and the control of States. On the other hand, the court extends the obligation to areas beyond national control instead of jurisdiction. Moreover, the court formulates a more general obligation to respect the environment instead of an obligation not to cause damage. See Brown Weiss, 'Opening the Door to the Environment and to Future Generations', p. 340.

[63] French, 'A Reappraisal of Sovereignty in the Light of Global Environmental Concerns', p. 385.

[64] International Court of Justice, Gabčíkovo–Nagymaros Project (*Hungary* v. *Slovakia*), Judgment, *I.C.J. Reports 1997*, p. 7, para. 53 and International Court of Justice, Case Concerning Pulp Mills on the River Uruguay (*Argentina* v. *Uruguay*), *I.C.J. Reports 2010*, para. 193.

[65] Permanent Court of Arbitration, Arbitration Regarding the Iron Rhine ('IJzeren Rijn') Railway (between the Kingdom of Belgium and the Kingdom of the Netherlands), Award of 24 May 2005, paras. 222–4.

[66] Author's emphasis added.

within the national jurisdiction of States and to activities undertaken by them outside their jurisdiction but within their control. As Louis Sohn noted, this implies that the obligation 'applies clearly to citizens of a state, to ships flying its flag, and perhaps even to corporations incorporated in its territory'.[67]

Furthermore, and highly relevant to the current book, it can be argued that the obligation applies to a State which exercises *de facto* control on (part of) the territory of another State as well. This can be inferred from the Commentary of the ILC to its Draft Articles on Prevention of Transboundary Harm from Hazardous Activities, which noted that '[t]he function of the concept of "control" in international law is to attach certain legal consequences to a State whose jurisdiction over certain activities or events is not recognised by international law; it covers situations in which a State is exercising de facto jurisdiction, even though it lacks jurisdiction de jure'.[68] If this is a correct interpretation of the term 'control', it implies that the obligation to prevent damage to the environment of other States applies in situations of occupation.[69]

The duty of prevention is central to the obligation to prevent damage to the environment of other States and to areas beyond national jurisdiction.[70] This duty of prevention, sometimes also designated as the principle of prevention, is referred to in several cases relating to the prohibition against causing transboundary environmental damage.

In the *Gabčíkovo–Nagymaros case*, for example, the International Court of Justice determined that 'in the field of environmental protection, vigilance and prevention are required on account of the often irreversible character of damage to the environment and of the limitations inherent in the very mechanism of reparation of this type of damage'.[71] In addition, in the Pulp Mills case, the Court even referred to the customary nature of 'the principle of prevention'. In this regard, the Court pointed out that 'the principle of prevention, as a customary rule, has its origins in the due

67 Sohn, 'The Stockholm Declaration on the Human Environment', p. 493.

68 Commentary of the ILC on its Draft Articles on Prevention of Transboundary Harm from Hazardous Activities, *Yearbook of the International Law Commission*, Vol. II, Part Two (2001), p. 151, para. 12.

69 This was expressly contemplated by the ILC, which referred to cases of 'unlawful intervention, occupation and unlawful annexation'. Ibid.

70 According to Handl, 'the obligation of prevention presents itself as an essential aspect of the obligation not to cause significant harm to the environment beyond national jurisdiction or control'. Handl, 'Transboundary Impacts', p. 539.

71 International Court of Justice, Gabčíkovo–Nagymaros Project (*Hungary* v. *Slovakia*), Judgment, *I.C.J. Reports 1997*, p. 78, para. 140.

diligence that is required of a State in its territory'.[72] Similarly, in the *Iron Rhine Arbitration*, the arbitral tribunal determined that 'where development may cause significant harm to the environment there is a duty to prevent, or at least mitigate, such harm. This duty, in the opinion of the Tribunal, has now become a principle of general international law'.[73]

It should be noted that the obligation to prevent transboundary environmental damage does not imply a complete prohibition against States engaging in activities that cause transboundary damage. Although not expressly indicated in Principle 21, it is generally acknowledged that the obligation of States only concerns the prevention of damage that exceeds a certain minimum threshold.[74] This threshold is usually considered to be damage that may be designated as 'significant'. According to the ILC commentary to the Draft Articles on Prevention of Transboundary Harm from Hazardous Activities, this may be defined as 'something more than "detectable", but need not be at the level of "serious" or "substantial"'.[75]

Furthermore, the obligation to prevent extraterritorial damage must be interpreted by States as an obligation to exercise due diligence with regard to activities undertaken by them.[76] In general, this implies that States are to 'use all the means at [their] disposal' or 'to take all appropriate measures' to prevent transboundary damage.[77] For this purpose, States

[72] International Court of Justice, Case Concerning Pulp Mills on the River Uruguay (*Argentina* v. *Uruguay*), *I.C.J. Reports 2010*, para. 101.

[73] Permanent Court of Arbitration, Arbitration Regarding the Iron Rhine ('IJzeren Rijn') Railway (between the Kingdom of Belgium and the Kingdom of the Netherlands), Award of 24 May 2005, para. 59.

[74] See Trouwborst, *Precautionary Rights and Duties of States*, p. 44; see also Brunnée, 'Common Areas, Common Heritage and Common Concern', p. 552.

[75] Draft articles on Prevention of Transboundary Harm from Hazardous Activities, with commentaries, *Yearbook of the International Law Commission*, vol. II, Part Two (2001), p. 152. See also Article 7 of the UN Convention on the Law of the Non-navigational Uses of International Watercourses, 21 May 1997, *36 ILM 700 (1997)*; and the judgment of the International Court of Justice in the Case Concerning Pulp Mills on the River Uruguay (*Argentina* v. *Uruguay*), *I.C.J. Reports 2010*, para. 101, where the court states that a State 'is thus obliged to use all the means at its disposal in order to avoid activities which take place in its territory, or in any area under its jurisdiction, causing *significant* damage to the environment of another State'. Author's emphasis added.

[76] See Birnie, Boyle and Redgwell, *International Law and the Environment*, 3rd edn., p. 147. Also see Hanqin, *Transboundary Damage in International Law*, pp. 162–87.

[77] International Court of Justice, Case Concerning Pulp Mills on the River Uruguay (*Argentina* v. *Uruguay*), Judgment of 20 April 2010, *I.C.J. Reports 2010*, para. 101; and Article 3 of the ILC Draft Articles on Prevention of Transboundary Harm from Hazardous Activities. See also Article 194(2) of the United Nations Convention on the Law of the Sea, 10 December 1982, *1833 UNTS 3*, which indicates an obligation for States to 'take

are not only to adopt appropriate rules and procedures, but also to take on 'a certain level of vigilance in their enforcement and the exercise of administrative control applicable to public and private operators'.[78]

Arguably, such an obligation to act with vigilance is also relevant for the situation of armed conflict, when armed groups operate in territory under the control of a foreign State. In the *Congo–Uganda case*, the International Court of Justice determined the existence of an obligation of vigilance incumbent upon Uganda in territories occupied by that State. According to the Court, this obligation of vigilance implied a duty for the occupant to prevent acts of looting and plundering of natural resources by armed groups acting on their own account.[79] Arguably, the obligation for States to prevent damage to the environment of other States therefore also includes a duty to prevent environmental damage caused by armed groups in territories under their control.

In addition to these obligations, the due diligence obligation entails several other procedural obligations, including an obligation to notify and to inform the affected States of the potential damage, an obligation to consult with them on actions to be taken and an obligation to conduct a so-called environmental impact assessment (EIA) in order to determine the risk and extent of the damage.[80]

These obligations are dealt with in Principles 17 and 19 of the 1992 Rio Declaration. Principle 17 states that '[e]nvironmental impact assessment, as a national instrument, shall be undertaken for proposed activities that are likely to have a significant adverse impact on the environment', while Principle 19 formulates a duty for States to 'provide prior and timely notification and relevant information to potentially affected States on activities that may have a significant adverse transboundary

all measures necessary to ensure that activities under their jurisdiction or control are so conducted as not to cause damage by pollution to other States and their environment'.

78 International Court of Justice, Case Concerning Pulp Mills on the River Uruguay (*Argentina* v. *Uruguay*), Judgment of 20 April 2010, *I.C.J. Reports 2010*, para. 197. See also Birnie, Boyle and Redgwell, *International Law and the Environment*, 3rd edn., pp. 147–50. See also Hanqin, *Transboundary Damage in International Law*, p. 163, who refers to an obligation to exercise 'good government', that is, 'evincing responsibility for its international obligation to exercise proper care so as not to cause such effects or to prevent others in its territory from causing such effects'.

79 International Court of Justice, Case Concerning Armed Activities on the Territory of the Congo (*Democratic Republic of the Congo* v. *Uganda*), Judgment of 19 December 2005, *I.C.J. Reports 2005*, p. 168, para. 179. This issue is discussed in more detail in the second part of this study.

80 For more details on these procedural obligations, see Hanqin, *Transboundary Damage in International Law*, pp. 165–78.

environmental effect and shall consult with those States at an early stage and in good faith'.

The obligation to notify and to inform other States has also been recognised in treaty law, *inter alia*, in Article 14(1)(d) of the 1992 Convention on Biological Diversity, and in the case law of international tribunals, including the judgment of the International Court of Justice in the *Pulp Mills case*, as well as the order of ITLOS in the Land Reclamation case for provisional measures to be taken.[81] The obligation to conduct an EIA to prevent transboundary damage to the environment has similarly attained a strong status in international law. It has been inserted in several treaties, including Article 4(2)(f) and Annex V(A) of the 1989 Basel Convention on the Control of Transboundary Movements of Hazardous Wastes and Their Disposal, Article 206 of UNCLOS and Article 12 of the 1997 UN Convention on the Law of the Non-navigational Uses of International Watercourses.[82]

Moreover, in its judgment in the *Pulp Mills case*, the International Court of Justice even went so far as to state that

> the obligation to protect and preserve [the aquatic environment] has to be interpreted in accordance with a practice, which in recent years has gained so much acceptance among States that it may now be considered a requirement under general international law to undertake an environmental impact assessment where there is a risk that the proposed industrial activity may have a significant adverse impact in a transboundary context, in particular, on a shared resource. Moreover, due diligence, and the duty of vigilance and prevention which it implies, would not be considered to have been exercised, if a party planning works liable to affect the régime of the river or the quality of its waters did not undertake an environmental impact assessment on the potential effects of such works.[83]

[81] See International Court of Justice, Case Concerning Pulp Mills on the River Uruguay (*Argentina* v. *Uruguay*), Judgment of 20 April 2010, *I.C.J. Reports 2010*, paras. 67–158 concerning the procedural obligations of the parties to the dispute; and International Tribunal for the Law of the Sea, Case Concerning Land Reclamation by Singapore in and around the Straits of Johor (*Malaysia* v. *Singapore*), Order of 8 October 2003, para. 99. In general on the topic of environmental information and related duties, see Sands and Peel, *Principles of International Environmental Law*, 3rd edn., pp. 624–64.

[82] See the Basel Convention on the Control of Transboundary Movements of Hazardous Wastes and Their Disposal, 22 March 1989, *1673 U.N.T.S. 126*; the UN Convention on the Law of the Non-navigational Uses of International Watercourses, 21 May 1997, *36 I.L.M. 715 (1997)*; and the UN Convention on the Law of the Sea, 10 December 1982, *1833 U.N.T.S. 3*. For other examples, also see Sands and Peel, *Principles of International Environmental Law*, 3rd edn., pp. 601–23.

[83] International Court of Justice, Case Concerning Pulp Mills on the River Uruguay (*Argentina* v. *Uruguay*), *I.C.J. Reports 2010*, para. 204.

As the obligation to conduct an EIA is not aimed specifically at preventing environmental damage in a transboundary context, it is discussed at greater length in the following section dealing with the obligation to adopt a precautionary approach to protect the environment and natural resources.

In conclusion, for the purposes of the present book, it is possible to identify three different situations in which the obligation to prevent harm to territories outside national jurisdiction or control entails specific responsibilities for States. First, the obligation is relevant for activities relating to resource exploitation which a State undertakes within its own jurisdiction and which result in transboundary damage, such as the pollution of an international river by chemical substances used for the extraction of minerals.

Second, the obligation applies to the situation in which a State exploits natural resources outside its jurisdiction but within its control, for example, when a State exploits the natural resources of another State over whose territory it exercises *de facto* control, including the situation in which it has occupied that territory. Moreover, in situations of occupation, the obligation of a State to prevent damage to the environment of other States includes an obligation to prevent other actors, including armed groups, from causing such damage.

The third situation in which the obligation becomes relevant is in the context of the exploitation of natural resources shared by two or more States, so-called shared or transboundary natural resources. Natural resources such as forests, oil fields and natural gas deposits, located on the border between two or more States, are particularly important in this respect.[84] In principle, a State is liable with respect to its neighbouring State(s) for damage caused to the shared resource either through its own activities or through the activities of private parties operating from within its jurisdiction.

4.3.4 The obligation to adopt a precautionary approach to protect the environment and natural resources

The obligation to prevent damage to the environment is also expressed in the precautionary principle, which requires States to act with caution, to prevent damage not only to the territory of other States, but also to

[84] For the rules relating to the management of shared natural resources, see Section 4.4.3 of this chapter.

their own domestic environment.[85] At the core of this principle – which is also referred to as an 'approach' by States preferring more flexibility, in particular the United States[86] – lies the need to anticipate environmental damage, even in the face of scientific uncertainty.[87]

The precautionary principle requires States, '[w]here there are threats of serious or irreversible damage [not to use] lack of full scientific certainty . . . as a reason for postponing cost-effective measures to prevent environmental degradation'.[88] In other words, if there are indications that particular activities or policies could cause severe damage to the environment, the precautionary principle requires States to take measures to prevent the damage, even if the scientific evidence does not make it possible to identify the precise risks concerned.

In this way the principle extends the obligation of States to use their natural resources in a sustainable way, in the sense that the precautionary principle requires States to take into account the risks involved in the exploitation of their natural wealth and resources.[89] Therefore, the principle significantly extends the standard of care expected of States when undertaking activities that could have a negative impact on the environment. More specifically, the precautionary principle extends the duty of prevention to situations of scientific uncertainty.[90]

At the same time, the principle is in some ways more restrictive than the principle of prevention. While the principle of prevention applies to 'significant' damage, the precautionary principle sets a higher

85 See Schrijver, 'The Status of the Precautionary Principle in International Law and Its Application and Interpretation in International Litigation', pp. 241–53; Sands and Peel, *Principles of International Environmental Law*, 3rd edn., pp. 217–28; Handl, 'Transboundary Impacts', pp. 539; Kiss and Shelton, *Guide to International Environmental Law*, pp. 90–94.

86 See Schrijver, 'The Status of the Precautionary Principle in International Law and Its Application and Interpretation in International Litigation', p. 243.

87 Ibid.

88 Principle 15 of the Rio Declaration on Environment and Development. On the precautionary principle, see in general Trouwborst, *Precautionary Rights and Duties of States*; Trouwborst, *Evolution and Status of the Precautionary Principle in International Law*; Schrijver, 'The Status of the Precautionary Principle in International Law and Its Application and Interpretation in International Litigation', pp. 241–53; Freestone and Hey, *The Precautionary Principle and International Law*.

89 In this respect, also see Birnie, Boyle and Redgwell, *International Law and the Environment*, 3rd edn., p. 199, who argue that '[t]he precautionary principle, endorsed by Principle 15 of the Rio Declaration is also an important element of sustainable utilization, because it addresses the key question of uncertainty in the prediction of environmental effects'.

90 In this respect, Kiss and Shelton argue that 'the precautionary principle can be considered as the most developed form of prevention that remains the general basis for environmental law'. Kiss and Shelton, *Guide to International Environmental Law*, p. 95.

standard. It applies only to situations where the potential damage is either 'serious' or 'irreversible'. In addition, precautionary action is required only when the measures to be taken are cost-effective and is dependent on the respective capabilities of States.[91] In a way, these additional requirements are understandable, as the element of scientific uncertainty makes it more difficult to assess the risks involved in the proposed activities.

The precautionary principle has found recognition in several international environmental conventions, covering such diverse fields as the international law for the protection of the ozone layer, biodiversity and the climate system, as well as freshwater law and fisheries law.[92] Precautionary considerations underlie many of these conventions and constitute a basis for action. This can be illustrated with reference to the legal regime to address climate change. Even though the 1992 Climate Change Convention notes in its preamble 'that there are many uncertainties in predictions of climate change', several parties to this Convention have agreed to take concrete measures to reduce the emission of greenhouse gases under the 1997 Kyoto Protocol.

In most environmental conventions the threshold for the application of the precautionary principle is serious or irreversible damage. Examples of conventions that set a lower threshold include the 1992 Biodiversity Convention which calls for precautionary action when there is a risk of

[91] For an analysis of the relationship between the precautionary principle and socioeconomic interests, including a detailed account of the ongoing debate on this issue, see Trouwborst, *Precautionary Rights and Duties of States*, pp. 229–81.

[92] See Article 3(3) of the 1992 UN Framework Convention on Climate Change, 9 May 1992, *1771 U.N.T.S.107*; paragraph 9 of the preamble to the 1992 Biodiversity Convention, 5 May 1992, *1760 U.N.T.S. 79*; Articles 1, 10.6 and 11.8 of the 2000 Cartagena Protocol on Biosafety, 29 January 2000, *2226 U.N.T.S. 208*; paragraph 4 of the preamble to the 2010 Nagoya Protocol on Access to Genetic Resources and the Fair and Equitable Sharing of Benefits Arising from Their Utilization, 29 October 2010; 2(5)(a) of the 1992 Convention on the Protection and Use of Transboundary Watercourses and International Lakes, 17 March 1992, *1936 U.N.T.S. 269*; Articles 5(c) and 6 of the 1995 United Nations Agreement for the Implementation of the Provisions of the United Nations Convention on the Law of the Sea of 10 December 1982 relating to the Conservation and Management of Straddling Fish Stocks and Highly Migratory Fish Stocks, 4 August 1995, *2167 U.N.T.S. 88*; and Paragraph 8 of the preamble, Articles 1 and 8(9) of the 2001 Stockholm Convention on Persistent Organic Pollutants, 22 May 2001, *2256 UNTS 119*. Precautionary language can also be discerned in older legal instruments, including paragraph 5 of the preamble of the 1985 Vienna Convention for the Protection of the Ozone Layer, 22 March 1985, *1513 U.N.T.S. 323*; paragraph 8 of the preamble to the 1987 Montreal Protocol on Substances that Deplete the Ozone Layer, 16 September 1987 (as amended in 1992), *26 ILM 1550 (1987)*; and Article IV of the 1968 African Convention on the Conservation of Nature and Natural Resources (revised 11 July 2003).

'significant reduction or loss of biological diversity' and its 2000 Cartagena Protocol on Biosafety which refers only to 'adverse effects'.[93]

Apart from these environmental treaties, elements of the precautionary principle can also be found in treaties in other fields of international law. UNCLOS Article 206 provides, for example, that States must assess the potential effects of planned activities under their jurisdiction or control when they have '*reasonable* grounds for believing' that such activities '*may* cause substantial pollution of or significant and harmful changes to the marine environment'.[94] Furthermore, the Agreement on the Application of Sanitary and Phytosanitary Measures (SPS Agreement), one of the treaties of the World Trade Organisation (WTO), also contains some references to precaution, in particular in Article 5.7, which permits members of the WTO to provisionally adopt measures to protect human, animal or plant life or health '[i]n cases where relevant scientific evidence is insufficient'.[95]

The concept of precaution is also found in IHL. In addition to provisions relating to precautions in situations of armed conflict, reference can be made to the environmental provisions of Additional Protocol I to the 1949 Geneva Conventions relating to the protection of victims of international armed conflicts. Both Articles 35(3) and 55 of Additional Protocol I prohibit parties to an armed conflict from employing 'methods or means of warfare which are intended, *or may be expected*, to cause widespread, long-term and severe damage to the natural environment'.[96] The more

[93] See paragraph 9 of the Preamble to the Biodiversity Convention and Article 1 of the Cartagena Protocol on Biosafety.

[94] Author's emphasis added.

[95] See Article 5.7 of the Agreement on the Application of Sanitary and Phytosanitary Measures, 15 December 1993, *1867 UNTS 154*. In the EC–Hormones case, the WTO Panel confirmed that 'the precautionary principle has been incorporated and given a specific meaning in Article 5.7 of the SPS Agreement'. See EC Measures Concerning Meat and Meat Products (Hormones) – Complaint by the United States – Report of the Panel, *Doc. WT/DS26/R/USA*, 18 August 1997. For a more detailed analysis of the role of the precautionary principle in WTO law, see Gehring and Cordonnier-Segger, *Precaution in World Trade Law*.

[96] Protocol Additional to the Geneva Conventions of 12 August 1949, and Relating to the Protection of Victims of International Armed Conflicts (Protocol I), Geneva, 8 June 1977, *1125 UNTS 3*. Author's emphasis added. It may be noted that IHL also contains a principle of precaution, but this principle has a meaning which is distinct from the precautionary principle discussed in this section. The IHL principle of precaution sees to the obligation of parties to an armed conflict to take constant care during military operations to protect the civilian population as far as possible from (the effects of) an attack. On this subject, see Kalshoven and Zegveld, *Constraints on the Waging of War*, 3rd edn., pp. 107–11.

restrictive approach that emerges from these provisions reflects battlefield practice and, more specifically, the need to give clear instructions to the military officers who make the decisions in the field.

Despite the fact that the principle is fairly firmly rooted in international environmental law, international courts have so far been hesitant to expressly apply the precautionary principle. The International Court of Justice, for example, could have taken the opportunity to pronounce on the principle in two cases relating to the management of shared watercourses. Both cases involved disputes regarding projects which could have affected the aquatic ecosystem of the river. However, in both cases the Court relied on the general obligation of prevention, without clarifying whether this obligation could entail precautionary action.

In the *case concerning the Gabčíkovo–Nagymaros Project*, the Court determined that 'in the field of environmental protection, vigilance and prevention are required on account of the often irreversible character of damage to the environment and of the limitations inherent in the very mechanism of reparation of this type of damage'.[97] However, the Court did not pronounce on the standards that parties should adopt in this respect. Instead, the Court insisted on the obligation for the parties to the dispute to look afresh at the matter and to negotiate with a view to finding a solution to the problem. As part of this obligation to negotiate, the Court stressed that parties must take into account modern norms and standards derived from the concept of sustainable development, but left it to the parties to decide which standards to apply.[98]

Similarly, in the *Pulp Mills case*, the International Court of Justice relied entirely on the 'principle of prevention, as a customary rule', interpreted as an obligation for States to stop their activities from causing damage to the territory of other States.[99] Moreover, although the Court did acknowledge that 'a precautionary approach may be relevant in the interpretation and application of the Statute' – the principal legal instrument referred to by the Court in the case – it did so only because both parties to the dispute agreed that the instrument itself adopted a precautionary approach.[100]

Arguably, the Court's hesitance to expressly rely on the precautionary principle in these cases can be explained with reference to the subject

[97] International Court of Justice, Gabčíkovo–Nagymaros Project (*Hungary* v. *Slovakia*), Judgment of 25 September 1997, *I.C.J. Reports 1997*, p. 7, para. 140.

[98] Ibid.

[99] International Court of Justice, Case Concerning Pulp Mills on the River Uruguay (*Argentina* v. *Uruguay*), Judgment of 20 April 2010, *I.C.J. Reports 2010*, para. 101.

[100] Ibid., paras. 160–64.

matter of the disputes. Both cases involved a dispute involving a shared natural resource and the obligation to prevent extraterritorial damage to the environment of other States applies to this. As explained earlier, this obligation has a firm status in international law, while the precautionary principle is still controversial. Generally, the Court adopts a conservative approach, meaning that it only embraces principles that are generally accepted by States. In these cases, the Court had such a principle at its disposal, i.e., the principle of prevention, interpreted as an obligation not to cause extraterritorial damage to the environment of other States. Therefore, the Court arguably did not feel the need to pronounce on the status or applicability of the precautionary principle to these disputes.

While the International Court of Justice was able to settle the disputes brought before it without pronouncing on the precautionary principle, the WTO dispute settlement mechanism was expressly called upon to apply the precautionary principle in two cases brought before it. In the *EC–Hormones case* the European Communities relied on the precautionary principle as a general customary rule of international law, or at least as a general principle of international law, in order to introduce an import ban on meat treated with hormones from the United States and Canada. Both the Panel and the Appellate Body confirmed that the precautionary principle is reflected in the SPS Agreement, in particular in Article 5.7 concerning the right of States to provisionally adopt sanitary and phytosanitary measures on the basis of available pertinent information. Moreover, the Appellate Body concluded that the precautionary principle is also reflected in the sixth paragraph of the preamble of the APS Agreement, as well as in its Article 3.3, which 'explicitly recognize the right of Members to establish their own appropriate level of sanitary protection, which level may be higher (i.e., more cautious) than that implied in existing international standards, guidelines and recommendations'.[101]

However, the Appellate Body did not accept the contention of the European Communities that other provisions of the SPS Agreement – i.e., concerning the assessment of risks – must be interpreted in light of the precautionary principle, because, in the view of the Appellate Body, the precautionary principle was not part of the general principles of

[101] EC Measures Concerning Meat and Meat Products (Hormones) – Complaint by the United States – Report of the Appellate Body, *Doc. WT/DS26/R/USA*, 16 January 1998, para. 124.

law and 'at least outside the field of international environmental law, still awaits authoritative formulation as a customary principle of international law'.[102] This was the point of view of the Appellate Body in 1998.

In 2006, in the *EC–Biotech case* the Panel gave ample consideration to the contention of the European Communities that the precautionary principle had '"by now" become a fully-fledged and general principle of international law'.[103] Nevertheless, the Panel still did not find sufficient evidence to conclude that the status of the precautionary principle had changed since the decision of the Appellate Body in the *EC–Hormones case*. Therefore, it decided to act with prudence and not to take a stand on this complex issue.[104]

Finally, ITLOS was also called upon to apply the precautionary principle in three cases relating to the effects of activities on the marine environment.[105] ITLOS did not explicitly pronounce on the status of the precautionary principle in any of these cases. However, it did refer to 'prudence and caution' as a legal basis for ordering precautionary measures.[106]

In the *Southern Bluefin Tuna cases*, the decision of ITLOS to impose provisional measures on the parties to the dispute in order 'to preserve the rights of the parties and to avert further deterioration of the southern bluefin tuna stock' was based on the existence of scientific uncertainty regarding measures to be taken to conserve the stock of southern bluefin

102 Ibid., para. 123. The Appellate Body refers more specifically to the rules for treaty interpretation as incorporated in Articles 31 and 32 of the Vienna Convention on the Law of Treaties. In this regard, Article 31(3)(c) stipulates that 'any relevant rules of international law applicable between the parties' should be taken into account when interpreting the treaty. However, according to the Appellate body, it is far from clear that the precautionary principle constitutes a principle of general or customary international law and that it thus constitutes such 'a rule of international law'.

103 EC – Approval and Marketing of Biotech Products, Panel Reports, *Docs. WT/DS/291/R, WT/DS/292/R, WT/DS/293/R*, 29 September 2006, para. 786.

104 Ibid., para. 789.

105 These are the Southern Bluefin Tuna cases (*New Zealand* v. *Japan*; *Australia* v. *Japan*), Request for Provisional Measures, Order of 27 August 1999; the Mox Plant Case (*Ireland* v. *United Kingdom*), Request for Provisional Measures, Order of 3 December 2001; and the Case Concerning Land Reclamation by Singapore In and Around the Straits of Johor (*Malaysia* v. *Singapore*), Request for Provisional Measures, Order of 8 October 2003.

106 See the Southern Bluefin Tuna Cases, para. 77; the Mox Plant case, para. 84; and the Land Reclamation case, para. 99. In its Advisory Opinion on Deep Seabed Mining, ITLOS explicitly recognised that it had applied a precautionary approach in these cases. See International Tribunal for the Law of the Sea, Responsibilities and Obligations of States Sponsoring Persons and Entities with respect to Activities in the Area, Advisory Opinion, 1 February 2011, para. 132.

tuna.[107] In addition, in the *Mox Plant case*, the tribunal used 'prudence and caution' as a legal basis for imposing an obligation on parties to exchange information concerning risks or effects from the operation of a radioactive plant.[108] Finally, in the case concerning the Straits of Johor, ITLOS itself advocated a broader application of the preventive approach when it considered that 'given the *possible* implications of land reclamation on the marine environment, prudence and caution require that Malaysia and Singapore establish mechanisms for exchanging information and assessing the risks or effects of land reclamation works and devising ways to deal with them in the areas concerned'.[109]

Although these judicial decisions demonstrate that international courts are hesitant to apply the precautionary principle *expressis verbis*, the decisions also demonstrate a general willingness of courts to apply precautionary measures. The reliance of ITLOS on 'prudence and caution', as well as the pronouncements of the WTO dispute settlement mechanism on the role of precaution in WTO law, attests to this.

Furthermore, as referred to in the previous section, the International Court of Justice considered in the *Pulp Mills case* that parties 'must, for the purposes of protecting and preserving the aquatic environment with respect to activities which may be liable to cause transboundary harm, carry out an environmental impact assessment'.[110] Although many uncertainties remain regarding the precise content of the obligation to conduct an EIA,[111] as the Court explicitly recognised in its judgement, it did acknowledge the existence of such a basic obligation for States to prevent extraterritorial damage to the environment.[112]

[107] International Tribunal for the Law of the Sea, Southern Bluefin Tuna Cases (*New Zealand* v. *Japan*; *Australia* v. *Japan*), Request for Provisional Measures, Order of 27 August 1999, paras. 79–80.

[108] International Tribunal for the Law of the Sea, Mox Plant Case (*Ireland* v. *United Kingdom*), Request for Provisional Measures, Order of 3 December 2001, para. 84.

[109] International Tribunal for the Law of the Sea, Case Concerning Land Reclamation by Singapore in and around the Straits of Johor (*Malaysia* v. *Singapore*), Request for Provisional Measures, Order of 8 October 2003, para. 99. Emphasis added. For a more thorough review of these cases, see Schrijver, 'The Status of the Precautionary Principle in International Law and Its Application and Interpretation in International Litigation', pp. 246–50; and Trouwborst, *Evolution and Status of the Precautionary Principle in International Law*, pp. 156–78.

[110] International Court of Justice, Case Concerning Pulp Mills on the River Uruguay (*Argentina* v. *Uruguay*), Judgment of 20 April 2010, *I.C.J. Reports 2010*, para. 204.

[111] Ibid., para. 205 and Trouwborst, *Precautionary Rights and Duties of States*, p. 175.

[112] Also see Trouwborst, *Precautionary Rights and Duties of States*, p. 175, who argues that an 'EIA . . . can either provide the basis for precautionary action or constitute a precautionary measure in itself'. In the first instance, the EIA aims to determine the scale of the potential

According to the Court, such an obligation exists prior to the implementation of a project, while it continues to exist once 'operations have started and, where necessary, throughout the life of the project' in the form of the continuous monitoring of the effects of the operations on the environment.[113]

Although the statement of the Court regarding the obligation to conduct an EIA is limited to the prevention of extraterritorial damage to the environment, the obligation to conduct an EIA also applies to other situations. This is clear from Principle 17 of the 1992 Rio Declaration, which states in general terms that '[e]nvironmental impact assessment, as a national instrument, shall be undertaken for proposed activities that are likely to have a significant adverse impact on the environment'. Furthermore, Article 14 of the 1992 Convention on Biological Diversity provides that each party shall

> [i]ntroduce appropriate procedures requiring environmental impact assessment of its proposed projects that are likely to have significant adverse effects on biological diversity with a view to avoiding or minimizing such effects and, where appropriate, allow for public participation in such procedures.

Guidelines were also adopted by the Conference of the Parties in the context of the 1971 Ramsar Convention on the Protection of Wetlands, calling on parties 'to ensure that any projects, plans, programmes and policies with the potential to alter the ecological character of wetlands in the Ramsar List . . . are subjected to rigorous impact assessment procedures'.[114] In addition, the World Bank prescribes that EIAs must be carried out 'to examine the potential environmental risks and benefits associated with Bank investment lending operations'.[115]

There is no standard procedure for conducting an EIA. As the International Court of Justice noted in the *Pulp Mills case*,

> it is for each State to determine in its domestic legislation or in the authorization process for the project, the specific content of the environmental impact assessment required in each case, having regard to the nature and

damage (significant, serious or severe) in order to decide on the measures to be taken. In the latter case, the EIA aims to determine whether at all a particular activity or policy carries a risk of causing of damage to the environment.

113 International Court of Justice, Case Concerning Pulp Mills on the River Uruguay (*Argentina* v. *Uruguay*), Judgment of 20 April 2010, *I.C.J. Reports 2010*, para. 205.

114 Resolution VII.16 of the Conference of the Parties on Impact Assessment (1999).

115 See http://web.worldbank.org under 'Environmental Assessment in Operational Policy'. Also see Sands and Peel, *Principles of International Environmental Law*, 3rd edn., pp. 617–19.

> magnitude of the proposed development and its likely adverse impact on the environment as well as to the need to exercise due diligence in conducting such an assessment.[116]

The flexibility of an EIA as an instrument for assessing risks to the environment resulting from proposed projects makes it suitable for application in situations of armed conflict as well. The precise requirements can be accommodated to the specific circumstances, while leaving intact the basic obligation to assess the impacts of a proposed project on the environment on the basis of available scientific information.

In conclusion, it can be argued that the legal status of the precautionary principle, either as a general principle of international law or as a principle of customary international law, has not yet fully materialised. Although it seems that an increasing number of States – including all the States belonging to the European Union – consider the principle to be part of customary international law, there is as yet no worldwide agreement on its precise content. Nevertheless, there is general agreement on the need to take precautions to preserve and protect the environment. A precautionary approach to environmental damage is reflected in many treaties and has also found recognition in international case law. Moreover, specialised procedures have been developed in order to assess the risks involved in particular projects. EIAs can be effective tools for implementing the precautionary principle.

4.4 Common regimes

International environmental law contains several specialised regimes aimed at protecting particular species or parts of the environment for the benefit of a larger community of States. Most of these treaties assign a special status to the objects they aim to protect. For example, international environmental law has designated specific areas and their natural resources as 'world heritage'. Some treaties deal with natural resources that are shared by two or more States. In addition, certain environmental processes such as climate change and the loss of biological diversity have been proclaimed a 'common concern of humankind'.

In all these cases, States are required to take special measures to protect a common interest. Some of these measures have a direct impact on the right of States to use their natural resources freely, while others are

[116] International Court of Justice, Case Concerning Pulp Mills on the River Uruguay (*Argentina* v. *Uruguay*), Judgment of 20 April 2010, *I.C.J. Reports 2010*, para. 205.

aimed at giving States a fair share in the benefits resulting from common resources. A distinction should be made in this respect between natural resources that are situated within the national territories of States and natural resources that fall outside State sovereignty. Natural resources that are situated within State territory fall under the permanent sovereignty of the State where they are located. If such natural resources are located in more than one territory – or, in the case of species, if they migrate from one territory to another – they should be regarded as shared natural resources. These natural resources fall under the permanent sovereignty of more than one State. Some natural resources do not belong to particular States, because they fall entirely outside State territory. These natural resources are shared by all States.[117]

Natural resources that are located within State territory are protected by regimes for 'world heritage', 'shared natural resources' and the 'common concern of mankind', while natural resources that are located outside the territory of a State are protected either by the notion of the 'common heritage of humankind'[118] or by the notion of the 'common concern of mankind'. This section discusses some of these specialised regimes, focusing on the measures they impose on States for the protection of the common interests of a larger community of States.

4.4.1 Natural resources situated within State territory with special importance for the international community

Some natural resources that are situated within the territory of a State have been attributed a special status because of their outstanding importance for the international community as a whole. Examples of such regimes include those for 'wetlands of international importance' under the Ramsar Convention on Wetlands of International Importance and 'world heritage' under the UNESCO Convention for the Protection of World Heritage. The primary aim of these regimes is to preserve sites either 'on account of their international significance in terms of ecology, botany, zoology, limnology or hydrology' or because of their 'outstanding universal value' from the point of view of science, conservation or natural beauty.[119]

[117] Also see Schrijver, *Development without Destruction*, pp. 34–113.

[118] The notion of the 'common heritage of mankind' is not discussed, because it applies only to natural resources that are located in areas beyond national jurisdiction.

[119] Article 2(2) of the Convention on Wetlands of International Importance Especially as Waterfowl Habitat, 2 February 1971, *996 UNTS 245*; Article 2 of the UNESCO Convention

The Ramsar and UNESCO Conventions both function on the basis of lists. Under the Ramsar Convention, it is the State itself which decides on the listing, while the UNESCO Convention has designated a committee for this purpose. However, the committee decides only on the basis of a proposal by the State party on whose territory the natural heritage is situated.[120] The primary characteristic of both regimes is that the protection of the sites is based on the principle of sovereignty. Both regimes place the primary responsibility for preserving the sites on the national State and reserve a complementary role for the international community to assist in the protection of the sites.[121]

Under the Ramsar Convention, the role of the international community is limited. International cooperation for the protection of wetlands consists mainly of mutual consultation and coordination of policies and regulations. The World Heritage Convention contains a more far-reaching system of cooperation. While Article 6(1) formulates a general duty of cooperation for the international community as a whole, Article 6(2) formulates an obligation for all States parties to help the State on whose territory the heritage is situated to implement its obligations under the convention, if that State so requests. In addition, the Convention establishes a fund for the protection of the world heritage, financed by the States parties to the Convention. This fund is used to provide assistance to States for the preservation of their world heritage.[122]

The World Heritage Convention also contains some provisions that have special relevance for the protection of world heritage in situations of armed conflict. First, States parties are prohibited from taking 'any deliberate measures which might damage directly or indirectly the

Concerning the Protection of the World Cultural and Natural Heritage, 16 November 1972, *1037 UNTS 151*. It should be noted that the UNESCO World Heritage Convention does not only protect natural but also cultural properties of special significance. In addition, the 1954 Hague Convention for the Protection of Cultural Property in the Event of Armed Conflict (14 May 1954, *249 U.N.T.S. 240*) has been specifically adopted to protect cultural properties in situations of armed conflict. A cultural property that is under threat at this moment is the ancient city of Aleppo in Syria, which requires protection under the UNESCO World Heritage Convention. In addition, Syria is a party to the 1954 Hague Convention, referred to above. No specific convention has been adopted to protect natural heritage in situations of armed conflict. See Hulme, *War Torn Environment*, pp. 113–16, on the relevance of the 1954 Hague Convention for the protection of the environment.

120 Article 2 of the Ramsar Convention; Article 11 of the World Heritage Convention.

121 Articles 2(3) and 5 of the Ramsar Convention; Articles 4, 6 and 7 of the World Heritage Convention.

122 See Part IV of the World Heritage Convention.

cultural and natural heritage... situated on the territory of other States Parties to this Convention'.[123] In other words, States may not deliberately harm the world heritage. A similar prohibition for States with regard to the world heritage situated within their own borders can be deduced from the general obligation contained in Article 4 for States parties to ensure 'the identification, protection, conservation, presentation and transmission to future generations' of the world heritage situated within their territories.[124]

The possibility provided by the Convention of entering natural heritage threatened by 'the outbreak or the threat of an armed conflict' on a list of 'World Heritage in Danger' is of particular interest for the protection of natural resources in situations of armed conflict.[125] The inclusion of a site in this list enables the World Heritage Committee to immediately allocate assistance to the endangered site from the Convention's Fund. Five nature reserves in the DR Congo have been placed on this list.[126]

The last treaty that should be mentioned in this category is the CITES.[127] This Convention is aimed at protecting endangered species of flora and fauna against overexploitation in international trade. Some of these species are migratory and therefore fall into the category of shared natural resources, while other species are found exclusively within the jurisdiction of a single State. The Convention recognises that wild fauna and flora are 'an irreplaceable part of the natural systems of the earth [and therefore] must be protected for this and the generations to come'.[128] The Convention therefore has a listing system similar to the systems of the Ramsar and World Heritage Conventions. It makes a distinction between three categories of species, based on their conservation status. The most threatened species are listed in Appendix I and are subject to particularly strict international regulation, while Appendix II and III species can be traded, provided that national authorities certify that the species have a legal origin and that trade is not detrimental to their survival.

[123] Article 6(3) of the World Heritage Convention.

[124] It should however be noted that this obligation can only be said to work *erga omnes partes*. See O'Keefe, 'World Cultural Heritage', pp. 189–209. Reference should further be made to the 1954 Hague Convention for the Protection of Cultural Property in the Event of Armed Conflict, referred to previously.

[125] Article 11(4) of the World Heritage Convention.

[126] For the role of the World Heritage Convention in protecting the Virunga Park in the DR Congo, see Sjöstedt, 'The Role of Multilateral Environmental Agreements in Armed Conflict', pp. 129–53.

[127] CITES, 3 March 1973, *993 UNTS 243*.

[128] Ibid., first paragraph of the preamble.

CITES is of particular relevance to this book, because it can be used to curtail the trade in specific conflict resources, especially wildlife and timber. Although the focus of CITES is on protecting endangered species, including commercial species in the lists covered by the Convention is certainly not out of the question. In fact, almost 200 commercial timber species have been listed in one of the CITES Appendices.[129] The CITES system works on the basis of export and import permits, which must be verified by management and scientific authorities in the countries of origin and destination. CITES can perform two different functions in preventing the trade in conflict resources. First, it can help national authorities to halt the trade in timber by rebel groups, as only the national authorities can grant export permits. Furthermore, the permit system of the Convention can assist the Security Council when it establishes a ban on timber originating from a particular country, provided that other States exporting the species under embargo adhere to CITES as well.[130] In that case, all the timber that is traded without an official permit must be considered suspicious.

4.4.2 *Common concern*

Other common regimes are based on the notion of 'common concern'.[131] Common concern regimes are aimed at creating a system of cooperation to address specific problems that concern the international community as a whole by dealing with matters of common concern at an international level. Common concern regimes qualify State sovereignty in a way similar to the World Heritage and Ramsar Conventions, in the sense that

[129] See International Tropical Timber Organization, Tracking Sustainability: Review of Electronic and Semi-electronic Timber Tracking Technologies, ITTO Technical Series 40, October 2012, p. 3.

[130] It is relevant to note that Article X of the Convention contains a provision on trade with non-parties to CITES. This provision stipulates as follows: 'Where export or re-export is to, or import is from, a State not a Party to the present Convention, comparable documentation issued by the competent authorities in that State which substantially conforms with the requirements of the present Convention for permits and certificates may be accepted in lieu thereof by any Party'. This means, for example, that a party to CITES that imports a particular species must ask the exporting State for documentation proving that the species is traded legally and has been harvested in a sustainable way.

[131] For a more detailed analysis of the notion of common concern, see Biermann, 'Common Concern of Humankind', pp. 426–81; Shelton, 'Common Concern of Humanity', pp. 83–90; Brunnée, 'Common Areas, Common Heritage and Common Concern', pp. 550–73; and Birnie, Boyle and Redgwell, *International Law and the Environment*, 3rd edn., pp. 128–30.

States retain primary responsibility for the protection of their natural resources.

The Convention on Biological Diversity is a good example. In its preamble, the Convention affirms that 'the conservation of biological diversity is a common concern of humankind', while reaffirming that 'States have sovereign rights over their own biological resources'. In addition, the preamble qualifies these sovereign rights by '[r]eaffirming also that States are responsible for conserving their biological diversity and for using their biological resources in a sustainable manner'. The provisions elaborate on this by imposing obligations upon States regarding the conservation and sustainable use of (components of) biological diversity, while defining 'the sovereign right [of States] to exploit their own resources pursuant to their own environmental policies' as a principle.

In addition to the conservation of biological diversity, the common concern concept has also been applied to climate change. In its preamble, the UNFCCC acknowledges that 'change in the Earth's climate and its adverse effects are a common concern of humankind', while it reaffirms 'the principle of sovereignty of States in international cooperation to address climate change'. Moreover, obligations for States concerning the formulation of policies regarding the mitigation of climate change have been inserted in the provisions. However, despite the application of the concept in these conventions, its significance as a system for international cooperation has remained modest. The concept has not been applied to other environmental problems.

Common concern regimes are important to this book because these regimes impose obligations upon States to protect their natural resources for the benefit of the entire community of States. Relevant obligations in the Convention on Biological Diversity and under the Climate Convention include monitoring and reporting obligations, as well as financial assistance and technology transfer to developing countries. The Convention on Biological Diversity, and in particular the constraints it places on the use of biological diversity and biological resources, are the most important for the purposes of the present book. As discussed in greater detail in Chapter 5, States involved in an armed conflict should at the very least refrain from actions that cause a serious threat to biological diversity.

4.4.3 Shared natural resources

Shared natural resources fall into two different categories. The first category concerns natural resources that are situated on the border between two or more States, such as transboundary forests or wetlands. The second category concerns natural resources that are present within different States' borders at different times, such as migratory (land) animals, straddling fish stocks and freshwater resources.[132] In both cases, States must take special protective measures and must cooperate to protect their interests in the shared natural resources. The protection of shared natural resources has two major objectives: (1) to preserve the natural resources and (2) to guarantee a fair share in the resources for the States where these natural resources are found. One major difference from the regimes discussed in the previous sections is therefore that the natural resources are not protected in order to protect a special interest of the international community as a whole, but rather to protect the rights of directly affected States.

Although the issue of shared natural resources is also addressed to some extent in older conventions,[133] the 1978 Draft Principles of Conduct in the Field of the Environment for the Guidance of States in the Conservation and Harmonious Utilization of Natural Resources Shared by Two or More States are the first to address the issue of shared natural resources in a systematic way. These principles were prepared by UNEP in response to a request by the UN General Assembly to report on measures to be adopted for the implementation of a system for the effective cooperation between States for the conservation and harmonious utilisation of shared natural resources.[134] In its Resolution 34/186 of 18 December 1979, the UN General Assembly took note of the principles while requesting States 'to

[132] See the Convention on the Conservation of Migratory Species of Wild Animals, 23 June 1979, *1651 UNTS 333*; the United Nations Agreement for the Implementation of the Provisions of the United Nations Convention on the Law of the Sea of 10 December 1982 relating to the Conservation and Management of Straddling Fish Stocks and Highly Migratory Fish Stocks, 4 August 1995, *2167 UNTS 88*; and the UN Convention on the Law of the Non-navigational Uses of International Watercourses, 21 May 1997, *36 ILM 700 (1997)*.

[133] See, in particular, Article 5 of the 1971 Ramsar Convention on Wetlands of International Importance Especially as Waterfowl Habitat, 2 February 1971, 996 UNTS 245, which emphasises that a duty of consultation about the implementation of obligations arising from the Convention exists 'especially in the case of a wetland extending over the territories of more than one Contracting Party or where a water system is shared by Contracting Parties'.

[134] Draft Principles of Conduct in the Field of the Environment for the Guidance of States in the Conservation and Harmonious Utilization of Natural Resources Shared by Two or More States, *17 ILM 1097 (1978)*. For the request of the UN General Assembly, see UNGA Resolution 3129 (XXVIII) of 13 December 1973 concerning Co-operation in the Field of the Environment Concerning Natural Resources Shared by Two or More States.

use the principles as guidelines and recommendations in the formulation of bilateral or multilateral conventions regarding natural resources shared by two or more States'.[135]

Many of the UNEP principles reflect modern obligations in international law, such as the obligation not to cause transboundary damage and the obligation to conduct an EIA. The principles also formulate standards for cooperation between States for the protection of shared natural resources, including the exchange of information, notification and consultation between States which share resources. In addition, they cover the peaceful settlement of disputes relating to shared natural resources and the liability of States for environmental damage resulting from violations of their international obligations with regard to the conservation and utilisation of shared natural resources.

Since the adoption of the UNEP principles, several treaties have been adopted that deal specifically with the management of shared natural resources. One of the most sophisticated legal regimes in this respect relates to the use of international rivers, lakes and groundwater sources. Specific reference can be made to the 1997 UN Convention on the Law of the Non-navigational Uses of International Watercourses, which formulates a dual obligation for States to utilise the watercourse in an equitable and reasonable manner and to cooperate in its protection and development.[136] Arguably, these obligations not only apply to the use of the watercourse itself, but also have implications for the use of the natural resources found within the watercourse, such as alluvial minerals. The obligation of equitable use implies, *inter alia,* that States must ensure that other States can enjoy the shared resource on the basis of equality.[137] It can be assumed that the obligation of equitable use implies

[135] UNGA Resolution 34/186 concerning Cooperation in the Field of the Environment Concerning Natural Resources Shared by Two or More States, 18 December 1979, especially paras. 2 and 3.

[136] See Article 5 of the UN Convention on the Law of the Non-navigational Uses of International Watercourses. For an analysis of international law relating to the non-navigational use of international watercourses, see McCaffrey, *The Law of International Watercourses*; and Boisson de Chazournes and Salman (eds.), *Les Ressources en Eau et le Droit International.*

[137] See the judgment of the International Court of Justice in the case concerning the Gabčíkovo–Nagymaros Project (*Hungary* v. *Slovakia*), Judgment of 25 September 1997, *I.C.J. Reports 1997*, p. 7, para. 85, in which the court determines the existence of 'a common legal right, the essential features of which are the perfect equality of all riparian States in the use of the whole course of the river and the exclusion of any preferential privilege of any one riparian State in relation to the others', referring to the 1929 *Lac Lanoux case*

a prohibition against States seriously upsetting the ecological balance of the watercourse, e.g., by causing pollution through exploitation of the natural resources found within the watercourse.

Furthermore, reference can be made to UNCLOS, which contains some basic rules for the protection of enclosed or semi-enclosed seas. Relevant obligations for States bordering on an enclosed or semi-enclosed sea include a duty to coordinate the management, conservation, exploration and exploitation of the living resources of the sea, as well as a duty to coordinate the implementation of their rights and duties with respect to the protection and preservation of the marine environment.[138] These rules complement the general provisions on the protection and preservation of the marine environment, included in Part XII of the Convention. This part deals primarily with the prevention of pollution in the marine environment.

There are several other regimes for the management and protection of shared natural resources. These include the Convention on the Conservation of Migratory Species of Wild Animals and the 1995 Straddling Fish Stocks Agreement.[139] For other shared natural resources, such as forests, oil or gas, there are still no specific rules. There are a few regional treaties concerning transboundary forests, including the Amazon Cooperation Treaty and the Congo Basin Conservation Treaty.[140] In contrast, controversy regarding the delimitation of geographical boundaries between States and political sensitivities have so far prevented the adoption of specific rules for shared oil and natural gas deposits altogether.[141]

In conclusion, legal regimes for the management and protection of shared natural resources are based on a dual obligation to protect these

rendered by the Permanent Court of Justice, and that 'Czechoslovakia, by unilaterally assuming control of a shared resource, and thereby depriving Hungary of its right to an equitable and reasonable share of the natural resources of the Danube . . . failed to respect the proportionality which is required by international law'.

138 See Part IX of the UN Convention on the Law on the Sea concerning enclosed or semi-enclosed seas, in particular Article 123. It should be noted that the nonliving resources of the sea, such as minerals, oil and gas, are exempted from the regime for cooperation.

139 Convention on the Conservation of Migratory Species of Wild Animals, 23 June 1979, *1651 UNTS 333*; United Nations Agreement for the Implementation of the Provisions of the United Nations Convention on the Law of the Sea of 10 December 1982 Relating to the Conservation and Management of Straddling Fish Stocks and Highly Migratory Fish Stocks, 4 August 1995, *2167 UNTS 88*.

140 For example, see the Amazon Cooperation Treaty of 3 July 1978, concluded between the States on whose territory the Amazon is situated.

141 The topic of oil and natural gas was originally envisaged by the ILC in 2002 as part of its work on shared natural resources, but in the end it was not considered feasible to draft articles relating to the use of such shared oil and gas deposits.

resources and to cooperate with regard to their protection. This obligation to cooperate with regard to the protection and management of shared natural resources is firmly rooted in international law. In the Pulp Mills case, the International Court of Justice stated that 'the procedural obligations of informing, notifying and negotiating . . . are all the more vital when a shared resource is at issue . . . which can only be protected through close and continuous co-operation' between the interested States.[142] In the *Mox Plant case*, ITLOS also indicated that 'the duty to cooperate is a fundamental principle . . . under . . . general international law'.[143] Arguably, as explored in more detail in Chapter 5, this obligation does not cease to exist in situations of armed conflict.

4.5 Conclusions

This chapter has discussed several principles arising from the field of international environmental law that qualify the right of States to exploit their natural resources. These principles formulate obligations of care for States with regard to the use of their own natural resources and those of other States. Relevant principles include the principle of conservation and sustainable use of natural resources, the principle of intergenerational equity, the principle of prevention and the precautionary principle.

Of the principles discussed in this chapter, two can be considered to have become part of customary international law. These are the principles of sustainable use and the principle of prevention. While the principle of sustainable use is aimed at preserving natural wealth and resources for long-term development, the principle of prevention formulates an obligation of due diligence for States with regard to the prevention of damage to the environment of other States. These principles apply even when States have not subscribed to the relevant treaties in which the principles are embodied.

The principles of intergenerational equity, as well as the precautionary principle, do not have such a firm status in international law. Nevertheless, the principle of intergenerational equity can be regarded as an important argument for most measures that aim at protecting the environment. The precautionary principle, for its part, has also become increasingly

[142] International Court of Justice, Case Concerning Pulp Mills on the River Uruguay (*Argentina* v. *Uruguay*), *I.C.J. Reports 2010*, para. 81.

[143] The Mox Plant case (*Ireland* v. *United Kingdom*), Request for Provisional Measures, Order of 3 December 2001, para. 82. The tribunal confirmed this judgment in its Case Concerning Land Reclamation by Singapore in and around the Straits of Johor (*Malaysia* v. *Singapore*), Provisional Measures, Order of 8 October 2003, para. 92.

important in the last decade. It has been inserted into several international environmental treaties, while elements of the principle can also be found in treaties in other fields of international law. Furthermore, international courts are cautiously starting to attach more weight to the principle. The most important development is that there is now an obligation under international law to perform an EIA in order to assess the risks of a proposed activity on the environment.

Arguably, these principles are not only relevant for the exploitation of natural resources by States in times of peace, but also in situations of armed conflict. Only a few of the armed conflicts examined in this book have amounted to full-scale wars affecting the whole territory of a State. In most of the armed conflicts examined in this book the violence was limited to specific parts of the State territory. In these situations, national authorities must continue to respect their obligations under international environmental law when conducting commercial activities in parts of the territory under their control.

In addition, some of the principles examined in this chapter are also relevant for territories that are occupied by other States. As explained in more detail in Part II of this book, occupants are *de facto* authorities whose legal position can be compared in many ways with that of the national authorities of a State. Although their legal position is primarily governed by IHL, international environmental law is relevant to situations of occupation as well, both directly and indirectly.

Furthermore, this chapter has examined legal regimes aimed at protecting a common interest of two or more States. Some of these common regimes are aimed at protecting natural resources that are only important to specific States, while others are aimed at protecting natural resources that are important to the international community as a whole. This chapter has examined three categories of common regimes. These are regimes aimed at protecting specific natural resources situated within the territory of a single State, but which have special importance for the international community as a whole, regimes that are aimed at addressing a concern that is common to the international community, and regimes for the management of shared natural resources. All these regimes are based on an obligation to individually and collectively protect the natural resources in the interests of all the States concerned. Arguably, this obligation does not cease to exist in situations of armed conflict. Furthermore, the common interest that these regimes are aimed at protecting entails a presumption that they will not be susceptible to unilateral suspension in situations of armed conflict.

Concluding remarks to Part I

This part has examined the legal framework for the governance of natural resources within sovereign States. Chapter 2 examined the principle of permanent sovereignty over natural resources, which is the organising principle for the governance of natural resources within States. This principle formulates a right for States and peoples to freely dispose of their natural resources. Normally this right is exercised by the government of a State on behalf of the State and its people. This only changes when a government is not or is no longer recognised by the international community.

The principle of permanent sovereignty over natural resources can first of all be upheld vis-à-vis other States. In this sense, the principle of permanent sovereignty over natural resources formulates a right for both States and peoples that have not yet organised themselves within sovereign States to exercise control over their natural resources, without interference from other States. This is the horizontal, or external, dimension of the principle of permanent sovereignty over natural resources.

A vertical – or internal – dimension can be added to this horizontal dimension. The 1962 Declaration on the Principle of Permanent Sovereignty over Natural Resources assigns permanent sovereignty not only to States but also to peoples. In addition, the 1962 Declaration formulates an important condition for the exercise of permanent sovereignty by States, namely, that natural resources must be exploited for national development and the well-being of the people of the State. This condition was repeated in several subsequent resolutions and treaties, including those relating to armed conflicts involving natural resources. On the basis of the 1962 Declaration and subsequent instruments, peoples can therefore be identified as subjects and beneficiaries of the principle of permanent sovereignty.

Chapter 3 examined the implications of peoples as subjects and beneficiaries of the principle of permanent sovereignty for the governance of natural resources within sovereign States. It did so from the perspective of human rights law, as this field of international law formulates rights for 'peoples', to be exercised in their relations with States. The chapter concluded that the notion of 'peoples' is a dynamic concept that can designate different groups depending on the precise right that is invoked. With regard to the right to external self-determination, the term 'peoples' is reserved for colonial peoples and peoples under foreign subjugation. As soon as these peoples have attained an international status, the right to self-determination becomes (1) a right of the State and its peoples to be free of foreign interference and (2) a right for the peoples living within the State to freely determine their political system, also referred to as internal self-determination.

Chapter 3 argued that the right to internal self-determination accrues in particular to four groups. These are first, the whole population of a State, both as the sum of the peoples living in that State and as succeeding the people who attained the right to external self-determination. Furthermore, the right to internal self-determination accrues to three specific communities within a State – including in particular, peoples, minorities and indigenous peoples.

The right to self-determination as enshrined in the identical Articles 1 of the ICESCR and the ICCPR entails a right for peoples 'to freely pursue their economic, social and cultural development'. It was argued that within an independent State, this right must be interpreted as a right to be involved in decision-making processes pertaining to development, including decision-making processes regarding the use of the State's natural resources as the capital for development.

The special position of peoples as subjects and beneficiaries of the principle of permanent sovereignty over natural resources therefore has two important implications for the governance of natural resources. First, it entails an obligation for the government to put in place procedures that allow for public participation in decision making regarding the exploitation of natural resources. Public participation can be defined broadly so as to include access to information and to justice. These participatory rights must be regarded as a logical consequence of the right to self-determination of peoples. In addition, the right to freely pursue economic, social and cultural development, as embodied in the right to self-determination and the emerging right to development, entails an additional obligation for governments not only to involve peoples and individuals in the process of development, but also to ensure that the population as a whole, as well as specific groups within society, benefit from the resulting development. The first obligation is firmly established in international law, *inter alia* in Security Council resolutions relating to particular conflicts, while the second obligation finds some resonance in relevant Security Council resolutions.

In addition to human rights law, international environmental law has developed principles that have an impact on the governance of natural resources within States. These principles were examined in Chapter 4.

This chapter demonstrated that international environmental law formulates duties of care for the environment which States must respect when they exploit their natural resources. Chapter 4 discussed the following principles: the principle of sustainable use, the principle of intergenerational equity, the principle of prevention and the precautionary principle.

The principle of sustainable use and the principle of intergenerational equity qualify the right of States to exploit their natural resources in order to safeguard a State's natural resource capital for future development. In addition, the principle of prevention formulates an obligation for States to take measures to prevent damage to the environment of other States. Furthermore, States must act with caution to prevent damage to the environment. Although the precautionary principle is not generally accepted, it entails an obligation to conduct an EIA for resource projects that are likely to cause significant damage to the environment. Today this obligation represents customary international law. All these principles qualify the right of States to exploit their natural resources.

In addition, Chapter 4 examined the concept of common regimes which have been set up to protect a specific interest of a broader community of States. Relevant common regimes include those for the protection of natural resources that have been designated 'world heritage' or 'wetlands of special importance', as well as those for the protection of endangered species. These common regimes share similar characteristics: (1) they were set up to protect natural resources that represent a special interest to the international community as a whole; and (2) they are situated within the territory of a State. Common regimes that were set up to address a 'common concern' of the international community share these characteristics. Finally, common regimes that were set up to protect natural resources shared by two or more States primarily serve to preserve the interests of States that have a share in the natural resources. However, in all cases these regimes protect natural resources because they are important to a broader community of States. It is for this reason that these regimes can be seen as qualifying the right of States to freely dispose of these natural resources.

In conclusion, it can be argued that the legal regime for the governance of natural resources within States is based on the right of States and peoples to freely dispose of their natural resources. This right is normally exercised by the government on behalf of the State and its people. However, the right of a government to dispose of the State's natural resources is qualified by several obligations arising from international human rights and environmental law. These obligations are aimed at ensuring that the government effectively exercises the right of the State to freely dispose of its natural resources for the purpose of promoting sustainable development, in the sense of long-term and inclusive development. It is argued that respect for this framework is paramount, both for the prevention of armed conflicts and for post-conflict reconstruction. Part II of this book examines the applicability of this legal framework in situations of armed conflict.

PART II

The governance of natural wealth and resources in situations of armed conflict

Introductory remarks to Part II

The current part of this book discusses the legal framework for the governance of natural resources in situations of armed conflict, which pose major challenges to the governance of natural resources within States. In many of the conflicts referred to in this book, parts of State territory were brought under the control of armed groups or foreign troops, making it impossible for the government to exercise control over the natural resources situated within these territories. The occupation of the eastern Congo by Uganda and Rwanda in the late 1990s is one example of this. The situation in Côte d'Ivore between 2002 and 2007, where the northern part of Côte d'Ivoire was under the control of the rebel forces that made up the Forces Nouvelles, is another example.

The extent to which contemporary international law is able to address these challenges is examined in this part of the book. To what extent does international law formulate obligations for non-State armed groups and foreign States regarding the use of their adversary's natural resources? In addition, to what extent does international law formulate obligations for States in relation to the exploitation of their own natural resources in situations of armed conflict?

The previous part of this book argued that it is the government of a State that should exploit the State's natural resources on behalf of the State and its people. However, it also demonstrated that the government cannot in all situations be considered to constitute the legitimate representative of the people of the State. Specific problems may arise in internal armed conflicts, where the government is a party to the armed conflict as well. As a party to an armed conflict, a government can have interests that do not coincide with the interests of the people living in the State.

All these situations – occupation by foreign States, territories under the control of armed groups and the exercise of permanent sovereignty over natural resources by governments that are parties to an armed conflict – pose challenges to the premises on which the legal framework for the governance of natural resources is based, in particular the basic premise that natural resources must be exploited for national development and the well-being of the people.

The current legal framework governing the exploitation of natural resources in situations of armed conflict is made up of rules from various fields of international law. Chapter 5 discusses the effects of armed conflict on the general legal framework for the governance of natural resources, as discussed in Part I of this book. The legal framework set out in Part I of this book defines the rights and obligations of governments with regard to the management of the State's natural resources, as well as the effects of particular exploitation activities on the environment of other States. For the purposes of this book, it is especially relevant to examine to what extent this legal framework continues to apply in situations of armed conflict for (1) the actions of governments involved in internal armed conflicts and (2) the actions of States intervening in an armed conflict on the territory of another State.

Chapter 6 discusses the rules of the law of armed conflict, or IHL. This field of international law sets out the rights and obligations of parties to an armed conflict. Although its principal focus is on regulating military operations and their effects on vulnerable groups, IHL does contain some rules that are relevant for the exploitation of natural resources by parties to an armed conflict. In the first place, it contains a well-developed body of rules to regulate the powers of occupants in occupied territory. Moreover, IHL is the only body of international law that applies directly to non-State armed groups.

5

The role of international human rights and environmental law in situations of armed conflict

5.1 Introductory remarks

Pursuant to the principle of permanent sovereignty over natural resources, States and peoples have the right to exploit their natural resources within the limits set by international law, including limits set by international human rights and environmental law. International human rights law formulates as a minimum obligation that '[i]n no case may a people be deprived of its own means of existence'.[1] In addition, both international human rights and environmental law formulate rights relating to public participation in decision making. Furthermore, international environmental law formulates several obligations of care with regard to the use of natural resources. These include an obligation to conserve and sustainably use particular natural resources that are considered important to several States or to the international community as a whole, including biological diversity, international watercourses, wetlands of international importance, threatened species and natural heritage.[2]

These obligations are relevant not only to States exploiting their own natural resources, but also to occupants. Although the rights and obligations of occupants are primarily regulated through IHL, it can be argued that international human rights and environmental law constitute additional sources of obligations for them because of the special responsibility of occupants as *de facto* authorities in occupied territory. This is also explicitly provided in Article 43 of the 1907 Hague Conventions, which

[1] See the identical Articles 1(2) of the ICESCR and the ICCPR, discussed in Chapter 1 of this study.

[2] Relevant obligations can be inferred from the following treaties: the 1992 Convention on Biological Diversity, the 1997 UN Convention on the Law of the Non-navigational Uses of International Watercourses, the 1971 Convention on Wetlands of International Importance Especially as Waterfowl Habitat, the 1973 Convention on International Trade in Endangered Species of Wild Fauna and Flora, the 1979 Convention on the Conservation of Migratory Species of Wild Animals and the 1972 Convention for the Protection of the World Cultural and Natural Heritage. Also see Chapter 4 of this study.

stipulates that occupants must respect the laws in force in occupied territory unless they are 'absolutely prevented' from doing so.

However, it is generally acknowledged that the outbreak of an armed conflict may alter the extent to which obligations under international law have to be fulfilled. The principal questions posed in this chapter are therefore to what extent norms of international human rights and environmental law continue to apply during armed conflict, and what the implications are for the legal framework regarding the exploitation of natural resources in situations of armed conflict.

The effects of armed conflict on treaties constitute a longstanding issue, which has not yet been fully resolved. The Institut de Droit International (IDI) issued a first set of draft articles dealing with the matter as early as 1912, followed by a second set in 1985.[3] Despite the early work of the IDI in this respect, the 1969 Vienna Convention on the Law of Treaties dodges the issue. Article 73 of the Vienna Convention stipulates that '[t]he provisions of the present Convention shall not prejudge any question that may arise in regard to a treaty . . . from the outbreak of hostilities between States'.

During the drafting of the Vienna Convention, the ILC took – in the words of Anthony Aust – an 'ostrich-like' position by arguing that the outbreak of hostilities between States should be considered as an 'entirely abnormal condition', which should not be regulated in a treaty dealing with 'the general rules of international law applicable in the normal relations between states'.[4] Indeed, the reports of the Special Rapporteurs on the law of treaties, Gerald Fitzmaurice and Humphrey Waldock, both repeatedly emphasise that the effect of armed conflict on treaties raises special issues which should be addressed in a separate study.[5]

In 2004, the ILC finally decided to include the topic in its long-term programme of work, a decision that was endorsed by the UN General Assembly.[6] It led to the drafting of eighteen articles on the effects of armed conflict on treaties. These draft articles were adopted at the

[3] See Règlement Concernant les Effets de la Guerre Sur les Traités, Christiania (1912); and The Effects of Armed Conflicts on Treaties, Helsinki (1985).

[4] Aust, *Modern Treaty Law and Practice*, p. 308.

[5] See the Second Report on the Law of Treaties of the Special Rapporteur, Sir Humphrey Waldock, *UN Doc. A/CN.4/156 and Add. 1–3*, Yearbook of the International Law Commission 1957, Vol. II, p. 79; and the Second Report on the Law of Treaties of the Special Rapporteur, Sir Gerald Fitzmaurice, *UN Doc. A/CN.4/107*, Yearbook of the International Law Commission 1957, Vol. II, p. 30.

[6] See UNGA Resolution 59/41 of 2 December 2004 on the Report of the International Law Commission on the work of its fifty-sixth session, para. 5.

sixty-third session of the ILC in 2011.[7] The UN General Assembly subsequently took note of the draft articles and decided to consider the form to be given to the articles at its session in 2014. However, to date, no further action has been taken.[8]

The draft ILC articles on the effects of armed conflict on treaties are clearly based on earlier work of the ILC, especially on its work in relation to the law on treaties and the law on State responsibility. The draft articles mirror several of the provisions of the Vienna Convention on the Law of Treaties, as well as the ILC Articles on the Responsibility of States for Internationally Wrongful Conduct, also known as the ILC Articles on State Responsibility. The close connection established by the ILC between its new draft articles on the effects of armed conflict on treaties and its earlier work considerably strengthens the authority of the draft articles and might prove conducive to their acceptance by States.

One innovative feature of the ILC draft articles is that they formulate the basic principle that the outbreak of an armed conflict does not *ipso facto* suspend or terminate the operation of treaties in force either between the parties to an armed conflict themselves or between parties to the conflict and third States. More specifically, the treaty relations between a belligerent State, on one hand, and third States, on the other, continue to be governed by the law of peace, supplemented by the law of neutrality in international armed conflict.[9] Thus, as a matter of principle, States involved in an armed conflict – whether international or internal[10] – remain under a duty to abide by their treaty obligations with

[7] Report of the International Law Commission on the work of its sixty-third session, *UN Doc. A/66/10* (2011), paras. 89–101.

[8] See UNGA Resolution 66/99 of 9 December 2011, paras. 3 and 4.

[9] See, *inter alia,* Bothe et al., 'International Law Protecting the Environment during Armed Conflict', p. 581; Koppe, *The Use of Nuclear Weapons and the Protection of the Environment during International Armed Conflict*, p. 336. Specifically on the law of neutrality, which is based on a duty of nonparticipation and impartiality for the neutral State as well as a right not to be adversely affected by the armed conflict, see Bothe, 'Neutrality, Concept and General Rules', pp. 617–34; Hostettler and Danai, 'Neutrality in Land Warfare', pp. 638–43, para. 1; Oppenheim, *International Law: A Treatise*, Vol. II, 7th edn.; and Chadwick, *Traditional Neutrality Revisited.* Of course, the general principle of the continued applicability of treaty relations between a State involved in armed conflict and third States does not imply that these treaty relations remain unaffected in all circumstances. The following section discusses the suspension of treaties during armed conflict as well as circumstances precluding the wrongfulness of a State's acts.

[10] A remarkable novelty of the ILC draft articles on the effects of armed conflict on treaties – as compared with those of the IDI – is that these cover not only international armed conflict, but also internal armed conflicts in which government authorities are involved. Compare Article 1 of the Helsinki Resolution of the IDI with Article 2 of the draft articles of the ILC, *UN Doc. A/CN.4/L.777* of 11 May 2011 on the Effects of Armed Conflicts

regard to third States. Moreover, the articles formulate the principle that even between belligerent States *inter se*, whose relations are of course primarily regulated by IHL, the operation of treaties is considered not to be terminated or suspended *ipso facto* upon the outbreak of armed conflict.[11]

This chapter examines the implications of the basic principle formulated by the ILC for the legal framework governing the management and protection of natural resources during armed conflict. The ILC draft articles on the effects of armed conflict on treaties serve as a guideline throughout this chapter. There are two specific reasons for taking the ILC articles as a point of reference. In the first place, the ILC is a committee set up by the UN General Assembly pursuant to Article 13 of the UN Charter with the specific mandate to promote 'the progressive development of international law and its codification'.[12] In accordance with its mandate, the ILC has been engaged in the preparation of a number of 'draft articles', some of which have subsequently been adopted by States in the form of treaties. The 1969 Vienna Convention on the Law of Treaties is a relevant example. Others, such as the ILC articles on State responsibility, are directly relied on by States and international courts, despite the fact that the articles are not contained in a legally binding document.

The second reason for taking the articles on the effects of armed conflict as a point of reference relates to the working method of the ILC, which is characterised by a constant dialogue with governments throughout the drafting process and which includes an extensive consideration of State practice. The drafting process of ILC articles – and in particular the views expressed by States with regard to the draft articles – therefore offers important insights into the process of customary international law making.

on Treaties: Titles and Texts of the Draft Articles on the Effects of Armed Conflicts on Treaties Adopted by the Drafting Committee on Second Reading. It should be noted that the ILC draft articles exclude armed conflicts between non-State armed groups without the involvement of government forces. This restriction relates to the scope of the draft articles as specified in draft Article 3, i.e., that the articles apply only to situations in which at least one State party to a treaty is also a party to the conflict. See draft Article 3 and the first report on the effects of armed conflict on treaties prepared by Special Rapporteur Mr. Lucius Caflisch, *UN Doc. A/CN.4/627* of 22 March 2010, para. 21.

[11] See, e.g., Lassa Oppenheim, who had already declared in 1912 that 'the opinion is pretty general that war by no means annuls every treaty'. See Oppenheim, *International Law: A Treatise*, Vol. II, 2nd edn., p. 129. Also see Greenwood, 'Scope of Application of Humanitarian Law', p. 73; and Aust, *Modern Treaty Law and Practice*, p. 310.

[12] Statute of the International Law Commission, UNGA Resolution 174 (II) of 21 November 1947, last amended by Resolution 36/39 of 18 November 1981, Article 1.

Section 5.2 examines the outbreak of armed conflict as grounds for the termination or suspension of treaties. Section 5.3 then takes a closer look at the general rules on the termination and suspension of treaties, codified in the Vienna Convention on the Law of Treaties. Section 5.4 examines circumstances precluding wrongfulness under the law of State responsibility for the nonperformance of treaty obligations. Section 5.5 assesses the effects of armed conflict on obligations under customary international law. Finally, Section 5.6 evaluates the role of international human rights and environmental law for the legal regime regarding the exploitation of natural resources in situations of armed conflict.

5.2 The outbreak of armed conflict as grounds for the termination or suspension of treaties

This section assesses the outbreak of armed conflict as autonomous grounds for the termination or suspension of the operation of treaties. It first assesses the general rules formulated in the ILC draft articles and then examines the effects of armed conflict on human rights and environmental treaties specifically, looking both at the rules formulated in the ILC draft articles and at relevant case law.

5.2.1 General principles concerning the effects of armed conflict on treaties

To assess the precise effects of armed conflict on the applicability of individual treaties, the ILC draft articles formulate guidelines on the susceptibility of treaties to suspension, withdrawal or termination as a consequence of the outbreak of an armed conflict.[13] According to Article 4 of the ILC draft Articles, reference should first be made to the provisions of the relevant treaty. It states that 'where a treaty itself contains provisions on its operation in situations of armed conflict, those provisions shall apply'. In this way, the ILC draft Articles follow the system set out in the 1969 Vienna Convention on the Law of Treaties, which determines that the termination, withdrawal from or suspension of the operation

[13] This may be considered one of the most innovative features of the ILC draft Articles on the Effects of Armed Conflict on Treaties, since it breaks away from the traditional approach consisting of a negative assumption that treaty relations will be discontinued during armed conflict.

of a treaty may take place 'in conformity with the provisions of the treaty'.[14]

Second, if the treaty does not contain an express provision on its operation, Article 5 of the ILC draft Articles prescribes that recourse must be made to the rules of international law on treaty interpretation in order to determine whether the treaty is susceptible to termination, withdrawal or suspension in the event of an armed conflict.[15] Thus the text of the provisions should be seen in context and in the light of the object and purpose of the treaty.[16]

If the treaty itself does not provide any indication of its susceptibility to termination, withdrawal or suspension in the event of an armed conflict, recourse should be made to Article 6 of the draft Articles. This provision determines that regard shall be had to external factors indicating the susceptibility of a treaty to termination, withdrawal or suspension in the event of an armed conflict, including the nature of the treaty – in particular its subject matter, its object and purpose, its content and the number of parties to the treaty – as well as the characteristics of the armed conflict, such as its territorial extent, its scale and intensity, its duration, and, in the case of a noninternational armed conflict, the degree of outside involvement.[17]

[14] See Article 54 of the 1969 Vienna Convention on the Law of Treaties (23 May 1969, *1155 U.N.T.S. 331*) on termination and withdrawal and Article 57 on suspension.

[15] This refers to the customary rules on treaty interpretation. Although these rules have been codified in Articles 31 and 32 of the Vienna Convention on the Law of Treaties, the ILC preferred to include a general reference to the customary rules in the draft articles rather than a specific reference to the Vienna Convention. The reason for including such a general reference is twofold. First of all, it is intended to ensure that the provision also addresses those States that are not a party to the Vienna Convention. Second, it is meant as a concession to the committee members favouring a subjective approach to the question of continued applicability of treaties, focusing on the intention of the parties to the treaty rather than on the objective question of whether the treaty is compatible with the situation of armed conflict. See The Effects of Armed Conflicts on Treaties, Statement of the Chairman of the Drafting Committee of 17 May 2011, pp. 9–10. For the customary international law status of these provisions, see, *inter alia*, the judgment of the International Court of Justice in *Oil Platforms* (*Islamic Republic of Iran* v. *United States of America*), Judgment of 6 November 2003, *I.C.J. Reports 2003*, p. 161, para. 41, in which the Court refers to 'the general rules of treaty interpretation, as reflected in the 1969 Vienna Convention on the Law of Treaties'. For references to other ICJ cases confirming the customary international law status of these provisions, see Villiger, *Commentary on the 1969 Vienna Convention on the Law of Treaties*, p. 440, note 121.

[16] Compare Article 31 of the Vienna Convention on the Law of Treaties. For a discussion of the rules on interpretation, see *inter alia* Gardiner, *Treaty Interpretation*; and Linderfalk, *On the Interpretation of Treaties*.

[17] The Commentary on the draft articles indicates that recourse to Article 6 may be made only when interpretation under Article 5 has not provided a conclusive answer. See the

This provision should be read together with Article 7 and the annex containing an indicative list of treaties 'the subject matter of which involves an implication that they continue in operation, in whole or in part, during armed conflict'. These treaties include international human rights and environmental treaties, but also treaties which may cover these subject matters, namely, treaties declaring, creating or regulating a permanent regime or status and multilateral lawmaking treaties.[18] It is ultimately the subject matter of the treaty which determines to what extent a treaty continues to apply during armed conflict. Special Rapporteur Lucius Caflisch indicates that 'the survival of a treaty belonging to a category included in the list may be limited to only some of its provisions'.[19] This implies that parties to an armed conflict must carefully consider to what extent they must continue to respect their obligations under a particular treaty.

Although the list of treaties included in Article 7 is merely indicative and has also met with some criticism,[20] the inclusion in the list of international human rights treaties and environmental treaties, as well as categories which may cover these subject matters, may be interpreted as a strong presumption in favour of the continued applicability of these types of treaties, in whole or in part, during an armed conflict. The following

Statement of the Chairman of the Drafting Committee on the Effects of Armed Conflict on Treaties of 17 May 2011, p. 11. The present author expresses serious doubts with regard to this approach. Several of the factors mentioned in Article 6 are already part of the interpretation exercise under Articles 31 and 32 of the Vienna Convention to which Article 5 of the draft articles refers, including the subject matter of the treaty, its object and purpose and its content.

[18] In this regard, see the comments made by Switzerland, arguing that international environmental treaties may be said to fall within the category of multilateral lawmaking treaties. See Effects of Armed Conflict on Treaties, Comments and Information Received from Governments, *UN Doc. A/CN.4/622*, 15 March 2010, comments concerning draft Article 5 and its annex. For a study of the effects of armed conflict on international environmental agreements in particular, see Vöneky, 'A New Shield for the Environment', pp. 20–32.

[19] International Law Commission, First Report on the Effects of Armed Conflicts on Treaties, by Mr. Lucius Caflisch, Special Rapporteur, *UN Doc. A/CN.4/627* of 22 March 2010, para. 69.

[20] For comments by governments in respect of the list, see Effects of Armed Conflict on Treaties, Comments and Information Received from Governments, *UN Doc. A/CN.4/622*, 15 March 2010, comments concerning draft Article 5 and its annex; and *UN Doc. A/C.6/60/SR.20* of 29 November 2005, para. 1, for critical remarks made by the United Kingdom in respect of the inclusion of international environmental treaties. See also the commentary of the United States in the Sixth Committee of the General Assembly: 'Such a categorization of treaties was problematic, since treaties did not automatically fall into one of several categories . . . It would be more useful, for the guidance of States, to enumerate the factors that might lead to the conclusion that a treaty or some of its provisions should continue or should be suspended or terminated in the event of armed conflict.' See *UN Doc. A/C.6/60/SR.2* of 29 November 2005, para. 34.

subsections examine the question of the continued applicability of these types of treaties in more detail.

5.2.2 *Human rights instruments*

This section discusses two issues. The first concerns the effects of armed conflict on human rights instruments in general, with particular emphasis on the effects of armed conflict on the rights protected under the ICESCR and the ICCPR. The second part discusses the implications of this general framework for the right of a people not to be deprived of its means of subsistence, while the third part focuses on rights relating to public participation in decision making.

General remarks concerning the effects of armed conflict on human rights instruments

The ILC draft articles on the effects of armed conflict suggest that human rights treaties continue to apply during armed conflict. This is supported first of all in the preamble of Additional Protocol II, which recalls that 'international instruments relating to human rights offer a basic protection to the human person'. The legal effect of armed conflict on the operation of international human rights treaties has also been dealt with extensively in the case law of international tribunals, in particular in the case law of the International Court of Justice.

With regard to the operation of the ICCPR, the ICJ made a distinction between the derogable and nonderogable rights listed in the Convention.[21] In its *Nuclear Weapons Advisory Opinion*, the Court observed that the

[21] Article 4(1) of the ICCPR permits States to derogate from their obligations under the Covenant '[i]n time of public emergency' – which may include an armed conflict. See General Comment No. 29 of the Human Rights Committee on Art. 4 (Derogations during a State of Emergency), *UN Doc. CCPR/C/21/Rev.1/Add.11*, 31 August 2001. It must be noted that derogation and suspension, strictly speaking, have different legal effects. Where suspension temporarily sets aside the legal obligation, derogation does not affect the binding nature of the legal obligation as such. In the former case, a State is completely exempted from compliance with the legal obligation, while in the latter case, it will have to justify noncompliance for each individual case. However, it may be argued that when a treaty provides for derogation from its provisions in situations of armed conflict, this must be interpreted as a strong indication against the susceptibility of the treaty to suspension in these particular circumstances. This conclusion is supported by the ILC in its commentary to the draft articles, which state that 'the competence to derogate' in time of war or other public emergency threatening the life of the nation 'certainly provides evidence that an armed conflict as such may not result in suspension or termination'. See Draft Articles on the Effects of Armed Conflicts on Treaties, with Commentaries, *Yearbook*

protection of the ICCPR 'does not cease in times of war, except by operation of Article 4 of the Covenant whereby certain provisions may be derogated from in a time of national emergency'.[22]

In the *Nuclear Weapons Advisory Opinion*, the Court also commented on the relationship between international human rights law and IHL. In this respect, it should be remembered that both IHL and international human rights law provide protection to human beings. However, they do so in very different ways. The primary aim of IHL is to regulate the horizontal relationship between parties to an armed conflict, and in doing so, to prevent unnecessary suffering for those not directly involved in the armed conflict. On the other hand, international human rights law regulates the vertical relationship between governmental authorities and the persons falling within their jurisdiction.

In this particular case, the Court was confronted with the application of a right from which no derogation is permitted during armed conflict under Article 4 of the ICCPR, i.e., the right to life. The Court determined that:

> the right not arbitrarily to be deprived of one's life applies also in hostilities. The test of what is an arbitrary deprivation of life, however, then falls to be determined by the applicable *lex specialis*, namely, the law applicable in armed conflict which is designed to regulate the conduct of hostilities. Thus whether a particular loss of life, through the use of a certain weapon in warfare, is to be considered an arbitrary deprivation of life contrary to Article 6 of the Covenant, can only be decided by reference to the law applicable in armed conflict and not deduced from the terms of the Covenant itself.[23]

It can be concluded from this case that – whenever obligations under human rights law are in conflict with obligations under IHL in situations of armed conflict – the relevant obligations under human rights law must be interpreted in the light of concurring rights or obligations under IHL.

In its *Advisory Opinion on the Legal Consequences of the Construction of a Wall in the Occupied Palestinian Territory*, the Court based its views on its previous opinion in *Nuclear Weapons* and considered that there are three possible scenarios with respect to the relations between international

of the International Law Commission (2011), Vol. II, Part Two, para. 50. Therefore, this section focuses on derogation rather than suspension of human rights treaties.

[22] International Court of Justice, Legality of the Threat or Use of Nuclear Weapons, Advisory Opinion of 8 July 1996, *I.C.J. Reports 1996*, para. 25.

[23] Ibid.

human rights law and IHL: IHL is exclusively applicable, international human rights law is exclusively applicable, or both these branches of international law are concurrently applicable.[24] The Court further extended the protection of human rights instruments, including the ICCPR and the ICESCR, to situations of occupation.[25]

The Court confirmed its earlier case law in its judgment in the *Case Concerning Armed Activities on the Territory of the Congo*, when it concluded that 'both branches of international law, namely international human rights law and international humanitarian law, would have to be taken into consideration' in situations of armed conflict and that 'international human rights instruments are applicable "in respect of acts done by a State in the exercise of its jurisdiction outside its own territory", particularly in occupied territories'.[26]

In addition to the case law of the International Court of Justice, several judgments of regional human rights courts have dealt with the application of human rights to conflict situations.[27] First, in its order for provisional measures against Libya issued during the internal conflict that broke

[24] International Court of Justice, Legal Consequences of the Construction of a Wall in the Occupied Palestinian Territory, Advisory Opinion of 9 July 2004, *I.C.J. Reports 2004*, p. 136, para. 106. Also see Koppe, *The Use of Nuclear Weapons and the Protection of the Environment During International Armed Conflict*, p. 347, who distinguishes a fourth situation, namely a situation in which neither international human rights law nor IHL would be applicable. The present author doubts whether such a situation would be possible, at least with regard to the rights protected under the ICCPR, because the possibility to derogate from particular human rights in situations of public emergency under this convention – including situations of internal disturbances not amounting to armed conflict – does not render the rights as such completely inoperative. After all, Article 4(1) determines that the provisions may only be derogated from 'to the extent strictly required by the exigencies of the situation'. In this respect, also see: Minimum Humanitarian Standards, Analytical Report of the Secretary-General Submitted Pursuant to Commission on Human Rights Resolution 1997/21, *UN Doc. E/CN.4/1998/87*, 5 January 1998, para. 54.

[25] International Court of Justice, Legal Consequences of the Construction of a Wall in the Occupied Palestinian Territory, Advisory Opinion of 9 July 2004, *I.C.J. Reports 2004*, p. 136, paras. 111–12.

[26] International Court of Justice, Case Concerning Armed Activities on the Territory of the Congo (*Democratic Republic of the Congo* v. *Uganda*), Judgment of 19 December 2005, *I.C.J. Reports 2005*, p. 168, para. 216. It is interesting to note that, by applying the ICCPR to situations of occupation, the International Court of Justice explicitly departs from the original intentions of the parties to the ICCPR. See on this Dennis, 'Application of Human Rights Treaties Extraterritorially in Times of Armed Conflict and Military Occupation', pp. 119–41.

[27] Where the current section deals with the application of human rights law to situations of armed conflicts by human rights bodies, see Byron, 'A Blurring of the Boundaries', 839–96 for an analysis of the application of IHL by human rights bodies.

out in February 2011, the newly set up African Court on Human and Peoples' Rights ordered the Gaddafi regime to 'immediately refrain from any action that would result in loss of life or violation of physical integrity of persons, which could be a breach of the provisions of the Charter or of other international human rights instruments to which it is a party'.[28] Similarly, the Inter-American Court of Human Rights consistently applies the Inter-American Convention on Human Rights in situations of internal armed conflict.[29] Finally, the European Court of Human Rights has also applied the rights protected under the European Convention on Human Rights in conflict situations, in particular in situations of internal armed conflict and occupation.[30]

Special reference should be made in this respect to the Chechnya cases before the European Court of Human Rights. Several cases have been filed before the Court against Russia for violations of the European Convention on Human Rights as a result of its military operations in Chechnya, including violations of the right to life.[31] The situation in Chechnya clearly suggests the application of both the common Articles 3 of the 1949 Geneva Conventions and the provisions of the 1977 Additional Protocol II. In other words, the situation can be characterised as an internal armed conflict to which the less stringent rules of IHL apply when it comes to the protection of human lives. Nevertheless, the European Court directly applied human rights standards to assess the legality of the conduct of the Russian security forces. In this respect, one of the important considerations of the Court was that Russia had not declared a state of 'war or other public emergency', as required under the European Convention for the Protection of Human Rights to derogate from the Convention's provisions.[32]

[28] *Commission on Human and Peoples' Rights* v. *Great Socialist People's Libyan Arab Jamahiria*, Application No. 004/2011, Order for Provisional Measures, 25 March 2011.

[29] See the judgments of the Inter-American Court of Human Rights in the Las Palmeras Case, Judgment of 4 February 2000 (preliminary objections), para. 32 and the Case of *Bámaca-Velasquez* v. *Guatemala*, Judgment of 25 November 2000 (merits), para. 207.

[30] For occupation, see, e.g., the judgments of the European Court for Human Rights in *Loizidou* v. *Turkey* (preliminary objections), Application No. 15318/89, Judgment of 23 March 1995 and in *Al-Skeini and Others* v. *the UK*, Application No. 55721/07, Judgment of 7 July 2011.

[31] See, e.g., the following cases before the European Court of Human Rights: *Khashiyev and Akayeva* v. *Russia*, Applications no. 57942/00 and 57945/00, Judgment of 24 February 2005; *Isayeva* v. *Russia*, Application no. 57950/00, Judgment of 24 February 2005; and *Estamirov and Others* v. *Russia*, Application no. 60272/00, Judgment of 12 October 2006.

[32] See, e.g., European Court of Human Rights, *Isayeva* v. *Russia*, Application no. 57950/00, Judgment of 24 February 2005, para. 191: 'The Court considers that using this kind of

It may therefore be concluded that human rights treaties continue to apply during armed conflict. This is particularly the case for situations of internal armed conflict and for situations of occupation. In situations of occupation, the case law of the ICJ shows that in occupied territory an occupant must respect its own obligations arising from treaties to which it is a party, at least those with extraterritorial effects. In addition, IHL – in particular, Article 43 of the 1907 Hague Regulations – provides that an occupant must respect the laws in force in occupied territory. This may include relevant treaties to which the occupied State is a party.[33]

Although the continued applicability of human rights treaties certainly covers the nonderogable rights protected under the ICCPR, a similar conclusion can be drawn with regard to the derogable rights protected under the ICCPR and, to a lesser extent, for economic, social and cultural rights protected under the ICESCR. As regards derogable rights under the ICCPR, it should be noted that derogation is permitted only under exceptional circumstances and to the extent necessary in view of the situation, which implies that derogation must be justified in each individual case.[34] In addition, as the Chechnya cases before the European Court for Human Rights show, a State may only derogate from its obligations under human rights treaties when it explicitly invokes this right. As regards rights protected under the ICESCR, the *Israeli Wall Opinion*

weapon in a populated area, outside wartime and without prior evacuation of the civilians, is impossible to reconcile with the degree of caution expected from a law-enforcement body in a democratic society. No martial law and no state of emergency has been declared in Chechnya, and no derogation has been made under Article 15 of the Convention (see § 133). The operation in question therefore has to be judged against a normal legal background.'

[33] See p. 232 on this.

[34] Article 4(1) of the ICCPR permits States to take measures derogating from their obligations under the Covenant in case of a public emergency which 'threatens the life of the nation', but these measures may not be inconsistent with their other obligations under international law – including under IHL – and may only be taken 'to the extent strictly required by the exigencies of the situation'. See General Comment No. 31 of the Human Rights Committee on the Nature of the General Legal Obligation Imposed on States Parties to the Covenant, *UN Doc. CCPR/C/21/Rev.1/Add.13*, 26 May 2004, para. 11 for an express confirmation that the Covenant applies also in situations of armed conflict. Also see General Comment No. 29 of the Human Rights Committee on Art. 4 (Derogations during a State of Emergency), *UN Doc. CCPR/C/21/Rev.1/Add.11*, 31 August 2001, para. 3, which stipulates that '[t]he Covenant requires that even during an armed conflict measures derogating from the Covenant are allowed only if and to the extent that the situation constitutes a threat to the life of the nation'. See also Koppe, *The Use of Nuclear Weapons and the Protection of the Environment during International Armed Conflict*, p. 347.

confirms their applicability to situations of occupation, depending on the nature and duration of the occupation. From the *Israeli Wall Opinion* it can be inferred that a State exercising jurisdiction over an occupied territory over a longer period of time is considered bound by the provisions of the ICESCR.[35]

It can be concluded from the case law examined in this section that international law contains two basic principles for determining the applicable law in situations where both IHL and international human rights law contain relevant rules. First, it is necessary to determine whether there is any conflict between the rules of international humanitarian and human rights law. A conflict occurs when the rules from the two fields of international law point in different directions. This was the case in the *Nuclear Weapons Advisory Opinion*, where the right to life protected under the ICCPR clashed with the rules regarding the use of weapons under IHL. In these situations, the *lex specialis* principle must be applied, implying that the relevant rules of IHL prevail over the rules of international human rights law. However, in many cases, rules of international humanitarian and human rights law that apply to similar situations complement each other. In these cases, the principle of harmonious interpretation must be applied, implying that the rules from the two fields of international law should be interpreted in such a way as 'to give rise to a single set of compatible obligations'.[36]

Implications for the prohibition against depriving a people of its means of subsistence

As regards the implications of these general rules set out in the case law of international tribunals for the right of peoples not to be deprived of their means of subsistence, as protected under Article 1(2) of the ICESCR and the ICCPR, it should first of all be noted that Article 1 of the ICCPR is not listed in Article 4 among the rights from which no derogation is permitted. Nevertheless, at the same time, the prohibition against depriving peoples of their means of subsistence is framed in absolute terms. The identical

[35] Legal Consequences of the Construction of a Wall in the Occupied Palestinian Territory, *I.C.J. Reports 2004*, Advisory Opinion of 9 July 2004, p. 136, para. 112. For more details, see Vité, 'The Interrelation of the Law of Occupation and Economic, Social and Cultural Rights', pp. 629–51.

[36] International Law Commission, Conclusions of the Work of the Study Group on the Fragmentation of International Law: Difficulties Arising from the Diversification and Expansion of International Law, *Yearbook of the International Law Commission*, 2006, Vol. II, Part Two, p. 408.

Articles 1(2) of the ICESCR and the ICCPR provide that *in no case* may a people be deprived of its means of subsistence. This may be regarded as a strong presumption in favour of its continued applicability during armed conflict.

This presumption is further strengthened by Article 25 of the ICESCR and Article 47 of the ICCPR, which expressly provide that '[n]othing in the present Covenant shall be interpreted as impairing the inherent right of all peoples to enjoy and utilize fully and freely their natural wealth and resources'. It may therefore be concluded that Article 1 has a special status compared to other rights protected under the Covenants.

The special status of the identical Articles 1 of the ICESCR and the ICCPR has been confirmed on several occasions. For example, in its General Comment No. 24 regarding reservations, the Human Rights Committee stated that a 'reservation to article 1 denying peoples the right to determine their own political status and to pursue their economic, social and cultural development, would be incompatible with the object and purpose of the Covenant'.[37] Furthermore, in its commentary on the draft articles on State responsibility the ILC argued that, in relation to the permissibility of countermeasures, the prohibition against depriving peoples of their means of subsistence constitutes a fundamental human right which may not be affected by – otherwise lawful – countermeasures.[38]

The question arises what the special status of Article 1(2) of the 1966 Covenants implies for the application of the provision in situations of armed conflict. Current case law of the International Court of Justice, and in particular the *Nuclear Weapons Advisory Opinion*, indicates that in situations of armed conflict, human rights law must be interpreted with reference to relevant rules of IHL. However, as explained in the previous section, this is only the case when there is a conflict between the relevant rules of these fields of law, as in the *Nuclear Weapons Advisory Opinion*, where the prohibition against arbitrarily depriving someone of his or her life under international human rights law was thought to be at odds with the right under IHL to use weapons that cause civilian casualties. The question is therefore whether there is a conflict between the prohibition

[37] Human Rights Committee, General Comment No. 24 on Issues Relating to Reservations Made Upon Ratification or Accession to the Covenant or the Optional Protocols Thereto, or in Relation to Declarations under Article 41 of the Covenant, 4 November 1994, *UN Doc. CCPR/C/21/Rev.1/Add.6 (1994)*, para. 9.

[38] Draft articles on Responsibility of States for Internationally Wrongful Acts, with commentaries, *UN Doc. A/56/10, Yearbook of the International Law Commission* 2001, Vol. II, Part Two, p. 132, para. 7.

against depriving peoples of their means of subsistence and a relevant rule of IHL. It is only then that the *lex specialis* principle applies.

International humanitarian law does not contain provisions that expressly allow parties to an armed conflict to deprive the civilian population of its means of subsistence. Rather, it contains several rules that are aimed at protecting the civilian population against such practices. As the very least, parties to an armed conflict may not attack, destroy, remove or render useless objects indispensable to the survival of the civilian population. In addition, IHL contains prohibitions against pillage and the seizure of property outside situations of military necessity that go beyond the prohibition to remove objects indispensable to the civilian population.[39]

It can therefore be argued that the prohibition against depriving peoples of their means of subsistence incorporated in Article 1(2) of the ICESCR and the ICCPR remains fully applicable in situations of armed conflict. The prohibition against attacking, destroying, removing or rendering useless objects indispensable to the survival of the civilian population must be regarded as a minimum guarantee, while the prohibitions against pillage and against seizing property outside situations of military necessity can be regarded as providing complementary protection.

Implications for rights relating to public participation in decision making

Chapter 3 discussed the right to internal self-determination and argued that this right entails a right for the population of a State and for specific groups within society to participate in decision making regarding exploitation projects. For indigenous peoples this right is inextricably linked to their right to enjoy their culture under Article 27 of the ICCPR. For individual members of the population, it can be argued that their right to be involved in decision making is expressed in the right to participate in the conduct of public affairs under Article 25 of the ICCPR.

As far as Article 27 of the ICCPR is concerned, the Human Rights Committee explicitly stated that 'a State may not reserve the right to . . . deny to minorities the right to enjoy their own culture, profess their own religion, or use their own language'.[40] The Committee also noted that

[39] These prohibitions are discussed in more detail in the following chapter.

[40] Human Rights Committee, General Comment No. 24: Issues Relating to Reservations Made upon Ratification or Accession to the Covenant or the Optional Protocols Thereto,

Article 27 of the ICCPR is a right 'of profound importance'.[41] However, the Committee's Comment relates to the subject of treaty reservations, rather than the issue of the suspension of treaties as a result of armed conflict. Moreover, the Comment relates to the right of minorities to enjoy their culture in general and not to the right to public participation arising from this.

Furthermore, none of the provisions cited earlier provides for a direct right to public participation. Pursuant to Article 1 of the ICCPR, States are required to establish procedures that allow the exercise of the right to internal self-determination in practice, but this obligation does not automatically afford citizens a direct right to participate in decision making. That right cannot be automatically inferred from Article 25 of the ICCPR either, as that provision deals only with the right to participate in the conduct of public affairs in a general way.

Generally speaking, it may be argued that the right of a State to derogate from relevant provisions of the human rights covenants providing indirectly for public participation in decision making, in particular, Articles 1, 25 and 27 of the ICCPR, is only permitted to the extent necessary in view of the situation. The right of a government to limit the exercise of specific rights in situations of armed conflict does not relieve a government of its obligations under human rights law in general. Therefore, arguably a State must respect its obligation to consult local communities regarding projects that directly affect them, but only insofar as this obligation is compatible with the situation of armed conflict.

5.2.3 *International environmental treaties*

The ILC draft articles on the effects of armed conflict on treaties not only formulate a presumption of continued applicability for international human rights instruments, but also for international environmental treaties. The decision of the ILC to include environmental treaties in the indicative list annexed to Article 7 is quite remarkable, as there is hardly any conclusive case law or practice to base this presumption on. The ICJ's *Nuclear Weapons Advisory Opinion* is an exception in this respect. In this opinion, the Court briefly touched upon the legal effects of armed conflict on international environmental treaties.

or in Relation to Declarations under Article 41 of the Covenant, 4 November 1994, *CCPR/C/21/Rev.1/Add.6*, para. 8.

[41] Ibid., para. 10.

The Court took a cautious view and only addressed the actual question put to it, namely, whether the obligations stemming from environmental treaties would preclude the threat or use of nuclear weapons in legitimate self-defence.[42] It argued 'that the issue is not whether the treaties relating to the protection of the environment are or are not applicable during an armed conflict, but rather whether the obligations stemming from these treaties were intended to be obligations of total restraint during military conflict'.[43]

The Court also stated that it did 'not consider that the treaties in question could have intended to deprive a State of the exercise of its right of self-defence under international law because of its obligations to protect the environment', but that nevertheless, 'States must take environmental considerations into account when assessing what is necessary and proportionate in the pursuit of legitimate military objectives.' It went on to consider that 'respect for the environment is one of the elements that go to assessing whether an action is in conformity with the principles of necessity and proportionality'. Therefore, this Opinion implies that environmental standards must be taken into account in the interpretation of the IHL principles of necessity and proportionality.

A similar approach was adopted by an ICTY Committee established to review the NATO bombing campaign against the Federal Republic of Yugoslavia.[44] This Committee used the IHL principles of necessity and proportionality in order to assess the legitimacy of the environmental damage inflicted by the NATO bombing campaign in former Yugoslavia.[45] It concluded that the principle of proportionality requires a balancing exercise between the military advantage obtained by an attack on the one

[42] The original request for an Advisory Opinion asked the Court to render its opinion on the following question: 'Is the threat or use of nuclear weapons in any circumstance permitted under international law?' See UNGA Resolution 49/75 of 15 December 1994. In this respect, also see the written statement of the United Kingdom to the request for an advisory opinion, which contains a clear exposé of the issues to be considered by the International Court of Justice.

[43] Legality of the Threat or Use of Nuclear Weapons, Advisory Opinion of 8 July 1996, *I.C.J. Reports 1996*, para. 30.

[44] Final Report to the Prosecutor by the Committee Established to Review the NATO Bombing Campaign against the Federal Republic of Yugoslavia, published on 14 June 2000, available through www.icty.org.

[45] The Committee considered in this regard that the environmental effects of the NATO bombing campaign 'are best considered from the underlying principles of the law of armed conflict such as necessity and proportionality'. Ibid., para. 15. For a critical assessment of the report on this point, see Bothe, 'The Protection of the Civilian Population and NATO Bombing on Yugoslavia', pp. 531–5.

hand, and damage to the environment on the other. The Committee stated in this respect that 'in order to satisfy the requirement of proportionality, attacks against military targets which are known or can reasonably be assumed to cause grave environmental harm may need to confer a very substantial military advantage in order to be considered legitimate'.[46] From the perspective of environmental protection, this interpretation of the principle of proportionality at first seems highly unsatisfactory. It implies that, when the stakes are sufficiently high, causing grave harm to the environment can be considered legitimate, as long as this harm does not reach the threshold of 'widespread, long-term and severe' damage to the environment. However, at the same time, it also implies that the threshold for environmental damage is considerably lower when such a 'very substantial military advantage' cannot be anticipated.

Both the *Nuclear Weapons Advisory Opinion* and the report of the ICTY Committee focus on environmental damage resulting from military attacks. The *Nuclear Weapons Advisory Opinion* addressed the question of permissible environmental damage only against the background of the right to self-defence, which is too narrow a context to deal with this question. Neither the ICJ nor the ICTY Committee addressed the broader question of the continued applicability of international environmental law as such in situations of armed conflict.

This question is highly relevant for the purposes of the present book, as international environmental treaties formulate obligations of care that may qualify the right of States to exploit natural resources in situations of armed conflict. In addition, combined environmental and trade treaties, like CITES, can be instrumental in curbing the trade in conflict resources. In the light of the general presumption of the ILC in favour of the continued applicability of international environmental law in situations of armed conflict and in the absence of specific guidelines arising from the case law of the ICJ or any other authority, the best way to proceed is to take a closer look at the relevant treaties themselves.

Looking at international environmental treaties, it becomes apparent first of all that these treaties rarely contain express provisions on their applicability in situations of armed conflict.[47] CITES, for example, is completely silent on the matter. However, there are a few

[46] Ibid., para. 22.

[47] A study by UNEP indicates that around 20 per cent of international environmental treaties provide for their discontinuance during armed conflict, while the remaining 80 per cent either do not provide any answer or are inconclusive on their operation during armed conflict. See UNEP, Protecting the Environment during Armed Conflict: An Inventory and Analysis of International Law (2009).

treaties that do contain provisions which implicitly provide for their applicability – or inapplicability – in situations of armed conflict. The UN Convention on the Law of the Non-navigational Uses of International Watercourses, which contains a *renvoi* to the relevant rules of IHL, is an example of this.[48] Article 29 of this Convention provides that 'international watercourses and related installations, facilities and other works shall enjoy the protection accorded by the principles and rules of international law applicable in international and non-international armed conflict and shall not be used in violation of those principles and rules'.

This provision can be interpreted in two ways. The first interpretation regards this provision as a confirmation of the complementary protection afforded by IHL to international waterways in situations of armed conflict. It should be noted that international waterways can have strategic relevance to parties to an armed conflict, e.g., as supply lines or transportation routes. In contrast, the second interpretation regards this provision as a confirmation of the inapplicability of the convention in situations of armed conflict in favour of the application of the relevant rules of IHL.

The Commentary of the ILC, which was responsible for drafting the convention, shows a preference for the first interpretation. The Commentary indicates in this respect that Article 29 'simply serves as a reminder that the principles and rules of international law applicable in international and internal armed conflict contain important provisions concerning international watercourses and related works', but that '[o]f course, the present articles themselves remain in effect even in time of armed conflict'.[49]

When there is no conflict between the relevant rules of IHL and the Watercourses Convention,[50] there is no reason to assume that the latter ceases to apply. The Watercourses Convention contains several obligations that are relevant for the protection of watercourses in situations of peace as well as in situations of armed conflict. For example, Article 5 of the Convention, formulates an obligation for watercourse States to

[48] UN Convention on the Law of the Non-navigational Uses of International Watercourses, 21 May 1997, *36 ILM 700 (1997)*.

[49] International Law Commission, Draft Articles on the Law of the Non-navigational Uses of International Watercourses and Commentaries Thereto, *Yearbook of the International Law Commission 1994*, Vol. II, Part Two, p. 131, paras. 1 and 3.

[50] A conflict may occur if an international watercourse is used by one of the parties to an armed conflict in a way as to make an effective contribution to an armed conflict, for example, when an international watercourse is used to transport weapons. In these cases, the watercourse can become a military objective, which means that it can be subject to a military attack. See Chapter 6 of this study for the definition of a military objective and the relevant rules that apply to these objectives.

utilise an international watercourse in their territories 'in an equitable and reasonable manner'. Furthermore, Article 7 stipulates that '[w]atercourse States shall, in utilizing an international watercourse in their territories, take all appropriate measures to prevent the causing of significant harm to other watercourse States'. These obligations qualify the right of States parties to the Watercourses Convention to exploit the natural resources of international watercourses, including alluvial diamonds.

The UNESCO World Heritage Convention is another example. It includes a provision on safeguarding of world heritage threatened by armed conflict. Article 11(4) of the UNESCO World Heritage Convention provides for the possibility of placing natural heritage threatened by 'the outbreak or the threat of an armed conflict' on a list of 'World Heritage in Danger'.[51] In this way, the convention implicitly provides for its own continued application in conflict situations. Several World Heritage sites in the DR Congo and Côte d'Ivoire have been placed on the list because of threats associated with the conflicts raging in those States.

The continued applicability of this convention in situations of armed conflict also directly affects the obligations of States involved in an international armed conflict. Article 6(3) of the UNESCO World Heritage Convention formulates a prohibition for States against taking 'any deliberate measures which might damage directly or indirectly' natural heritage 'situated on the territory of other States Parties to this Convention'. In the first place, this means that States may not deliberately launch an attack which could cause damage to World Heritage sites. However, it also implies that States may not exploit natural resources situated in world heritage parks, if such exploitation would cause damage to the natural heritage. This implies, for example, that Uganda and Rwanda may have acted in violation of the convention when they undertook the exploitation of natural resources within and around UNESCO World Heritage sites in the DR Congo, including ivory poaching, logging and mining. These activities have posed a significant threat to the integrity of these biodiversity reserves.[52]

In addition to provisions that indicate the continued applicability of environmental treaties, there may be conflict clauses in these treaties which indicate their operation during armed conflict. Article 22(1) of the

[51] UNESCO Convention Concerning the Protection of the World Cultural and Natural Heritage, 16 November 1972, *1037 UNTS 151*.

[52] Interim report of the Panel of Experts on the Illegal Exploitation of Natural Resources and Other Forms of Wealth of the Democratic Republic of the Congo, *UN Doc. S/2002/565*, paras. 50 and 52.

Biodiversity Convention, for example, determines that the provisions of the convention

> shall not affect the rights and obligations of any Contracting Party deriving from any existing international agreement, except where the exercise of those rights and obligations would cause a serious damage or threat to biological diversity.

It is relevant to note that the 1907 Hague Regulations, the 1949 Geneva Conventions and the 1977 Additional Protocols contain several rights for parties to an armed conflict which could be in conflict with their obligations under the Biodiversity Convention. Examples include the right of parties to an armed conflict to destroy property of the hostile party in cases of military necessity as well as the right of parties to launch an attack against parts of the environment that constitute military objectives. Article 22 of the Biodiversity Convention makes it clear that the exercise of these rights may not cause a serious damage or threat to biological diversity.[53]

It can be concluded that international environmental conventions generally remain applicable in situations of armed conflict, unless the relevant convention provides otherwise. However, it should be noted that the obligations of the parties to these conventions can change as a result of an armed conflict. Many international environmental conventions contain clauses which are more lenient towards States with regard to the implementation of their obligations in view of special circumstances. Article 6 of the 1992 Biodiversity Convention, for example, provides that parties have to implement the general measures for conservation and sustainable use 'in accordance with [their] particular conditions and capabilities'. Of course, such clauses could be invoked by parties to the convention in situations of armed conflict as a reason not to implement part of their obligations under the convention.

5.2.4 *Conclusions on the outbreak of armed conflict as a ground for the termination or suspension of treaties*

This section has shown that the outbreak of an armed conflict does not automatically suspend the obligations for States under relevant international human rights and environmental treaties. However, this

[53] What constitutes 'serious damage or threat' can be discerned from the ILC commentary to the Draft Articles on Prevention of Transboundary Harm from Hazardous Activities, discussed in Chapter 4 of this book. Damage to the environment can be considered 'serious' when it is substantial in the sense of encompassing 'significant' damage.

does not imply that these two fields of law apply fully in situations of armed conflict. In some cases international human rights law expressly grants States the right to derogate from their obligations under relevant conventions. The ICCPR contains an express provision allowing for the derogation of rights under the convention in cases of national emergency, including armed conflicts. For the purposes of this book, the right of States to derogate from their obligations under the ICCPR includes a right to derogate to a certain extent from provisions that indirectly provide for public participation by the population of a State.

Furthermore, some of the obligations of States under international human rights treaties may be at odds with rights formulated by IHL for parties to an armed conflict. This can be illustrated with reference to the ICJ's *Nuclear Weapons Advisory Opinion*, where the International Court of Justice had to consider whether the use of nuclear weapons in situations of armed conflict would constitute a violation of the right to life under international human rights law. In cases where a particular right under IHL (i.e., the right to cause casualties in situations of armed conflict) is at odds with an obligation under international human rights law (i.e., the prohibition against arbitrarily depriving someone of his life), the rules of human rights law must be applied in the light of the relevant provisions of IHL. No such express conflict was established in relation to the rights that are relevant to this book. In fact, it appears that the relevant prohibitions under international human rights law and IHL are complementary.

Whether particular obligations of international environmental law continue to apply must be established first of all with reference to the treaties themselves. It is relevant to note that some of the environmental conventions that contain relevant obligations for States with respect to the exploitation of natural resources contain provisions indicating their continued applicability in situations of armed conflict. The most relevant examples are the 1972 UNESCO World Heritage Convention and the 1992 Convention on Biological Diversity. Both conventions contain provisions that in practice qualify the right of States to exploit natural resources in situations of armed conflict, most notably by prohibiting certain forms of environmental damage. These apply in all circumstances.

Therefore, it can be concluded that the outbreak of an armed conflict has some effect on the applicability of international human rights law and international environmental law, but that most obligations continue to apply to some extent. The following section discusses other grounds for the termination or suspension of treaties under general international law and assesses their relevance to the applicability of international human rights and environmental law in situations of armed conflict.

5.3 Termination or suspension of treaties under the 1969 Vienna Convention on the Law of Treaties

Article 18 of the draft ILC articles on the effects of armed conflict on treaties provides that the draft articles 'are without prejudice to the termination, withdrawal or suspension of treaties as a consequence of, inter alia: (a) a material breach; (b) supervening impossibility of performance; or (c) a fundamental change of circumstances'. The current section addresses all these grounds for the termination, withdrawal or suspension of a treaty, which are codified in the 1969 Vienna Convention on the Law of Treaties.

5.3.1 Material breach

A material breach by a party to a treaty entitles the other parties to terminate or suspend the operation of the treaty. Article 60 of the 1969 Vienna Convention on the Law of Treaties defines a material breach as either 'a repudiation of the treaty not sanctioned by the present Convention', meaning *a contrario* that repudiations that are sanctioned by the Vienna Convention do not constitute material breaches for the purposes of Article 60,[54] or – and this is more relevant to the present book – 'the violation of a provision essential to the accomplishment of the object and purpose of the treaty'. A provision is considered 'essential' if it is 'considered by a party to be essential to the effective execution of the treaty'.[55] This includes provisions that touch directly on the central purposes of the treaty, as well as provisions of an ancillary character.

[54] Bruno Simma and Christian Tams state in this respect that '[t]he reference to repudiation "sanctioned by the present Convention" makes clear that claims of invalidity of treaties pursuant to Articles 46 to 53 of the Convention, or for the suspension and/or termination of treaties pursuant to Articles 54 to 64, do not constitute material breaches. In addition, it follows from Article 73 of the Convention that repudiations justified under the law of State responsibility or the United Nations Charter cannot bring Article 60 into operation either'. See Simma and Tams, 'Article 60: Termination or Suspension of the Operation of a Treaty as a Consequence of Its Breach', p. 1358.

[55] International Law Commission, Reports of the International Law Commission on the second part of its seventeenth session and on its eighteenth session, *UN Doc. A/6309/Rev.l*, in *Yearbook of the International Law Commission* (1966), Vol. II, p. 255.

Article 60 of the 1969 Vienna Convention clearly delineates the circumstances in which parties may invoke material breach as a reason to terminate a treaty or suspend its operation. In the case of multilateral treaties, which are most relevant to the current study, Article 60(2)(a) provides that a treaty may be suspended or terminated by all the parties to the treaty by unanimous agreement, either between themselves and the defaulting State only, or between all the parties. This possibility is of limited relevance to the current study, as it is not directly related to the circumstances regarding the outbreak of an armed conflict.

In addition, Article 60(2)(b) and (c) recognise two circumstances for unilateral responses, which are limited to suspension. A right to suspend the operation of a treaty in a case of material breach accrues first to specially affected parties under section 2(b). The pollution of a State's territory as a result of the violation of an obligation under a multilateral environmental treaty is a relevant example of this.[56]

Second, according to Article 60(2)(c) of the Vienna Convention, such a right accrues to other parties 'if the treaty is of such a character that a material breach of its provisions by one party radically changes the position of every party with respect to the further performance of its obligations under the treaty'. The drafting history of Article 60 shows that this provision specifically referred to so-called 'integral agreements', i.e., treaties which require the interdependent performance of obligations by all parties for the achievement of their objectives.[57] Typical examples include disarmament treaties.

For the purposes of the present study, the question arises of whether Article 60 allows a party to suspend the operation of a treaty in the case of a breach of *erga omnes* obligations. As argued previously, several environmental conventions contain *erga omnes partes* obligations. In this respect, Bruno Simma and Christian Tams argue that, for the purposes of Article 60(2)(b), the fact that all States can be held to have a legal interest in the observation of the treaty does not make these States specially affected in the case of a breach of the treaty.[58] Therefore, it can be argued that this provision cannot be invoked by a State as a ground to suspend the operation of environmental treaties.

[56] See Simma and Tams, 'Article 60: Termination or Suspension of the Operation of a Treaty as a Consequence of its Breach', pp. 1364–5 for this and other examples.

[57] Ibid., p. 1365. Simma and Tams define integral treaties as treaties 'the objective of which can only be achieved through the interdependent performance of obligations by all parties'.

[58] Ibid., p. 1366.

Article 60(2)(c) raises another question. Can a breach of an *erga omnes* obligation have the effect of 'radically changing the position of all other parties with respect to the performance of their obligations under the treaty'? This question could be rephrased to ask whether those environmental treaties that protect common goods can be considered to constitute integral treaties. In general this is not the case, as obligations under international environmental law are usually not interdependent, in the sense that the parties have made their performance of the treaty dependent on the performance by other parties, as is the case with regard to disarmament treaties. Therefore, it can be argued that Article 60(2)(c) does not provide grounds for the suspension of the operation of such treaties either.

There may, however, be exceptions to this rule, in particular when parties have agreed to achieve particular targets, as in the case of the 1997 Kyoto Protocol to the 1992 UN Framework Convention on Climate Change. This instrument could be considered an integral treaty in the sense of Article 60(2)(c) of the Vienna Convention. However, it should be noted that a material breach of a specialised instrument such as the Kyoto Protocol would not affect the general obligations of States under the Climate Convention itself.

The final issue relates to the suspension of humanitarian treaties. Article 60(5) of the 1969 Vienna Convention provides that a treaty cannot be suspended in the case of a material breach of 'provisions relating to the protection of the human person contained in treaties of a humanitarian character'. The term 'treaties of a humanitarian character' refers primarily to IHL treaties. However, arguably, it refers to human rights treaties as well.[59] This implies that human rights treaties cannot be suspended in response to a material breach by another party.

In conclusion, it may be argued that Article 60 of the 1969 Vienna Convention formulates the general rule that a treaty may be suspended – and in some cases terminated – in response to a material breach by one of the parties. However, the provision sets out clear and strict rules for the legality of such responses. Most importantly, suspension is mainly open to parties that are specially affected by the breach. For the purposes of the

[59] See the drafting history of Article 60(5) of the Vienna Convention, United Nations Conference on the Law of Treaties, Official Records, *UN Doc. A/CONF.39/11*, p. 354, para. 12. The Swiss delegate proposing the insertion of Article 60(5) mentioned not only the Geneva Conventions, but also 'conventions of equal importance concerning the status of refugees, the prevention of slavery, the prohibition of genocide and the protection of human rights in general'.

present book, the provision is therefore primarily relevant in situations of international armed conflict. It affords a belligerent State a right to suspend the operation of a treaty in the case of a material breach committed by another State, provided that the former State suffers damage from the breach of obligations. For the purposes of this book, such damage will usually concern extraterritorial damage to the environment.

5.3.2 *Supervening impossibility of performance*

According to Article 61 of the 1969 Vienna Convention, supervening impossibility of performance can be invoked as a reason to terminate, withdraw from or suspend the operation of a treaty if the performance of the treaty has become impossible because of the temporary or permanent disappearance or destruction of an object indispensable for the execution of the treaty.[60]

Thus the impossibility of performance must be directly linked to the disappearance or destruction of an object which was essential for the performance of the treaty.[61] Relevant examples for the purposes of the current book include the destruction of a particular site protected under the Ramsar or the World Heritage Convention or the extinction of a species protected by a wildlife treaty. Therefore, the mere loss of control by a State over territory in which the site or species is situated does not meet the requirements of the Vienna Convention.

One question that arises is whether the impossibility can be of a juridical nature as well. This possibility was originally rejected by the ILC. According to Fitzmaurice, admitting a juridical impossibility would have the result

> that a country could always obtain release from its treaty obligation by entering into other incompatible obligations. In such cases there is not impossibility in the sense that the treaty cannot be executed, but merely in the sense that it cannot be executed without involving a breach of another treaty.[62]

[60] In the case of the temporary disappearance of an object indispensable for the operation of a treaty, a party may only suspend the operation of the treaty.

[61] See Bodeau-Livinec and Morgan-Foster, 'Article 61: Supervening Impossibility of Performance', p. 1383.

[62] Second Report on the Law of Treaties of the Special Rapporteur, Sir Gerald Fitzmaurice, *UN Doc. A/CN.4/107*, *Yearbook of the International Law Commission* 1957, Vol. II, p. 50.

In other words, a State may not invoke supervening impossibility of performance as a ground to suspend its obligations under one treaty, for example, a human rights or environmental treaty, because of a perceived conflict with its obligations under another treaty, for example, an IHL treaty.

However, it is possible to envisage situations in which the juridical impossibility is not linked to a conflict of norms, but to the actual disappearance of a juridical object indispensable to the execution of the treaty. The termination of a legal regime or a radical change in the situation on which the performance of the treaty was based would be an example of this.

This issue was raised by Hungary before the International Court of Justice in the case concerning the *Gabčíkovo–Nagymaros Project.* Hungary argued that 'the essential object of the Treaty . . . had permanently disappeared and that the Treaty had thus become impossible to perform'.[63] Although the Court rejected Hungary's argument in this particular case, it did not as such refute the possibility that the disappearance of a juridical object could fall within the scope of Article 61 of the Vienna Convention.

According to Pierre Bodeau-Livinec and Jordan Morgan-Foster, 'What matters is that the impossibility of performance is material, due to the absence of a necessary element for the implementation of the treaty.'[64] Within these strict confines, it does not matter whether the object that disappeared was of a physical or juridical nature.

Furthermore, according to Article 61(2), a State may not invoke the ground if the impossibility results from its own behaviour, as the result of a breach by that State either of its obligations under the relevant treaty or of its other international law obligations. In the *case concerning the Gabčíkovo–Nagymaros Project,* the International Court of Justice expressly relied on this provision in response to Hungary's claim that the essential object of the treaty between itself and Slovakia had permanently disappeared.[65]

[63] International Court of Justice, case concerning the Gabčíkovo–Nagymaros Project (*Hungary* v. *Slovakia*), Judgment of 25 September 1997, *I.C.J. Reports 1997*, p. 7, para. 103.

[64] Bodeau-Livinec and Morgan-Foster, 'Article 61: Supervening Impossibility of Performance', p. 1391.

[65] This claim was refuted altogether by the ICJ. See the International Court of Justice, case concerning the Gabčíkovo–Nagymaros Project (*Hungary* v. *Slovakia*), Judgment of 25 September 1997, *I.C.J. Reports 1997*, p. 7, para. 103.

For the purposes of the present book, this limitation implies, *inter alia*, that an aggressor State cannot invoke supervening impossibility of performance as a ground for suspending its obligations under treaties to which it is a party.[66] It also implies that a State that destroys World Heritage sites within its own territory because these protected sites are used by non-State armed groups as a shelter, for example, cannot invoke the justification to terminate or suspend the operation of the UNESCO World Heritage Convention.

Therefore, it is clear that Article 61 of the Vienna Convention allows States to invoke supervening impossibility of performance as a justification for the termination, withdrawal or suspension of treaty obligations only in very exceptional circumstances. Indeed, it is hard to imagine situations relevant to this book that would meet the requirements set by this provision.

5.3.3 *Fundamental change of circumstances*

According to Article 62 of the Vienna Convention, the principle of *rebus sic stantibus* or fundamental change of circumstances can be invoked when the circumstances existing at the time that the treaty was concluded constituted an essential basis for the consent of the parties to be bound by the treaty *and* if the effect of the change is radically to transform the extent of obligations still to be performed under the treaty.[67] Furthermore, the fundamental change may not relate to circumstances which the parties to the treaty must have been able to foresee.

According to the ILC, the provision serves as a 'safety valve' for 'cases in which, failing any agreement, one party may be left powerless under the treaty to obtain any legal relief from outmoded and burdensome provisions'.[68] This was also recognised by the International Court of

[66] Compare in this regard Article 15 of the ILC draft Articles on the Effects of Armed Conflict to Treaties, *UN Doc. A/CN.4/L.777*, 11 May 2011, which prohibits an aggressor State from terminating or withdrawing from a treaty or suspending its operation as a consequence of an armed conflict that results from the act of aggression if the effect would be to the benefit of that State.

[67] For an explanation of these conditions, see the Second Report on the Law of Treaties of the Special Rapporteur, Sir Gerald Fitzmaurice, *UN Doc. A/CN.4/107*, *Yearbook of the International Law Commission* 1957, Vol. II, pp. 32–3.

[68] International Law Commission, *Document A/6309/Rev. l:* Reports of the International Law Commission on the Second Part of Its Seventeenth Session and on Its Eighteenth Session, *Yearbook of the International Law Commission (1966)*, Vol. II, p. 258. See also the Second Report on the Law of Treaties of the Special Rapporteur, Sir Gerald Fitzmaurice,

Justice in the *case concerning the Gabčíkovo–Nagymaros Project*, in which the Court reasoned that 'the stability of treaty relations requires that the plea of fundamental change of circumstances be applied only in exceptional cases'.[69] Thus a plea of fundamental change of circumstances can only be considered as a last resort.

The exceptional nature of a justification for the termination, withdrawal from or suspension of the operation of a treaty is reflected in the conditions set by Article 62 of the Vienna Convention. The conditions are cumulative and must be interpreted narrowly. First, the change of circumstances must be objective. It must refer to 'external elements independent of the will of the parties'.[70] Furthermore, the change must be *fundamental* in the sense of affecting circumstances which constituted the essential basis of the consent of the parties to be bound by the treaty and in the sense of radically transforming the extent of obligations still to be performed under the treaty.

Therefore, in the first place, the change must alter the core of the agreement between the parties. Second, the change must radically transform the obligations under the treaty, meaning that '[t]he change must have increased the burden of the obligations to be executed to the extent of rendering the performance something essentially different from that originally undertaken'.[71]

The last condition for invoking the plea of fundamental change of circumstances is that the change may not relate to circumstances that the parties to the treaty should have been able to foresee. The outbreak of an armed conflict is generally considered to constitute a circumstance that the parties were not able to foresee when they concluded a treaty, which makes the provision relevant to this book. Finally, Article 62 contains a provision similar to Article 61, providing that a party invoking the ground cannot take advantage of its own breach of an obligation.[72]

For the purposes of the current book, the question of whether the existence of a peaceful situation in a State 'constituted an essential basis

UN Doc. A/CN.4/107, Yearbook of the International Law Commission (1957), Vol. II, p. 32, which already recognised the residual nature of the justification.

69 International Court of Justice, Gabčíkovo–Nagymaros Project (*Hungary* v. *Slovakia*), Judgment of 25 September 1997, *I.C.J. Reports 1997*, p. 7, para. 104.

70 Shaw and Fournet, 'Article 62: Fundamental Change of Circumstances', p. 1424.

71 International Court of Justice, Fisheries Jurisdiction case (*Federal Republic of Germany* v. *Iceland*), Judgment of 2 February 1973, *I.C.J. Reports 1973*, para. 43.

72 Statement in Vienna by the Dutch delegation, reported in Villiger, *Commentary on the 1969 Vienna Convention on the Law of Treaties*, p. 776.

of the consent of the parties to be bound by the treaty' *and* of whether the effect of the outbreak of armed conflict radically transforms 'the extent of obligations still to be performed under the treaty' are both crucial. In these circumstances, the question of whether the outbreak of an armed conflict radically alters the relationships between the parties to the treaty is a decisive element.[73] This is not automatically the case. While the outbreak of an armed conflict can certainly affect the capacity of a State to respect its obligations under international environmental and human rights treaties, it does not necessarily affect the relationship between the belligerent State and other States to the treaty. Therefore, this ground for the suspension of a treaty is primarily relevant in the relationship between belligerents *inter se*.

5.3.4 Conclusions on the relevance of other grounds for the termination or suspension of treaties in situations of armed conflict

The previous section demonstrated that the outbreak of an armed conflict does not automatically suspend the operation of international human rights or environmental treaties, except where relevant treaties provide otherwise. States wishing to suspend the operation of their obligations under international human rights or environmental law therefore have to resort to the general grounds for the termination or suspension of treaties, codified in the 1969 Vienna Convention on the Law of Treaties.

This section has shown that the primary objective of the system established by the 1969 Vienna Convention for the termination and suspension of treaties is to maintain stability in treaty relations. Therefore, States can invoke the grounds for the termination or suspension of treaties only in exceptional circumstances. For the purposes of this book, there are some situations that would allow States to suspend their obligations under relevant treaties.

First, States can suspend their treaty obligations in response to a material breach by another State. However, this possibility exists only for a material breach that directly affects the State concerned. A material breach of a treaty that protects a natural resource shared by two or more States is an example of this. Second, supervening impossibility of performance can be invoked if the object of protection of a treaty has disappeared. The destruction of a wetland protected under the Ramsar Convention and

[73] See Shaw and Fournet, 'Article 62: Fundamental Change of Circumstances', p. 1430.

that of a natural heritage site protected under the UNESCO World Heritage Convention are relevant examples. Finally, a fundamental change of circumstances can be invoked if the outbreak of an armed conflict radically alters the relationships between the parties to a treaty and their mutual obligations. A treaty regulating the common use of a shared natural resource, concluded between States that have subsequently engaged in an armed conflict with each other, is an example of this.

It can therefore be concluded that in most cases States remain bound by their obligations under relevant treaties. The main exceptions are international environmental treaties and concern the relationship between belligerent States *inter se*. States must continue to respect their obligations to neutral States. In addition, internal armed conflicts do not generally entail a right for States to suspend their obligations under international environmental or human rights treaties.

5.4 Circumstances precluding wrongfulness

If a treaty cannot be terminated or suspended on the basis of one of the grounds discussed in the previous section, a State involved in an armed conflict may wish to preclude the wrongfulness of its conduct by invoking one of the circumstances discussed in this section. This argument lasts only as long as the circumstances persist. In the *Gabčíkovo–Nagymaros Project case*, the International Court of Justice emphasised that a State must resume its international obligations as soon as the situation changes.[74]

Circumstances precluding wrongfulness are based on the domain of State responsibility. Their function is not to affect treaty obligations as such, but rather to remove the responsibility of a State for the breach of an obligation. In its commentary on the Articles on State Responsibility, the ILC emphasised that circumstances precluding wrongfulness 'act as a shield rather than a sword.'[75]

The Articles on State Responsibility list six circumstances precluding the wrongfulness of an act that would otherwise constitute a breach of the international obligations of the State concerned. These are consent (Article 20), self-defence (Article 21), countermeasures (Article 22), *force*

[74] International Court of Justice, Gabčíkovo–Nagymaros Project (*Hungary* v. *Slovakia*), Judgment, *I.C.J. Reports 1997*, p. 7, para. 101.

[75] Draft articles on Responsibility of States for Internationally Wrongful Acts, with commentaries, *Yearbook of the International Law Commission* 2001, Vol. II, Part Two, p. 71.

majeure (Article 23), distress (Article 24) and necessity (Article 25). The situations of *force majeure* and necessity are the most relevant for this book.[76]

5.4.1 Force majeure

Force majeure is defined in Article 23 of the ILC Articles on State Responsibility as 'the occurrence of an irresistible force or of an unforeseen event, beyond the control of the State, making it materially impossible in the circumstances to perform the obligation'. There are three criteria that have to be met. First, the situation concerned must be brought about by an irresistible force or an unforeseen event. The outbreak of an armed conflict could qualify as such an 'unforeseen event' if it was not easily foreseeable.[77] Second, the unforeseen event must be beyond the control of the State concerned. This criterion is not elaborated in any further detail, but it implies that the State must be in a position in which it has no reasonable means at its disposal to alter the situation. Finally, there must be a direct link between the unforeseen event and the material impossibility of performance. The ILC Commentary explicitly mentions the loss of control over a portion of the State's territory as a result of an insurrection as an example of material impossibility.[78]

For the purposes of the present study, *force majeure* could therefore be invoked by a State for breaches of its obligations under international human rights and environmental conventions in territories under the control of armed groups. While these situations do not justify the suspension of a treaty based on supervening impossibility of performance, the State can preclude the wrongfulness of its acts by invoking *force majeure*. Of course, as soon as the State regains control over its territory, it must resume its obligations under the relevant conventions.

There is, however, one important additional condition that must be fulfilled for a State to be able to successfully appeal to *force majeure*. Article 61(2) of the ILC Articles excludes a plea of *force majeure* if the situation

[76] Self-defence, as relevant as it is in general to a situation of armed conflict, is left out of consideration. It seems too far-fetched to argue that the exploitation of the natural resources of another State constitutes a lawful measure of self-defence, as required by Article 21 of the Articles on State Responsibility.

[77] Draft articles on Responsibility of States for Internationally Wrongful Acts, with commentaries, *Yearbook of the International Law Commission* 2001, Vol. II, Part Two, p. 76.

[78] Ibid.

of *force majeure* is due, either solely or in combination with other factors, to the conduct of the State invoking it, or if the State has assumed the risk of that situation occurring. A considerable degree of responsibility is therefore required before a State can be assumed to have brought about the situation of *force majeure*. According to the ILC Commentary, the State must have either played a substantial role in bringing about the situation of *force majeure* or explicitly accepted responsibility for the occurrence of a particular risk.[79]

For the purposes of the present study, this would imply, for example, that a government that does not actively attempt to stop violations of international human rights and environmental treaties in territories under the control of armed groups could be barred from invoking a plea of *force majeure*. Côte d'Ivoire provides a relevant example. In 2003, a government of national unity was installed in the country as part of the peace process, which included the government in control of the south of the country and the rebel group Forces Nouvelles in control of the north of the country. However, the subsequent report of the Panel of Experts on Côte d'Ivoire concluded that the government of national unity's efforts to redeploy local government administration in the north of the country were inadequate, as a result of which local warlords were able to remain in control over this part of the territory.[80] This example illustrates that a government can indirectly be responsible for the occurrence of a situation of *force majeure* because of its lax attitude.

5.4.2 *Necessity*

Necessity arises only in exceptional circumstances where there is an irreconcilable conflict between an essential interest, either of the State invoking necessity or of the international community on the one hand, and a legal obligation on the other.[81]

According to Article 25 of the ILC Articles on State Responsibility, a plea of necessity must meet the following cumulative requirements. First, the breach of an international obligation must be 'the only way for the State to safeguard an essential interest against a grave and imminent peril'.

[79] Ibid., p. 78.

[80] See in particular the Final Report of the Group of Experts Submitted in Accordance with Paragraph 11 of Security Council Resolution 1842 (2008) of 9 October 2009, *UN Doc. S/2009/521*, paras. 30–41.

[81] Draft articles on Responsibility of States for Internationally Wrongful Acts, with commentaries, *Yearbook of the International Law Commission* 2001, Vol. II, Part Two, p. 80.

The question of what constitutes an 'essential interest' of a State must be determined on a case-by-case basis.[82] Obviously the national security of a State would certainly constitute such an interest. For the purposes of the present study, it is interesting to note that the preservation of the environment has expressly been recognised as an essential interest within the scope of this provision.[83]

In addition, the essential interest of the State must be protected against a 'grave and imminent peril'. In the *Gabčíkovo–Nagymaros Project case*, the International Court of Justice stated that the terms 'grave and imminent peril' imply that a state of necessity cannot exist without a peril 'duly established at the relevant point in time', although a degree of uncertainty about the future is permitted as long as the peril

> appearing in the long term might be held to be 'imminent' as soon as it is established, at the relevant point in time, that the realization of that peril, however far off it might be, is not thereby any less certain and inevitable.[84]

Moreover, the wrongful conduct must be the 'only way' open to the State to protect its essential interest. Therefore, necessity may not be invoked to excuse behaviour for which reasonable, and more proportionate, alternatives were available.

In addition to these requirements, Article 25 of the ILC Articles provides that a State invoking necessity may not 'seriously impair an essential interest of the State or States towards which the obligation exists, or of the international community as a whole'. Thus a State may not invoke necessity to justify a breach of obligations relating to the essential interests of other States or of the international community as a whole. Finally, according to Article 25, no appeal can be made to necessity if 'the international obligation in question excludes the possibility of invoking necessity' – which is, for example, the case for certain provisions under IHL – or if 'the State has contributed to the situation of necessity'.

These requirements entail two important consequences for the purposes of the present study. First, a State that breaches an international obligation in order to protect the environment against a grave and imminent danger could in principle invoke the plea of necessity. This is because the preservation of the environment has expressly been recognised to

[82] Ibid., p. 83.

[83] International Court of Justice, Gabčíkovo–Nagymaros Project (*Hungary* v. *Slovakia*), Judgment of 25 September 1997, *I.C.J. Reports 1997*, p. 7, para. 53.

[84] Ibid., para. 54.

constitute an 'essential interest'. In contrast, States cannot invoke necessity to justify particular actions that harm the environment for reasons of national security, because such actions would touch upon the essential interests of other States. This is particularly the case when their actions are directed against an object that is subject to a common regime, such as the regimes protecting natural heritage, endangered species or biological diversity.

Therefore, it can be concluded that necessity cannot be invoked by States to justify breaches of international environmental agreements which affect the essential interests of the international community, such as the Biodiversity Convention. Nor can it be invoked by States that have contributed to the occurrence of an armed conflict.[85] Furthermore, it is interesting to note that a plea of necessity could in theory be invoked by another State as a justification for taking action to safeguard a natural heritage site against its destruction by the parties to the armed conflict. However, whether such action would include entering the territory of a State involved in an armed conflict without its permission is doubtful, as the State that undertook such an operation would have to demonstrate that there was no other reasonable alternative to prevent the destruction of the natural heritage site.

5.5 Customary international law

The previous sections discussed the continued applicability of treaty law in situations of armed conflict. However, this book has also identified some principles that apply independent of treaties. Relevant principles of customary international law include the principle of permanent sovereignty over natural resources, the principle of sustainable use of natural resources and the principle of prevention of environmental damage. Arguably, these principles could continue to apply irrespective of the applicability of the treaty in which they are incorporated.[86]

[85] Compare Koppe, who asserts for the situation of international armed conflict that '[o]nly states using force in self-defense comply with the requirement that the non-performance of their obligations under conventional and customary international law is not the result of their own behavior'. See Koppe, *The Use of Nuclear Weapons and the Protection of the Environment during International Armed Conflict*, p. 364.

[86] Compare Article 10 (Obligations imposed by international law independently of a treaty) of the ILC draft articles on the effects of armed conflict on treaties and Article 43 of the Vienna Convention on the Law of Treaties.

5.5.1 *The principle of permanent sovereignty over natural resources*

The principle of permanent sovereignty is relevant to the situation of armed conflict in several ways. First, it entails an obligation for third States to respect a State's sovereignty over natural resources. This obligation imposes clear limits on what a State involved in an international armed conflict is permitted to do with the natural resources of its adversary. Second, the principle of permanent sovereignty entails obligations for the national government with regard to the exploitation of natural resources. One condition inherent in the principle of permanent sovereignty is the obligation to exercise sovereignty over natural resources for national development and the well-being of the people of the State. It is this condition that is of particular relevance for the current book.

The principle of permanent sovereignty over natural resources has been applied to situations of armed conflict on several occasions. First, it was referred to in several UN Security Council resolutions relating to the armed conflict in the DR Congo.[87] Furthermore, in a more general vein, the sovereign right of States to exploit their own natural resources was reaffirmed in a presidential statement of the Security Council concerning the maintenance of international peace and security.[88]

In addition, in its resolutions concerning the Israeli occupation of Palestinian territory, the UN General Assembly expressly declared the principle of permanent sovereignty over natural resources to be applicable to the natural resources of territories under occupation. Resolution 66/225 of 29 March 2012, in which the UN General Assembly reaffirms 'the principle of the permanent sovereignty of peoples under foreign occupation over their natural resources'[89] is one example.

[87] See, e.g., UNSC Resolutions 1291 (2000), 1304 (2000), 1332 (2000), 1341 (2001), 1355 (2001), 1493 (2003) and 1533 (2004).

[88] Statement by the President of the Security Council made in connection with the Council's consideration of the item entitled Maintenance of International Peace and Security, *UN Doc. S/PRST/2007/22*, 25 June 2007. See in this regard also 'The Plundering of Natural Resources and Destruction of the Environment in Times of Armed Conflict', in Genugten, Scharf and Radin (eds.), *Criminal Jurisdiction 100 Years after the 1907 Hague Peace Conference*, Proceedings of the 2007 Hague Joint Conference on Contemporary Issues of International Law, p. 242 (2009).

[89] UNGA Resolution 66/225 on 'Permanent Sovereignty of the Palestinian People in the Occupied Palestinian Territory, Including East Jerusalem, and of the Arab Population in the Occupied Syrian Golan over Their Natural Resources', adopted on 29 March 2012.

Similarly, in a report on the implications of the United Nations resolutions on permanent sovereignty over natural resources in the occupied Palestinian and other Arab territories and on the obligations of Israel concerning its conduct in these territories under international law, the UN Secretary-General stated that the principle of permanent sovereignty over natural resources and the law of belligerent occupation 'strengthen and reinforce each other'.[90]

The decision of the International Court of Justice in the Congo–Uganda case does not appear to be in line with this. In that case, the DR Congo had invoked the principle of permanent sovereignty as a principle relevant to the situation of the illegal exploitation, looting and plundering of natural resources by members of the Ugandan army. After the Court determined that the principle of permanent sovereignty was part of customary international law, it noted that there was nothing in the UNGA resolutions defining the principle of permanent sovereignty to suggest 'that they are applicable to the specific situation of looting, pillage and exploitation of certain natural resources by members of the army of a State militarily intervening in another State . . . The Court does not believe that this principle is applicable to this type of situation'.[91]

The precise meaning of the Court's judgment in this respect remains unclear. Does the Court say that the principle of permanent sovereignty is not applicable at all to the situation of armed conflict or is its inapplicability confined to the specific situation at hand?[92] In this respect, it should be noted that in general the Court does not exclude the applicability of the principle of permanent sovereignty to the situation of armed conflict. Instead, it refers to 'this' type of situation. The decision could therefore be determined by the specific circumstances of the case – i.e., that the looting, pillage, and exploitation were committed by individual members of the Ugandan army in the absence of sufficient evidence of a systematic policy of the Ugandan government aimed at the plunder of the natural resources of the DR Congo.[93]

90 UN Secretary-General, Report on the Implications, under International Law, of the United Nations Resolutions on Permanent Sovereignty over Natural Resources, on the Occupied Palestinian and other Arab Territories and on the Obligations of Israel Concerning Its Conduct in These Territories, *UN Doc. A/38/265*, 21 June 1983, para. 47.

91 Congo–Uganda case, *supra*, note 11 at para. 244.

92 Compare Schrijver, 'Natural Resources, Permanent Sovereignty over', para. 18.

93 Compare Ibid. and Okowa, 'Natural Resources in Situations of Armed Conflict', p. 2.

Moreover, the Court's decision does not appear to affect the rights and obligations inherent in the principle of permanent sovereignty. This conclusion follows, first of all, from the decision itself. When it comes to determining Uganda's international responsibility, the Court explicitly refers to Article 21 of the 1981 African Charter of Human and Peoples' Rights, which formulates the right of all peoples to freely dispose of their natural resources and, in cases of spoliation, formulates a right for a dispossessed people to the lawful recovery of its property, as well as to adequate compensation.[94]

In other words, the Court seems to acknowledge that the right of peoples to freely dispose of their natural resources does impose specific obligations on Uganda as an occupying power, if not on the basis of custom, then at least on the basis of treaty law. Furthermore, in his declaration, Judge Koroma stated that the rights and interests arising from the 1962 Declaration on Permanent Sovereignty over Natural Resources 'remain in effect at all times, including *during armed conflict and during occupation*'.[95]

Therefore, it can be argued that the principle of permanent sovereignty over natural resources continues to apply in times of armed conflict, both in relation to third States and in relation to a State's own natural resources. Of course, the obligation to exploit natural resources for the well-being of the people does not prohibit a government from using the proceeds of resource exploitation for military expenditure. Fighting rebel groups that undermine State authority can perfectly well be 'for the well-being of the people'. Nevertheless, the obligation for a government to act for the well-being of the people arguably does entail a general obligation for the government to account for its decisions in this respect.

5.5.2 The environmental principles of sustainable use and prevention of environmental damage

Other principles that are of particular relevance to the exploitation of natural resources in situations of armed conflict are the principles of sustainable use and prevention of environmental damage. Arguably these principles apply both to the exploitation by a State of its own natural resources and in relation to the natural resources of a third State. Despite their relevance to situations of armed conflict, there have not been many

[94] Congo–Uganda case, *supra*, note 11 at para. 245.

[95] Ibid. (declaration of Judge Koroma) [emphasis in original].

references to these principles in the practice of UN bodies in relation to specific armed conflicts. The UN Security Council has referred to the concept of sustainability only in a few of its resolutions, mainly by indirect references.[96] Nevertheless, the systematic exploitation of natural resources 'with little regard to sustainable . . . practices', as happened in Liberia under Charles Taylor, is arguably not permitted except in situations of military necessity.[97]

The obligation to prevent damage to the environments of other States has been explicitly applied to situations where a State exercises *de facto* control in another State. Arguably this principle therefore applies in situations of occupation.[98] Moreover, there is no reason that it would cease to apply in the relationship between a belligerent State and third States. In this respect, it should be noted that the law of neutrality even ensures the territorial inviolability of neutral States.[99]

One important implication of the obligation to prevent damage to the environment of other States concerns the related obligation to conduct an EIA, an obligation which, according to the International Court of Justice in the Pulp Mills case, constitutes a 'requirement under general international law . . . where there is a risk that the proposed industrial activity may have a significant adverse impact in a transboundary context'.[100] Arguably the obligation to conduct an EIA applies not only when there is a risk of damage to the environments of other States, but also when there is a risk of damage to natural resources or parts of the environment that are important to the larger community of States, even if these natural resources are found entirely within the territory of a single State. Reference can be made to natural resources that are subject to common regimes, such as biological diversity and particular ecosystems and species.

The obligation to conduct an EIA requires States to conduct an assessment of the risks of a project for the environment both before the start

96 These resolutions relate to armed conflicts in Cambodia and Liberia respectively. For more details, see Chapter 7 of this study.

97 Report of the Panel of Experts on Liberia Established Pursuant to Security Council Resolution 1343 (2001), Paragraph 19, Concerning Liberia, *UN Doc. S/2001/1015* of 26 October 2001, para. 33.

98 See the commentary of the ILC on its Draft articles on Prevention of Transboundary Harm from Hazardous Activities, *Yearbook of the International Law Commission*, Vol. II, Part Two (2001), p. 151, para. 12, as discussed in Chapter 4 of this study.

99 Koppe, *The Use of Nuclear Weapons and the Protection of the Environment during International Armed Conflict*, p. 361.

100 International Court of Justice, Case Concerning Pulp Mills on the River Uruguay (*Argentina* v. *Uruguay*), *I.C.J. Reports 2010*, para. 204.

of the project and during its exploitation. A situation of armed conflict does not relieve States of this responsibility, especially not for exploitation projects that are to be conducted in parts of the State territory where no fighting occurs. Moreover, an EIA is a flexible instrument that can be adapted to all circumstances. Therefore, the extent to which States have to assess the risks arising from a project will depend on the factual circumstances.

5.6 Concluding remarks on the role of international human rights and environmental law in situations of armed conflict

This chapter has examined whether and to what extent States remain bound by international human rights and environmental law when conducting exploitation activities in situations of armed conflict. It argued that the exploitation of natural resources by States as a commercial activity continues to be regulated by the legal framework that applies to the management of natural resources in situations of peace. This implies that States remain bound by their obligations under international human rights and environmental law in situations of armed conflict. There are two exceptions to this basic assumption.

First, as the case law of the International Court of Justice shows, situations of armed conflict are primarily governed by the rules of IHL. In cases where the relevant rules of international human rights and environmental law clash with this field of international law, there is a presumption that the rules of IHL prevail. However, in cases where there is no apparent clash between the relevant rules from the different fields of international law, the relevant rules complement each other. As the following chapter will show, IHL contains only a few specialised rules that apply to the management of natural resources. In addition, these rules do not directly conflict with relevant rules of international human rights and environmental law.

The existence of an armed conflict may alter the extent of the obligations to be fulfilled by States under international human rights and environmental law. There are factors inherent in international human rights and environmental treaties which have an impact on the performance of their obligations during an armed conflict. For obligations under international human rights law, the principal issue affecting the operation of human rights instruments during an armed conflict concerns the possibility of derogating from the provisions of the treaties. This applies particularly to the ICCPR, which contains an express provision on derogation.

Derogation permits States to deviate from their obligations under human rights treaties in situations of public emergency, including armed conflicts. Derogation is permitted in exceptional circumstances only after a situation of public emergency has been announced. Moreover, derogation does not annul the obligation itself. States have to justify not respecting their obligations in each individual case.

This chapter has argued that the possibility of derogating from particular human rights may have an impact on the rights of individuals and minorities to participate in decision making, but it does not affect the basic prohibition against depriving a people of their means of subsistence, incorporated into the identical Articles 1(2) of the ICCPR and the ICESCR. This prohibition is framed in absolute terms, which implies that derogation from the prohibition is not permitted under any circumstances.

As far as environmental obligations are concerned, it should be noted that many provisions in environmental treaties are lenient with regard to the implementation of the substantive obligations by States. This leniency can be seen at two levels. First, environmental obligations are generally not executed automatically. The implementation of environmental obligations often requires the formulation of plans and policies at the national level. Examples include the provisions of the Biodiversity Convention relating to the *in situ* (Article 8) and *ex situ* (Article 9) conservation of biological diversity, the provisions in the UNESCO World Heritage Convention on the protection, conservation and preservation of world heritage (in particular, Article 5) and the provisions in the Ramsar Convention on Wetlands on the listing and conservation of wetlands (i.e., Articles 2 and 4).

Second, the implementation of obligations under international environmental treaties is often conditional on the respective capabilities of States. Examples include obligations incorporated into the Convention on the Conservation of Migratory Species of Wild Animals, the Biodiversity Convention and the Climate Change Convention, which require implementation only as far as this is possible and appropriate.[101] This

[101] See, for example, Article III (4) of the Convention on the Conservation of Migratory Species of Wild Animals, which determines that Parties 'shall endeavour . . . where feasible and appropriate; . . . as appropriate . . . ; and to the extent feasible and appropriate'. Similarly, Articles 8 to 11 of the Biodiversity Convention formulate obligations for parties to be implemented 'as far as possible and appropriate'. Similarly, the principle of common but differentiated responsibilities, expressed in the Climate Change Convention, implies a degree of leniency as well.

implies that States could deviate from these obligations in situations of armed conflict if their implementation were not possible or appropriate.

However, as a minimum, it can be argued that States cannot act contrary to their core obligations under international environmental treaties. This results from their general obligation to act in good faith with regard to the implementation of their treaty obligations. This applies not only to exploitation activities in inter-State armed conflicts, but also to the exploitation of public natural resources in intra-State conflicts. In both cases, the *rationale* for the continued applicability of international environmental law is based on the need to protect the interests of third States. As argued previously, many obligations under international environmental law serve to protect the interests of a larger community of States. The occurrence of an armed conflict does not diminish these obligations.

This chapter also examined the possibilities for States to terminate or suspend the operation of treaties in situations of armed conflict. In particular, it examined three possibilities for suspension: the suspension of a treaty in the case of a material breach of that treaty by another party to the treaty; supervening impossibility of performance; and fundamental change in circumstances. Arguably States can only suspend their treaty obligations in exceptional circumstances. Therefore, in most cases, States remain bound by their obligations under relevant treaties. The exceptions mainly affect international environmental treaties and concern the relationship between belligerent States *inter se*.

In addition, this chapter examined circumstances precluding the wrongfulness of otherwise illegal conduct. In particular, it examined *force majeure* and necessity as circumstances that would preclude the wrongfulness of acts of States contrary to their treaty obligations under international human rights and environmental treaties. Most relevant to the current study is the conclusion that a State can invoke *force majeure* for breaches of its obligations under international human rights and environmental conventions in territories under the control of armed groups, but only to the extent that it is factually impossible for the State to prevent the violation of the relevant obligations.

Furthermore, States continue to be bound by their obligations under customary international law in situations of armed conflict. The most relevant example of a customary international law obligation concerns the principle of permanent sovereignty and the inherent condition that a government must exercise permanent sovereignty for national development and the well-being of the population. As a minimum, this implies that a government remains accountable for its use of the proceeds of natural resources exploitation. Another example concerns the obligation to conserve and sustainably use natural resources, as incorporated, *inter alia,* into the Ramsar Convention on the Protection of Wetlands, the UNESCO World Heritage Convention and CITES. Arguably, this principle qualifies the right of States to exploit their natural resources, even in situations of armed conflict.

Another customary international law obligation which continues to apply for States involved in an armed conflict is the obligation to prevent damage to the environment of other States resulting from exploitation activities, including an obligation to conduct an EIA when an activity could entail risks for the environment. These obligations continue to be relevant in situations of armed conflict.

In conclusion, it can be argued that international human rights and environmental law provide a basic framework qualifying the right of governments to freely dispose of the State's natural resources in situations of armed conflict. The extent to which these fields of international law can in fact regulate the commercial exploitation of natural resources by governments in situations of armed conflict in a meaningful way depends on a number of factors. This chapter has discussed several of these factors. In a more general vein, it can be argued that the extent to which international human rights and environmental law continue to effectively regulate the management of natural resources by governments depends on the gravity of the conflict situation, including the measure of control exercised by a government over the State's territory.

6

Protection of natural resources and the environment under international humanitarian law

6.1 Introductory remarks

The law of armed conflict – or IHL – regulates the conduct of parties to an armed conflict. It limits the methods and means they may use to weaken the adversary and it provides rules that aim to limit the effects of warfare on vulnerable groups, in particular the civilian population, as well as persons who are no longer taking part in hostilities. In other words, IHL primarily regulates the use of violence by parties to an armed conflict.[1] This specific focus of IHL is decisive for the way in which this field of international law addresses activities relating to the exploitation of natural resources by parties to an armed conflict. It also immediately reveals the limits of IHL in this respect.

The exploitation of natural resources by parties to an armed conflict is not an act of war in itself, but rather an activity that sustains conflict. Natural resources provide parties to an armed conflict with the means to finance their armed struggle. Therefore, IHL appears to be ill suited to regulate the exploitation of natural resources by parties to an armed conflict, in contrast with occupation law, which has a different aim, namely to define the rights and obligations for occupants as *de facto* State authorities. This field of IHL does include rules defining the rights of an occupant with regard to the natural resources situated in occupied territory.

The limits of IHL for the scope of this book are also evident from its environmental provisions. The few IHL provisions which were specifically

[1] See the definition provided by the International Committee of the Red Cross (ICRC), which defines IHL as 'the branch of international law limiting the use of violence in armed conflicts by: a) sparing those who do not or no longer directly participate in hostilities; b) restricting it to the amount necessary to achieve the aim of the conflict, which – independently of the causes fought for – can only be to weaken the military potential of the enemy'. See Sassòli, Bouvier and Quintin, *How Does Law Protect in War?* Vol. I, p. 1.

designed to protect the environment during armed conflict focus on the effects of military operations on the environment.[2] Their purpose is to prevent 'widespread, long-term and severe' damage to the environment resulting from acts of warfare.[3] They were not designed to protect the environment against other threats resulting from the conduct of parties to an armed conflict, such as environmental damage resulting from the exploitation of natural resources by parties to an armed conflict. Furthermore, it should be noted that these provisions were adopted in 1977, when modern international environmental law was at an early stage of development.

Despite all these apparent limitations, IHL is important for the protection of natural resources and the environment during armed conflict. First, it is the only field of international law that contains obligations directly binding for non-State armed groups. In addition, it is the primary field of international law that is applicable to States which occupy or intervene militarily in other States.

Therefore, the current chapter examines the few provisions of IHL which are relevant for the protection of natural resources and the environment during armed conflict. These are Article 23(g) of the 1907 Hague

[2] Articles 35(3) and 55, Protocol Additional to the Geneva Conventions of 12 August 1949, and Relating to the Protection of Victims of International Armed Conflicts (Protocol I), 8 June 1977, *1125 UNTS 3*. Besides these provisions, mention must be made of the Convention on the Prohibition of Military or Any Other Hostile Use of Environmental Modification Techniques (ENMOD), concluded on 10 December 1976 in New York (entry into force: 5 October 1978), *1108 UNTS 151*. This convention aims to prevent the environment being used as a weapon.

[3] For proposals regarding the current Article 55 of Additional Protocol I, see *CDDH/III/60* of 19 March 1974 (Proposal by Australia to insert a new provision, Article 49 bis, in Additional Protocol I) and *CDDH/III/64* of 19 March 1974 (Proposal by Czechoslovakia, the German Democratic Republic and Hungary to add a new paragraph to Article 48 of Additional Protocol I). For proposals with regard to current Article 35(3) of Additional Protocol I, see *CDDH/III/108* of 11 September 1974 (Amendment by the German Democratic Republic to Article 33 of Protocol I); *CDDH/III/222* of 24 February 1975 (Amendment by the Arab Republic of Egypt, Australia, Czechoslovakia, Finland, German Democratic Republic, Hungary, Ireland, Norway, Sudan, Yugoslavia to Article 33 of Additional Protocol I) and *CDDH/III/238 and Add. 1* of 25 February 1975 (Amendment by the Democratic Republic of Vietnam and Uganda to Article 33 of Additional Protocol I). *Official Records of the Diplomatic Conference on the Reaffirmation and Development of International Humanitarian Law Applicable in Armed Conflicts*, Geneva (1974–7), Vol. III, p. 220, 155–7. For a proposal regarding the insertion of a new paragraph to current Article 14 of Additional Protocol II, see *CDDH/III/55* of 19 March 1974 (proposal by Australia to insert a new provision, Article 28 bis, in Additional Protocol II). *Official Records of the Diplomatic Conference on the Reaffirmation and Development of International Humanitarian Law Applicable in Armed Conflicts*, Geneva (1974–7), Vol. IV, Amendments, p. 91.

Regulations, containing a prohibition against destroying or seizing the property of the enemy; Article 28 of the 1907 Hague Regulations, Article 33(2) of the 1949 Geneva Convention IV and Article 4(2)(g) of the 1977 Additional Protocol II to the Geneva Conventions on the prohibition against pillage; Article 55 of the 1907 Hague Regulations defining the right of usufruct of an occupant; Article 54 of the 1977 Additional Protocol I and Article 14 of the 1977 Additional Protocol II on the protection of objects indispensable to the survival of the civilian population; and finally, Articles 35(3) and 55 of the 1997 Additional Protocol I on the protection of the natural environment.

The current chapter aims to determine to what extent IHL contains rules that prohibit the illicit exploitation, looting and plundering of natural resources by parties to an armed conflict and address the related environmental damage. Of course, as explained earlier, IHL was not specifically designed to address instances of natural resource exploitation by parties to an armed conflict. As a specialised branch of international law, IHL is, however, part of the broader system of international law. This implies that it must be interpreted and applied in light of the relevant rules of general international law and other specialised branches of international law. International environmental and human rights law in particular can be instrumental in filling the gaps in IHL. This applies particularly to international environmental law, as the standards set by this field of law are more specific and more recent than those set by IHL.

Before embarking on an in-depth analysis of substantive IHL, Section 6.2 analyses the classical dichotomy made in IHL between international and noninternational armed conflicts from the perspective of resource-related armed conflicts. Section 6.3 then discusses the relevant rules of IHL, while Section 6.4 takes a closer look at the Martens clause as a means of integrating rules from international human rights and environmental law into the law of armed conflict. Finally, Section 6.5 assesses the protection provided by IHL to natural resources and the environment.

6.2 Qualification of the legal situation

IHL makes a fundamental distinction between international and noninternational armed conflicts. The classification of a conflict as international or noninternational determines which law is applicable to the conflict. Article 2 common to the 1949 Geneva Conventions defines 'international armed conflict' as a situation of 'declared war or . . . any other armed conflict which may arise between two or more of the High Contracting

Parties' or a situation of 'total or partial occupation of a territory'. Article 3 common to the 1949 Geneva Conventions defines 'non-international armed conflict' as an armed conflict 'occurring in the territory of one of the High Contracting Parties'.

Most of the armed conflicts discussed in this chapter are internal in nature. However, some are internationalised through the intervention of foreign States. This intervention is sometimes direct, in the sense that the foreign State sends its army into the territory of another State. This is what Uganda and Rwanda did during the 1990s, when they entered the territory of the DR Congo and even occupied parts of the DR Congo's territory. However, the intervention can also be indirect, in the sense that a foreign State provides support to armed groups engaged in an internal armed conflict. Again, Rwanda serves as an example. A recent report by the Group of Experts on the DR Congo revealed Rwanda's support for armed groups operating in the DR Congo.[4] Liberia's support for the RUF between 1998 and 2002 is another example of a State providing indirect support to armed groups.

The extent to which foreign States are involved in an internal armed conflict determines whether it is qualified as an international or internal conflict. The current section examines this distinction between internal and international armed conflicts. It looks in particular at the following questions: What constitutes an internal armed conflict? When can such an armed conflict be deemed to have become internationalised? What are the legal implications of the distinction between internal and international armed conflicts?

6.2.1 *Internal armed conflict*

For a long time, internal armed conflicts were not subject to international regulation. These conflicts were considered to fall within the *domaine réservé* of the State concerned.[5] The treatment of insurgents was left to

[4] Group of Experts on the DR Congo, Addendum to the Interim Report of the Group of Experts on the DRC Submitted in Accordance with Paragraph 4 of Security Council Resolution 2021 (2011), *UN Doc. S/2012/348/Add.1* of 27 June 2012.

[5] See Pictet and Uhler, *The Geneva Conventions of 12 August 1949*, pp. 26–30. There is one early instrument that regulates internal armed conflict, but this is a State's military manual rather than a legal instrument. The *Instructions for the Government of Armies of the United States in the Field (General Orders No. 100)* of 24 April 1863, also known as the 'Lieber Code', contains a section X on 'insurrection, civil war and rebellion'. For reasons of 'humanity' rather than out of a sense of legal obligation, this section proposed to apply

the discretion of the incumbent government, which could freely choose whether or not to grant its opponent rights by conferring belligerent status on him.[6] Third States were prohibited altogether from interfering in these 'internal affairs', which were subject to domestic regulation.[7]

This gradually changed during the course of the nineteenth century, when the duty of noninterference started to give way to the doctrine of recognition of belligerency. If the hostilities in the armed conflict had attained a certain level, close to that of an international armed conflict, third States declared recognition of belligerency of both parties, thus bringing into effect the corpus of IHL.[8] Recognition of belligerency required careful consideration, as the legal conditions were stringent and the legal consequences of premature or unfounded recognition could be severe.[9]

the rules of international armed conflict to the situation of internal armed conflict. This is reflected in Article 52, one of the key provisions of Section X, which provides as follows: 'When humanity induces the adoption of the rules of regular war toward rebels, whether the adoption is partial or entire, it does in no way whatever imply a partial or complete acknowledgement of their government, if they have set up one, or of them, as an independent and sovereign power. Neutrals have no right to make the adoption of the rules of war by the assailed government toward rebels the ground of their own acknowledgment of the revolted people as an independent power'. On this subject, see Perna, *The Formation of the Treaty Law of Non-international Armed Conflict*, pp. 31–3 and Moir, *The Law of Internal Armed Conflict*, p. 19. The Lieber Code is available through the International Humanitarian Law Database of the ICRC. See www.icrc.org/ihl.

6 On the subject of recognition of belligerency, see Lauterpacht, *Recognition in International Law*, pp. 175–200; Riedel, 'Recognition of Belligerency', pp. 47–50; Perna, *The Formation of the Treaty Law of Non-international Armed Conflict*, pp. 29–30; and Moir, *The Law of Internal Armed Conflict*, pp. 4–11. In most cases, the incumbent government was not willing to grant its opponents belligerent status, because doing so would give them extensive rights. See Perna, *The Formation of the Treaty Law of Non-international Armed Conflict*, p. 30.

7 Lauterpacht points to a resolution of the Institute of International Law, adopted in 1900, which clearly states that 'every third Power, at peace with an independent nation, is bound not to interfere with the measures which this nation takes for the re-establishing of internal peace'. See *Resolutions of the Institute*, Carnegie Endowment (1916), p. 156, quoted in Lauterpacht, *Recognition in International Law*, p. 230.

8 See Lauterpacht, *Recognition in International Law*, pp. 175–6 and Riedel, 'Recognition of Belligerency', p. 47. Lauterpacht mentions the following conditions (p. 176): 'First, there must exist within the State an armed conflict of a general (as distinguished from a purely local) character; secondly, the insurgents must occupy and administer a substantial portion of national territory; thirdly, they must conduct the hostilities in accordance with the rules of war and through organised armed forces acting under a responsible authority; fourthly, there must exist circumstances which make it necessary for outside States to define their attitude by means of recognition of belligerency'.

9 Premature or unfounded recognition constituted an internationally wrongful act against the incumbent government. See Lauterpacht, *Recognition in International Law*, p. 176.

This is the background against which the delegations at the 1949 Geneva Diplomatic Conference negotiated a special provision applicable to internal armed conflicts, which was to be inserted into all four Conventions. Article 3 common to the 1949 Geneva Conventions offered protection to all persons taking no active part in hostilities – including members of armed groups, whether they were recognised by their government or not.

Article 3 common to the 1949 Geneva Conventions defines internal armed conflicts as armed conflicts 'occurring in the territory of one of the High Contracting Parties'. There was considerable discussion about this definition during the drafting of common Article 3.[10] According to the Commentary on the Geneva Conventions, some States feared that the term 'conflict not of an international character' might be interpreted as covering any act committed by force of arms, including minor insurgencies or even plain banditry.[11] Therefore, several delegations proposed inserting amendments containing conditions for the applicability of the Conventions. These amendments were concerned with various aspects, including recognition of belligerency, the form of organisation of armed groups and even the recognition by the Security Council that the dispute constituted a threat to international peace, a breach of the peace or act of aggression.[12] Ultimately, none of these amendments were included in the Conventions, leaving a large measure of flexibility for application of the provision.

Thus what constitutes an internal armed conflict for the purposes of Article 3 is left wide open. However, as was clear from the start, a certain threshold must be met for Article 3 to apply. The Commentary on the Geneva Conventions states that 'it must be recognised that the conflicts referred to in Article 3 are armed conflicts, with armed forces on either side engaged in hostilities . . . In many cases, each of the Parties is in possession of a portion of the national territory, and there is often some sort of front'.[13] The ICRC description indicates that there are specific requirements relating to the organisation of the parties to the conflict and the intensity of the violence. Both requirements were identified and elaborated upon in subsequent case law of international criminal tribunals, in particular in the case law of the International Criminal Tribunal for the former Yugoslavia (ICTY).

[10] For a full account of the drafting history of Article 3, see Cullen, *The Concept of Non-international Armed Conflict in International Humanitarian Law*, pp. 27–51.

[11] See Pictet and Uhler, *The Geneva Conventions of 12 August 1949*, p. 35.

[12] Ibid., pp. 35–6. [13] Ibid., p. 36.

In this respect, the ICTY's *Tadić case*, which defined a noninternational armed conflict as '*protracted* armed violence between governmental authorities and *organised* armed groups or between such groups within a State' was a landmark case.[14] This definition was subsequently inserted in Article 8 of the ICC Statute, dealing with war crimes.[15] The term 'protracted armed violence' has become the standard for assessing the intensity of the violence. To distinguish armed conflict from internal disturbances, the violence must be carried out over a longer period of time. The violence must exceed sporadic acts of violence, but it does not have to involve sustained military operations.[16] As regards the degree of organisation of armed groups, reference can be made to indicators such as the command structure and the operational effectiveness of the group.[17]

All the conflicts discussed in the current book satisfy these requirements. In many resource-related armed conflicts, non-State armed groups even control a portion of State territory, in particular a region where natural resources are located. Examples include the conflict in Côte d'Ivoire between 2002 and 2007, where the Forces Nouvelles de Côte d'Ivoire occupied most of the northern part of the country. The RUF in Sierra Leone also exercised control over a region of Sierra Leone bordering Liberia, where most of the diamonds are located.

This means that these conflicts are governed by the rules stipulated in Article 3 common to the 1949 Geneva Conventions. This provision contains a set of fundamental rules for parties to an internal armed conflict regarding the humane treatment of persons taking no active part in hostilities. In the words of the International Court of Justice, these rules reflect 'elementary considerations of humanity', which can be interpreted as a recognition of their customary international law status.[18] The rules

[14] International Criminal Tribunal for the former Yugoslavia, *The Prosecutor* v. *Dusko Tadić*, Decision on the Defence Motion for Interlocutory Appeal on Jurisdiction, Case No. IT-94-1-A, Appeals Chamber Decision of 2 October 1995, para. 70. Emphasis added.

[15] Article 8(2)(f) of the ICC Statute defines internal armed conflicts as 'armed conflicts that take place in the territory of a State when there is protracted armed conflict between governmental authorities and organised armed groups or between such groups'. In the case against Thomas Lubanga, the ICC Trial Chamber clarified the concept of 'non-international armed conflict' for the purposes of the ICC Statute. See International Criminal Court, *The Prosecutor* v. *Thomas Lubanga Dyilo*, Trial Chamber I, Judgment pursuant to Article 74 of the Statute, 14 March 2012, *ICC-01/04-01/06-2842*, paras. 534–8.

[16] For a full discussion of relevant case law and literature, see Cullen, *The Concept of Non-international Armed Conflict in International Humanitarian Law*, pp. 122–33.

[17] Ibid.

[18] Military and Paramilitary Activities in and against Nicaragua (*Nicaragua* v. *United States of America*), judgment of 27 June 1986, *I.C.J. Reports 1986*, para. 218.

formulated in Article 3 of the Geneva Conventions apply automatically and without any requirement of reciprocity.[19] Other provisions of the Geneva Conventions apply only to noninternational armed conflicts with the express consent of all parties to the armed conflict.[20]

To increase the humanitarian protection offered by the common Article 3 of the 1949 Geneva Conventions, a second Protocol to the Geneva Conventions was adopted in 1977 after extensive negotiations. Today, Additional Protocol II has been ratified by the majority of States, including nearly all States which have been involved in resource-related armed conflicts in the last decades.[21] Based on the rules provided by common Article 3, the more detailed provisions of Additional Protocol II on the treatment of prisoners and civilians significantly raise the level of protection for these categories of persons.

At the same time, Additional Protocol II sets a much higher threshold for application than the common Articles 3. While Article 3 common to the 1949 Geneva Conventions is generally assumed to apply to all internal conflicts, whether the State army is involved or not, Additional Protocol II applies only to situations of armed conflict between governments on one hand, and non-State armed groups on the other. In addition, the conflict must take place within the territory of the government concerned. Finally, armed groups must be 'under responsible command' and 'exercise such control over a part of its territory as to enable them to carry out sustained and concerted military operations'.[22]

[19] In general, see Riedel, 'Recognition of Belligerency', pp. 47–50. See also Pictet and Uhler, *The Geneva Conventions of 12 August 1949*, p. 35.

[20] The common Article 3 to the Geneva Conventions urges parties to conclude 'special agreements' by means of which they bring into operation 'all or part of the other provisions of the Geneva Conventions'.

[21] As of November 2012, Protocol II has been ratified by 166 States. For an overview of the State parties to Protocol II, see www.icrc.org/ihl.nsf/CONVPRES?OpenView. It must be noted that the United States has not ratified the Protocol, but it did sign it. For its negotiating history, see Momtaz, 'Le droit international humanitaire applicable aux conflits armés non internationaux', pp. 30–33. Momtaz argues that the reason for many states to have ratified the Protocol in recent years is due to the formation of new customary rules which have made the provisions of Protocol II rather obsolete. At the same time, it could be argued that the formation of customary rules similar to the rules incorporated in the Protocol may also confirm the Protocols' legal significance. Its provisions may then to a certain extent be considered an expression of customary law.

[22] Article 1, Protocol Additional to the Geneva Conventions of 12 August 1949, and Relating to the Protection of Victims of Non-international Armed Conflicts (Protocol II), 8 June 1977, *1125 UNTS 609.*

This degree of organisation of armed groups that is required can pose difficulties in practice. Even if an armed group exercises control over part of the State territory, it may not have an adequate command structure or be unable to carry out 'sustained and concerted' military operations.[23] In the DR Congo, in particular, many different armed groups are active. Some of these are highly organised, but many do not satisfy the criteria set by Additional Protocol II. This leads to confusing situations, where different rules apply in the relationship between the State and different armed groups. The situation becomes even more complex when foreign States are involved. This situation is examined below.

6.2.2 *International armed conflict*

Article 2 common to the 1949 Geneva Conventions defines 'international armed conflict' as a situation of 'declared war or . . . any other armed conflict which may arise between two or more of the High Contracting Parties' or a situation of 'total or partial occupation of a territory'. A large body of IHL applies to these situations, including the 1907 Hague Conventions, the 1949 Geneva Conventions and the 1977 Additional Protocol I to the 1949 Geneva Conventions, as well as a large number of specialised conventions. Some of the rules contained in these instruments apply to international armed conflicts in general, while other rules are specific to the situation of invasion or occupation respectively.

The definition of international armed conflict set out in Article 2 of the 1949 Geneva Conventions is quite straightforward. An armed conflict is international when two or more States are fighting each other and/or when a State occupies (part of) the territory of another State. However, for the purposes of the present book the definition is not so clear. In the late 1990s, for example, Uganda and Rwanda were invited by the Congolese government to enter its territory in order to fight irregular Ugandan and Rwandese armed groups operating from Congolese territory. However, these States decided to stay in the DR Congo after the government had requested them to leave, and even occupied parts of Congolese territory.

How should this situation be characterised? There are no particular problems as regards the term 'occupation'. Occupation is a factual

[23] Also see Momtaz, 'Le Droit International Humanitaire Applicable aux Conflits Armés Non Internationaux', pp. 49–51.

situation which is determined on the basis of the transfer of *de facto* State authority.[24] As soon as a State exercises *de facto* authority in a particular region, the law on occupation applies. However, in other parts of Congolese territory, the classical definition does pose some difficulties. Uganda and Rwanda were not actually fighting the Congolese government, but were fighting armed groups launching attacks on these countries from Congolese territory. Does this mean that the law on international armed conflict does not apply?

The International Court of Justice had the opportunity to pronounce on this issue in the *case concerning Armed Activities in the Territory of the Congo* (hereafter the *Congo–Uganda case*), at least in relation to Uganda.[25] In that case, the Court considered whether Uganda was responsible for acts committed by its troops during its military intervention in the DR Congo. The Court concluded that 'a party to an armed conflict shall be responsible for all acts by persons forming part of its armed forces'.[26] Therefore, it found that Uganda was 'internationally responsible for violations of international human rights law and international humanitarian law committed by the UPDF and by its members in the territory of the DRC'.[27] Provisions of IHL mentioned by the Court were all part of the body of law regulating international armed conflict. This case implies that a State intervening in a foreign State is bound by the law regulating international armed conflict, even if the foreign State is not its opponent as such.

An internal armed conflict can also be internationalised as a result of a State providing support to armed groups, either directly, by means of armed intervention on behalf of a non-State armed group, or indirectly, in the form of financial and strategic military support for operations

[24] Article 43 of the 1907 Hague Regulations, annexed to Convention (IV) respecting the Laws and Customs of War on Land, 18 October 1907, determines in this regard, '[t]he authority of the legitimate power having in fact passed into the hands of the occupant, the latter shall take all the measures in his power to restore, and ensure, as far as possible, public order and safety, while respecting, unless absolutely prevented, the laws in force in the country'.

[25] It must be noted that a similar case instituted by the DR Congo against Rwanda was dismissed on the basis of jurisdiction. See International Court of Justice, Armed Activities on the Territory of the Congo (New Application: 2002) (*Democratic Republic of the Congo* v. *Rwanda*), Judgment of 3 February 2006, *I.C.J. Reports 2006*, p. 6.

[26] International Court of Justice, Case Concerning Armed Activities in the Territory of the Congo (*Democratic Republic of the Congo* v. *Uganda*), Judgment of 19 December 2005, *I.C.J. Reports 2005*, para. 214.

[27] Ibid., para. 220.

of armed groups.[28] In the case of indirect intervention, a conflict can be qualified as international if it is determined that the armed group is acting on behalf of the foreign State.

There are two different criteria by which to establish whether an armed group is acting on behalf of a foreign State. To determine the criminal responsibility of individuals, the International Criminal Tribunal for the former Yugoslavia introduced the 'overall control' test. In the 1999 *Tadić Case* the ICTY determined that an armed group can be considered to act on behalf of a State when that State exercises general strategic control over the operations of the armed group.[29] This is the case when the foreign State '*has a role in organizing, co-ordinating or planning the military actions* of the military group, in addition to financing, training and equipping or providing operational support to that group'.[30]

By introducing this test, the ICTY departed from the more stringent 'effective control' test introduced by the International Court of Justice in the 1986 *Nicaragua Case*. This test was established to determine the responsibility of a State for the actions of an armed group; in other words, to determine whether an armed group was acting as a *de facto* State organ. According to the 'effective control' test, a State is responsible only for those violations of international law committed by an armed group in the course of military operations over which the State exercised effective control.[31]

In the 2007 *Genocide Case*, the International Court of Justice pronounced on the relationship between the two tests. The Court considered that the effective control test must be applied in order to attribute responsibility to a State for actions committed by an armed group. However, to determine 'whether or not an armed conflict is international', the ICJ

[28] See Fleck (ed.), *The Handbook of International Humanitarian Law*, p. 606; and Stewart, 'Towards a Single Definition of Armed Conflict in International Humanitarian Law', p. 315. See International Court of Justice, *Application of the Convention on the Prevention and Punishment of the Crime of Genocide* (*Bosnia and Herzegovina* v. *Serbia and Montenegro*), Judgment of 26 February 2007, *I.C.J. Reports 2007*, paras. 402–6.

[29] International Criminal Tribunal for the Former Yugoslavia, *The Prosecutor* v. *Dusko Tadić, Case No. IT-94-1-AR72*, Appeals Chamber Judgment of 15 July 1999, para. 131.

[30] Ibid., para. 137. Emphasis in original. These criteria have been confirmed in other cases before the ICTY as well. See, e.g., International Criminal Tribunal for the Former Yugoslavia, *The Prosecutor* v. *Dario Kordić and Mario Čerkez, Case No. IT-95-14/2-A*, Appeals Chamber Judgment of 17 December 2004, paras. 306–8.

[31] International Court of Justice, Military and Paramilitary Activities in and against Nicaragua (*Nicaragua* v. *United States*), Judgment of 27 June 1986, *I.C.J. Reports 1986*, para. 115.

stated that the overall control test 'may well be applicable and suitable'.[32] According to the Court, each test has its own purpose. In this respect, it considered that

> the degree and nature of a State's involvement in an armed conflict on another State's territory which is required for the conflict to be characterised as international, can very well, and without logical inconsistency, differ from the degree and nature of involvement required to give rise to that State's responsibility for a specific act committed in the course of the conflict.[33]

Thus a conflict can be characterised as being international if it is established that a State is exercising overall control over the operations of an armed group, which means that the State has a role in organising, coordinating or planning the military actions.

However, the following question arises regarding the implications for the law that is applicable in a conflict between a government and an armed group that is supported by a third State. In the *Military and Paramilitary Activities in and against Nicaragua case*, the International Court of Justice made a clear distinction between two conflict situations:

> The conflict between the Contras' forces and those of the Government of Nicaragua is an armed conflict which is 'not of an international character'. The acts of the Contras towards the Nicaraguan Government are therefore governed by the law applicable to conflicts of that character; whereas the actions of the United States in and against Nicaragua fall under the legal rules relating to international conflicts.[34]

Thus the case implies that indirect third State intervention does not alter the classification of the conflict between the State and the opposing armed group. Arguably, this definition cannot be distinguished from the earlier conclusion reached by the Court that the United States did not exercise effective control over the Contras. If the Court had reached a different conclusion on the issue of control, it might well have reached a different conclusion regarding the classification of the armed conflict.

[32] International Court of Justice, Application of the Convention on the Prevention and Punishment of the Crime of Genocide (*Bosnia and Herzegovina* v. *Serbia and Montenegro*), Judgment of 26 February 2007, *I.C.J. Reports 2007*, paras. 402–6.

[33] Ibid., para. 405.

[34] International Court of Justice, Military and Paramilitary Activities in and against Nicaragua (*Nicaragua* v. *United States of America*), Merits, Judgment, *I.C.J. Reports 1986*, para. 219.

Case law does not fully clarify the implications of indirect State intervention for the law applicable to the relationship between a State and a rebel group. The Special Court for Sierra Leone, for example, did not deal in any of its cases with the question of whether the support from the Liberian President, Charles Taylor, internationalised the armed conflict in Sierra Leone, although there was sufficient evidence of Taylor's financial and strategic involvement in the operations of the RUF. In these cases it was not necessary to deal with the question of the internationalisation of the armed conflict, because the Statute of the SCSL does not distinguish between crimes committed in the course of an international or an internal armed conflict.

The ICC has dealt with the issue in a few cases, especially in the case against Thomas Lubanga, the leader of a Congolese rebel group that received support from Uganda. In an early decision, the ICC Pre-trial Chamber discussed the issue extensively. The Chamber applied the overall control test of the ICTY to the situation. It also relied on the judgment of the ICJ in the *Congo–Uganda case* to establish that Uganda had effectively intervened in the armed conflict in the DR Congo, turning it into an international armed conflict. The Pre-trial Chamber decided to apply Article 8(2)(b) of the ICC Statute on war crimes committed in the context of an international armed conflict to Lubanga's acts committed between July 2002 and June 2003, when Uganda occupied parts of Congolese territory.[35]

However, the Trial Chamber reversed the earlier judgment of the Pre-trial Chamber. Although it stated that the 'overall control' test was decisive for establishing whether armed groups were acting under the control of a foreign State, the Trial Chamber decided that it had not been demonstrated that either Rwanda or Uganda exercised sufficient control over the Congolese rebel groups to turn the conflict into an international armed conflict.[36] Arguably the decision of the Trial Chamber can be interpreted

[35] See International Criminal Court, *The Prosecutor* v. *Thomas Lubanga Dyilo*, Pre-Trial Chamber I, Decision on the Confirmation of Charges, 29 January 2007, *ICC-01/04-01/06-803-tEN*, paras. 205–26. The Pre-trial Chamber made a similar determination in the cases against Katanga and Chui, more than a year later. See International Criminal Court, *Prosecutor* v. *Germain Katanga and Mathieu Ngudjolo Chui*, Pre-trial Chamber I, Decision on the Confirmation of Charges, 30 September 2008, *Case No. ICC- 01/04-01/07-717*. Also see Heinsch, 'Legal Maxims: Summaries and Extracts from Selected Case Law of the International Criminal Court', pp. 394–403.

[36] International Criminal Court, *The Prosecutor* v. *Thomas Lubanga Dyilo*, Trial Chamber I, Judgment pursuant to Article 74 of the Statute, 14 March 2012, *ICC-01/04-01/06-2842*, paras. 541–2 (on the law) and 552–67 (on the facts).

as providing support for the thesis that indirect third State intervention changes the relationship between the government and an armed group. In these situations, the law applicable to international rather than internal armed conflicts applies. However, the decision also demonstrates that the evidentiary standards are high.

The last way in which an internal armed conflict can be internationalised is when third States grant recognition to an armed group as a formal belligerent. The theory of recognition of belligerency has become outdated as a result of the adoption of rules regulating the situation of internal armed conflict. Since the adoption of the 1949 Geneva Conventions, internal armed conflicts are no longer considered to be a matter of domestic concern, but are properly regulated under international law. However, even today, recognition of belligerency is more than a theoretical option. Chapter 2 argued that the recognition of the opposition forces as the official representative of the people by a large number of States, both in the recent armed conflict in Libya in 2011 and in the ongoing armed conflict in Syria, can be considered as implied acts of recognition of belligerency by these States. These examples show that recognition of belligerency is still one of the principal ways in which an internal armed conflict can be internationalised.

6.2.3 The relevance of the distinction between international and internal armed conflict

The relevance of the distinction between international and internal armed conflict has declined in recent years. Three developments have been instrumental in bridging the gaps between the rules applicable to international and internal armed conflicts. The first development concerns the harmonisation of the treaty rules relevant to the two types of armed conflict, especially those relating to the use of weapons in international and internal armed conflicts. Since the 1990s several conventions prohibiting the use of certain weapons have been amended either to encompass the situation of noninternational conflict or with an express provision to this effect. Relevant examples include the 1993 Chemical Weapons Convention and the 1997 Anti-personnel Mines Convention, which prohibit 'in any circumstances' the development, production, stockpiling, transfer and use of chemical weapons and of anti-personnel mines, respectively.[37]

[37] Convention on the Prohibition of the Development, Production, Stockpiling and Use of Chemical Weapons and on Their Destruction, 13 January 1993, *1974 UNTS 45*, Article 1;

Both types of weapons are particularly harmful to the environment and seriously hamper post-conflict reconstruction.

Furthermore, in 2001, the scope of application of the 1980 Convention on Certain Conventional Weapons and its five protocols was extended to the situation of noninternational armed conflict.[38] The 1996 Amended Protocol II on Mines, Booby-Traps and Other Devices and the 1980 Protocol III on Incendiary Weapons are particularly relevant to the protection of the environment during armed conflict.[39] Protocol III on Incendiary Weapons, for example, includes an express prohibition against making 'forests or other kinds of plant cover the object of attack by incendiary weapons'.[40]

More relevant to the current study, however, is the second development, the crystallisation of relevant treaty rules into customary international law. There has been increasing recognition in recent years that particular rules applicable to international armed conflicts have also become applicable to internal armed conflicts. An important study by the ICRC on customary IHL demonstrated that many rules regulating international armed conflict are applied to internal armed conflicts as well.[41] Although the ICRC study is contentious in some respects and therefore cannot be relied upon directly, it provides a wealth of information regarding the application of IHL in practice.[42]

In this respect, the case law of international criminal tribunals is especially relevant. This case law has applied and interpreted rules of IHL

Convention on the Prohibition of the Use, Stockpiling, Production and Transfer of Antipersonnel Mines and on Their Destruction (Ottawa Convention), 18 September 1997, *2056 UNTS 241*, Article 1.

[38] Convention on Prohibitions or Restrictions on the Use of Certain Conventional Weapons Which May Be Deemed to be Excessively Injurious or to Have Indiscriminate Effects, 10 October 1980, *19 ILM 1823 (1980)*.

[39] Protocol II to the 1980 Conventional Weapons Convention on Prohibitions or Restrictions on the Use of Mines, Booby-Traps and Other Devices as amended on 3 May 1996, 3 May 1996, *35 ILM 1209 (1996)*; Protocol III to the 1980 Convention on Conventional Weapons on Prohibitions or Restrictions on the Use of Incendiary Weapons, 10 April 1981, *1342 U.N.T.S. 171*.

[40] Article 2(4) of Protocol III.

[41] See Henckaerts and Doswald-Beck (eds.), *Customary International Humanitarian Law*, Vols. I and II.

[42] Criticism on the methodology has been voiced notably by the United States. See Joint Letter from John Bellinger and William Haynes to Jakob Kellenberger on Customary International Law Study, *46 ILM 514 (2007)*. For critical assessments of the study, see Bothe, 'Customary International Humanitarian Law', pp. 143–78; Newalsing, 'Customary International Humanitarian Law', pp. 255–79.

in the context of particular conflict situations. While the postwar criminal tribunals dealt exclusively with international armed conflict, many of the present day international criminal tribunals deal with internal armed conflicts as well. Examples include the International Tribunal for the Former Yugoslavia (ICTY), the Special Court for Sierra Leone (SCSL) and, of course, the International Criminal Court (ICC).

The interpretation of rules of IHL by these international criminal tribunals is closely linked to the third development that has been instrumental in bridging the gaps between the law applicable to international and internal armed conflicts. This development is related to the evolution of international criminal law as a distinct branch of international law. Not all of the war crimes listed in Statutes of international criminal tribunals that apply to situations of internal armed conflict are directly based on express provisions in IHL conventions.

One example concerns the war crime of destroying or seizing the property of an adversary, unless such destruction or seizure be imperatively demanded by the necessities of the conflict, as codified in Article 8(2)(e)(xii) of the Rome Statute of the International Criminal Court (ICC Statute).[43] This war crime, which applies to internal armed conflicts, follows from Article 23(g) of the 1907 Hague Regulations, applicable only to international armed conflicts. There is no IHL equivalent for this war crime related to internal armed conflicts. In this way, international criminal law can be said to progressively develop IHL as well.

6.3 International humanitarian law protection of natural resources and the environment

This section assesses the protection afforded by IHL to natural resources and to the environment against (the effects of) the exploitation and plundering of natural resources. Protection is provided primarily by provisions on the protection of property and civilian objects.

This section starts with the provisions on the protection of property and in particular with the prohibition against pillage, which is the most cited provision in relation to the plundering of natural resources by parties to an armed conflict. It argues that the prohibition against pillage is primarily applicable to the plundering of natural resources for the purposes of self-enrichment. It then turns to the prohibition against destroying or

[43] Rome Statute of the International Criminal Court, adopted 17 July 1998 (entry into force: 1 July 2002), *2187 UNTS 90*.

seizing property to see if this provision can fill the gap left open by the prohibition against pillage. Furthermore, this section discusses the right of an occupant to exploit natural resources on the basis of *usufruct*.

The section goes on to discuss two provisions which provide protection to civilian objects. It looks at the extent to which the prohibition against attacking, destroying, removing or rendering useless objects indispensable to the survival of the civilian population provides residual protection to natural resources because of their significance to the civilian population. Second, it examines to what extent the duty of care with regard to protecting the natural environment applies to environmental damage caused by the exploitation of natural resources by parties to an armed conflict.

It should be noted that the rules of IHL which have a bearing on the exploitation of natural resources are deficient in several respects. The most important deficiency is their lack of precision. They are not specifically designed to address instances of natural resource exploitation by parties to an armed conflict. This is partly due to the fact that most of the rules of the law of armed conflict predate important developments in international environmental law which qualified the right of States to exploit natural resources. It is therefore important to interpret the relevant rules of IHL in the broader context of public international law and, more specifically, to take more recent developments in international law into account in the interpretation of the provisions.

Therefore, the current section interprets the provisions of IHL in the light of relevant provisions of international human rights and environmental law. The means of interpretation used in this section include a dynamic evolutionary method of interpreting treaty terms, as well as a systemic method of interpretation for the substantive rules contained in the provisions.[44]

[44] The dynamic–evolutionary method refers to intertemporal interpretation of treaty provisions. See Ress, 'The Interpretation of the Charter', p. 23. For various approaches to evolutionary interpretation, see Dupuy, 'Evolutionary Interpretation of Treaties', pp. 123–37. For an early critical perspective on the evolutionary approach, see Yasseen, 'L'Interprétation des Traités d'après la Convention de Vienne sur le Droit des Traités', p. 27. The systemic method refers to interpretation of treaty provisions in the light of different subsets of international law and general international law based on Article 31(3)(c) of the Vienna Convention. The ICJ applied this method in the Oil Platforms case, when it considered that 'under the general rules of treaty interpretation, as reflected in the 1969 Vienna Convention on the Law of Treaties, interpretation must take into account "any relevant rules of international law applicable in the relations between the parties" (Art. 31, para. 3 (c)). The Court cannot accept that Article XX, paragraph 1 (d), of the 1955 Treaty was

6.3.1 *The protection of property*

IHL conventions contain several provisions aimed at protecting property against unjustified destruction or appropriation by parties to an armed conflict. In international law property can be broadly defined to include movable and immovable, as well as public and private property.[45] In addition, the case law of the Nuremberg Tribunal established that property includes both physical and intangible property.[46] The term 'property' is therefore sufficiently broad to capture all types of natural resources, whether State-owned or privately held, extracted natural resources or natural resources which have not yet been removed, as well as rights relating to the exploitation of natural resources, such as concessions.

The term 'property' is presumed to cover natural resources. Despite the lack of a formal definition, the conventions provide sufficient indications to support this. Article 55 of the 1907 Hague Regulations, for example, expressly defines forests as property. Moreover, the relevant provisions have all been considered to be applicable to the protection of the environment.[47] *Mutatis mutandis* they must also cover materials which are part of that environment.

The current book proposes making a further distinction between natural resources *in situ* and *ex situ*.[48] As long as the natural resources are not extracted (*in situ*), they are part of the environment and therefore qualify

intended to operate wholly independently of the relevant rules of international law on the use of force'. See International Court of Justice, Oil Platforms Case (*Iran* v. *United States of America*), Judgment of 6 November 2003, *I.C.J. Reports 2003*, p. 161, para. 41.

45 See Sandoz, Swinarski and Zimmermann (eds.), *Commentary on the Additional Protocols of 8 June 1977 to the Geneva Conventions of 12 August 1949*, p. 1376.

46 See the I.G. Farben case, *Trials of War Criminals before the Nuremberg Military Tribunals under Control Council Law No. 10*, vol. VIII (1952), p. 1134.

47 See the Report of the Secretary-General on the Protection of the Environment in Times of Armed Conflict, *UNGA Document A/48/269* of 29 July 1993, pp. 5–6; and the Memorandum on International Law Providing Protection of the Environment in Times of Armed Conflict, Annex to a Letter Dated 28 September 1992 from the Permanent Missions of the Hashemite Kingdom of Jordan and of the United States of America Addressed to the Chairman of the Sixth Committee of the General Assembly, *UN Doc. A/C.6/47/3* of 28 September 1992.

48 See the 1956 judgment from the Court of Appeal of Singapore in the Singapore Oil Stocks Case, regarding the exploitation of oil in the Netherlands Indies by the Japanese occupant during the Second World War. In this case, the Court determined that crude oil in the ground constituted immovable property. *N.V. De Bataafsche Petrolium Maatschappij and Ors.* v. *The War Damage Commission*, Court of Appeal, Singapore, April 13, 1956, reprinted in the *American Journal of International Law*, Vol. 51 (1957), p. 809. For more details, see Scobbie, 'Natural Resources and Belligerent Occupation', pp. 235–7.

as immovable property. However, as soon as they have been extracted (*ex situ*), natural resources become tangible objects and therefore fall into the category of movable property. This means that the exploitation of natural resources is governed by the rules concerning immovable property, while the rules on movable property regulate the (il)legality of the appropriation of natural resources which have already been extracted.

Prohibition against pillage

The prohibition against pillage is codified in Articles 28 and 47 of the 1907 Hague Regulations, Article 33(2) of 1949 Geneva Convention IV and Article 4(2)(g) of 1977 Additional Protocol II. Some of these provisions are aimed at providing protection for particular persons, especially civilians and persons who no longer take part in hostilities, while others have a more general scope.[49] In addition, the prohibition has been recognised as having customary international law status, both for international and for noninternational armed conflicts.[50]

Traditionally the prohibition against pillage was applied to acts of theft during armed conflict, either by individual soldiers or in the form of organised plundering.[51] The main purpose of the drafters of the 1907

[49] General protection is provided through Article 28 of the Hague Regulations, applicable to international armed conflicts, which provides that 'the pillage of a town or place, even when taken by assault, is prohibited' and Article 47 of the Hague Regulations, applicable to occupation, which provides that 'pillage is formally forbidden'. Specific protection is provided to civilian persons through Article 33(2) of Geneva Convention IV, applicable to international armed conflicts, and to civilians as well as persons who do not actively take part in hostilities through Article 4(2)(g) of Additional Protocol II, applicable to noninternational armed conflicts.

[50] For international armed conflict, the customary nature of the prohibition stems primarily from its inclusion in the 1907 Hague Regulations, which have been affirmed to constitute customary law. The customary status of the Regulations has been affirmed by the International Court of Justice in its *Advisory Opinion on the Construction of a Wall in the Occupied Palestinian Territory*, Advisory Opinion of 9 July 2004, *I.C.J. Reports 2004*, p. 172, para. 89, where the Court considered 'that the provisions of the Hague Regulations have become part of customary law'. For noninternational armed conflict, both the Appeals Chamber of the ICTY and the SCSL have expressly held this prohibition to be part of customary law applicable to noninternational armed conflict. ICTY, Hadzihasanovic, Alagic and Kubura (IT-01–47), Decision on Joint Defence Interlocutory Appeal of Trial Chamber Decision on Rule 98bis Motions for Acquittal, para. 37; SCSL, *The Prosecutor* v. *Moinina Fofana and Allieu Kondewa*, Appeal Chamber Judgment of 28 May 2008, para. 390.

[51] See Sandoz, Swinarski and Zimmermann (eds.), *Commentary on the Additional Protocols of 8 June 1977 to the Geneva Conventions of 12 August 1949*, p. 1376; and Carducci, 'Pillage', pp. 299–304.

Hague Regulations was to ban the practice of rewarding troops for their services by authorising them to loot villages and towns. The Nuremberg Tribunal cast the net much wider. The Tribunal applied the war crime of plunder to all forms of appropriation of public or private property – whether this concerns physical property or rights attached to property[52] – without the consent of the owner, in the context of an armed conflict. The prohibition against pillage is also the most cited provision in relation to the illegal exploitation, looting and plundering of natural resources by foreign troops and armed groups.[53]

The prohibition against pillage is one of the few provisions of IHL that prohibit the appropriation of a State's natural resources by parties acting without the consent of the State. However, despite the broad scope of the prohibition, it is important to remember its original purpose, which was to prohibit theft. The prohibition therefore contains an important restriction: it applies only to the appropriation of property for personal gain. This restriction is based on the system of IHL itself, which makes a distinction between 'pillage' on one hand, and 'seizure' and 'requisition' on the other. While pillage is prohibited in absolute terms, the seizure or requisition of property is permitted under particular circumstances. The ICRC Commentary to Article 33 of Geneva Convention IV explicitly states that the prohibition against pillage 'leaves intact the right of requisition or seizure'.[54]

This distinction is retained in international criminal law as well. The ICC Statute lists pillage on one hand, and the destruction or seizure of the property of the hostile party outside a situation of military necessity on the other, as two separate war crimes.[55] Furthermore, the Elements of Crime defining the crimes listed in the ICC Statute restrict pillage to appropriation for private or personal use.[56] This interpretation of pillage is confirmed in the case law of the Special Court for Sierra Leone. According to the Appeals Chamber of the SCSL, 'pillage' refers to the appropriation

[52] See the *I.G. Farben* case, *Trials of War Criminals before the Nuremberg Military Tribunals under Control Council Law No. 10*, Vol. VIII (1952), p. 1134.

[53] See, e.g., Stewart, *Corporate War Crimes*; Lundberg, 'The Plunder of Natural Resources during War', pp. 495–526; and Van den Herik and Dam-de Jong, 'Revitalizing the Antique War Crime of Pillage', pp. 237–73.

[54] Pictet and Uhler, *The Geneva Conventions of 12 August 1949*, p. 227.

[55] See Article 8(2)(b)(xiii) and (xvi) and Article 8(2)(e)(v) and (xii) of the ICC Statute.

[56] Elements of Crimes, *Official Journal of the International Criminal Court*, available at www.icc-cpi.int/library/about/officialjournal/Element_of_Crimes_English.pdf. Also see Dörmann, *Elements of War Crimes under the Rome Statute of the International Criminal Court*.

of property for private purposes.[57] It is also in this context that the prohibition against pillage was considered by the International Court of Justice in the case of the DR Congo against Uganda. In that case, the DR Congo claimed that members of the Ugandan army had systematically exploited the DR Congo's natural resources for their personal benefit.[58] The International Court of Justice concluded that 'whenever members of the UPDF were involved in the looting, plundering and exploitation of natural resources in the territory of the DRC', they acted in violation of the prohibition against pillage.[59]

There is no specific case law from modern international criminal tribunals which has determined that the war crime of pillage applies to the exploitation of natural resources. Up to now, none of these tribunals has applied the provision to instances of natural resource exploitation. Despite the fact that the war crime could cover them, instances of pillage before modern international criminal tribunals have been limited to the appropriation of personal belongings of civilians, mainly in relation to the raiding of villages.[60] Even in the cases against Charles Taylor and the leaders of the RUF and the AFRC before the Special Court for Sierra Leone, where there was a close connection between the exploitation of natural resources and the commission of other crimes, the pillage of natural resources was not one of the charges.[61]

In the absence of modern case law from international criminal tribunals which may provide more specific guidance for the interpretation of pillage in relation to natural resources, it may be concluded from the judgment of the International Court of Justice in the *Congo–Uganda case* that the prohibition against pillage applies first and foremost to the exploitation

[57] Special Court for Sierra Leone, *The Prosecutor* v. *Moinina Fofana and Allieu Kondewa*, Appeals Chamber Judgment of 28 May 2008, para. 392, note 770. The Appeals Chamber departed from the decision of the Trial Chamber on this point, which held that 'the inclusion of the requirement that the appropriation be for private or personal use is an unwarranted restriction on the application of the offence of pillage'. Special Court for Sierra Leone, *The Prosecutor* v. *Moinina Fofana and Allieu Kondewa*, Trials Chamber Judgment of 2 August 2007, para. 160.

[58] Armed Activities on the Territory of the Congo *(Democratic Republic of the Congo* v. *Uganda)*, I.C.J., 19 December 2005, Judgment, *I.C.J. Reports 2005*, paras. 222–9.

[59] Ibid., para. 245.

[60] For examples of relevant practice by international criminal tribunals, see the *ICRC Customary International Humanitarian Law Database*, Rule 52, available through www.icrc.org/customary-ihl/eng/docs/home.

[61] For a detailed discussion of the crime of pillage and its applicability to the exploitation of natural resources, see Van den Herik and Dam-de Jong, 'Revitalizing the Antique War Crime of Pillage', pp. 237–73.

of natural resources by members of rebel groups or foreign armies for the purpose of self-enrichment. Arguably, it applies equally to the misappropriation of natural resources or their proceeds by public officials of the domestic State, including members of the government or the State's armed forces, in view of the fact that natural resources belong to the State and not to its representatives. Furthermore, pillage may be interpreted broadly to include all appropriation of property that does not – directly or indirectly – serve a military purpose. As the case law of the Nuremberg Tribunal showed, appropriation of property by a foreign army to benefit the economy of the foreign State therefore also constitutes pillage. However, it seems less appropriate to apply the prohibition against pillage to the exploitation of natural resources for military purposes, including the funding of an armed conflict. In the light of the system of IHL as a whole, these instances are covered by the prohibition against seizing the property of the adversary, which is discussed in the following section.

Prohibition against destroying or seizing the property of a hostile party

Article 23(g) of the 1907 Hague Regulations formulates a prohibition against destroying or seizing 'enemy property' in situations of international armed conflict 'unless imperatively demanded by the necessities of war'. In addition, Article 53 of Geneva Convention IV contains an express prohibition against occupants destroying 'real or personal property belonging individually or collectively to private persons, or to the State, or to other public authorities, or to social or cooperative organizations . . . , except where such destruction is rendered absolutely necessary by military operations'.[62]

Although there is no express provision for internal armed conflicts, the applicability of the prohibition against destroying or seizing the property of a hostile party in internal armed conflicts can be deduced from international criminal law, and more specifically from Article 8(2)(e)(xii) of the

62 One of the main differences between the two provisions is their formal scope of application. Whereas Article 23(g) of the Hague Regulations applies to international armed conflict in general, including the situation of occupation, Article 53 of Geneva Convention IV applies exclusively to the situation of occupation. Thus the prohibition contained in Article 23(g) extends to all phases of an armed conflict, while Article 53 of Geneva Convention IV does not bind a party to an armed conflict until it actually takes authority over (part of) its enemy's territory. After all, Article 42 of the Hague Regulations determines that 'territory is considered occupied when it is actually placed under the authority of the hostile army'.

ICC Statute, which criminalises the destruction and seizure of the property of an 'adversary', unless such destruction or seizure be imperatively required by the necessities of the conflict. Both the ICTY and the SCSL also expressly determined that the prohibition against destroying the property of a hostile party is part of customary international law applicable to both international and noninternational armed conflict.[63] By analogy, the customary international law status of the prohibition could also extend to the appropriation of property. Furthermore, as the customary international law prohibition addresses parties to an armed conflict in general, it can be interpreted as binding non-State armed groups.[64]

These provisions, as well as the system of IHL as a whole, imply that the prohibition against seizing or destroying the property of a hostile party is aimed at prohibiting the destruction or seizure of property only outside situations of military necessity. *Mutatis mutandis*, the prohibition formulates an indirect right for belligerents to destroy or seize the property of the hostile party when it is imperative from a military perspective.

It is important to note beforehand that the right of belligerents to destroy or seize particular property in cases of imperative military necessity does not depend upon the characteristics of the property itself. Whereas IHL generally distinguishes between civilian objects and military objectives, determining that civilian objects may not be the subject of attack, this distinction does not affect the application of the current provisions.

The question of whether an object is civilian or military depends on the nature, location, purpose or use of the object. If the object does not make an effective contribution to military action by any of these factors, it may normally not be the subject of attack.[65] However, for the application of the current provisions, it does not matter whether or not the objects make an effective contribution to military action. The decisive criterion is the existence of a situation of imperative military necessity. In these circumstances, belligerents may seize or destroy the property of the hostile party, whether this property is a military objective or a

[63] International Criminal Tribunal for the Former Yugoslavia, Kordić and Čerkez case, Judgment of 26 February 2001, para. 205; Special Court for Sierra Leone, *The Prosecutor* v. *Moinina Fofana and Allieu Kondewa*, Appeals Chamber Judgment of 28 May 2008, para. 390.

[64] On the binding nature of customary international law in relation to non-State armed groups, see Chapter 1 of this study.

[65] See Section 6.3.2 of this chapter.

civilian object. This must be regarded as an exception to the general rule prohibiting attack on civilian objects.

Given the exceptional nature of the right that ensues from the prohibition of seizing or destroying the property of a hostile party, it is of great importance to carefully delineate the objects covered by the provisions and the circumstances that allow the exception to be invoked. The first question that arises concerns the interpretation of the terms 'enemy property' in international armed conflicts and 'property of an adversary' in internal armed conflicts. Although both terms cover all types of property – whether movable or immovable, public or private[66] – there are important differences as regards the scope of the two terms. In international armed conflicts, all property situated within the territory of the 'enemy' State is considered to be 'enemy property' for the purposes of IHL. In other words, in international armed conflicts, belligerents are prohibited from seizing or destroying any property found within the territory of their adversary, including both publicly and privately owned property, unless the seizure or destruction is strictly necessary from a military perspective.

In internal armed conflicts, the situation is more complex, as ownership of the property must be determined by national law.[67] Whereas international law attributes ownership of natural resources to the State on the basis of the principle of permanent sovereignty over natural resources, it is for the State to decide on issues of ownership within the national context. In relation to natural resources, many national constitutions vest the ownership of natural resources in the State, which is formally represented by the government. This means that in internal armed conflicts the prohibition against destroying or seizing the property of an adversary primarily covers natural resources that belong to the State or to private persons affiliated with the State. In other words, the prohibition against

[66] See Article 53 of Geneva Convention IV, which expressly prohibits the destruction of 'real' and 'personal' property. Also see the judgment of the Nuremberg Military Tribunal in the Hostage case, which determined that Article 23(g) of the Hague Regulations applied to such diverse objects as 'railways, lines of communication, or any other property that might be utilized by the enemy' as well as 'private homes and churches'. *Trials of War Criminals before the Nuremberg Military Tribunals under Control Council Law No. 10*, Nuremberg, October 1946–April 1949, Vol. XI, Washington, DC: Government Printing Office (1959), p. 1254.

[67] According to Zimmerman, in the context of Article 8(2)(e)(xii) of the ICC Statute, the term 'adversary' refers to 'any person, who is considered to belong to another party to the conflict, such as the government, insurgents or, as article 8 para. 2(f) of the Statute demonstrates, belongs to an opposing organised armed group'. Zimmerman, 'Article 8 – Para. 2(e)', margin no. 326–7, p. 284.

seizing or destroying natural resources, except in cases of imperative military necessity, will therefore primarily apply to non-State armed groups, provided that they are actually fighting the government.[68] Conversely, it also means that these armed groups can justify the seizure or destruction of natural resources in cases of imperative military necessity.

The second question that must be addressed concerns the interpretation of 'imperative military necessity'. The concept of military necessity can be traced back to the American Lieber Code of 1863, which defined military necessity as 'those measures which are indispensable for securing the ends of the war, and which are lawful according to the modern law and usages of war'.[69] In other words, military necessity excuses actions that are otherwise prohibited if the relevant provision provides for such an excuse and if the actions would help the belligerent party to gain a military advantage.[70]

Although the concept of military necessity was inserted into all subsequent legal instruments regulating the conduct of hostilities, the definition was not retained. This makes it difficult to determine the precise content and limits of the exception contained in the prohibition against seizing or destroying the property of the hostile party. Some guidance on the interpretation of military necessity can be found in the case law of the Nuremberg Tribunals. The exception of military necessity to excuse particular behaviour was invoked in several proceedings before the Nuremberg Tribunals. The tribunals also dealt with the interpretation of the phrase 'imperative military necessity' as part of the prohibition against destroying or seizing the property of a hostile party.

Reference can be made in particular to the *Hostage case*, which dealt, *inter alia*, with charges against high-ranking officers in the German army for wanton destruction of cities, towns and villages, as well as other acts of devastation. In this case the Military Tribunal considered that '[m]ilitary necessity permits a belligerent, subject to the laws of war, to apply any

[68] Since natural resources generally do not belong to armed groups, a right to seize or destroy natural resources in cases of military necessity does not apply to conflicts between armed groups. *Mutatis mutandis*, the prohibition of seizing or destroying the natural resources of the adversary does not apply to these situations either.

[69] Instructions for the Government of Armies of the United States in the Field (Lieber Code), 24 April 1863. Available through www.icrc.org/ihl.nsf.

[70] Of course, implicit in the notion of military necessity is further that property of the hostile party can be seized or destroyed solely for military purposes. See Dinstein, 'Military Necessity', pp. 201–7, paras. 25–6. This requirement that the property be appropriated for military purposes is also what distinguishes the qualified prohibition of seizing the property of a hostile party from the absolute prohibition of pillage.

amount and kind of force to compel the complete submission of the enemy with the least possible expenditure of time, life and money. In general, it sanctions measures by an occupant necessary to protect the safety of his forces and to facilitate the success of his operations'.[71] It also considered that the Hague Regulations require the military necessity to be 'urgent' and that there must be a 'reasonable connection between the destruction of property and the overcoming of the enemy forces'.[72]

Two principal requirements can be derived from this case law. First, the seizure or destruction of property must make an effective contribution to military action.[73] Second, whether the seizure or destruction of property is permitted in particular circumstances depends on the urgency of the situation. The requirement of 'urgency' concerns both the time element and the existence of alternatives to attain the objective. As regards the time element, reference can be made to the *Caroline* criteria generally used to assess the need for an act of self-defence. According to the *Caroline* criteria, military action can be justified if the necessity is 'instant, overwhelming, leaving no choice of means and no moment for deliberation'.[74] As regards proportionality, 'urgency' means, at the very least, that the belligerent did not have any less injurious alternatives at his disposal to achieve the objective.[75] According to Otto Triffterer, military necessity even implies that 'there are no other means to secure military safety'.[76]

For the purposes of the present study, the excuse of imperative military necessity is of limited relevance to armed groups seeking to justify the

[71] The Tribunal also recognised that destruction as an end in itself is a violation of international law. Hostage case, Judgment of 19 February 1948, *Trials of War Criminals before the Nuremberg Military Tribunals under Control Council Law No. 10*, Nuremberg, October 1946–April 1949, Vol. XI, Washington, DC: Government Printing Office (1959), pp. 1253–4.

[72] Ibid. Also see Triffterer (ed.), *Commentary on the Rome Statute of the International Criminal Court*, margin no. 105, p. 232.

[73] See International Criminal Tribunal for the Former Yugoslavia, Strugar Case, *Case No. IT-01-42*, Trial Judgment of 31 January 2005, para. 295. The Chamber defined 'military necessity' with reference to the definition of military objects in Article 52 of Additional Protocol I to the Geneva Conventions, discussed in the following section.

[74] Correspondence between Great Britain and the United States, Respecting the Arrest and Imprisonment of Mr. McLeod, for the Destruction of the Steamboat *Caroline*, March, April 1841.

[75] See Werle and Jessberger, *Principles of International Criminal Law*, p. 340, margin no. 1003, who argue that military necessity implies that destruction is not permitted if alternative means of achieving the military goal are open.

[76] Triffterer (ed.), *Commentary on the Rome Statute of the International Criminal Court*, p. 232, margin nos. 154 and 155.

appropriation or destruction of natural resources. The contribution of natural resources to an armed conflict is in most cases indirect, in the sense that they cannot be directly used in military operations or to guarantee the safety or survival of members of an armed group. Rather, they provide the means to finance military operations and to provide food and shelter. Therefore, their destruction or appropriation may secure a military advantage, but does not satisfy the requirement of urgency. The *Krupp case* before Nuremberg Military Tribunal III confirms this interpretation. In that case, the Tribunal quoted and approved the following passage from *Garner's International Law and the World War*:

> it is quite clear from the language and context of Article 23(g) as well as the discussions on it in the Conference that *it was never intended to authorize a military occupant to despoil on an extensive scale the industrial establishments of occupied territory or to transfer their machinery to his home country for use in his home industries. What was intended merely was to authorize the seizure or destruction of private property only in exceptional cases when it was an imperative necessity for the conduct of military operations* in the territory under occupation. This view is further strengthened by Article 46 which requires belligerents to respect enemy private property and which forbids confiscation, and by Article 47 which prohibits pillage.[77]

In conclusion, the excuse of imperative military necessity is primarily relevant in emergency situations, where there is a reasonable connection between the appropriation or destruction of natural resources and a military purpose. This means that it may be a justification for the appropriation of natural resources that can be directly used to satisfy the basic needs of members of armed groups, such as the poaching of wild animals or the cutting of trees in a State forest for firewood. However, the excuse of imperative military necessity is too narrowly formulated to justify the systematic exploitation of natural resources for the purpose of financing military operations.

Administration of public property in territories under occupation

The most detailed regime for the protection of property is set out for territories under foreign occupation. One of the basic tenets of occupation

[77] *Trials of War Criminals before the Nuremberg Tribunals under Control Council Law No. 10*, Vol. IX, the Krupp case, Washington, DC: Government Printing Office (1950), pp. 1344–5. Author's emphasis added.

law is that private property must be respected.[78] An occupant may only appropriate private property in exceptional circumstances, and must provide financial compensation. In contrast, as the principal governmental authority in territory under occupation,[79] an occupant may to a certain extent dispose of public property. First, Article 53 of the 1907 Hague Regulations authorises the occupant to take possession of particular objects, such as State-owned cash, funds and realisable securities, as well as all public movable property 'which may be used for military operations' and munitions of war.[80] Second, Article 55 of the 1907 Hague Regulations grants the occupant a right of usufruct over immovable public property.

The latter provision is key to the occupant's right to exploit natural resources. It reads in full,

> The occupying State shall be regarded only as administrator and usufructuary of public buildings, real estate, forests, and agricultural estates belonging to the hostile State, and situated in the occupied country. It must safeguard the capital of these properties, and administer them in accordance with the rules of usufruct.

[78] Bothe, 'Occupation, Belligerent', p. 766. Article 46(2) of the 1907 Hague Regulations prohibits the confiscation of such property and Article 47 prohibits pillage of property in general. The Hague Regulations contain only two exceptions to the principle of the inviolability of private property. First, Article 52 of the Hague Regulations permits the occupant to requisition private property against financial compensation in order to satisfy 'the needs of the army of occupation', provided such requisitions 'shall be in proportion to the resources of the country, and of such a nature as not to involve the inhabitants in the obligation of taking part in military operations against their own country'. The second exception concerns property which may be qualified as 'munitions of war' under Article 53(2) of the Hague Regulations – which applies equally to public property. These properties may be seized without offering immediate compensation, provided the objects are restored and compensation is fixed after the war.

[79] This authority is based on *de facto* rather than *de jure* power. See Dinstein, *The International Law of Belligerent Occupation*, p. 49; and Bothe, 'Occupation, Belligerent', p. 764. Furthermore, according to Bothe, 'international law does not grant rights to the occupying power, but limits the occupant's exercise of its *de facto* powers' (p. 764). Also see Benvenisti, *The International Law of Occupation*, 1st edn., pp. 5–6. Benvenisti compares the occupant's status to that of a trustee. According to Benvenisti, the occupant administers the territory on behalf of the sovereign.

[80] Article 53 of the Hague Regulations reads in full: 'An army of occupation can only take possession of cash, funds, and realizable securities which are strictly the property of the State, depots of arms, means of transport, stores and supplies, and, generally, all movable property belonging to the State which may be used for military operations.

All appliances, whether on land, at sea, or in the air, adapted for the transmission of news, or for the transport of persons or things, exclusive of cases governed by naval law, depots of arms, and, generally, all kinds of munitions of war, may be seized, even if they belong to private individuals, but must be restored and compensation fixed when peace is made'.

The right of *usufruct*, as set out in Article 55 of the 1907 Hague Regulations, grants the occupant the right to administer the immovable properties of the occupied State, including State-owned forests and mines, and to enjoy their proceeds as long as he 'safeguards the capital of these properties'.

Thus it is clear that the concept of usufruct imposes limits on the right of an occupant to use the property of the territory under occupation. As Lassa Oppenheim noted as early as 1952, the occupant is 'prohibited from exercising its right [of usufruct] in a wasteful or negligent way so as to decrease the value of the stock and plant. Thus, for instance, he must not cut down a whole forest, unless the necessities of war compel him'.[81] This is still the prevailing view in academic literature today.[82]

Arguably, the requirement that an occupant must safeguard the capital of the properties it administers should be interpreted in light of the relevant obligations of the occupant under customary international law, including customary international law obligations arising from other fields of international law. This would require an occupant to use the natural resources in a sustainable way and to exploit them with respect for the principle of permanent sovereignty over natural resources and the right to self-determination of the people under occupation, meaning that an occupant must exploit the natural resources in occupied territory for the benefit of the occupied territory and its population.[83]

Furthermore, the principle of sustainable use is today one of the basic tenets underlying the obligation of an occupant to safeguard the capital of the State's natural resources. The principle creates a balance between the right of an occupant to use the natural resources in occupied territory to cover the costs of the occupation and the obligation to safeguard these resources for the benefit of future generations.

One longstanding issue in international law concerns the right of an occupant to exploit nonrenewable natural resources. This issue received much scholarly attention, especially in relation to Israel's right to exploit

[81] Oppenheim, *International Law: A Treatise*, Vol. II, 7th edn., p. 398. Obviously the obligation to safeguard the capital of the properties in occupied territory does not impede the right of an occupant to destroy property in occupied territory in cases of military necessity as incorporated into Article 23(g) of the Hague Regulations and Article 53 of Geneva Convention IV.

[82] See, e.g., Arai-Takahashi, *The Law of Occupation*, pp. 209–15; Dinstein, *The International Law of Belligerent Occupation*, p. 214.

[83] For the impact of the principle of permanent sovereignty on the interpretation of the right of usufruct, see Arai-Takahashi, *The Law of Occupation*, pp. 215–16.

oil resources in the occupied Sinaï Peninsula in the 1970s.[84] Nico Schrijver remarks that 'while usufruct of renewable resources may give no rise to particular problems, its application to non-renewable resources such as minerals is controversial'.[85] Indeed, opinions differ considerably in this respect. An examination of the scholarly debate reveals that the obligation to safeguard the capital of nonrenewable natural resources may be interpreted either narrowly to prohibit the exploitation of nonrenewable natural resources altogether, based on the idea that exploitation would *ipso facto* reduce their capital, or broadly to prohibit only excessive exploitation.[86] Based on the principle of sustainable use, this book argues that contemporary international law allows an occupant to exploit the natural resources of occupied territory, including its nonrenewable natural resources, insofar as this would not harm the options of future generations for exploiting the natural resources for their development.

On the other hand, the principle of permanent sovereignty serves to emphasize the obligation of occupants to administer the natural resources in occupied territory for the benefit of the people.[87] This implies that the right of usufruct precludes exploitation of the natural resources of a country by an occupant for its own benefit,[88] a prohibition that is also confirmed in the relevant case law of the Nuremberg tribunals. The International Military Tribunal at Nuremberg considered that 'the economy of an occupied country can only be required to bear the expense(s) of

[84] See in particular Sloan, 'Study on the Implications, under International Law, of the United Nations Resolutions on Permanent Sovereignty over Natural Resources, on the Occupied Palestinian and Other Arab Territories and on the Obligations of Israel Concerning Its Conduct in These Territories', *UN Doc. A/38/85*, 21 June 1983; and US Department of State, 'Memorandum of Law on Israel's Right to Develop New Oil Fields in Sinai and the Gulf of Suez', *17 ILM 2 (1978)*, pp. 432–44.

[85] Schrijver, *Sovereignty over Natural Resources*, p. 268.

[86] See ibid., pp. 268–9; Sloan, 'Study on the Implications, under International Law, of the United Nations Resolutions on Permanent Sovereignty over Natural Resources, on the Occupied Palestinian and Other Arab Territories and on the Obligations of Israel Concerning Its Conduct in These Territories', *UN Doc. A/38/85*, 21 June 1983, in particular pp. 15 and 16; Cassese, 'Powers and Duties of an Occupant in Relation to Land and Natural Resources', pp. 419–42; Benvenisti, *The International Law of Occupation*, 2nd edn., pp. 81–2.

[87] See Arai-Takahashi, *The Law of Occupation*, pp. 215–16.

[88] See, e.g., Cassese, 'Powers and Duties of an Occupant in Relation to Land and Natural Resources', p. 426, who argues that the principle of permanent sovereignty over natural resources, in the context of belligerent occupation, 'tends to support a restrictive interpretation of the occupant's powers to exploit and dispose of immovable property. Even if the occupant has reservations about the "statehood" of its enemy, this principle should serve to restrain the occupant from exploiting resources in contravention of the rights of an alien people in occupied territory'.

the occupation, and these should not be greater than the economy of the country can reasonably be expected to bear'.[89] This judgment should be read in conjunction with the *Krupp case*, decided by a lower military tribunal at Nuremberg. This tribunal considered that an occupied country's economic assets could never be used for military operations against the occupied territory.[90] The International Military Tribunal at Nuremberg also considered that excessive exploitation of natural resources could even amount to plunder. According to the Tribunal, Germany had exploited the occupied territories for the German war effort 'in the most ruthless way, without consideration of the local economy, and in consequence of a deliberate design and policy'. The Tribunal held that this amounted in reality to 'a systematic "plunder of public and private property"'.[91]

A modern interpretation of these judgments suggests that an occupant is permitted to use the proceeds from exploiting resources for the purposes of maintaining a civilian administration in occupied territory, but not to cover the costs associated with military operations. This can be illustrated with reference to the Development Fund for Iraq, set up and administered by the US–UK occupying authority in Iraq in 2003 with the specific purpose of meeting 'the humanitarian needs of the Iraqi people, for the economic reconstruction and repair of Iraq's infrastructure, for the continued disarmament of Iraq, and for the costs of Iraqi civilian administration, and for other purposes benefiting the people of Iraq'.[92] The Development Fund was primarily funded with proceeds from the sale of Iraqi oil.[93] Although it may be questioned whether all the stated purposes of the fund are in conformity with the limited powers conferred

[89] *Trial of the Major War Criminals before the International Military Tribunal*, Nuremberg, 14 November 1945–1 October 1946, Official Documents, Vol. I, Nuremberg (1947), p. 239.

[90] *Trials of War Criminals before the Nuremberg Tribunals under Control Council Law No. 10*, Vol. IX, the Krupp case, Washington, DC: Government Printing Office (1950), p. 1341. The tribunal held in relevant part: 'Just as the inhabitants of the occupied territory must not be forced to help the enemy in waging the war against their own country or their own country's allies, so must the economic assets of the occupied territory not be used in such a manner'.

[91] Ibid. Today, as a consequence of the narrow definition of pillage in the ICC *Elements of Crime*, the conduct of Germany would be more likely to fall under the war crime of destruction or seizure of the property of a hostile party, a crime which was not included in the Statute of the Nuremberg Tribunal.

[92] UNSC Resolution 1483 (2003), especially para. 14.

[93] UNSC Resolution 1483 (2003) determined that 'all proceeds from [export sales of petroleum, petroleum products, and natural gas from Iraq] shall be deposited into the Development Fund for Iraq until such time as an internationally recognized, representative government of Iraq is properly constituted'.

upon an occupant by the international law on occupation,[94] it is relevant to note that the Development Fund underlines the basic idea that the natural resources in occupied territory must be exploited for the benefit of the people of the occupied territory.

Thus Article 55 of the 1907 Hague Regulations formulates a right for occupants to exploit the natural resources within occupied territory, but only for the benefit of the population. The proceeds from the exploitation of natural resources may therefore be used to cover costs related to civilian administration, but not to cover costs associated with the occupation itself. An occupant cannot escape this restriction by claiming that particular natural resources are 'munitions of war' under Article 53 of the Hague Regulations, which would mean that they could be seized by the occupant at all times. In this respect, Elihu Lauterpacht remarks that

> belligerent occupation is essentially a temporary affair. For that reason, an Occupant is not entitled to diminish or retard the prospects of the economic recovery of the territory by draining it of its resources of minerals and raw materials on the pretext that they constitute *munitions de guerre.* It is this factor which underlies, for example, the limitation of powers of an Occupant in respect of public immovable property to the rights of an usufructuary and no more.[95]

It is generally accepted that the term 'munitions de guerre' has a narrow scope and only includes objects which can be of direct military use, in the sense that they can be used for military operations.[96] Precious minerals, such as diamonds, cobalt or tin, are therefore excluded from the definition. After all, these minerals do not have any direct military use, as opposed to

[94] Article 43 of the 1907 Hague Regulations, which sets out the general obligations of an occupant, prescribes that an occupant should 'take all the measures in his power to restore, and ensure, as far as possible, public order and safety, while respecting, unless absolutely prevented, the laws in force in the country'. Whether the measures regarding Iraq are in conformity with the law of occupation depends on the interpretation of Article 43. Does it imply an obligation for the occupant to preserve as much as possible the *status quo ante bellum* or does the obligation to 'ensure . . . public order and safety' also bring about positive obligations for occupants to enact legislation and to set up economic and social policies? See on this issue, e.g., Benvenisti, *The International Law of Occupation,* 2nd edn.; and Roberts, 'Transformative Military Occupation', pp. 580–622. On the occupation of Iraq and the relationship between international occupation law and UN Security Council Resolutions, see Scheffer, 'Beyond Occupation Law', pp. 842–60; and Zwanenburg, 'Existentialism in Iraq', pp. 745–68. On the management of Iraqi natural resources, in particular oil and water, see Benvenisti, *The International Law of Occupation,* pp. 264–6.

[95] E. Lauterpacht, 'The Hague Regulations and the Seizure of *Munitions de Guerre*', p. 240.

[96] See, e.g., ibid., pp. 219–43; Dinstein, *The International Law of Belligerent Occupation,* p. 233.

oil, which can serve as fuel for military vehicles. In this respect, reference can be made to the distinction made in the often-cited 1956 Singapore Oil Stocks Case between natural resources *in situ* (immovable property) and *ex situ* (movable property).[97] This case implies that only extracted oil – as a movable property – can qualify as *munitions de guerre*. Furthermore, only processed oil can actually be used directly for military purposes and thus qualifies as *munitions de guerre*.

It is also important to note, as indicated in Chapter 5, that occupants have a general obligation to respect the laws in force of the occupied State 'unless absolutely prevented'.[98] Arguably, this also implies an obligation to respect the treaties to which the occupied State is a party, including relevant environmental and human rights treaties.[99] For example, this implies that an occupant must respect the rights of indigenous peoples over their lands and the resources situated in their lands, ensuing from Article 27 of the ICCPR, provided that the occupied State is a party to this treaty.

Finally, an occupant is responsible not only for its own conduct in occupied territory, but also for the conduct of other actors operating in the territory, including non-State armed groups. Its role as the principal governmental authority in occupied territory entails an obligation for the occupant to prevent other actors operating in the territory from violating IHL. In the *Congo–Uganda Case*, the ICJ determined that, as Uganda was an occupying power in part of the territory of the DR Congo at the relevant time,

[97] Singapore Court of Appeal, *N.V. De Bataafsche Petrolium Maatschappij and Ors.* v. *The War Damage Commission*, Judgment of 13 April 1956, reprinted in the *American Journal of International Law*, Vol. 51 (1957), p. 809.

[98] Article 43 of the 1907 Hague Regulations reads in full, 'The authority of the legitimate power having in fact passed into the hands of the occupant, the latter shall take all the measures in his power to restore, and ensure, as far as possible, public order and safety, while respecting, unless absolutely prevented, the laws in force in the country'.

[99] Some support for this proposition can be found in Meron, 'Applicability of Multilateral Conventions to Occupied Territories', pp. 550–51. He argues that an occupant must respect a Convention ratified by the sovereign authorities of the occupied territory if the authorities have adopted the necessary implementing legislation. If they have not done so, Meron argues that the 'ratification should be regarded as determining that the convention is suitable for the local social and economic conditions'. However, in these circumstances, he does not consider the occupant bound to apply the Convention. Actually, this position is not very helpful, since it can be argued that a treaty that is implemented through national legislation has automatically become part of 'the laws in force'. In these circumstances, it is not the treaty that has to be respected by the occupant, but rather the domestic legislation.

> Uganda's responsibility is engaged both for any acts of its military that violated its international obligations and for any lack of vigilance in preventing violations of human rights and international humanitarian law by other actors present in the occupied territory, including rebel groups acting on their own account.[100]

According to the Court, Uganda was under an obligation to 'take appropriate measures to prevent the looting, plundering and exploitation of natural resources in the occupied territory to cover private persons in the district'. Thus the 'duty of vigilance' of an occupant seems to entail an obligation to prevent other actors from exploiting, looting or plundering natural resources in occupied territory.

6.3.2 *The protection of civilian objects*

Parts IV of Additional Protocols I and II deal with the protection of the civilian population. Both protocols contain provisions that provide protection for objects that are important to the civilian population. In international armed conflicts, a general provision provides protection for civilian objects. Article 52 of Additional Protocol I provides that hostilities may only be directed at military objectives. It defines civilian objects as 'all objects which are not military objectives'. According to paragraph 2 of the same provision, 'military objectives' are 'those objects which by their nature, location, purpose or use make an effective contribution to military action and whose total or partial destruction, capture or neutralization, in the circumstances ruling at the time, offers a definite military advantage'.

Thus Article 52 of Additional Protocol I sets a dual standard for determining whether objects are military objectives. They must 'make an effective contribution to military action' in relation to one of the factors mentioned in the provision,[101] and in addition, their 'destruction, capture or neutralization' must offer 'a definite military advantage'.[102] If

[100] Armed Activities on the Territory of the Congo (*Democratic Republic of the Congo* v. *Uganda*), Judgment of 19 December 2005, *I.C.J. Reports 2005*, para. 179.

[101] According to the Commentary on the Additional Protocols, objects which by their nature make an effective contribution to military action comprise all objects directly used by armed forces, such as weapons, means of transport or buildings used by the armed forces. Objects which by their location make an effective contribution to military action include strategic objects such as bridges. Furthermore, according to the commentary, 'purpose' refers to 'the intended future use of an object', while 'use' refers to 'its present function'. Sandoz, Swinarski and Zimmermann (eds.), *Commentary on the Additional Protocols of 8 June 1977 to the Geneva Conventions of 12 August 1949*, Art. 52, p. 636.

[102] Ibid., p. 636.

these conditions are satisfied, civilian objects are no longer protected and become military objectives.

It is not difficult to imagine instances where natural resources constitute military objectives rather than civil objects. This is the case particularly when natural resources are exploited by parties to an armed conflict to finance their armed struggle. In these cases, natural resources make an effective contribution to military action, in terms both of their use and of their purpose. In addition, destroying or capturing those natural resources offers a definite military advantage, because such action cuts off the financial means of the hostile party. Thus, for the purposes of the current study, the general protection provided by Article 52 of Additional Protocol I to civilian objects is of little relevance.

In addition to the general protection afforded to civilian objects, Additional Protocols I and II also identify particular objects for which special protection is provided, regardless of whether such objects constitute civilian objects or military objectives. Objects that are deemed indispensable for the survival of the civilian population are protected under Article 54 of Additional Protocol I and Article 14 of Additional Protocol II, while the natural environment is protected under Article 55 of Additional Protocol I. These provisions are more relevant to the protection of natural resources and the environment than those providing general protection to civilian objects, since they also apply to natural resources or parts of the environment that are considered to be military objectives.

Prohibition against attacking, destroying, removing or rendering useless objects indispensable to the survival of the civilian population

Article 54(2) of Additional Protocol I and Article 14 of Additional Protocol II contains a prohibition which states that parties to an armed conflict may not 'attack, destroy, remove or render useless objects indispensable to the survival of the civilian population'. The provisions are aimed at providing a safety net for the population of a State involved in an armed conflict, ensuring their right to retain access to the basic needs for survival.

The reason for providing protection to objects which are indispensable to the civilian population is therefore to ensure the survival of the population. According to Article 54(2) of Additional Protocol I, parties to an armed conflict may not attack, destroy, remove or render useless such objects 'for the specific purpose of denying them for their sustenance value to the civilian population or to the adverse Party'. The provisions are therefore primarily aimed at prohibiting practices such as targeting water supply systems and destroying crops, as the rebel group RUF reportedly did during the conflict in Sierra Leone.[103]

In order to establish whether and to what extent the provisions qualify the right of parties to an armed conflict to exploit natural resources, it is necessary to consider three different issues. The first concerns the limitations related to the objective of the provisions, the second concerns the types of objects that are protected, and the third concerns the exceptions formulated in the provisions.

Both provisions formulate a prohibition against attacking, destroying, removing or rendering useless objects that are indispensable for the *survival* of the population. More specifically, Article 14 of Additional Protocol II makes the protection of such objects subordinate to the all-encompassing prohibition against starving the population as a method of combat.[104] The prohibition is formulated more loosely for international armed conflict. Article 54(2) of Additional Protocol I provides that such objects may not be attacked, destroyed, removed or rendered useless 'for the specific purpose of denying them *for their sustenance value* to the civilian population . . . *whatever the motive*.'[105] In both cases, the provisions imply a certain degree of immediacy, in the sense that the survival of the civilian population must be at stake. Furthermore, it therefore has to be established that parties to an armed conflict have the intention of starving the population (internal armed conflict) or denying the population certain objects for their sustenance value (international armed conflict).

It is not clear to what extent these requirements qualify the prohibition. If specific intent is required, it must be assumed that the prohibition does not cover the appropriation of natural resources for the purpose of financing an armed conflict or for personal gain, as in these cases the removal of natural resources is not carried out with the specific intent to deprive the population of their means of subsistence. A similar conclusion can be drawn with regard to damage to the environment caused by such

[103] UNEP, Sierra Leone: Environment, Conflict and Peacebuilding Assessment, Technical Report, February 2010, p. 45.

[104] The original draft provision did not subordinate the protection of objects indispensable to the survival of the civilian population to the prohibition to use starvation of the population as a method of combat. It simply prohibited parties attacking or destroying those objects with the intention 'to starve out civilians, to cause them to move away or for any other reason'. *Official Records of the Diplomatic Conference on the Reaffirmation and Development of International Humanitarian Law Applicable in Armed Conflicts*, Geneva (1974–77), Vol. I, Part 3, pp. 16 and 40.

[105] Author's emphasis added.

activities, if such damage has the effect of destroying objects indispensable to the civilian population. If, however, it is accepted that reckless disregard by a party to an armed conflict of the consequences of its actions can be considered to reflect intent, the provisions may cover the removal of natural resources for economic purposes, as well as environmental damage caused by such activities. From the perspective of protecting the civilian population, a broad interpretation of 'intent' is therefore to be preferred.

Although State practice is not uniform, the customary IHL study conducted by the International Committee of the Red Cross (ICRC) shows that the majority of military manuals do not state that the prohibition requires a specific intent to starve the civilian population or prevent it from being supplied.[106] Although the extent to which military manuals accurately reflect State practice is still open to debate, these manuals do provide indications in favour of a broad rather than a stringent interpretation of the provisions.

The second issue concerns the types of objects that are covered by the provisions. The ICRC Commentary indicates that the provisions apply to objects that are 'of basic importance for the population from the point of view of providing the means of existence'.[107] The notion of 'basic importance' is not defined in any further detail. The provisions refer to objects such as foodstuffs, agricultural areas for the production of foodstuffs, crops and drinking water installations, but this list is by no means exhaustive. The Diplomatic Conference that adopted the Additional Protocols did not want to narrow down the categories of objects to which the provisions should apply, as 'an exhaustive list might well have resulted in omissions or in making a somewhat arbitrary choice of objects'.[108]

It is evident from the express reference in the provisions to objects such as foodstuffs and drinking water installations that particular natural resources, such as lakes and rivers, which provide drinking water and fish,

[106] See Henckaerts and Doswald-Beck (eds.), *Customary International Humanitarian Law*, Vol. I, p. 190.

[107] See Sandoz, Swinarski and Zimmermann (eds.), *Commentary on the Additional Protocols of 8 June 1977 to the Geneva Conventions of 12 August 1949*, Art. 14, p. 1458.

[108] Ibid., Art. 14, p. 1458. It is interesting to note that the original draft provision proposed by the ICRC contained an exhaustive list of objects, consisting of 'food stuffs and food-producing areas, crops, livestock, drinking water supplies and irrigation works'. *Official Records of the Diplomatic Conference on the Reaffirmation and Development of International Humanitarian Law Applicable in Armed Conflicts*, Geneva (1974–7), Vol. I, Part 3, pp. 16 and 40.

should fall within the ambit of the provisions.[109] Arguably, forests, which provide food, timber, firewood and medicinal plants, may also constitute indispensable 'objects' in the sense of the provisions.[110]

One interesting question in this respect is whether the prohibition also covers economically valuable natural resources that cannot be directly consumed, such as diamonds or coltan. Can such natural resources be considered 'indispensable to the survival of the population'? Although this may initially seem far-fetched, it must be remembered that many civilians in conflict regions are highly dependent on particular natural resources to generate a basic income. In fact, it seems that the dependency of the local population on artisanal mining in the DR Congo was one of the principal reasons for the Security Council to abstain from imposing commodity sanctions to curb the trade in natural resources originating from the DR Congo.[111]

It should also be noted that the provisions themselves leave ample discretion for the parties to an armed conflict to interpret the objects they consider 'indispensable for the survival of the population' in their own way. During the negotiations on the draft text of Article 54 of Additional Protocol I, Egypt and several other oil-producing States proposed including fuel reservoirs and refineries in the text of the provision 'since fuel concerned the whole international community, which depended on oil in all spheres'.[112] Therefore, it can be argued that the phrase 'objects

[109] Compare Mollard-Bannelier, *La Protection de l'Environnement en Temps de Conflit Armé*, p. 189. Mollard-Bannelier argues that certain natural resources could clearly be considered to constitute indispensable objects, but she does not provide examples.

[110] The Democratic Republic of Vietnam explicitly mentioned the destruction of forests 'for the purpose of starving the civilian population and forcing them to become refugees'. *Official Records of the Diplomatic Conference on the Reaffirmation and Development of International Humanitarian Law Applicable in Armed Conflicts*, Geneva (1974–77), Vol. XIV, CDDH/III/SR.17, p. 143. Furthermore, the Additional Protocols themselves consider objects such as medicines and means of shelter essential to the survival of the civilian population. In this regard, Article 18(2) of Additional Protocol II mentions medical supplies, while Article 69(1) of Additional Protocol I also points to clothing, bedding, means of shelter and other supplies. See Henckaerts and Doswald-Beck (eds.), *Customary International Humanitarian Law*, Vol. I, p. 193.

[111] A report prepared by the Secretary-General had warned against the negative impacts of such sanctions on the local population. See the *Report of the Secretary-General Pursuant to Paragraph 8 of Resolution 1698 (2006) Concerning the Democratic Republic of the Congo*, UN Doc. S/2007/68 of 8 February 2007, paras. 62–3.

[112] Egypt and several other oil-producing States proposed to include fuel reservoirs and refineries in Article 54 of Protocol I 'since fuel concerned the whole international community, which depended on oil in all spheres'. *Official Records of the Diplomatic Conference on the Reaffirmation and Development of International Humanitarian Law*

indispensable to the survival of the civilian population' in Article 54(2) of Additional Protocol I and in Article 14 of Additional Protocol II should be broadly interpreted to cover natural resources that provide a basic income for the local population.

This broad interpretation also follows from the interpretation of Article 54(2) of Additional Protocol I and Article 14 of Additional Protocol II in light of the identical Articles 1(2) of the ICESCR and the ICCPR. This provision is of particular relevance because it determines that '*in no case*, may a people be deprived of its own means of subsistence'.[113] An interpretation of Article 54(2) of Additional Protocol I and Article 14 of Additional Protocol II in the light of Article 1(2) of the ICESCR and the ICCPR would extend the protection provided by the provision to all objects which provide the population with the means of subsistence, including particular natural resources that generate a basic income for the local population. Following this interpretation, parties to an armed conflict may, under certain circumstances, be prohibited from cutting off the civilian population from the mining sites or forests under their control.

The last relevant issue concerns the exceptions formulated in Article 54 of Additional Protocol I. The first exception is formulated in Article 54(3) of Additional Protocol I and is also implicit in Article 14 of Additional Protocol II. This provision determines that the prohibition does not apply to objects which are used 'as sustenance solely for the members of its armed forces' or 'in direct support of military action'. The latter phrase is particularly relevant to the subject of this book. The ICRC Commentary to the Additional Protocols points to the following examples: a food-producing area which the enemy uses as it advances through it, or a food storage barn used by the enemy for cover or as an arms depot.[114] Objects

Applicable in Armed Conflicts, Geneva (1974–7), Vol. III, CDDH/III/63, p. 218 and Vol. XIV, CDDH/III/SR.16, p. 139. Also see Mollard-Bannelier, *La Protection de l'Environnement en Temps de Conflit Armé*, pp. 188–9. The interpretation of what constitute 'indispensable' objects is largely left to the discretion of the parties to an armed conflict. Despite the major advantage of flexibility, this system has some important drawbacks. Mollard-Bannelier argues that it creates legal uncertainty for parties to an armed conflict regarding the application of the provision. One could also argue that it gives parties to an armed conflict a loophole with regard to the obligations incumbent on them.

113 Author's emphasis added.

114 Sandoz, Swinarski and Zimmermann (eds.), *Commentary on the Additional Protocols of 8 June 1977 to the Geneva Conventions of 12 August 1949*, Art. 54, p. 657. These exceptions were inserted at the proposal of the United States, which wanted to prevent 'combatants to seek protection under provisions intended solely for the protection and benefit of the

used in these ways lose their immunity unless actions against these objects could 'leave the civilian population with such inadequate food or water as to cause its starvation or force its movement'. This implies that Article 54 of Additional Protocol I does not prohibit parties to an international armed conflict from destroying areas where natural resources are exploited by the hostile party, unless this could lead to the starvation or forced removal of the population. Of course, it should be noted that such a right should be interpreted consistently with Article 23(g) of the 1907 Hague Regulations, which allows parties to an armed conflict to destroy property of a hostile party only in situations of imperative military necessity.[115]

The second exception concerns the defence of national territory against invasion by a foreign State. In these circumstances, Article 54(5) of Additional Protocol I allows a party to an armed conflict to derogate from the prohibitions of paragraph 2 on its own territory if 'imperative military necessity' so requires. *De facto*, this permits a party to an armed conflict to resort to a 'scorched earth' policy.[116] However, the exception is formulated in such a restrictive way as to apply only in exceptional circumstances. It only covers the situation of *defence* of national territory which is under the *control* of the party to the armed conflict against *invasion*.[117] Furthermore, such action may under no circumstances result in the starvation of the population.[118] For the purposes of the present study, it is hard to imagine a situation where a State would destroy its own natural resources to defend itself against an invasion by a third State.

Prohibition of causing widespread, long-term and severe damage to the environment

Articles 35(3) and 55 of Additional Protocol I formulate a prohibition against causing widespread, long-term and severe damage to the

civilian population'. *Official Records of the Diplomatic Conference on the Reaffirmation and Development of International Humanitarian Law Applicable in Armed Conflicts*, Geneva (1974–7), Vol. XIV, CDDH/III/SR.16, p. 138.

115 As discussed in Section 6.3.1, Article 23(g) of the Hague Regulations contains a prohibition of destroying the property of a hostile party, except in cases of imperative military necessity.

116 Sandoz, Swinarski and Zimmermann (eds.), *Commentary on the Additional Protocols of 8 June 1977 to the Geneva Conventions of 12 August 1949*, Art. 54, p. 659. For an analysis of military necessity, see Section 6.3.1 of this study.

117 Emphasis added.

118 The prohibition of starvation is formulated in Article 54(1) of Additional Protocol I, while the current provision derogates from Article 54(2) only. Also see Mollard-Bannelier, *La Protection de l'Environnement en Temps de Conflit Armé*, p. 190.

environment.[119] Article 35(3) of Additional Protocol I provides that 'it is prohibited to employ methods or means of warfare which are intended, or may be expected, to cause widespread, long-term and severe damage to the natural environment', while Article 55 provides that 'care shall be taken in warfare to protect the natural environment against widespread, long-term and severe damage'. In addition, Article 55 specifies that 'this protection includes a prohibition of the use of methods or means of warfare which are intended or may be expected to cause such damage to the natural environment and thereby to prejudice the health or survival of the population'. It also prohibits attacks against the environment in the form of reprisals.

The prohibition against causing widespread, long-term and severe damage to the environment applies exclusively to the situation of international armed conflict. A proposal from Australia to introduce a similar provision to Articles 35(3) and 55 of Additional Protocol I in Additional Protocol II relating to internal armed conflicts met with resistance from several delegations.[120] For example, Canada considered the provision superfluous, as it considered that both the government and rebels would have good reason not to risk alienating the population by causing ecological damage.[121]

Furthermore, it is doubtful whether the prohibition can be considered to apply to internal armed conflicts as a matter of customary international law, as argued by the ICRC in its customary IHL study.[122] The prohibition

[119] Only Article 55 on the protection of the natural environment is actually part of Chapter III on the protection of civilian objects. Article 35, on the other hand, lays down the basic rules of armed conflict and is part of Section I of Part III on the 'Methods and means of warfare'. However, despite these different perspectives, the two provisions both incorporate the prohibition to cause widespread, long-term and severe damage to the environment. Therefore, this study deals with both provisions.

[120] The amendment provided that 'It is forbidden to despoil the natural environment as a technique of warfare'. *Official Records of the Diplomatic Conference on the Reaffirmation and Development of International Humanitarian Law Applicable in Armed Conflicts*, Geneva (1974–7), Vol. IV, Amendments, p. 91, Doc. CDDH/III/55, 19 March 1974.

[121] For this and other comments, see *Official Records of the Diplomatic Conference on the Reaffirmation and Development of International Humanitarian Law Applicable in Armed Conflicts*, Geneva (1974–7), Vol. XIV, CDDH/III/SR.12, pp. 176–9 and CDDH/III/SR.18, p. 153.

[122] See Henckaerts and Doswald-Beck (eds.), *Customary International Humanitarian Law*, Vol. I, pp. 151–5. The ICRC customary law study argues that, for international armed conflicts, the prohibition has attained customary law status and posits that a similar conclusion can be drawn for internal armed conflicts. It should, however, be noted that for a rule to become part of customary international law, there should be, in the words of Article 38 of the Statute of the International Court of Justice, 'a general practice accepted as law'. The ICRC study argues that the prohibition has been inserted into many military

is referred to in only two other IHL conventions, of which only one applies to the situation of internal armed conflict.[123] In addition, in its 1996 *Advisory Opinion on the Legality of the Threat or Use of Nuclear Weapons*, the International Court of Justice expressly stated that Articles 35(3) and 55 were 'powerful constraints for all the States *having subscribed to these provisions*.'[124] This is indicative of the Court's belief that neither of the provisions has attained customary international law status, not even for international armed conflicts. At most, there are indications that the prohibition expresses an emerging custom.[125]

Thus Articles 35(3) and 55 of Additional Protocol I are the only provisions which formulate the prohibition against causing widespread, long-term and severe damage to the environment. They do so in different ways. While Article 35(3) sets limits on the means and methods of warfare, Article 55 provides protection to the environment because of its importance to human beings.[126] Most importantly, Article 55 formulates a general

manuals of States, but, as argued before, insertion into a military manual does not prove that States consider themselves legally bound by the prohibition. On the contrary, the United States, for example, has inserted the prohibition into its military manual, but it has also explicitly stated that it does not consider the prohibition to be part of customary international law.

123 See the Convention on Prohibitions or Restrictions on the Use of Certain Conventional Weapons Which May Be Deemed to Be Excessively Injurious or to Have Indiscriminate Effects, adopted in Geneva on 10 October 1980, *1342 UNTS 163*, as amended in 2001, which recalls in its preamble 'that it is prohibited to employ methods or means of warfare which are intended, or may be expected, to cause widespread, long-term and severe damage to the natural environment'. See also, for the situation of international armed conflict only, the Convention on the prohibition of military or any other hostile use of environmental modification techniques (ENMOD), concluded on 10 December 1976 in New York (entry into force: 5 October 1978), *1108 UNTS 151*. Article 1 of this convention determines that 'each State Party to this Convention undertakes not to engage in military or any other hostile use of environmental modification techniques having *widespread, long-lasting or severe effects* as the means of destruction, damage or injury to any other State Party'. Author's emphasis added.

124 International Court of Justice, *Advisory Opinion on the Legality of the Threat or Use of Nuclear Weapons*, 8 July 1996, para. 30, *I.C.J. Reports 1996*. Author's emphasis added.

125 Koppe, *The Use of Nuclear Weapons and the Protection of the Environment during International Armed Conflict*, p. 235. For an extensive analysis regarding the status of the prohibition, see pp. 177–97.

126 It must be noted that this does not imply that the environment is protected only insofar as damage would prejudice the health or survival of the population, as argued by some authors. See, e.g., Verwey, 'Protection of the Environment in Times of Armed Conflict', p. 13, who argues that the reference to the health or survival of the population in the second part of Article 55 must be read as a limitation on the protection afforded to the environment under this provision. However, the official records of the diplomatic conference that adopted the provisions note that 'the first sentence enjoining the taking of care lays down a general norm, which is then particularized in the second sentence.

duty of care for the environment.[127] In this sense, Article 55 is broader in scope than Article 35(3) of Additional Protocol I, because it encompasses all activities that cause 'widespread, long-term and severe damage' to the environment, not only damage caused by the means and methods of warfare. Furthermore, it includes a positive obligation to protect the environment.[128] This makes this provision more relevant to the purposes of the current study.

One important question that arises with respect to Article 55 of Additional Protocol I is what this 'duty of care' for the environment actually implies. In this respect, Karen Hulme argues that the duty of care first and foremost serves as 'a lasting reminder of th[e] recognition that humankind must continue to protect the environment in armed conflict'.[129] From this perspective, the duty of care formulated in Article 55 of Additional Protocol I should be achieved on the basis of the general standards of care formulated in international environmental law. The principles of prevention and precaution are most relevant in this regard. Both require States to exercise due diligence in the activities they undertake.[130] As indicated in Chapter 4 of this book, 'due diligence' implies that States are to 'use all the means at [their] disposal' or 'to take all appropriate measures' to prevent

Care must be taken to protect the natural environment against the sort of harm specified even if the health or survival of the population is not prejudiced'. See the *Official Records of the Diplomatic Conference on the Reaffirmation and Development of International Humanitarian Law Applicable in Armed Conflicts*, Geneva (1974–7), Vol. XV, Report to the Third Committee on the Work of the Working Group, Committee 3, April 1975, CDDH/III/275, p. 4. Also see Koppe, *The Use of Nuclear Weapons and the Protection of the Environment during International Armed Conflict*, p. 148, who argues that the prohibition formulated in the second sentence of Article 55(1) 'is illustrative and exemplary for the duty of care of Article 55(1), first sentence'; Sandoz, Swinarski and Zimmermann (eds.), *Commentary on the Additional Protocols of 8 June 1977 to the Geneva Conventions of 12 August 1949*, Art. 55, p. 663, who note that 'the expression "care shall be taken" is not used in Article 35 paragraph 3, which is therefore more stringent'; and Dinstein, 'Protection of the Environment in International Armed Conflict', pp. 531–2, who argues that the first phrase of Article 55 is not reduced to cases in which damage to the natural environment prejudices human health or survival. In his opinion, 'the injury to human beings should be regarded not as a condition for the application of the injunction against causing environmental damage, but as the paramount category included within the bounds of a larger injunction'.

[127] See Hulme, 'Taking Care to Protect the Environment against Damage', pp. 675–91. Also see Koppe, *The Use of Nuclear Weapons and the Protection of the Environment during International Armed Conflict*, p. 148; and Dinstein, 'Protection of the Environment in International Armed Conflict', p. 530.

[128] Hulme, *War Torn Environment*, p. 73.

[129] See Hulme, 'Taking Care to Protect the Environment against Damage', p. 677.

[130] See Hulme, *War Torn Environment*, pp. 80–88.

damage.[131] Of course, what is considered 'appropriate' in situations of armed conflict can differ significantly from what is expected in situations of peace.

The next question is whether this provision applies to the exploitation of natural resources by parties to an armed conflict, and if so, what this entails. First, it is relevant to note that Article 55 provides that 'care shall be taken *in warfare*.'[132] The exploitation of natural resources by parties to an armed conflict for financial purposes cannot in itself be considered to constitute an act of warfare. However, the exploitation of the natural resources that belong to the hostile party could be regarded as a form of economic warfare aimed at strengthening its own military capacity, while weakening the capacity of the enemy with economic measures.[133] Thus Article 55 arguably covers instances of resource exploitation. This means that a party to an armed conflict that engages in the exploitation of the natural resources of the enemy must take appropriate measures to prevent 'long-term, widespread and severe' damage to the environment.

The last relevant question concerns the kind of standard implied by the terms 'long-term, widespread and severe'. At the very least, the cumulative criteria rule out the possibility that the prohibition applies to incidental damage resulting from conventional military operations.[134] However, there is no general understanding regarding the threshold that does apply. Neither the provision itself nor the *travaux préparatoires* give any further indication of how the criteria are interpreted. The *travaux* merely indicate that the term 'long-term' refers to damage lasting several decades.[135]

[131] Case Concerning Pulp Mills on the River Uruguay (*Argentina* v. *Uruguay*), *I.C.J. Reports 2010*, para. 101; and Article 3 of the *ILC Draft articles on Prevention of Transboundary Harm from Hazardous Activities*. See also Article 194(2) of the United Nations Convention on the Law of the Sea, 10 December 1982, *1833 UNTS 3*, which indicates an obligation for States to 'take all measures necessary to ensure that activities under their jurisdiction or control are so conducted as not to cause damage by pollution to other States and their environment'.

[132] Author's emphasis added.

[133] On the notion of economic warfare, see Lowe and Tzanakopoulos, 'Economic Warfare'.

[134] *Official Records of the Diplomatic Conference on the Reaffirmation and Development of International Humanitarian Law Applicable in Armed Conflicts*, Geneva (1974–7), Vol. XV, CDDH/215/Rev.1, para. 27, pp. 268–9. It should be noted that Articles 35(3) and 55 of Additional Protocol I both embody the precautionary principle to a certain extent, by allowing a degree of latitude as to the actual occurrence of damage. See Chapter 4 of this study for a more comprehensive discussion on this principle.

[135] Ibid.

Only ENMOD provides some indications, although the *travaux* do indicate that the threshold for damage envisaged for Protocol I was to be higher than that for ENMOD.[136] The *Understandings* which States adopted regarding certain provisions of the ENMOD Convention defined 'widespread' as 'encompassing an area on the scale of several hundred square kilometres' and 'severe' as involving 'serious or significant disruption or harm to human life, natural and economic resources or other assets'.[137]

Thus if these definitions can be considered to provide a minimum threshold for the prohibition contained in Additional Protocol I, as a minimum the prohibition seems to require an impact that covers a considerable area, encompasses serious damage and lasts for several decades.[138] These requirements limit the scope of application of the prohibition against causing widespread, long-term and severe damage to the more extreme cases of environmental damage. Therefore, Phoebe Okowa, among others, argues that 'the so-called natural resource/environmental protection provisions in Additional Protocol I, in particular Articles 35(3) and 55, are set at such a high threshold with a wide margin of discretion during military operations, making them of marginal relevance as effective constraints in most conflicts'.[139]

On the other hand, they do not rule out that certain damage caused by natural resource exploitation, such as large-scale deforestation and loss of biodiversity caused by timber extraction or the poisoning of groundwater in a region caused by the extraction of minerals, may be included in the scope of this prohibition. This applies particularly if the damage

[136] *Official Records of the Diplomatic Conference on the Reaffirmation and Development of International Humanitarian Law Applicable in Armed Conflicts*, Geneva (1974–7), Vol. VI, CDDH/SR.39, Annex, pp. 113–18. Also see Hulme, *War Torn Environment*, pp. 89–91.

[137] Report of the Conference of the Committee on Disarmament, Volume I, General Assembly Official records, Thirty-first session, Supplement No. 27, *Doc. A/31/27*, New York, United Nations, 1976, pp. 91–2.

[138] The terms have also been incorporated into Article 20(g) of the 1996 *Draft Code of Crimes against the Peace and Security of Mankind* of the International Law Commission and into Articles 8(2)(b)(iv) of the *ICC Statute*. Unfortunately, the preparatory works of these instruments fail to clarify the meaning of the threshold. It should further be noted that the protocol does not define the meaning of the term 'damage'. It is therefore not clear what constitutes 'damage' for the purposes of the protocol and whether 'damage' includes alterations to the environment. For a thorough analysis of the damage criteria, see Hulme, *War Torn Environment*, pp. 17–40.

[139] Okowa, 'Natural Resources in Situations of Armed Conflict', p. 250.

threshold is interpreted in a dynamic and evolutionary way. Arguably, a correct interpretation of the provision and its damage threshold would take into account modern views on environmental protection, calling for the adoption of an ecosystem approach. The starting point for this is that damage to components of an ecosystem can disrupt the balance of the ecosystem as a whole. From this perspective, environmental damage can be considered to be widespread, long-term and severe if it seriously upsets the balance of an ecosystem that encompasses a considerable area in such a way that the damage lasts for several decades.

Of course, this still is a fairly high threshold. Therefore, Article 55 of Additional Protocol I cannot be expected to provide meaningful protection to the environment against damage resulting from the commercial exploitation of natural resources in situations of armed conflict. Moreover, since the provision does not apply to internal armed conflicts, its use is relatively limited. In view of these limitations, the provision can be considered to be of relatively little use for the purposes of this study.

6.4 The Martens Clause

The previous section showed how standards in international human rights and environmental law impact upon obligations of parties to an armed conflict under IHL. In addition, reference can be made to another way of incorporating external norms in IHL treaties, i.e., by way of express provisions in the treaty itself. In this respect, the so-called 'Martens Clause' is of particular interest. It was named after the Russian delegate at the 1899 Hague Peace Conference who introduced the clause in order to break a deadlock in the negotiations concerning the right of populations in occupied territories to rebel against the occupying forces.[140] Since then it has been inserted into a number of IHL treaties.

The original clause, as included in the preamble of the 1899 Hague Convention, states as follows:

> Until a more complete code of the laws of war is issued, the High Contracting Parties think it right to declare that in cases not included in the Regulations adopted by them, populations and belligerents remain under the protection and empire of the principles of international law, as they

[140] For a thorough analysis of the genesis of the Martens Clause, see Cassese, 'The Martens Clause', pp. 187–216.

> result from the usages established between civilised nations, from the laws of humanity, and the requirements of the public conscience.[141]

Over time, the Martens Clause has been used to avoid a legal vacuum in the protection of human beings in cases not dealt with in IHL conventions and to prevent these cases being left – in the words of the 1899 Hague Convention – to 'the arbitrary judgment of the military commanders'.[142] The clause was mainly interpreted in this way by the Nuremberg Military Tribunal III in the *Krupp case*. The Nuremberg Tribunal used the Martens Clause to reject the argument of the defence that certain provisions applicable to occupied territories did not apply in cases of 'total war', referring to a conduct of war that leaves no room for considerations of humanity. With regard to the Martens Clause the tribunal stated,

> It is a general clause, making the usages established among civilized nations, the laws of humanity and the dictates of public conscience into the legal yardstick to be applied if and when the specific provisions of the Conventions . . . do not cover specific cases occurring in warfare, or concomitant to warfare.[143]

Although this passage of the judgment does not specifically refer to the protection of human beings, it is clear from the context of the passage that the Nuremberg Tribunal did not intend to apply the Martens Clause to all cases occurring in or concomitant to warfare. The Martens Clause was invoked directly in relation to the protection of private property.

Providing protection to the civilian population was also the rationale for the International Court of Justice to apply the Martens Clause in its *Nuclear Weapons Advisory Opinion*. In this Advisory Opinion, the International Court of Justice referred to the Martens Clause to interpret the humanitarian law principles of distinction and necessity in the light of new technological developments in warfare not dealt with in the relevant conventions. The Court considered that the Martens Clause 'has proved to be an effective means of addressing the rapid evolution of military technology'.[144] In other words, the Court used the Martens Clause to

[141] Convention (II) with Respect to the Laws and Customs of War on Land and its annex: Regulations Concerning the Laws and Customs of War on Land. The Hague, 29 July 1899.

[142] Ibid.

[143] *Trials of War Criminals before the Nuremberg Tribunals under Control Council Law No. 10*, Vol. IX, the *Krupp* case, Washington, DC: Government Printing Office (1950), p. 1341.

[144] See Legality of the Threat or Use of Nuclear Weapons, Advisory Opinion, *I.C.J. Reports 1996*, p. 226, para. 78.

justify a dynamic-evolutionary interpretation of two of the core principles of IHL.

Furthermore, the Martens Clause has been relied on in case law to confirm the applicability of customary international law principles alongside treaty law. It is in this sense that the Martens Clause was relied on in the *Nicaragua case.* The Court referred to the version of it inserted into the Geneva Conventions, dealing with the legal effects of denunciation of the conventions.[145] In this case, it was principally called upon to confirm that the core principles of IHL could be applied, even when the conventions of which they are part could not.[146]

However, the primary significance of the Martens Clause is not so much its confirmation of the applicability of customary international law in situations of armed conflict in general. Today it is generally accepted that armed conflicts are regulated not only by treaty law, but also by customary international law. Many rules that were codified in the 1907 Hague Regulations and the 1949 Geneva Conventions have been recognised as reflecting customary international law in international case law. In addition, modern criminal tribunals have confirmed the existence of principles of customary international law applicable to situations of international and internal armed conflicts.

The primary significance of the Martens Clause is rather its reference to 'the laws of humanity' and 'the requirements of the public conscience' – or, in their modern formulations, 'the principles of humanity' and 'the dictates of the public conscience', as foundations of the principles of international law that provide protection to populations and belligerents in cases not covered by treaty law.[147] The question is what is meant by

[145] See Article 158 of Geneva Convention IV: 'The denunciation shall have effect only in respect of the denouncing Power. It shall in no way impair the obligations which the Parties to the conflict shall remain bound to fulfil by virtue of the principles of the law of nations, as they result from the usages established among civilized peoples, from the laws of humanity and the dictates of the public conscience'.

[146] International Court of Justice, Case Concerning Military and Paramilitary Activities in and against Nicaragua, Judgment of 27 June 1986, *I.C.J. Reports 1986*, p. 14, para. 218.

[147] See Article 1(2) of Additional Protocol I and the preamble of Additional Protocol II. It is further to be noted that Additional Protocol II contains a shortened version of the Martens Clause. It simply states that 'in cases not covered by the law in force, the human person remains under the protection of the principles of humanity and the dictates of the public conscience'. The Commentary to Additional Protocol II indicates that the absence of a reference to custom 'should not be interpreted as a rejection on the part of the Conference, as the ICRC had not made a proposal to that effect in its initial draft'. See Sandoz, Swinarski and Zimmermann (eds.), *Commentary on the Additional Protocols of 8 June 1977 to the Geneva Conventions of 12 August 1949*, p. 1337. The reasons for the

these terms. The wording of the Martens Clause as a whole clearly shows that the principles of humanity and the dictates of public conscience are not to be considered as 'new' or additional sources of international law. Rather, their purpose is to help shape the content of the customary international law principles to be applied whenever a particular situation is not covered by the existing treaty rules – either because the treaty rules are imprecise or incomplete or, as in the case of the Geneva Conventions, because a party to an armed conflict has denounced the treaty in question.

The emphasis placed by the Martens Clause on the moral foundations of legal principles has two significant implications.[148] First, as argued by both Meron and Cassese, the emphasis in the Martens Clause on the moral foundations of legal principles raises the conceptual element of the customary international law process to a higher level, while relaxing the requirements prescribed for State practice.[149] In addition, these authors argue that the reference to the 'law' or 'principles' of 'humanity' denotes a strong presumption in favour of applying IHL consistently with human rights norms, as well as using human rights law to fill the gaps in IHL treaties.[150]

It is for these reasons that the Martens Clause retains its relevance in modern armed conflicts. The Martens Clause recognises the paramount importance of providing protection to human beings in situations of armed conflict, even in cases where the law of armed conflict is silent. Most importantly, it applies to international as well as internal armed conflicts.

absence of such a proposal in the draft Convention are not entirely clear. They could be related to the particular nature of internal armed conflicts as compared to the one-sided focus of the process of international customary norm creation on *State* practice and *State opinio juris*, or there could be other reasons. In any case, the absence of a reference to established custom should not be interpreted as a rejection of the applicability of international customary law to internal armed conflicts.

148 For a discussion of the moral imperatives of the Martens Clause, see also Salter, 'Reinterpreting Competing Interpretations of the Scope and Potential of the Martens Clause', pp. 433–6.

149 Cassese argues that the Martens Clause '*loosens* the requirements prescribed for *usus*, while at the same time *elevating opinio* (*iuris* or *necessitates*) to a rank higher than that normally admitted'. See Cassese, 'The Martens Clause', p. 214. Meron argues that the Martens Clause 'reinforces a trend . . . toward basing the existence of customary law primarily on *opinio juris* (principles of humanity and dictates of public conscience) rather than actual battlefield practice'. See Meron, 'The Martens Clause, Principles of Humanity, and Dictates of Public Conscience', p. 88.

150 Cassese further argues in favour of deducing the principles of humanity from existing international human rights standards. See Cassese, 'The Martens Clause', p. 212.

The body of IHL is much less developed for internal armed conflicts than for international armed conflicts. Therefore, the Martens Clause can play an important role in ensuring basic protection to civilian populations in internal armed conflicts in addition to the protection provided by Article 3 of the 1949 Geneva Conventions and, if applicable, the provisions of 1977 Additional Protocol II. At the very least, the Martens Clause clearly shows that even though they are not formally bound by international human rights law, armed groups may not abuse gaps in the law of armed conflict to commit human rights violations.

The Martens Clause could also be relevant for a coherent reading of IHL. For example, one issue that is not adequately addressed in current IHL applicable to internal armed conflicts concerns the protection of private property. In the law applicable to international armed conflicts, private property has a special status. This is most apparent in international occupation law, which prohibits the taking of private property altogether. In contrast, in internal armed conflicts, private property is only expressly protected by the prohibition against pillage, which, as argued earlier, does not apply to the taking of property for military purposes. The prohibition against seizing the property of an adversary, which does apply to the taking of property for military purposes, is, however, more difficult to apply to the protection of private property in internal armed conflicts because one needs to determine that the owner is somehow affiliated to a party to the armed conflict, something which is far less problematic in relation to international armed conflicts.[151] A consistent reading of IHL would result in the assumption that taking private property in internal armed conflicts is not permitted for military purposes either, regardless of any particular affiliation to a party to an armed conflict, except in situations of imperative military necessity. It is in these cases that the Martens Clause is useful, in the sense that the dictates of public conscience prescribe that the law applicable to the protection of private property in internal armed conflicts is interpreted consistently with the relevant provisions relating to the protection of private property in international armed conflicts.

In conclusion, the Martens Clause provides protection to human beings in situations not dealt with by IHL treaties. Its purpose is to provide basic protection to civilians and combatants in the conduct of hostilities, where such protection is not provided by relevant IHL treaties. The question

[151] For international armed conflicts one can rely on the general assumption that all private property that belongs to citizens of one of the belligerent States constitutes property of the 'enemy'.

arises whether the Martens Clause could be used to fill other gaps in the law of armed conflict.

Certainly some authors propose using the Martens Clause as a tool to protect the environment and natural resources. Iain Scobbie, for example, refers to the seemingly broad interpretation given to the Martens Clause by the Nuremberg Tribunal in the *Krupp* case, quoted earlier, to support his argument that the Martens Clause 'is a dynamic mechanism by which general international law is imported into the [Hague] Regulations in matters "concomitant to warfare"'. Therefore, in his opinion '[g]eneral international law regarding natural resources, as it has developed since 1907, must now accordingly form part of the provisions set out in Section III of the Regulations [relating to the law of occupation]'.[152] However, as argued earlier, the relevant passage in the *Krupp* case should not be interpreted as an attempt to broaden the application of the Martens Clause. Moreover, such an overly broad interpretation would run counter to a textual interpretation of the Martens Clause, as inserted in both prior and subsequent legal instruments.

The Martens Clause cannot be seen as a magic wand which can be used to fill all the gaps in IHL. The principal objective of the clause is to provide protection to human beings against unnecessary suffering or abuse during an armed conflict in cases not dealt with in relevant treaties. This is also clear from the emphasis placed by the clause on the laws of humanity and the dictates of public conscience, both of which have strong humanitarian connotations. Thus, insofar as general natural resources law provides protection to human beings where IHL does not, it can be applied by virtue of the Martens Cause. However, in general, it should be concluded that the Martens Clause is not the appropriate mechanism for the introduction of norms other than those with a humanitarian character into IHL.

6.5 Preliminary conclusions

IHL contains a number of obligations for parties to an armed conflict which are applicable to the exploitation and plundering of natural resources in situations of armed conflict. These obligations follow from

[152] See, e.g., Scobbie, who argues that general international law regarding natural resources, as it has developed since 1907, must be inserted through the Martens Clause into the section of the 1907 Hague Regulations covering occupation. Scobbie, 'Natural Resources and Belligerent Occupation', p. 247. Also see Simonds, 'Conventional Warfare and Environmental Protection', p. 188.

provisions which afford protection to property and to civilian objects. However, upon closer examination, three problems immediately become apparent. The first concerns the general ability of IHL to regulate the exploitation of natural resources, which is principally a commercial activity and not an act of warfare. IHL is not designed to address these types of activities. This is only different for occupation law, which regulates the position of an occupant as a *de facto* authority. Most importantly, the right of an occupant to exploit natural resources is limited to a right of 'usufruct' to cover the costs of civilian administration in occupied territory.

The second issue that immediately becomes apparent concerns the enormous range of obligations under IHL. Although there actually are not many rules that apply to the exploitation of natural resources in situations of armed conflict, different rules apply to different conflict situations. Moreover, some of the rules target only one party to the conflict. This asymmetry of obligations for parties to an armed conflict is most apparent in situations of internal armed conflict. For example, the prohibition against seizing or destroying the property of an 'adversary' restricts its application to the exploitation of natural resources by non-State armed groups, while the prohibition has no direct relevance to governments.

The final problem that is apparent is the failure of IHL to provide adequate protection to the environment in situations of armed conflict. The prohibition against causing widespread, long-term and severe damage to the environment applies only to situations of international armed conflict. Moreover, it has such a high threshold that it would only cover the most extreme cases of environmental damage resulting from the exploitation of natural resources. The massive pollution of a river caused by the use of chemicals or the cutting down of a forest encompassing at least several hundred square kilometres are examples of this. More general provisions regarding the protection of property or of objects that are indispensable to the civilian population could fill some of the gaps, but these provisions do not primarily serve environmental purposes.

Some possibilities for the reform of IHL have been proposed in order to provide better protection to the environment. Michael Bothe et al., for example, propose the creation of protected zones and non-defended localities under Articles 59 and 60 of Additional Protocol I in order to provide protection to the environment in situations of armed conflict.[153] Such protected zones may not be the subject of attack. However, this does

[153] Bothe et al., 'International Law Protecting the Environment during Armed Conflict', p. 577.

not seem to be a viable option in areas of high economic importance, which form the subject matter of this book.

Other options include the adoption of a new legal instrument to protect the environment during armed conflict. Reference can be made to specific calls for the adoption of a fifth Geneva Convention on the protection of the environment or of a 'green' Additional Protocol.[154] Although these proposals focus mainly on the effects of warfare on the environment, their scope could be broadened to encompass environmental damage caused by parties to an armed conflict by other activities as well. In this sense it could be construed as a legally binding code of conduct for parties to an armed conflict with regard to the environment.

However, it remains to be seen whether the adoption of a new legal instrument to protect the environment in situations of armed conflict is a viable option. Discussions on this subject date back to 1991, when a round table debate was organised by the London School of Economics. Since then, the subject has remained on the agenda, but the debate has been confined to academic and civil society circles.

Apart from these policy considerations, a more fundamental objection can be made to this sort of legislative effort in relation to the subject matter of this book. A Convention focusing on the protection of the environment in situations of armed conflict could be very useful in providing better protection to the environment in these situations. From this perspective, the initiative is to be applauded. However, it does not solve the other problems identified in this chapter, in particular the lack of clarity with regard to the existing rules for the exploitation of natural resources by parties to an armed conflict. A convention focusing on the protection of the environment is not an appropriate instrument to address issues related to an essentially economic activity. Furthermore, what is needed is not so much a codification of relevant rules belonging to the field of IHL relating to the exploitation of natural resources, but rather a reassessment of the existing rules from all relevant fields of international law. This issue is explored in greater detail in the final conclusions to this part of the book.

Finally, it can be argued that IHL contributes to the protection of natural resources in two important ways. First, it contains an elaborate regime for the situation of occupation which explicitly deals with the exploitation of natural resources in occupied territories. Second, it is the only field of international law that contains binding obligations for

[154] Plant, *Environmental Protection and the Law of War.*

non-State armed groups, including rules that are relevant for the exploitation of natural resources. According to these rules, armed groups are not allowed to exploit natural resources, except in cases of imperative military necessity. However, in reality it is difficult to imagine situations where the exploitation of natural resources could ever satisfy the criteria of imperative military necessity, in particular the 'urgency' requirement. Although these restrictions are understandable from the point of view of the States that have negotiated the relevant treaties which embody these rules, the question arises of whether these restrictions are effective. If there is a quasi-prohibition against armed groups exploiting natural resources to finance their armed struggle, why should they then bother to abide by the law at all? From the point of view of environmental protection, it may therefore be more useful to provide those armed groups that satisfy the criteria of Additional Protocol II with a qualified right to exploit natural resources in territories under their control. This point is taken up in greater detail in the concluding remarks to this part of the book.

Concluding remarks to Part II

This part of the book has examined the legal framework governing the exploitation of natural resources in situations of armed conflict. Chapter 5 showed that the foundations of the general legal framework for the governance of natural resources are only partially affected in situations of armed conflict. The ILC draft articles on the effects of armed conflict on treaties show a strong presumption in favour of the continued applicability of both international human rights and environmental treaties. Furthermore, the rules for the suspension of treaties, as well as the circumstances precluding wrongfulness, are sufficiently stringent to preclude any easy ways out. However, there are other factors that affect the operation of international human rights and environmental treaties in situations of armed conflict. First, human rights treaties provide for the possibility of derogating from obligations in situations of public emergency. This means that domestic governments can, for example, derogate from provisions on public participation in these treaties. Second, international environmental treaties often contain clauses that are lenient with regard to States implementing their obligations. Such clauses call on States to implement their obligations as far as this is appropriate or depending on their capabilities.

As a minimum requirement, States remain bound by their core obligations under these treaties. These include a prohibition against depriving a people of its means of subsistence under the 1966 Human Rights Covenants, as well as a prohibition against inflicting harm on particular natural resources that are protected under relevant environmental conventions, including the 1972 UNESCO World Heritage Convention and the 1992 Convention on Biological Diversity. Furthermore, States remain bound by their obligations under customary international law. These include the principle of permanent sovereignty and the inherent condition that a government must exercise permanent sovereignty for national development and the well-being of the population, as well as the principle of sustainable use, which qualifies the right of States to exploit their natural resources, even in situations of armed conflict.

One major deficiency of international human rights and environmental law is that these fields of international law do not contain direct obligations for armed groups. Furthermore, their obligations are only partially relevant for the conduct of foreign States in situations of armed conflict. Therefore, Chapter 6 has addressed the role of IHL in providing relevant rules. It demonstrated that on the whole, IHL does not directly address issues related to the exploitation of natural resources by parties to an armed conflict. This is different only for the situation of occupation, which does contain express rules for occupants relating to the exploitation of natural resources. The key provision in this respect is Article 55 of the 1907 Hague Regulations, which provides occupants with a right to usufruct on the natural resources situated in occupied territory. According to the right of usufruct, occupants are allowed to exploit natural resources in occupied territory for two purposes: (1) to cover the costs of civilian administration, within reasonable limits and in proportion to the available natural resources; and (2) for other purposes benefitting the population living in occupied territory.

Rules that apply to other States with a military presence on the territory of a foreign State, as well as to armed groups, must be derived from more general provisions relating to the protection of property and civilian objects. Protection of natural resources is provided first of all by the prohibition against pillage, which prohibits the taking of property for personal gain. Furthermore, parties to an armed conflict are prohibited from taking or destroying property that belongs to a hostile party for military purposes, except in situations of 'imperative military necessity'. Although the categories of situations to which the exception of 'imperative military necessity' applies are not expressly listed, an exception can be made only if the following conditions are met: (1) there must be a reasonable connection between the taking or destruction of property and the accomplishment of a military advantage; and (2) there must be a degree of urgency. It is particularly this degree of urgency that is absent in the majority of cases involving the exploitation of natural resources by parties to an armed conflict.

In internal armed conflicts, the IHL prohibitions mainly focus on armed groups. However, this asymmetry of obligations for armed groups and the government is not a problem when considered in a broader context, and in particular in the light of the view that governments remain bound by the general framework for the exploitation of natural resources. The virtual absence of provisions protecting the environment in IHL is more problematic.

There are only two provisions that expressly prohibit parties to an armed conflict from causing damage to the environment. They prohibit parties to an armed conflict from causing long-term, widespread and severe damage to the environment. It has been argued that these provisions suffer from two major deficiencies. The first is that they apply only to international armed conflict. The second is that they set a cumulative threshold for environmental damage, which means that the provisions apply only to environmental damage that is widespread, long-term *and* severe. This is a very high threshold, even when it is interpreted in the light of modern developments in international environmental law.

Other provisions that are relevant to the protection of the environment include the prohibition against taking or destroying the property of a hostile party, except in cases of imperative military necessity, and the prohibition against destroying or rendering useless objects that are considered indispensable to the civilian population. Chapter 6 has demonstrated that the protection provided to the environment by these provisions is far less than what is necessary to prevent environmental degradation.

Two main conclusions can be drawn from these findings to address the challenges involved in resource-related armed conflicts. First, it is necessary to develop clear rules for the commercial exploitation of natural resources in situations of armed conflict. Second, there is a need for adequate rules for the protection of the environment in situations of armed conflict, particularly internal armed conflicts. These rules can mainly be based on existing international law, but new rules also need to be developed.

The task of evaluating the existing rules and developing new rules can best be assigned to the ILC. Despite the lengthy procedures involved in drafting its articles, it is the only international body that combines expertise in all the relevant fields of international law with an official mandate to progressively develop and codify international law. The ILC could undertake this work as part of its study on the 'Protection of the Environment in Relation to Armed Conflicts', a topic which it recently included in its programme of work.[155] Special Rapporteur Marie Jacobsson proposed to include in this study an analysis of the existing rules applicable in situations of armed conflict, with a particular emphasis on internal armed conflicts.[156] As regards the development of new rules, the Special Rapporteur indicated that 'it was suggested that it was not the task of the Commission to modify ... existing legal regimes [regulating the law of armed conflict]'.[157] It is argued, however, that the task of the ILC includes progressive development of international law. Therefore, the ILC should not limit its work to an analysis of the existing rules, but should also progressively develop those rules.

This book suggests that the mandate of the ILC should first of all include the clarification of the implications of the existing rules of international

155 See International Law Commission, Report on the work of its sixty-fifth session (2013), *UN Doc. A/68/10*, Chap. IX.

156 Ibid., paras. 136 and 141.

157 Ibid., para. 136.

humanitarian, environmental and human rights law for the commercial exploitation of natural resources during armed conflict, an issue that has not been systematically addressed in existing legal instruments. The ILC should address several questions, including the meaning of 'imperative military necessity' in relation to the prohibition against appropriating or destroying the property of a hostile party under IHL. What does this exception entail? Does it include the exploitation of natural resources to provide for the basic needs of hostile parties? Arguably, it does not. It is only when natural resources can be directly consumed, such as firewood, that the condition of urgency is satisfied.

Furthermore, the ILC should assess the existing rules in their totality; i.e., it should take the existing rules from international humanitarian, human rights and environmental law together. All too often the rules of IHL are looked at in isolation when assessing activities that take place in situations of armed conflict. However, rules from international human rights and environmental law are equally important, especially when assessing the rights and obligations of domestic governments in relation to the exploitation of natural resources. Chapters 5 and 6 have shown that IHL primarily creates obligations for non-State armed groups and foreign States, while international human rights and environmental law create obligations for domestic governments and, to a lesser extent, for foreign States as well. For the sake of clarity and comprehensiveness, it is therefore essential to list all the relevant rules, not only those of IHL.

In addition, the ILC should clarify the position of armed groups in relation to the exploitation of natural resources in situations of armed conflict. The relevant provisions of IHL applicable to internal armed conflicts formulate an absolute prohibition against armed groups exploiting natural resources. However, as soon as a conflict is internationalised, armed groups which are recognised as belligerents by third States or acting under the control of a foreign State become subject to the law applicable to international armed conflict. For those armed groups that control portions of a State's territory, this means that they are granted a limited right to exploit natural resources under international occupation law. From an environmental and human rights perspective, a case could be made for the elimination of this distinction for armed groups that satisfy the criteria of Additional Protocol II. These armed groups should be accorded a right similar to that of occupants, whether or not the armed conflict is internationalised.[158] It is then at the discretion of

[158] For a similar plea for purposes of criminal prosecution, see Stewart, 'Corporate War Crimes', p. 61.

the UN Security Council to decide whether exploitation activities pose a risk to international peace and security in specific instances and therefore must be prevented altogether.

This position is reflected to some extent in the KPCS, discussed in Chapter 8. This Scheme defines 'conflict diamonds' as 'rough diamonds used by rebel movements or their allies to finance conflict aimed at undermining legitimate governments, as described in relevant United Nations Security Council resolutions'.[159] This definition implies that the determination of what constitutes 'conflict diamonds' is left to the discretion of the UN Security Council.

Furthermore, the major advantage of taking occupation law as a point of reference for rules regulating the behaviour of armed groups in control of portions of the State territory is that this field of law is well developed and is susceptible to interpretation in the light of relevant human rights and environmental norms. Some rights are accorded to armed groups in this way, but at the same time, these armed groups must also meet stringent obligations. Arguably this balancing of rights and obligations is the best way to provide protection to the environment and the civilian population in territories that are controlled by armed groups. Furthermore, granting armed groups some rights may give these groups a positive incentive to respect the corresponding obligations.

Finally, the ILC should evaluate the existing rules for the protection of the environment in internal armed conflict and formulate proposals to improve these rules. One of the major gaps in the existing rules relate to the absence of binding rules for armed groups in relation to environmental protection. Arguably, governments remain bound by international environmental law, but armed groups are not. Therefore, the ILC should examine the extent to which existing rules of IHL protect the environment and develop new rules in relation to environmental damage caused by acts of warfare. It is argued that the prohibition against destroying the property of an adversary provides basic protection to the environment, but this protection needs to be strengthened. The proposals for the adoption of a fifth Geneva Convention on the protection of the environment or of a 'green' Additional Protocol could be taken as a starting point for the ILC in this respect.

Most relevant to the purposes of the present study, the ILC should define the implications of existing rules for preventing more serious environmental damage caused by the exploitation of natural resources by

[159] Kimberley Process Certification Scheme, Section I.

parties to an armed conflict, including the provisions of the 1977 Additional Protocols relating to the protection of objects indispensable to the civilian population. For example, do these rules cover situations such as the poisoning of groundwater as a result of irresponsible dumping of chemical substances used in the mining sector? Arguably, they do cover such situations if the poisoning of groundwater results in the starvation or forced movement of people.

One of the aspects that an ILC study should further address concerns the effects on the environment of the exploitation of natural resources by parties to an armed conflict. It is of the essence that the ILC clarifies the threshold of damage to the environment as laid down in Articles 35(3) and 55 of Additional Protocol I. The evolution of international environmental law as well as our improved knowledge of natural processes in the past decades should be taken into account when interpreting these provisions. This should result in the adoption of an ecosystem approach when interpreting these provisions, meaning that the effects of military and conflict-sustaining activities on the environment should be measured on the basis of the interdependency of natural processes. It is essential that the ILC sheds some light on these issues and develops the law in this field.

PART III

The governance of natural resources as part of conflict resolution and post-conflict peacebuilding efforts

Introductory remarks to Part III

This part discusses two distinct but interrelated issues. The first concerns approaches to stopping trade in natural resources that is used to finance armed conflicts. Addressing this issue is a prerequisite for resolving those armed conflicts. The second concerns the governance of natural resources in countries that are recovering from resource-related armed conflicts. While economic reconstruction must be an inherent part of any peacebuilding strategy, specific challenges must be addressed when natural resources play a role in armed conflicts, to either finance or sustain them. In these situations, it is often necessary to implement institutional changes regarding the governance of natural resources in order to prevent a relapse into armed conflict.

Notwithstanding the paramount importance of addressing natural resources governance as part of peacebuilding efforts, this issue has not been included in the official mandate of the UN Peacebuilding Commission, an intergovernmental advisory body established in 2005 by the UN Security Council, together with the UN General Assembly. The principal objective of the UN Peacebuilding Commission is 'to address the special needs of countries emerging from conflict towards recovery, reintegration and reconstruction and to assist them in laying the foundation for sustainable development'.[1] As part of its general mandate, the UN Peacebuilding Commission has recently started to consider issues related to natural resources management, both in a general sense and in its country specific configurations.[2] However, the practice of the UN Peacebuilding

[1] UNSC Resolution 1645 (2005), preambular para. 6; UNGA Resolution 60/180 (2005), sixth preambular paragraph. For this purpose, the UN Peacebuilding Commission has received three main tasks: (1) to bring together all relevant actors to marshal resources and to advise on and propose integrated strategies for post conflict peacebuilding and recovery; (2) to focus attention on the reconstruction and institution-building efforts necessary for recovery from conflict and to support the development of integrated strategies in order to lay the foundation for sustainable development; and (3) to provide recommendations and information to improve the coordination of all relevant actors within and outside the United Nations, to develop best practices, to help to ensure predictable financing for early recovery activities and to extend the period of attention given by the international community to postconflict recovery.

[2] The need for the UN Peacebuilding Commission to address these issues was emphasised in a 2009 UNEP report, entitled 'From Conflict to Peacebuilding: The Role of Natural Resources and the Environment'. The UNEP Report further contains a number of recommendations for the Peacebuilding Commission on the integration of natural resources management and environmental protection into its peacebuilding strategies. In response to the UNEP report, the UN Peacebuilding Commission's Working Group on Lessons Learned has issued a background paper in July 2011 on 'Economic Revitalization and Youth Employment for

Commission is still limited, preventing a systematic analysis of its work in this field. Furthermore, the Commission becomes involved at a relatively late stage, when the situation in a former conflict country has, to a certain extent, stabilised. It is submitted that, to enhance the success of the peace process in countries emerging from armed conflict, changes in the governance of natural resources must be initiated already in the phases of conflict resolution and immediate post-conflict reconstruction, which is the principal focus of this part of the study.

Recent attempts to address the governance of natural resources, and, as a prerequisite, the trade in natural resources that finance armed conflicts as part of conflict resolution and immediate post-conflict reconstruction efforts have evolved around two distinctive but interrelated approaches, namely sanctions by the Security Council under Chapter VII of the United Nations Charter on the one hand, and voluntary agreements between States and other entities related to the management of natural resources in States experiencing an armed conflict, on the other.

The United Nations Charter assigns the Security Council the primary responsibility for maintaining international peace and security.[3] It gives the Security Council a wide range of powers to perform its functions effectively. In this respect, the principal powers of the Security Council relate to its role in the pacific settlement of disputes under Chapter VI of the UN Charter and its authority to adopt coercive measures in response to threats to the peace, breaches of the peace and acts of aggression under Chapter VII of the UN Charter. Together these chapters assign the Security Council a variety of options to effectively address specific situations which constitute a threat to international peace and security.

In practice, resource-related economic measures under Article 41 of the UN Charter have been the principal means used by the Security Council to address links between natural resources and armed conflict.[4] Before the end of the Cold War, the Council only used its powers under Chapter VII once to impose resource-related coercive measures aimed at ending a

Peacebuilding', identifying natural resources management as one of the priority areas for the Peacebuilding Commission to focus on in the near future. This background paper expanded on preliminary work undertaken by this Working Group in cooperation with UNEP on 'Environment, Conflict and Peacebuilding'. Nonetheless, the proposals of the Working Group have not yet been adopted as part of the overall strategy of the Peacebuilding Commission.

[3] The legal basis for this function of the Security Council may be found in Article 24 of the UN Charter.

[4] See Le Billon, 'Natural Resources, Armed Conflicts, and the UN Security Council', p. 2.

conflict, namely in the case of natural resources originating in Southern Rhodesia.[5] Since 1990 the Council has increasingly used its powers for this purpose. Examples include diamond sanctions in the cases of Angola, Sierra Leone, Liberia and Côte d'Ivoire, petroleum sanctions in the case of Iraq and timber sanctions in the case of Liberia.[6] This practice of the Security Council reveals the recent trend towards 'smart' or 'targeted' rather than comprehensive sanctions.[7]

The Council has secured the implementation of its sanctions regimes partly through UN peace operations. The mandates of several of these operations include measures related to the enforcement of resource-related sanctions. In addition, the Council expressly included issues related to the management of natural resources in the mandate of some of these missions, most notably in those of the UN Mission in Liberia (UNMIL) and the UN Organization Stabilization Mission in the Democratic Republic of the Congo (MONUSCO).[8]

A second approach to address the link between natural resources and armed conflict, both as an alternative and complementary to Security Council sanctions, is through informal normative processes bringing together States, the business community and civil society. Examples of these include the Kimberley Process for the Certification of Rough Diamonds (KPCS), a certification mechanism which aims to curb the trade in conflict diamonds; the Extractive Industries Transparency Initiative (EITI), a mechanism which aims to increase transparency in the management of public natural resources; and the OECD Due Diligence Guidance for Responsible Supply Chains of Minerals from Conflict-Affected and High-Risk Areas, a set of guidelines which aims to increase corporate responsibility for companies operating in or sourcing from the minerals sector in fragile States.

By way of their standard-setting function, these informal normative processes can make an important contribution to reinstating and/or

[5] See UNSC Resolution 232 (1966) concerning an import ban on certain natural resources, including iron ore and copper and Resolution 253 (1968) concerning an import ban on all commodities and products.

[6] See, e.g., UNSC Resolution 1173 (1998) concerning an import ban on diamonds originating in Angola; Resolution 1306 (2000) concerning an import ban on diamonds originating in Sierra Leone and Resolution 1521 (2003) concerning an import ban on diamonds and timber products from Liberia.

[7] Cortright and Lopez (eds.), *Smart Sanctions: Targeting Economic Statecraft*.

[8] For more details on these and other peacekeeping missions, see a report issued by UNEP, 'Greening the Blue Helmets: Environment, Natural Resources and UN Peacekeeping Operations' (2012). See also Section 7.6.

improving governance of natural resources in conflict-torn States. At the same time, they signify a move away from formal treaty-making procedures, creating 'commitments' rather than legal obligations for States. This can partly be explained by a genuine desire of States to actively involve other stakeholders, principally civil society and the private sector, in efforts to address issues of general concern. However, this practice also raises more fundamental questions, particularly in relation to the efficacy of nonbinding standards to address issues of general concern as compared to binding norms resulting from formal treaty processes. In other words, are these informal normative processes credible alternatives to formal treaty processes?

Chapter 7 examines the approach of the Security Council in stopping natural resources from financing or fuelling armed conflicts and in improving the governance of natural resources in conflict-torn States, with an emphasis on sanctions regimes. The chapter discusses the contribution of sanctions to conflict resolution and, ultimately, post-conflict peacebuilding. It also examines the role of peacekeeping operations in supporting the implementation of sanctions regimes and that of the Peacebuilding Commission in consolidating the processes initiated by the Security Council. Chapter 8 examines three categories of informal normative processes. These are certification mechanisms, anti-corruption initiatives and corporate responsibility tools. Each category is discussed from the perspective of one instrument which is of particular interest for the purposes of this study.

One question that is central to both chapters concerns the ways in which these mechanisms contribute to providing structural solutions for preventing future conflicts involving natural resources in States that have experienced armed conflicts. Throughout this book it has been argued that the issue of resource governance is of central importance to prevent conflicts involving natural resources. In other words, the question is how and to what extent these mechanisms contribute to promoting adequate resource governance in countries that have experienced armed conflict. And what does 'adequate' resource governance mean in this context?

Of course, the current book can only give a glimpse into the enormous range of initiatives that – directly or indirectly – contribute to breaking the link between natural resources and armed conflict. The purpose of this book is not to give an exhaustive summary of all the initiatives, but rather to provide insight into the contribution of those approaches that have been at the forefront of efforts to break the link between natural resources and armed conflict.

7

The UN Security Council and resource-related armed conflicts

7.1 Introductory remarks

Sanctions constitute one of the principal tools of the Security Council for addressing the links between natural resources and armed conflict. Pursuant to Article 25 of the UN Charter, UN member States are obliged to implement measures taken by the Security Council under Article 41 of the UN Charter. This makes sanctions *prima facie* a particularly effective tool for addressing instances in which natural resources finance or even fuel armed conflicts.

Sanctions can involve a variety of measures, ranging from import and export embargoes and the freezing of assets to travel bans and reducing diplomatic relations. While older sanctions regimes were mainly comprehensive, covering all sorts of measures, most of the modern sanctions regimes apply so-called 'smart' sanctions. These consist of specific measures taking account of the potential impact of sanctions on vulnerable groups.[9]

Smart sanctions comprise 'targeted sanctions' designed to target specific persons or organisations and 'selective sanctions' which impose restrictions on trade in specific products.[10] Obviously this implies that commodity sanctions exclusively against particular organisations are both selective *and* targeted. However, for clarity, this chapter refers to commodity sanctions as selective sanctions, while reserving the term 'targeted' for measures that involve designating particular individuals or organisations on a sanctions list.

[9] Cortright and Lopez (eds.), *Smart Sanctions: Targeting Economic Statecraft*, p. 2.

[10] For the distinction between 'targeted' and 'selective' sanctions, see, e.g., ibid., p. 172, defining selective sanctions as less-than-comprehensive measures involving restrictions on particular products or financial flows, while targeted sanctions are described as a subset of selective sanctions, specifically aiming at narrower and more precise effects, usually directed at a particular segment of the population in the targeted State.

The Security Council has imposed several sanctions regimes to address the contribution of natural resources to armed conflict, including both selective and targeted sanctions. Examples of selective sanctions imposed by the Security Council include diamond sanctions in the cases of Angola, Sierra Leone, Liberia and Côte d'Ivoire and timber sanctions in the cases of Cambodia and Liberia. Examples of targeted sanctions imposed in relation to natural resources include travel bans and asset freezes in the cases of the DR Congo and Libya. In addition, in the case of the DR Congo, the Security Council developed an innovative approach, consisting of the direct targeting of companies which do not respect due diligence requirements.

In the Presidential Statement of 25 June 2007, the President of the Security Council clarified the objectives of the sanctions regimes adopted by the Security Council in order to address the link between natural resources and armed conflict:

> [t]he Security Council, through its resolutions, has taken measures on [the issue of natural resources contributing to armed conflict], more specifically to prevent illegal exploitation of natural resources, especially diamonds and timber, from fuelling armed conflicts and to encourage transparent and lawful management of natural resources, including the clarification of the responsibility of management of natural resources.[11]

This chapter aims to explore to what extent the Security Council resolutions have actually gone beyond merely sanctioning the illegal trafficking of natural resources and have addressed issues relating to the governance of natural resources. In particular, the question arises of whether these resolutions have set standards for the management of natural resources. If so, is the Security Council the appropriate body to do so or is the Council exceeding its authority here?

To answer these questions, this chapter traces the evolution of the Security Council's approach to addressing the role of natural resources in financing armed conflicts. It analyses several sanctions regimes established by the Security Council to address specific conflicts financed by natural resources from the 1960s to the present. The chapter examines the overall structure and objectives of the sanctions regimes, as well as the targets and addressees of the sanctions obligations. In addition, it takes a closer

[11] Statement by the President of the Security Council of 25 June 2007, *UN Doc. S/PRST/2007/22*, para. 6.

look at the ways in which the mandates of UN peacekeeping missions and the practice of the UN Peacebuilding Commission implement and consolidate the decisions and recommendations included in the Council's resolutions.

Section 7.2 defines the role of sanctions in the particular context of resource-related armed conflicts. Section 7.3 then takes a closer look at two older sanctions regimes which paved the way for the new generation of smart sanctions. These are the 232 Southern Rhodesia Sanctions Regime and the 661 Iraq Sanctions Regime. Section 7.4 examines selective commodity sanctions imposed by the Security Council in relation to resource-related armed conflicts. These are the 792 Cambodia Sanctions Regime, the 864 UNITA Sanctions Regime, the 1132 Sierra Leone Sanctions Regime, the 1343 and 1521 Liberia Sanctions Regimes, and the 1572 Côte d'Ivoire Sanctions Regime. Section 7.5 takes a closer look at the Security Council's use of targeted sanctions in order to put an end to resource driven conflicts. This section discusses the 1493 DR Congo Sanctions Regime and the 1970 Libya Sanctions Regime. Section 7.6 focuses on the role of peacekeeping operations in giving effect to the Council's decisions and recommendations, while Section 7.7 examines the role of the UN Peacebuilding Commission in consolidating the approach set out by the UN Security Council in the conflict resolution phase. Finally, Section 7.8 discusses the evolution of the Security Council's approach to sanctions in the context of resource-related armed conflicts. It also examines the implications of the approach developed by the Security Council for its contribution to promoting sustainable resource governance in specific conflict situations.

7.2 General remarks concerning sanctions

Georges Abi-Saab provided a generally accepted definition of sanctions as 'coercive measures taken against a target State or entity in application of a decision by a socially competent organ'.[12] Most of the elements of this definition accurately reflect the sanctions regimes discussed in this chapter, which target States, individuals or non-State entities, such as non-State armed groups and corporations. They are imposed by the Security Council on the basis of the role assigned to it by Article 24 of the UN Charter. In addition, most of the sanctions regimes examined in this

[12] Abi-Saab, 'The Concept of Sanction in International Law', p. 39.

chapter are imposed pursuant to decisions of the Security Council taken under Chapter VII of the UN Charter.[13]

On the basis of Chapter VII of the UN Charter, the Security Council may adopt measures pursuant to Article 41 of the UN Charter once it has determined the existence of a threat to the peace, a breach of the peace or an act of aggression under Article 39 of the UN Charter. Furthermore, it may do so only in order to 'maintain or restore international peace and security'. These requirements have two important implications for the Security Council's ability to act.

First of all, Article 39 defines the purposes and legal basis for Security Council action. As Hans Kelsen had already noted in 1950, '[t]he purpose of the enforcement action under Article 39 is not: to maintain or restore the law, but to maintain, or restore peace, which is not necessarily identical with the law'.[14] In other words, the authority of the Security Council to take measures under Chapter VII of the UN Charter is not dependent on

[13] It is relevant to note here that only *decisions* of the Security Council are binding on Member States pursuant to Article 25 of the UN Charter. Several factors should be taken into account in order to determine whether particular measures imposed by the Security Council are binding on States or not. In this respect, see the approach set out by the International Court of Justice in its Namibia and Kosovo Opinions. In the Namibia Advisory Opinion, the Court determined that a conclusion regarding the binding nature of a Security Council Resolution can only be made after careful analysis of its language. According to the Court, the question of whether the powers under Article 25 of the UN Charter have been exercised 'is to be determined in each case, having regard to the terms of the resolution to be interpreted, the discussions leading to it, the Charter provisions invoked and, in general, all circumstances that might assist in determining the legal consequences of the resolution of the Security Council'. International Court of Justice, Legal Consequences for States of the Continued Presence of South Africa in Namibia (South West Africa) notwithstanding Security Council Resolution 276 (1970), Advisory Opinion of 21 June 1971, *I.C.J. Reports 1971*, p. 53, para. 114. In the Kosovo Advisory Opinion, the Court explained the differences between the interpretation of treaties and the interpretation of Security Council resolutions, determining that other factors must be taken into account in interpreting Security Council resolutions, especially in relation to their drafting process and legal effects. International Court of Justice, Accordance with International Law of the Unilateral Declaration of Independence in Respect of Kosovo, Advisory Opinion of 22 July 2010, *I.C.J. Reports (2010)*, p. 403, para. 94. Also see M.C. Wood, 'The Interpretation of Security Council Resolutions', in *Max Planck Yearbook of United Nations Law* (1998), pp. 73–95. *Security Council Report, Special Research Report 2008, No. 1* on Security Council Action under Chapter VII: Myths and Realities, 23 June 2008, pp. 9–12, available at www.securitycouncilreport.org, consulted on 24 June 2008. For a discussion of the Namibia opinion, see Greig, *Invalidity and the Law of Treaties*, London: British Institute of International and Comparative Law (2006), pp. 166–80.

[14] Kelsen, *The Law of the United Nations*, p. 294. Also see Crawford, 'The Relationship between Sanctions and Countermeasures', pp. 58–9; and Van den Herik, Individualizing Enforcement in International Law.

determining that there has been a violation of international law, but rather that a particular situation constitutes a threat to international peace and security.

This means that the Security Council can address situations that are perfectly legal – such as the exploitation of natural resources by a State and the use of the proceeds to finance an armed conflict – but which pose a threat to international peace and security anyway. For the purposes of the present study, this means that the Security Council may qualify the right of a State to exercise permanent sovereignty over its natural resources when it considers this necessary to maintain or restore international peace and security. An internal uprising against the government of a State is another relevant example. International law does not formally oppose waging a civil war. However, such a situation may constitute a threat to peace and security, and the Council can act against that – for example, by imposing sanctions against natural resources used by the rebel forces to finance their armed struggle.

The second implication of Article 39 of the UN Charter regarding the Security Council's ability to act is that it limits the powers of the Security Council. Article 39 provides that the Security Council can only take measures pursuant to Articles 41 and 42 of the UN Charter 'in order to maintain or restore international peace and security'. For internal armed conflicts, this means that the Security Council can, in principle, impose sanctions only if these armed conflicts pose a threat to *international* peace and security. In practice, the Security Council has adopted a flexible approach in this respect. It has imposed sanctions to address threats arising from internal situations with a potential cross-border impact, as well as to address threats ensuing from purely 'internal' situations, such as the large-scale violation of human rights by governments.[15]

Furthermore, Security Council measures do not necessarily have to target States.[16] The behaviour of non-State entities, such as armed groups, can also trigger Security Council action. Many of the sanctions regimes

[15] This is linked to the doctrine of the responsibility to protect, as recognised in paras. 138 and 139 of the 2005 World Summit Outcome Document, which formulates a responsibility for States to protect their populations from genocide, war crimes, ethnic cleansing and crimes against humanity as well as a responsibility for the international community to intervene when a State does not respect his responsibilities. See World Summit Outcome Document, *UN Doc. A/60/L.1* of 15 September 2005.

[16] See Pellet and Miron, 'Sanctions', para. 22, who argue that 'the elasticity of the notion of a threat to, or breach of, the peace was accompanied by an enlargement of the category of targeted entities; as a consequence, it is no longer necessary that a violation of international law amounting to a threat to the peace be attributable to a State in order to justify the

discussed in this chapter target non-State armed groups. Examples include the sanctions regime imposed against the National Union for the Total Independence of Angola (UNITA) in Angola and against the RUF and other rebel groups in Sierra Leone.

This targeting of entities other than States also has implications for the definition of sanctions itself. It highlights an important problem inherent in Abi-Saab's definition, at least for the purposes of the current study. This problem arises from the interpretation of the term 'coercive'. According to Abi-Saab, 'coercive' implies that measures are 'taken against the will of the target State at least without its consent' and 'to the detriment of the target State'.[17] However, this view of sanctions, based on the idea that sanctions are measures that intend to cause harm to a particular State, does not correspond very well with the *rationale* behind many of the sanctions regimes discussed in the present chapter.

Many of the sanctions regimes discussed in this chapter are in fact imposed to assist governments in regaining control over a State's natural resources. Examples include the diamond sanctions imposed against UNITA in Angola and against the RUF and other rebel groups in Sierra Leone. In some cases, sanctions have even been imposed at the request of the government of a target State. The diamond sanctions imposed in relation to the conflicts in Angola, Sierra Leone and Côte d'Ivoire are examples of this.[18] Another example concerns the endorsement by the Security Council of a national ban on timber in Cambodia, imposed to cut off the Khmer Rouge from timber revenues.

Instead of being defined as 'coercive measures' as Abi-Saab does, sanctions can therefore be regarded in a less intrusive way in this context as economic or diplomatic measures aimed at constraining the actors against which they are imposed, whether these actors are States or non-State actors. More in general, the sanctions imposed by the Security Council in this context could be described as measures aimed at assisting a particular State to address a threat to the peace coming from within its borders.

Some final remarks can be made with regard to the operation of sanctions regimes, in particular with respect to the role of Expert Panels and Sanctions Committees. Most contemporary sanctions regimes discussed in this chapter make use of 'smart sanctions' which are tailored to address a specific situation. To make an informed decision about the type of

imposition of sanctions. Individuals or groups can violate international law and be subject to sanctions'.

[17] Ibid. [18] These examples are discussed in more detail in Section 7.4.

measures to impose, the Security Council has increasingly relied on Expert Panels to provide the information necessary to tailor its sanctions. These Expert Panels are established on the basis of Article 29 of the UN Charter, which permits the Security Council to establish subsidiary bodies to assist it in the performance of its functions.[19]

Panel reports have extensively documented the role played by natural resources in the conflicts discussed in this chapter. In addition, their findings on sanctions busting in particular conflicts, such as those in Angola, Sierra Leone and the DR Congo, have been instrumental in the Security Council's embracing new approaches to tackle the trade in 'conflict resources'. These include the KPCS and the due diligence requirements formulated by the Group of Experts on the DR Congo, discussed later in this chapter.

In addition to Panels of Experts, the Security Council has established Sanctions Committees, mandated with the monitoring and implementation of sanctions regimes. The composition of the Sanctions Committees is similar to that of the Security Council itself. These committees play an important role in the application of sanctions. They are often entrusted with the task of designating persons or entities to apply targeted sanctions. Furthermore, they provide the Security Council with information on the implementation of the sanctions regime by States. Their regular reports to the Security Council, supplemented by the reports of the Panels of Experts, are vital to the proper functioning of sanctions regimes.

7.3 Early examples of resource-related sanctions regimes

The current section discusses two early sanctions regimes imposed by the Security Council which rely principally on comprehensive sanctions, and which involve natural resources.[20] In the case of Southern Rhodesia, selective sanctions against natural resources were imposed as a first measure, before the sanctions regime was made comprehensive. In the case of Iraq, the sanctions regime provided a conditional exemption from the comprehensive regime for the export of limited quantities of oil.

[19] For an overview of committees established pursuant to this provision, see Farrall, *United Nations Sanctions and the Rule of Law*, pp. 146–81.

[20] The link with natural resources is what distinguishes these sanctions regimes from other regimes which contain import prohibitions, such as the sanctions regime imposed against the Federal Republic of Yugoslavia (Serbia and Montenegro) through UNSC Resolution 757 (1992).

7.3.1 The 232 Southern Rhodesia Sanctions Regime

Structure and objectives of the sanctions regime

The sanctions regime issued against Southern Rhodesia in 1966 was the first ever imposed by the Security Council.[21] Its aim was to put an end to the white minority regime established in Southern Rhodesia in 1965 and to enable the population of Southern Rhodesia to exercise their right to self-determination. The first resolution adopted by the Security Council with regard to the situation in Southern Rhodesia called upon all States to break off all economic relations with Southern Rhodesia, but the associated measures did not comprise any import prohibitions and were not taken pursuant to Chapter VII of the UN Charter.[22]

It was only a year later, with the adoption of Resolution 232 (1966), that the Security Council imposed mandatory sanctions based on Article 41 of the UN Charter against the illegal authorities in Southern Rhodesia. These sanctions included an import embargo for UN member States on a range of commodities, including several minerals, sugar, tobacco, meat and other animal products, targeting not only the direct import of these commodities, but also all activities undertaken by UN member States within their territory or by their nationals that would promote the export of the banned commodities from Southern Rhodesia.[23] The import embargo was accompanied by export embargos for UN member States with regard to the supply of oil or oil products, arms and military and transport material to Southern Rhodesia.[24]

Resolution 253 (1968) subsequently transformed the selective regime set up by Resolution 232 into a comprehensive regime, extending sanctions to all products and commodities originating from or destined to Southern Rhodesia, with the exception of some products that were very

[21] For more details regarding this sanctions regime, see Kuyper, *The Implementation of International Sanctions*; and Farrall, *United Nations Sanctions and the Rule of Law*, pp. 247–53.

[22] See UNSC Resolution 217 (1965), especially para. 8, and Farrall, *United Nations Sanctions and the Rule of Law*, p. 248, who labels these sanctions as voluntary in nature. Earlier, the UN General Assembly had already called upon all States to refrain from rendering assistance to the white minority regime and had, subsequently, condemned the unilateral declaration of independence made by the racialist minority regime. See UNGA Resolutions 2022 (XX) of 5 November 1965 and 2024 (XX) on the Question of Southern Rhodesia of 11 November 1965.

[23] See UNSC Resolution 232 (1966), especially paras. 2(a) and (b).

[24] Ibid., especially paras. 2(d), (e) and (f).

important for the local population,[25] such as medical supplies, educational materials and, under certain conditions, foodstuffs.[26]

The same resolution established a committee to monitor the implementation of the sanctions regime, also known as the 'Watchdog Committee'.[27] The mandate of this committee, which was to examine reports and seek information from States and specialised agencies regarding the implementation of Resolution 253 (1968), was rather modest compared to modern sanctions committees.[28] Nevertheless, the establishment of the Committee provided the Security Council with the opportunity to experiment with the implementation of sanctions by subsidiary bodies.

In subsequent years the Security Council adopted several resolutions building on the sanctions regime established in Resolutions 232 and 253. Unfortunately the sanctions were not particularly effective. Many countries, including Portugal and South Africa, continued to trade with the illegal white minority regime.[29] In 1979, the sanctions were finally lifted after a political solution to the situation had been reached and when Zimbabwe emerged as a newly independent State.[30]

Targets and addressees of the sanctions obligations

The sanctions regime against Southern Rhodesia targeted in particular the *de facto* government in that country, i.e., the illegitimate white minority regime. It was aimed at strengthening the efforts of the United Kingdom to end the illegal situation in its former colony in order to realise the right of the black majority in the country to self-determination pursuant to the UN Charter and the UN General Assembly's Decolonisation Declaration. In this way, the sanctions regime indirectly provided support not only to the United Kingdom, but also to armed groups within the country opposing the political authorities.

The obligation to implement the sanctions was imposed on all States. In the first place, it was imposed on UN member States by Article 25 of the UN Charter. However, the resolutions also urged non-UN member

25 See UNSC Resolution 253 (1968), especially para. 3.

26 Ibid., especially para. 3(d).

27 Ibid., especially para. 20. See on this committee, Kuyper, 'The Limits of Supervision', pp. 159–94.

28 Ibid.; and De Wet, Nollkaemper and Dijkstra (eds.), *Review of the Security Council by Member States*, pp. 50–51.

29 See Schrijver, 'The Use of Economic Sanctions by the UN Security Council', p. 130.

30 See UNSC Resolution 460 (1979).

States to implement the measures with a general appeal to the principles stated in Article 2 of the UN Charter.[31]

Appraisal of the sanctions regime

The sanctions regime imposed against Southern Rhodesia was the first time the Security Council adopted sanctions in order to apply economic pressure to an entity as a response to a threat to the peace. It did so in the first instance by imposing selective commodity sanctions. In this respect, it can be seen as a predecessor of later sanctions regimes targeting particular commodities in order to restore international peace and security.

However, there are also important differences from later sanctions regimes. While the sanctions regime started with the imposition of selective sanctions, it soon became comprehensive. Furthermore, even the selective sanctions imposed by the Security Council in relation to Southern Rhodesia were rather blunt compared to later sanctions regimes. The Security Council simply targeted all primary export products from the Southern Rhodesian State, without examining their precise contribution to keeping the illegal minority regime in power.

Therefore, the aim of the sanctions was simply to put pressure on the Rhodesian authorities by targeting all their sources of income. It did not take into account the impact of the commodity sanctions on the civilian population. The humanitarian exemptions introduced by the Security Council were not related to the commodity sanctions, as these were introduced only after the sanctions regime had become comprehensive.[32]

The sanctions regime imposed against Southern Rhodesia can therefore be considered as the first experiment of the Security Council with the instrument of economic sanctions. Arguably, the poor compliance of States with the sanctions constituted an important lesson for the Security Council. It laid the foundations for a more active role of the Security Council in the enforcement of sanctions applied subsequently in the sanctions regime imposed against Iraq in 1990.

[31] See UNSC Resolution 232 (1966), especially para. 7 and Resolution 253 (1968), especially para. 14. It must be remembered that Article 2(6) of the UN Charter states that the United Nations 'shall ensure that states which are not Members of the United Nations act in accordance with [the] Principles [set out in Article 2 of the UN Charter] so far as may be necessary for the maintenance of international peace and security'.

[32] See UNSC Resolution 253 (1968), especially para. 3(d).

7.3.2 *The 661 Iraq Sanctions Regime*

Structure and objectives of the sanctions regime

The sanctions regime against Iraq was imposed in 1990 after Iraq's unlawful invasion and occupation of neighbouring Kuwait.[33] Its original purpose was to put pressure on Iraq to withdraw from Kuwait and to restore Kuwait's sovereignty, independence and territorial integrity.[34] The measures imposed by the Security Council included a comprehensive import and export embargo, as well as an assets freeze.[35] Humanitarian exemptions were provided for medicines and health supplies, as well as essential foodstuffs strictly meant for the civilian population.[36] A Sanctions Committee was established to monitor the implementation of the sanctions.[37]

After Operation Desert Storm, the sanctions regime against Iraq was maintained but its purposes were modified to accommodate the new situation. The new objectives included the disarmament of Iraq and the creation of a fund to pay reparations for damage inflicted by Iraq during the Gulf War.[38] In addition, the exemptions from the export embargo were broadened to cover all foodstuffs submitted to a special committee under a 'no objections procedure'.[39] Furthermore, Resolution 687 (1991) provided specifically for the possibility of lifting the import embargo when Iraq fully complied with the requirements set out in the resolution.[40]

A further relaxation of the sanctions regime was realised with the adoption of the so-called Oil-for-Food programme, which allowed Iraq

33 For more details regarding this sanctions regime, see Manusama, *The United Nations Security Council in the Post-Cold War Era*, pp. 138–49; Farrall, *United Nations Sanctions and the Rule of Law*, pp. 261–81; and Cortright, Lopez and Gerber-Stellingwerf, 'Sanctions', pp. 350–52. See also the report of the Dutch Commission of Inquiry upon Iraq, *Rapport Commissie van onderzoek besluitvorming Irak* (Commissie Davids), Amsterdam: Boom Publishers, pp. 229–36.

34 See UNSC Resolution 661 (1990), second paragraph of the preamble.

35 Ibid., especially para. 3. 36 Ibid., especially para. 3(c). 37 Ibid., especially para. 6.

38 See UNSC Resolutions 686 and 687 (1991). Reference is made in particular to Iraq's liability for environmental damage and the depletion of natural resources as a result of the setting on fire of Kuwaiti oil wells by Iraq during the conflict. See UNSC Resolution 687 (1991), especially para. 16.

39 See UNSC Resolution 687 (1991), especially para. 20. The committee is further referred to as 'the 661 sanctions committee'.

40 These requirements include the destruction, removal or rendering harmless of chemical and biological weapons as well as a prohibition on acquiring or developing nuclear weapons. See UNSC Resolution 687 (1991), especially paras. 7–14 and 22.

to export controlled quantities of oil in order to provide the population with the basic means of subsistence.[41] States wishing to import oil from Iraq were to ask the 661 Sanctions Committee to approve each individual purchase,[42] and payment was to be made to an escrow account established by the Secretary-General exclusively to meet the purposes of Resolution 986 (1995).[43]

The responsibility for the distribution of humanitarian goods to the civilian population was left with the government of Iraq, provided that Iraq effectively guaranteed an equitable distribution of goods to every sector of the Iraqi population throughout the country.[44] However, an exception was made for three provinces in northern Iraq, where the UN would resume responsibility for the distribution of humanitarian goods.[45]

The Oil-for-Food programme was revised once more in Resolution 1409 (2002), which introduced a Goods Review List. The new scheme allowed all goods to be exported to Iraq, except those listed in the Goods Review List.[46] The programme and the sanctions regime ended shortly after the fall of the Hussein regime in 2003.[47]

Targets and addressees of the sanctions obligations

The sanctions regime against Iraq targeted the government of Iraq. Although it originally also comprised products from Kuwait, it was adjusted as soon as Kuwait was liberated from Iraqi occupation in early 1991. Furthermore, like the regime against Southern Rhodesia, all States, including nonmember States of the United Nations, were requested to implement the regime.[48]

However, the most notable feature of the sanctions regime was the role of international organisations in the implementation of the sanctions. Even at an early stage, international organisations were expressly called upon to implement the arms embargo.[49] The role of United

[41] This was a concession to the government of Iraq, which had not accepted the original proposal for an Oil-for-Food-Programme as envisaged by the Security Council. The original proposal, set out in UNSC Resolutions 706 (1991) and 712 (1991), granted full control over the sale of Iraqi oil to the United Nations.

[42] See UNSC Resolution 986 (1995), especially para. 1(a).

[43] Ibid., especially paras. 1(b), 7 and 8.

[44] Ibid., preamble and especially para. 8(a)(ii).

[45] Ibid., especially para. 8(b).

[46] See UNSC Resolutions 1409 (2002) and 1382 (2001). For the Goods Review List, see *UN Doc. S/2002/515*.

[47] See UNSC Resolution 1483 (2003), especially paras. 10 and 16.

[48] See UNSC Resolution 661 (1990), para. 5.

[49] See, e.g., UNSC Resolution 687 (1991), especially para. 25.

Nations organs – in particular of the Sanctions Committee and the Secretary-General – is the most significant with regard to implementing the commodity-related sanctions. The responsibilities of the Sanctions Committee established pursuant to Resolution 661 (1990) to monitor the implementation of the sanctions included monitoring the export of oil from Iraq.[50] The Secretary-General was also requested to open an escrow account for the administration of the oil revenues and to appoint independent and certified public accountants to audit the account.[51]

The account was to be used by the United Nations for several purposes, *inter alia*, to provide humanitarian relief to the Iraqi population and to ensure reparation for the damage caused by Iraq to Kuwait during the first Gulf War. In this respect, it is interesting to note that in addition to damage caused to Kuwaiti assets, Iraq was also held liable for the depletion of natural resources and environmental damage resulting from its unlawful invasion and occupation of Kuwait. For this reason, a special compensation fund was established, supervised by the United Nations Compensation Commission.[52]

Appraisal of the sanctions regime

The sanctions regime in Iraq is an example of a comprehensive sanctions regime. However, as in the case of Southern Rhodesia, specific exemptions to the sanctions regime were provided for humanitarian purposes. Interestingly, these exemptions related to the export of oil, a conflict-sustaining commodity. This was done through the Oil-for-Food programme, which was aimed at mitigating the negative effects of the sanctions on the Iraqi population and ensuring that the Iraqi population had the basic means of subsistence at its disposal.

One interesting aspect of the sanctions regime against Iraq as it evolved is that it upheld the sovereignty and territorial integrity of Iraq, as well as the principle of permanent sovereignty over natural resources.[53] The Oil-for-Food programme permitted the Iraqi government to export small

50 See UNSC Resolutions 986 (1995), especially para. 6.

51 Ibid., especially para. 7. For more details on the administration of the escrow account, see Memorandum of understanding between the Secretariat of the United Nations and the Government of Iraq on the implementation of Security Council Resolution 986 (1995), *UN Doc. S/1996/356* of 20 May 1996.

52 For more details, see Elias, 'Sustainable Development, War Reparations and Environmental Damage', pp. 67–90 and Schrijver, *Development without Destruction*, pp. 179–80.

53 See, e.g., UNSC Resolutions 986 (1995), fifth preambular paragraph, which makes general reference to the sovereignty and territorial integrity of Iraq.

quantities of oil in order to provide the Iraqi population with the basic means of subsistence. This was not a deliberate choice based on the principle of permanent sovereignty, but one dictated by political reality. Saddam Hussein refused to accept the scheme unless he retained a minimum of control over the oil resources.

Another interesting aspect of the sanctions regime against Iraq is that it was the first to envisage an active role for the United Nations in the management of natural resources as part of conflict resolution. Although watered down to accommodate the wishes of Saddam Hussein, the sanctions regime still assigned a significant role to the UN. The UN assumed full responsibility for the administration of the revenues obtained from the export of oil from Iraq. A special fund was created for this purpose, which was maintained even after the sanctions regime was lifted as a result of the removal of the Saddam Hussein regime. It was then renamed 'Development Fund for Iraq' and its administration was placed in the hands of the Central Bank of Iraq, monitored by representatives of the UN, the IMF, the Arab Fund for Social and Economic Development and the World Bank.[54]

Arguably, the sanctions regime proved to be instrumental in removing the threat posed by Iraqi weapons of mass destruction.[55] The best proof of this was delivered in 2003 after the US-led invasion of Iraq. Despite suspicions that Iraq had a vast arsenal of weapons, no such weapons were actually found. However, it remains unclear in what way the sanctions contributed to this result. Were the sanctions successful because they curtailed Saddam Hussein's ability to stockpile weapons of mass destruction or were they successful in compelling Iraq to comply with the conditions set out in Resolution 687 (1991) for the removal of the sanctions, which included the destruction of the existing arsenal of weapons of mass destruction?

The administration of the Oil-for-Food programme by the UN proved problematic. An Independent Inquiry Committee, established to assess the performance of the UN in this respect, issued a very critical report in 2005 regarding the UN's management of Iraqi oil. The Inquiry Committee found gross irregularities in the administration of the oil proceeds. In addition, it concluded that the operational structure of the programme

[54] See UNSC Resolution 1483 (2003), especially para. 12.

[55] See Cortright, Lopez and Gerber-Stellingwerf, 'Sanctions', p. 351. For a different view, see the Report of the Dutch Committee of Inquiry on Iraq (Commissie Davids). This report signals the problem of sanctions busting by States.

had several deficiencies, including a lack of clarity about the distribution of responsibilities for the implementation of the programme.[56] Other reports highlighted the manipulation of the Oil-for-Food programme by Saddam Hussein and the impact of the programme on the Iraqi population. All in all, the reports did not paint a rosy picture of the Oil-for-Food programme.[57]

Despite its many deficiencies, the Oil-for-Food programme served as a model for subsequent sanctions regimes. It was a precedent for the more active involvement of the United Nations, and especially of the Security Council, in the management of natural resources in the context of conflict resolution.

7.3.3 *Comparing the sanctions regimes*

The sanctions regime against Iraq, like the regime against Southern Rhodesia, targeted the behaviour of a State rather than non-State actors. However, the objective of the sanctions regime against Iraq differed significantly from that of the sanctions regime imposed against Southern Rhodesia. While the latter was aimed at resolving an essentially internal situation, i.e., to bring the rebellion in Southern Rhodesia to an end,[58] the former was aimed first and foremost at reducing the threat of Iraq to other States.[59]

Another major difference concerns the operation of the sanctions regimes, in particular with respect to the role of commodities. In the case of Southern Rhodesia, the sanctions regime originally targeted selective commodities that supported the Rhodesian economy, but the measures themselves were all-inclusive. No exemptions were provided for humanitarian purposes. It was only after the regime became comprehensive that exemptions were provided, but these exemptions concerned the import into Rhodesia of humanitarian goods – including educational materials – and were unrelated to the targeted commodities. In contrast, the

[56] See Independent Inquiry Committee into the United Nations Oil-for-Food Programme, The Management of the United Nations Oil-for-Food Programme, Report of the Committee, Vol. I (2005), in particular pp. 60–62.

[57] All reports are available through www.iic-offp.org/documents.htm.

[58] See UNSC Resolution 232 (1966), second paragraph of the preamble.

[59] See UNSC Resolution 661 (1990), second paragraph of the preamble and Resolution 687 (1991), para. 24 of the preamble. However, it must be noted that Resolution 687 also mentions Iraq's threat to use chemical weapons amongst the reasons for imposing sanctions. This must be read against the background of Saddam Hussein's earlier attacks against the Kurdish population in the North.

sanctions regime was comprehensive from the beginning in Iraq, but it did provide specific exemptions for humanitarian purposes for the export of oil, a conflict-sustaining commodity.

In other words, the sanctions regime in Iraq established a direct link between the sanctions themselves and exemptions to the regime. As shown in this chapter, this direct link between sanctions and exemptions became a characteristic of the approach developed by the Security Council in subsequent sanctions regimes. However, the sanctions regime imposed against Iraq also taught the Security Council some important lessons. The comprehensive regime might have been effective, but it also led to a humanitarian crisis in Iraq. For these reasons, the Security Council further refined its methods as part of its policy of 'smart sanctions'.[60]

7.4 Selective commodity sanctions

This section discusses sanctions regimes that have been imposed for specific natural resources which were believed to contribute directly to sustaining armed conflicts. Some of the decisions to impose sanctions against particular commodities were based on reports by investigative bodies, such as Panels of Experts and Monitoring Mechanisms established by the Security Council. However, public concern raised by campaigns by NGOs such as Global Witness and Partnership Africa Canada has also played a significant role in convincing the Security Council to take action in particular cases, notably in Angola and Sierra Leone. Finally, it is striking that in most situations, the Council's action was triggered by the national State itself requesting the Security Council to take measures targeting particular commodities.

7.4.1 The 792 Cambodia Sanctions Regime

Structure and objectives of the sanctions regime

The sanctions regime imposed in relation to the conflict in Cambodia differs significantly from all other sanctions regimes discussed in this

[60] Mention must be made in this regard of the Interlaken, Bonn and Stockholm processes which delivered the necessary input for the Security Council's policy reforms. On these processes, see the Watson's Institute background paper on targeted sanctions, available through www.watsoninstitute.org/pub/Background_Paper_Targeted_Sanctions.pdf as well as the white paper prepared by this same institute, entitled 'Strengthening Targeted Sanctions through Fair and Clear Procedures', 30 March 2006, available through www.watsoninstitute.org/pub/Strengthening_Targeted_Sanctions.pdf.

chapter. The most important difference is to be found in its legal basis. The sanctions regime imposed in relation to the conflict in Cambodia was not imposed by the Security Council itself. Rather, the Security Council expressed support for sanctions imposed by the national authorities of Cambodia. This explains also why the Security Council did not invoke Chapter VII of the UN Charter, which provides the legal basis for imposing sanctions.[61] Furthermore, the Security Council refrains from using hortatory language in relation to the measures regarding natural resources, which suggests that these measures are not legally binding on States. These choices are explained by the political background of the conflict.

The internal armed conflict in Cambodia started in the late 1960s. In 1975, the Khmer Rouge took control and renamed the country 'Democratic Kampuchea'. The Khmer Rouge established a regime of terror and committed many international crimes.[62] In response to the brutalities committed by the Khmer Rouge regime against the Cambodian population, Vietnamese troops invaded the country in 1978 to assist Cambodian opposition forces in removing the Khmer Rouge regime from power. In 1979, the opposition forces installed a new government and renamed the country 'People's Republic of Kampuchea', while the ousted Khmer Rouge regime – together with two other resistance groups – formed the Coalition Government of Democratic Kampuchea.[63]

Vietnam's intervention in Cambodia created a difficult situation for the UN and the General Assembly was deeply divided on the issue. It finally adopted a resolution greatly regretting the Vietnamese armed intervention and calling for the immediate withdrawal of all foreign forces from Cambodia.[64] However, this resolution was adopted with 91 in favour,

[61] It must be noted that the Security Council can only impose sanctions pursuant to Article 41 of the UN Charter, which is part of Chapter VII of the UN Charter. Obviously, the Security Council need not expressly invoke Chapter VII when it imposes sanctions. Moreover, the Security Council can also take binding decisions other than sanctions, pursuant either to Chapter VI or to Chapter VII of the UN Charter. Whether measures imposed by the Security Council are legally binding has to be determined through a careful analysis of the text of the resolution, its objectives and the context of its adoption. See supra, note 13.

[62] These international crimes, including genocide and crimes against humanity, are currently being investigated by a hybrid criminal tribunal, set up by the UN and the Cambodian government. This tribunal is officially called the Extraordinary Chambers in the Courts of Cambodia for the Prosecution of Crimes Committed during the Period of Democratic Kampuchea.

[63] For more details on the situation in Cambodia, see Vickery, *Cambodia 1975–82*.

[64] UNGA Resolution 34/22 of 14 November 1979, para. 2 of the preamble and especially para. 7.

while 50 States voted against or abstained.[65] Meanwhile, the UN Security Council was paralysed due to serious tensions between China and the Soviet Union, both supporting their respective allies.[66] China, supported by the West, submitted two draft resolutions addressing the situation in Cambodia, calling on all parties to cease combat and to withdraw all foreign forces from Cambodia. Neither was put to the vote.[67]

This deadlock lasted until the end of the Cold War in 1989, when the five permanent members of the Security Council, together with all the Cambodian factions and the Association of Southeast Asian Nations, participated in a peace conference in Paris in order to resolve the Cambodian conflict.[68] This was the first of several meetings aimed at reaching a political settlement. In an unprecedented move, the five permanent members of the Security Council issued a statement in 1990 introducing the framework for the Cambodian peace process.[69] The framework consisted of five key elements necessary for the restoration of peace in Cambodia. These included transitional arrangements for the administration of Cambodia during the pre-election period, military arrangements during the transitional period, the preparation of elections under the auspices of the United Nations and special measures to assure the protection of human rights.[70]

The framework document also outlined two important institutional arrangements. The first was the establishment of a Supreme National

[65] See Benvenisti, *The International Law of Occupation*, 2nd edn., pp. 185–7. In addition, Falk, 'The Complexities of Humanitarian Intervention', pp. 504–5.

[66] China supported the Coalition Government, while the Soviet Union supported the new government. Tensions ran extremely high when China invaded Vietnam on 17 February 1979 as a countermeasure to Vietnam's foreign politics, including its invasion of Cambodia. Chinese troops withdrew a month later. For more details on this conflict and on the difficult relationship between China and Vietnam during these years, see Chen, *China's War with Vietnam, 1979.*

[67] See *Repertoire of the Practice of the Security Council 1975–1980*, Chapter XI, p. 396.

[68] See Keller, 'Cambodia Conflicts (Kampuchea)', para. 12.

[69] Letter Dated 30 August 1990 from the Permanent Representatives of China, France, the Union of Soviet Socialist Republics, the United Kingdom of Great Britain and Northern Ireland and the United States of America to the United Nations Addressed to the Secretary-General, *UN Doc. A/45/472 and S/21689*, 31 August 1990. For more details on the Paris Agreements, see Ratner, 'The Cambodia Settlement Agreements', pp. 1–41.

[70] For more details, see the Letter Dated 30 August 1990 from the Permanent Representatives of China, France, the Union of Soviet Socialist Republics, the United Kingdom of Great Britain and Northern Ireland and the United States of America to the United Nations Addressed to the Secretary-General, *UN Doc. A/45/472 and S/21689*, 31 August 1990.

Council of Cambodia (SNC), consisting of all the Cambodian factions, as the legitimate representative of Cambodia.[71] The second was the proposal to increase the role of the United Nations in the peace process with the establishment of a United Nations Transitional Authority in Cambodia (UNTAC), comprising a military and a civilian component.[72] After being accepted by the Cambodian factions, the Security Council adopted Resolution 668 (1990), in which it endorsed the framework and welcomed the commitment of the Cambodian parties to work together with the participants of the Paris conference to elaborate the framework for a comprehensive political settlement.[73] This led to the signing of the Paris Peace Agreements in 1991.

Despite the progress made in many fields, the peace process proved cumbersome. One of the major factions, the Khmer Rouge, withdrew from the peace process and continued fighting. It financed its activities by issuing timber concessions to Thai logging companies and by smuggling gems.[74] The Security Council repeatedly stressed the need for all the factions to comply with the peace agreements, but it did not take any further action.[75]

It was only after the SNC adopted a moratorium on the export of logs from Cambodia to put pressure on the Khmer Rouge that the Security Council took further action, although, as stated previously, without invoking Chapter VII of the UN Charter. In Resolution 792 (1992), the Security Council expressed support for the moratorium. It also requested other States to respect the moratorium by not importing logs from Cambodia and requested UNTAC to take appropriate measures to ensure the implementation of the moratorium.[76] In addition, the Council requested the SNC to adopt a similar moratorium on the export of minerals and

[71] Ibid., Section 1 on transitional arrangements regarding the administration of Cambodia during the pre-election period.

[72] Ibid., Section 2 on military arrangements during the transitional period. For more details on UNTAC's mandate and its role in the peace process, see, e.g., Ratner, 'The Cambodia Settlement Agreements', pp. 1–41; Stahn, *The Law and Practice of International Territorial Administration*, pp. 269–79; and Dobbins et al., *The UN's Role in Nation-Building*, pp. 69–91.

[73] UNSC Resolution 668 (1990), especially paras. 1 and 3.

[74] See Le Billon and Springer, 'Between War and Peace', p. 24.

[75] See, e.g., UNSC Resolution 766 (1992), especially para. 2; Resolution 783 (1992), paras. 5 and 6.

[76] UNSC Resolution 792 (1992), especially para. 13.

gems – another important source of income for the Khmer Rouge rebels – 'in order to protect Cambodia's natural resources'.[77]

Despite the nonmandatory nature of these measures, a number of countries followed suit by imposing import embargos on logs from Cambodia. In addition, UNTAC took several measures to implement the moratorium, including the deployment of border control teams to monitor violations of the moratorium on the export of logs by land or sea and by raising the number of its checkpoints along the Cambodia–Thailand border.[78] Subsequently the SNC adopted a moratorium on minerals and gems, as requested by the Security Council.

The Security Council commended the decision of the SNC to adopt the moratorium on minerals and gems in its Resolution 810 (1993). It also commended the SNC on its decision to consider limits to the export of sawn timber from Cambodia in order to protect its natural resources.[79] Furthermore, it expressed support for steps taken by the Technical Advisory Committee on Management and Sustainable Exploitation of Natural Resources established by UNTAC to implement these measures.[80]

These were the last references made by the Security Council to natural resources. Subsequent resolutions relating to Cambodia focused on the elections that were organised. After the establishment of a democratically elected government in Cambodia, the Security Council ended the peacekeeping mission with Resolution 880 (1993).

Targets and addressees of the sanctions

The commodity measures clearly targeted the Khmer Rouge because of its failure to cooperate in the peace process. However, in practice, the scope of the sanctions was broader. The measures did not distinguish between natural resources traded by the Khmer Rouge and natural resources traded by the government. Instead, the measures banned all round logs, minerals and gems originating from Cambodia. In this respect, they were rather blunt. In subsequent sanctions regimes, including those for Angola, Sierra Leone and Liberia, the Security Council refined its commodity measures in more detail.

[77] Ibid., especially para. 14. [78] *Yearbook of the United Nations* 1993, p. 363.

[79] UNSC Resolution 810 (1993), especially para. 16 read in conjunction with the sixth paragraph of the preamble.

[80] UNSC Resolution 810 (1993), especially para. 16. For more details on this Advisory Committee, see Dobbins et al., *The UN's Role in Nation-Building*, p. 87.

The commodity measures were addressed to States. They were to respect the moratorium imposed by the SNC. In addition, the Security Council assigned an important role to UNTAC, the peacekeeping mission operating in Cambodia, to take appropriate measures to secure the implementation of the moratorium.[81] This is the first time that a peacekeeping mission received an express mandate to assist in implementing measures related to natural resources.[82]

Appraisal of the sanctions regime

The Security Council resolutions related to the Cambodian conflict were remarkable in several respects. For the first time the Security Council focused directly on those commodities that were primarily associated with the funding of an armed conflict. Second, the resolutions related to Cambodia were the first to target a non-State armed group rather than a State.

Another remarkable aspect concerns the references in the Security Council's resolutions to the protection of Cambodia's natural resources as a reason for the measures.[83] This is the only occasion on which the Security Council based the adoption of commodity measures on the need to protect natural resources for their intrinsic value.

Furthermore, none of the resolutions adopted by the Security Council to address the situation in Cambodia invoked Chapter VII of the UN Charter. This was the case not only for the resolutions containing commodity measures, but also for all the resolutions adopted to further the Paris Peace Agreements. It seems that the legal basis for the measures of the Security Council in relation to Cambodia, which include binding as well as nonbinding measures, was Chapter VI of the UN Charter rather than Chapter VII. The Security Council was enacting its role as facilitator and adjudicator in the pacific settlement of disputes, rather than its role as guardian of collective security.

[81] UNSC Resolution 792 (1992), especially para. 13.

[82] For an excellent overview of peacekeeping missions with a mandate including natural resources, see UNEP, 'Greening the Blue Helmets Environment, Natural Resources and UN Peacekeeping Operations', Part II (2012). See also Section 7.6 for a discussion of selected peacekeeping missions.

[83] UNSC Resolution 792 (1992), especially para. 14; UNSC Resolution 810 (1993), especially para. 16 read in conjunction with the sixth paragraph of the preamble.

These facilitating and adjudicating roles characterised the approach of the Security Council throughout the resolution of the Cambodian conflict. During the entire peace process, the Security Council struck a careful balance between collective UN action in the form of a peace support mission and local ownership of the peace process through the establishment of the Supreme National Council of Cambodia. This is reflected in the mandate of UNTAC, which was based on the SNC delegating the UN 'all powers necessary to ensure the implementation' of the peace agreement.[84] In other words, the mandate of UNTAC was not based on the exercise of mandatory powers under the UN Charter but on State consent.

The commodity measures should also be considered in this context. Rather than imposing sanctions itself, the Security Council supported measures taken at the national level; the measures were not imposed from the 'outside' but from the 'inside'. The reason for the Security Council to proceed in this way must be attributed to a large extent to ideological differences between the permanent members regarding the Cambodian conflict. These ideological differences prevented the Security Council from taking firmer action. China, for example, abstained from voting in favour of Resolution 792 (1992) because it feared that the commodity measures laid down in the resolution would destroy the already very fragile peace process by alienating the Khmer Rouge faction from it.[85] These considerations explained the Council's decision not to impose mandatory commodity sanctions in relation to Cambodia.

However, this decision could also explain why the logging embargo was not particularly effective. The nonmandatory nature of the commodity measures did not sufficiently convince neighbouring countries, particularly Thailand, to follow suit. It was until 1995 that Thailand finally closed its borders to logs originating from Cambodia. Once it did, the effects on the military capacity of the Khmer Rouge became immediately clear. The logging embargo considerably weakened them. However, it still took years before their resistance was finally broken down. Although the logging embargo did significantly reduce the Khmer Rouge's military capability, small groups remained active until the early 2000s.[86]

[84] Article 6 of the Paris Peace Agreement.

[85] Resolution 792 not only expressed support for the moratorium on logs, but also contained a call on States to prevent the supply of petroleum products to Khmer Rouge occupied areas (para. 10). China feared that the adoption of such measures 'would further increase differences and sharpen contradictions, and thus could lead to new, complicated problems'. See *Yearbook of the United Nations* 1992, p. 259.

[86] See Le Billon and Springer, 'Between War and Peace', pp. 17–36.

7.4.2 *The 864 UNITA Sanctions Regime*

The structure and objectives of the sanctions regime

The sanctions regime imposed in relation to the conflict in Angola was intended to put an end to the civil war between the Angolan government and the National Union for the Total Independence of Angola (UNITA) that had devastated the country since its independence in 1975.[87] During most of the conflict, the country had been trapped by the rivalry between the Cold War powers, with the United States financing UNITA and the Soviet Union backing the Angolan government. After the end of the Cold War, with revenues drying up, the parties found new ways of financing their armed struggle in revenues generated from the extraction of natural resources such as oil and diamonds.[88]

Nevertheless, when the Security Council imposed a sanctions regime in 1993 to compel UNITA to cooperate with the implementation of the peace agreements concluded two years earlier with the Angolan government, the sanctions regime did not cover natural resources.[89] Furthermore, when the Security Council imposed additional measures on UNITA in 1997, it did not address the trade in natural resources to fund the armed conflict.[90]

It was not until 1998 that the Security Council decided, as part of a larger package of financial and representative sanctions, to directly target the trade in natural resources. In Resolution 1173 (1998), the Security Council decided to impose an embargo on 'all diamonds that are not controlled through the Certificate of Origin regime of the [Angolan government]', as well as a prohibition against selling or supplying mining equipment to persons or entities in 'areas of Angola to which State administration has not been extended'.[91] The diamond embargo was the first of its kind in the history of the Security Council.

[87] For more details regarding this sanctions regime, see Farrall, *United Nations Sanctions and the Rule of Law*, pp. 334–44.

[88] See Ballentine and Sherman (eds.), *The Political Economy of Armed Conflict*, pp. 23–4.

[89] In Resolution 864 (1993), the Security Council decided under Chapter VII that all States were to prevent the sale or supply to UNITA of weapons and related materiel as well as of petroleum and petroleum products. See UNSC Resolution 864 (1993), especially paras. 16 and 19.

[90] Resolution 1127 (1997) complemented the sanctions regime with travel and aviation sanctions and further provided for additional measures to be taken against UNITA if it failed to implement its obligations under the Lusaka Protocol and relevant Security Council Resolutions.

[91] UNSC Resolution 1173 (1998), especially paras. 12(b) and (c). The diamond embargo was brought in effect through UNSC Resolution 1176 (1998).

Following reports on States' violations of the sanctions on arms, petroleum and diamonds, particularly by African and Eastern European countries, the Security Council decided to establish a panel of experts, under the chairmanship of Robert Fowler, to look into the matter.[92] This panel of experts investigated the alleged violations of the sanctions regime in great detail, outlining the involvement of several African and European States in busting the arms and petroleum sanctions. In relation to diamonds, the Panel came to the damning conclusion that the 'extremely lax controls and regulations governing the Antwerp market facilitate and perhaps even encourage illegal trading activity'.[93]

The Panel also issued several recommendations, including some with regard to diamonds. It considered that possibilities should be explored to devise a system of controls 'that would allow for increased transparency and accountability in the control of diamonds from the source of origin to the bourses'. In addition, the panel recommended that 'the diamond industry develop and implement more effective arrangements to ensure that its members worldwide abide by the relevant sanctions against UNITA'.[94]

The Fowler Report was an important trigger for further developments to curtail the trade in 'conflict diamonds'. First of all, the Report's policy of naming and shaming, namely, the explicit identification of particular States and companies as sanctions busters, was an important motivation for these States and companies to stop trading with UNITA, thus depriving UNITA of its funding.[95] Second, it inspired the creation of an international certificate system for rough diamonds, the Kimberley Process for the Certification of Rough Diamonds.[96]

In its Resolution 1295 (2000), the Security Council implicitly endorsed the recommendations of the Panel of Experts. It also emphasised that the implementation of the diamond embargo required 'an effective Certificate of Origin regime' and welcomed steps towards devising a more

[92] UNSC Resolution 1237 (1999), especially para. 6. This panel of experts was formally replaced by a monitoring mechanism consisting of a maximum of five experts. See UNSC Resolution 1295 (2000).

[93] Report of the Panel of Experts on Violations of Security Council Sanctions against UNITA, 10 March 2000, *UN Doc. S/2000/203*, para. 87.

[94] Ibid., paras. 113 and 114.

[95] See Winkelmann, 'Angola', pp. 400–408, para. 26.

[96] The Kimberley Process is discussed in more detail in the following chapter. It can be noted here that the Kimberley Process is a voluntary certification regime for rough diamonds, developed by States, civil society and the diamond business in order to address the issue of diamonds used by armed groups to fuel conflicts.

comprehensive system of controls, 'including arrangements that would allow for increased transparency and accountability in the control of diamonds from their point of origin to the bourses'.[97] In this respect, the Council explicitly referred to the first meeting that led to the adoption of the KPCS in 2002, which was scheduled to be held in May 2000 in Kimberley, South Africa.

In the same resolution the Security Council established a 'Monitoring Mechanism' to replace the Panel of Experts. This body published a total of six reports, disclosing in great detail the structures for the mining of and trade in diamonds from UNITA-controlled regions.[98] One of the principal contributions of the reports is that they helped to provide an understanding of the methods used by UNITA to circumvent the Security Council sanctions regarding rough diamonds. Together with the report of the Panel of Experts, the reports of the Monitoring Mechanism contributed greatly to the design of more effective Certificate of Origin regimes.

The sanctions regime finally came to an end in December 2002, when UNITA started to cooperate with the implementation of the peace accords.[99] By then the national certificate of origin had been replaced by membership of Angola in the KPCS. The introduction of this scheme, backed by relevant Security Council resolutions, together with the Fowler Report's policy of naming and shaming, can be regarded as important factors that contributed to weakening UNITA, leading to the solution of the conflict.

Targets and addressees of the sanctions obligations

The sanctions regime was adopted at the request of the Angolan government and consisted entirely of measures imposed against UNITA.[100] It was the first sanctions regime to directly target a non-State actor pursuant to Chapter VII of the UN Charter. The reason for imposing sanctions on UNITA was that it was failing to implement the peace accords concluded

[97] UNSC Resolution 1295 (2000), especially paras. 16–19. For the Kimberley Process Certification Scheme, see the following chapter.

[98] For the reports of the Monitoring Mechanism, see Documents Relating to the Committee Established Pursuant to Resolution 864 (1993) Concerning the Situation in Angola.

[99] See UNSC Resolution 1448 (2002).

[100] *Repertoire of the Practice of the Security Council* (1993–5), Chap. XI, 'Consideration of the Provisions of Chapter VII of the Charter, Part III on Article 41, Section B, Case 4', available through www.un.org/en/sc/repertoire. See also *UN Doc. S/PV.3277* of 15 September 1993 for the speech of the Angolan government representative at the Security Council on the occasion of the adoption of Resolution 864 (1993).

between UNITA and the Angolan government. After losing the democratic elections held following the peace accords which were concluded in 1991, UNITA continued to fight the government. A second peace agreement concluded in 1994, the Lusaka Protocol, did not change the situation in any way. The sanctions regime was intended to put pressure on UNITA to cooperate in reaching a political settlement to the conflict in Angola, *inter alia,* by curtailing its ability to pursue its objectives by military means.

The Security Council measures adopted in relation to diamonds addressed a variety of actors. Obviously States were the primary addressees responsible for the implementation of the sanctions and also the only entities that were addressed in mandatory terms. According to Resolution 1173 (1998), States were to take 'the necessary measures' to prohibit the 'direct or indirect import' of Angolan diamonds to their territory.[101]

In order to make the diamond embargo more effective, the Security Council called upon States in Resolution 1295 (2000) 'to cooperate with the diamond industry to develop and implement more effective arrangements' to ensure that members of the diamond industry worldwide abide by the embargo against UNITA. The Security Council also addressed the diamond industry, though mainly to invite the Belgian High Diamond Council to continue its efforts to work with the Sanctions Committee and States in order to 'devise practical measures to limit access by UNITA to the legitimate diamond market'.[102]

Appraisal of the sanctions regime

The sanctions regime adopted in relation to Angola is special for several reasons. It is the first in a series of sanctions regimes addressing the trade in rough diamonds from conflict regions. It is also the first sanctions regime in which the Security Council experimented with commodity sanctions targeting specific entities, in the sense that the commodity sanctions targeted only the trade in diamonds by rebel groups and not by the Angolan authorities. Such a distinction was made possible by the use of a certificate of origin regime to provide exemptions to the sanctions. This is an innovation compared with the sanctions regime adopted in relation to Cambodia, which had also targeted one particular commodity, but

[101] UNSC Resolution 1173 (1998), especially para. 12(b).
[102] UNSC Resolution 1295 (2000), especially para. 17.

the moratorium on round logs had extended to all logs originating from Cambodia, whether exported by the Khmer Rouge or by the Cambodian authorities.

Furthermore, the sanctions regime against UNITA can be seen as a catalyst for the Security Council's structural approaches to curbing the illicit flow in natural resources. The problem of diamond smuggling in contravention of the Angolan sanctions regime motivated the Security Council to look beyond its own powers and search for alternative solutions to address the problem. The Council's endorsement of the proposal to convene a meeting of experts in Kimberley, South Africa to devise 'a system of controls . . . including arrangements that would allow for increased transparency and accountability in the control of diamonds from their point of origin to the bourses' should be seen in this light.[103] This was a first – cautious – movement towards what later became the Kimberley Process for the Certification of Rough Diamonds.

The last point of interest is that the Council set explicit requirements for a system of controls for rough diamonds. In this respect, the Security Council mentioned the elements of effectiveness, transparency and accountability.[104] The Kimberley meeting in 2000 explicitly referred to these requirements.[105] Moreover, the Angolan sanctions regime set an example for all subsequent sanctions regimes relating to the trade in particular commodities, which all draw on these requirements of effectiveness, transparency and accountability. The following sections show that the Security Council has continued to develop and refine criteria for the management of natural resources from conflict regions.

7.4.3 The 1132 Sierra Leone Sanctions Regime

Structure and objectives of the sanctions regime

The 1132 sanctions regime imposed in relation to the conflict in Sierra Leone aimed to put pressure on the military junta which had taken over power there following a coup d'état in 1997, to restore the democratically elected government.[106] The military junta was composed of two rebel

[103] Ibid., especially para. 18. [104] Ibid., especially paras. 16 and 18.
[105] See Kimberley Process, Third Year Review, November 2006, p. 12, available through www.kimberleyprocess.com.
[106] See UNSC Resolution 1132 (1997), para. 7 of the preamble and especially para. 1.

groups, the Armed Forces Revolutionary Council (AFRC) and the RUF. The AFRC was a rebel group of soldiers of the Sierra Leonean army, set up in 1997 by Johnny Paul Koroma to take over power in Sierra Leone. The RUF was a rebel group sponsored by the Liberian Charles Taylor, which had spread terror throughout Sierra Leone since its establishment in 1991.[107]

The sanctions regime imposed under Resolution 1132 (1997) consisted of a travel ban, an arms embargo and a prohibition against exporting petroleum and petroleum products to Sierra Leone.[108] It did not comprise sanctions related to the import of natural resources from Sierra Leone, despite ample indications that diamonds constituted an important source of income for the rebel groups united in the military junta.[109] It was not until after the armed conflict escalated that the Security Council resorted to diamond sanctions, consisting of an import embargo on rough diamonds from Sierra Leone for all States.[110]

The embargo was based on Chapter VII of the UN Charter and was to be supervised by the Sanctions Committee established pursuant to Resolution 1132 (1997).[111] In addition, the Security Council called for an exploratory hearing to assess the role of diamonds in the Sierra Leone conflict and the link between the trade in Sierra Leone diamonds and the trade in arms and related matériel in violation of Resolution 1171 (1998).[112] The Council also created a Panel of Experts, *inter alia*, to collect information on the link between the trade in diamonds and the trade in arms, and to report on strengthening the implementation of the sanctions with observations and recommendations.[113] The Panel issued a

[107] On 18 May 2012, the Trial Chamber of the Special Court for Sierra Leone sentenced Charles Taylor to a prison term of 50 years for his involvement in the armed conflict in Sierra Leone.

[108] See UNSC Resolution 1132 (1997), especially paras. 5 and 6.

[109] It was an NGO report, issued in January 2000 by Partnership Africa Canada (PAC), entitled *The Heart of the Matter: Sierra Leone, Diamonds, and Human Security*, that spurred the debate on Sierra Leone. A report issued in December 2000 by the Panel of Experts established pursuant to Security Council Resolution 1306 (2000) confirms that, at least from 1995 on, diamonds have been a major source of funding for the RUF. The report also shows that the AFRC, during its short reign, benefitted from the exploitation of natural resources as well. See the Report of the Panel of Experts appointed pursuant to Security Council Resolution 1306 (2000), para. 19, in relation to Sierra Leone of 20 December 2000, *UN Doc. S/2000/1195*, paras. 65–111.

[110] See UNSC Resolution 1306 (2000), especially para. 1.

[111] Ibid., especially para. 7.

[112] Ibid., especially para. 12.

[113] Ibid., especially para. 19.

report later that year, revealing in great detail the ways in which diamonds funded the activities of the RUF.[114]

The sanctions regime comprised all rough diamonds originating in Sierra Leone, but it exempted from the measures those rough diamonds controlled by the government of Sierra Leone with a certificate of origin regime to be set up by the government in cooperation with other States and relevant organisations.[115] As in the case of Angola, the Security Council required that the regime should be 'effective'.[116]

The diamond embargo was renewed twice before it was lifted in 2003 'in the light of the Government of Sierra Leone's increased efforts to control and manage its diamond industry and ensure proper control over diamond mining areas, and the Government's full participation in the Kimberley Process'.[117] The arms embargo and the travel ban were maintained until 2010, when the Security Council finally terminated the sanctions regime, after the government of Sierra Leone had fully reestablished its control over the territory, and when all nongovernmental forces had been disarmed and demobilised.

Targets and addressees of the sanctions obligations

The sanctions regime generally prohibited the import of all rough diamonds originating from Sierra Leone, with an exception for diamonds the origin of which could be properly established with a Certificate of Origin. As subsequent reports by both the Sanctions Committee and the Panel of Experts showed,[118] the primary targets of the sanctions regime were non-State armed groups fighting against the government of Sierra Leone, in particular the RUF.[119]

114 See the Report of the Panel of Experts appointed pursuant to Security Council Resolution 1306 (2000), para. 19, in relation to Sierra Leone of 20 December 2000, *UN Doc. S/2000/1195*, paras. 65–111.

115 See UNSC Resolution 1306 (2000), especially paras. 2–5.

116 Ibid., especially para. 2.

117 See Resolutions 1385 (2001) and 1446 (2002) for the extensions of the diamond sanctions and UN Doc. SC/7778 of 5 June 2003 for the press statement by the president of the Security Council commenting upon the decision not to renew diamond sanctions against Sierra Leone.

118 See, e.g., Report of the Panel of Experts Appointed Pursuant to Security Council Resolution 1306 (2000), para. 19, in relation to Sierra Leone, *UN Doc. S/2000/1195*, December 2000.

119 UNSC Resolution 1306 (2000) refers to a report of the Secretary-General recommending the Security Council to strengthen its sanctions regime by including 'measures which would prevent RUF commanders from reaping the benefits of their illegal exploitation

The obligation to implement the sanctions was imposed on States. They were to take 'the necessary measures to prohibit the direct or indirect import of all rough diamonds from Sierra Leone to their territory'.[120] Furthermore, one novel feature of the sanctions regime was that other entities, including in particular the diamond industry, were to play an active role in devising structural approaches to solving the problem of conflict diamonds.

The Security Council therefore requested States, international organisations and other bodies, including representatives from the diamond industry, to provide assistance to the government of Sierra Leone to set up an effective Certification of Origin Regime and invited them to 'offer assistance to the Government of Sierra Leone to contribute to the further development of a well-structured and well-regulated diamond industry that provides for the identification of the provenance of rough diamonds'.[121]

Appraisal of the sanctions regime

The 1132 Sierra Leone sanctions regime resembles the 864 Angola regime in several respects. First, both sanctions regimes used diamond sanctions to stop the flow of revenues to a non-State armed group. In the case of Angola, the targeted group was UNITA; in the case of Sierra Leone, it was principally the RUF. In addition, both regimes exempted diamonds controlled by a Certificate of Origin Regime. Finally, both regimes welcomed the efforts of the diamond industry to devise practical solutions to the issue of conflict diamonds.

The 1132 Sierra Leone sanctions regime went a step further than the 864 Angola sanctions regime. Resolution 1306 explicitly encouraged the diamond industry 'to work with the Government of Sierra Leone and the Committee to develop methods and working practices to facilitate the effective implementation of this resolution'.[122] As noted by the United Kingdom upon the adoption of the resolution, this direct appeal to the diamond industry was an unusual feature of Resolution 1306.[123]

of mineral resources, in particular diamonds'. Fourth Report of the Secretary General on the United Nations Mission in Sierra Leone, *UN Doc. S/2000/455* of 19 May 2000, para. 94.

[120] UNSC Resolution 1306 (2000), especially para. 1.

[121] Ibid., especially paras. 3 and 11.

[122] Ibid., especially para. 10.

[123] See *UN Doc. S/PV.4168 (2000)*, p. 4: 'The draft resolution is unusual in its direct appeal to the diamond trade'.

Arguably, it shows the Security Council's growing awareness of the need to involve the business community in the implementation of sanctions.

In addition, the Security Council took the unprecedented step of calling for an exploratory hearing on the issue of diamonds in Sierra Leone, involving representatives of interested States and regional organisations, the diamond industry and other relevant experts. This was the first time the Security Council organised a hearing for the purpose of gaining a better understanding on an issue related to the perpetuation of an armed conflict. Moreover, the aim was not only to gain a better understanding of the causes of the conflict, but also to find solutions for the problem of diamonds funding it. The topics discussed at the hearing included the ways and means of developing a sustainable and well-regulated diamond industry in Sierra Leone.[124]

Another exceptional feature of the sanctions regime is that the Security Council established a Panel of Experts only after imposing the diamond sanctions. This implies that the decision of the Security Council to impose the diamond sanctions was based on information from third sources, including NGO reports.[125] The Council also acted on the request of the Sierra Leonean government, which had asked it to impose a trade embargo on Sierra Leonean diamonds as early as 1999.[126]

7.4.4 The 1343 Liberia Sanctions Regime

Structure and objectives of the sanctions regime

The sanctions regime imposed in relation to Liberia by Resolution 1343 was the second sanctions regime to be imposed against Liberia. It immediately followed and replaced the first sanctions regime established in 1992 with the aim of ending the civil war between the government of Liberia and the National Patriotic Front of Liberia (NPFL), an opposition

124 See the summary report, along with observations from the Chairman on the exploratory hearing on Sierra Leonean diamonds, held on 31 July and 1 August 2000, Annex to *UN Doc. S/2000/1150* of 4 December 2000.

125 See notably the report released by Partnership Africa Canada, *The Heart of the Matter*, January 2000.

126 See the remarks of the representative of Sierra Leone at the Council debate, which preceded the adoption of Resolution 1306 (2000) as well as the letter sent to the Council by the Sierra Leonean government, both identifying diamonds as a root cause of the conflict in Sierra Leone. See *UN Doc. S/PV.4168* of 5 July 2000 and *UN Doc. S/2000/641* of 28 June 2000.

movement led by Charles Taylor.[127] When Charles Taylor took power in the country, this sanctions regime was terminated and replaced by the new 1343 sanctions regime.[128] While the previous sanctions regime had consisted only of an arms embargo, the new sanctions regime included diamond sanctions.

The aim of the 1343 sanctions regime was to address Liberia's support for the Sierra Leonean Revolutionary United Front (RUF) and other rebel groups operating in the West African region.[129] Therefore, in Resolution 1343 (2001), the Security Council determined 'that the active support provided by the Government of Liberia for armed rebel groups in neighbouring countries, and in particular its support for the RUF in Sierra Leone, constitutes a threat to international peace and security in the region'.[130] In pursuance of Chapter VII of the UN Charter, the Security Council demanded that the government of Liberia 'cease all direct or indirect import of Sierra Leone rough diamonds which are not controlled through the Certificate of Origin regime of the Government of Sierra Leone' and called upon the government 'to establish an effective Certificate of Origin regime for trade in rough diamonds that is transparent and internationally verifiable'.[131]

In addition, other States were to 'take the necessary measures to prevent the direct or indirect import of all rough diamonds from Liberia, whether or not such diamonds originated in Liberia' and were called upon to 'take appropriate measures to ensure that individuals and companies in their jurisdiction . . . act in conformity with United Nations embargoes . . . and, as appropriate, take the necessary judicial and administrative action to end any illegal activities by those individuals and companies'.[132] Furthermore, the Security Council urged diamond-exporting countries in West Africa to

[127] See UNSC Resolution 788 (1992). For more details regarding this sanctions regime, see Farrall, *United Nations Sanctions and the Rule of Law*, pp. 316–19.

[128] See UNSC Resolution 1343 (2001).

[129] See the preceding section of this chapter and the Report of the Panel of Experts Appointed Pursuant to Security Council Resolution 1306 (2000), para. 19, in relation to Sierra Leone, *UN Doc. S/2000/1195* of December 2000. This report concluded that the illicit trade in Sierra Leonean diamonds through Liberia was not possible without the involvement of high Liberian officials. On 18 May 2012, the Trial Chamber of the Special Court for Sierra Leone sentenced Charles Taylor to a prison term of 50 years for his involvement in the armed conflict in Sierra Leone.

[130] UNSC Resolution 1343 (2001), para. 9 of the preamble.

[131] Ibid., especially paras. 2(c) and 15. For more information on the sanctions regime imposed in relation to the conflict in Sierra Leone, see the preceding section of this chapter.

[132] Ibid., especially paras. 6 and 21.

adopt Certificate of Origin regimes for the trade in rough diamonds with the assistance of other States and of relevant international organisations and bodies.[133]

The supervision of these sanctions was assigned to a sanctions committee established by the same resolution.[134] In addition, the Security Council requested the Secretary-General to establish a Panel of Experts with the mandate to investigate, *inter alia,* violations of the sanctions and 'possible links between the exploitation of natural resources and other forms of economic activity in Liberia, and the fuelling of conflict in Sierra Leone and neighbouring countries'.[135]

In 2002, following two reports of the Panel of Experts which both concluded that the exploitation of timber provided the government of Liberia with large amounts of money used to provide support to the (former) RUF and other rebel groups,[136] the Security Council decided to extend the 1343 regime to include timber sanctions.

The first resolution adopted by the Security Council in this respect provided that 'the active support provided by the Government of Liberia to armed rebel groups in the region, in particular to former Revolutionary United Front (RUF) combatants who continue to destabilize the region, constitutes a threat to international peace and security in the region'.[137] In pursuance of Chapter VII of the UN Charter, the Council called upon the government of Liberia to 'take urgent steps, including through the establishment of transparent and internationally verifiable audit regimes, to ensure that revenue derived by the Government of Liberia from the . . . Liberian timber industry is used for legitimate social, humanitarian and development purposes'.[138]

As this resolution had no effect on the Liberian government's practices, the Security Council adopted a second resolution that included the timber sanctions. Resolution 1478 (2003) considered that the government of Liberia had not demonstrated that the revenue derived from the Liberian timber industry 'is used for legitimate social, humanitarian and

133 Ibid., especially para. 16.
134 Ibid., especially para. 14.
135 Ibid., especially para. 19.
136 Report of the Panel of Experts Pursuant to Security Council Resolution 1343 (2001), Paragraph 19, Concerning Liberia, 17 October 2001, *UN Doc. S/2001/1015*, paras. 309–15 and 319–50; Report of the Panel of Experts Appointed Pursuant to Security Council Resolution 1395 (2002), Paragraph 4, in Relation to Liberia, 11 April 2002, *UN Doc. S/2002/470*, paras. 138–50.
137 UNSC Resolution 1408 (2002), para. 11 of the preamble.
138 Ibid., especially para. 10.

development purposes, and is not used in violation of Resolution 1408 (2002)'.[139] Therefore, the Security Council decided in pursuance of Chapter VII that 'all States shall take the necessary measures to prevent . . . the import into their territories of all round logs and timber products originating in Liberia'.[140]

In addition, in response to reports indicating that the sanctions targeting the transit of Sierra Leonean diamonds through Liberia had caused a reverse flow of Liberian rough diamonds being smuggled out of the country and into neighbouring certification schemes,[141] the Security Council reiterated its earlier call for the Liberian government to establish a Certificate of Origin regime for Liberian rough diamonds.[142] The Security Council explicitly called upon the Liberian government to bear in mind 'the plans for the international certification scheme under the Kimberley Process' and proposed to exempt from the embargo those rough diamonds controlled by a transparent and internationally verifiable Certificate of Origin regime.[143]

In a resolution adopted after the official launch of the Kimberley Process for the Certification of Rough Diamonds, the Security Council reiterated its appeal to the Liberian government to adopt a transparent and internationally verifiable Certificate of Origin Regime and also demanded that the regime be 'fully compatible with the Kimberley Process'.[144]

The 1343 sanctions regime was terminated later that year in response to political changes in Liberia, in particular the departure of President Taylor and the installation of a new transitional government. Nevertheless, in the light of the fragile situation in the country, the timber and diamond sanctions were brought under a new sanctions regime. As this sanctions regime had a completely different character, it is discussed in the following section.

Targets and addressees of the sanctions obligations

The 1343 sanctions regime was aimed at preventing the Liberian government from financing non-State armed groups, in particular the RUF. The sanctions regime directly addressed the government of Liberia led by Charles Taylor, which was held responsible for financing these rebel

139 UNSC Resolution 1478 (2003), especially para. 16.

140 Ibid., especially para. 17(a).

141 See the Report of the Panel of Experts Appointed Pursuant to Security Council Resolution 1395 (2002), Paragraph 4, in Relation to Liberia, *UN Doc. S/2002/470*, para. 136.

142 UNSC Resolution 1408 (2002), especially para. 7.

143 Ibid., especially paras. 7 and 8.

144 UNSC Resolution 1478 (2003), especially para. 13.

factions. Obviously the sanctions regime indirectly targeted the rebel factions sponsored by the Taylor government.

The responsibility for the implementation of the diamond and timber sanctions was placed first and foremost on States. All States were to implement the embargos on rough diamonds and round logs. Furthermore, in order to stop the busting of sanctions on diamonds originating from Liberia when they were smuggled to neighbouring countries, additional appeals were made to diamond-exporting countries in West Africa. These States were requested to adopt Certificate of Origin regimes for the trade in rough diamonds, assisted by other States and relevant international organisations and bodies. Except for providing assistance to States, the resolutions did not impose obligations on international organisations or non-State actors, such as civil society and corporations.

Appraisal of the sanctions regime

The 1343 sanctions regime addressed the role of States in providing support to non-State armed groups. In this sense, the sanctions regime differs from earlier sanctions regimes imposed against States. The sanctions regimes against Southern Rhodesia and Iraq also targeted States, but primarily as parties to an armed conflict. In the case of Liberia, the link with an armed conflict is indirect. The sanctions regime was aimed at preventing the Liberian State from interfering in other conflicts in the region to which Liberia itself was not a party.

However, subsequent Panel reports concluded that the sanctions barely had any effect on the trade in diamonds and timber. This could partly explain why the Security Council resorted to other initiatives to strengthen the effectiveness of the sanctions, especially to the Kimberley Process. In fact, it is interesting to note that the Security Council explicitly recognised the Kimberley Process Certification Scheme as the regime of preference for the certification of rough diamonds. This is a new development compared to the sanctions regimes adopted for Angola and Sierra Leone. Furthermore, as in the earlier sanctions regimes, the Security Council linked the adoption of a certification scheme to the lifting of sanctions.

The emphasis placed by the Security Council on the need to ensure that revenue derived by the Government of Liberia from the Liberian timber industry was used for legitimate social, humanitarian and development purposes was another interesting aspect.[145] The Security Council could have confined itself to addressing the link between timber and the fuelling

[145] UNSC Resolution 1408 (2002), especially para. 10.

of the armed conflict. However, the Security Council implicitly established a link between the timber sanctions and the obligation of a State to use its natural resources for national development and the well-being of the population, as a corollary to its right to exercise permanent sovereignty over its natural resources, thus going much further than the traditional context of peace and security. This link was confirmed in the subsequent sanctions regime in relation to Liberia, discussed below. Thus the Security Council showed that it is prepared to withhold respect for the principle of permanent sovereignty over natural resources if a State fails to respect the corollary obligation to use the natural resources for national development.

The final interesting aspect is related to the many references made by the Security Council to improvements in governance over natural resources. In relation to diamonds, the Security Council referred to an *effective* Certificate of Origin regime that is *transparent* and *internationally verifiable*. Similarly, in relation to the timber sanctions, the Security Council referred to the establishment of *transparent* and *internationally verifiable* audit regimes. In the latter case, these audit regimes served to introduce more general improvements in governance in the timber sector. In both cases, these improvements in governance were linked to the possibility of lifting sanctions. These references to effective, transparent and internationally verifiable regimes reveal a growing tendency of the Security Council to rely on improvements in governance over natural resources as an effective means to address the link between natural resources and armed conflicts.

7.4.5 The 1521 Liberia Sanctions Regime

Structure and objectives of the sanctions regime

Resolution 1521 (2003) ended the sanctions regime imposed against the government of Liberia for its support to rebel groups in the West African region and imposed a new one aimed at addressing the threat to international peace and security in West Africa posed by the proliferation of illegal arms financed by the illegal exploitation of timber and diamonds.[146] One of the aims of the sanctions regime was to assist the new transitional government of Liberia to regain control over the diamond and timber industries in order to stop these natural resources from fuelling armed conflict in the region.

[146] UNSC Resolution 1521 (2003), paras. 7 and 8 of the preamble.

Resolution 1521 (2003) was adopted under Chapter VII of the UN Charter. It included both diamond and timber sanctions. In relation to diamonds, the Security Council instructed all States 'to take the necessary measures to prevent the direct or indirect import of all rough diamonds from Liberia to their territory, whether or not such diamonds originated in Liberia'.[147] Furthermore, the resolution called upon the National Transitional Government of Liberia 'to establish an effective Certificate of Origin regime for trade in Liberian rough diamonds that is transparent and internationally verifiable' and encouraged the government 'to take steps to join the Kimberley Process as soon as possible'.[148]

In relation to timber, Resolution 1521 (2003) stipulated that all States were to take the necessary measures 'to prevent the import into their territory of all round logs and timber products originating in Liberia'.[149] The Security Council also urged the government 'to establish its full authority and control over the timber producing areas, and to take all necessary steps to ensure that government revenues from the Liberian timber industry are not used to fuel conflict or otherwise in violation of the Council's resolutions but are used for legitimate purposes for the benefit of the Liberian people, including development'.[150] To this end, the Liberian government was encouraged 'to establish oversight mechanisms for the timber industry that will promote responsible business practices, and to establish transparent accounting and auditing mechanisms'.[151]

The Security Council called upon States, international organisations and other relevant bodies to offer assistance to the Liberian government to achieve these objectives, including assistance with regard to 'the promotion of responsible and environmentally sustainable business practices in the timber industry',[152] in order to ensure that the diamond and timber sanctions could eventually be lifted.

In response to the Security Council's call to assist the Liberian government in achieving the objectives set for the timber industry, the United States, together with the World Bank, the International Monetary Fund, the European Commission, the International Union for the Conservation of Nature, the United Nations Food and Agriculture Organisation and several other international organisations and NGOs set up the Liberia Forest Initiative (LFI). The aim of the LFI was to assist the Liberian government to adopt the necessary reforms in its forestry sector to allow the

[147] Ibid., para. 6 of the preamble. [148] Ibid., especially paras. 7 and 9.
[149] Ibid., especially para. 10. [150] Ibid., especially para. 11.
[151] Ibid., especially para. 13. [152] Ibid., especially para. 15.

sustainable and transparent management of its forest resources for the benefit of the Liberian population.[153]

The LFI programmes focused on every aspect of sustainable forest management, including the three internationally recognised components of sustainable forest management.[154] The economic component of forestry was addressed with a commercial forestry programme, the social component through a communal forestry programme, and the environmental component through a forest conservation programme. The LFI also addressed several interrelated issues, including governance-related issues. Thus the LFI can be considered to have adopted an integrated approach to forest management.

The Security Council expressed its support for the LFI in its subsequent resolutions. In Resolution 1579 (2004), the Security Council noted with some concern that 'despite having initiated important reforms', the Liberian government had made only limited progress towards improving its governance of the timber industry.[155] It therefore encouraged the government to 'intensify its efforts to meet these conditions, in particular by implementing the Liberia Forest Initiative and the necessary reforms in the Forestry Development Authority'.[156]

The Security Council reiterated its call to the Liberian government to continue the implementation of the LFI and related reforms in subsequent resolutions. It added that these reforms would 'ensure transparency, accountability and sustainable forest management'.[157] Furthermore, the Security Council encouraged the Liberian government to implement the Governance and Economic Management Assistance Program (GEMAP) as a means of expediting the lifting of the sanctions.[158] This programme was initiated by the same organisations as the LFI in order to enhance

[153] For more information on this initiative, see the website of the UN Food and Agriculture Organization at www.fao.org/forestry/lfi/en. Also see Altman, Nichols and Woods, 'Leveraging High-Value Natural Resources to Restore the Rule of Law', pp. 337–65.

[154] The Non-legally Binding Instrument on All Types of Forests, *UN Doc. A/C.2/62/L.5*, of 22 October 2007 defines sustainable forest management in its Article III(4) as 'a dynamic and evolving concept, [which] aims to maintain and enhance the economic, social and environmental values of all types of forests, for the benefit of present and future generations'.

[155] UNSC Resolution 1579 (2004), para. 11 of the preamble.

[156] Ibid., especially para. 3. For more details on the Liberia Forest Initiative, see Altman, Nichols and Woods, 'Leveraging High-Value Natural Resources to Restore the Rule of Law', pp. 337–65.

[157] UNSC Resolution 1607 (2005), especially para. 4; and Resolution 1647 (2004), especially para. 3(a).

[158] See UNSC Resolution 1647 (2005), especially para. 4.

transparency and accountability in Liberia's public administration, also in relation to the granting of natural resources concessions.[159] Reported irregularities in the granting of diamond concessions by the Liberian authorities, preventing Liberia's accession to the Kimberley Process,[160] had been a cause of concern and led to the launch of this programme.

The effective implementation of the proposed reforms by the Liberian government finally led to the lifting of the commodity sanctions. The timber sanctions were lifted in 2006 after extensive reforms of the forestry sector, including the adoption of legislation and the establishment of independent audits.[161] The diamond sanctions were lifted almost a year later, upon Liberia's accession to the KPCS.[162]

Targets and addressees of the sanctions regime

The 1521 sanctions regime principally targeted non-State armed groups threatening the peace process in Liberia and in the wider West African region. However, these armed groups were also represented in the newly established transitional government of Liberia.[163] This led to a rather paradoxical situation. On one hand, the sanctions regime was set up to assist the new government to gain control over the timber industry and the diamond fields as part of the peace process, while on the other hand, the sanctions aimed to prevent members of that government using Liberian natural resources to fund their war efforts.[164]

The burden of implementing the diamond and timber sanctions was placed on States. International organisations and other relevant bodies were assigned an additional role. Their role was not so much related to the implementation of the sanctions as it was to assist the government of

[159] For more details on the GEMAP programme, see www.gemap-liberia.org.

[160] In this respect, see, e.g., the Preliminary Report of the Panel of Experts on Liberia Submitted Pursuant to Resolution 1579 (2004) (On Diamonds) of 17 March 2005, *UN Doc. S/2005/176*, in particular paras. 17–24; and the Report of the Panel of Experts on Liberia Submitted Pursuant to Resolution 1579 (2004) of 13 June 2005, *UN Doc. S/2005/360*, paras. 97–119.

[161] See UNSC Resolution 1689 (2006), especially para. 1.

[162] UNSC Resolution 1753 (2007), para. 2 of the preamble and especially paras. 1–3.

[163] The National Transitional Government of Liberia consisted of the former Government of Liberia, Liberians United for Reconciliation and Democracy (LURD) and the Movement for Democracy in Liberia (MODEL). See Resolution 1521 (2003), fourth paragraph of the preamble.

[164] See the Report of the Panel of Experts Appointed Pursuant to Paragraph 25 of Security Council Resolution 1478 (2003) Concerning Liberia, *UN Doc. S/2003/937* of 28 October 2003.

Liberia in satisfying the criteria for the lifting of sanctions. Their responsibilities included providing assistance to set up a Certificate of Origin regime for diamonds and to promote responsible and environmentally sustainable business practices in the timber industry. For diamonds, this international action was coordinated mainly through the Kimberley Process for the Certification of Rough Diamonds, while for the timber industry action was coordinated mainly through the LFI programme.

Appraisal of the sanctions regime

The commodity sanctions in the 1521 sanctions regime served two distinct but interrelated purposes. The first was to stop timber and diamonds from fuelling armed conflict in Liberia and the West African Region as part of a strategy to resolve the conflict. The second purpose was to prevent natural resources from contributing to a relapse into armed conflict as part of a strategy for post-conflict reconstruction. This second purpose explains why the sanctions regime aimed to achieve real structural reforms of the diamond and timber industries. Beyond the direct contribution of diamonds and timber to the armed conflict, it also sought to address threats to the peace resulting from underlying problems of governance in the Liberian diamond and timber industries.

Thus the Security Council used sanctions as a means of putting pressure on the Liberian government to bring about important structural reforms in Liberia's key economic sectors as part of a comprehensive peacebuilding process. The Security Council's approach was very innovative in this respect, especially in relation to the proposed reforms for the timber sector. The first innovative feature was that it explicitly adopted the basic principle that 'government revenues from the Liberian timber industry are [to be] used for legitimate purposes for the benefit of the Liberian people, including development'.[165] In this way it implicitly emphasised that States must use their sovereignty over their natural resources for the benefit of their people. In this respect, the 1521 sanctions regime went one step further than the 1343 regime, which stated in more general terms that timber revenues should be used for legitimate social, humanitarian and development purposes.

Another innovative feature of the sanctions regime was its explicit recognition of the need to integrate environmental protection in regulatory mechanisms for the timber sector. The Security Council encouraged

[165] UNSC Resolution 1521 (2003), especially para. 11.

the Liberian government 'to establish oversight mechanisms for the timber industry that will promote responsible business practices' and called upon States, international organisations and other bodies to offer assistance to the Liberian government to achieve this objective, including assistance with regard to 'the promotion of responsible and environmentally sustainable business practices in the timber industry'.[166]

These are major improvements in comparison with earlier sanctions regimes, which focused principally on stopping the trade in conflict resources. By placing emphasis on every aspect of the governance of natural resources, the Liberian sanctions regime contributed to peacebuilding efforts in a more structural way, ensuring that Liberian natural resources were managed in a sustainable way for the purposes of development rather than conflict.

The 1521 sanctions regime is one of the few regimes discussed in this chapter that actually succeeded in achieving the necessary changes. The success of the sanctions regime can largely be attributed to the political will of the newly established Liberian President, Ellen Johnson Sirleaf. She has been one of the driving forces behind the reform of the Liberian natural resource sectors, as well as of government administration in general.[167] This demonstrates that a commitment to good governance that is rooted in the political system of a country itself is very important in bringing about change.

7.4.6 The 1572 Côte d'Ivoire Sanctions Regime

Structure and objectives of the sanctions regime

The sanctions adopted by the Security Council in relation to Côte d'Ivoire were imposed in order to end hostilities between government forces under the command of the elected president Laurent Gbagbo and the opposition forces (the Forces Nouvelles).[168] Two peace agreements between the government and the Forces Nouvelles were signed in 2003 (the Linas–Marcoussis Agreement) and 2004 (the Accra III Agreement) respectively, providing, *inter alia,* for the establishment of a government of national reconciliation and a program of disarmament. These peace agreements

166 UNSC Resolution 1521 (2003), especially paras. 13 and 15.

167 See Altman, Nichols and Woods, 'Leveraging High-Value Natural Resources to Restore the Rule of Law', pp. 353–4.

168 For more details regarding this sanctions regime, see Farrall, *United Nations Sanctions and the Rule of Law*, pp. 439–47.

were supplemented with a third agreement (the Pretoria Agreement) in 2005. The aim of the Security Council sanctions was precisely to secure the implementation of these peace agreements.

The sanctions regime was imposed first with Resolution 1572 (2004). The Security Council, determining that the situation in Côte d'Ivoire continued to pose a threat to international peace and security in the region and acting under Chapter VII of the UN Charter, decided to impose an arms embargo as well as a travel ban and an assets freeze on designated individuals and entities.[169] Furthermore, the Security Council established a Sanctions Committee to monitor the sanctions, to be assisted by a Group of Experts.[170] A year later, with Resolution 1643 (2005), the Security Council decided to expand the sanctions regime to include diamond sanctions, targeting the whole diamond industry in Côte d'Ivoire.[171]

The diamond sanctions were taken because of the links between the illicit exploitation of and trade in diamonds on the one hand, and the arms trade and use of mercenaries on the other, 'as one of the sources of fuelling and exacerbating conflicts in West Africa'.[172] However, interestingly, the reports of the Group of Experts revealed that diamonds were not the only natural resources directly linked to the arms trade and the financing of the conflict in general. The Group of Experts also examined the role of other commodities, with a particular emphasis on cocoa and oil, in relation to the funding of the conflict in Côte d'Ivoire.[173]

The Group reported several ways in which these natural resources were used to violate the arms embargo by both parties to the armed conflict, e.g., by diverting tax revenues to finance extra-budgetary military spending by the government.[174] Despite ample indications that natural resources

[169] UNSC Resolution 1572 (2004), especially paras. 7, 9 and 11.

[170] Ibid., especially paras. 14 and 17. This group of experts was established through Resolution 1584 (2005), para. 7.

[171] UNSC Resolution 1643 (2005), especially para. 6.

[172] UNSC Resolution 1643 (2005), para. 9 of the preamble.

[173] See, e.g., Midterm Report of the Group of Experts Submitted in Accordance with Paragraph 11 of Security Council Resolution 1842 (2008), *UN Doc. S/2009/188*, paras. 59–72; Final Report of the Group of Experts on Côte d'Ivoire, Prepared in Accordance with Paragraph 14 of Security Council Resolution 1980 (2011), *UN Doc. S/2012/196*, para. 113.

[174] See, e.g., Report of the Group of Experts Submitted in Accordance with Paragraph 7 of Resolution 1584 (2005), *UN Doc. S/2005/699*, paras. 22–46; Report of the Group of Experts Submitted in Accordance with Paragraph 9 of Resolution 1643 (2005), *UN Doc. S/2006/735*, paras. 113–28; Final Report of the Group of Experts on Côte d'Ivoire, Prepared in Accordance with Paragraph 14 of Security Council Resolution 1980 (2011), *UN Doc. S/2012/196*, paras. 92–110. The Group further identified instances in which natural resources were offered directly in exchange for arms and noted the existence of

such as cocoa and oil were prolonging the conflict in Côte d'Ivoire in the same way as diamonds,[175] the Security Council did not impose sanctions on these natural resources.

This is characteristic of the Security Council's approach, which focuses mainly on curtailing the trade in natural resources by or for the benefit of rebel groups. In general the Council does not look into the ways in which the national authorities use the revenues from natural resources. In itself this is understandable from a legal perspective, especially in the light of the principles of State sovereignty and permanent sovereignty over natural resources, but not in the current case, where the national authorities openly used the proceeds from the cocoa and oil sectors to violate the arms embargo. Therefore, there was good cause to address the irregularities in the cocoa and oil sectors, either with an embargo or with formal requests for the reform of those sectors.

The Security Council renewed the diamond sanctions several times before it introduced an exemption to the sanctions regime in Resolution 1893 (2009),[176] though only for diamond samples necessary for scientific research, in order to facilitate the implementation of the Kimberley Process. In Resolution 1893 (2009), the Security Council decided to exclude from the embargo diamond imports 'that will be used solely for the purposes of scientific research and analysis to facilitate the development of specific technical information concerning Ivorian diamond production'.[177] This research was to be coordinated by the Kimberley Process.[178] In addition, a request to exempt from the embargo particular imports of diamonds was to be submitted to the Committee 'jointly by the Kimberley Process and the importing Member State'.[179]

parallel taxation systems as well as practices of racketeering and looting. For all these instances, see the Final Report of the Group of Experts on Côte d'Ivoire, Prepared in Accordance with Paragraph 14 of Security Council Resolution 1980 (2011), *UN Doc. S/2012/196*, paras. 92–110.

[175] See in particular the Report of the Group of Experts Submitted in Accordance with Paragraph 7 of Resolution 1584 (2005), *UN Doc. S/2005/699*, paras. 22–46; the Midterm Report of the Group of Experts Submitted in Accordance with Paragraph 11 of Security Council Resolution 1842 (2008) of 8 April 2009, *UN Doc. S/2009/188*, paras. 59–64; and the Final Report of the Group of Experts Submitted in Accordance with Paragraph 11 of Security Council Resolution 1842 (2008) of 9 October 2009, *UN Doc. S/2009/521*, paras. 170–88, which establish direct links between the trade in natural resources by the government and the violation of the arms embargo, e.g., through extra-budgetary military spending.

[176] The sanctions were renewed through UNSC Resolution 1727 (2006); Resolution 1782 (2007); and Resolution 1842 (2008).

[177] UNSC Resolution 1893 (2009), especially para. 16.

[178] Ibid., especially para. 16. [179] Ibid., especially para. 17.

In November 2010, elections were finally held in Côte d'Ivoire as part of the implementation of the Ouagadougou peace agreement concluded in March 2007. However, when the defeated president, Laurent Gbagbo, refused to step down, a crisis broke out. It was only after the crisis was ended with the help of UNOCI and ECOWAS troops that Alassane Dramane Ouattara could be installed as the newly elected President of Côte d'Ivoire in April 2011. From then on, the sanctions regime entered a new phase. The measures were no longer intended to contribute to ending the conflict in Côte d'Ivoire, but instead to support the peace process.[180]

In Resolution 1980 (2011), adopted soon after the installation of President Ouattara, the Security Council emphasised the contribution that the diamond sanctions had made to achieving stability in Côte d'Ivoire and encouraged the Ivorian authorities 'to work with the Kimberley Process Certification Scheme to conduct a review and assessment of Côte d'Ivoire's internal controls system for trade in rough diamonds and a comprehensive geologic study of Côte d'Ivoire's potential diamond resources and production capacity, with a view to possibly modifying or lifting [the diamond sanctions]'.[181] Resolution 2045 (2012) extended the diamond sanctions even further and urged the Ivorian authorities to 'create and implement an action plan to enforce the Kimberley Process rules in Côte d'Ivoire'.[182]

In response to a report by the Group of Experts indicating that diamond smuggling by military–economic networks in Côte d'Ivoire continued to pose a threat to the stability of the country,[183] the UN Security Council decided to extend the diamond sanctions until 30 April 2014.[184] However, the Council did express its 'readiness to review measures in light of progress made towards Kimberley Process implementation', thus making the lifting of the diamond sanctions conditional upon effective implementation of the minimum requirements of the Kimberley Process in Côte d'Ivoire.[185] Furthermore, the Council requested the Kimberley Process and national and international agencies to help the Group of Experts with 'its enquiries concerning the individuals and networks involved in the production, trading and illicit export of diamonds from Côte d'Ivoire' and to communicate such matters to the Sanctions Committee.[186]

180 UNSC Resolution 1980 (2011), para. 4 of the preamble. 181 Ibid., especially para. 19.

182 UNSC Resolution 2045 (2012), especially paras. 6 and 21.

183 Final Report of the Group of Experts Submitted in Accordance with Paragraph 16 of Security Council Resolution 2045 (2012), *UN Doc. S/2013/228* of 17 April 2013.

184 UNSC Resolution 2101 (2013), especially para. 6. 185 Ibid.

186 Ibid., especially paras. 23 and 24.

In addition to the diamond measures, the Resolution also addressed the threats to the peace process resulting from the smuggling and illegal taxation of other natural resources by military networks. Although the Resolution did not impose any concrete measures with respect to these natural resources, it is relevant to note that the Security Council did express its concern about the smuggling of cocoa, cashew nuts, cotton, timber and gold, thus paving the way for the adoption of more concrete measures in the future.[187]

Furthermore, in response to a recommendation by the Group of Experts regarding the problems faced by Côte d'Ivoire with regard to artisanal mining in its gold and diamond sectors,[188] the Security Council 'encourages the Ivorian authorities to participate in the OECD-hosted implementation programme with regard to the due diligence guidelines for responsible supply chains of minerals from conflict-affected and high-risk areas'.[189] This recommendation refers to the OECD Due Diligence Guidance that was developed for companies as a tool to mitigate the risk that their mineral procurement policies could contribute to instability and armed conflict in a country. The Security Council's reference to this programme indicates its commitment to the promotion of more structural solutions for the illegal exploitation of natural resources beyond the financing of conflict.[190]

Resolution 2153 (2014) consolidated some of these measures, while the Council also lifted the diamond embargo 'in light of progress made towards Kimberley Process Certification Scheme (KPCS) implementation and better governance of the sector'.[191] In particular, the Council reiterated its call on the authorities to participate in the OECD-hosted implementation programme.[192] It also noted that persons or entities 'determined to be a threat to the peace and national reconciliation process in Côte d'Ivoire through the illicit trafficking of natural resources, including diamonds and gold, may be designated by the Committee' to be placed on a sanctions list pursuant to paragraph 12(a) of Resolution 1727 (2006).[193] In this way, the Council replaced the selective diamond

[187] Ibid., para. 14 of the preamble.

[188] Final Report of the Group of Experts Submitted in Accordance with Paragraph 16 of Security Council Resolution 2045 (2012), *UN Doc. S/2013/228* of 17 April 2013.

[189] UNSC Resolution 2101 (2013), especially para. 25.

[190] For more details on the OECD Due Diligence Guidance, see the following section and Chapter 8.

[191] See UNSC Resolution 2153 (2014), para. 13.

[192] Ibid., para. 31. [193] Ibid., para. 25.

sanctions by targeted sanctions against persons directly responsible for hampering the peace process through illegal trade in diamonds and gold.

Targets and addressees of the sanctions obligations

The diamond embargo imposed against Côte d'Ivoire targets all diamonds originating from the country. During the armed conflict, this meant that the embargo *de facto* exclusively targeted the Forces Nouvelles, since they were in control of diamond production. In fact, the embargo issued by the Security Council complemented an already existing national ban on the export of diamonds, issued by the Ivorian government in 2002.[194]

The primary addressees of the sanctions regime were States. However, in relation to the diamonds sanctions, the Security Council also assigned a prominent role to the Kimberley Process. To prevent the introduction of diamonds from Côte d'Ivoire into the legitimate diamond trade, the Security Council expressly referred to measures taken within the framework of the Kimberley Process Certification Scheme.[195] Although Côte d'Ivoire has been a formal participant in the Kimberley Process since its launch in 2003, the country has never exported diamonds under the scheme.[196]

In addition, the Security Council directly addressed the Kimberley Process. The primary role of the Kimberley Process was to provide the Council with information concerning the production and illicit export of diamonds from Côte d'Ivoire, as well as information about possible violations of the arms and diamond embargoes.[197] In addition, the Kimberley Process was assigned the task of coordinating research on diamonds exempted from the regime 'for the purposes of scientific research and analysis to facilitate the development of specific technical information concerning Ivorian diamond production'.[198]

[194] Report of the Group of Experts Submitted in Accordance with Paragraph 7 of Resolution 1584 (2005), *UN Doc. S/2005/699*, para. 48.

[195] UNSC Resolution 1893 (2009), especially para. 16; Resolution 1980 (2011), para. 19; and Resolution 2045 (2012), para. 21.

[196] Report of the Group of Experts Submitted in Accordance with Paragraph 7 of Resolution 1584 (2005), *UN Doc. S/2005/699*, para. 48.

[197] See, e.g., UNSC Resolution 1727 (2006), especially paras. 10–11; Resolution 1782 (2007), paras. 13–14; Resolution 1842 (2008), paras. 14–15; and Resolution 2045 (2012), para. 20.

[198] UNSC Resolution 1893 (2009), especially para. 16. See also Resolution 1946 (2010), para. 14, which confirms that the export of Ivorian diamonds for scientific research is to be seen as an exemption to the ban.

Appraisal of the sanctions regime

The sanctions regime imposed in relation to the conflict in Côte d'Ivoire clearly builds upon earlier sanctions regimes addressing the trade in diamonds. There are some differences, but most of these can be based on the particularities of the situation in Côte d'Ivoire. The first difference relates to the scope of the diamond embargo. While earlier sanctions regimes exempted from the ban diamonds controlled by a certificate of origin regime, the 1572 Côte d'Ivoire sanctions regime covered all diamonds originating from that country. The reason for this difference can be traced back to the internal situation in Côte d'Ivoire. The lack of government control over the diamond mining sites necessitated a comprehensive ban on diamonds.

The second difference relates to the role of the Kimberley Process in the sanctions regime. While earlier sanctions regimes made the modification or lifting of sanctions conditional upon the implementation of an effective certificate of origin regime, the 1572 Côte d'Ivoire sanctions regime required the implementation of the Kimberley Process. Again this difference can be understood in the light of Côte d'Ivoire's membership of the Kimberley Process. Côte d'Ivoire had already joined the Kimberley Process in 2003, but has only recently been able to meet the requirements of the process.

Furthermore, it is important to note that throughout the conflict in Côte d'Ivoire the Security Council never addressed the role of other natural resources besides diamonds in fuelling the conflict, despite ample indications that the government used the proceeds from these natural resources to violate the arms embargo. It is only now, in the phase of post-conflict reconstruction, that the Security Council has started to consider the role of natural resources such as cocoa and gold in perpetuating the violence in Côte d'Ivoire. The attention devoted by the Security Council to the role of key economic sectors in hampering the prospects for sustainable peace is encouraging, as reforms in the governance of these sectors would make a significant contribution to the reconstruction of Côte d'Ivoire.

7.4.7 Comparing the sanctions regimes

The sanctions regimes discussed in this section all applied sanctions targeting selected commodities which were thought to make a direct contribution to the financing of armed conflicts. In all cases, the ultimate objective of the sanctions was to cut off revenues for armed groups. This was even the case for Liberia, the only sanctions regime targeting a State. The objective of the 1343 Liberia sanctions regime was to stop the Liberian authorities from actively providing financial support to armed groups operating in the region, while the 1521 Liberia sanctions regime was aimed at preventing Liberian natural resources beyond the control of the Liberian authorities from being used to finance these armed groups.

Thus the sanctions regimes discussed in this section show that the Security Council is prepared to address the contribution of natural resources to armed conflict, but only insofar as a link can be established between natural resources and the funding of non-State armed groups. There seems to be a general reluctance on the part of the Security Council to address a government's mismanagement of natural resources revenues in the absence of a link with rebel funding. This explains why the Security Council resorted to the use of sanctions on natural resources exploited by the national authorities in the case of Liberia, while it did not in the case of Côte d'Ivoire. The sanctions regarding Côte d'Ivoire exclusively targeted diamonds, the main source of rebel funding. In contrast, the Security Council did not act against the government, which used revenues from the oil and cocoa industries to fund extra-budgetary military expenditure in contravention of the UN arms embargo. These examples show that the Security Council is prepared to uphold the principle of permanent sovereignty over natural resources in most circumstances, even when a State contravenes Security Council Resolutions.

Most of the sanctions regimes discussed in this section targeted diamonds. With the exception of Côte d'Ivoire, the Security Council in each case provided for the possibility of exempting from the sanctions regime diamonds regulated by a certificate of origin regime. The Security Council also set standards for such a regime; namely, it had to be effective, transparent and accountable. In later sanctions regimes, these requirements were complemented with the requirement that the certificate of origin must be fully compatible with the Kimberley Process.

Two of the sanctions regimes discussed in this section also included timber sanctions. It is interesting to note that these are also the only cases – and during quite different periods of time – that had regard for environmental sustainability. In the case of Cambodia, the protection of Cambodia's natural resources was an underlying reason for the adoption of the measures. In the case of Liberia, the measures aimed to enhance sustainable forest management and to promote responsible and environmentally sustainable business practices in the timber sector.

7.5 From commodity sanctions to targeted sanctions

This section discusses sanctions regimes that have addressed the links between natural resources and armed conflict through sanctions targeting individuals and entities rather than commodities.

7.5.1 The 1493 DR Congo Sanctions Regime

Structure and objectives of the sanctions regime

The 1493 DR Congo sanctions regime was adopted in 2003, when the armed conflict in the DR Congo had entered the phase of a gradual transition to peace.[199] Joseph Kabila had succeeded his father as president of the DR Congo. Under his leadership, agreements had been signed with Rwanda and Uganda, and international troops from neighbouring countries had started to withdraw from Congolese territory.[200] In addition, Kabila had signed a peace agreement with different Congolese militias, the Global and All Inclusive Agreement on the Transition in the Democratic Republic of the Congo, and had established a Government of National Unity and Transition. In this context, the adoption of the sanctions regime should therefore be seen as an attempt by the Security Council to support the peace process in the DR Congo.

The sanctions regime consisted of an arms embargo targeting particular armed groups.[201] The Council also condemned the illegal exploitation of the natural resources and other sources of wealth of the DR Congo and expressed its intention to consider possible ways of ending it.[202] However, it did not adopt specific measures in this regard.

In 2004, the Security Council established a Sanctions Commission to oversee the implementation of the arms embargo, as well as a Group of Experts to assist the Commission.[203] It again condemned the continuing

[199] For an overview of the different phases in the armed conflict in the DR Congo between March 1993 and June 2003, see the *Report of the Mapping Exercise Documenting the Most Serious Violations of Human Rights and International Humanitarian Law Committed within the Territory of the Democratic Republic of the Congo between March 1993 and June 2003*, United Nations Human Rights Office of the High Commissioner, August 2010.

[200] The Pretoria Accord with Rwanda was signed on 30 July 2002, while the Luanda Agreement with Uganda was signed on 6 September 2002.

[201] UNSC Resolution 1493 (2003), especially para. 20. For an overview of the sanctions regime, see Farrall, *United Nations Sanctions and the Rule of Law*, pp. 411–18. See also Schrijver, *Development without Destruction*, pp. 184–6.

[202] UNSC Resolution 1493 (2003), especially para. 28.

[203] UNSC Resolution 1533 (2004), especially paras. 8 and 10.

illegal exploitation of natural resources in the DR Congo. Furthermore, it reaffirmed 'the importance of bringing an end to these illegal activities, including by applying the necessary pressure on the armed groups, traffickers and all other actors involved' and urged 'all States, and especially those in the region, to take the appropriate steps to end these illegal activities, including through judicial means where possible, and, if necessary, to report to the Council'.[204] However, no mandatory measures were introduced.

A year later Resolution 1596 (2005) renewed and broadened the arms embargo to include all recipients on the territory of the DR Congo.[205] In addition, it contained several auxiliary measures to strengthen the embargo, including measures concerning aviation and border controls, as well as travel and financial sanctions against persons suspected of violating the arms embargo.[206] A subsequent resolution extended the travel and financial sanctions to all political and military leaders of armed groups who were preventing the demobilisation of their members.[207]

Moreover, this resolution contained measures relating to the transit of Congolese natural resources through neighbouring countries. The Security Council demanded that neighbouring States as well as the Congolese government 'impede any kind of support to the illegal exploitation of Congolese natural resources, particularly by preventing the flow of such resources through their respective territories'.[208] The Security Council reaffirmed its demand in Resolution 1698 (2006).[209] However, neither of these resolutions contained any specific measures that States should take to implement the obligation, and they did not specify the types of natural resources that were targeted by the resolutions.

Nevertheless, it seems that from that moment on, the Security Council started to address the illegal exploitation of Congolese natural resources in a more coherent manner, looking for more direct ways to stop the exploitation of natural resources from financing armed groups in the DR Congo. The first step can be found in Resolution 1698 (2006), in which the Council expressed its intention to consider possible measures to stem the flow of financing of armed groups and militias operating in the eastern part of the DR Congo, including commodity sanctions.[210]

The Council requested two reports in order to make an informed decision on the type of measures to impose. The Group of Experts was

[204] Ibid., especially paras. 6 and 7. [205] UNSC Resolution 1596 (2005), especially para. 1.
[206] Ibid., especially paras. 6, 10, 13 and 15.
[207] UNSC Resolution 1649 (2005), especially para. 2. [208] Ibid., especially para. 16.
[209] UNSC Resolution 1698 (2006), especially para. 1. [210] Ibid., especially para. 9.

requested to report on feasible and effective measures that the Council could impose, and the Secretary-General was asked to assess the economic, humanitarian and social impacts of such measures on the Congolese population.[211] On the basis of the recommendations contained in these reports, the Security Council decided to address the illegal exploitation of natural resources principally through the existing financial and travel sanctions.[212]

The Security Council specifically decided to extend these sanctions to 'individuals or entities supporting the illegal armed groups [operating] in the eastern part of the Democratic Republic of the Congo through the illicit trade of natural resources'.[213] In this way it intended to directly target those responsible for the illicit trade in natural resources from the DR Congo.

This decision has had major consequences for companies operating in or sourcing from the DR Congo, because it set in motion a process leading to the adoption of due diligence guidelines for companies. Where Resolution 1857 (2008) encouraged States to take measures 'to ensure that importers, processing industries and consumers of Congolese mineral products under their jurisdiction exercise due diligence on their suppliers and on the origin of the minerals they purchase',[214] Resolution 1896 (2009) addressed the minerals industry directly. It recommended that importers and processing industries adopt policies and practices to prevent their businesses from providing indirect support to armed groups.[215] More importantly, the Council mandated the Group of Experts to draw up guidelines for the exercise of due diligence by importers, processing industries and consumers of mineral products from the DR Congo.[216]

211 Ibid., especially paras. 6 and 8.

212 The Security Council acted here upon a recommendation of the Group of Experts. See the Report of the Group of experts submitted pursuant to resolution 1654 (2006), *UN Doc. S/2006/525*, para. 159; and the Interim report of the Group of Experts submitted pursuant to resolution 1698 (2006), *UN Doc. S/2007/40*, para. 52. The Group of Expert had also recommended the imposition of selective commodity sanctions, but the report of the Secretary-General dissuaded the Security Council from imposing such sanctions. This report concluded that commodity sanctions would have negative impacts on artisanal miners and on the fragile peace process in the DR Congo. See the Report of the Secretary-General Pursuant to Paragraph 8 of Resolution 1698 (2006) Concerning the Democratic Republic of the Congo, *UN Doc. S/2007/68* of 8 February 2007, paras. 62–3.

213 UNSC Resolution 1857 (2008), especially para. 4(g).

214 Ibid., especially para. 15.

215 UNSC Resolution 1896 (2009), especially para. 16, which reads in full: '*Recommends* that importers and processing industries adopt policies and practices, as well as codes of conduct, to prevent indirect support to armed groups in the Democratic Republic of the Congo through the exploitation and trafficking of natural resources.'

216 Ibid., especially para. 7.

In its final report of 2010 the Group of Experts presented two sets of due diligence guidelines. The first focused exclusively on preventing the purchase of minerals from individuals and entities suspected of providing support to illegal armed groups through the illicit trade in natural resources. The other set also addressed purchases from criminal networks and perpetrators of serious human rights abuses within the Congolese army. Both sets of guidelines followed the same five-step risk-based approach to due diligence. These five steps consisted of strengthening company management systems, identifying and assessing supply chain risks, designing and implementing strategies to respond to identified risks, conducting independent audits and publicly disclosing supply chain due diligence and findings.[217]

The guidelines required companies to adopt appropriate procedures to identify the risk of their purchases of minerals providing any sort of support to armed groups, sanctioned individuals or entities or criminal networks or perpetrators of serious human rights abuses in the eastern part of the DR Congo. If a risk was identified, the guidelines required that companies suspend their contracts with their suppliers until the risk was removed. Furthermore, independent audits had to be performed to verify that the due diligence applied by the company was sufficient to identify and prevent the risk of providing support to an individual or entity identified by the Group as contributing to the violence in the eastern part of the DR Congo. Finally, companies had to publish their due diligence policies as part of their annual sustainability or corporate responsibility reports.[218]

These due diligence guidelines received the express support of the Security Council.[219] In this respect, it is interesting to note that the Council opted for the second and more far-reaching set of guidelines, thus targeting not only the trade with armed groups, but also the trade with subversive elements within the Congolese army.[220] In addition, the Council made several decisions regarding the implementation of the

[217] See the Final Report of the Group of Experts Prepared Pursuant to Paragraph 6 of Security Council Resolution 1896 (2009), *UN Doc. S/2010/596*, para. 318. For more details on this five-step approach, see the following chapter of this study.

[218] For more details, see the Final Report of the Group of Experts Prepared Pursuant to Paragraph 6 of Security Council Resolution 1896 (2009), *UN Doc. S/2010/596*, paras. 328–55 for the first set of guidelines and paras. 356–69 for the second set.

[219] The Security Council supported 'taking forward the Group of Experts' recommendations on guidelines for due diligence for importers, processing industries and consumers of Congolese mineral products'. See UNSC Resolution 1952 (2010), especially para. 7.

[220] Ibid.

guidelines. First, it called upon States 'to take appropriate steps to raise awareness of the due diligence guidelines' presented by the Group of Experts, 'to urge importers, processing industries and consumers of Congolese mineral products to exercise due diligence by applying the aforementioned guidelines, or equivalent guidelines' and to regularly report to the Sanctions Committee on the actions they were taking to implement these recommendations.[221]

More significantly, the Security Council established an express link between compliance with the due diligence guidelines on one hand and the imposition of financial and travel sanctions on the other. It decided that the failure of individuals or entities to exercise due diligence consistent with the steps set out in the resolution could be a reason for them to be placed on the sanctions list.[222] This meant that companies operating in or sourcing from the DR Congo were obliged to adhere to the due diligence guidelines.

So far the Sanctions Committee has only placed two companies involved in the trade in minerals on the sanctions list. These are two gold trading companies located in neighbouring Uganda. It justified placing these companies on the list because they 'bought gold through a regular commercial relationship with traders in the DRC tightly linked to militias [which] constitutes "provision of assistance" to illegal armed groups in breach of the arms embargo of resolutions 1493 (2003) and 1596 (2005)'.[223]

The Security Council's subsequent resolutions focused strongly on ways to implement the due diligence guidelines adopted by the Group of Experts. Two particular measures taken by the Security Council deserve special attention. The first concerns the question of traceability of the minerals supply chain, 'a key element of any due diligence exercise' according to the Group of Experts.[224] The Council did not take any specific measures in this regard, but rather expressed its support for the efforts of the Congolese government and the wider region 'to address the tracing and certification of minerals'.[225] Thus it implicitly referred to instruments adopted under the auspices of the International Conference for the Great

[221] Ibid., especially paras. 8 and 20. [222] Ibid., especially para. 9.

[223] List of Individuals and Entities Subject to the Measures Imposed by Paragraphs 13 and 15 of Security Council Resolution 1596 (2005) as Renewed by Paragraph 3 of Resolution 2021 (2011), last updated on 12 November 2012, available through www.un.org/sc/committees/1533/pdf/1533_list.pdf.

[224] See the Interim Report of the Group of Experts Prepared in Pursuance of Paragraph 5 of Security Council Resolution 1952 (2010), *UN Doc. S/2011/345*, para. 77.

[225] UNSC Resolution 1991 (2011), especially para. 17.

Lakes Region and showed its willingness to let the affected countries decide for themselves on the design of an instrument addressing the tracing and certification of minerals.

The second measure concerns the decision of the Security Council to include the inspection of mining sites in the mandate of the UN military operation in the DR Congo, MONUSCO.[226] This measure is not directly related to the implementation of the due diligence guidelines, but is part of a broader package of measures involving MONUSCO – and before that, MONUC – aimed at preventing the provision of support to illegal armed groups.[227] Another measure in this package relating to the measures discussed in the current section was the involvement of MONUSCO in a project of the Congolese government to bring together all State services in a limited number of trading counters in order to improve the traceability of mineral products.[228]

Targets and addressees of the sanctions

The 1493 DR Congo sanctions regime has consistently targeted individuals and entities impeding the peace process in the DR Congo. All the measures taken by the Security Council, including the due diligence guidelines, should be seen in this light. The Security Council gradually increased the number of individuals against whom the sanctions were imposed. The adoption of the due diligence guidelines had two important implications in this respect. It showed that the sanctions targeted not only members of non-State armed groups, but also subversive elements from within the Congolese army. In addition, the Council clearly indicated that 'providing support to armed groups' must be broadly interpreted, including providing indirect support to these groups by irresponsible mineral sourcing practices.

The addressees of the sanctions were primarily States, including the Congolese State. They were to implement the arms embargo, as well as the travel and financial sanctions. Indirectly, companies were also addressees of the sanctions. They were to implement the due diligence guidelines, thus preventing armed groups from obtaining the revenues to violate

[226] See UNSC Resolution 2021 (2011), especially para. 10. The UN operation in the DR Congo was originally called MONUC but was renamed in 2010 to reflect the new situation in the DR Congo's transition to peace. For more information on the mission, see www.un.org/en/peacekeeping/missions/monuc/ and www.un.org/en/peacekeeping/missions/monusco/.

[227] See, e.g., UNSC Resolution 1756 (2007), especially para. 2(l) and Resolution 1856 (2008), para. 3(g). See also Section 7.6.2.

[228] UNSC Resolution 1925 (2010), especially para. 12.

the arms embargo. The final addressee of the sanctions was the United Nations Organization (Stabilization) Mission in the Democratic Republic of the Congo (MONUC/MONUSCO). The relevant tasks include military action aimed at 'preventing the provision of support to illegal armed groups, including support derived from illicit economic activities'.[229]

Appraisal of the sanctions regime

In order to break the link between the exploitation of natural resources and the ongoing violence in the DR Congo, the Security Council opted for a new approach, compared with earlier sanctions regimes. Instead of imposing commodity sanctions, the Security Council opted for targeted sanctions against individuals and companies in order to address the link between natural resources and armed conflict. In this way, the Security Council broke away from the trend it had set with its earlier sanctions regimes.

Another striking aspect of the sanctions regime is that it paved the way for imposing sanctions on the business community for conducting irresponsible business practices. Companies that did not respect the due diligence guidelines risked being added to the sanctions list. Although this was not the first sanctions regime to directly target companies, it was the first to target companies further up the supply chain as well. Earlier sanctions regimes imposed sanctions only on companies that were directly implicated in the busting of sanctions. Examples include asset freezes imposed against aviation companies suspected of transporting arms in violation of the arms embargo imposed in relation to Liberia.[230]

In the 1493 DR Congo sanctions regime the Security Council went a step further. It stretched the causal link between the practices of companies and the violation of sanctions by armed groups. This was an interesting development, especially in light of the earlier sanctions regimes addressing the trade in rough diamonds, which relied on voluntary measures to engage the diamond industry in the proper implementation of sanctions.

In the case of the DR Congo, the Security Council moved away from a voluntary approach to industry self-regulation as articulated in Resolution 1896 (2009) in favour of sanctions to induce the minerals industry to modify their sourcing practices. However, it is too early to tell whether

[229] UNSC Resolution 1756 (2007), especially para. 2(l); and Resolution 1856 (2008), para. 3(g).

[230] See the List of Individuals and Entities Subject to the Measures Contained in Paragraph 1 of Security Council Resolution 1532 (2004) Concerning Liberia (The Assets Freeze List), last updated on 20 July 2012, available through www.un.org/sc/committees/1521/aflist.shtml.

this move away from voluntary measures to sanctions can be regarded as a response to the particular circumstances in the DR Congo, or whether it indicates a change in the approach of the Security Council which extends beyond the specific case of the DR Congo.

Similarly, it is too early to tell whether this new approach adopted by the Council in relation to the DR Congo will actually lead to a change in the behaviour of companies sourcing from the DR Congo. The 2011 Final Report of the Group of Experts reveals a mixed picture. On one hand, it concluded that the implementation of the due diligence guidelines by the Congolese government has halted nearly all tin, tantalum and tungsten exports from the eastern DR Congo. On the other hand, it concluded that these minerals were increasingly being smuggled into neighbouring countries, impairing the objective of the due diligence guidelines.[231] The 2014 Final Report of the Group of Experts drew a similar conclusion for gold. It estimated that, during 2013, 98% of artisanally produced gold was smuggled out of the country.[232] Therefore, the success of the due diligence guidelines is impaired by smuggling practices and lax controls in neighbouring countries. This indicates that the due diligence guidelines can only be successfully implemented when improvements are carried out in the transparency of the extractive industry in the DR Congo and in neighbouring countries as well. An effective tracing and certification system for minerals is a first requirement in this respect. However, other factors are important as well, especially combating corruption in the minerals sectors.

7.5.2 The 1970 Libya Sanctions Regime

Structure and objectives of the sanctions regime

The sanctions regime imposed by the Security Council against Libya in 2011 was not the first sanctions regime imposed against the Libyan authorities. An earlier sanctions regime had addressed the alleged role of the Libyan government in supporting terrorist groups, as part of the response to the Lockerbie incident.[233] However, the 2011 sanctions regime

[231] Final Report of the Group of Experts on the DRC Submitted in Accordance with Paragraph 4 of Security Council Resolution 2021 (2011), *UN Doc. S/2012/843*, 15 November 2012, paras. 159–242.

[232] Final Report of the Group of Experts on the Democratic Republic of the Congo, *UN Doc. S/2014/42*, 23 January 2014, para. 171.

[233] For more details, see Farrall, *United Nations Sanctions and the Rule of Law*, pp. 297–305.

differed from the earlier one in the sense that it was directly related to a situation of armed conflict.

In February 2011, civil protests against the regime of Colonel Muammar Gaddafi resulted in an internal armed conflict between Gaddafi's forces on the one side, and an insurrectional movement labelling itself the National Transitional Council (NTC) on the other.[234] Reports on gross and systematic violations of human rights committed by the Libyan government, including widespread and systematic attacks against the civilian population, prompted the Security Council to take action.

On 26 February 2011, the Security Council adopted Resolution 1970. This resolution referred the situation in Libya to the ICC and imposed 'biting' sanctions against the Gaddafi government as 'a clear warning to the Libyan Government that it must stop the killing'.[235] These sanctions included an arms embargo, a travel ban and an asset freeze.[236] The asset freeze applied to all persons 'involved in or complicit in ordering, controlling, or otherwise directing, the commission of serious human rights abuses' against the Libyan population.[237] The sanctions list annexed to the resolution targeted exclusively members of Colonel Gaddafi's family. The Security Council further appointed a Sanctions Committee to oversee the implementation of the sanctions and to designate other individuals subject to the sanctions.[238]

A few weeks later, Resolution 1973 was adopted in response to Gaddafi's failure to put an end to the violence and to fulfil the legitimate demands of the population. Resolution 1973 established a Panel of Experts to assist the Sanctions Committee and further strengthened the sanctions, including the asset freeze.[239] From that moment on, the asset freeze applied to all assets belonging to the Libyan authorities, including the assets of

[234] For a timeline of the conflict in Libya, see *The Economist*, 'The Birth of Free Libya', 25 August 2011; and BBC, 'Libya: The Fall of Gaddafi', available through www.bbc.co.uk.

[235] See the statement of the representative of the United States in the Security Council Meeting that adopted Resolution 1970, *UN Doc S/PV.6491*: 'Tonight, acting under Chapter VII, the Security Council has come together to condemn the violence, pursue accountability and adopt biting sanctions targeting Libya's unrepentant leadership. This is a clear warning to the Libyan Government that it must stop the killing. Those who slaughter civilians will be held personally accountable. The international community will not tolerate violence of any sort against the Libyan people by their Government or security forces.'

[236] See UNSC Resolution 1970 (2011), 26 February 2011, paras. 9–14 (arms embargo); 15–16 (travel ban); and 17–21 (asset freeze).

[237] Ibid., para. 22. [238] Ibid., para. 24.

[239] UNSC Resolution 1973 (2011), 17 March 2011, para. 24.

high government officials and entities under the control of the Libyan authorities.[240]

Most interesting in this respect is the inclusion in the list of the Libyan National Oil Corporation (LNOC) as a 'potential source of funding for [Gaddafi's] regime'.[241] In addition, the Security Council decided that States must require all individuals and entities under their jurisdiction doing business with Libya to exercise vigilance if they have reasonable grounds to believe that such business could contribute to violence and use of force against civilians.[242] Since the oil business constituted Libya's principal source of income, these measures first and foremost addressed the responsibilities of foreign oil companies operating in Libya.[243]

One of the principal questions that arise in relation to these measures concerns their implications for the trade in Libyan oil. The asset freeze targeted only one of the parties to the conflict, i.e., the Libyan authorities. In other words, the assets freeze did not affect the trade in Libyan oil to the benefit of other actors, such as the NTC. At the same time, the assets freeze against the Libyan authorities was comprehensive: it applied to all assets of the Libyan authorities that were located abroad and it included a prohibition against foreign individuals and entities making assets available to the Libyan authorities. This prohibition extended to payments

[240] The Security Council decides that the asset freeze 'shall apply to all funds, other financial assets and economic resources . . . which are owned or controlled, directly or indirectly, by the Libyan authorities . . . or by individuals or entities acting on their behalf or at their direction, or by entities owned or controlled by them'. See UNSC Resolution 1973 (2011), 17 March 2011, para. 19.

[241] Ibid., Annex II. On 24 June 2011, the Sanctions Committee extended the assets freeze to a subsidiary of the LNOC. See in this regard the following press release: 'Security Council Committee Concerning Libya Adds Names of Individuals and Entities to Its Travel Ban and Assets Freeze List', *UN Doc. SC/10302*, 28 June 2011.

[242] The resolution stated that 'all States shall require their nationals, persons subject to their jurisdiction and firms incorporated in their territory or subject to their jurisdiction to exercise vigilance when doing business with entities incorporated in the Libyan Arab Jamahiriya or subject to its jurisdiction, and any individuals or entities acting on their behalf or at their direction, and entities owned or controlled by them, if the States have information that provides reasonable grounds to believe that such business could contribute to violence and use of force against civilians'. See UNSC Resolution 1973 (2011), 17 March 2011, para. 21.

[243] The Panel of Experts concerning Libya observed that Libya was one of the 'less diversified oil-producing economies in the world'. It further noted that the oil sector was responsible for 93 per cent of government revenues and 95 per cent of Libya's export earnings. See the Final Report of the Panel of Experts Established Pursuant to Security Council Resolution 1973 (2011) Concerning Libya, *UN Doc. S/2012/163*, para. 163.

made by foreign companies to the Libyan authorities or entities under their control, including payments made to the National Oil Corporation.

The effects of this prohibition should not be underestimated, since the National Oil Corporation was implicated in most oil operations in Libya, mostly through joint ventures with foreign oil companies. In addition, Resolution 1973 (2011) decided that States must require their companies to 'exercise vigilance' when doing business in Libya in order to prevent these companies from contributing to 'violence and use of force against civilians'.[244] This requirement amounts to an obligation of 'due care' for companies. Although not watertight, it entails an obligation for companies doing business in Libya to choose their business partners carefully, irrespective of the inclusion of these companies on the sanctions list or not.

The sanctions against the LNOC and its subsidiaries were lifted after the NTC had taken over power in Libya. Resolution 2009, adopted on 16 September 2011, determined that the LNOC and Zueitina Oil Company were no longer to be subject to the asset freeze.[245] Sanctions against other entities, including financial institutions, have been lifted subsequently. Some remaining sanctions, notably against Libyan investment companies, are still in place.

Targets and addressees of the sanctions regime

As noted above, the sanctions regime against Libya exclusively targeted the Gaddafi regime. No measures were imposed against the opposition forces. The sanctions regime was to be implemented by all States. Specific obligations relating to the implementation of the asset freeze included the freezing of all assets belonging to the Libyan authorities that were found on their territories and preventing their nationals from making available funds to the Libyan authorities.[246] In addition, States were to require all persons and entities under their jurisdiction to exercise vigilance when doing business with Libyan persons and entities.[247]

Interestingly enough, the resolutions do not directly call upon individuals or companies to exercise vigilance. Instead, the resolutions ask the home States of these companies to enact relevant legislation. This is a departure from other sanctions regimes, discussed in this chapter, which have made direct calls upon individuals and companies to assist in implementing sanctions. Examples include the sanctions regimes

244 UNSC Resolution 1973 (2011), especially para. 21.
245 UNSC Resolution 2009, 16 September 2011, para. 14.
246 See UNSC Resolution 1973 (2011), especially para. 19.
247 Ibid., especially para. 21.

imposed against Sierra Leone and Liberia. The sanctions regime against the DR Congo even went a step further through the designation of persons and companies on a sanctions list for not respecting due diligence in the choice of their business partners.

How can this departure from earlier sanctions regimes be explained? A closer look at the objectives and targets of the sanctions regimes may provide a partial answer. Whereas the sanctions regime against Libya was adopted in order to put pressure on the Gaddafi government to end the violence, the sanctions regimes for Sierra Leone, Liberia and the DR Congo were adopted in order to assist these States in addressing a threat to their peace. The due diligence measures in relation to the DR Congo, for example, were adopted at the request of the International Conference for the Great Lakes Region and in support of national legislation. In other words, the sanctions were there to help these States in enforcing national legislation, which was of course not the case in Libya. Nevertheless, the differences in nature between the sanctions regimes only provide a partial explanation. In addition to the adoption of measures addressing the home States of companies doing business with the Gaddafi regime, the Security Council could have addressed companies directly. In this sense, the sanctions regime imposed against Libya can be regarded as a step back in the process of involving individuals and companies in sanctions implementation.

Appraisal of the sanctions regime

In the case of Libya, the Security Council opted for an asset freeze rather than an oil embargo in order to curtail the oil revenues of the Libyan authorities. The reasons for the Security Council to refrain from imposing an oil embargo on Libya may have been manifold. Some of these may have been politically motivated. It is not a secret that foreign oil companies operating in Libya have conducted fierce lobbying in order to safeguard their business interests. Nevertheless, this would only partially explain the motivation of the Security Council to choose an asset freeze as a lesser means of achieving its objectives.[248]

Another reason may be found in the effects of the sanctions on the Libyan population. In view of the prime significance of oil revenues for

[248] This may be exemplified by the position of the European Union as one of the main consumers of Libyan oil. The European Union has extended the asset freeze to include almost the entire Libyan oil industry. See 'Libya: EU Imposes Additional Sanctions Following the Adoption of UNSCR 1973', Council of the European Union Press Release, 24 March 2011, *Doc. 8110/11 PRESSE 79.*

the Libyan economy, full-fledged oil sanctions would have had severe consequences for the Libyan population. A further reason could be related to the objectives of the sanctions regime. The Security Council's main concern was to target the Gaddafi regime in order to stop the violence against the Libyan civilian population. An asset freeze is a more appropriate instrument for targeting a specific actor than an oil embargo, since such an embargo would have affected both sides in the conflict.

Even if the Security Council could have solved this problem by exempting oil extracted under authorisation of the NTC from the embargo, it would have encountered both practical and legal problems. The practical problem relates to determining the distinction between 'legitimate' and 'illegitimate' oil. Certification measures, like those used in the diamond sanctions regimes discussed above, would not have been a viable option in this situation, because these are normally implemented by the government of a State. The legal problem relates to the question of sovereignty. Providing exemptions to an oil embargo for oil traded by an insurrectional movement would have required the Security Council to make a formal statement recognising this movement as the new Libyan government.[249] The asset freeze avoids these problems while at the same time contributing to the overall objectives of the sanctions regime, i.e., putting an end to the violence in Libya.

A further aspect of interest in relation to the sanctions regime is that the Security Council in both resolutions explicitly expressed its intention to make available at a later stage the frozen assets 'to and for the benefit of the people of the Libyan Arab Jamahiriya'.[250] This reference arguably constitutes an implicit recognition that the assets belonging to the Libyan authorities belong to and must be used for the benefit of the Libyan people. The reference is reiterated in subsequent resolutions that gradually terminate the asset freeze. In Resolution 2040 (2012), for example, the Security Council decides that the Sanctions Committee must lift the freezing of assets of particular entities 'as soon as practical to ensure the assets are made available to and for the benefit of the people of Libya'.[251]

It is further interesting to note that the Security Council emphasizes the importance of making the assets available 'in a transparent and responsible manner in conformity with the needs and wishes of the Libyan

[249] For a more detailed analysis of the legal impacts of recognition of the NTC during the Libyan civil war, see Chapter 2 and Talmon, 'Recognition of the Libyan National Transitional Council'.

[250] UNSC Resolution 1970 (2011), especially para. 18; and S/RES/1973 (2011), para. 20.

[251] See UNSC Resolution 2040 (2012), para. 9. Also see UNSC Resolution 2009 (2011), paras. 14–19.

people'.[252] Moreover, the Council requests the International Monetary Fund and the World Bank 'to work with the Libyan authorities on an assessment of Libya's public financial management framework, which would recommend steps to be taken by Libya to ensure a system of transparency and accountability with respect to the funds held by Libyan governmental institutions'.[253] These statements demonstrate the Security Council's adherence to the principles of transparency and accountability.

7.5.3 Comparing the sanctions regimes

The sanctions regimes against the DR Congo and Libya use targeted sanctions rather than commodity sanctions to achieve their purposes. In addition, both sanctions regimes cover natural resources. However, the roles of natural resources in the sanctions regimes differ significantly. In the case of the DR Congo, individuals and entities are targeted because of their involvement in the illegal trade in natural resources. In the case of Libya, natural resources are targeted because they are owned by individuals placed on the sanctions list.

The regimes also present differences in other respects. One example concerns the targets of the sanctions. In the case of the DR Congo, the sanctions regime targets non-State armed groups and subversive elements of the Congolese army as well as individuals and entities that provide support to these groups. In the case of Libya, the sanctions target the Libyan authorities and those associated with them.

The final difference concerns the role of the private sector in the sanctions regimes. Both regimes target the private sector, but the extent to which and the way in which they do so differs considerably. The 1493 DR Congo sanctions regime targets all companies providing support to armed groups, whether directly or through their mineral procurement policies. If there are grounds for believing that a company is providing support to armed groups and the company has not exercised due diligence, it can be placed on the sanctions list. This implies that the sanctions have a potentially broad reach, targeting companies worldwide that source minerals from the DR Congo. In the case of Libya, the sanctions list includes only those companies that have a direct connection to the Libyan authorities. The guiding principle for placing a company on the list is 'ownership' or 'control'. The Security Council insists that States require their companies

252 See UNSC Resolution 2009 (2011), para. 14 of the preamble.
253 Ibid., especially para. 18.

to exercise due care in the choice of their business partners, but the Council does not provide for the possibility of placing these companies on the sanctions list. Thus in this respect the Security Council can be considered to have watered down the 1970 Libya sanctions regime compared to the 1493 DR Congo regime.

7.6 Peacekeeping operations and sanctions implementation

In several of the conflict situations analysed in this chapter, the UN Security Council deployed peacekeeping operations to help bringing the conflict to an end. Some of these were also mandated to support the government in implementing the sanctions imposed by the UN Security Council. The current section assesses their contribution to realising the aims of the respective sanctions regimes. The section first briefly sets out the conceptual framework for peacekeeping operations. Subsequently, it discusses the role of UN peace operations in eliminating the trade in conflict resources and in creating the conditions for transparent and accountable management of natural resources.

7.6.1 General remarks concerning peacekeeping operations

The deployment of peacekeeping operations by the UN Security Council has a longstanding tradition within the history of the organisation. In the absence of an explicit legal basis in the UN Charter, these operations have grown out of the practice of the UN, dating back to as early as 1948.[254] The primary objective of peacekeeping operations is to support States in the implementation of a cease-fire or peace agreement, once these States have started the transition from armed conflict to peace. Generally, peacekeeping operations are therefore deployed from the moment the parties to an armed conflict have agreed to end the violence. This does not, however, necessarily imply the actual ending of violence. On the contrary, many peacekeeping operations have been deployed in highly volatile settings.

[254] The United Nations Truce Supervision Organization (UNTSO) was deployed for the purpose of monitoring the Armistice Agreement between Israel and its Arabic neighbouring countries after the 1948 Arab–Israeli war following the proclamation of the Israeli State. See http://untso.unmissions.org.

Over time, peacekeeping operations have undergone considerable changes, notably in relation to their legal basis and mandates.[255] Traditionally associated with Chapter VI of the UN Charter and based on explicit consent of the host State to the deployment of an operation, most modern peacekeeping operations are authorised on the basis of Chapter VII in order to strengthen the operation's mandate.[256] Although consent of the host State is still the cornerstone of modern peacekeeping, the Chapter VII basis seeks to accommodate a reality where (some of the) parties to an armed conflict are reluctant to cooperate in the implementation of a peace agreement.[257] In these instances, the Chapter VII basis provides legal certainty where consent can no longer be presumed.[258] Furthermore, it provides the Council leeway to assign peace enforcement tasks to the operations if required by the circumstances.

In addition to modifications in their legal basis, the mandates of peacekeeping operations have also gradually changed over time. Whereas the principal responsibility of traditional peacekeeping operations was to monitor a cease-fire agreed upon by the parties to the conflict, the

[255] A distinction is normally made between 'generations' of peacekeeping operations. In the early years of the United Nations, 'first generation' or 'traditional' peacekeeping operations were deployed with a mandate limited to maintaining ceasefires. After the Cold War ended, 'second generation' or 'multidimensional' operations were deployed with a mandate to assist States in implementing comprehensive peace agreements. Around the turn of the century, 'third generation' multidimensional peacekeeping operations increasingly started to include peacebuilding tasks in their mandates combined with enhanced law enforcement tasks. See Doyle and Sambanis, 'Peacekeeping Operations', pp. 323–48; and Bothe, 'Peacekeeping', pp. 1171–99. For an overview of peacekeeping operations in relation to territorial administration, see Stahn, *The Law and Practice of International Territorial Administration*. See also the following reports, which set out the framework for modern peacekeeping operations: Report of the Secretary-General on an Agenda for Peace, Preventive Diplomacy, Peacemaking and Peacekeeping, *UN Doc. A/47/277 – S/24111* (1992); Report of the Panel on United Nations Peace Operations (Brahimi Report), *UN Doc. A/55/305 – S/2000/809* (2000); and Report of the Secretary-General on No Exit without Strategy: Security Council Decision-Making and the Closure or Transition of United Nations Peacekeeping Operations, *UN Doc. S/2001/394* (2001).

[256] See United Nations Department of Peacekeeping Operations, *United Nations Peacekeeping Operations: Principles and Guidelines* (2008), pp. 13–14.

[257] See Fox, *Humanitarian Occupation*, pp. 63–5.

[258] It can be argued that the withdrawal of consent by the host State after the deployment of the operation would have no legal effect, since the government agreed on the fulfillment of particular tasks by the operation. The government would therefore not have the right to come back to its earlier decision. See Orakhelashvili, *Collective Security*, pp. 315–18. On the other hand, mandates of peacekeeping operations are generally not static. The Council often adds new responsibilities to the mandate of an operation in the course of its deployment and consent would not encompass these new responsibilities.

mandates of modern peacekeeping operations are far more ambitious. These often include responsibilities related to governance assistance and statebuilding for the purpose of laying the foundations for sustainable peace in conflict-torn States. In other words, peacebuilding tasks addressing the structural causes of the armed conflict and the impediments for a lasting peace have become an integral part of modern peacekeeping operations.[259]

The foundations for the contemporary architecture of peacekeeping operations, combining traditional peacekeeping, peace enforcement and peacebuilding tasks, can be traced back to the 1992 Agenda for Peace.[260] In this landmark document former Secretary-General Boutros Boutros-Ghali introduced the concept of post-conflict peacebuilding, arguing that peacekeeping operations 'to be truly successful, must come to include comprehensive efforts to identify and support structures which will tend to consolidate peace'.[261] Subsequent reports, including the 2000 Brahimi report, have developed this idea of integrated multidimensional operations.[262] The operations discussed in the following section are all examples of such multidimensional operations, even though the extent to which they incorporate elements of peace enforcement and peacebuilding differs.

7.6.2 Peacekeeping operations and natural resources

In its Presidential Statement of 25 June 2007, the Security Council explicitly recognised that 'UN missions and peacekeeping operations deployed in resource-endowed countries experiencing armed conflict could play a role in helping the governments concerned, with full respect of their sovereignty over their natural resources, to prevent the illegal exploitation of those resources from further fuelling the conflict'. The Council further emphasised 'the importance of taking this dimension of conflict

[259] These tasks would fall under 'support to the restoration and extension of State authority', one of the five critical peacebuilding activities identified in the 2008 DPKO Report. See United Nations Department of Peacekeeping Operations, *United Nations Peacekeeping Operations: Principles and Guidelines* (2008), pp. 26–8.

[260] Report of the Secretary-General on an Agenda for Peace, Preventive Diplomacy, Peacemaking and Peacekeeping, *UN Doc. A/47/277 – S/24111* (1992).

[261] Ibid., para. 55.

[262] Report of the Panel on United Nations Peace Operations (Brahimi Report), *UN Doc. A/55/305 – S/2000/809* (2000).

into account, where appropriate, in the mandates of UN and regional peacekeeping operations'.

Peacekeeping operations address the role of natural resources in armed conflict in two principal ways. First, these operations may offer on-the-ground assistance in the implementation of resource sanctions. Important tasks include the securing of mining sites and effectuating border controls in order to prevent the smuggling of natural resources into neighbouring countries. The Security Council has included tasks related to sanctions monitoring in the mandate of several peacekeeping operations. The most prominent examples include UNTAC in Cambodia, UNAMSIL in Sierra Leone, UNMIL in Liberia and MONUC (and later MONUSCO) in the DR Congo. A second purpose these operations may fulfil is to assist the government of a State with institutional and legal reforms in order to break the link between natural resources and conflict financing. The Council has explicitly included such tasks in the mandates of UN peace operations only in two situations. These are UNMIL in Liberia and MONUC/MONUSCO in the DR Congo.

The following sections discuss the operations in Cambodia, Sierra Leone, Liberia and the DR Congo for the purpose of assessing their contribution to implementing the sanctions regimes imposed – or, in the case of Cambodia, supported – by the Security Council. Special emphasis is placed on their contribution to laying the foundations for sustainable peace.

The United Nations Transitional Authority in Cambodia

The United Nations Transitional Authority (UNTAC) was established pursuant to the 1991 Agreement on a Comprehensive Political Settlement of the Cambodia Conflict, concluded between the Cambodian factions represented in the Supreme National Council of Cambodia (SNC) and the different States participating in the Paris Conference.[263] In Article 2 of this Agreement, the signatories invite the Security Council 'to establish a United Nations Transitional Authority in Cambodia . . . with civilian and military components under the direct responsibility of the Secretary-General of the United Nations'. UNTAC therefore relied on consent as the legal basis for its operations. Article 3 further recognises the SNC as

[263] Agreement on a Comprehensive Political Settlement of the Cambodia Conflict, *UN Doc. S/23177* of 30 October 1991, Annex 1. For more details, see Section 7.4.1. See also Ratner, 'The Cambodia Settlement Agreements', pp. 1–41; Stahn, *The Law and Practice of International Territorial Administration*, pp. 269–79; and Dobbins et al., *The UN's Role in Nation-Building*, pp. 69–91.

'the unique legitimate body and source of authority in which, throughout the transitional period, the sovereignty, independence and unity of Cambodia are enshrined', while Article 6 of the Agreement stipulates that the SNC 'delegates to the United Nations all powers necessary to ensure the implementation of this Agreement', including the relevant aspects of the administration of Cambodia.[264]

In Resolution 717 (1991) the Security Council decided to establish a UN advance mission to assist the Cambodian parties in maintaining the ceasefire until UNTAC could be deployed.[265] UNTAC was established four months later by Resolution 745 (1992) for a period not to exceed eighteen months.[266] The main purpose of the operation was to create an enabling environment for elections to take place in Cambodia, based on the mandate set out in the 1991 Agreement. For this purpose, all administrative agencies, bodies and offices acting in the field of foreign affairs, national defence, finance, public security and information as well as other administrative agencies, bodies and offices that could directly influence the outcome of elections were placed under the direct control of UNTAC.[267] In addition, UNTAC was to supervise, monitor and verify the cease-fire and the withdrawal of foreign forces, as well as organising and conducting the elections.[268]

UNTAC was structured into seven components in order to fulfil its mandate.[269] Issues related to natural resources management were primarily addressed within the rehabilitation component, which was mandated to coordinate international development aid and to assist the SNC with the provision of basic services to the Cambodian population.[270] An assessment of Cambodia's natural resource base was part of this mandate, for the purpose of establishing their potential to promote development.

[264] See Ratner, 'The Cambodia Settlement Agreements', pp. 9–12.

[265] UNSC Resolution 717 (1991), para. 2. [266] UNSC Resolution 745 (1992), para. 2.

[267] See Annex 1, Section B 1 and 2 of the 1991 Agreement on a Comprehensive Political Settlement of the Cambodia Conflict. Ratner refers to this as 'the most exceptional feature of the Paris Accords', since it was the first time that the international community empowered the UN 'to undertake key aspects of the civil administration of a member state'. See Ratner, 'The Cambodia Settlement Agreements', p. 12.

[268] See Annex, Sections C and D of the 1991 Agreement.

[269] These are human rights, electoral activities, military, civil administration, civil police, repatriation and rehabilitation. See Findlay, *Cambodia: The Legacy and Lessons of UNTAC*, p. 28.

[270] See the 1991 Declaration on the Rehabilitation and Reconstruction of Cambodia. It was understood that in this first phase leading up to the elections, particular attention was to be given to food security, health, housing, training, education, the transport network and the restoration of Cambodia's existing basic infrastructure and public utilities.

Based upon evidence that the country's timber stock and gem mines had been rapidly depleted, UNTAC advised the SNC to adopt a mechanism for reviewing and examining the different contractual arrangements relating to the exploitation of natural resources.[271]

In response, the SNC established a Technical Advisory Committee on the Management and Sustainable Exploitation of Natural Resources, chaired by the UNTAC Director of Rehabilitation, to formulate and recommend to the SNC specific measures for dealing with the problem of overexploitation of Cambodia's natural resources.[272] Among the recommendations of the Committee were the adoption of moratoria on round logs and on gems, which the SNC ultimately approved in September 1992 and February 1993, respectively. UNTAC subsequently played an important role in implementing the moratoria,[273] including deploying border controls to monitor violations of the moratoria and overseeing the legitimate export of sawn timber.[274]

UNTAC's contribution to this effect was crucial, even though it encountered many difficulties in performing its tasks, especially those relating to enforcing the moratoria.[275] More important, however, was UNTAC's role in the territorial administration of Cambodia, based on a delegation of powers by the transitional government. As an administering authority, UNTAC's mandate included peacebuilding tasks. The establishment of a rehabilitation unit within UNTAC, addressing the management of natural resources in Cambodia from a developmental and environmental perspective, was very innovative. However, the relatively short period of UNTAC's deployment and its narrow focus on the organisation of elections prevented it from addressing the management of natural resources in a structural way.

The United Nations Mission in Sierra Leone

The United Nations Mission in Sierra Leone (UNAMSIL) was established pursuant to UN Security Council Resolution 1270 (1999) *inter alia* to cooperate with the government of Sierra Leone and the RUF to implement

[271] See the Second Progress Report of the Secretary-General, *UN Doc. S/24578 (1992)*, para. 57.

[272] Ibid., para. 58.

[273] For a direct reference, see UNSC Resolution 792 (1992), in which the Security Council requested UNTAC to secure the implementation of the embargo on logs.

[274] See the Fourth Progress Report of the Secretary-General, *UN Doc. S/25289 (1993)*, Sect. V.

[275] See Section 7.4.1.

the Lomé Peace Agreement concluded between them on 7 July 1999.[276] The Agreement specifically requested a UN presence for this purpose,[277] while Chapter VII of the UN Charter served as an additional legal basis for the deployment of UNAMSIL.[278]

At start, UNAMSIL's mandate did not include resource-related issues. The Lomé Agreement reserved issues related to the management of the State's natural resources to State sovereignty. Article VII of the Lomé Agreement provided for the establishment of a special Commission for the Management of Strategic Resources, National Reconstruction and Development, charged with the responsibility of securing and monitoring the legitimate exploitation of Sierra Leone's gold and diamonds and other resources that were determined to be of strategic importance for national security and welfare on behalf of the government of Sierra Leone. The Commission was to be chaired by Mr. Sankoh, one of the leaders of the RUF.[279] This proved to be a major error, since it allowed the RUF to continue with the illegal exploitation of diamonds in territory under its control. Almost a year after the signing of the Lomé Agreement, the Commission was still not established, while the RUF retained control over the diamonds fields and refused UNAMSIL access to these regions.[280]

The reaction of the international community was cautious. The Secretary-General emphasised in his March 2000 progress report that 'UNAMSIL has neither the mandate nor the intention to stop or interfere with any economic activity'. He reassured that 'the exploitation of natural resources falls entirely within the responsibility of the Government and its relevant organs, in particular the Commission for the Management of Strategic Resources, National Reconstruction and Development under the chairmanship of Mr. Sankoh'. At the same time, he recommended to the international community 'to consider measures to help curtail the sale of illegally mined diamonds from Sierra Leone'.[281]

276 UNSC Resolution 1270 (1999), para. 8. Other relevant tasks included disarmament and demobilization and the organisation of elections.

277 The parties to the Agreement requested the Security Council to expand the mandate for the observer mission operating in Sierra Leone. See Peace Agreement between the Government of Sierra Leone and the Revolutionary United Front, 7 July 1999, Article XIV.

278 In Resolution 1270 (1999), the Council determines that the situation in Sierra Leone continues to constitute a threat to international peace and security in the region.

279 See UN Secretary-General, First Report on the United Nations Mission in Sierra Leone, *UN Doc. S/1999/1223 (1999)*, para. 5.

280 See UN Secretary-General, Third Report on the United Nations Mission in Sierra Leone, *UN Doc. S/2000/186 (2000)*, paras. 48–9.

281 Ibid.

The Security Council waited and only when the conflict escalated did it take further action. In May 2000, RUF leader Foday Sankoh was arrested after the RUF had taken 500 peacekeepers hostage.[282] In response to these events and in light of the RUF's refusal to implement the ceasefire agreement, the Security Council decided to take stronger measures to restore peace and security. The Council's measures included the adoption of an embargo on diamonds in July 2000,[283] backed up by a revision of UNAMSIL's mandate. In Resolution 1313 (2000) the Council mandated UNAMSIL 'to assist, through its presence and within the framework of its mandate, the efforts of the Government of Sierra Leone to extend state authority, restore law and order and further stabilize the situation progressively throughout the entire country', while in subsequent resolutions it explicitly referred to reestablishing State authority over the diamond producing areas.[284]

Pursuant to its mandate, UNAMSIL focused principally on providing physical security by deploying troops in the diamond producing areas. In addition, its civilian police component played an important role in the development of local capacity by providing advise and training to the Sierra Leonean police forces, which included the establishment of a diamonds crime intelligence and investigation unit.[285] UNAMSIL was not actively involved, however, in legal or institutional reforms for the diamonds sector. Its role in implementing the Security Council's embargo against diamonds was therefore limited to providing the necessary logistical support for bringing the diamond mines under effective control of the government.

The United Nations Mission in Liberia

The United Nations Mission in Liberia (UNMIL) was established by the Security Council in September 2003 to relieve the ECOMIL forces that

282 See UN Secretary-General, Fourth Report on the United Nations Mission in Sierra Leone, *UN Doc. S/2000/455 (2000).*

283 See Section 7.4.3 for more details.

284 See UNSC Resolution 1313 (2000), para. 3(c); Resolution 1346 (2001), para. 15; and Resolution 1400 (2002), para. 7. The direct references to the diamond-producing areas follow from the provisions of the Abuja Cease Fire Agreement, concluded between the government of Sierra Leone and the RUF in November 2000, in which they agreed that 'UNAMSIL shall have full liberty to deploy its troops and other personnel throughout Sierra Leone including the diamond producing areas in the discharge of its responsibilities.'

285 See UN Secretary-General, Twenty-First Report on the United Nations Mission in Sierra Leone, *UN Doc. S/2004/228 (2004)*, para. 8.

were already deployed in Liberia. It was not the first UN peacekeeping operation in Liberia, but it was the most ambitious in terms of mandate and functions as well as the only operation that received an explicit mandate to assist the transitional government in restoring proper administration of natural resources.[286] It is for this reason that this section focuses exclusively on UNMIL.

UNMIL was established pursuant to Chapter VII of the UN Charter, as requested by the Liberian factions that concluded the Accra Comprehensive Peace Agreement.[287] In addition to typical law enforcement tasks including border inspection controls and surveillance of mining areas,[288] UNMIL was also given an important advisory function. In order to give effect to its mandate to assist the government in restoring proper administration of natural resources, UNMIL was given specific tasks, including providing assistance to the government in working 'towards establishing an official Certificate of Origin regime for trade in rough diamonds that is transparent and internationally verifiable, with a view to joining the Kimberley Process'.[289] Another important task that was given to UNMIL was to assist the Liberian government and the Panel of Experts in the monitoring of sanctions.[290]

Most of these tasks were undertaken by the civil affairs component of the operation, which was given a role in assisting the Liberian government in 'developing a strategy and setting up mechanisms for monitoring and controlling the exploitation of [natural] resources' as well as in 'devising mechanisms for ensuring accountability and transparency in the collection and disbursement of revenues accruing from the exploitation of natural resources'.[291] For this purpose, a specific Environment and Natural

[286] UNSC Resolution 1509 (2003), para. 3(r). It is interesting to note that this task was not envisaged in the proposal of the Secretary-General. See Report of the Secretary-General to the Security Council on Liberia, *UN Doc. S/2003/875 (2003).*

[287] Comprehensive Peace Agreement between the Government of Liberia and the Liberians United for Reconcilation and Democracy (LURD) and the Movement for Democracy in Liberia (MODEL) and Political Parties, Accra, 18 August 2003. Article IV of this Agreement states, 'The GOL, the LURD, the MODEL and the Political Parties agree on the need for the deployment of an International Stabilization Force (ISF) in Liberia. Accordingly, the Parties hereby request the United Nations in collaboration with ECOWAS, the AU and the ICGL to facilitate, constitute, and deploy a United Nations Chapter VII force in the Republic of Liberia to support the transitional government and to assist in the implementation of this Agreement.'

[288] See, e.g., UNSC Resolutions 1607 and 1647 (2005).

[289] UNSC Resolution 1607 (2005), para. 2.

[290] Ibid., para. 11.

[291] UN Secretary-General, First Progress Report on the United Nations Mission in Liberia, *UN Doc. S/2003/1175 (2003)*, paras. 38 and 40.

Resources Unit was created. In addition, a Working Group on Sanctions was established to coordinate sanctions-related activities undertaken by this and other Units.[292]

Pursuant to its mandate set out above, UNMIL provided advice and assistance to the government in such areas as sanctions compliance, drafting and implementing legislative reforms in the minerals and timber sectors as well as the implementation of the GEMAP and LFI programmes.[293] Other tasks included training, equipping and deploying mineral inspectors and mining agents to institute Kimberley Process certification scheme procedures, establishing regional Kimberley Process offices as well as advising artisanal miners on the formation of cooperatives for the purpose of legalising small-scale mining.[294] Finally, UNMIL was responsible for providing technical and logistical support to the Environmental Protection Agency, established by the newly elected government in 2006 as the principal authority for the protection of the environment and the sustainable use of natural resources.[295]

When the timber and diamond sanctions were lifted in 2006 and 2007, UNMIL remained active in Liberia, providing the necessary support to the government in initiating and consolidating reforms in those sectors for the purpose of achieving a durable peace. It performs these tasks up until today, although its focus has shifted to more general assistance in promoting transparency and accountability in public administration.

UNMIL was the first peacekeeping operation that received an explicit mandate encompassing natural resources management, thus enabling the operation to address this issue as a matter of priority. In the performance

[292] UN Secretary-General, Report Pursuant to Security Council Resolution 1579 (2004) Regarding Liberia, *UN Doc. S/2005/376 (2005)*, para. 20.

[293] Ibid., paras. 24–5; UN Secretary-General, Twelfth Progress Report on the United Nations Mission in Liberia, *UN Doc. S/2006/743 (2006)*, para. 33. UNMIL assisted the programmes in several ways. As a member of the Governance Steering Committee of the GEMAP, UNMIL was responsible for overseeing the implementation of the programme. In addition, UNMIL's Legal and Judicial System Support Division assisted the GEMAP partnership in combating corruption. Furthermore, UNMIL worked with the LFI partnership to draft a working plan for the protection of Liberia's forest resources. See UN Secretary-General, Ninth Progress Report on the United Nations Mission in Liberia, *UN Doc. S/2005/764 (2005)*, paras. 55 and 61. For more information on the GEMAP and LFI programmes, see Section 7.4.4.

[294] UN Secretary-General, Report Pursuant to Security Council Resolution 1579 (2004) Regarding Liberia, *UN Doc. S/2005/376 (2005)*, para. 41; Eleventh Progress Report on the United Nations Mission in Liberia, *UN Doc. S/2006/376 (2006)*, para. 30.

[295] UN Secretary-General, Thirteenth Progress Report on the United Nations Mission in Liberia, *UN Doc. S/2006/958*, para. 27.

of its functions, UNMIL greatly contributed to implementing the necessary reforms to improve the management of natural resources in a State without properly functioning institutions. It performed a crucial role in assisting the government and international partners to fulfil the stringent and extensive conditions set by the Security Council for the lifting of the timber and diamond sanctions. Importantly, UNMIL's role went far beyond providing assistance in restoring the authority of the government over Liberia's natural resources and encompassed tasks related to the administration of natural resources and their revenues. In these ways, UNMIL effectively contributed to the implementation of structural solutions to improving natural resources management in Liberia, paving the way for the country's post-conflict reconstruction process.

The UN Organization (Stabilization) Mission in the Democratic Republic of the Congo

The United Nations Organization Mission in the Democratic Republic of the Congo (MONUC) was established by the Security Council, acting under Chapter VII of the UN Charter, in November 1999 to assist the parties to the Lusaka Ceasefire Agreement, concluded earlier that year by the DR Congo, Angola, Namibia, Rwanda, Uganda, Zambia, and Zimbabwe, in its implementation,[296] as specifically provided for under the Agreement.[297] The Security Council refrained from including resource related tasks in MONUC's mandate at that stage, even though it was aware of illegal resource exploitation activities in the DR Congo when it established MONUC.[298]

It was only in 2007 that resource-related tasks were included in MONUC's mandate, albeit indirectly. In its Resolution 1756 (2007), the Council instructed MONUC 'to assist the Government of the Democratic Republic of the Congo in establishing a stable security environment in the country, and, to that end, to . . . support operations [of the Congolese

[296] See UNSC Resolution 1279 (1999).

[297] Article 11(a) of the Lusaka Agreement states that the Security Council 'acting under Chapter VII, shall be requested to constitute, facilitate and deploy an appropriate peacekeeping force in the DRC to ensure implementation of this Agreement; and taking into account the peculiar situation of the DRC, mandate the peacekeeping force to track down all armed groups in the DRC'.

[298] Only seven months after it established MONUC, the Council requested the Secretary-General to establish an expert panel on the illegal exploitation of natural resources and other forms of wealth of the Democratic Republic of the Congo. See Security Council Presidential Statement of 2 June 2000, *UN Doc. S/PRST/2000/20.*

army] with a view to . . . prevent the provision of support to illegal armed groups, including support derived from illicit economic activities'.[299]

A year later, this mandate was broadened to include monitoring and inspection tasks to curtail the provision of support to illegal armed groups derived from illicit trade in natural resources.[300] MONUC was authorised to use all necessary means to carry out these tasks, although, in light of its limited capacities, priority was given to its primary task to protect the civilian population.[301] This resulted in a pilot project undertaken by the Congolese government and MONUC to bring together all State services in a limited number of trading counters in the eastern part of the DR Congo with a view to enable the tracing of minerals for the purpose of reinstating government control over the key mining sites. In Resolution 1906 (2009) the Security Council urged MONUC to 'consolidate and assess, jointly with the Government of the Democratic Republic of the Congo, its pilot project . . . in order to improve the traceability of mineral products'.[302]

In 2010, MONUC was renamed MONUSCO in order to reflect the new phase of the DR Congo's transition to peace.[303] MONUSCO's tasks remained essentially the same, focusing *inter alia* on providing assistance to the Congolese government in reinstating government control over the key mining sites. Its mandate included consolidating the five trading counters set up to facilitate tracing the origin of minerals as well as to carry out spot checks and regular visits to mining sites, trade routes and markets, in the vicinity of the five pilot trading counters.[304] In addition, MONUSCO was given a role in assisting the government in strengthening its justice system in order to prosecute those responsible for illegal resource exploitation.[305] Throughout its operation, MONUSCO made considerable progress in realising this part of its mandate. It assisted the government in establishing the mineral trading counters, in validating mining sites as well as in training mining staff and local police to secure the counters.[306]

[299] UNSC Resolution 1756 (2007), para. 2.

[300] UNSC Resolution 1856 (2008), para. 3. [301] Ibid., paras. 5 and 6.

[302] UNSC Resolution 1906 (2009), para. 28.

[303] See UNSC Resolution 1952 (2010), establishing MONUSCO.

[304] See UNSC Resolutions 1952 (2010), para. 16 and 1991 (2011), para. 17.

[305] UNSC Resolution 1952 (2010), para. 16.

[306] See, e.g., the Reports of the Secretary-General on the United Nations Organization Stabilization Mission in the Democratic Republic of the Congo, *UN Doc. S/2011/20 (2011)*, para. 54; *UN Doc. S/2011/656 (2011)*, para. 53; and *UN Doc. S/2012/838 (2012)*, para. 75.

In 2013, a special Intervention Brigade was established within MONUSCO with a mandate to neutralise armed groups, to contribute in reducing the threat posed by armed groups to state authority and civilian security in eastern DR Congo and to make space for stabilization activities.[307] The Brigade did not receive specific instructions in relation to the mining sites. Likewise, the overall mandate of MONUSCO remained largely the same.[308]

More importantly from the perspective of providing structural solutions to break the interlinkage between natural resources and armed conflict in the DR Congo, MONUC/MONUSCO was also given the mandate to assist the Congolese government in its endeavours towards improving transparent and accountable economic management, including the management of the State's natural resources and revenues.[309] In 2005, the Council already encouraged and later requested MONUC 'to provide advice and assistance as well as the necessary support to the setting up by the Transitional Government, international financial institutions and donors, of an arrangement to strengthen support for good governance and transparent economic management'.[310] However, capacity problems prevented MONUC from giving effect to this recommendation. This remained a problem throughout the operation's deployment. Even after the Council decided in Resolution 1856 (2008) that 'MONUC will also have the mandate, in close cooperation with the Congolese authorities, the United Nations Country Team and donors, to support the strengthening of democratic institutions and the rule of law and, to that end, to . . . contribute to the promotion of good governance and respect for the principle of accountability',[311] the operation did not effectively implement this part of its mandate. MONUSCO's focus remained on its core

307 UNSC Resolution 2098 (2013), para. 9.

308 See, e.g., UNSC Resolution 2136 (2014), para. 25. In its most recent resolutions, the Council expanded the civilian mandate of MONUSCO to include 'the consolidation of an effective national civilian structure to control key mining activities and to manage in an equitable manner the extraction and trade of natural resources in eastern DRC'. However, the Council formulated this task in the form of a recommendation and tied it to the use of good offices. See UNSC Resolutions 2098 (2013), para. 14 and 2147 (2014), para. 5.

309 A 2013 Report by the UN Secretary-General stated that '[i]nternational independent indicators have persistently ranked the Democratic Republic of the Congo as one of the most corrupt countries in the world'. See UN Secretary-General, Special Report on the Democratic Republic of the Congo and the Great Lakes Region, *UN Doc. S/2013/119 (2013)*, para. 24.

310 UNSC Resolution 1621 (2005), para. 4 and Resolution 1635 (2005), para. 7.

311 See UNSC Resolution 1856 (2008), para. 4.

tasks, particularly protecting the civilian population and reinstating State authority in the mining areas.

MONUC/MONUSCO received an explicit mandate to assist the government in improving the management of its natural resources. The operation's principal contribution to this purpose consisted of reorganising the infrastructure for the tracing of minerals exploited in the conflict regions of the DR Congo. Even though MONUC/MONUSCO's contribution in this respect is very valuable for the purpose of implementing the Security Council's due diligence measures, it is too limited for the purpose of improving the management of natural resources in the DR Congo. The focus of MONUC/MONUSCO is principally on eliminating the trade in conflict resources, without addressing some of the underlying problems, notably malfunctions in the public administration of natural resources and their revenues. The operation's failure to address these issues is not related to the Security Council mandate, which is sufficiently broad to encompass these tasks. The principal problem therefore seems to be the limited capacity of MONUC/MONUSCO to implement the full package of tasks which the Security Council has assigned to it. This demonstrates that the capacity of a peacekeeping operation needs to be tailored to its ambitions.

7.6.3 Appraisal

This section discussed four different operations, two of which received an explicit mandate to assist the State in improving the management of its natural resources. All operations combined elements of traditional peacekeeping, peace enforcement and peacebuilding. While peace enforcement, notably for the purpose of restoring State authority over mining sites, was an important component for all operations, the extent to which these operations addressed natural resources management for the purpose of peacebuilding beyond restoring State authority over the mining sites differed significantly.

UNMIL's mandate was the most ambitious one in this respect. It did not only assist in initiating the reforms necessary to stop the trade in conflict resources, but it also assisted the government in establishing the mechanisms necessary to improve public administration of natural resources. It performed these tasks directly on the basis of its mandate and indirectly through its involvement in the GEMAP and LFI programmes. As an early example, UNTAC's role in initiating the moratoria on timber and gems is of interest as well. Principally motivated by environmental and developmental reasons, the purposes of the moratoria included safeguarding Cambodia's natural resource base for sustainable development.

In conclusion, it is to be noted that all four peacekeeping operations contributed to implementing the necessary conditions for the lifting of sanctions imposed by the Security Council. In addition, except for the overstretched MONUC/MONUSCO, they realised the mandate that was given to them by the Council. The current section further demonstrated that the principal purpose of peacekeeping operations is to provide security, for example, by clearing mining sites. In most cases, additional reform tasks undertaken by these operations can be directly related to this overarching purpose. The regrouping of trading counters in the DR Congo is a relevant example.

This leaves open one remaining question: to what extent can peacekeeping operations be expected to restore legal and institutional arrangements for the management of natural resources in the host State for the purposes of post-conflict reconstruction and conflict prevention? Arguably, the contribution of peacekeeping operations in instituting the necessary reforms should be further enhanced. The work of UNMIL in Liberia can serve as an example for other operations in this respect. UNMIL greatly contributed to remedying institutional failures that facilitated illegal exploitation of natural resources as a driver for armed conflict. At the same time, the example of UNMIL demonstrates that these tasks cannot be fulfilled by a peacekeeping operation alone. The key to UNMIL's success in Liberia is related to its cooperation with other partners, most notably the international partnership instituting the GEMAP and LFI programs as well as informal mechanisms such as KPCS and EITI. This calls for early coordination of peacebuilding tasks, from the point of view of both conflict resolution and post-conflict reconstruction.

7.7 From conflict resolution to peacebuilding: the role of the UN Peacebuilding Commission

In 2005, the Security Council and the General Assembly established the UN Peacebuilding Commission as an intergovernmental advisory body to help States recovering from armed conflict to build a sustainable peace. It was established as a subsidiary organ of both the General Assembly and the Security Council pursuant to Articles 7, 22 and 29 of the UN Charter for the purpose of filling an institutional gap between the mandates of the Security Council – i.e., the maintenance of international peace and security – and ECOSOC, responsible for promoting development in stable countries.[312]

Its origins can be traced back to the 1992 Agenda for Peace, which introduced the concept of post-conflict peacebuilding and indicated the need for the UN to integrate this more directly into its work.[313] In the following years, peacebuilding tasks were increasingly included in the mandates of peacekeeping operations, yet an institutional structure was lacking. Therefore, in its 2004 report, the High-Level Panel on Threats, Challenges and Change proposed to establish a 'single intergovernmental organ dedicated to peacebuilding, empowered to monitor and pay close attention to countries at risk, ensure concerted action by donors, agencies, programmes and financial institutions, and mobilize financial resources for sustainable peace'.[314]

At the 2005 World Summit, States recognised the need for such an institutional mechanism and resolved to establish the Peacebuilding Commission for this purpose, albeit with a more limited objective than envisaged by the High-Level Panel.[315] The purpose of this new mechanism was 'to address the special needs of countries emerging from conflict towards recovery, reintegration and reconstruction and to assist them in laying the foundation for sustainable development', thereby leaving out the early warning and monitoring function recommended by the High-Level Panel.[316]

The official mandate of the Peacebuilding Commission, as set out in the relevant resolutions of the General Assembly and the Security Council, is broadly formulated. It does not refer to specific priorities the Commission should address. Instead, it consists of three principal tasks: to

[312] See Baetens and Kohoutek, 'United Nations Peacebuilding Commission', pp. 406–14. See also on this topic, e.g., Baetens, 'Facilitating Post-conflict Reconstruction', pp. 346–75; Salomons, 'On the Far Side of Conflict', pp. 195–211; Otobo, 'The New Peacebuilding Architecture', pp. 212–34; Stahn, 'Institutionalizing Brahimi's Light Footprint', pp. 403–15.

[313] Report of the Secretary-General on an Agenda for Peace, Preventive Diplomacy, Peacemaking and Peacekeeping, *UN Doc. A/47/277 – S/24111* (1992), paras. 55–9.

[314] Report of the High-Level Panel on Threats, Challenges and Change, *A More Secure World*, para. 225.

[315] UNGA Resolution 60/1 of 24 October 2005, para. 97.

[316] In his 2005 report 'In Larger Freedom: Towards Development, Security and Human Rights For All', the Secretary-General had advised against equipping the Commission with early warning and monitoring functions. See *UN Doc. A/59/2005* of 21 March 2005, para. 115.

bring together the different actors in the field to marshal resources and to advise on and propose integrated strategies for post-conflict peacebuilding and recovery; to focus attention on the necessary reconstruction and institution-building efforts and to support the development of integrated strategies in order to lay the foundation for sustainable development; and, last, to provide recommendations and information to improve the coordination of all relevant actors within and outside the UN, to develop best practices, to help to ensure predictable financing for early recovery activities and to extend the period of attention given by the international community to post-conflict recovery.[317]

In order to fulfil its mandate, the Commission operates in three principal formations. The Organizational Committee is the principal steering body of the Commission, consisting of representatives of the principal UN bodies that have a direct stake in the working domain of the Commission, i.e., the General Assembly, Security Council and ECOSOC, as well as those of the principal troop contributing and donor countries.[318] This constellation aims to ensure that the Peacebuilding Commission can fulfil one of its principal functions, namely to coordinate the activities of different actors both within and outside the UN system in the field of peacebuilding.

The principal focus of this section is on the two other formations, namely the country-specific configurations, which oversee peacebuilding activities in the countries that are on the Commission's agenda, and the Working Group on Lessons Learned, which develops best practices for peacebuilding strategies. The current section assesses the extent to which these two bodies have addressed issues relating to natural resources management.

7.7.1 Country-specific configurations

There are currently six countries on the agenda of the Commission, including Sierra Leone and Liberia.[319] The first has been included in the agenda of the Commission since 2007 at the request of the Security

[317] UNGA Resolution 60/180 and UNSC Resolution 1645 (2005).

[318] See www.un.org/en/peacebuilding/orgcommittee.shtml. It is notable that the States that are on the agenda of the Peacebuilding Commission are not represented in the Organizational Committee.

[319] The four other countries are Burundi, Guinea, Guinea-Bissau and the Central African Republic.

Council, while the latter has been included in 2010 at its own request.[320] Country-specific configurations are composed of all members of the Organizational Committee, complemented with representatives of the State under consideration, regional States, relevant regional and subregional organisations, the major financial, troop and civilian police contributors involved in the recovery effort, senior UN officials involved in the peacebuilding effort and international and regional financial organisations.

The relationship between the Commission and the State concerned is governed by a flexible agreement, which can be changed over time if considered necessary by the parties, containing priorities for peacebuilding as well as the mutual commitments of the Commission and the State concerned. It is important to note here that the basic principle governing these documents is national ownership, meaning that the primary responsibility and ownership for the peacebuilding process lies with the State concerned. This also implies that it is for the State to set the priorities for the peacebuilding process. For Sierra Leone, the peacebuilding priorities and commitments have been included in the Sierra Leone Peacebuilding Cooperation Framework, while for Liberia the Commission adopted a Statement of Mutual Commitments on Peacebuilding in Liberia. The following sections discuss these documents and their implementation in more detail, with an emphasis on their relevance for natural resources management.

Sierra Leone Peacebuilding Cooperation Framework

The Sierra Leone Peacebuilding Cooperation Framework was developed through a consultative process with national and international stakeholders in Sierra Leone and through deliberations within the Peacebuilding Commission.[321] It identifies the following five priorities as the basis for specific commitments: youth employment and empowerment, consolidation of democracy and good governance, justice and security sector reform, capacity-building and energy sector development.

Natural resources management is addressed first of all under the heading of 'consolidation of democracy and good governance' in relation to

[320] A country can be included in the PBC's agenda via a request for advice by the Security Council, the General Assembly, ECOSOC, the Secretary-General or by the country itself. See www.un.org/en/peacebuilding/countryconfig.shtml.

[321] Sierra Leone Peacebuilding Cooperation Framework, adopted on 3 December 2007, *UN Doc. PBC/2/SLE/1*, para. 7.

combating corruption. The Cooperation Framework stipulates that 'further efforts are needed to strengthen the capacity of the Government of Sierra Leone, in accordance with the Extractive Industries Transparency Initiative, for the management and governance of natural resources for the benefit of the people of Sierra Leone'.[322] For this purpose, the Government of Sierra Leone is to '[r]eview the Core Minerals Policy and related regulations to improve the Governance and management of natural resources, including on current contracts and revenue collection, to prevent smuggling and illicit trade, and to ensure participation at the local and community levels'.

Relevant commitments for the Peacebuilding Commission relate to capacity building and its general mandate to coordinate peacebuilding activities. Pursuant to its general mandate, the Commission commits itself to '[s]upport the efforts of the Government and the people of Sierra Leone, taking into account existing instruments, such as the Extractive Industries Transparency Initiative and the Kimberley Process, by advocating for appropriate action in the engagement of the relevant stakeholders, in ensuring national ownership for effective, transparent and sustainable exploitation and management of Sierra Leone's natural resources'. Capacity building as a priority for peacebuilding laid down in the Cooperation Framework includes the need to ensure adequate economic and financial management.[323] For this purpose, the Commission is to 'support capacity-building to enhance the Government's efforts in the management of natural resources, in particular the Ministries of Marine and Mineral Resources'.[324]

From a legal point of view, the Peacebuilding Cooperation Framework is interesting in three respects. The first aspect relates to the operation of the principle of national ownership in the Framework. Respect for this principle is guaranteed by giving the government the primary responsibility for instituting legal reforms in the mining sector, while the Peacebuilding Commission has a supportive role, focusing on general capacity building and coordination tasks. Another point of interest is the observation that the Peacebuilding Cooperation Framework relies heavily on the implementation of informal mechanisms to achieve its goals, most notably EITI and KPCS.[325]

Last, it is interesting to take a closer look at the peacebuilding priorities formulated in the Cooperation Framework, on one hand, and relevant

[322] Ibid., para. 19. [323] Ibid., para. 20. [324] Ibid., Part IV Sect. B paras. 26(g) and (z).
[325] These mechanisms are discussed in the following chapter.

resolutions of the Security Council and reports of the Secretary-General, on the other. An analysis of these documents indicates perfect harmony between the priorities formulated for the United Nations Integrated Office in Sierra Leone (UNIOSIL), established to replace UNAMSIL for the purpose of consolidating peace in Sierra Leone, and the priorities formulated in the Peacebuilding Cooperation Framework.[326] The latter document clearly builds upon the approach set out by the Security Council and the Secretary-General, making it apparent that the work of the Peacebuilding Commission in Sierra Leone was intended as a follow-up to the process initiated by the Security Council. This is also apparent from subsequent institutional arrangements. From the moment that the Security Council referred Sierra Leone to the agenda of the Peacebuilding Commission, it instructed UNIOSIL to provide active support to the work of the Commission.[327]

After the adoption of the Peacebuilding Cooperation Framework, the peacebuilding process was subsequently streamlined on the basis of policy documents adopted by the government of Sierra Leone and the UN. Relevant documents include two poverty reduction strategies adopted by the government of Sierra Leone, the Agenda for Change (2008–12) and the Agenda for Prosperity (2013–17), which address natural resources management as a central issue. These documents served as the peacebuilding frameworks of reference for the UN and were complemented by the United Nations Joint Vision for Sierra Leone, adopted with the support of all relevant UN organisations and the World Bank.[328]

Natural resources management received high priority in the Sierra Leone configuration throughout the process. Effective cooperation between the Commission and UNIOSIL was achieved by relevant Security Council resolutions mandating UNIOSIL to provide support to the Commission. One may question, however, whether the Peacebuilding Commission was indeed able to assume the principal role assigned to it

[326] See UNSC Resolution 1620 (2005), para. 1 and UN Secretary-General, Second Addendum to the Twenty-Fifth Report on the United Nations Mission in Sierra Leone, *UN Doc. S/2005/273/Add.2 (2005)*, para. 6 on the proposed mandate for UNIOSIL.

[327] See UNSC Resolution 1793 (2007), para. 3.

[328] See, e.g., the Outcome of the Peacebuilding Commission High-Level Special Session on Sierra Leone of 12 June 2009, where the Commission decides to align its future engagement with Sierra Leone with the Agenda for Change; and the Second Review of the Outcome of the High-Level Special Session of the Peacebuilding Commission on Sierra Leone of 2 October 2012, *UN Doc. PBC/6/SLE/2*, where the Commission reaffirms the importance of providing necessary support for the full implementation of the instruments referred to above.

by the international community, i.e., to advise on and propose integrated strategies for post-conflict peacebuilding and recovery. The Peacebuilding Cooperation Framework added little to the existing post-conflict strategy for Sierra Leone, initiated by the Security Council and the Secretary-General. The principal role of the Peacebuilding Commission was therefore to provide support to the implementation of this strategy.

Statement of Mutual Commitments on Peacebuilding in Liberia

The Statement of Mutual Commitments on Peacebuilding in Liberia was adopted on 29 October 2010.[329] It contains the following peacebuilding priorities: the rule of law, security sector reform and national reconciliation. The Statement contains no specific references to natural resources management. This omission is remarkable in light of the high importance attached to this issue by the Security Council, both in the phase of conflict resolution and as part of peacebuilding efforts. Until March 2014, the Security Council actively monitored the progress made by the government of Liberia in relation to the management of its natural resources,[330] while UNMIL is still mandated to provide assistance to the Liberian government on issues related to public finance and natural resources management. It was therefore to be expected that the Peacebuilding Commission would assume a role in coordinating this process, in close cooperation with other actors, most notably the Kimberley Process and EITI.

In the peacebuilding strategy, natural resources management is partially addressed through issues related to land reform, which falls under the priorities 'rule of law' and 'national reconciliation'. Most notably, attention is focused on ways to improve transparency and accountability

[329] Statement of Mutual Commitments on Peacebuilding in Liberia, *UN Doc. PBC/4/LBR/2* of 16 November 2010.

[330] In Resolution 1279 (2012) the Council mandated the Panel of Experts on Liberia inter alia to conduct assessment missions in Liberia and neighbouring countries to investigate violations of the arms embargo 'including the various sources of financing, such as from natural resources, for the illicit trade of arms'. In addition, the Panel was to assess 'the extent to which forests and other natural resources are contributing to peace, security and development rather than to instability and to what extent relevant legislation (National Forestry Reform Law, Lands Commission Act, Community Rights Law with respect to Forest Land, and Liberia Extractive Industries Transparency Initiative Act) and other reform efforts are contributing to this transition, and to provide recommendations on how such natural resources could better contribute to the country's progress towards sustainable peace and stability' as well as 'the Government of Liberia's compliance with the Kimberley Process Certification Scheme'.

as well as to enhance public participation of local communities in natural resources concession procedures, since this is directly related to (disputes over) the use of land.[331] All other aspects of natural resources management, including Liberia's implementation of informal mechanisms such as EITI, are however coordinated by the World Bank by country partnership strategies, without any significant involvement of the Peacebuilding Commission.[332] To a certain extent, this makes sense. The World Bank has assumed an important role in the reforms in Liberia's natural resources sectors since the end of the conflict. There is therefore no need for the Peacebuilding Commission to address this issue. From the point of view of the Peacebuilding Commission's mandate to coordinate the peacebuilding process, it is however more problematic, since it prevents the Peacebuilding Commission from assuming the role assigned to it, namely to support the development of integrated strategies in order to lay the foundation for sustainable development and to improve the coordination of all relevant actors within and outside the UN.

Similar problems occur in the cooperation between the Commission and the Security Council. The Resolutions of the Security Council only marginally refer to the work of the Peacebuilding Commission. Resolution 2079 (2012), for example, refers only once to the Peacebuilding Commission, welcoming its engagement in supporting the Liberian government in its efforts to meet the conditions set out in the Council's primary sanction resolution 1521 (2003). In contrast, the operative part of the resolution contains multiple references to the work of the Kimberley Process. This questions the ability of the Commission to coordinate the peacebuilding process effectively.

7.7.2 Working Group on Lessons Learned

The Working Group on Lessons Learned is an informal platform aimed at identifying lessons to be learned from previous post-conflict peacebuilding experiences. Throughout its existence, it has given systematic consideration to natural resources management, both in relation to economic revitalisation and environmental protection. The issue was first discussed

[331] See, e.g., Peacebuilding Commission, Informal Meeting of the Liberian Country Specific Configuration, 24 February 2014, Chair's Summary of the Discussion, para. 16. For this purpose, the government established a commission entrusted with the task of resolving claims to land. The Peacebuilding Commission is to advise this commission. See Statement of Mutual Commitments, paras. 9 and 32.

[332] See the Liberia Country Partnership Strategy, available through http://worldbank.org.

in 2008 at a meeting jointly organised with UNEP on 'Environment, Conflict and Peacebuilding'. The participants to this meeting explored the links between natural resources scarcity and abundance in relation to armed conflict and considered the role of the Peacebuilding Commission in addressing these issues. The overall conclusion of the debate was that building national capacities, institutions and policies to strengthen the equitable use of natural resources and the environment was considered to constitute an important component of peacebuilding.[333] The debate further highlighted the interlinkages between resource exploitation and rule of law reforms, the need for the Peacebuilding Commission to give proper attention to problems related to the exploitation of natural resources as well as to mainstream environmental issues into peacebuilding efforts. Furthermore, the meeting highlighted the lessons to be learned from international policy responses to natural resource issues, particularly the Kimberley Process and EITI. These conclusions were reiterated in subsequent reports of the Working Group.[334]

Furthermore, natural resources management was discussed at a meeting organised in 2011 on economic revitalisation, focusing on youth unemployment and natural resources management. There are significant links between these topics, since some of the States on the agenda of the Peacebuilding Commission have significant natural resources sectors that generate considerable employment. This is particularly so for Sierra Leone and Liberia. Although the meeting did not formulate best practices for natural resources management, it did contain two important conclusions. It first highlighted the importance of reviewing concession systems, introducing more transparency in the allocation of concessions as well as equitable conditions in natural resources contracts. In addition, it reiterated the need to use natural resources revenues to ensure peace dividends to the local population.

7.7.3 *Appraisal*

In its 2007 Presidential Statement, the Security Council acknowledged 'the crucial role that the Peacebuilding Commission, together with other

[333] Peacebuilding Commission, Working Group on Lessons Learned, 'From Conflict to Peacebuilding: The Role of Natural Resources and Environment', 8 May 2008, Chair's Summary.

[334] See, e.g., Report of the Working Group on Lessons Learned of the Peacebuilding Commission, Emerging Lessons and Practices in Peacebuilding, 2007–2009 (May 2010).

UN and non-UN actors, can play, in post-conflict situations, in assisting governments, upon their request, in ensuring that natural resources become an engine for sustainable development'. However, it follows from the review in the previous sections that the Peacebuilding Commission, in its functioning, has so far not realised its potential. The current section discusses the two principal impediments for the Peacebuilding Commission's effective functioning, with an emphasis on its capacity to consolidate the processes initiated by the Security Council in relation to reforms in the governance of natural resources.

A first impediment is the weak mandate of the Commission. As an advisory body, the Peacebuilding Commission has limited possibilities to shape its role as a coordinating instance. The Peacebuilding Commission in its current form is a meagre reflection of the ambitions formulated by the High-Level Panel on Threats, Challenges and Change in its 2004 Report. It is highly dependent on other actors to realise its mandate, including the recovering State itself. The principle of national ownership has been generally recognised as cardinal to the peacebuilding process, since post-conflict recovery can only be successful if it is rooted in national commitment. While this is true, it prevents the Peacebuilding Commission from addressing particular issues, such as natural resources governance, if the State does not request it to do so.[335] The question can therefore be posed whether this principle should continue to operate in the way it has so far. A strong argument can be made for the Peacebuilding Commission to condition its assistance on the adoption of peacebuilding priorities which the Commission deems essential for the successful completion of the process. This would give it the possibility to designate priorities which would help the State in its efforts to achieve a sustainable peace.

At the same time, the importance attached to the principle of national ownership is not adequately reflected in the composition of the organisational committee, the Commission's principal steering body. States that are on the Commission's agenda should be given the opportunity to be represented in this body, if not as members than at least as participants in its meetings.[336] Currently, they can only participate if elected as members of one of the principal UN organs.

[335] See, on the principle of ownership and its application to the context of territorial administration, Chesterman, 'Ownership in Theory and in Practice', pp. 3–26.

[336] Similar arrangements are already in place for the World Bank and the International Monetary Fund. See UNGA Resolution 60/180 (2005), para. 9 and UNSC Resolution 1645 (2005), para. 9.

A second impediment preventing the Commission from realising its potential flows from its dependence on other actors, most notably from the difficult relationship between the Peacebuilding Commission and one of its co-founders, the Security Council. Where the cooperation between the Commission and the Council was relatively successful in the case of Sierra Leone, it was much more troublesome in the case of Liberia. There, the Council followed its own course, focusing on the relationship between natural resources and violations of the arms embargo, while largely ignoring the Peacebuilding Commission.

A 2010 report reviewing the performance of the Commission in the first years of its existence confirmed that interaction with the Security Council had been limited and felt short of the expectations of 2005.[337] A debate held within the Security Council on post-conflict peacebuilding on 25 April 2013 supports this conclusion. Several delegates indicated that the two bodies acted as separate compartments and that there was a lack of communication between them.[338] Even though the Peacebuilding Commission is a subsidiary body, it should be more directly involved in the work of the Security Council and vice versa if it is to perform its functions effectively.

If the Peacebuilding Commission is to be a coordinating body for all efforts relating to post-conflict reconstruction, it should be made responsible for those aspects of the Council's work which have a clear peacebuilding dimension, including issues relating to the governance of natural resources. This would also have implications for the relationship between peacekeeping operations employed in these States and the Peacebuilding Commission, implying that the Commission should be actively involved in the design and implementation of their mandate. The need for this has recently been confirmed by the Security Council itself, in a resolution dealing with peacekeeping operations. There the Council emphasised the need for further harnessing the advisory, advocacy and resource mobilisation roles of the Peacebuilding Commission 'in advancing and supporting an integrated and coherent approach with respect to multidimensional peacekeeping mandates in countries on its agenda'.[339]

There are no clear institutional impediments for strengthening the Commission's functions in relation to the coordination of the peacebuilding process, since the Security Council with its mandatory powers

[337] Review of the United Nations peacebuilding architecture, *UN Docs. A/64/868 – S/2010/393*, 21 July 2010, Executive Summary.

[338] See *UN Doc. SC/10989* of 25 April 2013.

[339] UNSC Resolution 2086 (2013), para. 19.

is formally represented in the Peacebuilding Commission's Organizational Committee and in the country-specific configurations. The question is therefore rather to what extent should the Peacebuilding Commission assume these functions? The Commission is set up as an advisory body which has among its principal objectives to coordinate peacebuilding activities undertaken by other actors and to marshall the necessary resources to this effect. It is therefore neither designed nor equipped for the purpose of taking on a leading role in the peacebuilding process: not only is its function of an advisory nature, but it is also largely dependent on outside support for the exercise of its functions.

Given these constraints, the best solution for the short term would be to strengthen the relationship between the Security Council and the Peacebuilding Commission in relation to formulating early peacebuilding strategies, while leaving the responsibility for the coordination of peacebuilding aspects that are closely related to the maintenance of international peace and security to the Council. For the longer term, it might prove necessary to reconsider the peacebuilding architecture as it is currently construed. Given the wide range of actors involved, each with their own mandate and priorities, it is necessary to appoint one organisation to coordinate the process. Since the Security Council's role is limited to addressing threats to international peace and security, it is not the appropriate body to deal with all aspects of the peacebuilding process. Given its broad institutional structure the Peacebuilding Commission is therefore a more suitable candidate, provided it is equipped with a stronger mandate and its membership is expanded by including the World Bank and the IMF in its organisational committee. One of the issues that should further be addressed is the funding of peacebuilding initiatives. The current Peacebuilding Fund that was created for the purpose of funding peacebuilding initiatives is managed by the office of the UN Secretary-General rather than by the Peacebuilding Commission. If the Peacebuilding Commission is to be the primary instance for the coordination of peacebuilding initiatives, it should also be made responsible for the management of the Peacebuilding Fund.

7.8 Appraisal of the Security Council's approach to addressing the links between natural resources and armed conflict

This chapter has analysed the sanctions regimes imposed by the Security Council to address the links between natural resources and armed conflict as well as the contribution of peacekeeping operations and the Peacebuilding Commission in implementing and consolidating the regimes. In most of the cases discussed in this chapter natural resources were at the heart of the conflict. Relevant examples include Angola, Sierra Leone, Liberia and the DR Congo. In other cases, the links between natural resources and conflict can be considered more remote. The sanctions regime in Southern Rhodesia is an example of a regime targeting natural resources merely because of their general contribution to the Southern Rhodesian economy.

7.8.1 Legal basis

In all cases except Cambodia, the legal basis for imposing sanctions can be found in Chapter VII of the UN Charter. In most cases, the Security Council referred to Chapter VII in a general sense, while in relation to Southern Rhodesia the Council based the sanctions explicitly on Article 41 of the UN Charter. In the case of Cambodia, no reference was made to Chapter VII. Furthermore, the Security Council did not impose sanctions itself, but merely expressed support for a national moratorium. Therefore, the commodity measures imposed in relation to Cambodia do not qualify as sanctions in the sense of Article 41 of the Charter.

In addition, in all cases except Iraq and Cambodia, the Security Council determined the existence of a threat to the peace under Article 39 of the UN Charter before imposing sanctions. In the case of Iraq, the Council referred to 'a breach of the peace' because of Iraq's unlawful invasion in Kuwait. In the case of Cambodia, no reference was made to Article 39 of the UN Charter.

Furthermore, in all cases except Cambodia, the legal basis for the peacekeeping operations discussed in Section 7.6 is based on a request formulated in a peace agreement concluded between the warring factions, backed up with a Chapter VII mandate of the Security Council. In the case of Cambodia, a peace agreement constituted the sole legal basis for the establishment of the transitional authority.

7.8.2 Objectives

In its Presidential Statement of 11 February 2011 on the maintenance of international peace and security, the Security Council stated that

> The Security Council recalls the role played by the illegal exploitation of natural resources in fuelling some past and current conflicts. In this regard, it recognises that the United Nations can play a role in helping the States concerned, as appropriate, upon their request and with full respect for their sovereignty over natural resources and under national ownership, to prevent illegal access to those resources and to lay the basis for their legal exploitation with a view to promoting development, in particular through the empowerment of governments in post-conflict situations to better manage their resources.[340]

This Presidential Statement clearly formulates two of the most important objectives of the Security Council measures discussed in this chapter. The first is to help States involved in an internal armed conflict to prevent illegal access by armed groups to the States' natural resources, while the second objective seeks to strengthen the State's governance over natural resources with a view to promoting development.

Curtailing 'conflict resources'

The majority of the sanctions regimes discussed in this chapter address trade in so-called 'conflict resources'. These are natural resources traded by armed groups in order to finance their armed struggle. Examples of these sanctions regimes include Cambodia, Angola, Sierra Leone, Côte d'Ivoire and the DR Congo. Therefore, in many cases, sanctions regimes are in fact established to help governments restore the State's sovereignty over its natural resources. The sanctions regimes are often even imposed at the request of the national authorities. In these instances the Council has also mandated peacekeeping operations to help the State regain control over natural resources production areas. Relevant examples include the operations in Cambodia, Sierra Leone and the DR Congo.

In internal armed conflicts, the Security Council has been hesitant to impose sanctions targeting the national authorities and has done so only in the cases of Southern Rhodesia and Libya. In Southern Rhodesia, sanctions were imposed against a regime that was considered illegal. Similarly, the sanctions imposed in the case of Libya targeted a regime that had lost its legitimacy due to its own actions.

However, in other similar cases, the Security Council refrained from imposing sanctions against the national authorities. In Côte d'Ivoire, it did not take any action against the national authorities during the armed

[340] Presidential Statement on Maintenance of International Peace and Security: The Interdependence between Security and Development, 11 February 2011, *UN Doc. S/PRST/2011/4.*

conflict, despite ample evidence of the government violating the arms embargo. Another example concerns the armed conflict in the Darfur region of Sudan between 2003 and 2011, which has not been discussed previously in this chapter.

In the Darfur region, government-supported militias, notably the Janjaweed, were carrying out gross and systematic attacks on the civilian population.[341] To put an end to the humanitarian crisis in the Darfur Region, the Security Council imposed an arms embargo against the Janjaweed and provided for the possibility of lifting these sanctions on condition that the government of Sudan fulfilled its commitments to 'disarm the Janjaweed militias and apprehend and bring to justice Janjaweed leaders and their associates who have incited and carried out human rights and international humanitarian law violations and other atrocities'.[342] In a subsequent resolution, the Security Council expressly contemplated 'actions to affect Sudan's petroleum sector' in order to put pressure on the Sudanese government to disarm the militias and stop the atrocities, but the Council never actually imposed such sanctions.[343] Instead, it extended the arms embargo to include the Sudanese government.[344]

These examples show that the Security Council is committed to upholding the principle of a State's sovereignty over its natural resources in most circumstances, even in cases where governments use the proceeds from natural resources in ways that threaten international peace and security. However, they also show that political motivations sometimes prevent the Security Council from taking appropriate action. There is no objective reason that explains the difference in the approach used in Libya on the one hand, where the Security Council did impose sanctions against the national oil company, and in Sudan on the other, where the Security Council did not impose such targeted sanctions. In both situations, the government was involved in gross human rights violations. This arbitrary approach undermines the credibility of the Security Council.

Strengthening governance over natural resources

Another relevant issue for the purposes of this chapter is the Security Council's approach to the governance of natural resources. In several

341 For more details on the Darfur conflict, see Straus, 'Darfur and the Genocide Debate', pp. 123–33; and Abass, 'The United Nations, the African Union and the Darfur Crisis', pp. 415–40.

342 UNSC Resolution 1556 (2004).

343 Ibid., especially para. 14.

344 UNSC Resolution 1591 (2005), especially para. 7. See also Abass, 'The United Nations, the African Union and the Darfur Crisis', p. 429.

cases discussed in this chapter, the Security Council referred to improvements in governance as a reason to exempt natural resources from the sanctions or to lift the sanctions altogether. In the case of diamond sanctions, the Security Council exempted from the sanctions those diamonds that were controlled with an effective, transparent, accountable and internationally verifiable certificate of origin regime. Furthermore, in the case of Liberia, the Security Council made the lifting of the sanctions dependent on the implementation of reform plans for the forestry sector and for public administration in general. Liberia in particular is an example of a sanctions regime where the Security Council used sanctions as a tool to bring about great structural reforms in the governance of natural resources. These reforms also addressed environmental protection as a way of safeguarding the natural resources of Liberia for development.

Another relevant example concerns the DR Congo, where the Security Council is engaged in structural reforms of the minerals sector. However, the methods used by the Security Council in relation to the DR Congo differ from the sanctions regimes discussed above. The Council aims to restore the governance of the Congolese State over its mines through a combination of measures, including the introduction of due diligence requirements to companies. Indirectly, the implementation of these due diligence requirements by companies will increase transparency in the Congolese mineral sector.

Both in Liberia and in the DR Congo, the Council made effective use of peacekeeping operations to implement these measures. These operations were given explicit mandates to assist the States in improving the management of their natural resources. In the case of Liberia, UNMIL played an essential role in initiating legal and institutional reforms as well as in creating the conditions for the government to effectively implement the Kimberley Process as a condition for the lifting of the diamond sanctions. Even though the role of MONUC/MONUSCO was more limited because of capacity problems, the operation did provide essential assistance in the implementation of the Panel of Experts' due diligence guidelines by creating the conditions for an effective due diligence assessment.

The approach of the Security Council in these cases is commendable. Its engagement in structural reforms of natural resources sectors is an essential part of strategies aimed at addressing the links between natural resources and armed conflict. The role of sanctions is important in this respect. They can serve as a catalyst for improvements in the governance of natural resources in States affected by conflicts. The 1521 Liberia sanctions regime serves as an example for future action by the Security Council in this respect. The sanctions against Liberia have prompted important changes in the governance of Liberian resources, mainly by supporting reforms undertaken by other organisations.

7.8.3 Evolution in the approach of the Security Council

The sanctions regimes signal an important evolution in the approach of the Security Council in addressing the links between natural resources and armed conflict. This evolution is linked to the Council's efforts to find ways to address these links effectively, while minimising the negative effects of the sanctions on the civilian population. Thus whereas the earlier sanctions regimes were mainly comprehensive in nature, the Security Council soon switched to more selective sanctions regimes. These commodity sanctions regimes targeted specific commodities based on their particular contribution to an armed conflict. In addition, peacekeeping operations, mandated to reinstate State control over its natural resources, were employed to support the implementation of these sanctions.

The first time the Security Council used such selective commodity sanctions was in Cambodia, where it particularly targeted round logs and gems. In subsequent sanctions regimes, it refined its approach, at least in relation to diamonds. The Council introduced a distinction between diamonds traded by armed groups and by a State's authorities. Diamonds traded by the latter were exempted from the regime. The Security Council introduced an important innovation for this purpose: the Certificate of Origin Regime. This enabled it to directly target those responsible for causing a threat to the peace, while minimising the negative effects of the sanctions on the civilian population. At the same time, peacekeeping operations were increasingly mandated to assist the government in implementing the necessary reforms, culminating in full-scale assistance to implementing the Kimberly Process Scheme requirements in Liberia.

However, more recent sanctions regimes imposed by the Security Council started to move away from commodity sanctions in favour of sanctions targeting individuals and organisations. In 2008 when the Security Council decided to impose measures to address the illegal exploitation of natural resources in the DR Congo, it opted for an assets freeze and a travel ban targeting individuals and entities supporting illegal armed groups with the illicit trade of natural resources. Similarly, in the case of Libya, the Security Council opted for a freezing of the assets of the national oil company rather than imposing an oil embargo. At the same time, the mandate of the peacekeeping operation in the DR Congo devoted some attention to institutional reforms by giving it a role in the reorganisation of the State's administrative structure with regard to the minerals trade.

MONUC/MONUSCO was given the responsibility to assist the government in establishing trading counters to trace the origin of minerals.

One major advantage of targeted sanctions is that individuals and entities responsible for provoking a threat to the peace are targeted directly. This prevents a major problem encountered in the commodity-based sanctions regimes. In the cases of Liberia and Côte d'Ivoire, for example, the Taylor government and the Forces Nouvelles respectively switched from one natural resource to another in order to escape the sanctions.[345] Sanctions targeting individuals and entities avoid this problem, but also have major disadvantages, such as the risk of the arbitrary application of sanctions. This can be illustrated with reference to the reforms in recent years with regard to appeal procedures regarding the delisting of individuals.[346] Another important disadvantage is the sophisticated level of knowledge required and the administrative burden placed on the Sanctions Committee responsible for the listing and delisting of individuals and entities. In order to apply targeted sanctions effectively, it is necessary to have detailed knowledge of those individuals and entities directly and indirectly involved in the illegal trade of natural resources. From this perspective, commodity sanctions exempting from the embargo those natural resources that are traded with a certificate of origin regime are preferable.[347]

Perhaps the best option for the Security Council would be to apply a combination of the two types of sanctions, strengthened by a peacekeeping operation providing assistance on the ground in implementing those sanctions. Recently, in a resolution relating to the situation in Somalia, the Security Council did resort to imposing both types of sanctions. In Resolution 2036 (2012), the Security Council imposed an embargo on the export of charcoal from Somalia in order to prevent this natural resource from financing armed groups operating in the country. At the same time, it decided that individuals and entities engaged in the trade in charcoal may become subject to targeted measures upon designation by the Sanctions Committee.[348] In addition, ANISOM, a regional peacekeeping operation

345 See Wallensteen, Eriksson and Strandow, 'Sanctions for Conflict Prevention and Peace Building', p. 31.

346 See, e.g., Eckert et al., *Due Process and Targeted Sanctions, Update of the Watson Report*; and Van den Herik, 'The Security Council's Targeted Sanctions Regimes', pp. 797–807.

347 In the case of the DR Congo, a regional tracking-and-tracing system for minerals is currently being developed under the auspices of the International Conference for the Great Lakes Region.

348 UNSC Resolution 2036 (2012), paras. 22 and 23.

deployed by the African Union with the support by the UN, provides the necessary security as well as assistance to the government in restoring functioning state institutions for development purposes.[349]

7.8.4 *Sustainability: a missed opportunity*

The Security Council has only referred to the protection of natural wealth and resources in a few resolutions. In its resolutions relating to Cambodia, it simply endorsed measures imposed by the national authorities to protect the environment, while in the case of Liberia it referred to the promotion of environmentally sustainable business practices as a reason to lift the timber sanctions. However, in the case of Liberia the Security Council's measures should be viewed in relation to the Liberian Forest Initiative. In other words, it was not the Security Council that took the initiative to impose measures aimed at environmental protection, but rather the organisations responsible for implementing the LFI. This is also clear from UNMIL's mandate, which does not expressly include environmental matters. The environmental protection related tasks that UNMIL undertook were in pursuance of its general mandate to assist in the implementation of the LFI.

Thus the Security Council does not actively include environmental protection in its strategies for conflict resolution and post-conflict peacebuilding. A study of relevant reports of UN Panels of Experts does reveal some attention to the issue of environmental protection. For example, some references to this issue can be found in the reports of the Panels of Experts on Liberia and the DR Congo. The main focus of these panels is the issue of (over)exploitation of natural resources and its effect on the environment.

The Panel of Experts on the Illegal Exploitation of Natural Resources and Other Forms of Wealth of the Democratic Republic of the Congo, for example, designates the 'illicit exploitation of wildlife, forest and other resources' in national nature reserves and 'intensive and unsustainable mining and logging activities' outside these reserves as the causes of the ecological destruction resulting from the armed conflict.[350] It reports 'highly organized and systematic exploitation activities at levels never

[349] For ANISOM's mandate, see, e.g., ibid. and Resolution 1744 (2007).

[350] Interim report of the Panel of Experts on the Illegal Exploitation of Natural Resources and Other Forms of Wealth of the Democratic Republic of the Congo, *UN Doc. S/2002/565*, para. 50.

before seen'. According to the Panel, these activities include 'poaching for ivory, game meat and rare species, logging, and mining for coltan, gold and diamonds'.[351] Similarly, the Panel of Experts on Liberia explicitly refers to the problem of overexploitation of forest resources by the parties to the armed conflict in Liberia.[352]

In addition, both Panels assess the impact of sanctions on the environment. In this respect, the Panel of Experts on Liberia assesses the impact of the timber sanctions imposed by the UN Security Council on the long-term viability of the forest and advises the UN Security Council to declare a moratorium on all commercial activities in the extractive industries.[353] In contrast, the Panel of Experts on the Illegal Exploitation of Natural Resources and Other Forms of Wealth of the Democratic Republic of the Congo assesses the desirability of imposing sanctions on particular commodities and concludes that 'an embargo or a moratorium banning the export of raw materials originating in the Democratic Republic of the Congo does not seem to be a viable means of helping to improve the situation of the [. . .] natural environment'.[354]

In addition to these general references to the environment and to sustainability, the reports of the Panel of Experts on the Illegal Exploitation of Natural Resources and Other Forms of Wealth of the Democratic Republic of the Congo also contain indications that parties to an armed conflict must respect the rules of international environmental law. In two of its reports, the Panel of Experts explicitly refers to the Convention on International Trade in Endangered Species of Wild Fauna and Flora (CITES) in relation to poaching activities. In its interim report, the panel states that it 'has indications that, in most cases, poaching of elephants *in violation of international law* (Convention on International Trade in Endangered Species of Wild Fauna and Flora (CITES)) was well organized'.[355] It goes on to specify that the violations of CITES were committed by the parties themselves: '[e]ither soldiers hunted directly with

[351] Ibid., para. 52.

[352] Report of the Panel of Experts Pursuant to Paragraph 25 of Security Council Resolution 1478 (2003) Concerning Liberia, *UN Doc. S/2003/779*, para. 14 and paras. 66–9.

[353] Ibid., para. 17.

[354] Final report of the Panel of Experts on the Illegal Exploitation of Natural Resources and Other Forms of Wealth of the Democratic Republic of the Congo, *UN Doc. S/2002/1146*, para. 155.

[355] Report of the Panel of Experts on the Illegal Exploitation of Natural Resources and Other Forms of Wealth of the Democratic Republic of the Congo, *UN Doc. S/2001/357*, para. 62. Author's emphasis added.

the consent of the commander or they provided equipment and protection to local villagers to execute the task with the objective of collecting elephant tusks'.[356] In its final report, the panel asks Member States to ensure 'that their National Bureaus, established under the [Lusaka Agreement on Cooperative Enforcement Operations Directed at Illegal Trade in Wild Fauna and Flora], intensify their investigations into the criminal traffic in endangered species of wild animals and plants as outlined by CITES'.[357]

In many cases the Security Council expressly relies on information from reports issued by the Panels of Experts that it established, but it does not show any particular sensitivity with regard to the environmental findings of the Panels of Experts. These findings do not seem to play any role in decisions of the Security Council to either impose or to refrain from imposing sanctions, neither do they find resonance in the mandates of peacekeeping operations. This is unfortunate, as environmental protection is essential for creating an enduring peace in a country. It is therefore of the utmost importance for the Security Council to start devoting more explicit attention to environmental protection as part of its strategies regarding the economic reconstruction of States that have experienced armed conflict.

7.8.5 The role of the Security Council

With regard to the conflicts discussed in this chapter, the Security Council acts principally in a coordinating capacity. Sanctions serve mainly to prompt reforms that have to be implemented by means of other forms of cooperation. The role of the private sector is of paramount importance in this respect. The trade in natural resources that finance armed conflict can only be curbed by engaging the private sector in reforms. The diamond sanctions, as well as the due diligence standards, reveal the Security Council's awareness of the need to engage the private sector in reforms.

The role of governments is of course equally important. Reforms in the natural resources sectors can only be achieved with the full support of the government of a State. Sanctions serve only as a tool to bring about the necessary changes. The Security Council therefore often leaves

[356] Ibid.

[357] Final report of the Panel of Experts on the Illegal Exploitation of Natural Resources and Other Forms of Wealth of the Democratic Republic of the Congo, *UN Doc. S/2002/1146*, para. 185.

the initiative to implement changes to the States themselves, aided by peacekeeping operations providing assistance to these States. Examples include the certificate-of-origin regimes proposed for rough diamonds. The Security Council has left it to the States themselves to choose the appropriate mechanism for this purpose.

In most cases, the Security Council keeps its distance while using sanctions to put pressure on governments to implement the necessary changes. This can even benefit the respective governments when it gives the national authorities the necessary support to push for changes. For example, this was the case in Liberia. The sanctions strengthened the efforts of President Johnson Sirleaf to implement changes in Liberia's administrative system.

The principle of national ownership of strategies for post-conflict peacebuilding is central to the Security Council's efforts in this respect. In a 2009 Presidential Statement on post-conflict peacebuilding, the Security Council explicitly emphasised the importance of this principle for peacebuilding efforts and priorities, while at the same time emphasising 'the vital role of the United Nations in supporting national authorities to develop an early strategy, in close consultation with international partners, to address these priorities'.[358] The sanctions regimes discussed in this chapter demonstrate the will of the Security Council to respect national ownership as much as possible, even in relation to sanctions regimes. Although this is commendable, the principle also has its limits, as demonstrated in relation to the country-specific configurations of the Peacebuilding Commission. National ownership should not impede the consolidation of measures introduced in the phase of conflict resolution. Strategies for post-conflict reconstruction should therefore directly build on those instituted as part of conflict resolution efforts. It is for the Security Council to ensure that its strategies are adequately reflected in the peacebuilding priorities of States on the agenda of the Peacebuilding Commission.

Finally, it is of paramount importance for the Security Council to continue its efforts to address the role of natural resources in financing armed conflict. In fact, its role should even be strengthened in this respect. The current sanctions regimes focus mainly on preventing the trade in natural resources by armed groups. However, to achieve a lasting peace, the underlying governance structures should be addressed as

[358] UNSC Presidential Statement of 22 July 2009, S/PRST/2009/23. The importance of the principle was confirmed in subsequent presidential statements regarding post-conflict peacebuilding. See S/PRST/2010/7 and S/PRST/2010/20.

well. The Security Council should use sanctions more often to push for structural changes in the governance of natural resources in countries recovering from armed conflict. These changes should be aimed at introducing transparency, accountability and sustainability in the governance of natural resources as a tool to prevent future conflicts in countries that have suffered from armed conflict. For this purpose, the civilian mandate of peacekeeping operations should also be strengthened in order to assist States in implementing the necessary reforms in their domestic institutions for the purpose of achieving a lasting peace.

The Security Council has wide discretionary powers to act under Chapter VII of the UN Charter, and greater use should be made of these. It is precisely because of its authority to impose mandatory measures that the Security Council is the appropriate body to do so. This approach is in line with the broader acceptance of the Council's role beyond immediate crisis management. In addition, as one of its co-founders, the Council should work more closely with the Peacebuilding Commission to consolidate the long-term strategies which it sets out in the conflict resolution phase. Even though the Council's discretionary powers are wide, they are still limited to addressing threats to international peace and security. Achieving sustainable peace requires a more integrated approach.

8

Addressing resource-related armed conflicts with informal normative processes

8.1 Introductory remarks

The preceding chapter discussed the ways in which sanctions regimes imposed by the Security Council address the links between natural resources and armed conflict. It demonstrated that several of the resolutions adopted by the Security Council encouraged States to participate in voluntary initiatives aimed at improving resource transparency.

Some of these resolutions established a direct link between the participation of States in voluntary initiatives and the implementation of the sanctions regimes. Resolution 2045 (2012), related to Côte d'Ivoire, is one example. This resolution explicitly offers the government of Côte d'Ivoire the possibility of modifying or lifting sanctions, provided that the Ivorian authorities 'create and implement an action plan to enforce the Kimberley Process rules in Côte d'Ivoire' and that they 'closely work with the Kimberley Process Certification Scheme to conduct a review and assessment of Côte d'Ivoire's internal controls system for trade in rough diamonds and a comprehensive geologic study of Côte d'Ivoire's potential diamond resources and production capacity'.[1] Another example concerns the sanctions regime imposed to address the armed conflict in the DR Congo, where the Security Council expressed its intention to impose sanctions for noncompliance by corporate entities with the voluntary due diligence guidelines developed by the UN Group of Experts.[2]

The Security Council also expressed its support for these voluntary initiatives in a more general fashion. In its Presidential Statement of 25 June 2007 on Natural Resources and Conflict, it emphasised the important contribution of commodity monitoring and certification schemes, such as the Kimberley Process, to preventing and combating trafficking,

[1] UNSC Resolution 2045 (2012), especially paras. 6 and 21.

[2] See UNSC Resolution 1952 (2010), especially para. 9.

illicit trade and illegal exploitation of natural resources.[3] It also recognised the role of voluntary initiatives aimed at improving revenue transparency, such as EITI, in ensuring that natural resources stimulate sustainable development.[4] Furthermore, the Security Council referred to the role of voluntary initiatives aiming at encouraging multinational enterprises to adopt responsible business practices, such as the OECD Guidelines for Multinational Enterprises and the UN Global Compact.[5] Last, in its Presidential Statement of 15 April 2013 on Peace and Security in Africa, the Security Council recognised 'the importance of commodity monitoring and certification schemes, such as the Kimberley Process, and the role of voluntary initiatives aimed at improving revenue transparency, such as the Extractive Industries Transparency Initiative', as tools for the prevention of conflicts.[6]

The current chapter aims to identify the contribution of these voluntary initiatives to the development of a regulatory framework for the management of natural resources in post-conflict environments. More specifically, the purpose of this chapter is to assess whether and to what extent these voluntary initiatives respond to the call made in the report of the High-Level Panel on Threats, Challenges and Change to the United Nations, national authorities, international financial institutions, civil society organisations and the private sector 'to develop norms governing the management of natural resources for countries emerging from or at risk of conflict'.[7]

This call did not receive express follow-up in subsequent formal documents. Instead, the 2005 World Summit Outcome Document focused exclusively on the process of peacebuilding and its procedural modalities, most notably the establishment of the UN Peacebuilding Commission as the principal institution to coordinate action in this field. From a substantive perspective, the call therefore remains very relevant. This is illustrated by the fact that the UN Peacebuilding Commission itself has recently started to consider issues relating to the management of natural resources in its work programme, showing the continued need for a regulatory framework, as called for by the High-Level Panel.

[3] UNSC Presidential Statement on Natural Resources and Conflict, *UN Doc. S/PRST/2007/22*, 25 June 2007, para. 8.

[4] Ibid., para. 9.

[5] Ibid., para. 10.

[6] UNSC Presidential Statement on Peace and Security in Africa, *UN Doc. S/PRST/2013/4*, 15 April 2013, para. 18.

[7] Report of the High-Level Panel on Threats, Challenges and Change, *A More Secure World*, para. 92.

For this purpose, the current chapter first examines the substantive contributions made by voluntary initiatives to the governance of natural resources in countries emerging from armed conflict. To what extent do voluntary initiatives create standards for the management of natural resources in post-conflict situations? In particular, to what extent do such initiatives effectively incorporate elements of sustainable development into their methods of operation, and how do these elements contribute to shaping the governance of natural resources in countries recovering from armed conflict?

Furthermore, given their increasing popularity, this chapter addresses the question of whether these informal instruments provide a credible alternative to legally binding instruments. Even though these instruments do not impose legally binding obligations on participants, these participants have committed themselves to strive for the achievement of particular objectives. The question is therefore whether these voluntary instruments contain effective mechanisms to monitor and enforce the implementation of the instruments by the participants.

The current chapter discusses three initiatives that are representative of the categories of voluntary initiatives mentioned in the Presidential Statement. The Kimberley Process for the Certification of Rough Diamonds is an example of a commodity monitoring and certification initiative. The EITI is an initiative aimed at improving resource transparency. Finally, the OECD Due Diligence Guidance for Responsible Supply Chains of Minerals from Conflict-Affected and High-Risk Areas is an example of an initiative aimed at encouraging responsible business conduct.

These initiatives share some common characteristics that make them particularly useful for the purposes addressed in this chapter. First, all three specifically focus on issues related to natural resource governance. This gives them added value compared to the broad range of other initiatives that address revenue transparency and corporate responsibility in a more general fashion. They include the UN Anti-corruption Convention and the UN Global Compact. In addition, all three are multistakeholder initiatives, which have been developed by representatives of States, civil society and the business community. Thus these initiatives represent a relatively new category of instruments for setting standards, in the sense that they have not been developed by traditional State-centred standard-setting processes. Furthermore, the effective implementation of the initiatives depends not only on States, but also on companies. Finally, the ambition of all three initiatives is to become universal in their application. Therefore, they go further than initiatives specific to a particular country or region, such as the Mineral Certification Scheme of the International Conference on the Great Lakes Region.

The following sections discuss the three mentioned initiatives. Section 8.2 discusses the Kimberley Process, Section 8.3 examines the EITI and Section 8.4 looks at the OECD Due Diligence Guidance. Section 8.5 discusses the substantive contribution of the three initiatives to the development of a regulatory framework for the management of natural resources in conflict-affected States, with particular emphasis on the role of these initiatives in promoting sustainable resource governance. Finally, Section 8.6 examines the effectiveness of these instruments.

8.2 The Kimberley Process for the Certification of Rough Diamonds

8.2.1 Context

The Kimberley Process Certification Scheme was developed in response to the armed conflicts raging in Angola and Sierra Leone, where diamonds were used to finance the military campaigns of rebel groups opposing the legitimate government.[8] The Security Council had adopted sanctions targeting the export of diamonds originating from these States.[9] However, neither Angola nor Sierra Leone had an effective system in place to track the origin of diamonds mined in these States.[10] Therefore, the sanctions could easily be busted by armed groups smuggling the diamonds into neighbouring countries, from which they were reexported and sold on the international market.[11]

[8] For more details on these conflicts, see Chapter 7 of this study.

[9] See UNSC Resolutions 1173 (1998) and 1295 (2000) concerning the armed conflict in Angola; Resolution 1306 (2000) concerning the armed conflict in Sierra Leone; and Resolution 1343 (2001) concerning Liberia's involvement in the smuggling of diamonds from Sierra Leone. For a more detailed discussion of these resolutions, see Chapter 5 of this study. It should be noted that the first meeting leading to the Kimberley Certification Scheme took place before the Security Council adopted diamond embargoes for Sierra Leone and Liberia.

[10] See for example the following reports for an account of the difficulties experienced by the government of Angola in setting up a certification mechanism that would effectively control the trade in Angolan diamonds: Final Report of the Panel of Experts, *UN Doc. S/2000/203*, paras. 94–8; and the 2000 Interim Report of the Monitoring Mechanism, *UN Doc. S/2000/1026*, p. 12.

[11] For more information, see the report of the Panel of Experts on Angola (the Fowler report), *UN Doc. S/2000/203*, paras. 75–114; and the report of the Panel of Experts on Sierra Leone, *UN Doc. S/2000/1195*, paras. 65–166.

The origin of the Kimberley Process for the Certification of Rough Diamonds is therefore linked to UN sanctions. It was set up in order to find an effective international solution to the problem of diamond smuggling in contravention of UN sanctions. The aim of the process was quite innovative: to design a universal certification scheme for rough diamonds that would be applied by all States producing and purchasing diamonds. The scheme was to be based on national certification schemes, supplemented by international minimum standards. Because of its universal membership, the scheme would stop so-called 'blood diamonds' from entering the international diamond market by closing the trade routes for armed groups.

Another innovative feature of the process concerns the diversity of its membership. The Kimberley Process was initiated not only by governments but also by the diamond industry and NGOs. The involvement of all the interested actors, and especially of the diamond industry, was considered crucial to the success of the scheme. For example, in relation to Angola, the report of the Panel of Experts concluded that lax controls in diamond-selling centres were one of the factors that made it easy for UNITA to gain access to the international diamond market.[12]

The Kimberley Process Certification Scheme was launched in November 2002, only two and a half years after the first meeting in Kimberley, South Africa. The Scheme was adopted with a ministerial declaration at a conference held in Interlaken.[13] The process is based on voluntary commitments undertaken by participants, i.e., countries producing and trading diamonds. These commitments include the adoption of appropriate national legislation and reporting requirements concerning the volume of their trade in rough diamonds. The implementation of the commitments is monitored by the participating NGOs.[14] The Kimberley Process is paralleled by a system of self-regulation for the diamond industry under the auspices of the World Diamond Council.[15]

[12] Final Report of the Panel of Experts, *UN Doc. S/2000/203*, paras. 87–93.

[13] Interlaken Declaration of 5 November 2002 on the Kimberley Process Certification Scheme for Rough Diamonds.

[14] For more details, see Wetzel, 'Targeted Economic Measures to Curb Armed Conflict?' pp. 170–71.

[15] The World Diamond Council was established in 2000 with the purpose of 'represent[ing] the diamond industry in the development and implementation of regulatory and voluntary systems to control the trade in diamonds embargoed by the United Nations or covered by the Kimberley Process Certification Scheme'. See www.worlddiamondcouncil.com for more details.

8.2.2 *Scope and objectives of the scheme*

The Kimberley Process is premised on the idea that 'urgent international action is imperative to prevent the problem of conflict diamonds from negatively affecting the trade in legitimate diamonds, which makes a critical contribution to the economies of many of the producing, processing, exporting and importing states, especially developing states'.[16] The Kimberley Process Certification Scheme was designed 'to exclude conflict diamonds from the legitimate trade'.[17] As its objectives show, it is a very practical initiative with the primary aim of protecting the legitimate diamond trade.

To gain a proper understanding of the scope of the Kimberley Process, it is essential to take a closer look at its definition of 'conflict diamonds'. This may help to understand what the scheme covers and, more importantly, what it does not. The Kimberley Process defines conflict diamonds as

> rough diamonds used by rebel movements or their allies to finance conflict aimed at undermining legitimate governments, as described in relevant United Nations Security Council (UNSC) resolutions insofar as they remain in effect, or in other similar UNSC resolutions which may be adopted in the future, and as understood and recognized in United Nations General Assembly (UNGA) Resolution 55/56, or in other similar UNGA resolutions which may be adopted in future.[18]

The first element that reveals the scope of the Kimberley Process is the reference to 'rough diamonds', defined as 'diamonds that are unworked or simply sawn, cleaved or bruted'.[19] In other words, as soon as diamonds have undergone any form of modification from their natural state, they are no longer covered by the Kimberley Process Certification Scheme. Of course, this considerably narrows the scope of the scheme. In addition, it provides loopholes for bypassing it. In fact, in 2007 the participating NGO Global Witness reported a significant number of suspicious shipments of polished diamonds from countries with no diamond industry.[20] One possible explanation for this is that these shipments were deliberately misclassified.

[16] Kimberley Process Certification Scheme, fourth paragraph of the preamble.
[17] Kimberley Process Certification Scheme, ninth paragraph of the preamble.
[18] Kimberley Process Certification Scheme, Sect. I.
[19] Kimberley Process Certification Scheme, Sect. I.
[20] Global Witness, 'Loopholes in the Kimberley Process', October 2007.

Second, the Kimberley Process covers only diamonds that are used by rebel movements or their allies. Thus the definition covers rebel movements and all those who provide support to these movements, either by trading with them or by other means, including foreign governments, such as the Taylor administration, which supported the RUF in Sierra Leone, as well as companies.[21] Therefore, the definition is broader than an earlier one proposed by the General Assembly in its Resolution 55/56, which focused exclusively on the role of rebel movements themselves.[22]

However, diamonds mined by national authorities are excluded from the definition, even when the mining is associated with gross human rights violations. This turns out to be a very problematic limitation, threatening the very survival of the Kimberley Process. The 2011 Plenary decision to allow Zimbabwe to resume export of its diamonds,[23] after an earlier decision of the Plenary in 2009 to temporarily block the export of diamonds from Zimbabwe, was a cause of great concern. The reasons for blocking Zimbabwe's diamond exports in 2009 were reports of human rights abuses committed by the Zimbabwean army at particular mining sites, as well as reports of smuggling in contravention of the scheme.[24] The 2011 Plenary decision provoked a great deal of anger, notably among the NGOs involved in the Process. Some of them even walked out of the Process.[25]

The last element of the definition is very interesting, as it indirectly touches on the question of the legitimacy of the armed conflict itself. According to the definition, conflict diamonds are diamonds that are used to finance conflicts aimed at undermining *legitimate* governments. The term 'legitimate' with respect to governments seems to imply that the definition excludes diamonds that are used by rebel movements to overthrow governments that are not – or are no longer – recognised by the international community. In this respect, reference can be made to

[21] See also Wetzel, 'Targeted Economic Measures to Curb Armed Conflict?' pp. 173–4.

[22] The General Assembly defined rough diamonds as 'diamonds which are used by rebel movements to finance their military activities, including attempts to undermine or overthrow legitimate Governments'. UNGA Resolution 55/56 (2000), second paragraph of the preamble.

[23] Final Communiqué from the Kimberley Process Plenary Meeting, 3 November 2011, available through www.worlddiamondscouncil.org, resources section, para. 19.

[24] See the Final report of the Kimberley Process Certification Scheme Review Mission to Zimbabwe from 30 June to 4 July 2009, available through http://graphics8.nytimes.com/packages/pdf/world/ZimFinaldraft020909.pdf.

[25] See in this regard, e.g., the Press release of Global Witness, one of the founding NGOs, on www.globalwitness.org.

Chapter 2 of this book, which discussed the position of governments under international law. The reference to legitimate governments in the Kimberley definition of conflict diamonds lends support to the conclusion reached there, in the sense that armed groups that aim to overthrow an illegitimate government are considered to have a right to exploit the State's natural resources.

Furthermore, the definition indicates that it is up to the Security Council to determine whether rough diamonds used by armed groups constitute 'conflict diamonds'. The definition explicitly refers to existing and future Security Council resolutions: 'as described in relevant United Nations Security Council resolutions'. This reference could be interpreted to mean that the Security Council must determine in advance whether diamonds used by armed groups in particular situations are 'conflict diamonds'. This implies that the Kimberley scheme only covers diamonds that have explicitly been labelled as 'conflict diamonds' by the Security Council.

Therefore, the definition of conflict diamonds in the context of the Kimberley Process is very specific and very limited. This is understandable, as the original objective of the Kimberley Process was to stop diamonds from financing horrific conflicts such as those in Angola and Sierra Leone, where diamonds were mined by rebel groups such as UNITA and the RUF.

However, the Kimberley Process scheme entered into force ten years ago, and it is time to rethink its objectives. Is it an initiative that aims at reestablishing sovereignty over natural resources by helping governments to regain control over the State's natural resources? Or is the objective of the process rather human-rights-oriented; i.e., is its objective to exclude from the market all diamonds that are associated with violence and human rights abuses in general? In the latter case, the term 'conflict diamonds' urgently needs to be redefined.

The United States, which chaired the Kimberley Process in 2012,[26] was certainly in favour of increasing the scope of the definition. It proposed a new definition of conflict diamonds which would include all diamonds associated with violence and human rights abuses, whether committed by rebel movements or States, in or outside the context of an armed conflict.[27]

[26] The Chair of the Kimberley Process rotates on an annual basis. The current Chair is China, while Angola (the current Vice-chair) will become the Chair in 2015.

[27] In this respect, see the Chair Vision Statement of 7 August 2012, available through www.kimberleyprocess.com. See also the commentary to the Chair Vision Statement, which sets out in more detail a proposition to change the definition for conflict diamonds so as to apply to 'diamond-related conflicts that meet generally agreed-upon standards of armed conflicts, such as a resort to armed force between States or protracted armed violence

The advocates of this broader definition include not only civil society groups and State members of the Kimberley Process, but also companies in the diamond industry. The reason for the diamond industry to engage in the Kimberley Process in the first place was the damage to the industry's reputation after reports involving 'blood diamonds' in the late 1990s. Examples such as Zimbabwe pose a similar problem for the industry. However, there are also a number of opponents of a new definition, especially – and not surprisingly – in States that produce diamonds. In the light of the controversy surrounding a new definition, the 2012 Plenary meeting, held in December 2012 in Washington, delayed the adoption of a new definition until at least 2013. The Plenary subsequently assigned the task to assess the definition of conflict diamonds to the KPCS Review Committee (CKR), but to no avail. At the end of its mandate, the Committee had not been able to reach consensus on this issue.[28] No further action has been taken at the time of publication of this book.

8.2.3 *Participants and institutional structure*

The Kimberley Process has 54 participants, representing 80 States.[29] Although it is not an international organisation, State participants are referred to as 'members'. Producing members account for 99.8% of the worldwide production in rough diamonds, and the process includes all the major diamond trading countries. Other participants in the process include the World Diamond Council, representing the diamond industry, and civil society. Global Witness and Partnership Africa Canada are among the founding NGOs.

The institutional structure of the Kimberley Process is very basic. Its operation largely depends on the contribution of the participants and

between governmental authorities and organized armed groups or between such groups within a State. This would also apply to circumstances of systematic violence, such as protracted and violent internal disturbances and tensions, grave acts of violence or acts of a similar nature over an extended period. Such a definition would not apply to individual or isolated cases. Neither would this apply to violence that is unrelated to diamonds'. See Chair Vision Statement of 7 August 2012 FAQs, p. 4.

[28] See the Final Communiqué from the Kimberley Process Plenary Meeting of 22 November 2013, in which the Plenary noted that the CKR could not reach consensus on the definition of conflict diamonds and in which it encouraged the Chair, Participants and Observers to continue dialogue on these areas.

[29] See www.kimberleyprocess.com. The European Union and its member States count as one single participant. In December 2012, Panama, Kazakhstan and Cambodia were admitted as new participants following the admission of Cameroon in August.

observers to the scheme. The Kimberley Process does not have a permanent secretariat at its disposal, although there are plans to establish a so-called administrative support mechanism.[30] Furthermore, the principal organ of the Kimberley Process is the Plenary, which meets once a year and consists of all the Kimberley Process participants and observers, i.e., the participating States, as well as the diamond industry and civil society. Decisions regarding the functioning of the system are adopted by this organ on the basis of consensus.[31] It may also set up ad hoc working groups and subsidiary bodies to refine particular aspects of the system, i.e., to prepare guidelines on internal controls or to look into specific situations.[32]

The Kimberley Process is supervised by a Chair, a function that rotates amongst the participants on a yearly basis. In addition to directing the working groups and administering the Process, the Chair's functions include the resolution of disputes between participants regarding the implementation of the scheme.[33] This dispute resolution mechanism could constitute an important tool to ensure compliance by members, if used effectively. It is triggered by a form of 'whistle blowing'. Participants can inform the Chair of concerns regarding compliance with the scheme by other participants. The Chair will then try to find a solution to the problem with a form of mediation. So far, the dispute settlement mechanism has been used once, leading to the suspension of a participant from the process.[34]

8.2.4 *Operation of the scheme*

The Kimberley Process Certification Scheme functions on the basis of export and import permits for shipments of rough diamonds. Each

30 See the 2010 Administrative Decision on the Establishment of an Ad Hoc Committee for Exploring the Modalities of Enhancing the Efficiency of the Kimberley Process with a View to Provide Administrative Support for Its Activities and the 2011 amendment to this decision, available through www.kimberleyprocess.com, documents section. In December 2012, the Plenary agreed to accept the offer of the World Diamond Council to supply administrative support to the body for one year, starting January 1, 2013.

31 2003 Rules of Procedure of Meetings of the Plenary, and its Ad Hoc Working Groups and Subsidiary Bodies [hereafter: Rules of Procedure], available through www.kimberleyprocess.com, Rule 42.

32 Rules of Procedure, Rules 1 and 19.

33 Kimberley Process Certification Scheme, Sect. VI.

34 In this respect, see The Kimberley Process Certification Scheme: Third Year Review, p. 6, available through www.kimberleyprocess.com, documents section.

shipment of rough diamonds must be accompanied by a duly validated Certificate.[35] This Certificate must meet a number of minimum requirements, including a statement that the rough diamonds in the shipment have been handled in accordance with the provisions of the Kimberley Process Certification Scheme. Furthermore, it must be tamper- and forgery-proof, it must identify the issuing authority as well as the exporter and importer, it must state the carat weight, the number of parcels and the value of the shipment, and it must include a validation of the Certificate by the Exporting Authority.[36] In addition, a confirmation of receipt must be sent to the relevant Exporting Authority, with reference to the Certificate number, the number of parcels, the carat weight and the details of the importer and exporter.[37]

To meet these requirements, participants must establish a system of internal controls designed to eliminate conflict diamonds from shipments of rough diamonds imported into or exported from their territory.[38] For this purpose, participants must meet a number of minimum requirements. They must designate Importing and Exporting Authorities, ensure that rough diamonds are imported and exported in tamper-proof containers, adopt appropriate legislation to implement and enforce the Certification Scheme, and collect, maintain and exchange official production, import and export data with other participants.[39] Finally, participants should cooperate with each other through the exchange of information and best practices.[40] Over the course of time, these requirements have been further refined with administrative decisions and declarations adopted in the plenary sessions.[41]

In addition to these minimum requirements, the Kimberley Process Certification Scheme provides a number of recommendations

[35] Kimberley Process Certification Scheme, Sect. III(a).

[36] Kimberley Process Certification Scheme, Annex I A.

[37] Kimberley Process Certification Scheme, Sect. III(b).

[38] Kimberley Process Certification Scheme, Sect. IV(a).

[39] Kimberley Process Certification Scheme, Sects. IV(b)–(f).

[40] Kimberley Process Certification Scheme, Sect. V.

[41] See, e.g., the 2005 Moscow Declaration, which sets out a number of recommendations concerning internal controls over alluvial diamond mining. Similarly, the 2007 Brussels Declaration contains recommendations on internal controls for participants with rough diamonds trading and manufacturing which directly affect companies. See also the 2009 Administrative Decision on Implementation and Enforcement, which builds on Section V of the Kimberley Process Certification Scheme concerning cooperation and transparency, inter alia, to counter fraudulent certificates and suspect shipments. For all these documents, see the documents section of www.kimberleyprocess.com.

for the establishment of a system of internal controls. These include recommendations relating to the transparency of payments for rough diamonds, the licensing of mines and miners, and the registration and licensing of diamond buyers, sellers, exporters, agents and courier companies.[42]

The proper functioning of the Kimberley Process is therefore largely dependent on national implementation. Decisions on the operation of the internal controls are left to the national States participating in the scheme. The prosecution of infringements of the scheme is also a domestic issue. The Kimberley Process Third Year Review Report of November 2006 mentions a number of seizures of diamond parcels, as well as the instigation of criminal proceedings by countries, but the report fails to give a real insight into the proper functioning of the Process. The significant number of reported seizures by trading countries such as the European Union, Australia and Canada is a hopeful sign, but does not provide much information on the overall success of the scheme.

Although the scheme relies on national implementation, the Kimberley Process has introduced a system of international monitoring. This system is based primarily on a peer review system and works largely on a voluntary basis. States have to consent to the use of a review mission.[43] Despite the voluntary nature of the monitoring system, the majority of Kimberley members have accepted review missions. In some cases, these have had a considerable impact. In the case of Zimbabwe, for example, a review mission in 2009 provided essential information resulting in a temporary blocking of Zimbabwean diamonds and the adoption of a working plan by the Zimbabwean government to address the findings of the review team.

Despite the emphasis on national implementation and the voluntary nature of the commitments, States do have to satisfy a number of requirements in order to be eligible to participate in the Kimberley Process. Participation in the process is dependent on the implementation of the minimum requirements set out above. If States do not meet these minimum requirements, they can be suspended from the Process.[44]

[42] Kimberley Process Certification Scheme, Annex II.

[43] See the 2003 Administrative Decision on the Implementation of Peer Review in the KPCS, available through www.kimberleyprocess.com, documents section. The peer review system has been revised several times; the last revision dates from 2007, through Administrative Decision 16.

[44] Guidelines for the Participation Committee in Recommending Interim Measures as regards Serious Non-compliance with KPCS Minimum Requirements, adopted on 5 November 2008, available through www.kimberleyprocess.com.

In practice there have been some cases of suspension or self-suspension under the Process. In 2004, the Republic of the Congo was suspended because it could not provide sufficient details on its diamond production. It was suspected of being a transit country for smuggling diamonds from the DR Congo and Angola. The suspension was lifted in 2007, after the Republic of the Congo had demonstrated that it had introduced reforms in its diamond sector.[45] In addition, the Central African Republic was suspended in 2013, following a coup d'état and the outbreak of hostilities.[46]

Venezuela and Côte d'Ivoire are examples of participants that opted for self-suspension. Côte d'Ivoire opted for suspension as soon as the requirements were introduced in 2003. It lasted until 2014 for the suspension to be lifted, but this is largely due to the UN Security Council sanctions imposed in 2005 against diamonds originating from the country. The Kimberley Process and the UN Panel of Experts on Côte d'Ivoire have cooperated closely to reinstate Côte d'Ivoire as an active member of the Kimberley Process. Venezuela announced in 2008 that it would suspend its export of rough diamonds until it had taken the necessary reforms to control its diamond sector. However, Venezuela has not yet rejoined the Kimberley Process.

Since the launch of the Kimberley Process, the number of 'conflict diamonds' traded on the international market has dropped significantly. It is estimated that conflict diamonds represent about 1 per cent of the international trade in diamonds today, compared to estimates of up to 15 per cent in the 1990s.[47] Nevertheless, it is difficult to measure the precise contribution the Kimberley Process has made to this success. Some of the conflicts that were financed with diamonds, in particular the conflicts in Angola and Sierra Leone which triggered the development of the Kimberley Process in the first place, had already come to an end by the time the Kimberley Process entered into force in early 2003. As a result, the total number of 'conflict diamonds' traded on the international market obviously declined as well.

Thus it is difficult to measure the impact of the Kimberley Process on the elimination of the trade in conflict diamonds. One important function of the Kimberley Process is related to conflict prevention. The improved governance of diamonds, with the introduction of internal

[45] See Grant, 'The Kimberley Process at Ten', p. 165.

[46] See the Administrative Decision of the Plenary of 23 May 2013.

[47] See www.kimberleyprocess.com, 'About' section.

controls, the licensing of mines and increased transparency in export data and payments, can fulfil an important role in preventing rebel groups from gaining access to diamond mines. Furthermore, a functioning system of internal controls can be a disincentive for rebel groups to consider diamonds as a source of funding or financial gain. The certificate requirements, as well as the almost universal membership to the scheme, make it more difficult for rebel groups to find buyers for conflict diamonds.[48]

In the case of Sierra Leone, the Kimberley Process has certainly played an important role in capacity building, making the diamond sector in that country more resilient against future attempts by rebel groups to gain control over the sector. Moreover, the proportion of diamonds exported through government channels in that country has increased significantly due to implementation of the Kimberley Process.[49]

8.2.5 *International recognition of the Kimberley Process*

From the beginning, the Kimberley Process received the support of the principal UN organs. In its Resolution 55/56, adopted in December 2000, the UN General Assembly enthusiastically welcomed the Kimberley Process initiative and encouraged the development of an international certification scheme.[50] Moreover, the General Assembly issued a number of recommendations on the design of such a scheme.[51] These included recommendations to base it primarily on national certification schemes to ensure the widest possible participation. They emphasised the need for appropriate arrangements to help to ensure compliance and the need for transparency. Since then, the General Assembly has issued several resolutions endorsing the process and the resulting certification scheme.[52]

From the start of the process, the Security Council also emphasised the importance of States working together with the diamond industry to devise effective arrangements to ensure that members of the diamond industry worldwide abide by the diamond sanctions imposed by it.[53] In

48 See Grant, 'The Kimberley Process at Ten', p. 175.

49 Ibid., pp. 166–73.

50 UNGA Resolution 55/56 of 1 December 2000 (date of publication 29 January 2001) on the role of diamonds in fuelling conflict: breaking the link between the illicit transaction of rough diamonds and armed conflict as a contribution to prevention and settlement of conflicts, para. 10 of the preamble and especially para. 5.

51 Id., para. 3.

52 See, *inter alia*, UNGA Resolution 56/263 of 13 March 2002, Resolution 57/302 of 15 April 2003, Resolution 58/290 of 14 April 2004 and subsequent resolutions. The most recent resolution is Resolution 66/252 of 25 January 2012.

53 UNSC Resolution 1295 (2000), especially para. 19.

this respect the Council welcomed the initiatives that led to the Kimberley Process Certification Scheme.[54] In addition, soon after the official launch of the certification scheme in 2002, the Security Council expressed its strong support for the scheme and urged all member States to actively participate in it.[55] Moreover, as discussed in the preceding chapter, the Security Council embraced the mechanism in several of its subsequent sanctions regimes as the primary way of implementing the sanctions. This gave significant added authority to the Kimberley Process.

In addition, the Kimberley Process has received support from organisations outside the UN – most notably recognition by the WTO through its waiver procedure. This waiver grants WTO members participating in the Kimberley Process the right to adopt measures to regulate the trade in rough diamonds that deviate from the trading rules of the WTO.[56] In this way, the WTO expresses its support for the Kimberley Process. It should be noted that it is exceptional for the WTO to express support for an initiative that addresses ethical concerns. In most cases where States have invoked ethical concerns as a reason to deviate from the WTO rules, the WTO has adhered to its nondiscrimination policy.[57]

8.2.6 Appraisal of the initiative

The Kimberley Process is a voluntary initiative which does not impose legally binding obligations on participating States. However, as stated before, States wishing to participate in the initiative must meet the minimum requirements of the Process. If they do not meet these requirements, they either cannot join or risk suspension from the Process. This is one of the major strengths of the Process, as the participants, including almost all the diamond-producing States, as well as all States hosting major diamond markets, such as Belgium, South Africa and Israel, are barred from trading with nonparticipants.[58] Therefore, expulsion from the process implies exclusion from the international diamond market.

[54] Ibid., especially paras. 17–18. [55] UNSC Resolution 1459 (2003), especially paras. 1–3.

[56] Waiver Concerning Kimberley Process Certification Scheme for Rough Diamonds, Decision of the WTO General Council of 15 May 2003, *Doc. WT/L/518* (27 May 2003). The waiver was extended in 2006 by General Council Decision of 15 Dec. 2006, *Doc. WT/L/676* (19 December 2006) and again in 2012 by General Council Decision of 11 December 2012, *Doc. G/C/W/675/Rev.2*. The waiver expires on 31 December 2018.

[57] See Bossche, Schrijver and Faber, 'Unilateral Measures Addressing Non-trade Concerns'.

[58] This is the characteristic of the scheme that has inspired most debates concerning the compatibility of the scheme with WTO trade law and especially with the principle of nondiscrimination. Although in practice this problem is solved through a waiver by the WTO,

The implementation of the Kimberley Process and its standards is achieved through the adoption of national legislation and procedures. Thus, while the Kimberley Process itself does not impose legally binding obligations on its participants, standards set by the Kimberley Process acquire legal force through implementation in national legislation. Participants expressly commit themselves to implementing Kimberley's minimum requirements regarding internal controls in their national legislation.

Moreover, the international recognition of the scheme, especially the strong support from the Security Council, adds considerable weight to the credibility and effectiveness of the initiative. In its sanctions regimes in relation to Angola, Sierra Leone and Liberia, the Security Council expressly provided for exemptions from the sanctions for rough diamonds traded with an effective certificate of origin regime, and expressed a preference for the Kimberley Process Certification Scheme. In its sanctions regime in relation to Côte d'Ivoire, the Security Council even made the lifting of sanctions conditional on Côte d'Ivoire's participation in the Kimberley Process.

However, from an institutional point of view, the Kimberley Process also has some significant weaknesses. The most important concerns the monitoring mechanism of the scheme. The Kimberley Process relies principally on national monitoring. There is no independent international body responsible for monitoring the implementation of the Kimberley Process requirements by the participants. International monitoring is conducted on the basis of a peer review system and largely on a voluntary basis. This system diminishes the credibility of the Kimberley Process and increases the possibilities for rebel groups to find loopholes to bypass the scheme.

Another weakness of the system is related to the decision-making process. As indicated previously, decisions are taken in the Plenary, which is composed of the participants in the Process. This means that the participants have to decide on each other's performance. Decisions are taken on the basis of consensus, which means that States can effectively block controversial decisions. This makes enforcing the requirements much more

many authors question the necessity of such a waiver. The main argument of these authors is that the Kimberley Process can be exempted under one of the general exceptions to the principle of nondiscrimination under GATT. For more details on this discussion, see, e.g., Pauwelyn 'WTO Compassion or Superiority Complex?' pp. 1177–1207; Schefer, 'Stopping Trade in Conflict Diamonds', pp. 391–450; Wetzel, 'Targeted Economic Measures to Curb Armed Conflict?' pp. 171–3.

difficult. The Group of Experts on Côte d'Ivoire mentioned this problem when it concluded that 'the Kimberley Process fails to take action when its participants do not, or cannot, adhere to its principles. This problem is not restricted to the region, but applies to Kimberley Process participants more generally'.[59]

Thus, on the whole, the Kimberley Process could be seen as an example of a voluntary agreement with compulsory elements, albeit not from a purely legal perspective. In countries that are committed to implementing the scheme, the results have been impressive. Sierra Leone serves as an example in this respect. The country has seen its official diamond exports growing considerably, while a recurrence of the armed conflict has so far been prevented. However, in countries that do not have such a direct interest in implementing the scheme, the results have not always been so positive. Countries such as Venezuela and Côte d'Ivoire, which are notorious for large-scale diamond smuggling and circumvention of the Kimberley Process requirements, illustrate the weaknesses of a non-legally binding regulatory regime such as the Kimberley Process.

From a legal point of view, the significance of the Kimberley Process could be further improved by reforms in its institutional structure. The monitoring mechanism would benefit from greater impartiality with the introduction of independent audits. The functioning of the enforcement mechanism could be improved by the introduction of a more refined set of sanctions. The only formal sanction that exists at the moment is suspension from the scheme. This is such a robust measure that it is hardly ever applied.

The introduction of more moderate sanctions would give the participants more options to deal with issues of noncompliance, and in practice, such options already exist. The diamond exports of a country can, for example, be blocked without this resulting in the official suspension of the participant. This was the case in Zimbabwe in 2009. The system would benefit from formalising and refining these options.

In spite of its weaknesses, the Kimberley Process has proved to be an invaluable tool in eliminating conflict diamonds. It has provided a universal template for the certification of rough diamonds which can be applied in all countries trading in them. Therefore, one important contribution of the Kimberley Process is that it has increased transparency in

[59] Midterm Report of the Group of Experts on Côte d'Ivoire Pursuant to Paragraph 12 of Security Council Resolution 1893 (2009) of 18 March 2010, *UN Doc. S/2010/179*, para. 77.

the diamond industry. Another important contribution of the Kimberley Process is that it has provided a platform for dialogue for States, companies and civil society to draw up plans for the elimination of the trade in conflict diamonds.

It is precisely this latter function that determines the future relevance of the Kimberley Process. In order to continue to be relevant, the participants should carefully reconsider the objectives of the Process. Currently, its principal function is related to conflict resolution, in the sense that it provides a tool to stop armed groups from financing their armed struggle with the trade in rough diamonds. Its function as a tool for conflict prevention is limited to discouraging armed groups from turning to diamonds to finance their armed struggle. Arguably, the participants should continue to develop the role of the Kimberley Process in the prevention of conflicts by adopting a broader definition of conflict diamonds, as proposed by the United States. This definition should include rough diamonds that are associated with violence and human rights abuses, whether they are committed by rebel movements or governments, in or outside the context of an armed conflict. Obviously, this policy change has major implications, not only for the Kimberley Process itself, but also for its relationship with other institutions, most notably with the Security Council. The Kimberley Process would become more independent from the Security Council as a result of this change, since it would allow Kimberley to address situations that do not directly pose a threat to international peace and security. Nonetheless, in order to improve its credibility as a tool to break the link between diamonds and armed violence, it is imperative for Kimberley to embark upon that route.

8.3 Extractive Industries Transparency Initiative

8.3.1 Context

EITI results from an NGO-driven campaign introduced in 1999 with the aim of increasing transparency in the natural resources sectors of poor States which are rich in resources by publishing company payments and government revenues. This 'Publish What You Pay' campaign inspired the British government to initiate EITI, based on a multistakeholder initiative involving governments, the extractive industry and NGOs.[60] EITI

[60] For more information on the 'Publish What You Pay Campaign', consult www.publishwhatyoupay.org.

was introduced during the 2002 Johannesburg Summit on Sustainable Development and a pilot phase was launched a year later. In the following years, both the institutional structure and the implementation process were developed in more detail. A Secretariat and a Board were established, and EITI principles, criteria and a validation guide were adopted. EITI has been fully operational since 2009.[61] Moreover, the EITI Standard is updated on a regular basis in order to increase the effectiveness of the initiative. The most recent version of the Standard was adopted in May 2013.

8.3.2 Scope and objectives of the initiative

The objective of EITI is to strengthen governance in resource-rich States by increasing transparency and accountability in the extractive industries. In the first place this involves the oil, gas and mining sectors, but it may also include other natural resources industries. Liberia, for example, has included the forestry and rubber industries in its EITI programme.[62]

The initiative is based on twelve principles which clearly demonstrate a broader commitment to sustainable development.[63] This is especially clear from the first principle, which formulates the premises on which the initiative is built. This is the belief that 'the prudent use of natural resource wealth should be an important engine for sustainable economic growth that contributes to sustainable development and poverty reduction' and that the improper management of natural resource wealth 'can create negative economic and social impacts'.

The principles reaffirm the sovereignty of States over their natural resources, while emphasising the responsibility of governments to manage natural resources for the benefit of the country's population and in the interests of national development. In this respect, the principles reflect the idea of stewardship for revenue streams and public expenditure.[64] In addition, the principles articulate the relationship between the

[61] For more details, see the Extractive Industries Transparency Initiative, *The EITI Standard*, EITI International Secretariat (May 2013), available through http://eiti.org.

[62] See http://eiti.org/Liberia.

[63] These principles can be found in the EITI Standard, p. 9.

[64] See Principle 2: 'We affirm that management of natural resource wealth for the benefit of a country's citizens is in the domain of sovereign governments to be exercised in the interests of their national development', and Principle 8: 'We believe in the principle and practice of accountability by government to all citizens for the stewardship of revenue streams and public expenditure.'

accountability of governments for the management of natural resources and for sustainable development.[65]

EITI's main tool for increasing transparency and accountability for the management of natural resources revenues is the regular publication of reports, including full government disclosure of all extractive industry revenues on one hand, and of all material payments to governments by extractive companies on the other. These publications must be made available to a wide audience in a publicly accessible, comprehensive and comprehensible manner. Other tools for increasing transparency and accountability include external audits and the active engagement of civil society.[66]

Although EITI is not designed specifically to stop natural resources from fuelling armed conflict, the mechanism can be extremely useful in restoring effective government control and improving governance over natural resources in situations of (immediate) post-conflict reconstruction. In this way, EITI can help to prevent resource revenues from provoking a relapse into armed conflict. In fact, its broader ambit does not preclude its being one of the principal tools to break the link between natural resources and armed conflict. Many countries where major resource-related conflicts have taken place in the last twenty years have joined the Initiative.[67] In addition, a concept note prepared by the United Kingdom for the Security Council's thematic open debate of 19 June 2013 on natural resources and conflict prevention refers to EITI as one of four risk-mitigating initiatives, together with the Kimberley Process, the OECD Due Diligence Guidance and the Ruggie Framework for responsible business practices.[68] During the Open Debate, several delegations confirmed this position.[69] Last, EITI is among the principal tools

[65] See Principle 4, which states that 'a public understanding of government revenues and expenditure over time could help public debate and inform choice of appropriate and realistic options for sustainable development'.

[66] See the seven EITI Requirements as set out in the EITI Standard 2013, p. 10.

[67] EITI-compliant countries include Liberia, while candidate countries include the DR Congo, Sierra Leone, Iraq and Côte d'Ivoire. See http://eiti.org/countries for up-to-date information.

[68] See the annex to the letter dated 6 June 2013 from the Permanent Representative of the United Kingdom of Great Britain and Northern Ireland to the United Nations addressed to the Secretary-General on 'Conflict prevention and natural resources: how can the effective and transparent management of natural resources in conflict-affected States contribute to international peace and security?' *UN Doc. S/2013/334*, 6 June 2013, para. 6.

[69] See, e.g., the United States, which emphasised that '[m]ultiple stakeholder partnerships among Governments, the private sector and civil society, such as the Extractive Industries

of the International Conference on the Great Lakes Region to curb illegal exploitation of natural resources, as set out in the 2010 Lusaka Declaration.

8.3.3 *Participants and institutional structure*

EITI has 39 implementing countries, of which 23 are recognised as EITI-compliant countries while 16 have the status of candidate countries.[70] Compliant countries meet all the requirements of the EITI standard, while candidate countries implement the EITI standard but do not yet meet all the requirements. Liberia, Nigeria, Iraq and Côte d'Ivoire are examples of compliant countries, while Afghanistan is a candidate country. In addition to implementing countries, EITI recognises stakeholders. These are 'supporting' countries, including the Netherlands and the United States, but also NGOs, companies and international organisations. Relevant examples of NGOs include Global Witness, the Open Society Institute, Publish What You Pay and Transparency International. Participating companies include De Beers, BP, Shell and Tata Steel. Finally, international organisations involved in EITI include the African and European Union, the OECD, the IMF and the World Bank Group.

EITI's institutional structure is well-developed. EITI is governed by an association, which is registered as a nonprofit organisation under Norwegian law. Its governance structure is codified in Articles of Association.[71] The EITI Association comprises three permanent institutional bodies. First, the EITI's Members' Meeting, consisting of personal representatives of States, companies and civil society organisations.[72] This is EITI's governing body.[73] The second body is the EITI Board, which is the executive body of the Association. The EITI Board consists of an independent Chair, eight State members, six members from industry and five members from civil society.[74] The members of the Board are elected by the Members' Meeting.[75] The third institutional body is the EITI Secretariat, which

Transparency Initiative (EITI), are making significant progress in addressing the link between extracted resources and conflict'.

[70] See http://eiti.org/countries. [71] See the EITI Standard 2013, pp. 43–52.

[72] Articles of Association, Articles 4, 8 and 9. As regards States' representatives, these are mostly civil servants or independent experts. There is no formal State representation in the Members' Meeting.

[73] Ibid., Article 8. [74] Ibid., Articles 4 and 10. [75] Ibid., Articles 9 and 10.

supports the EITI Board in running the organisation.[76] The Secretariat is funded on a voluntary basis by supporting governments and participating companies.[77]

The well-developed institutional structure of the EITI Association, with organs that can act independent of the Association's members, is one of the principal strengths of the initiative, since it effectively allows EITI to perform its oversight function. It makes EITI less susceptible to inside pressure from member countries.

8.3.4 *Operation*

States wishing to join EITI have to meet four registration requirements. These include a public announcement of the State's intention to implement EITI and the creation of a multistakeholder group at the national level consisting of representatives from the private sector, civil society and relevant government ministries to prepare and supervise the implementation of the EITI programme.[78] When States have satisfied these requirements, they can apply to the EITI Board for admission as candidate countries. To ensure the participation of all the relevant actors in the implementation process, the application cannot take place without the full support of the multistakeholder group.

After admission as candidate countries, States have to meet yet another set of minimum requirements before being accepted as full members or 'compliant countries'.[79] Among other things, all the relevant actors must be included in the process of implementation, and all relevant companies and government entities must submit reports which are based on accounts audited to international standards.

Furthermore, governments and companies, including State-owned companies, must comprehensively disclose all material payments and revenues. These are published in an EITI report, drawn up by an independent organisation. The report must be 'comprehensible, actively promoted, publicly accessible, and contribute to public debate'.[80] One important innovation in the 2013 Standard, compared to the 2011 EITI rules, is that the reports must include contextual information about the extractive industry in the EITI participant's State.[81] This information must include details about the legal framework and fiscal regime, production data of the

[76] Ibid., Articles 4 and 16. [77] Ibid., Article 18. [78] EITI Standard 2013, p. 11.
[79] Ibid., p. 10. [80] Ibid., pp. 32–3, Requirement 6. [81] Ibid., pp. 21–5, Requirement 3.

extractive industries, government involvement in extractive companies, and the allocation of licences to extractive companies. The inclusion of this requirement in the EITI 2013 Standard is an important step in raising public awareness, as contextual information about the sector enables citizens to see the individual data from a broader perspective. The last requirement of interest is that EITI implementation must be on a 'stable, sustainable footing'.[82] However, the Standard does not elaborate on this requirement.

Candidate countries must submit their first EITI reports within 18 months after their admission. After that, countries must report annually. However, in order to be accepted as EITI-compliant countries, candidate countries must take one final step. Within two and one-half years after admission as candidates, countries must submit validation reports to the EITI Board for approval. This is an external review that assesses a country's compliance with the EITI Principles and Criteria.[83] Again, the process comprises a number of checks and balances: the validator is selected by the EITI Secretariat from a list of accredited organisations preapproved by the EITI Board, and the national multistakeholder group must give its consent to the proposed validator.

The validation process has to be repeated every three years once a country has been accepted as compliant. The validation requirements, together with the annual reporting procedure, ensure that States continue to comply with the requirements after their recognition as compliant countries. If the EITI Board considers at any given moment that a country has stopped complying, it can take several measures, ranging from temporary suspension from the process to the delisting of a State. At the moment only one country has been suspended from the process, namely the Central African Republic.[84]

The effectiveness of EITI was subject to a review in 2011, undertaken by an independent bureau.[85] However, the review report was based on a very limited case study of three countries, Nigeria, Gabon and Mongolia. Moreover, the report showed mixed results. In all three countries, reforms had been undertaken for the purpose of implementing the EITI

[82] Ibid., p. 33.

[83] For more details on the validation process, see the Validation Guide, included in the EITI Standard 2013, pp. 35–9.

[84] Status as of 1 October 2014. The CAR is suspended for not being able to implement EITI as a result of the coup d'état in March 2013.

[85] Scanteam, Evaluation of the Extractive Industries Transparency Initiative, May 2011, available through http://eiti.org/files/2011-EITI-evaluation-report.pdf.

Standard. However, there were important differences between the countries, notably with regard to the inclusiveness of the process and the institutional structure put in place to ensure the proper implementation of the process. Moreover, the report showed that the EITI process had hardly had any impact on society, in the sense of creating more accountability in government administration or promoting development. Other case studies on the Nigerian and Liberian EITI programmes have reached similar conclusions.[86]

Joining EITI is regarded as an important step in creating a platform for dialogue and for building trust in government institutions, but it does not directly contribute to creating more accountability in government administration. The 2013 review of the EITI requirements is specifically intended to address these deficiencies, notably with the introduction of the requirement to publish contextual information on the extractive sector and by requiring more detailed information regarding individual payments by companies to governments.

In conclusion, EITI's most important functions so far have been to provide a framework for changes in the administration of natural resources revenues, to create a level playing field for companies in the extractive industries, and to create a platform for dialogue. However, when it comes to bringing about changes in government administration in general, and especially in fostering accountability and sustainable development, it has not yet generated any tangible results. As a tool for conflict prevention and resolution, EITI's role is therefore limited to improving the basic structure for resource governance, while it is not sufficiently equipped to eliminate grievances over resource distribution and to promote sustainable peace.

8.3.5 *International recognition of the initiative*

Although the launch of EITI had been announced in 2002, it was not until 2009 that it became fully operational. Since then, it has steadily been gaining support. Early support for EITI was voiced by the leaders of the G8, who referred to the importance of the initiative for increasing transparency in the extractive industries in all their declarations since 2007. In their most recent declaration, adopted at the 2013 summit

[86] See Ocheje, 'The Extractive Industries Transparency Initiative (EITI)' on Nigeria, pp. 222–39; and Rich and Warner, 'Addressing the Roots of Liberia's Conflict through the Extractive Industries Transparency Initiative' on Liberia, pp. 201–9.

held in Northern Ireland, the G8 expressly encouraged countries to join EITI.[87]

Furthermore, several international organisations participate directly in the initiative, including the African and European Unions, the IMF, the World Bank and the OECD. It is relevant to note that the World Bank administers EITI's so-called Multi-Donor Trust Fund, which provides technical and financial assistance to implementing States.[88] In addition, the OECD has integrated EITI into its own policy tools, such as its Due Diligence Guidance, examined in the following section.[89] The International Conference on the Great Lakes Region also endorsed EITI in its Lusaka Declaration of 15 December 2010 as one of six tools developed to curb the illegal exploitation of natural resources.[90]

EITI has encouraged the implementation of disclosure requirements for the extractive industries in the national legislations of several States, including those where major extractive companies are located. The United States, for example, has included a section in its Dodd–Frank Wall Street Reform and Consumer Protection Act, which requires oil, gas and mining companies listed on Wall Street to include in their annual report information relating to any payment made by the company or any of its subsidiaries to a government for the purpose of the commercial development of oil, natural gas, or minerals.[91] This legislation affects all companies listed on the American stock market, including foreign companies such as BP and Shell.

Similarly, the European Union has amended its 2004 Transparency Directive and 1978 and 1983 Accounting Directives to introduce mandatory disclosure requirements in EU legislation. Under the new Directives, both extractive and timber companies must publicly disclose their tax and revenue payments to governments worldwide.[92] The EU legislation

[87] G8, 2013 Lough Erne G8 Leaders' Communiqué, 18 June 2013, paras. 34–9.

[88] See the Memorandum of Understanding between the MDTF and the EITI International Secretariat of 20 March 2008, available through http://eiti.org.

[89] *OECD Due Diligence Guidance for Responsible Supply Chains of Minerals from Conflict-Affected and High-Risk Areas*, OECD Publishing (2011), p. 24.

[90] Declaration of the ICGLR Special Summit to Fight Illegal Exploitation of Natural Resources in the Great Lakes Region, Lusaka, 15 December 2010, especially para. 2.

[91] Dodd–Frank Wall Street Reform and Consumer Protection Act, *H. R. 4173*, 21 July 2010, Sect. 1504.

[92] Directive 2013/50/EU of the European Parliament and of the Council of 22 October 2013 amending Directive 2004/109/EC of the European Parliament and of the Council on the Harmonisation of Transparency Requirements in Relation to Information about Issuers Whose Securities Are Admitted to Trading on a Regulated Market, Article 6; and Directive

goes beyond Section 1504 of the Dodd–Frank Act in two respects. First, unlike the Dodd–Frank Act, the EU legislation applies to timber companies as well. In addition, unlike the Dodd–Frank Act, which applies only to companies listed on the stock market, the EU proposals apply both to companies listed on the European stock markets and to large unlisted companies.[93]

Furthermore, the UN's principal organs have expressed their support for EITI. In a resolution on strengthening transparency in industries, the UN General Assembly emphasised that permanent sovereignty over natural resources must be exercised in the interests of national development and the well-being of the people of the State concerned.[94] It is in this context that the General Assembly encouraged the international community 'to strengthen, as appropriate, upon request, the capacity of States endowed with natural resources, especially those emerging from conflict situations' and that it noted 'the efforts of countries that are participating in all relevant voluntary initiatives to improve transparency and accountability in industries, including in the Extractive Industries Transparency Initiative in the extractive sector'.[95]

Similarly, the Security Council has expressed its support for EITI, both in a general fashion and in the specific case of Liberia.[96] In its Presidential Statement of 25 June 2007, the Security Council recognised the role of voluntary initiatives aimed at improving revenue transparency, such as EITI, in ensuring that natural resources become an engine for sustainable development.[97] In addition, in Resolution 1854

2013/34/EU of the European Parliament and of the Council of 26 June 2013 on the Annual Financial Statements, Consolidated Financial Statements and Related Reports of Certain Types of Undertakings, Amending Directive 2006/43/EC of the European Parliament and of the Council and Repealing Council Directives 78/660/EEC and 83/349/EEC Text with EEA Relevance, Articles 41–8. Oil, gas, mining and forestry companies are required to disclose their payments to governments not only country by country, but also on a project-to-project basis. Furthermore, it has set a relatively low threshold by requiring disclosure of all payments of €100,000 and over.

93 Large companies are those that exceed two of the following three criteria: annual turnover of €40 million, total assets €20 million and employees 250. An important consequence of bringing large unlisted companies under the directive is that State-owned companies also fall under the directives.

94 UNGA Resolution 62/274 of 11 September 2008, para. 4 of the preamble.

95 UNGA Resolution 62/274 of 11 September 2008, especially paras. 3 and 4.

96 See the Statement by the President of the Security Council of 25 June 2007, *UN Doc. S/PRST/2007/22*, p. 2; and UNSC Resolution 1854 (2008), para. 5 of the preamble.

97 UNSC Presidential Statement on Natural Resources and Conflict, *UN Doc. S/PRST/2007/22*, 25 June 2007, para. 9.

(2008) concerning Liberia the Security Council expressed its support for Liberia's decision to take part in EITI and encouraged 'Liberia's continued progress in implementing their EITI work plan to improve revenue transparency'.[98]

Nevertheless, it should be noted that the Security Council has never made use of the initiative to support its sanctions regimes, as it did with the Kimberley Process. This is remarkable, as there have been several cases where the Security Council had the occasion to do so. The first example concerns the conflict in Côte d'Ivoire, where revenues from natural resources were used by both sides to the conflict in order to acquire arms in contravention of the embargo.[99]

The second example concerns the situation in the DR Congo. In its Resolution 2053 (2012), the Security Council encouraged the Congolese Government 'to further increase transparency in the administration of contracts for mining rights and the collection and accounting for taxes'.[100] These recommendations were made in connection with broader efforts to stop the trade in conflict resources from the DR Congo and to restore governance over the natural resources sectors. However, the Security Council did not refer to EITI as a tool to help the Congolese government to increase the transparency of its administration. Therefore, the support for EITI expressed by the Security Council is not unequivocal.

The hesitancy of the Security Council to embrace an initiative such as EITI can be linked to the diverging views of members of the UN Security Council with regard to the role of the UN Security Council in preventing armed conflicts. EITI is primarily an initiative aimed at improving public management of natural resources, and in this way helps to eliminate some of the root causes of armed conflict. An open debate held in the Security Council on the topic of 'Conflict prevention and natural resources' on 19 June 2013 revealed that many countries support

[98] UNSC Resolution 1854 (2008), para. 5 of the preamble.

[99] See, e.g., the Midterm Report of the Group of Experts Submitted in Accordance with Paragraph 11 of Security Council Resolution 1842 (2008) of 8 April 2009, *UN Doc. S/2009/188*, paras. 61–72; Final Report of the Group of Experts Submitted in Accordance with Paragraph 11 of Security Council Resolution 1842 (2008) of 9 October 2009, *UN Doc. S/2009/521*, paras. 171–210; Final Report of the Group of Experts Submitted in Accordance with Paragraph 12 of Security Council Resolution 1893 (2009) of 27 April 2011, *UN Doc. S/2011/271*, paras. 118–219. The indications of the Group of Experts were confirmed after the conflict had ended. See Final Report of the Group of Experts on Côte d'Ivoire, Prepared in Accordance with Paragraph 14 of Security Council Resolution 1980 (2011), *UN Doc. S/2012/196*, paras. 92–100.

[100] UNSC Resolution 2053 (2012), especially para. 25.

a stronger role for the Security Council in addressing the root causes of armed conflict. France, for example, emphasised the responsibility of the Security Council 'to encourage initiatives that ensure proper, lasting and responsible management' of natural resources. In France's view, the Security Council 'must support measures that can establish the basis for lasting peace'.[101] France explicitly referred to EITI as one of those measures, which, according to it, 'has as a goal to ensure that [natural] resources serve development and not fuel ongoing conflicts'.[102]

At the same time, Russia opposed strengthening the role of the UN Security Council. In Russia's view, the Security Council can adopt sanctions 'only in the case of specific violators whose actions fuel hotspots of instability. Such measures should be introduced on the basis of the Charter of the United Nations, be targeted in nature and take account of the negative humanitarian consequences thereof for the population as a whole'. Russia also emphasised the danger of 'attempts to introduce automaticity in the sanctions mechanisms or to introduce, through the Security Council and not in line with its mandate, quasi-sanction instruments by broadening the practice of the certification of raw materials'.[103]

It is this difference of opinion of the permanent members of the UN Security Council with respect to the role of the Security Council in addressing the root causes of armed conflict which to a large extent explains the Council's position with respect to EITI. During the open debate, many delegations emphasised the significance of EITI in preventing armed conflicts involving natural resources. However, the debate also reveals that opinions diverge as to the role of the Security Council in promoting EITI as part of its sanctions mechanisms. This is unfortunate, because instruments such as EITI can and do make a valuable contribution to preventing a relapse into armed conflict.

8.3.6 *Appraisal of the initiative*

EITI is an initiative based on voluntary participation and States decide for themselves whether they are willing to participate. However, as soon as a State has decided to implement EITI, it has to satisfy a large number of compulsory requirements, both before joining and after admission.

[101] United Nations Security Council, Open Debate on Conflict Prevention and Natural Resources, *UN Doc. S/PV.6982*, p. 13.

[102] Ibid. [103] Ibid., p. 16.

These requirements may not be legally binding, but compliance is essential for participation in the initiative. Furthermore, States that do not – or no longer – satisfy the criteria can lose their membership. One of the major strengths of the initiative lies in its system for the verification of compliance with the EITI requirements. Compliance is verified with an independent third party audit and the process is supervised by the EITI Board.

However, the initiative also has some weaknesses; for example, it relies exclusively on national reporting. EITI therefore relies completely on national multistakeholder groups to provide reliable information concerning both government revenues and company payments. Even the validation process cannot guarantee that the information that is provided is wholly accurate. This weakness could be partly remedied by requiring governments and companies to report directly to EITI.

Furthermore, EITI has so far not been able to improve accountability in government administration. However, the evaluation reports predate the 2013 adaptation of the EITI requirements. Previous EITI Standards did not include any requirements regarding the distribution of revenues from the extractive sectors. The focus of the initiative was one-sided, in the sense that it dealt only with resources revenues and not with issues relating to the expenditure of revenues from the extractive sector. This meant that EITI could be instrumental only in showing where the money came from, but not what it was spent on. The 2013 EITI Standard, on the other hand, does include requirements related to the distribution of revenues from the extractive industries. Requirement 3.7, in particular, determines that the EITI Report 'should indicate which extractive industry revenues, whether cash or in-kind, are recorded in the national budget. Where revenues are not recorded in the national budget, the allocation of these revenues must be explained'. Although framed as a recommendation rather than as a mandatory requirement, the inclusion of a reporting requirement for revenue expenditure is encouraging. Broadening the scope of EITI to mandatory public expenditure reporting does not seem to be a viable option, as this would mean that States would have to accept a third party audit on their expenditure. This could be a bridge too far for many countries participating in the initiative.

In conclusion, EITI is the only global initiative that specifically addresses problems related to public administration in the extractive industry. This makes it an important tool for the prevention and resolution of armed conflicts which have grievances over natural resources among their root causes. EITI has successfully highlighted the importance of transparent and accountable public administration in a sector that is of great economic importance to many developing countries, including developing countries emerging from armed conflict. The subsequent adoption of national and regional legislation to address these issues attests to EITI's success in this respect.

At the same time, the adoption of the US Dodd–Frank Act and the revision of the European Transparency Directives, each with its own standards and modes of operation, also present a risk of the duplication of efforts. Therefore, there is a clear need to develop a single global reporting standard for the extractive industries, which was also recognised by the G8 at its 2013 Summit. In their final declaration, the leaders of the G8 committed themselves to 'raise global standards for extractives transparency and make progress towards common global reporting standards, both for countries with significant domestic extractive industries and the home countries of large multinational extractives corporations'.[104] EITI should play an important role in the implementation of these commitments. As the initiative brings together all the relevant actors and has a well-developed institutional structure, it constitutes a convenient forum for the synchronisation of further international action, both in relation to improving the governance of natural resources in general and, specifically, as part of post-conflict reconstruction efforts. Its primary role in improving resource transparency in conflict-affected States has been expressly acknowledged in specific instruments. Amongst these are the Lusaka Declaration of the International Conference on the Great Lakes Region, referred to above, and the OECD Due Diligence Guidance for Responsible Supply Chains of Minerals from Conflict-Affected and High-Risk Areas, examined next.

8.4 OECD Due Diligence Guidance for Responsible Supply Chains of Minerals from Conflict-Affected and High-Risk Areas

8.4.1 Context

The OECD Due Diligence Guidance is a voluntary code of conduct for companies in the minerals sector that either import from or operate in conflict-affected or otherwise politically unstable regions. The Guidance refers to 'high-risk areas', which are characterised by the presence of widespread violence or other risks of harm to people.[105] They include areas

[104] G8, 2013 Lough Erne G8 Leaders' Communiqué, 18 June 2013, para. 36.

[105] See the *OECD Due Diligence Guidance for Responsible Supply Chains of Minerals from Conflict-Affected and High-Risk Areas*, OECD Publishing (2013), p. 13.

of political instability or repression, institutional weakness, insecurity, collapse of civil infrastructure and widespread violence.[106]

In other words, the OECD Due Diligence Guidance applies both to companies operating in States where there is ongoing armed conflict and to companies operating in fragile States. Thus the Guidance is a tool to address not only the responsibility of companies for fuelling conflicts but also their responsibility in other situations where gross human rights violations occur.

The Guidance elaborates on earlier OECD initiatives in the context of the OECD Declaration on International Investment and Multilateral Enterprises. These initiatives include in particular the OECD Guidelines for Multinational Enterprises and the OECD Risk Awareness Tool for Multinational Enterprises in Weak Governance Zones.[107] The 2011 revision of the OECD Guidelines for Multinational Enterprises includes general due diligence requirements for all companies adhering to the OECD Guidelines.[108] The OECD Due Diligence Guidance develops these requirements specifically for some of the minerals that have contributed most to contemporary armed conflicts. These are tin, tantalum, tungsten and gold (3TG).

The OECD Due Diligence Guidance was developed to address the responsibility of corporations with respect to trade in conflict minerals, in particular from the DR Congo. In 2009, the Security Council mandated the Group of Experts on the DR Congo to draw up guidelines for the exercise of due diligence by importers, processing industries and consumers of mineral products from the DR Congo, taking advantage of work carried out in other forums.[109] To implement this resolution, the Group of Experts turned to the OECD, member States of the International Conference on the Great Lakes Region, industry and civil society. This collaboration resulted in two instruments: the OECD Due Diligence Guidance as a general tool for companies in the minerals sector

[106] *OECD Due Diligence Guidance for Responsible Supply Chains of Minerals from Conflict-Affected and High-Risk Areas*, OECD Publishing (2013), p. 13.

[107] For a discussion of the OECD Guidelines for Multinational Enterprises, see, e.g., Černič, *Human Rights Law and Business*, pp. 184–207. For a discussion of the 2011 update of the guidelines, from the same author, see 'The 2011 Update of the OECD Guidelines for Multinational Enterprises'.

[108] Ibid. for a discussion of these requirements.

[109] UNSC Resolution 1896 (2009), especially para. 7. The UN Security Council thus implicitly referred to the work undertaken by the OECD, in particular the 2006 Risk Awareness Tool for Multinational Enterprises in Weak Governance Zones; and by the International Conference on the Great Lakes Region, in particular to its 2006 Protocol Against the Illegal Exploitation of Natural Resources and related initiatives.

operating in conflict-affected or high-risk regions, and a more specific set of guidelines to address the problem of conflict minerals originating from the DR Congo, which was presented to the Security Council by the Group of Experts.

The OECD Council endorsed the Guidance with a recommendation that members and nonmembers adherent to the Declaration on Investment and Multilateral Enterprises 'actively promote the observance of the Guidance by companies', that they 'take measures to actively support the integration into corporate management systems' of the framework, and that they 'ensure the widest possible dissemination of the Guidance and its active use by other stakeholders including professional associations, financial institutions, and civil society organizations'.[110] Furthermore, the OECD Council instructed the Investment Committee and the Development Assistance Committee to monitor the implementation of the recommendation.[111]

8.4.2 *Scope and objectives of the initiative*

The aim of the Guidance is to ensure that companies procuring minerals from conflict-affected and high-risk areas 'respect human rights, avoid contributing to conflict and successfully contribute to sustainable, equitable and effective development'.[112] The Guidance provides a framework for these companies to help them assess the risk of their activities contributing to armed conflict or human rights abuses. Companies are to observe 'due diligence', defined as 'an on-going, proactive and reactive process through which companies can ensure that they respect human rights and do not contribute to conflict'.[113] The due diligence framework applies to companies throughout the mineral supply chain, from the extraction of the minerals to their incorporation into the final consumer product.[114] The Guidance currently covers tin, tantalum and tungsten, including their ores or mineral derivatives, as well as gold sources.[115]

110 See the Recommendation of the OECD Council on Due Diligence Guidance for Responsible Supply Chains of Minerals from Conflict-Affected and High-Risk Areas, adopted on 25 May 2011 (amended on 17 July 2012), *Doc. C(2012)93*, especially paras. 1–3.

111 Ibid., especially para. 5. 112 Ibid., especially para. 1.

113 *OECD Due Diligence Guidance for Responsible Supply Chains of Minerals from Conflict-Affected and High-Risk Areas*, OECD Publishing (2013), p. 13.

114 *OECD Due Diligence Guidance for Responsible Supply Chains of Minerals from Conflict-Affected and High-Risk Areas*, OECD Publishing (2013), p. 14.

115 Recommendation of the OECD Council on Due Diligence Guidance for Responsible Supply Chains of Minerals from Conflict-Affected and High-Risk Areas, adopted on 25 May 2011 (amended on 17 July 2012), *Doc. C(2012)93.*

The framework for due diligence aims to provide practical guidance to companies to help them assess the risks of their activities contributing to armed conflict or human rights violations and find adequate responses to eliminate these risks. This raises important questions regarding the nature of the risks the OECD Guidance aims to address. The OECD Guidance incorporates a Model Supply Chain Policy which sets out principles and standards for responsible mineral sourcing.[116] Companies adhering to the OECD Guidance must ensure that their own supply chain policies are consistent with the standards set out in this model. A discussion of the principles and standards set out in the Model Supply Chain Policy helps to gain a proper understanding of the OECD's definition of responsible mineral sourcing.

First of all, the Model Supply Chain Policy determines that companies 'sourcing from, or operating in conflict-affected and high-risk areas are not to tolerate nor by any means profit from, contribute to, assist with or facilitate the commission by any party' of serious abuses associated with the extraction, transport or trade in minerals. The first paragraph of the Model Supply Chain Policy identifies the following serious abuses: any forms of torture, cruel, inhuman or degrading treatment, any forms of forced or compulsory labour, the worst forms of child labour, other gross human rights violations and abuses such as widespread sexual violence, war crimes or other serious violations of IHL, and crimes against humanity or genocide.

In other words, the Model Supply Chain Policy requires companies engaged in the minerals sector in fragile States to ensure that neither they nor their business partners are in any way involved in the violation of fundamental human rights or the commission of international crimes. Thus the Model Supply Chain Policy sets a very high standard. It is also interesting to note that the Guidance does not require companies to respect relevant conventions, although it specifically refers to particular conventions and also uses legal terminology. It explicitly refers to the ILO Convention on the Worst Forms of Child Labour and uses the ILO's definition of forced and compulsory labour.[117] In addition, it uses such

[116] Model Supply Chain Policy for a Responsible Global Supply Chain of Minerals from Conflict-Affected and High-Risk Areas, *OECD Due Diligence Guidance for Responsible Supply Chains of Minerals from Conflict-Affected and High-Risk Areas*, OECD Publishing (2013), Annex II.

[117] ILO Convention No. 182 on the Worst Forms of Child Labour, concluded on 17 June 1999, *2133 UNTS 161*; ILO Convention No. 29 Concerning Forced or Compulsory Labour, concluded on 28 June 1930, *39 UNTS 55*.

legal terms as 'war crimes' or 'other serious violations of international humanitarian law', 'crimes against humanity' and 'genocide'.

The second form of irresponsible mineral sourcing that the OECD Guidance seeks to prevent is the provision of support to non-State armed groups or public or private security forces that illegally control mining sites. In this respect, the Model Supply Chain Policy requires companies not to tolerate any direct or indirect support of non-State armed groups or of public or private security forces through the extraction, transport, trade, handling or export of minerals. Direct or indirect support is defined broadly to include not only the procurement of minerals themselves, but also any indirect payments to such groups (e.g., by paying them illegal taxes) and providing them with logistical assistance or equipment.

In other words, the OECD Guidance seeks to prevent the involvement of companies in the trade in conflict minerals. It is interesting to note that the Guidance not only targets non-State armed groups, but also other actors such as mercenaries, private security companies and members of the national army involved in illegal mining. In this way, the Guidance aims to cover situations such as that in the DR Congo, where criminal bands in the national army are involved in illegal mining.[118]

Finally, the Model Supply Chain Policy requires companies to refrain from engaging in bribery or fraudulent misrepresentation of the origin of minerals. They must support efforts to eliminate money laundering and they must ensure that all taxes, fees and royalties related to mineral extraction, trade and export are paid to the government and disclosed in accordance with the EITI principles.

In this way, the OECD Guidance seeks to prevent illegal taxation in all its forms by non-State armed groups and criminal bands in conflict-affected and high-risk areas. This was a major issue in several of the conflicts discussed in this book. The conflict in Côte d'Ivoire is a good example. The Group of Experts on Côte d'Ivoire uncovered the existence of parallel taxation systems in that country, operated by the opposition forces.[119] A second point of interest is the reliance of the OECD Guidance on EITI as a means to ensure that taxes, fees and royalties paid to the

[118] Final Report of the Group of Experts on the Democratic Republic of the Congo Prepared Pursuant to Paragraph 6 of Security Council Resolution 1896 (2009), *UN Doc. S/2010/596* of 29 November 2010, pp. 47–76.

[119] Final Report of the Group of Experts on Côte d'Ivoire, Prepared in Accordance with Paragraph 14 of Security Council Resolution 1980 (2011), *UN Doc. S/2012/196*, paras. 92–110.

government are accounted for. This can be seen as a form of direct support for EITI.

It can be concluded from the above that the OECD has opted for a very broad definition of 'responsible supply chains of minerals'. The responsibility of mineral companies is not limited to their role in fuelling armed conflicts. The OECD Guidance also seeks to address the broader responsibility of mineral companies and their policies on society in conflict-affected and high-risk areas, in particular with the provisions on serious abuses and bribery.

However, at the same time, the OECD Guidance sets a very high standard with regard to abuses in the minerals sector that are not directly related to the issue of providing support to armed groups. For the Guidance to become relevant, these abuses must be of a serious nature, in the sense of amounting to complicity in the violation of fundamental human rights and the commission of international crimes. Therefore, the relevance of the Guidance is limited to addressing only the most serious irregularities in the extractive sector. It is not an instrument that addresses responsible business conduct in the extractive sector in a broad sense.

8.4.3 Participants and institutional structure

The OECD Due Diligence Guidance is part of a broader framework of instruments adopted by the OECD in relation to the (revised) OECD Declaration on International Investment and Multinational Enterprises. All OECD members, as well as nine nonmembers (Argentina, Brazil, Colombia, Egypt, Latvia, Lithuania, Morocco, Peru and Romania), have signed this declaration. For the purposes of the present study, it is relevant to note that these countries do not include any African States.

The Guidelines for Multinational Enterprises are annexed to the Declaration on International Investment and Multinational Enterprises.[120] They contain recommendations on responsible business conduct for multinational companies. Since 2011, the Guidelines have included detailed recommendations on supply chain due diligence. Under the new Guidelines, companies should 'carry out risk-based due diligence . . . to identify, prevent and mitigate actual and potential adverse impacts . . . and account for how these impacts are addressed'.[121] The impacts referred

[120] *OECD Guidelines for Multinational Enterprises*, OECD Publishing, 2011 edition.

[121] *OECD Guidelines for Multinational Enterprises*, OECD Publishing, 2011 edition, Chap. II, para. A 10.

to in the Guidelines include both adverse impacts caused by a company's own activities and adverse impacts caused by their business relations.[122]

In addition to this general due diligence requirement, companies must also carry out human rights due diligence in relation to their own activities and those of their business partners.[123] These requirements were inserted in response to the 'Protect, Respect and Remedy Framework for Business and Human Rights', developed by John Ruggie, the Special Representative of the Secretary-General on the issue of human rights and transnational corporations and other business enterprises.[124] This framework formulates human rights standards for companies. Guiding Principle 17, which sets out a human rights due diligence standard, is particularly relevant in this respect.[125]

It is also relevant to note that States adhering to the Guidelines for Multinational Enterprises must set up so-called National Contact Points (NCPs). The role of the NCPs is to increase the effectiveness of the

[122] *OECD Guidelines for Multinational Enterprises*, OECD Publishing, 2011 edition, Chap. II, paras. A 11–12. The OECD Official Commentary to these Guidelines define business relationships as including 'relationships with business partners, entities in the supply chain and any other non-State or State entities directly linked to its business operations, products or services'. *OECD Guidelines for Multinational Enterprises*, OECD Publishing, 2011 edition, p. 23.

[123] *OECD Guidelines for Multinational Enterprises*, OECD Publishing, 2011 edition, Chap. IV, paras. 2, 3 and 5.

[124] This framework has been developed on the initiative of the UN Human Rights Council (then: Commission) in order to improve corporate responsibility for the protection of human rights. It was subsequently endorsed by the Human Rights Council. Also see the Report on the 'Protect, Respect and Remedy Framework for Business and Human Rights' by John Ruggie, the Special Representative of the Secretary-General on the issue of human rights and transnational corporations and other business enterprises, *UN Doc. A/HRC/8/5*, 7 April 2008. See also the Report on the Guiding Principles on Business and Human Rights: Implementing the United Nations 'Protect, Respect and Remedy' Framework, *UN Doc. A/HRC/17/31*, 21 March 2011.

[125] Guiding Principle 17 states, 'In order to identify, prevent, mitigate and account for how they address their adverse human rights impacts, business enterprises should carry out human rights due diligence. The process should include assessing actual and potential human rights impacts, integrating and acting upon the findings, tracking responses, and communicating how impacts are addressed. Human rights due diligence:

(a) Should cover adverse human rights impacts that the business enterprise may cause or contribute to through its own activities, or which may be directly linked to its operations, products or services by its business relationships;
(b) Will vary in complexity with the size of the business enterprise, the risk of severe human rights impacts, and the nature and context of its operations;
(c) Should be ongoing, recognizing that the human rights risks may change over time as the business enterprise's operations and operating context evolve'.

Guidelines, for example, by resolving issues that arise in relation to the implementation of the Guidelines.[126] These issues can be raised by all the interested parties, including worker organisations and NGOs.[127] Although the NCPs cannot take binding decisions, the dispute resolution mechanism has proved to be a valuable resource for NGOs challenging the human rights policies of individual companies.

As the Due Diligence Guidance was a specific result of the general due diligence requirements set out in the Guidelines for Multinational Enterprises, its implementation is subject to the same institutional structure. This means that the dispute resolution mechanism set up under the Guidelines is also able to address alleged violations of the Due Diligence Guidance. This is a promising possibility for challenging the supply chain policies of mineral companies operating in conflict regions. In the 2000 version of the Guidelines, several complaints had already been filed against mineral trading companies operating in the DR Congo.[128] These complaints were triggered by a report of the Panel of Experts on the Illegal Exploitation of Natural Resources and Other Forms of Wealth of the Democratic Republic of the Congo on business enterprises considered by the Panel to be in violation of the OECD Guidelines for Multinational Enterprises.[129]

Most of these complaints alleged that the company had failed to observe sufficient due diligence in the supply chain. Despite the rudimentary provision of the 2000 version of the Guidelines on supply chain due diligence, stating merely that '[e]nterprises should encourage, where practicable, business partners, including suppliers and sub-contractors, to apply principles of corporate conduct compatible with the Guidelines',[130] some of the cases brought before NCPs have been quite successful.

One of these complaints related to the practices of Afrimex, a British mineral trading company operating in the DR Congo. The complaint brought to the British NCP by Global Witness accused Afrimex of

[126] *OECD Guidelines for Multinational Enterprises*, OECD Publishing, 2011 edition, p. 68, Sect. I(1).

[127] *OECD Guidelines for Multinational Enterprises*, OECD Publishing, 2011 edition, p. 72, Sect. C.

[128] See, e.g., *Global Witness* v. *Afrimex* (filed on 20 February 2007); *11.11.11 et al* v. *Cogecom* (filed on 24 November 2004); *11.11.11 et al.* v. *Nami Gems* (filed on 24 November 2004); *RAID* v. *Das Air* (filed on 28 June 2004); and *NiZA et al.* v. *CPH* (filed on 3 July 2003).

[129] Final Report of the Panel of Experts on the Illegal Exploitation of Natural Resources and Other Forms of Wealth of the Democratic Republic of the Congo, *UN Doc. S/2002/1146*, Annex III.

[130] *OECD Guidelines for Multinational Enterprises*, OECD Publishing, 2000 edition, Chap. II, para. I I.10.

paying taxes to rebel forces in the DR Congo and of practising insufficient due diligence in the supply chain, sourcing minerals from mines that use child and forced labour. According to the NCP, Afrimex failed to fulfil the due diligence requirements in two ways. In the first place, the NCP concluded that the reliance of Afrimex on statements by its suppliers on the origin of the minerals purchased by Afrimex did not reflect sufficient due diligence.[131] Second, Afrimex practised insufficient due diligence in the supply chain, because it 'did not take steps to influence the supply chain and to explore options with its suppliers exploring methods to ascertain how minerals could be sourced from mines that do not use child or forced labour or with better health and safety'.[132]

The UK National Contact Point applied the Guidelines in a very forward-looking way in the Afrimex case, taking into account new developments in corporate responsibility for human rights abuses emanating from the Protect, Respect and Remedy Framework developed by John Ruggie, Special Representative of the Secretary-General on the issue of human rights and transnational corporations and other business enterprises. The implementation of this framework in the 2011 version of the Guidelines for Multinational Enterprises will hopefully raise the awareness of both companies and implementing States about the responsibility of companies to carefully assess the risks of their activities contributing to armed conflict or human rights abuses. Furthermore, it is to be expected that when assessing whether companies in the extractive sector have satisfied the due diligence requirements of the 2011 Guidelines, National Contact Points will turn to the Due Diligence Guidance for more specific indications.

8.4.4 Operation

The OECD Due Diligence Guidance was developed to ensure that companies procuring minerals from conflict-affected and high-risk areas 'respect human rights, avoid contributing to conflict and successfully contribute to sustainable, equitable and effective development'.[133] The

[131] *Final Statement by the UK National Contact Point for the OECD Guidelines for Multinational Enterprises: Afrimex (UK) LTD*, Summary of NCP Decision, 28 August 2008, para. 51.

[132] *Final Statement by the UK National Contact Point for the OECD Guidelines for Multinational Enterprises: Afrimex (UK) LTD*, Summary of NCP Decision, 28 August 2008, para. 62.

[133] Recommendation of the OECD Council on Due Diligence for Responsible Supply Chains of Minerals from Conflict-Affected and High-Risk Areas, adopted on 25 May 2011, para. 17.

Guidance attempts to realise these objectives by introducing transparency and accountability into the minerals supply chain. It does so predominantly by using two main tools. The first involves putting in place mechanisms to ensure that "downstream companies", referring to companies in the supply chain from smelters/refiners to retailers, obtain information from their suppliers about the origin of the minerals purchased by them and that "upstream companies", referring to companies in the supply chain from the mine to smelters/refiners, provide such information to their business partners.[134] The second concerns requiring independent audits from companies in order to ensure the credibility of the information relied on by downstream companies, as well as the information provided to them by upstream companies.

The OECD Guidance is based on a five-step approach to due diligence. The basic components of the five-step approach are the establishment of strong company management systems, the identification and assessment of supply chain risks, the design and implementation of strategies to respond to identified risks, the performance of independent third-party audits and annual reporting on supply chain due diligence.

Therefore, the approach focuses on the management of risks associated with business transactions in the mineral and gold sectors. The Guidance provides individual companies with the tools to reduce the risks of their business practices contributing to armed conflict and other forms of violence. To ensure the proper implementation of the due diligence policies, the approach has also built in some safeguards. These consist of independent third-party audits and disclosure requirements, which permit business partners, as well as the general public, to verify the company's mineral policies.

The OECD has also developed two separate supplements which provide specific guidance to companies on how to implement the five steps in their particular sectors, as referred to earlier. One supplement focuses on supply chain due diligence for companies trading in tin, tantalum and tungsten, while the other focuses on gold. The two supplements make a distinction between upstream and downstream companies. Specific recommendations apply to these categories of companies. Neither of the supplements applies to small-scale mining by individuals, informal working groups or communities.

[134] For these definitions, see the *OECD Due Diligence Guidance for Responsible Supply Chains of Minerals from Conflict-Affected and High-Risk Areas, Supplement on Tin, Tantalum and Tungsten and Supplement on Gold*, OECD Publishing (2013).

Both supplements require companies to review their sourcing practices in advance in order to determine whether the Guidance applies to them. The supplement on tin, tantalum and tungsten contains a set of 'red flags' triggering the due diligence standards and processes contained in the Guidance. Red flags apply to certain locations of mineral origin or transit (minerals originating from or transported via a conflict-affected or high-risk area, minerals that are alleged to originate from a country with very low production levels of the mineral concerned, and minerals that are alleged to originate from a known transit country) and to particular suppliers (suppliers with ties to companies operating in one of the red flag locations, the suppliers or their business partners who are known to have recently sourced minerals from a red flag location). If one of these red flags applies or if a company cannot determine whether this is the case, it should proceed with the implementation of the Guidance.

The supplement on gold does not contain such a red flag system. To determine whether they actually or potentially source gold from conflict-affected and high-risk areas, all companies in this sector should immediately start carrying out the first steps of the process. These involve establishing strong management systems and identifying and assessing risks in the supply chain.[135] One important first step in this respect is the adoption of a supply chain policy, consistent with the Model Supply Chain Policy discussed above. The objective of this policy is to set forth common principles and standards against which the company can assess its own policies, as well as the activities and relationships of its suppliers.[136]

8.4.5 *International recognition of the initiative*

The OECD Due Diligence Guidance has had extensive backup from the international community. As mentioned previously, both the International Conference on the Great Lakes Region and the UN Group of Experts on the Democratic Republic of Congo were involved in drafting the guidelines. This cooperation resulted in the development of mutually supporting initiatives.

[135] *OECD Due Diligence Guidance for Responsible Supply Chains of Minerals from Conflict-Affected and High-Risk Areas, Supplement on Gold*, OECD Publishing (2013).

[136] *Supplement on Tin, Tantalum and Tungsten*, Step 1 (A); *Supplement on Gold*, Step 1, Sect. 1(A).

First, the International Conference on the Great Lakes Region endorsed the OECD Due Diligence Guidance in its Lusaka Declaration and directed its Secretariat to integrate the processes and standards of the OECD Guidance in the six tools of the Regional Initiative against the Illegal Exploitation of Natural Resources.[137] Second, the Group of Experts on the DR Congo developed a set of due diligence guidelines specifically for minerals originating from the DR Congo, which relies on the OECD Guidance. This was acknowledged by the Group of Experts, which recommended in its final report of 2010 'that relevant individuals and entities refer to the OECD guidance for further details on due diligence requirements'.[138]

The Security Council also expressed support for the OECD Guidance, both directly and indirectly, on several occasions. Most importantly, it did so by endorsing the Group of Experts Guidelines for the DR Congo. More specifically, the Security Council mandated that the exercise of due diligence by a company be taken into account when the DR Congo Sanctions Committee decided whether to place it on the sanctions list. In this respect, the Security Council specifically referred to the guidelines developed by the Group of Experts or 'equivalent guidelines' as a means of appraising the exercise of due diligence by companies.[139] The five-step approach to due diligence examined above is essential to the Security Council in this respect. Thus, at least in relation to the DR Congo, the Security Council expressed strong support for the approach to due diligence set out in the OECD Guidance. In its Resolution 2101 (2013) in relation to the situation in Côte d'Ivoire, the UN Security Council confirmed its support for the OECD Guidance. In this resolution it expressly encouraged the government of Côte d'Ivoire to participate in the OECD-hosted implementation programme with regard to the due diligence guidelines for responsible supply chains of minerals from conflict-affected and high-risk areas.[140] This reference to the OECD Guidance in relation to Côte d'Ivoire confirms

[137] Declaration of the ICGLR Special Summit to Fight Illegal Exploitation of Natural Resources in the Great Lakes Region, Lusaka, 15 December 2010, especially paras. 12 and 13. These six tools are a Regional Certification Mechanism; harmonisation of national legislation; a regional database on mineral flows; formalisation of the artisanal mining sector; promotion of EITI; and a whistle-blowing mechanism.

[138] Final Report of the Group of Experts Prepared Pursuant to Paragraph 6 of Security Council Resolution 1896 (2009), *UN Doc. S/2010/596*, para. 319.

[139] UNSC Resolution 1952 (2010), especially para. 8.

[140] UNSC Resolution 2101 (2013), especially para. 25.

the willingness of the Security Council to promote the implementation of the OECD Guidance in a more general fashion.

Furthermore, the OECD Guidance was put forward as a tool to implement national legislation, such as the obligations imposed by Section 1502 of the US Dodd–Frank Wall Street Reform and Consumer Protection Act.[141] Section 1502 of that Act requires companies listed on Wall Street to determine whether their products contain conflict minerals originating in the DR Congo or neighbouring countries, and to report this to the Securities and Exchange Commission (SEC).[142] A proposal for a European Regulation on this topic is currently under discussion. In October 2010 the European Parliament requested the European Commission and Council to examine a legislative initiative similar to Section 1502 of the US Dodd–Frank Act.[143] In March 2014, the European Commission submitted a proposal to this end.[144] Unlike the Dodd–Frank Act, which introduces mandatory reporting for all companies sourcing from the DR Congo, the European Draft Regulation introduces a system of self-regulation for all companies sourcing minerals from conflict-affected and high risk States. The strength of the European proposal is its broad application. Where the Dodd–Frank Act applies exclusively to minerals sourced from the DR Congo, the European Draft Regulation applies to minerals sourced from fragile States in general. The principal weakness of the European proposal is, however, its noncommittal approach. Where the Dodd–Frank Act contains a mandatory reporting component, the European Draft Regulation applies only to companies that voluntarily opt for self-certification. This could well mark a missed opportunity.

141 See Joint Letter of the International Conference on the Great Lakes Region, the OECD and the UN Group of Experts on the Democratic Republic of Congo to the U.S. Securities and Exchange Commission, 29 July 2011, available through www.oecd.org. The transparency requirements regarding the provenance of minerals sourced in the DR Congo, included in Section 1502 of the Dodd–Frank Act, must be distinguished from the transparency requirements regarding the payments of oil, gas and mining companies to governments under Section 1504 of the Dodd–Frank Act, discussed earlier. Although these sections complement each other in some ways, they deal with different issues.

142 Dodd–Frank Wall Street Reform and Consumer Protection Act, *H.R. 4173*, adopted on 21 July 2010, Section 1502.

143 European Parliament Resolution of 7 October 2010 on Failures in Protection of Human Rights and Justice in the Democratic Republic of Congo, *P7_TA(2010)0350*.

144 Proposal for a Regulation of the European Parliament and of the Council Setting Up a Union System for Supply Chain Due Diligence Self-Certification of Responsible Importers of Tin, Tantalum and Tungsten, Their Ores, and Gold Originating in Conflict-Affected and High-Risk Areas, COM(2014) 111 final, 2014/0059 (COD), 5 March 2014.

8.4.6 Appraisal of the initiative

The OECD Guidance is a voluntary initiative that aims to increase corporate responsibility in the minerals sector, operating on the basis of supply chain due diligence. Assigning responsibility throughout the supply chain is one of the ways of contributing to the effectiveness of the OECD Guidance as a framework for industry self-regulation. By requiring companies throughout the supply chain to conduct due diligence, it gives every company a stake in the due diligence process. Companies cannot hide behind each other or deny knowledge of what is happening further down the supply chain. Every company in the supply chain has a responsibility to check whether its business partners comply with the due diligence requirements in order to be able to fulfil its own obligations.

Another major strength of the Guidance is that it does not stand by itself, but can be used to give effect to other initiatives on social corporate responsibility. The OECD Due Diligence Guidance primarily provides mineral companies with a sophisticated set of guidelines which can be used to implement the due diligence requirements formulated in the OECD Guidelines for Multinational Enterprises. Companies can also ask the National Contact Points established pursuant to the OECD Guidelines for assistance with regard to the implementation of the Guidance. In addition, the Guidance can be instrumental in helping companies to implement their due diligence obligations pursuant to other initiatives, in particular the due diligence requirements that were imposed in relation to the DR Congo by the UN Security Council sanctions regime and by the US Dodd–Frank Act. The close coordination between these initiatives has resulted in mutually supportive regimes.

Another advantage of the complementary nature of the OECD Guidance is related to its enforcement. Although companies implement the due diligence requirements on a voluntary basis, there are ways of holding companies to account for their failure to exercise due diligence. The principal option for this is to file a complaint with the National Contact Points established pursuant to the OECD Guidelines. Although the decisions of the NCPs are not legally binding, their role in mediating disputes should not be underestimated. In addition, and exclusively in relation to the DR Congo, companies can be placed on a UN Security Council sanctions list for their failure to exercise due diligence and can be subjected to fines under the US Dodd–Frank Act.

The Due Diligence Guidance is a promising tool for increasing the responsibility of companies in the minerals sector and for preventing these companies from contributing to human rights violations and/or armed conflict. The principal contribution of the Guidance is that it provides companies with a comprehensive due diligence model which they can integrate into their policies. Furthermore, the Guidance sets standards for the protection of human rights and combating corruption. Although these standards are for the most part based on existing legal instruments, including ILO and OECD Conventions, the Guidance is one of the few instruments that are directly addressed to companies.

To increase corporate responsibility in the minerals sector, some issues need further consideration. The Guidance currently covers tin, tantalum and tungsten, including their ores or mineral derivatives, as well as gold sources.[145] Despite the broad reach of the Guidance, there is one striking omission from the list of minerals. The OECD Guidance does not cover diamonds, a mineral that has financed several contemporary armed conflicts. At first sight, it could be argued that this is obvious, as diamonds are already covered by the Kimberley Process. However, a closer look reveals that there is no clear explanation for this omission. Although the core objective of both initiatives is to exclude conflict minerals from the international market, they use different methods to achieve this objective. The Kimberley Process focuses on government-controlled certification, while the OECD Guidance focuses on the role of companies throughout the supply chain. This makes these initiatives mutually compatible. Moreover, the OECD Guidance could strengthen the Kimberley Process. After all, the Guidance covers every phase of the process, from rough minerals to end products, while the Kimberley Process focuses exclusively on rough diamonds. In addition, the Guidance applies not only to countries where there is an ongoing armed conflict, but also to countries where there is widespread violence. In these ways, the OECD Guidance could fill some of the existing gaps in the Kimberley Process. Therefore, it is imperative to increase the scope of the Guidance by adding a supplement on diamonds, as suggested by the Kimberley Process Civil Society Coalition.[146] This suggestion has not yet been followed up.

[145] *OECD Due Diligence Guidance for Responsible Supply Chains of Minerals from Conflict-Affected and High-Risk Areas*, OECD Publishing (2013).

[146] Kimberley Process Civil Society Coalition, Communiqué, Brussels, 19 November 2011, para. 3, available through www.pacweb.org.

Furthermore, it is necessary to coordinate initiatives such as the OECD Guidance with other corporate responsibility initiatives. In this respect, special mention can be made of the Voluntary Principles on Security and Human Rights, a multistakeholder initiative that formulates due diligence requirements for companies in the extractive sector in relation to their security arrangements. These principles overlap with the requirements formulated under the OECD Guidance in relation to security forces.

It is therefore clear that the OECD Due Diligence Guidance is an important step in addressing the contribution of companies to resource-related armed conflicts. The years to come will show whether the Guidance can succeed in changing corporate behaviour in the extractive sector in conflict regions. A recent pilot project in the Great Lakes region produced some encouraging results, although it also revealed that the success of the OECD Guidance is largely dependent on external factors, two of which are particularly important. First, the final report revealed that the success of the pilot project was in large part due to the adoption of relevant national legislation, as well as to the formulation of requirements by the industry itself.[147] In addition, the effective implementation of due diligence by companies can only be achieved if the origin of the minerals can be traced. The most recent reports of the Group of Experts on the DR Congo show that smuggling had increased considerably in the past years.[148] This shows that the implementation of corporate responsibility tools is highly dependent on the efficient functioning of a certification mechanism, as well as on law enforcement efforts in the border regions.

8.5 Substantive contribution of the initiatives to improving resource governance

This section aims to assess the substantive contribution of the initiatives to the governance of natural resources in conflict-affected States. In this respect, it is important to note that the three initiatives have different objectives and methods, but a common aim, to increase transparency in the management of natural resources. For this purpose, the initiatives

[147] See OECD, 'Upstream Implementation of the OECD Due Diligence Guidance for Responsible Supply Chains of Minerals from Conflict-Affected and High-Risk Areas', Final Report on One-Year Pilot implementation of the Supplement on Tin, Tantalum, and Tungsten (2013), p. 9.

[148] See e.g. Final Report of the Group of Experts on the DRC Submitted in Accordance with Paragraph 4 of Security Council Resolution 2021 (2011), *UN Doc. S/2012/843*, 15 November 2012, paras. 159–242; Final Report of the Group of Experts on the DRC, *UN Doc. S/2014/42*, 23 January 2014, para. 171.

set standards with regard to their management, both for States and for companies. The overall objective of the Kimberley Process is to introduce transparency in the trade in rough diamonds in order to eliminate the trade in conflict diamonds by rebel groups. Relevant standards set by the Kimberley Process include the establishment of internal controls, as well as the collection, maintenance and exchange of data relevant to diamond production, import and export. Additional standards relating to the management of rough diamonds include the licensing of mines and tracking cash purchases of rough diamonds through official banking channels. It is relevant to note that the Kimberley Process does not address companies directly.

EITI's contribution to increasing transparency in the management of natural resources consists of setting standards for the public administration of natural resources, which could be part of broader reforms in post-conflict peacebuilding strategies. To comply with EITI, States must publish the revenues obtained from contracts with the oil, gas and mining industries, while companies in these sectors must publish their payments to governments. In this way, EITI contributes more directly to improving governance over natural resources. In addition, the 2013 review of the EITI Standard introduced requirements aimed at improving transparency, in particular by formulating requirements relating to the publication of relevant information and to public administration. In this way, EITI has moved closer to achieving its basic objective, promotion of sustainable development in resource-rich States.

Finally, the contribution of the OECD Guidance in increasing transparency in the management of natural resources consists of setting standards for companies that extract, handle or procure minerals from countries that suffer from armed conflict or internal tensions in order to ensure that these companies source their minerals in a responsible manner. Responsible mineral sourcing implies, *inter alia,* respect for international human rights standards for the prevention of the most serious violations of human rights, as well as standards for the procurement of minerals and transparency in payments.

However, there is one aspect that is neglected in all three initiatives. None includes any direct sustainability requirements in its scheme. This is strange, as both EITI and the OECD Guidance include a reference to sustainable development as part of their objectives.[149] The absence of

[149] EITI is based on the principle that 'the prudent use of natural resources should be an important engine for sustainable economic growth that contributes to sustainable

requirements ensuring that natural resources are sourced in an environmentally sustainable way is regrettable, as environmental protection is essential for the proper management of natural resources and for the prevention of a relapse into armed conflict. To contribute more directly to achieving sustainable development, it is necessary for the initiatives to include some minimal requirements for environmental protection in future revisions of their standard-setting documents. The Kimberley Process could include a commitment adopting the ISO standards for environmental protection of diamond mines. The OECD Guidance could include recommendations on the prevention of serious environmental pollution related to the extraction of minerals.

8.6 Effectiveness of the initiatives

The initiatives discussed in this chapter can be characterised as voluntary agreements between States and other relevant stakeholders, notably civil society and the business community, aimed at creating standards for the governance of particular natural resources, which are to be implemented by States and/or companies. In other words, the initiatives discussed in this chapter create commitments for the actors involved, but on a voluntary basis only.

It is relevant to note that all the basic documents relating to the three initiatives emphasise the voluntary nature of the commitments, either expressly or in their formulation. The Kimberley Process Certification Scheme *recommends* that participants adopt the scheme. Furthermore, it consistently provides that participants *should* ensure that they meet all the requirements. The EITI Rules formulate minimum requirements for States to be EITI compliant. Finally, the OECD Guidance recommends that OECD members ensure the widest possible dissemination of the Guidance. In addition, the Five Step Framework for Due Diligence contains a number of measures that companies *should* take. Therefore, it is clear that none of the initiatives was intended to create legally binding obligations for participants.

development'. See EITI Standard 2013, p. 9. The OECD Guidance formulates as its objective that companies procuring minerals from conflict-affected and high-risk areas 'respect human rights, avoid contributing to conflict and successfully contribute to sustainable, equitable and effective development'. See the Recommendation of the OECD Council on Due Diligence Guidance for Responsible Supply Chains of Minerals from Conflict-Affected and High-Risk Areas, adopted on 25 May 2011 (amended on 17 July 2012), *Doc. C(2012)93*, para. 1.

Considerable differences can also be seen in the nature of the commitments. For the Kimberley Process and EITI, domestic implementation of the commitments is a prerequisite for participation in the initiatives. States that do not implement the commitments are suspended from the initiatives. However, even between the Kimberley Process and EITI, there are differences as regards the monitoring of compliance with the initiatives. While the Kimberley Process relies principally on a peer review system for the monitoring of compliance with the Kimberley requirements, EITI uses an independent third-party monitoring system. The OECD Guidance operates in a different way. It formulates guidelines to assist companies in implementing responsible sourcing practices, while respect for the Guidance must be ensured through the OECD National Contact Points.

Finally, the effectiveness of the initiatives hinges on five factors: (1) a dedication by those concerned to implement the commitments; (2) an inclusive system, in which all the relevant actors participate; (3) an effective monitoring system to ensure compliance; (4) effective national legislation to implement the commitments; and (5) external recognition of the initiatives. These factors can be illustrated with reference to the OECD Guidance. Even though it is principally a code of conduct, the OECD Guidance does provide companies with a set of guidelines to comply with OECD requirements, as well as with external requirements, such as US and Congolese legislation, with respect to conflict minerals originating from the DR Congo, as well as the due diligence requirements set by the UN Security Council with respect to minerals sourced from the DR Congo. As a result, companies operating in the DR Congo have started to implement the guidance.

This example reveals that the effectiveness of voluntary initiatives depends to a large extent on their inclusion in broader initiatives to tackle problems that grow out of resource-related armed conflicts. It is relevant to note in this respect that the OECD Guidance is the only initiative that is embedded in an international organisation, while the Kimberley Process and EITI stand alone. Obviously, it is a great advantage for the OECD Guidance to benefit from the institutional structure of the OECD, but that fact alone does not make it necessarily more effective than the Kimberley Process or EITI, since these initiatives rely on other mechanisms to ensure their effectiveness. Last, it must be noted that broad participation, not only of producing States, but also of transit and consuming States, is essential to ensure the effectiveness of the initiatives. When these conditions are satisfied, voluntary initiatives can play an important role in addressing the problems associated with resource-related armed conflicts.

8.7 Concluding remarks

The principal question that must be answered here is how and to what extent the initiatives discussed in this chapter respond to the recommendation of the High-Level Panel on Threats, Challenges and Change to the United Nations 'to develop norms governing the management of natural resources for countries emerging from or at risk of conflict'.[150] It should be noted that all three initiatives address aspects relating to the management of natural resources. Although the initiatives do not develop legal norms, they do develop standards for the management of natural resources for countries emerging from or at risk of conflict. Their main contribution is that they introduce elements of transparency, accountability and corporate responsibility in the management of natural resources in States that have experienced armed conflict. In this respect, the voluntary initiatives do respond to the call made by the High-Level Panel.

It should also be noted that the three initiatives discussed in this chapter are representative of particular categories of mechanisms which are essential components of a regulatory framework for resolving armed conflicts involving natural resources. These are certification mechanisms, anti-corruption mechanisms and corporate responsibility mechanisms. One major contribution of the initiatives discussed in this chapter is that they have resulted in best practices for the development of other regulatory initiatives. For example, reference can be made to the scheme for tracking and tracing minerals that is currently being developed under the auspices of the International Conference for the Great Lakes Region. This scheme is modelled on the Kimberley Process, but also takes into account the failures of the Kimberley Process, including its failure to properly address the issuing of false certificates. Furthermore, this scheme recognises the limited use of certification mechanisms such as Kimberley for the elimination of the root causes of armed conflict relating to the governance of natural resources.[151] The best practices resulting from these mechanisms

[150] Report of the High-Level Panel on Threats, Challenges and Change, *A More Secure World*, p. 35, para. 92.

[151] For more information on the design of this scheme, see Partnership Africa Canada, *Taming the Resource Curse: Implementing the ICGLR Certification Mechanism for Conflict-Prone Minerals*, March 2011.

can also assist the UN Peacebuilding Commission in devising new strategies for peacebuilding.

However, the existence of all these initiatives does not eliminate the need to develop general standards for the management of natural resources for countries emerging from or at risk of conflict, as called for by the High-Level Panel. The focus of such general standards should be on promoting a participatory and sustainable management of natural resources for the purpose of conflict prevention and resolution.

The first part of this book, dealing with the general legal framework for the management of natural resources, revealed several obligations for States with respect to the management of their natural resources. Amongst the principal obligations for States were, first, an obligation to exploit natural resources for the benefit of the population and, for this purpose, to establish constitutional and political processes which allow for public participation in decision making, and, second, an obligation to exploit natural resources in a sustainable way. General standards for the management of natural resources for countries emerging from or at risk of conflict should be based on these two obligations, as they constitute the very foundations of contemporary natural resources law.

It is a fact that these obligations are not adequately reflected in the initiatives examined in this chapter. Nevertheless, important lessons can be learned from these initiatives. A general regulatory framework for the management of natural resources in countries emerging from armed conflict should include standards relating to transparency, accountability and corporate responsibility in the management of natural resources. These standards are important prerequisites for conflict resolution and prevention, as they can be instrumental in eliminating the trade in conflict resources and improve the governance of natural resources.

Last, the question arises of who should develop such general standards. The High-Level Panel called on national authorities, international financial institutions, civil society organisations and the private sector to do this. The most likely option would be to set up an ad hoc mechanism for this purpose. Participants would have to include the Peacebuilding Commission, the World Bank, UNEP, UNDP, regional organisations including the OECD and the International Conference on the Great Lakes Region, representatives from the extractives industry and NGOs such as Partnership Africa Canada and Global Witness. Such an effort should be coordinated from within the UN system, preferably by the UN Secretariat, because of its general oversight function and its ability to bring together the key players, including the private sector represented in the UN Global Compact.

Concluding remarks to Part III

This part has discussed the two principal approaches adopted to address the links between natural resources and armed conflict during the phase of conflict resolution. Specific emphasis was given to the ways in which these approaches contribute to improving effective governance over natural resources in States that have experienced armed conflict.

Chapter 7 discussed the approach of the Security Council to resource-related armed conflicts, with a particular emphasis on sanctions regimes imposed in specific conflict situations to resolve armed conflicts involving natural resources. It demonstrated that these sanctions regimes focus mainly on the role of natural resources in financing and perpetuating armed conflicts. Underlying governance problems are primarily addressed from this perspective as well. It also showed that the aim of most sanctions regimes was to assist governments in restoring sovereignty over parts of their territory under the control of armed groups, which is reflected in the mandate of peacekeeping operations deployed by the Council. In general the Security Council is reluctant to impose sanctions against national authorities when their actions pose a threat to international peace and security.

A similar bias can be seen in the voluntary initiatives developed by States and other entities to address the challenges resulting from resource-related armed conflicts. Both the Kimberley Process and the OECD Guidance (mostly) target the trade in natural resources by armed groups. EITI can be seen as an exception in this respect because it focuses on enhancing transparency in government revenues from the extractive industries. However, it should be noted that EITI was not developed for the specific purpose of addressing resource-related armed conflicts, but as an instrument for combating corruption in the extractive industries. Its significance for addressing the root causes of resource-related armed conflict is nevertheless clear and its role in preventing these armed conflicts was raised by several participants in the Security Council's Open Debate on Natural Resources and Conflict Prevention of 19 June 2013.

Despite their general emphasis on the role of natural resources in financing armed groups, both approaches – i.e., Security Council sanctions regimes and voluntary initiatives – develop standards for the governance of natural resources as a tool for conflict resolution. Effectiveness, transparency and accountability are common elements of resource governance that can be identified in both approaches.

The focus of both approaches is therefore on promoting responsible or 'good' governance of natural resources as an element of conflict resolution. These approaches also contribute to preventing a relapse into armed conflict in countries that have experienced armed conflicts involving natural resources. However, to achieve lasting peace and promote long-term development, it is also necessary to prevent the overexploitation of natural resources and ensure that exploitation activities do not place too great a burden on the environment. This is an element that is largely lacking in existing approaches which address the links between natural resources and armed conflict. The existing mechanisms devote little or no attention to issues of sustainability or environmental protection. The Security Council's approach to Cambodia and Liberia constitutes an exception. It is argued here that this exception should become the norm.

Furthermore, the existing mechanisms devote much attention to transparency and accountability as means of preventing a relapse into armed conflict. However, to reduce the risks of dormant or renewed grievances flaring up, it is necessary to involve the population more directly in the process of conflict resolution and post-conflict recovery. This is not adequately reflected in the current initiatives.

In a more general vein, it is necessary to develop more structural solutions to prevent natural resources from financing or fuelling future armed conflicts. Promoting effectiveness, transparency and accountability in the governance of natural resources is important in conflict resolution strategies, but these elements in themselves are not sufficient to promote responsible governance over natural resources for the purposes of conflict resolution and prevention. It is essential to integrate sustainability and public participation requirements more directly in strategies to promote responsible resource governance for the purpose of conflict resolution and post-conflict peacebuilding. Addressing these elements from an early stage increases the chances of creating a lasting peace in countries that are recovering from armed conflicts involving natural resources.

9

The contribution of international law to addressing the challenges ensuing from resource-related armed conflicts

9.1 Introductory remarks

Resource-related armed conflicts pose considerable challenges to the premises on which the international legal framework for the governance of natural resources is based. This book demonstrated that the general legal framework for the governance of natural resources relies on a stable government that is in full control of the State's natural resources and exploits these for the benefit of all. However, resource-related armed conflicts often show a different reality in which governments are unable to exercise sovereignty over portions of the State territory, foreign States and armed groups plunder the State's natural wealth, and/or governments use the proceeds from natural resource exploitation to fund destructive military campaigns.

In order to resolve resource-related armed conflicts and to prevent future armed conflicts fuelled by natural resources, two principal challenges need to be addressed. The first concerns stopping natural resources from financing or fuelling armed conflict. Addressing this challenge requires the adoption of a two-pronged strategy aimed at stopping the illegal exploitation of natural resources as well as the trade in these resources on the one hand and returning the control over the State's natural resources to the lawful government on the other.[1] Strategies that

[1] The current chapter focuses on eliminating the trade in natural resources that finance armed conflict, since this issue raises the most relevant legal questions. For both issues, the legal position of the government is of primary importance, especially when this position is contested. See Chapter 2 for a more detailed discussion of this issue. Reinstating government control over natural resources is mostly achieved by mandating law enforcement tasks to peacekeeping operations. See Chapter 7 for more details.

address these issues aim primarily at removing the opportunities for parties to an armed conflict to derive an income from natural resources and are therefore linked to the feasibility and greed theories formulated by political economists to explain the relationship between natural resources and armed conflict, as introduced in Chapter 1. The second challenge consists of improving the governance of natural resources within States as part of post-conflict reconstruction efforts with the aim of preventing these States from relapsing into armed conflict. Strategies that address this issue focus both on removing the opportunities for parties to an armed conflict to derive an income from natural resources and address issues related to maldistribution of natural resources wealth as a cause of armed conflict. They are therefore linked to the feasibility and grievances theories formulated by political economists, as introduced in Chapter 1.

The objective of this book was to analyse the role of international law in addressing these challenges. More specifically, it has attempted to identify and assess the role of international law in ensuring that natural resources are used to promote development and achieve sustainable peace in countries that have experienced armed conflicts that were either caused, financed or fuelled by natural resources. For this purpose, this book first analysed the general legal framework for the governance of natural resources within States (Chapters 2–4), as well as the effects of armed conflict on this legal regime (Chapter 5). It then examined the additional protection provided to natural resources and the environment under the law of armed conflict (Chapter 6). Finally, it analysed the legal and extra-legal approaches to severing the link between natural resources and armed conflict. More in particular, this book examined the approach of the UN Security Council with regard to resource-related armed conflicts (Chapter 7) and the role of voluntary initiatives that have been developed alongside Security Council action (Chapter 8).

This chapter aims to bring to the fore the most important conclusions that can be drawn from this book for the purpose of addressing the two principal challenges referred to, building on the intermediate conclusions formulated for the various parts of this book. Section 9.2 outlines the contribution of international law to stopping natural resources from financing and fuelling armed conflicts, while Section 9.3 assesses international law's contribution to improving the governance of natural resources within States. Finally, Section 9.4 formulates proposals to address particular issues that encompass both challenges.

9.2 Stopping natural resources from financing and fuelling armed conflict

Natural resources have provided a source of conflict financing for States and armed groups alike. However, current practice addressing this challenge focuses mainly on eliminating the trade in so-called 'conflict resources', designating natural resources traded by armed groups to finance their armed struggle. The narrow focus on armed groups becomes most of all apparent from the definition of 'conflict diamonds' adopted within the Kimberley Process for the Certification of Rough Diamonds, which defines conflict diamonds as 'rough diamonds used by rebel movements or their allies to finance conflict aimed at undermining legitimate governments'.[2] However, a similar bias can be observed in the practice of the UN Security Council, which has adopted a number of sanctions regimes to stop the trade in natural resources that finance armed conflict. The Council's approach has proven dynamic, in the sense that it has continuously tried to improve its methods for the purpose of addressing specific threats to the peace more effectively. It embraced innovations such as a certificate-of-origin regime to distinguish between diamonds traded by armed groups and by governments and it adopted due diligence requirements for companies sourcing from the DR Congo. In each instance, these measures were backed up by assistance from peacekeeping operations.

However, the readiness of the UN Security Council to adopt measures is often linked to a particular type of threat to peace and security. Most of the sanctions regimes examined in this book were aimed at assisting the government of a State to restore governance over natural resources that had fallen into the hands of subversive entities. In the few cases in which the Security Council directly targeted the government of a State, the legitimacy of the government itself was at stake. These were the sanctions regimes imposed against Southern Rhodesia and Libya. Moreover, in the case of Liberia under the presidency of Charles Taylor, the Council targeted the Liberian government in order to cut off support provided by the government to rebel movements, notably the RUF.

The question is therefore if and to what extent this practice of the Security Council and the extra-legal initiatives reflect the rules that apply to the exploitation of natural resources in situations of armed conflict. As

[2] Kimberley Process Certification Scheme, Sect. I.

discussed in Part II of this book, the commercial nature of the exploitation of natural resources has clear implications for the applicable legal framework. IHL is normally considered to be the *lex specialis* in situations of armed conflict, but this field of international law is primarily concerned with acts of warfare and their implications for the population of a State. It only marginally addresses commercial activities such as natural resources exploitation. Therefore, other fields of international law are equally important for the regulation of natural resources exploitation in situations of armed conflict, at least for States. These are, in particular, international economic, environmental and human rights law.

Even though the international legal framework is fragmented and difficult to oversee, it does contain rules relating to the exploitation of natural resources for all parties to an armed conflict. The basic principle underlying the legal framework is that of permanent sovereignty over natural resources, which permits governments to exploit the State's natural resources on behalf of their people. In contrast to this extensive right for governments to exploit natural resources, international law contains a complete prohibition on non-State armed groups exploiting a State's natural resources as well as on third States doing so, except in situations of occupation. In these situations, third States have a right to exploit natural resources pursuant to the right of *usufruct*, subject to stringent conditions.

However, a closer analysis of the applicable rules and their operation reveals two inherent difficulties which shed a different light on the international legal framework. The first ensues from the specific nature of internal armed conflicts. In these armed conflicts, the government does not only represent the State; it is also a party to the armed conflict. In light of these specific circumstances, it is unrealistic to expect an armed group to comply with rules of IHL formulating a complete prohibition on exploiting natural resources, while the opposing party has a broadly defined right to exploit natural resources. This makes even more sense if one considers that every conflict dynamics is different: just as governments do not necessarily represent a good cause, armed groups do not necessarily struggle for a bad cause.

This book does not argue in favour of granting armed groups the same rights and obligations with regard to the exploitation of natural resources as governments, nor does it propose assigning all armed groups the right to exploit natural resources. However, it does propose granting those armed groups that are in control of a portion of the State territory a qualified right to exploit natural resources, based on the right of *usufruct* that is central to international occupation law. In the absence of effective control over these territories by the *de jure* government, the armed groups that exercise control can be considered to constitute *de facto* authorities in the territories under their control. Therefore, the armed group that is in control should at least be provided the opportunity to show that it is willing to assume governmental responsibilities.

It is furthermore essential to note that granting a *prima facie* right to exploit natural resources to armed groups that are in effective control over portions of a State's territory does not in any way rule out the possibility of the UN or States adopting enforcement action in individual cases, most notably of the UN Security Council imposing sanctions in situations which pose a threat to the peace. To a certain extent, support for this position can be derived from current practice. The Kimberley Process definition of 'conflict diamonds' refers explicitly to Security Council resolutions, which implies that it only covers diamonds that have been labelled 'conflict diamonds' by the Security Council.[3]

One of the principal reasons for proposing to grant the right of *usufruct* to armed groups that control portions of a State territory is that it protects the civilian population and the environment more adequately than the current rules do. In the first place, granting armed groups a right of *usufruct* gives them an incentive to respect the rules of IHL. Second, the concept of *usufruct* does not entail a right to use the proceeds from the exploitation of natural resources to buy weapons. It merely grants armed groups a right to set up and maintain a civilian administration for the benefit of the population.[4] The qualified nature of the concept of *usufruct* strikes a careful balance between the realities of armed conflict and the

[3] The definition reads in full, 'rough diamonds used by rebel movements or their allies to finance conflict aimed at undermining legitimate governments, *as described in relevant United Nations Security Council (UNSC) resolutions* insofar as they remain in effect, or in other similar UNSC resolutions which may be adopted in the future, and as understood and recognized in United Nations General Assembly (UNGA) Resolution 55/56, or in other similar UNGA resolutions which may be adopted in future'. Emphasis added by the present author. See Kimberley Process Certification Scheme, Sect. I.

[4] Arguably, compliance by armed groups to these conditions is difficult to oversee. Nonetheless, measuring compliance with the rules of IHL in general is one of the more troublesome aspects of this field of international law. For internal armed conflicts, Article 3 of the 1949 Geneva Conventions provides for an impartial humanitarian body, such as the ICRC, to 'offer its services to the Parties to the conflict'. This is the most commonly used option for measuring compliance by parties to an armed conflict with IHL. It should further be emphasised that resort to enforcement action, such as sanctions, remains open if there are indications of noncompliance to the rules.

provisional character of the situation. Moreover, the concept can be interpreted in the light of relevant human rights and environmental norms. This balancing of rights and obligations is the best way to protect the environment and the civilian population in territories that are controlled by armed groups.

The second issue that casts a different light on the international legal framework is related to the scope of the right of governments to exploit the State's natural resources. The right of governments to exploit natural resources pursuant to the principle of permanent sovereignty over natural resources has clear limits. It is restricted by obligations derived from several fields of international law, including international humanitarian, human rights and environmental law, as discussed in Parts I and II of this book. One of the obligations that qualify the right of governments to exploit the State's natural resources is that the government must act on behalf of the people. Governments therefore have a right to use the proceeds obtained from natural resources exploitation to fund a military campaign, as long as they act for the benefit of the people.

This people-oriented conception of the principle of permanent sovereignty over natural resources is partly derived from international human rights law.[5] In addition, it is reflected in the resolutions of the UN Security Council with regard to specific resource-related armed conflicts as well as in the extra-legal initiatives discussed in Chapter 8, which emphasise that natural resources should be exploited for the benefit of the people and for national development. The question is therefore to what extent this people-oriented conception is further reflected in the measures adopted by the Security Council and the extra-legal initiatives.

It is clear from the practice of the Security Council that a government which uses the proceeds from natural resources exploitation to fund a military campaign against its own people or which uses these proceeds to support foreign rebel groups is considered to pose a threat to the peace.[6] The sanctions imposed against the Gaddafi government in Libya and the Taylor government in Liberia attest to this. There are, however, also situations in which the Security Council refrained from imposing commodity sanctions against a government, even where this government used the proceeds of natural resources exploitation for purposes that were clearly

[5] See Chapters 2 and 3 and Section 9.3 for more details.

[6] It should be recalled that the concern of the Security Council is not directly related to ensuring respect for international law but rather to addressing threats to peace.

not in the interest of peace – or of the people of the State. The armed conflict in Côte d'Ivoire between the government and the Forces Nouvelles in the first decade of this century constitutes a striking example of such a situation. In this situation, the Security Council adopted sanctions in order to secure the implementation of the peace agreements concluded between the parties to the armed conflict. However, the commodity sanctions exclusively targeted the Forces Nouvelles, while no such measures were adopted to stop the government from violating its commitments pursuant to the peace agreements.

If the Security Council truly adheres to a people-oriented conception of permanent sovereignty, it should therefore be ready to use its powers under Chapter VII more readily to ensure that all parties to an armed conflict, including governments, use the proceeds of natural resources for the benefit of the people – or, at least, do not use them in ways that harm the people, as was the case in Côte d'Ivoire. This might entail the adoption of sanctions in specific instances. Likewise, the extra-legal initiatives that are designed to eliminate the trade in conflict resources should not shy away from addressing the contribution of governments to fuelling armed conflicts through the proceeds of natural resources exploitation. The OECD Due Diligence Guidance does address this issue to some extent, by addressing companies' responsibility in preventing the commission of gross human rights violations and international crimes. The Guidance does not restrict companies' due diligence to preventing such acts from being committed by armed groups alone. At the same time, the threshold of the OECD Guidance is extremely high, exactly because it addresses only the most serious violations of international law. It does not address the responsibility of companies to exercise due diligence in relation to situations in which it is apparent that a government uses the proceeds from its extractive industries to fuel internal armed conflict. In addition, the Kimberley Process does not address the issue of governments fuelling armed conflict at all; it focuses exclusively on stopping the trade in diamonds by armed groups.

There is an obvious logic in the failure of these mechanisms to address the contribution of governments to fuelling armed conflict. Besides sovereignty-related issues, the causal link between natural resources exploitation and conflict financing is more remote when it concerns the government. It is difficult to assess the contribution of natural resources to fuelling armed conflict separately from government public financing in general. Nevertheless, it is submitted that the Security Council as well as voluntary mechanisms should address instances where it is apparent that a government uses the proceeds from natural resources exploitation to fuel armed conflict.

9.3 Improving the governance of natural resources within States

The second challenge associated with resource-related armed conflicts is to improve the governance over natural resources within States, both to resolve existing armed conflicts and to prevent these States from relapsing into armed conflict. Natural resources endowment can certainly constitute an engine for development, provided that the resources are used wisely. The primary responsibility for the governance of natural resources lies with the State in which they are located, based on the principle of permanent sovereignty over natural resources. This principle is partly rooted in the right to self-determination of peoples. Although the principle of permanent sovereignty is considered to be attached to the sovereignty of the State, its roots in the right to self-determination are not without significance. As already referred to in the preceding section, it demonstrates that the State's natural resources should be exploited for the benefit of the people of the State. It further demonstrates that peoples are not only beneficiaries of the principle of permanent sovereignty over natural resources but subjects as well. This can also be derived from the landmark 1962 Declaration on Permanent Sovereignty over Natural Resources, which designates both peoples and States as holders of the right to exercise permanent sovereignty over natural resources and stipulates that they must exercise this right 'in the interest of their national development and of the well-being of the people of the State concerned'.[7] This is also reflected in the identical Articles 1 of the 1966 Human Rights Covenants.

As the organising principle of natural resources governance, permanent sovereignty over natural resources is a rights- and duties-based concept, as already alluded to in the previous section.[8] Most importantly, States have a right to exploit their natural resources pursuant to their own developmental priorities. This is a fundamental right for States, which the international community should respect at all times. At the same time, current practice in the context of resource-related armed conflict increasingly qualifies the principle of permanent sovereignty over natural resources by setting procedural standards for resource governance related

[7] Declaration on Permanent Sovereignty over Natural Resources, *UNGA Resolution 1803 (XVII)* of 14 December 1962.

[8] See Schrijver, *Sovereignty over Natural Resources.*

to 'good governance'. Both UN Security Council resolutions and extra-legal initiatives require States to manage their natural resources in an effective, transparent and accountable way. However, this book argued that 'good governance' for the purpose of preventing and resolving armed conflicts related to natural resources is broader and also encompasses standards related to public participation and sustainability.

Therefore, this book defined 'good governance' as follows:

> the sustainable, transparent and accountable management of natural resources for the purposes of equitable and sustainable development. It entails clear and participatory decision-making procedures at the level of public authorities, transparent and accountable institutions and the primacy of law in the management and distribution of natural resources and their revenues, as well as capacity building for elaborating and implementing measures aimed in particular at preventing and combating corruption in the public administration of revenues from natural resources.

One of the objectives of this book was to assess whether and to what extent these requirements for good governance are reflected in international law as well as in current approaches to addressing the links between natural resources and armed conflict.

It is notable that current approaches to improve governance of natural resources for the purposes of conflict prevention and resolution focus mainly on transparent and accountable management of natural resources. This book argues that, in addition, international law contains an emerging obligation for States to inform and consult local communities and the general population of proposed projects involving the exploitation of natural resources and to grant them access to justice. This obligation can first of all be derived from international environmental law, particularly the principle of public participation, which can be found in several international environmental conventions, including in the 1992 Convention on Biological Diversity. In addition, a right to public participation can partly be derived from international human rights law, most notably from identical Articles 1 of the ICESCR and the ICCPR as well as from Articles 25 and 27 of the ICCPR. These provisions have been extensively interpreted by human rights bodies and courts with respect to the protection of the rights of indigenous peoples. This book argues that these provisions also provide the basis for a more general right for the population to be more actively involved in decisions regarding resource exploitation projects, including in relation to the allocation of concessions and the management of revenues derived from these projects. Involving the population actively in these decisions creates a sense of ownership among the population and prevents (renewed) grievances over the distribution of natural resources wealth, which is essential to prevent a relapse into armed conflict.

Furthermore, international law requires States to use their natural resources in a sustainable way and to prevent damage to the environment. This obligation is enshrined in several international environmental conventions as well as increasingly in customary international law. Although these conventions do not formulate a general obligation for States to protect their own environments, they do establish standards of due care. In addition, significant parts of the environment are protected under 'common regimes' established for the purpose of protecting parts of the environment that are of interest to a larger community of States. Examples include the obligations to protect 'world heritage' and to conserve biological diversity. In addition, States are under a general obligation to conduct an EIA to assess the risks of resource exploitation projects on the environment. The obligation to use natural resources in a sustainable way and to prevent damage to the environment is particularly important for the purpose of preventing grievances among local communities in relation to their living environment as well as to improve prospects to achieve long-term development.

This book argues that current approaches to improving the governance of natural resources within States should integrate requirements relating to sustainability and public participation more closely into their strategies. Moreover, it is essential to move from ad hoc to more structural approaches towards improving the governance of natural resources in conflict-torn States. Much has been done already to improve the governance of natural resources in conflict-torn States, notably by UN peacekeeping operations, by specific programs such as the Liberian GEMAP and LFI programs and by the UN Peacebuilding Commission. Their work has greatly contributed to improving the governance of natural resources in specific States, including Cambodia, Sierra Leone and Liberia. It is now time to build upon the best practices developed for these countries and to develop a systematic approach to improving resource governance in conflict-torn States.

It is argued that a working group composed of the most relevant actors, including the UN Peacebuilding Commission and the World Bank, under the direction of the UN Secretariat, should develop general standards for the management of natural resources in States recovering from armed conflict for the purpose of achieving sustainable peace. These standards should build upon the definition of good governance as provided above and reflect more fully the obligations of States under international law, most notably obligations relating to public participation and sustainable use of natural resources.

Finally, to ensure a more coherent approach to improving resource governance in conflict-torn States in the future, it is essential to appoint one institution to coordinate the peacebuilding process. The UN Peacebuilding Commission would be a logical candidate, given its advisory function relating to post-conflict peacebuilding. For this purpose, the current peacebuilding architecture should however be amended in some respects. First of all, it is essential that the UN Security Council involves the UN Peacebuilding Commission directly in the phase of conflict resolution, e.g., by asking the Commission for advice in relation to the design and mandate of UN peacekeeping operations. Second, the international financial institutions, most notably the World Bank, should be more directly involved in the work of the UN Peacebuilding Commission by giving them a seat in the Commission's organisational committee. Last, and most important, the UN Peacebuilding Commission should receive a stronger mandate in order to perform its functions effectively. This mandate should reflect the Commission's role as a coordinating rather than a purely advisory instance, e.g. by linking the available funds for peacebuilding more directly to the Commission.

9.4 Proposals for strengthening the international legal framework

The principal question that this book aimed to answer is related to the contribution of international law to ensuring that natural resources are used to promote development and to achieve sustainable peace. The previous sections argued that international law addresses the challenges to resource-related armed conflicts fairly well. However, the system as it exists today is not perfect. The previous sections formulated specific recommendations to better address the two principal challenges ensuing from resource-related armed conflicts. The current section formulates two additional proposals that encompass both challenges.

A first proposal is to strengthen the contribution of existing treaties to addressing the problems associated with resource-related armed conflicts. There are several treaties that could play an important role in addressing the challenges ensuing from resource-related armed conflicts. Examples include mixed trade-environmental treaties such as CITES and ITTA that could be more directly relied on in efforts to stop natural resources from being used for the financing of armed conflicts. In addition, conventions such as the Biodiversity Convention and the UNESCO World Heritage Convention are of great value in assisting States to protect their environment in situations of armed conflict and to restore their environment in the immediate aftermath of armed conflict. Both conventions have funds dedicated to assisting States in protecting their biological diversity and natural heritage respectively.

In addition, these conventions benefit from strong institutional structures, which could be called upon to assist in addressing particular problems. Both the World Heritage Committee and the Conference of the Parties of the Biodiversity Convention, for example, issue guidelines and recommendations for State parties to give content and meaning to the provisions of the respective conventions. Specific guidelines could be issued to address challenges ensuing from resource-related armed conflicts. Also, in a more practical sense, these conventions could make a difference. The World Heritage Committee, for example, can provide practical assistance to States in protecting their natural heritage in situations of armed conflict. The institutional bodies of CITES and the ITTA for their part could play an important role in developing tracking and tracing systems for conflict timber. These mechanisms should be used more systematically and should address resource-related armed conflicts.

A second issue concerns the responsibility of the international community to assist States in their efforts to achieve a sustainable peace and to prevent resource-related armed conflicts, including most importantly in relation to building strong and accountable institutions for public administration. An additional responsibility can be discerned for the home States of multinational companies, the latter having occasionally contributed to fuelling past and present armed conflicts through their procurement policies. There is an urgent need for the international community to address the role of the private sector in fuelling armed conflicts by adopting more stringent legislation in relation to its compliance with international norms and the transparency of its business practices, with regard both to companies' procurement policies and to their contracts with the governments of the host States.

The US Dodd–Frank Act and the revised EU Transparency Directives are encouraging trends in this respect, but their geographical scope and their objectives are limited. In addition, informal mechanisms such as those of the OECD and the UN Guiding Principles on Business and Human Rights are important initiatives in addressing corporate social responsibility, but their noncommittal nature stands in the way of effectively regulating corporate behaviour. There is a need for a global effort to address the responsibility of the private sector, even though this will be a long and politically sensitive process. The adoption of the due diligence guidelines by the UN Security Council for minerals procured in the DR Congo can be regarded as a first precedent, since it applies to all companies sourcing from the DR Congo and is partly binding. An initiative addressing the responsibility of the private sector should, however, have a wider geographical and subject-matter scope. It should address broader concerns relating to the mineral procurement policies of companies globally, including the contribution of the private sector to fostering corruption.

It is finally through a concerted effort of the international community that natural resource endowment can again be associated with development. The first steps have been taken. The large number of ad hoc initiatives to address resource-related armed conflicts clearly shows the determination of the international community to address these issues. The time has come to build upon these approaches and to devise more comprehensive solutions, based on the existing legal framework for the management of natural resources. International law has proven sufficiently flexible to accommodate new global concerns and its dynamics should be used more systematically to stop natural resources from fuelling armed conflicts.

BIBLIOGRAPHY

Abass, A., 'The United Nations, the African Union and the Darfur Crisis: Of Apology and Utopia', *Netherlands International Law Review* 54(3) (2007), pp. 415–40.

Abi-Saab, G., 'The Concept of Sanction in International Law', in V. Gowland-Debbas (ed.), *United Nations Sanctions and International Law*, The Hague/London/Boston: Kluwer Law International (2001), pp. 29–41.

'Droits de L'Homme et Développement: Quelques Eléments de Réflexion', *African Yearbook of International Law* 3 (1995), pp. 3–10.

Alston, P., 'Ships Passing in the Night: The Current State of the Human Rights and Development Debate Seen through the Lens of the Millennium Development Goals', *Human Rights Quarterly* 27 (2005), pp. 755–829.

(ed.), *Peoples' Rights*, Academy of European Law, Oxford: Oxford University Press (2001).

'Peoples' Rights: The State of the Art at the Beginning of the 21st Century', in P. Alston (ed.), *Peoples' Rights*, Academy of European Law, Oxford: Oxford University Press (2001), pp. 259–93.

'Peoples' Rights: Their Rise and Fall', in P. Alston (ed.), *Peoples' Rights*, Academy of European Law, Oxford: Oxford University Press (2001), pp. 262–4.

'The Shortcomings of a "Garfield the Cat" Approach to the Right to Development', *California Western International Law Journal* 15 (1985), pp. 510–18.

Altman, S.L., Nichols, S.S., and Woods, J.T., 'Leveraging High-Value Natural Resources to Restore the Rule of Law: The Role of the Liberia Forest Initiative in Liberia's Transition to Stability', in P. Lujala and S.A. Rustad (eds.), *High-Value Natural Resources and Post-Conflict Peacebuilding*, Oxford/New York: Earthscan (2012).

Amede Obiora, L., 'Beyond the Rhetoric of a Right to Development', *Law and Policy* 18(3 and 4) (1996), pp. 355–418.

Anaya, S.J., 'The Human Rights of Indigenous Peoples', in F.G. Isa and K. De Feyter (eds.), *International Protection of Human Rights: Achievements and Challenges*, Bilbao: University of Duesto, Humanitarian Net (2006), pp. 604–5.

Andreopoulos, G.J., 'On the Accountability of Non-State Armed Groups', in G.J. Andreopoulos, Z.F. Kabasakal Arat, and P. Juviler (eds.), *Non-State Actors in the Human Rights Universe*, Bloomfield: Kumarian Press (2006).

Arai-Takahashi, Y., *The Law of Occupation: Continuity and Change of International Humanitarian Law, and its Interaction with Human Rights Law*, The Hague: Martinus Nijhoff Publishers (2009).

Atapattu, S.A., *Emerging Principles of International Environmental Law*, Transnational Publishers, Series on International Law and Development, New York (2006).

Aust, A., *Modern Treaty Law and Practice*, 2nd edn., Cambridge: Cambridge University Press (2007).

Austin, J.E. and Bruch, C.E., *The Environmental Consequences of War: Legal, Economic, and Scientific Perspectives*, Cambridge: Cambridge University Press (2000).

Auty, R., *Sustaining Development in Mineral Economies: The Resource Curse Thesis*, London: Routledge (1993).

Baetens, F., 'Facilitating Post-conflict Reconstruction: Is the UN Peacebuilding Commission Successfully Filling an Institutional Gap or Marking a Missed Opportunity?' in C. Stahn, J.S. Easterday, and J. Iverson (eds.), *Jus Post Bellum: Mapping the Normative Foundations*, Oxford: Oxford University Press (2014), pp. 346–75.

Baetens, F. and Kohoutek, K., 'United Nations Peacebuilding Commission', in R. Wolfrum (ed.), *Encyclopedia of Public International Law*, Vol. X, Max Planck Institute for Comparative Public Law and International Law, Oxford: Oxford University Press (2012), pp. 406–14.

Baetens, F., 'Muddling the Waters of Treaty Interpretation? Relevant Rules of International Law in the MOX Plant OSPAR Arbitration and EC–Biotech Case', *Nordic Journal of International Law* 77 (2008), pp. 197–216.

Ballentine, K. and Nitzschke, H. (eds.), *Profiting from Peace: Managing the Resource Dimensions of Civil War*, Boulder, CO: Lynne Rienner Publishers (2005).

Ballentine, K. and Sherman, J. (eds.), *The Political Economy of Armed Conflict: Beyond Greed and Grievance*, International Peace Academy, Boulder, CO/London: Lynne Rienner Publishers (2003).

Bannon, I. and Collier, P. (eds.), *Natural Resources and Violent Conflict: Options and Actions*, Washington, DC: World Bank (2003).

Barrera-Hernandez, L., 'Sovereignty over Natural Resources under Examination: The Inter-American System for Human Rights and Natural Resource Allocation', *Annual Survey of International and Comparative Law*, 12 (2006), pp. 43–58.

Bedjaoui, M., 'The Right to Development', in M. Bedjaoui (ed.), *International Law: Achievements and Prospects*, Paris: UNESCO (1991), pp. 1177–1203.

Beevers, M.D., 'Forest Resources and Peacebuilding: Preliminary Lessons from Liberia and Sierra Leone', in P. Lujala and S.A. Rustad (eds.), *High-Value Natural Resources and Post-Conflict Peacebuilding*, Oxford/New York: Earthscan (2012), pp. 367–90.

Bell, C., *On the Law of Peace: Peace Agreements and the Lex Pacificatoria*, Oxford: Oxford University Press (2008).

Benvenisti, E., *The International Law of Occupation*, 2nd edn., Oxford: Oxford University Press (2013).

The International Law of Occupation, 1st edn., Princeton, NJ/Oxford: Princeton University Press (2004).

'"Common Concern of Humankind": The Emergence of a New Concept of International Environmental Law', *Archiv des Völkerrechts*, 34(4) (1996), pp. 426–81.

Birnie, P.W., Boyle, A.E., and Redgwell, C., *International Law and the Environment*, 3rd edn., Oxford: Oxford University Press (2009).

Birnie, P.W. and Boyle, A.E., *International Law and the Environment*, 2nd edn., Oxford: Oxford University Press (2002).

Bodansky, D., Brunnée, J., and Hey, E., 'International Environmental Law: Mapping the Field', in D. Bodansky, J. Brunnée, and E. Hey (eds.), *The Oxford Handbook of International Environmental Law*, Oxford: Oxford University Press (2007), pp. 1–25.

The Oxford Handbook of International Environmental Law, Oxford: Oxford University Press (2007).

Bodeau-Livinec, P. and Morgan-Foster, J., 'Article 61: Supervening Impossibility of Performance', in O. Corten and P. Klein (eds.), *The Vienna Convention on the Law of Treaties: A Commentary*, Oxford: Oxford University Press, Vol. II (2011), pp. 1382–1408.

Boerefijn, I., 'Establishing State Responsibility for Breaching Human Rights Treaty Obligations: Avenues under UN Human Rights Treaties', *Netherlands International Law Review* 56(2) (2009), pp. 167–205.

Boisson de Chazournes, L. and Salman, S.M.L. (eds.), *Les Ressources en Eau et le Droit International*, The Hague: Nijhoff Publishers (2005).

Boisson de Chazournes, L. and Sands, P., *International Law, the International Court of Justice and Nuclear Weapons*, Cambridge: Cambridge University Press (1999).

Bossche, P. van den, Schrijver, N.J., and Faber, G., *Unilateral Measures Addressing Non-trade Concerns, a Study on WTO Consistency, Relevance of Other International Agreements, Economic Effectiveness and Impact on Developing Countries of Measures Concerning Non-product-related Processes and Production Methods*, The Hague: OBT/The Ministry of Foreign Affairs of the Netherlands (2007).

Bothe, M., 'Neutrality, Concept and General Rules', in R. Wolfrum (ed.), *Encyclopedia of Public International Law*, Vol. VII, Max Planck Institute for Comparative Public Law and International Law, Oxford: Oxford University Press (2012), pp. 617–34.

'Peacekeeping', in B. Simma et al. (eds.), *The Charter of the United Nations: A Commentary*, 3rd edn., Vol. I, Oxford: Oxford University Press (2012), pp. 1171–99.

Bothe, M., Bruch, C., Diamond, J., and Jensen, D., 'International Law Protecting the Environment during Armed Conflict: Gaps and Opportunities', *International Review of the Red Cross* 92 (879) (2010), pp. 569–92.

Bothe, M., 'Customary International Humanitarian Law: Some Reflections on the ICRC Study', in *Yearbook of International Humanitarian Law* 8 (2005), pp. 143–78.

'The Protection of the Civilian Population and NATO Bombing on Yugoslavia: Comments on a Report to the Prosecutor of the ICTY', *European Journal of International Law* 12(3) (2001), pp. 531–5.

'Occupation, Belligerent', in R. Bernhardt, *Encyclopedia of Public International Law*, Vol. III, Max Planck Institute for Comparative Public Law and International Law, Amsterdam: Elsevier (2000), pp. 763–6.

Bowen, S. (ed.), *Human Rights, Self-Determination and Political Change in the Occupied Palestinian Territories*, The Hague: Martinus Nijhoff Publishers, International Studies in Human Rights (1997).

Boyle, A. and Chinkin, C., *The Making of International Law*, Oxford: Oxford University Press (2007).

Boyle, A. and Freestone, D. (eds.), *International Law and Sustainable Development: Past Achievements and Future Challenges*, Oxford: Oxford University Press (1999).

Brown-Weiss, E. and Sornarajah, A., 'Good Governance', in R. Wolfrum (ed.), *Encyclopedia of Public International Law*, Vol. IV, Max Planck Institute for Comparative Public Law and International Law, Oxford: Oxford University Press (2012), pp. 516–28.

Brown-Weiss, E., 'Opening the Door to the Environment and to Future Generations', in L. Boisson de Chazournes and P. Sands, *International Law, the International Court of Justice and Nuclear Weapons*, Cambridge: Cambridge University Press (1999), pp. 338–53.

Brown-Weiss, E., 'Our Rights and Obligations to Future Generations for the Environment', *American Journal of International Law* 84 (1990), pp. 198–207.

In Fairness to Future Generations: International Law, Common Patrimony, and Intergenerational Equity, Tokyo: United Nations University (1989).

Brunnée, J., 'Common Areas, Common Heritage and Common Concern', in D. Bodansky, J. Brunnée, and E. Hey (eds.), *The Oxford Handbook of International Environmental Law*, Oxford: Oxford University Press (2007), pp. 550–73.

Brunner, L. and Quintana, K., 'The Duty to Consult in the Inter-American System: Legal Standards after Sarayaku', *ASIL Insight* 16(35) (2012).

Bunker, A.L., 'Protection of the Environment during Armed Conflict', *RECIEL* 13(2) (2004), pp. 201–13.

Bunn, I.D., 'The Right to Development: Implications for International Economic Law', *American University International Law Review* 15 (2000), pp. 1425–67.

Burgt, N.M.J. van der, *The Contribution of International Fisheries Law to Human Development: An Analysis of Multilateral and ACP-EC Fisheries Instruments*, The Hague: Martinus Nijhoff Publishers (2012).

Byron, 'A Blurring of the Boundaries: The Application of International Humanitarian Law by Human Rights Bodies', *Virginia Journal of International Law* 47(4) (2006–7), pp. 839–96.

Cannizzaro, E. (ed.), *The Law of Treaties Beyond the Vienna Convention*, Oxford: Oxford University Press (2011).

Carducci, G., 'Pillage', in R. Wolfrum (ed.), *Encyclopedia of Public International Law*, Vol. VIII, Max Planck Institute for Comparative Public Law and International Law, Oxford: Oxford University Press (2012), pp. 299–304.

Cassese, A., 'The Martens Clause: Half a Loaf or Simply Pie in the Sky?', *EJIL* 11 (2000), pp. 187–216.

Self-Determination of Peoples: A Legal Appraisal, Hersch Lauterpacht Memorial Lecture Series, Cambridge: Cambridge University Press (1995).

'Powers and Duties of an Occupant in Relation to Land and Natural Resources', in E. Playfair (ed.), *International Law and the Administration of Occupied Territories: Two Decades of Israeli Occupation of the West Bank and Gaza Strip*, Proceedings of a Conference Organized by al-Haq in Jerusalem in January 1988 (1992), pp. 419–42.

Černič, J.L., 'The 2011 Update of the OECD Guidelines for Multinational Enterprises', *ASIL Insight* 16(4), February 2012.

Human Rights Law and Business: Corporate Responsibility for Fundamental Human Rights, Groningen: Europa Law Publishing (2010).

Chadwick, E., *Traditional Neutrality Revisited: Law, Theory and Case Studies*, The Hague: Kluwer Law International (2002).

Chen, K.C., *China's War with Vietnam, 1979: Issues, Decisions, and Implications*, Hoover Institution Publication 357, Stanford University (1987).

Cheng, B., *General Principles of Law as Applied by International Courts and Tribunals*, Cambridge: Cambridge University Press (2006).

Chesterman, S., 'Ownership in Theory and in Practice: Transfer of Authority in UN Statebuilding Operations', *Journal of Intervention and Statebuilding* 1 (2007), pp. 3–26.

Churchill, R.R. and Lowe, A.V., *The Law of the Sea*, 3rd edn., Yonkers, NY: Juris Publishing (1999).

Clapham, A., 'Human Rights Obligations of Non-State Actors in Conflict Situations', *International Review of the Red Cross* 88(863) (2006), pp. 491–523.

Collier, P., Hoeffler, A., and Rohner, D., Beyond Greed and Grievance: Feasibility and Civil War, Working Paper (November 2007).

Collier, P., *The Bottom Billion: Why the Poorest Countries Are Failing and What Can Be Done about It*, New York [etc.]: Oxford University Press (2007).

Collier, P. and Hoeffler, A., 'Resource Rents, Governance, and Conflict', *Journal of Conflict Resolution* 49(4) (2005), pp. 625–33.

'Greed and Grievance in Civil War', *Oxford Economic Papers* 56 (2004), pp. 563–95.

'On Economic Causes of Civil War', *Oxford Economic Papers* 50 (1998), pp. 563–73.

Corten, O. and Klein, P. (eds.), *The Vienna Convention on the Law of Treaties: A Commentary*, Oxford: Oxford University Press (2011).

Cortright, D., Lopez, G.A., and Gerber-Stellingwerf, L., 'Sanctions', in T.G. Weiss and S. Daws (eds.), *The Oxford Handbook on the United Nations*, Oxford: Oxford University Press (2007), pp. 349–69.

Cortright, D. and Lopez, G.A. (eds.), *Smart Sanctions: Targeting Economic Statecraft*, Lanham: Rowman and Littlefield (2002).

The Sanctions Decade: Assessing UN Strategies in the 1990s, Boulder, CO: Lynne Reinner Publishers (2000).

Cot, J.-P., Pellet, A., and Forteau, M. (eds.), *La Charte des Nations Unies: Commentaire Article par Article*, 3rd edn., Paris: Economica (2005).

Crawford, J., *The Creation of States in International Law*, 2nd ed., Oxford: Oxford University Press (2006).

'The Relationship between Sanctions and Countermeasures', in V. Gowland-Debbas (ed.), *United Nations Sanctions and International Law*, Graduate Institute of International Studies Geneva, The Hague/London/Boston: Kluwer Law International (2001), pp. 57–68.

'The Right of Self-Determination in International Law', in P. Alston (ed.), *Peoples' Rights*, Academy of European Law, Oxford: Oxford University Press (2001), pp. 7–67.

Cullen, A., *The Concept of Non-international Armed Conflict in International Humanitarian Law*, Cambridge: Cambridge University Press (2010).

D'Amato, A., 'Do We Owe a Duty to Future Generations to Preserve the Global Environment?' *American Journal of International Law* 84 (1990), pp. 190–98.

De Frouville, O., 'Article 1 Paragraphe 3', in J.-P. Cot, A. Pellet, and M. Forteau (eds.), *La Charte des Nations Unies: Commentaire Article par Article*, 3rd edn., Paris: Economica (2005), pp. 357–78.

Dennis, M.J., 'Application of Human Rights Treaties Extraterritorially in Times of Armed Conflict and Military Occupation', *American Journal of International Law* 99(1) (2005), pp. 119–41.

Dinstein, Y., 'Booty in Warfare', in R. Wolfrum (ed.), *Encyclopedia of Public International Law*, Vol. I, Max Planck Institute for Comparative Public Law and International Law, Oxford: Oxford University Press (2012), pp. 990–93.

'Military Necessity', in R. Wolfrum, *Encyclopedia of Public International Law*, Vol. VII, Max Planck Institute for Comparative Public Law and International Law, Oxford: Oxford University Press (2012), pp. 201–7.

The International Law of Belligerent Occupation, Cambridge: Cambridge University Press (2009).

'The Interaction between Customary International Law and Treaties', *Recueil des Cours* 322 (2006), pp. 243–427.

'Protection of the Environment in International Armed Conflict', *Max Planck Yearbook of United Nations Law* 5 (2001), pp. 523–49.

Dinstein, Y. and Tabory, M. (eds.), *The Protection of Minorities and Human Rights*, The Hague: Martinus Nijhoff Publishers (1992).

Dinstein, Y., 'Collective Human Rights of Peoples and Minorities', *International and Comparative Law Quarterly* 25 (1976), pp. 102–20.

Dobelle, J.-F., 'Article 1 Paragraphe 2', in J.-P. Cot, A. Pellet, and M. Forteau (eds.), *La Charte des Nations Unies: Commentaire Article par Article*, 3rd edn., Paris: Economica (2005), pp. 337–56.

Dobbins, J. et al., *The UN's Role in Nation-Building : From the Congo to Iraq*, Santa Monica, CA [etc.]: RAND Corporation (2005).

Donnelly, J., 'In Search of the Unicorn: The Jurisprudence and Politics of the Right to Development', *California Western International Law Journal* 15 (1985), pp. 473–509.

Dörmann, K., *Elements of War Crimes under the Rome Statute of the International Criminal Court: Sources and Commentary*, International Committee of the Red Cross, Cambridge: Cambridge University Press (2002).

Doyle, M.W. and Sambanis, N., 'Peacekeeping Operations', in T.G. Weiss, and S. Daws (eds.), *The Oxford Handbook on the United Nations*, Oxford: Oxford University Press (2007), pp. 323–48.

Driest van den, S., *Remedial Secession: A Right to External Self-Determination as a Remedy to Serious Injustices?* School of Human Rights Research Series, Vol. 61, Cambridge: Intersentia (2013).

Dupuy, P.-M., 'Evolutionary Interpretation of Treaties', in E. Cannizzaro (ed.), *The Law of Treaties beyond the Vienna Convention*, Oxford: Oxford University Press (2011), pp. 123–37.

'Soft Law and the International Law of the Environment', *Michigan Journal of International Law* 12 (1990–91), pp. 420–35.

Dupuy, R.-J. (ed.), *Le développement du rôle du Conseil de sécurité*, Académie de droit international, Dordrecht/Boston/London: Martinus Nijhoff (1993).

Dupuy, R.J., *Droit déclaratoire et droit programmatoire de la coutume sauvage a la "soft law"*, Toulouse: Société française pour le droit international (1974).

Duruigbo, E., 'Permanent Sovereignty and Peoples' Ownership of Natural Resources in International Law', *George Washington International Law Review*, 38 (2006), pp. 33–100.

Ebeku, K.S.A., 'Constitutional Right to a Healthy Environment and Human Rights Approaches to Environmental Protection in Nigeria: Gbemre v. Shell Revisited', *RECIEL* 16(3) (2007), pp. 312–20.

Eckert, S., Biersteker, T., Herik, L.J. van den, and Cuyvers, A., *Due Process and Targeted Sanctions, Update of the Watson Report*, Brown University: Watson Institute (2012).

Elian, G., *The Principle of Sovereignty over Natural Resources*, Alphen aan den Rijn: Sijthoff and Noordhoff (1979).

Elias, O., 'Sustainable Development, War Reparations and Environmental Damage', in M. Fitzmaurice and M. Szuniewicz (eds.), *Exploitation of Natural Resources in the 21st Century*, The Hague: Kluwer Law International (2003), pp. 67–90.

Ellis, J., 'Shades of Grey: Soft Law and the Validity of Public International Law', *Leiden Journal of International Law* 25 (2012), pp. 313–34.

Emmerij, L., Jolly, R., and Weiss, T.G., *Ahead of the Curve? UN Ideas and Global Challenges*, Bloomington: Indiana University Press (2001).

Evans, M.D. (ed.), *International Law*, 3rd edn., Oxford: Oxford University Press (2010).

Falk, R., 'The Complexities of Humanitarian Intervention: A New World Order Challenge', *Michigan Journal of International Law* 17 (1995–6), pp. 491–513.

Farrall, J.-M., *United Nations Sanctions and the Rule of Law*, Cambridge: Cambridge University Press (2007).

Farmer, A., 'Towards a Meaningful Rebirth of Economic Self-Determination: Human Rights Realization in Resource Rich Countries', *International Law and Politics* 39, pp. 417–73.

Feichtner, I., 'The Waiver Power of the WTO: Opening the WTO for Political Debate on the Reconciliation of Competing Interests', *European Journal of International Law* 20(3), pp. 615–45.

Findlay, T., *Cambodia: The Legacy and Lessons of UNTAC*, SIPRI Research Report No. 9, Oxford: Oxford University Press (1995).

Fischer, H., 'Grave Breaches of the Geneva Conventions of 1949', in G.K. McDonald and O. Swaak-Goldman (eds.), *Substantive and Procedural Aspects of International Criminal Law*, The Hague: Kluwer Law International (2000), pp. 65–93.

Fitzmaurice, M., Elias, O., and Merkouris, P. (eds.), *Treaty Interpretation and the Vienna Convention on the Law of Treaties: 30 Years On*, Queen Mary Studies in International Law, Leiden: Martinus Nijhoff Publishers (2010), pp. 39–58.

Fitzmaurice, M. and Marshall, J., 'The Human Right to a Clean Environment – Phantom or Reality? The European Court of Human Rights and English Courts Perspective on Balancing Rights in Environmental Cases', *Nordic Journal of International Law* 76 (2007), pp. 103–51.

Fitzmaurice, M., 'International Protection of the Environment', in *Recueil des cours* 293 (2001), The Hague, Boston, London: Martinus Nijhoff Publishers (2002), pp. 9–488.

Fleck, D. (ed.), *The Handbook of International Humanitarian Law*, 2nd edn., Oxford: Oxford University Press (2008).

Fox, G.H., *Humanitarian Occupation*, Cambridge: Cambridge University Press (2008).

Freestone, D., Barnes, R., and Ong, D.M. (eds.), *The Law of the Sea: Progress and Prospects*, Oxford: Oxford University Press (2006).

Freestone, D. and Hey, E., *The Precautionary Principle and International Law: The Challenge of Implementation*, The Hague: Kluwer Law International (1996).

French, D., *International Law and Policy of Sustainable Development*, Melland Schill Studies in International Law, Manchester: Manchester University Press (2005).

'A Reappraisal of Sovereignty in the Light of Global Environmental Concerns', *Legal Studies* 21 (2001), pp. 377–99.

Gardiner, R.K., *Treaty Interpretation*, Oxford: Oxford University Press (2008).

Gehring, M.W. and Cordonnier-Segger, M.-C., *Precaution in World Trade Law: The Precautionary Principle and Its Implications for the World Trade Organization*, Montreal: CISDL (2002).

Gehring, T., 'Treaty-Making and Treaty Evolution', in D. Bodansky, J. Brunnée, and E. Hey (eds.), *The Oxford Handbook of International Environmental Law*, Oxford: Oxford University Press (2007), pp. 469–97.

Genugten, W.J.M. van, Scharf, M.P., and Radin, S.E. (eds.), *Criminal Jurisdiction 100 Years after the 1907 Hague Peace Conference*, Proceedings of the 2007 Hague Joint Conference on Contemporary Issues of International Law, The Hague: T.M.C. Asser Press (2009).

Gess, K.N., 'Permanent Sovereignty over Natural Resources: An Analytical Review of the United Nations Declaration and Its Genesis', *International and Comparative Law Quarterly* 13 (1964), pp. 398–449.

Ghai, Y., 'Whose Human Right to Development?' Human Rights Unit Occasion Paper, Commonwealth Secretariat (1989).

Ginther, K., Denters, E., and de Waart, P.J.I.M. (eds.), *Sustainable Development and Good Governance*, Dordrecht: Nijhoff (1995).

Global Witness, Loopholes in the Kimberley Process, Briefing Document (2006).
The Sinews of War: Eliminating the Trade in Conflict Resources (2006).
A Rough Trade: The Role of Companies and Governments in the Angolan Conflict (1998).
Goldmann, M., 'We Need to Cut Off the Head of the King: Past, Present, and Future Approaches to International Soft Law', *Leiden Journal of International Law* 25 (2012), pp. 335–68.
Gowland-Debbas, V. (ed.), *United Nations Sanctions and International Law*, Graduate Institute of International Studies Geneva, The Hague/London/Boston: Kluwer Law International (2001).
Grant, J.A., 'The Kimberley Process at Ten: Reflections on a Decade of Efforts to End the Trade in Conflict Diamonds', in P. Lujala and S.A. Rustad (eds.), *High-Value Natural Resources and Post-conflict Peacebuilding*, Oxford/New York: Earthscan (2012), pp. 159–79.
Greenwood, C., 'Scope of Application of Humanitarian Law', in D. Fleck (ed.), *The Handbook of International Humanitarian Law*, 2nd edn., Oxford: Oxford University Press (2008).
'The Advisory Opinion on Nuclear Weapons and the Contribution of the International Court to International Humanitarian Law', *International Review of the Red Cross* No. 316 (1997).
Greig, D.W., *Invalidity and the Law of Treaties*, London: British Institute of International and Comparative Law (2006).
Halperin, D.J., 'Human Rights and Natural Resources', *William and Mary Law Review* 9 (1967–8), pp. 770–87.
Handl, G., 'Transboundary Impacts', in D. Bodansky, J. Brunnée, and E. Hey (eds.), *The Oxford Handbook of International Environmental Law*, Oxford: Oxford University Press (2007), pp. 531–49.
Hanqin, X., *Transboundary Damage in International Law*, Cambridge: Cambridge University Press (2003).
Heinsch, R., 'Legal Maxims: Summaries and Extracts from Selected Case Law of the International Criminal Court', in G. Capaldo (ed.), *The Global Community Yearbook of International Law and Jurisprudence*, Volume I, Oxford: Oxford University Press (2009), pp. 385–407.
Henckaerts, J.-M. and Doswald-Beck, L. (eds.), *Customary International Humanitarian Law*, International Committee of the Red Cross, Cambridge: Cambridge University Press (2005), Vols. I and II.
Henckaerts, J.-M., 'Towards Better Protection for the Environment in Armed Conflict: Recent Developments in International Humanitarian Law', *Review of European Community & International Environmental Law* 9(1) (2000), pp. 13–19.
Herdegen, M., 'Interpretation in International Law', in R. Wolfrum, *Encyclopedia of Public International Law*, Vol. VI, Max Planck Institute for Comparative

Public Law and International Law, Oxford: Oxford University Press (2012), pp. 260–68.

Herik, L.J. van den, Individualizing Enforcement in International Law: Progress or Peril? Inaugural Lecture, Leiden University, 29 June 2012.

Herik, L.J. van den and Dam-de Jong, D.A., 'Revitalizing the Antique War Crime of Pillage: The Potential and Pitfalls of Using International Criminal Law to Address Illegal Resource Exploitation during Armed Conflict', *Criminal Law Forum* 22(3) (2011), pp. 237–73.

Herik, L.J. van den, 'The Difficulties of Exercising Extraterritorial Criminal Jurisdiction: The Acquittal of a Dutch Businessman for Crimes Committed in Liberia', *International Criminal Law Review* 9 (2009), pp. 211–26.

'The Security Council's Targeted Sanctions Regimes: In Need of Better Protection of the Individual', *Leiden Journal of International Law* 20(4) (2007), pp. 797–807.

Higgins, R., *Problems and Process: International Law and How We Use It*, Oxford: Clarendon Press (1994).

High-Level Panel on Threats, Challenges and Change, *A More Secure World: Our Shared Responsibility*, United Nations: New York (2004).

Hillgenberg, H., 'A Fresh Look at Soft Law', *European Journal of International Law* 10 (1999), p. 499–515.

Holt, J.C., *Magna Carta*, Cambridge: Cambridge University Press (1992).

Homer-Dixon, T. F., *Environment, Scarcity and Violence*, New York: Princeton University Press (1999).

Hostettler, P. and Danai, O., 'Neutrality in Land Warfare', in R. Wolfrum (ed.), *Encyclopedia of Public International Law*, Vol. VII, Max Planck Institute for Comparative Public Law and International Law, Oxford: Oxford University Press (2012), pp. 638–43.

Hulme, K., 'Taking Care to Protect the Environment against Damage: A Meaningless Obligation?' *International Review of the Red Cross* 92(879) (2010), pp. 675–91.

War Torn Environment: Interpreting the Legal Threshold, International Humanitarian Law Series, Leiden: Martinus Nijhoff (2004).

Human Rights Watch, *Sierra Leone: Sowing Terror: Atrocities against Civilians in Sierra Leone* (1998).

Kalshoven, F. and Zegveld, L., *Constraints on the Waging of War : An Introduction to international Humanitarian Law*, 3rd edn., Geneva: International Committee of the Red Cross (2001).

Kalshoven, F., 'The Undertaking to Respect and to Ensure Respect in All Circumstances: From Tiny Seed to Ripening Fruit', *Yearbook of International Humanitarian Law* 2 (1999), pp. 3–61.

Kamminga, M.T. and Zia-Zarivi, S., *Liability of Multinational Corporations under International Law*, The Hague: Kluwer Law International (2000).

Keller, L., 'Cambodia Conflicts (Kampuchea)', in R. Wolfrum (ed.), *Max Planck Encyclopedia of Public International Law*, Vol. I, Max Planck Institute for Comparative Public Law and International Law, Oxford: Oxford University Press (2012), pp. 1093–1104.

Kelsen, H., *The Law of the United Nations: A Critical Analysis of Its Fundamental Problems*, London: Stevens and Sons (1950).

Kirton, J.J. and Trebilcock, M.J., *Hard Choices, Soft Law: Voluntary Standards in Global Trade, Environment and Social Governance*, Aldershot etc.: Ashgate (2004).

Kiss, A. and Shelton, D., *Guide to International Environmental Law*, Leiden/Boston: Martinus Nijhoff Publishers (2007).

Kiss, A., 'Réflexions sur l'Intérêt Général de l'Humanité', in Z.R. Ribeiro Leão and A.A. Cançado Trindade (eds.), *Studies in Honour of Professor Antônio Augusto Cançado Trindade*, Porto Alegre: Fabris (2005).

'International Humanitarian Law and the Environment', *Environmental Policy and Law* 31(4–5) (2001).

Kiwanuka, R.N., 'The Meaning of "People" in the African Charter on Human and Peoples' Rights', *American Journal of International Law* 82(1) (1988), pp. 80–101.

'Developing Rights: The UN Declaration on the Right to Development', *Netherlands International Law Review* XXXV (1988), pp. 257–72.

Klabbers, J., 'Beyond the Vienna Convention: Conflicting Treaty Obligations', in E. Cannizzaro (ed.), *The Law of Treaties beyond the Vienna Convention*, Oxford: Oxford University Press (2011), pp. 192–205.

'The Redundancy of Soft Law', *Nordic Journal of International Law* 65 (1996), pp. 167–82.

Klare, M.T., *Resource Wars: The New Landscape of Global Conflict*, New York: Metropolitan Books (2001).

'The New Geography of Conflict', *Foreign Affairs* May/June 2001.

Knight, W.A., 'Democracy and Good Governance', in T.G. Weiss and S. Daws (eds.), *The Oxford Handbook on the United Nations*, Oxford: Oxford University Press (2008), pp. 620–33.

Koppe, E.V., *The Use of Nuclear Weapons and the Protection of the Environment during International Armed Conflict*, Studies in International Law, Vol. 18, Oxford: Hart (2008).

Koyame, M., 'United Nations Resolutions and the Struggle to Curb the Illicit Trade in Conflict Diamonds in Sub-Saharan Africa', *African Journal of Legal Studies* 2 (2005), pp. 80–101.

Kuyper, P.J., *The Implementation of International Sanctions: The Netherlands and Rhodesia*, Alphen aan den Rijn: Sijthoff and Noordhoff (1978).

'The Limits of Supervision: The Security Council Watchdog Committee on Rhodesian Sanctions', *Netherlands International Law Review* 25 (1978), pp. 159–94.

Ladeur, K.H., 'Governance, Theory of', in R. Wolfrum (ed.), *Encyclopedia of Public International Law*, Vol. IV, Max Planck Institute for Comparative Public Law and International Law, Oxford: Oxford University Press (2012), pp. 541–53.

Large, D., 'China and the Changing Context of Development in Sudan', *Development* 50(3) (2007), pp. 57–62.

Lauterpacht, E., 'The Hague Regulations and the Seizure of Munitions de Guerre', 32 *British Yearbook of International Law* 218 (1955–6), pp. 219–43.

Lauterpacht, H., *Recognition in International Law*, Cambridge: Cambridge University Press (1947).

Le Billon, P. and Springer, S., 'Between War and Peace: Violence and Accommodation in the Cambodian Logging Sector', in W. de Jong, D. Donovan, and K. Abe (eds.), *Extreme Conflict and Tropical Forests*, New York: Springer (2007), pp. 17–36.

Le Billon, P., *Wars of Plunder: Conflicts, Profits and the Politics of Resources*, New York: Columbia University Press (2012).

Natural Resources, Armed Conflicts, and the UN Security Council, Briefing Paper No. 07–001, Liu Institute for Global Issues, 30 May 2007.

Fuelling War: Natural Resources and Armed Conflict, 2nd edn., Adelphi Paper 373, The International Institute for Strategic Studies, Abingdon: Routledge (2005).

Lepard, B.D., *Customary International Law: A New Theory with Practical Applications*, ASIL Studies in International Legal Theory, Cambridge, New York, etc.: Cambridge University Press (2010).

Linderfalk, U., 'Who Are "the Parties"? Article 31, Paragraph 3(c) of the 1969 Vienna Convention and the "Principle of Systemic Integration" Revisited?' *Netherlands International Law Review* 55(3) (2008), pp. 343–64.

On the Interpretation of Treaties: The Modern International Law as Expressed in the 1969 Vienna Convention on the Law of Treaties, Law and Philosophy Library, Vol. 83, Dordrecht: Springer (2007).

Lowe, V. and Tzanakopoulos, A., 'Economic Warfare', in R. Wolfrum (ed.), *Encyclopedia of Public International Law*, Vol. VII, Max Planck Institute for Comparative Public Law and International Law, Oxford: Oxford University Press (2012).

Lowe, V., 'Sustainable Development and Unsustainable Arguments', in A. Boyle and D. Freestone (eds.), *International Law and Sustainable Development*, Oxford: Oxford University Press (1999), pp. 19–38.

Lujala, P. and Rustad, S.A. (eds.), *High-Value Natural Resources and Post-Conflict Peacebuilding*, Oxford/New York: Earthscan (2012).

Lundberg, M.A., 'The Plunder of Natural Resources during War: A War Crime (?)' *Georgetown Journal of International Law* 39(3) (2008), pp. 495–526.

Manusama, K.M., *The United Nations Security Council in the Post-Cold War Era : Applying the Principle of Legality*, Leiden: Nijhoff (2006).

Marceau, G., 'Conflicts of Norms and Conflicts of Jurisdictions: The Relationship between the WTO Agreement and MEAs and Other Treaties', *Journal of World Trade* 35(6) (2001), pp. 1081–1131.

Marks, Stephan, 'The Human Right to Development: Between Rhetoric and Reality', *Harvard Human Rights Journal* 17 (2004), pp. 137–68.

Marks, Susan, 'Nightmare and Noble Dream: The 1993 World Conference on Human Rights', *Cambridge Law Journal* 53 (1994), pp. 54–62.

McCaffrey, S.C., *The Law of International Watercourses*, 2nd edn., Oxford: Oxford University Press (2007).

McLachlan, C., 'The Principle of Systemic Integration and Article 31(3)(c) of the Vienna Convention', *International Comparative Law Quarterly* 54 (2005), pp. 279–320.

McNair, A.D., *The Law of Treaties*, Oxford: Clarendon Press (1961).

Meron, T., 'The Martens Clause, Principles of Humanity, and Dictates of Public Conscience', *American Journal of International Law* 94(1) (2000), pp. 78–89.

'Applicability of Multilateral Conventions to Occupied Territories', *American Journal of International Law* 72 (1978), pp. 542–57.

Moir, L., 'Towards the Unification of International Humanitarian Law?' in R. Burchill, N.D. White, and J. Morris (eds.), *International Conflict and Security Law: Essays in Memory of Hilaire McCoubrey*, Cambridge: Cambridge University Press (2005), pp. 108–28.

The Law of Internal Armed Conflict, Cambridge: Cambridge University Press (2002).

Mollard-Bannelier, K., *La Protection de l'Environnement en Temps de Conflit Armé*, Publication de la Revue Générale de Droit International Public, Nouvelle Série No. 53, Paris: Editions A. Pedone (2001).

Momtaz, D., 'Le Droit International Humanitaire Applicable aux Conflits Armés Non Internationaux', *Recueil des Cours* 292 (2001), pp. 9–145.

Munro, R.D. and Lammers, J.G., *Environmental Protection and Sustainable Development: Legal Principles and Recommendations*, Report Adopted by the Experts Group on Environmental Law of the World Commission on Environment and Development, London/Dordrecht/Boston: Graham and Trotman/Martinus Nijhoff (1986).

Newalsing, E., 'Customary International Humanitarian Law', *Leiden Journal of International Law* 21(1) (2008), pp. 255–79.

Ocheje, P.D., 'The Extractive Industries Transparency Initiative (EITI): Voluntary Codes of Conduct, Poverty and Accountability in Africa', *Journal of Sustainable Development in Africa* 8(3) (2006), pp. 222–39.

Oda, S., 'Fisheries under the United Nations Convention on the Law of the Sea', *American Journal of International Law* 77(4) (Oct. 1983), pp. 739–55.

O'Keefe, R., 'World Cultural Heritage: Obligations to the International Community as a Whole?' *International and Comparative Law Quarterly* 53 (Jan. 2004), pp. 189–209.

Okowa, P.N., 'Natural Resources in Situations of Armed Conflict: Is There a Coherent Framework for Protection?' *International Community Law Review* 9 (2007), pp. 237–62.

'Case Concerning Armed Activities on the Territory of the Congo (Democratic Republic of the Congo v. Uganda)', *International and Comparative Law Quarterly* 55(3) (2006), pp. 742–53.

Oppenheim, L., *International Law: A Treatise*, Vol. II, *Disputes, War and Neutrality*, 7th edn., edited by H. Lauterpacht, London/New York/Toronto: Longmans, Green and Co (1952).

International Law: A Treatise, Vol. II, *War and Neutrality*, 2nd edn., New York/Bombay/Calcutta: Longmans, Green and Co. (1912).

Collective Security, Oxford: Oxford University Press (2011).

Orford, A., 'Globalization and the Right to Development', in P. Alston (ed.), *Peoples' Rights*, Academy of European Law, Oxford: Oxford University Press (2001), pp. 127–84.

Otobo, E.E., 'The New Peacebuilding Architecture: An Institutional Innovation in the United Nations', in P.G. Danchin and H. Fischer (eds.), *United Nations Reform and the New Collective Security*, Cambridge: Cambridge University Press (2010), pp. 212–34.

Partnership Africa Canada, *The Heart of the Matter: Sierra Leone, Diamonds, and Human Security* (2000).

Pauwelyn, J., Wessel, R.A., and Wouters, J. (eds.), *Informal International Lawmaking*, Oxford: Oxford University Press (2012).

Pauwelyn, J., *Conflict of Norms in Public International Law: How WTO Law Relates to Other Rules of International Law*, Cambridge: Cambridge University Press (2003).

'WTO Compassion or Superiority Complex? What to Make of the WTO Waiver for "Conflict Diamonds"', *Michigan Journal of International Law* 24 (2002–3), pp. 1177–1207.

Pellet, A. and Miron, A., 'Sanctions', in R. Wolfrum (ed.), *Encyclopedia of Public International Law*, Max Planck Institute for Comparative Public Law and International Law, Vol. IX, Oxford: Oxford University Press (2012), pp. 1–15.

Pellet, A., 'Article 55, alinéas a et b', in J.-P. Cot, A. Pellet, and M. Forteau (eds.), *La Charte des Nations Unies: Commentaire Article par Article*, 3rd edn., Paris: Economica (2005), pp. 1451–80.

Pellet, A. and Sorel, J.-M. (eds.), *Le Droit International du Développement Social et Culturel*, 1st edn., Paris: L'Hermès (1997).

Pellet, A., *Le Droit International du Développement*, Collection 'Que sais-je ?' 2nd edn., Paris: Presses Universitaires de France (1987).

Perna, L., *The Formation of the Treaty Law of Non-international Armed Conflict*, International Humanitarian Law Series, Vol. 14, Leiden/Boston: Martinus Nijhoff (2006).

Pictet, J. and Uhler, O.M., *The Geneva Conventions of 12 August 1949: Commentary, Part 4 on the Geneva Convention Relative to the Protection of Civilian Persons in Time of War*, Geneva: International Committee of the Red Cross (1958).

Plant, G., *Environmental Protection and the Law of War: A 'Fifth Geneva' Convention on the Protection of the Environment in Time of Armed Conflict*, London: Belhaven Press (1992).

Post, H.G.H. (ed.), *International Economic Law and Armed Conflict*, The Hague: Martinus Nijhoff (1994).

Quénivet, N. and Shah-Davis, S. (eds.), *International Law and Armed Conflict: Challenges in the 21st Century*, The Hague: T.M.C. Asser Press (2010).

Ragazzi, M., *The Concept of International Obligations Erga Omnes*, Oxford: Clarendon Press (1997).

Raič, D., *Statehood and the Law of Self-Determination*, PhD. Thesis, Leiden University (2002).

Ratner, S.R., 'The Cambodia Settlement Agreements', *American Journal of International Law* 87(1) (Jan. 1993), pp. 1–41.

Rawls, J., *A Theory of Justice*, revised ed., Oxford: Oxford University Press (1999).

Renner, M., The Anatomy of Resource Wars, Worldwatch Paper 162, Worldwatch Institute, Washington, DC (2002).

Ress, G. 'The Interpretation of the Charter', in B. Simma (ed.), *The Charter of the United Nations. A Commentary*, Oxford: Oxford University Press (2002).

Rich, E. and Warner, N., 'Addressing the Roots of Liberia's Conflict through the Extractive Inustries Transparency Initiative', in P. Lujala and S.A. Rustad (eds.), *High-Value Natural Resources and Post-conflict Peacebuilding*, Oxford/New York: Earthscan (2012), pp. 201–9.

Riedel, E.H., 'Recognition of Belligerency', in R. Bernhardt, *Encyclopedia of Public International Law*, Vol. IV, Max Planck Institute for Comparative Public Law and International Law, Amsterdam: Elsevier (2000), pp. 47–50.

Roberts, A., 'Transformative Military Occupation: Applying the Laws of War and Human Rights', *American Journal of International Law* 100 (2006), pp. 580–622.

Rosenberg, D., *Le Principe de Souveraineté des Etats sur Leurs Ressources Naturelles*, Paris: Librairie Générale de Droit et de Jurisprudence (1983).

Rosenstock, R., 'The Declaration of Principles of International Law Concerning Friendly Relations: A Survey', *American Journal of International Law* 65(5) (1971), pp. 713–35.

Ross, M., 'How Do Natural Resources Influence Civil War? Evidence from Thirteen Cases', *International Organization* 58(1) (2004), pp. 35–67.

Ross, M., 'What Do We Know about Natural Resources and Civil War?' *Journal of Peace Research* 41 (2004), pp. 337–56.

Roth, B.R., *Governmental Illegitimacy in International Law*, Oxford: Clarendon Press (1999).

Ryngaert, C., 'Human Rights Obligations of Armed Groups', *Revue Belge de Droit International* 41(1–2) (2008), pp. 355–81.

Sachs, J.D. and Warner, A.M., 'The Curse of Natural Resources', *European Economic Review* 45 (2001), pp. 827–38.

Šahović, M., 'Codification des Principes du Droit International des Relations Amicales et de la Coopération entre les Etats', *Recueil des Cours* 137 (1972), pp. 243–310.

Salomon, M.E., *Global Responsibility for Human Rights: World Poverty and the Development of International Law*, Oxford: Oxford University Press (2007).

Salomons, D., 'On the Far Side of Conflict: The UN Peacebuilding Commission as Optical Illusion', in P.G. Danchin and H. Fischer (eds.), *United Nations Reform and the New Collective Security*, Cambridge: Cambridge University Press (2010), pp. 195–211.

Salter, M., 'Reinterpreting Competing Interpretations of the Scope and Potential of the Martens Clause', *Journal of Conflict and Security Law* 17(3) (2012), pp. 403–37.

Samson, M., 'High Hopes, Scant Resources: A Word of Scepticism about the Anti-fragmentation Function of Article 31(3)(c) of the Vienna Convention on the Law of Treaties', *Leiden Journal of International Law* 24 (2011), pp. 701–14.

Sand, P.H., 'The Evolution of International Environmental Law', in D. Bodansky, J. Brunnée, and E. Hey (eds.), *The Oxford Handbook of International Environmental Law*, Oxford: Oxford University Press (2007), pp. 29–43.

Sandoz, Y., Swinarski, C., and Zimmermann, B. (eds.), *Commentary on the Additional Protocols of 8 June 1977 to the Geneva Conventions of 12 August 1949*, Dordrecht: Nijhoff Publishers (1987).

Sands, P. and Peel, J., *Principles of International Environmental Law*, 3rd edn., Cambridge: Cambridge University Press (2012).

Sands, P. and Commission, J., 'Treaty, Custom and Time: Interpretation/ Application?' in M. Fitzmaurice, O. Elias, and P. Merkouris (eds.), *Treaty Interpretation and the Vienna Convention on the Law of Treaties: 30 Years On*, Queen Mary Studies in International Law, Leiden: Martinus Nijhoff Publishers (2010), pp. 39–58.

Sands, P., *Principles of International Environmental Law*, 2nd edn., Cambridge: Cambridge University Press (2003).

'Treaty, Custom and the Cross-Fertilization of Law', *Yale Human Rights and Development Law Journal* 1 (1999), pp. 85–106.

Sassòli, M., Bouvier, A.A., and Quintin, A., *How Does Law Protect in War? Cases, Documents and Teaching Materials on Contemporary Practice in International Humanitarian Law*, 3rd edn., Geneva: ICRC (2011).

Sassòli, M. and Olson, L.M., 'The Relationship between International Humanitarian and Human Rights Law', *International Review of the Red Cross*, 90 (871) (2008), pp. 599–627.

Schefer, K.N., 'Stopping Trade in Conflict Diamonds: Exploring the Trade and Human Rights Interface with the WTO Waiver for the Kimberley Process', in T. Cottier, J. Pauwelyn, and E. Bürgi (eds.), *Human Rights and International Trade*, Oxford: Oxford University Press (2006), pp. 391–450.

Scheffer, D.J., 'Beyond Occupation Law', *American Journal of International Law* 97 (2003), pp. 842–60.

Schermers, H.G. and Blokker, N.M., *International Institutional Law*, 5th revised edn., The Hague: Martinus Nijhoff (2011).

Schindler, D., 'Le Droit International Humanitaire et les Conflits Armés Internes Internationalisés', *Revue Internationale de la Croix Rouge* 64(737) (1982), pp. 263–72.

Schrijver, N.J., 'Natural Resources, Permanent Sovereignty over', in R. Wolfrum (ed.), *Encyclopedia of Public International Law*, Vol. VII, Max Planck Institute for Comparative Public Law and International Law, Oxford: Oxford University Press (2012), pp. 535–44.

Development without Destruction: The UN and Global Resource Management, United Nations Intellectual History Project Series, Bloomington and Indianapolis: Indiana University Press (2010).

Schrijver, N.J. and Prislan, V., 'From Mare Liberum to the Global Commons: Building on the Grotian Heritage', in *Grotiana* 30 (2009), pp. 168–206.

'After Us, the Deluge? The Position of Future Generations of Humankind in International Environmental Law', in M.A.M. Salih (ed.), *Climate Change and Sustainable Development: New Challenges for Poverty Reduction*, Cheltenham: Edward Elgar (2009), pp. 59–78.

'The Status of the Precautionary Principle in International Law and Its Application and Interpretation in International Litigation', in *Liber Amicorum Jean-Pierre Cot: Le Procès International*, Brussels: Bruylant (2009), pp. 241–53.

'Unravelling State Sovereignty? The Controversy on the Right of Indigenous Peoples to Permanent Sovereignty over Their Natural Wealth and Resources', in I. Boerefijn and J. Goldschmidt (eds.), *Changing Perceptions of Sovereignty and Human Rights: Essays in Honour of Cees Flinterman*, Antwerp/Oxford/Portland: Intersentia (2008), pp. 85–98.

'The Evolution of Sustainable Development in International Law: Inception, Meaning and Status', *Recueil des Cours* 329 (2007), Leiden/Boston: Martinus Nijhoff Publishers (2008), pp. 221–412.

Schrijver, N.J. and Weiss, F. (eds.), *International Law and Sustainable Development: Principles and Practice*, Leiden: Nijhoff Publishers (2004).

Schrijver, N.J., 'De verankering en betekenis van duurzame ontwikkeling in het internationale recht', *Volkenrecht en duurzame ontwikkeling*, Mededelingen van de Nederlandse Vereniging voor Internationaal Recht 127, Den Haag: T.M.C. Asser Press (2003), pp. 1–98.

Sovereignty over Natural Resources: Balancing Rights and Duties, Cambridge: Cambridge University Press (1997).

'The Use of Economic Sanctions by the UN Security Council: An International Law Perspective', in H.G.H. Post (ed.), *International Economic Law and Armed Conflict*, The Hague: Martinus Nijhoff (1994), pp. 123–62.

Schwarzenberger, G., 'The Fundamental Principles of International Law', *Recueil des Cours* 87, pp. 191–385.

Scobbie, I., 'Natural Resources and Belligerent Occupation: Mutation through Permanent Sovereignty', in S. Bowen (ed.), *Human Rights, Self-Determination and Political Change in the Occupied Palestinian Territories*, International Studies in Human Rights, The Hague: Martinus Nijhoff (1997), pp. 221–90.

Sengupta, A., 'Implementing the Right to Development', in N.J. Schrijver and F. Weiss (eds.), *International Law and Sustainable Development: Principles and Practice*, Leiden: Martinus Nijhoff (2004), pp. 341–77.

'On the Theory and Practice of the Right to Development', *Human Rights Quarterly* 24 (2002), pp. 837–89.

Shambaugh, J., Oglethorpe, J., and Ham, R. (with contributions from Sylvia Tognetti), 'The Trampled Grass: Mitigating the Impacts of Armed Conflict on the Environment', Washington, DC: Biodiversity Support Program (2001).

Shaw, M.N. and Fournet, C., 'Article 62: Fundamental Change of Circumstances', in O. Corten and P. Klein (eds.), *The Vienna Convention on the Law of Treaties: A Commentary*, Vol. II, Oxford: Oxford University Press (2011), pp. 1411–33.

Shelton, D., 'International Law and "Relative Normality"', in M. Evans (ed.), *International Law*, 3rd edn., Oxford: Oxford University Press (2010).

'Common Concern of Humanity', *Environmental Policy and Law* 39(2) (2009), pp. 83–90.

'Equity', in D. Bodansky, J. Brunnée, and E. Hey, *The Oxford Handbook of International Environmental Law*, Oxford: Oxford University Press (2007), pp. 639–62.

Simma, B. and Tams, C.J., 'Article 60: Termination or Suspension of the Operation of a Treaty as a Consequence of Its Breach', in O. Corten and P. Klein (eds.), *The Vienna Convention on the Law of Treaties: A Commentary*, Vol. II, Oxford: Oxford University Press (2011), pp. 1351–78.

Simonds, S.N., 'Conventional Warfare and Environmental Protection: A Proposal for International Legal Reform', *Stanford Journal of International Law* 29 (1992–3), pp. 165–221.

Sivakumaran, S., 'Binding Armed Opposition Groups', *International and Comparative Law Quarterly* Vol. 55 (2006), pp. 369–94.

Sjöstedt, B., 'The Role of Multilateral Environmental Agreements in Armed Conflict: "Green-Keeping" in Virunga Park. Applying the UNESCO World Heritage Convention in the Armed Conflict of the Democratic Republic of the Congo', *Nordic Journal of International Law* 82 (2013), pp. 129–53.

Sloan, B., 'Study on the Implications, under International Law, of the United Nations Resolutions on Permanent Sovereignty over Natural Resources, on the Occupied Palestinian and Other Arab Territories and on the Obligations of Israel Concerning Its Conduct in These Territories', reproduced in *UN Doc. A/38/85*, 21 June 1983.

Sohn, L.B., 'The Stockholm Declaration on the Human Environment', *Harvard International Law Journal* 14(3) (1973), pp. 423–515.

Spieker, H., 'The Conduct of Hostilities and the Protection of the Environment', in M. Bothe and A. Fischer-Lescano (eds.), *Frieden in Freiheit: Festschrift für Michael Bothe zum 70. Geburtstag*, Baden-Baden: Nomos (2008), pp. 741–68.

Völkergewohnheitsrechtlicher Schutz der Natürlichen Umwelt im Internationalen Bewaffneten Konflikt, Bochumer Schriften zur Friedenssicherung und zum Humanitären Völkerrecht, Band 10, Bochum: UVB Universitätsverlag Dr. N. Brockmeyer (1992).

Spijkers, O., *The United Nations, the Evolution of Global Values and International Law*, School of Human Rights Research Series, Vol. 47, Cambridge/Antwerp/Portland: Intersentia (2011).

Stahn, C., *The Law and Practice of International Territorial Administration: Versailles to Iraq and Beyond*, Cambridge Studies in International and Comparative Law, Cambridge [etc.]: Cambridge University Press (2008).

'Institutionalizing Brahimi's Light Footprint: A Comment on the Role and Mandate of the Peacebuilding Commission', *International Organizations Law Review* 2 (2005), pp. 403–15.

Stewart, J.G., *Corporate War Crimes: Prosecuting the Pillage of Natural Resources*, New York: Open Society Justice Initiative Publication (2011).

'Towards a Single Definition of Armed Conflict in International Humanitarian Law: A Critique of Internationalized Armed Conflict', *International Review of the Red Cross* 85(850) (2003), pp. 313–50.

Stoett, P., 'Wildlife Conservation: Institutional and Normative Considerations', in N.J. Schrijver and F. Weiss (eds.), *International Law and Sustainable Development: Principles and Practice*, Leiden: Nijhoff Publishers (2004), pp. 501–18.

Straus, S., 'Darfur and the Genocide Debate', *Foreign Affairs* 84(1) (Jan.–Feb. 2005), pp. 123–33.

Summers, J., *The Idea of the People: The Right of Self-Determination, Nationalism and the Legitimacy of International Law*, Doctoral Dissertation, University of Helsinki (2004).

Talmon, S., 'Recognition of the Libyan National Transitional Council', *ASIL Insights* 15(16) (16 June 2011).

Recognition of Governments in International Law: With Particular Reference to Governments in Exile, Oxford: Clarendon Press (1998).

Tarasofsky, R.G., 'Legal Protection of the Environment during International Armed Conflict', *Netherlands Yearbook of International Law* 24 (1993), pp. 17–79.

Thio, L.A., *Managing Babel: The International Legal Protection of Minorities in the Twentieth Century*, Leiden: Martinus Nijhoff (2005).

Thornberry, P., *International Law and the Rights of Minorities*, reprint, Oxford: Oxford University Press (2001).

Thürer, D. and Burri, T., 'Self-Determination', in R. Wolfrum (ed.), *Encyclopedia of Public International Law*, Vol. IX, Max Planck Institute for Comparative Public Law and International Law, Oxford: Oxford University Press (2012), pp. 113–28.

Triffterer, O. (ed.), *Commentary on the Rome Statute of the International Criminal Court: Observers' Notes, Article by Article*, Baden-Baden: Nomos (1999).

Trouwborst, A., *Precautionary Rights and Duties of States*, Leiden: Martinus Nijhoff (2006).

Evolution and Status of the Precautionary Principle in International Law, International Environmental Law and Policy Series, Vol. 62, The Hague: Kluwer Law International (2002).

Verri, P., *Dictionary of the International Law of Armed Conflict*, Geneva: International Committee of the Red Cross (1992).

Verwey, W.D., 'Protection of the Environment in Times of Armed Conflict: In Search of a New Legal Perspective', *Leiden Journal of International Law* 8(1) (1995), pp. 7–40.

Vickery, M., *Cambodia 1975–82*, Boston: South End Press (1984).

Villiger, M.E., *Commentary on the 1969 Vienna Convention on the Law of Treaties*, Leiden/Boston: Martinus Nijhoff (2009).

Vité, S., 'The Interrelation of the Law of Occupation and Economic, Social and Cultural Rights', *International Review of the Red Cross* 90(871) (2008), pp. 629–51.

Vöneky, S., 'A New Shield for the Environment: Peacetime Treaties as Legal Restraints of Wartime Damage', *Review of European Community and International Environmental Law* 9(1) (2000), pp. 20–32.

Vukas, B., 'States, Peoples and Minorities', *Recueil des Cours* 231 (1991), pp. 263–524.

Wallensteen, P., Eriksson, M., and Strandow, D., *Sanctions for Conflict Prevention and Peace Building: Lessons Learned from Côte d'Ivoire and Liberia*, Department of Peace and Conflict Research, Uppsala University (2006).

Weil, P., 'Towards Relative Normativity in International Law?' *American Journal of International Law* 77(3) (1983), pp. 413–42.

Weiss, T.G. and Daws, S., *The Oxford Handbook on the United Nations*, Oxford: Oxford University Press (2007).

Weiss, T.G. 'Governance, Good Governance and Global Governance: Conceptual and Actual Challenges', *Third World Quarterly* 21(5) (2000), pp. 795–814.

Werle, G. and Jessberger, F., *Principles of International Criminal Law*, The Hague: T.M.C. Asser Press (2005).

Wet, E. de, *The Chapter VII Powers of the United Nations Security Council*, Oxford: Hart Publishing (2004).

Wet, E. de, Nollkaemper, A., and Dijkstra, P. (eds.), *Review of The Security Council by Member States*, Utrecht: Intersentia (2003).

Wetzel, J.E., 'Targeted Economic Measures to Curb Armed Conflict? The Kimberley Process on the Trade in "Conflict Diamonds"', in N. Quénivet and S. Shah-Davis (eds.), *International Law and Armed Conflict: Challenges in the 21st Century*, The Hague: T.M.C. Asser Press (2010), pp. 161–81.

Wheatley, S., *Democracy, Minorities and International Law*, Cambridge: Cambridge University Press (2005).

Winkelmann, I., 'Angola', in R. Wolfrum (ed.), *Encyclopedia of Public International Law*, Vol. I, Max Planck Institute for Comparative Public Law and International Law, Oxford: Oxford University Press (2012), pp. 400–8.

Wolfrum, R., 'Iraq – From Belligerent Occupation to Iraqi Exercise of Sovereignty: Foreign Power versus International Community Interference', in A. van Bogdandy and R. Wolfrum (eds.), *Max Planck Yearbook of United Nations Law* 9 (2005), pp. 1–45.

Wood, M.C., 'The Interpretation of Security Council Resolutions', in *Max Planck Yearbook of United Nations Law* (1998), pp. 73–95.

World Commission on Environment and Development, *Our Common Future*, Oxford: Oxford University Press (1987).

Xanthaki, A., *Indigenous Rights and United Nations Standards: Self-Determination, Culture and Land*, Cambridge Studies in International and Comparative Law, Cambridge: Cambridge University Press (2007).

Yasseen, M.K., 'L'Interprétation des Traités d'Après la Convention de Vienne sur le Droit des Traités', *Recueil des Cours* 151 (1976), pp. 1–114.

Zegveld, L., *Accountability of Armed Opposition Groups in International Law*, Cambridge: Cambridge University Press (2002).

Zimmermann, A., 'Human Rights Treaty Bodies and the Jurisdiction of the International Court of Justice', *The Law and Practice of International Courts and Tribunals* 12 (2013), pp. 5–29.

Zimmerman, A., 'Article 8 – Para. 2(e)', in O. Triffterer (ed.), *Commentary on the Rome Statute of the International Criminal Court: Observers' Notes, Article by Article* (1999), pp. 276–84.

Zwanenburg, M., 'Existentialism in Iraq: Security Council Resolution 1483 and the Law of Occupation', *International Review of the Red Cross* 86 (2004), pp. 745–68.

Zyberi, G., *The Humanitarian Face of the International Court of Justice: Its Contribution to Interpreting and Developing International Human Rights and Humanitarian Law Rules and Principles*, School of Human Rights Research Series, Vol. 26, Antwerp, Oxford, Portland: Intersentia (2008).

UNITED NATIONS DOCUMENTS

Survey of UN Security Council practice in relation to natural resources

Resolutions

Situations	Principal resolutions and overview of relevant decisions
General	Resolution 1459 (2003): expresses its support for the Kimberley Process Certification Scheme
Angola	Resolution 864 (1993): installs an arms embargo and an embargo on the export of petroleum to Angola Resolution 1127 (1997): installs travel and aviation sanctions Resolution 1173 (1998): installs an import ban on diamonds that are not controlled through the Certificate of Origin regime of the Angolan government Resolution 1176 (1998): brings into effect the diamond sanctions Resolution 1237 (1999): establishes the Fowler Commission Resolution 1295 (2000): welcomes steps in the direction of devising a more comprehensive system of controls in relation to diamonds Resolution 1448 (2002): terminates the sanctions regime
Cambodia	Resolution 668 (1990): endorses the framework for a comprehensive political settlement of the conflict Resolution 792 (1992): expresses support for the national moratorium on logs; requests UNTAC to take appropriate measures to secure the implementation of the moratorium; and requests the Cambodian authorities to adopt a similar moratorium on minerals and gems Resolution 810 (1993): commends the decision of the Cambodian authorities to adopt a moratorium on minerals and gems; commends the authorities for their decision to consider limits on the export of sawn timber; and expresses support for steps taken by the Technical Advisory Committee on Management and Sustainable Exploitation of Natural Resources to implement these measures

(*cont.*)

(*Cont.*)

Situations	Principal resolutions and overview of relevant decisions
Côte d'Ivoire	Resolution 1572 (2004): installs an arms embargo, travel ban and assets freeze and establishes the Sanctions Committee Resolution 1584 (2005): establishes the Group of Experts Resolution 1643 (2005): installs diamond sanctions Resolution 1727 (2006): requests the Kimberley Process to communicate information about the production and illicit export of diamonds Resolution 1782 (2007): renews the sanctions until 31 October 2008 and decides to review the sanctions in light of progress achieved in the implementation of the peace process Resolution 1842 (2008): renews the sanctions until 31 October 2009 and decides to review the sanctions in light of progress achieved in the implementation of the peace process Resolution 1893 (2009): renews the sanctions until 31 October 2010 and introduces an exemption for diamonds that will be used solely for scientific research and analysis coordinated by the Kimberley Process Resolution 1946 (2010): renews the sanctions Resolution 1980 (2011): renews the diamond sanctions and conditions the lifting of the diamond sanctions on cooperation with the Kimberley Process Resolution 2045 (2012): renews the diamond sanctions and urges the authorities to adopt an action plan for the implementation of the Kimberley Process Resolution 2101 (2013): renews the sanctions until 30 April 2014; reiterates the conditions set out in Resolution 2045; and encourages the authorities to participate in an OECD-hosted programme with regard to the implementation of the Due Diligence Guidance Resolution 2153 (2014): lifts the diamond embargo and imposes targeted sanctions on those who hamper the peace process through the illicit trafficking of diamonds and gold.
DR Congo	Resolution 1291 (2000): expresses its serious concern at reports of illegal exploitation of natural resources in the DR Congo Resolution 1355 (2001): expresses its concern over the findings of the Panel of Experts on the Illegal Exploitation of Natural Resources and Other Forms of Wealth of the Democratic Republic of the Congo Resolution 1457 (2003): strongly condemns the illegal exploitation of the natural resources of the DR Congo and

Situations	Principal resolutions and overview of relevant decisions
	demands that all States concerned take immediate steps to end these illegal activities
	Resolution 1493 (2003): installs an arms embargo and expresses its intention to consider means to end the illegal exploitation of natural resources
	Resolution 1533 (2004): establishes a Sanctions Committee and Group of Experts
	Resolution 1596 (2005): amends and expands the arms embargo; imposes targeted travel and financial measures on particular leaders of armed groups; demands neighbouring States to impede the flow of illegal natural resources through their territories
	Resolution 1698 (2006): requests the Group of Experts and the Secretary-General reports relating to the illegal exploitation of natural resources and expresses its intention to consider measures with respect to natural resources
	Resolution 1857 (2008): extends the travel ban and asset freeze to individuals providing support to armed groups through the illicit trade of natural resources
	Resolution 1896 (2009): mandates the Group of Experts to produce recommendations to the Committee for guidelines for the exercise of due diligence by the importers, processing industries and consumers of mineral products regarding the purchase, sourcing, acquisition and processing of mineral products from the DR Congo
	Resolution 1925 (2010): includes natural resources related tasks in MONUSCO's mandate
	Resolution 1952 (2010): supports taking forward the Group of Experts' recommendations on guidelines for due diligence; calls upon all States to take appropriate steps to raise awareness of the due diligence guidelines and to urge importers, processing industries and consumers of Congolese mineral products to exercise due diligence by applying the aforementioned guidelines, or equivalent guidelines; and decides that the Sanctions Committee, in determining whether to designate an individual or entity supporting the illegal armed groups in the eastern part of the DR Congo through illicit trade of natural resources, should consider, amongst other things, whether the individual or entity has exercised due diligence consistent with the steps set out in the resolution.

(*cont.*)

(*Cont.*)

Situations	Principal resolutions and overview of relevant decisions
	Resolution 1991 (2011): expresses its support of the efforts of the DR Congo and the Great Lakes Region to address the tracing and certification of minerals Resolution 2021 (2011): includes inspection of mining sites in mandate MONUSCO Resolution 2078 (2012): welcomes the measures taken by the Congolese Government to implement the due diligence guidelines on the supply chain of minerals and calls on all States to assist the DR Congo, the ICGLR and the countries in the Great Lakes Region in the implementation of the guidelines
Iraq	Resolution 661 (1990): installs a comprehensive import and export embargo and an asset freeze; introduces humanitarian exemptions Resolution 687 (1991): affirms that Iraq is liable under international law for the depletion of natural resources in Kuwait; decides to create a compensation fund to pay for the damage inflicted by Iraq; broadens the exemptions to the export embargo to cover foodstuffs notified pursuant to the 'no-objections procedure' Resolution 986 (1995): establishes the 'Oil-for-Food Programme' Resolution 1409 (2002): revises the 'Oil-for-Food Programme' through the introduction of a Goods Review List Resolution 1483 (2003): terminates the 'Oil-for-Food Programme'; notes the establishment of a Development Fund for Iraq; and underlines that the Development Fund shall be used in a transparent manner to meet the humanitarian needs of the Iraqi people, for the economic reconstruction and repair of Iraq's infrastructure, for the continued disarmament of Iraq, and for the costs of Iraqi civilian administration, and for other purposes benefiting the people of Iraq
Liberia	Resolution 788 (1992): installs an arms embargo Resolution 1343 (2001): establishes a Sanctions Committee and a Panel of Experts; renews the arms embargo and installs diamond sanctions; demands the government of Liberia to cease import of Sierra Leone rough diamonds which are not controlled through the Sierra Leonean Certificate of Origin regime; and calls upon the government to establish an

Situations	Principal resolutions and overview of relevant decisions
	effective Certificate of Origin regime for trade in rough diamonds that is transparent and internationally verifiable Resolution 1408 (2002): calls upon the government to take urgent steps to ensure that revenue from the timber industry is used for legitimate social, humanitarian and development purposes Resolution 1478 (2003): installs a timber embargo; reiterates its call upon the government to establish a Certificate of Origin regime for Liberian rough diamonds; refers to the Kimberley Process; proposes to exempt from the embargo rough diamonds controlled by a transparent and internationally verifiable Certificate of Origin regime Resolution 1521 (2003): terminates the previous sanctions regime; installs sanctions on diamonds and timber products from Liberia; encourages the government to join the Kimberley Process; encourages the government to establish oversight mechanisms for the timber industry that will promote responsible business practices, and to establish transparent accounting and auditing mechanisms Resolution 1579 (2004): encourages the government to implement the Liberia Forest Initiative and the necessary reforms in the Forest Development Authority in order to meet the conditions for the lifting of the timber sanctions Resolution 1647 (2004): encourages the Liberian government to implement the Governance and Economic Management Assistance Program as a means to expedite the lifting of the sanctions Resolution 1689 (2006): lifts the timber sanctions Resolution 1753 (2007): lifts the diamond sanctions Resolution 1854 (2008): supports the decision of Liberia to take part in EITI
Libya	Resolution 1970 (2011): installs an arms embargo, a travel ban and an asset freeze, targeting Gaddafi's family members Resolution 1973 (2011): extends the asset freeze to all entities under the control of Libyan authorities, including the Libyan National Oil Corporation Resolution 2009 (2011): terminates the asset freeze in relation to the National Oil Corporation
Sierra Leone	Resolution 1132 (1997): installs a travel ban, an arms embargo and a petroleum embargo; establishes a Sanctions Committee

(*cont.*)

(*Cont.*)

Situations	Principal resolutions and overview of relevant decisions
	Resolution 1306 (2000): installs an import ban on diamonds, exempting from the measures diamonds controlled by an effective Certificate of Origin regime; calls for an exploratory hearing to assess the role of diamonds in the Sierra Leonean conflict and the link between diamonds and the violation of the arms embargo Resolution 1385 (2001): renews the diamond embargo Resolution 1446 (2002): renews the diamond embargo
Southern Rhodesia	Resolution 217 (1965): calls upon all States to break all economic relations with Southern Rhodesia Resolution 232 (1966): installs sanctions, including an import embargo on several commodities Resolution 253 (1968): extends the sanctions to all products and commodities originating from or destined to Southern Rhodesia, exempting humanitarian goods Resolution 460 (1979): lifts the sanctions

Principal Reports by Panels of Experts

Angola

Final Report of the Monitoring Group on Angola, *UN Doc. S/2000/1225.*

Report of the Panel of Experts on Violations of Security Council Sanctions against UNITA, *UN Doc. S/2000/203*, 10 March 2000.

Interim Report of the Monitoring Mechanism, *UN Doc. S/2000/1026.*

Côte d'Ivoire

Report of the Group of Experts Submitted in Accordance with Paragraph 7 of Resolution 1584 (2005), *UN Doc. S/2005/699.*

Report of the Group of Experts Submitted in Accordance with Paragraph 9 of Resolution 1643 (2005), *UN Doc. S/2006/735.*

Midterm Report of the Group of Experts on Côte d'Ivoire Submitted in Accordance with Paragraph 11 of Security Council Resolution 1842 (2008), *UN Doc. S/2009/188.*

Final Report of the Group of Experts on Côte d'Ivoire Submitted in Accordance with Paragraph 11 of Security Council Resolution 1842 (2008) of 9 October 2009, *UN Doc. S/2009/521.*

Midterm Report of the Group of Experts on Côte d'Ivoire Pursuant to Paragraph 12 of Security Council Resolution 1893 (2009) of 18 March 2010, *UN Doc. S/2010/179.*

Final Report of the Group of Experts Submitted in Accordance with Paragraph 12 of Security Council Resolution 1893 (2009) of 27 April 2011, *UN Doc. S/2011/271.*

Final Report of the Group of Experts on Côte d'Ivoire, Prepared in Accordance with Paragraph 14 of Security Council Resolution 1980 (2011), *UN Doc. S/2012/196.*

Final Report of the Group of Experts Submitted in Accordance with Paragraph 16 of Security Council Resolution 2045 (2012), *UN Doc. S/2013/228* of 17 April 2013.

Democratic Republic of the Congo

Report of the Panel of Experts on the Illegal Exploitation of Natural Resources and Other Forms of Wealth of the Democratic Republic of the Congo, *UN Doc. S/2001/357.*

Interim Report of the Panel of Experts on the Illegal Exploitation of Natural Resources and Other Forms of Wealth of the Democratic Republic of the Congo, *UN Doc. S/2002/565.*

UN Panel of Experts on the Illegal Exploitation of Natural Resources and Other Forms of Wealth of the Democratic Republic of the Congo, Final Report of 16 October 2002, *UN Doc. S/2002/1146.*

Report of the Group of Experts Submitted Pursuant to Resolution 1654 (2006), *UN Doc. S/2006/525.*

Interim Report of the Group of Experts Submitted Pursuant to Resolution 1698 (2006), *UN Doc. S/2007/40.*

Final Report of the Group of Experts on the Democratic Republic of the Congo Prepared in Accordance with Paragraph 8 of Security Council Resolution 1857 (2008), *UN Doc. S/2009/603.*

Final Report of the Group of Experts Prepared Pursuant to Paragraph 6 of Security Council Resolution 1896 (2009), *UN Doc. S/2010/596.*

Interim Report of the Group of Experts Prepared in Pursuance of Paragraph 5 of Security Council Resolution 1952 (2010), *UN Doc. S/2011/345.*

Group of Experts on the DR Congo, Addendum to the Interim Report of the Group of Experts on the DRC Submitted in Accordance with Paragraph 4 of Security Council Resolution 2021 (2011), *UN Doc. S/2012/348/Add.1* of 27 June 2012.

Final Report of the Group of Experts on the DR Congo, Prepared in Pursuance of Paragraph 4 of Security Council Resolution 2021 (2011), *UN Doc. S/2012/843*, 15 November 2012.

Liberia

Report of the Panel of Experts Pursuant to Security Council Resolution 1343 (2001), Paragraph 19, Concerning Liberia, *UN Doc. S/2001/1015*, 26 October 2001.

Report of the Panel of Experts Appointed Pursuant to Security Council Resolution 1395 (2002), Paragraph 4, in Relation to Liberia, 11 April 2002, *UN Doc. S/2002/470.*

Report of the Panel of Experts Pursuant to Paragraph 25 of Security Council Resolution 1478 (2003) Concerning Liberia, *UN Doc. S/2003/779.*

Report of the Panel of Experts Appointed Pursuant to Paragraph 25 of Security Council Resolution 1478 (2003) Concerning Liberia, *UN Doc. S/2003/937* of 28 October 2003.

Preliminary Report of the Panel of Experts on Liberia Submitted Pursuant to Resolution 1579 (2004) (on Diamonds) of 17 March 2005, *UN Doc. S/2005/176.*

Report of the Panel of Experts on Liberia Submitted Pursuant to Resolution 1579 (2004) of 13 June 2005, *UN Doc. S/2005/360.*

Libya

Final Report of the Panel of Experts Established Pursuant to Security Council Resolution 1973 (2011) Concerning Libya, *UN Doc. S/2012/163.*

Sierra Leone

Report of the Panel of Experts Appointed Pursuant to Security Council Resolution 1306 (2000), Paragraph 19, in Relation to Sierra Leone, *UN Doc. S/2000/1195,* December 2000.

Presidential Statements

Statement Regarding Sierra Leone, 27 May 1997, *UN Doc. S/PRST/1997/29.*

Statement Regarding Sierra Leone, 11 July 1997, *UN Doc. S/PRST/1997/36.*

Statement Regarding Sierra Leone, 6 August 1997, *UN Doc. S/PRST/1997/42.*

Statement Made in Connection with the Council's Consideration of the Item Entitled Maintenance of International Peace and Security: Natural Resources and Armed Conflict, 25 June 2007, *UN Doc. S/PRST/2007/22.*

Statement on Post-conflict Peacebuilding, 22 July 2009, *UN Doc. S/PRST/2009/23.*

Statement Made in Connection with the Council's Consideration of the Item Entitled Maintenance of International Peace and Security: The Interdependence between Security and Development, 11 February 2011, *UN Doc. S/PRST/2011/4.*

Statement on Peace and Security in Africa, 15 April 2013, *UN Doc. S/PRST/2013/4.*

General Assembly Resolutions

Resolution 174 (II) of 21 November 1947: Statute of the International Law Commission (last amended by Resolution 36/39 of 18 November 1981).

UNGA Resolution 217 (III) on an International Bill of Human Rights of 10 December 1948: Universal Declaration of Human Rights.

Resolution 626 (VII) of 21 December 1952: Right to Exploit Freely Natural Wealth and Resources.

Resolution 837 (IX) of 14 December 1954: Recommendations Concerning International Respect of the Right of Peoples and Nations to Self-Determination.

Resolution 1314 (XIII) of 12 December 1958: Recommendations Concerning International Respect of the Right of Peoples and Nations to Self-Determination.

Resolution 1514 (XV) of 14 December 1960: Declaration on the Granting of Independence to Colonial Countries and Peoples.

Resolution 1541 (XV) of 15 December 1960: Principles Which Should Guide Members in Determining Whether or Not an Obligation Exists to Transmit the Information Called for under Article 73e of the Charter.

Resolution 1803 (XVII) of 14 December 1962: Declaration on Permanent Sovereignty over Natural Resources.

Resolution 2158 (XXI) of 6 December 1966: Permanent Sovereignty over Natural Resources.

Resolution 2542 (XXIV) of 11 December 1969: Declaration on Social Progress and Development.

Resolution 2625 (XXV) of 24 October 1970: Declaration on Principles of International Law Concerning Friendly Relations and Co-operation among States in Accordance with the Charter of the United Nations.

Resolution 2692 (XXV) of 11 December 1970: Permanent Sovereignty over Natural Resources of Developing Countries and Expansion of Domestic Sources of Accumulation for Economic Development.

Resolution 3129 (XXVIII) of 13 December 1973: Co-operation in the Field of the Environment Concerning Natural Resources Shared by Two or More States.

Resolution 3171 (XXVIII) of 17 December 1973: Permanent Sovereignty over Natural Resources.

Resolution 3201 (S-VI) of 1 May 1974: Declaration on the Establishment of a New International Economic Order.

Resolution 3202 (S-VI) of 1 May 1974: Programme of Action for the Establishment of a New International Economic Order.

Resolution 3281 (XXIX), 12 December 1974: Charter of Economic Rights and Duties of States.

Resolution 34/22 of 14 November 1979: The Situation in Kampuchea.

Resolution 34/186 of 18 December 1979: Cooperation in the Field of the Environment Concerning Natural Resources Shared by Two or More States.

Resolution 41/128 of 4 December 1986: Declaration on the Right to Development.

Resolution 59/41 of 2 December 2004: Report of the International Law Commission on the Work of Its Fifty-Sixth Session.

Resolution 49/75 [K] of 15 December 1994: Request for an Advisory Opinion from the International Court of Justice on the Legality of the Threat or Use of Nuclear Weapons.

Resolution 55/2 of 18 September 2000: Millennium Declaration.

Resolution 55/56 of 1 December 2000: Role of Diamonds in Fuelling Conflict.

Resolution 60/1 of 24 October 2005: World Summit Outcome.

Resolution 62/274 of 26 September 2008: Strengthening Transparency in Industries.

Resolution 61/295, 2 October 2007: United Nations Declaration on the Rights of Indigenous Peoples.

Resolution 66/99 of 9 December 2011: Effects of Armed Conflict on Treaties.

Resolution 66/225 of 29 March 2012: Permanent Sovereignty of the Palestinian People in the Occupied Palestinian Territory, Including East Jerusalem, and of the Arab Population in the Occupied Syrian Golan over Their Natural Resources.

Resolution 66/288 of 11 September 2012: Outcome Document of the 2012 United Nations Conference on Sustainable Development 'The Future We Want'.

Other UN documents and reports

United Nations Committee of Jurists, Documents of the United Nations Conference on International Organization, Sixth Meeting of Committee I, 16 May 1945.

Report of the Secretary-General on Respect for Human Rights in Armed Conflicts, *UN Doc. A/7720* of 20 November 1969.

Declaration of the United Nations Conference on the Human Environment, Stockholm, 16 June 1972, *11 I.L.M. 1416 (1972).*

UNCTAD Integrated Programme for Commodities, *UNCTAD Resolution 93(IV)* (1976).

UN Commission on Human Rights, Resolution 4 (XXX-III), *UN Doc. E/CN.4/SR.1389 (1977)* of 21 February 1977.

Draft Principles of Conduct in the Field of the Environment for the Guidance of States in the Conservation and Harmonious Utilization of Natural Resources Shared by Two or More States, *17 ILM 1097 (1978).*

Report of the Secretary-General on the International Dimensions of the Right to Development, *UN Doc. E/CN.4/1334 (1979).*

The Study of the Historical and Current Development of the Right to Self-Determination, prepared by A. Cristescu (Romania), special rapporteur of the UN Sub-commission on Prevention of Discrimination and Protection of Minorities, *UN Publication, Sales No. E.80.XIV.3 (1980).*

Report of the Secretary-General on the Regional and National Dimensions of the Right to Development, *UN Doc. E/CN.4/1421(Part I)* and *E/CN.4/1488 (PART II and III) (1981).*

Secretary-General, Report on the Implications, under International Law, of the United Nations Resolutions on Permanent Sovereignty over Natural Resources, on the Occupied Palestinian and Other Arab Territories and on the Obligations of Israel Concerning Its Conduct in These Territories, *UN Doc. A/38/265*, 21 June 1983.

Human Rights Committee, General Comment No. 12: The Right to Self-Determination of Peoples (Art. 1), adopted by the Human Rights Committee at its twenty-first session, Office of the High Commissioner for Human Rights, 13 March 1984.

Commission on Human Rights, 'The Right to Self-Determination: Implementation of United Nations Resolutions', study prepared by H. Gros Espiell (Uruguay), special rapporteur of the UN Sub-commission on Prevention of Discrimination and Protection of Minorities (1980), *UN Doc. E/CN.4/Sub.2/405/Rev.1.*

Brundtland Commission, *Our Common Future*, Report of the World Commission on Environment and Development (1987).

UNESCO, Final Report and Recommendations of the International Meeting of Experts on Further Study of the Concept of the Rights of Peoples, *Doc. SHS-89/CONF.602/7*, 22 February 1990.

Committee on Economic, Social and Cultural Rights, General Comment 3 on the Nature of States Parties Obligations (art. 2, para. 1 of the Covenant), para. 14, Report of the Fifth Session, *UN Doc. E/1991/23*, 14 December 1990.

Declaration of the United Nations Conference on Environment and Development, Rio de Janeiro, 13 June 1992, *31 I.L.M. 874 (1992).*

Special Rapporteur Mr. Gaetano Arangio-Ruiz, Fourth Report on State Responsibility, *UN Doc A/CN.4/444 and Add. 1–3*, para. 92, in Yearbook of the International Law Commission 1992, Vol. II, Part One.

Memorandum on International Law Providing Protection of the Environment in Times of Armed Conflict, annex to a letter dated 28 September 1992 from the permanent missions of the Hashemite Kingdom of Jordan and of the United States of America addressed to the Chairman of the Sixth Committee of the General Assembly, *UN Doc. A/C.6/47/3* of 28 September 1992.

Report of the Secretary-General on the Protection of the Environment in Times of Armed Conflict, *UN Doc. A/48/269* of 29 July 1993.

Vienna Declaration and Programme of Action, *UN Doc. A/CONF.157/23*, adopted on 12 July 1993.

Human Rights Committee General Comment No. 23: The Rights of Minorities (Art. 27), *UN Doc. CCPR/C/21/Rev.1/Add.5*, 8 April 1994.

International Law Commission, Draft Articles on the Law of the Non-navigational Uses of International Watercourses and Commentaries thereto, *Yearbook of the International Law Commission 1994*, Vol. II, Part Two.

Human Rights Committee, General Comment No. 24 on Issues Relating to Reservations Made Upon Ratification or Accession to the Covenant or the Optional Protocols thereto, or in Relation to Declarations under Article 41 of the Covenant, 4 November 1994, *UN Doc. CCPR/C/21/Rev.1/Add.6 (1994).*

Human Rights Committee, General Comment No. 25: The Right to Participate in Public Affairs, Voting Rights and the Right of Equal Access to Public Service (Art. 25), 12 July 1996, *UN Doc. CCPR/C/21/Rev.1/Add. 7 (1996).*

Committee on Economic, Social and Cultural Rights, General Comment 7 on the Right to Adequate Housing (art. 11.1 of the Covenant): Forced Evictions, 20 May 1997.

Committee on Economic, Social and Cultural Rights, General Comment No. 12: The Right to Adequate Food (Art. 11), *UN Doc. E/C.12/1999/5* of 12 May 1999.

Final Report to the Prosecutor by the Committee Established to Review the NATO Bombing Campaign against the Federal Republic of Yugoslavia, published on 14 June 2000, available through www.icty.org.

International Law Commission, draft articles on Prevention of Transboundary Harm from Hazardous Activities, with commentaries, *Yearbook of the International Law Commission*, vol. II, Part Two (2001).

International Law Commission, draft articles on Responsibility of States for Internationally Wrongful Acts, with commentaries, *Yearbook of the International Law Commission* 2001, Vol. II, Part Two.

Human Rights Committee, General Comment No. 29 on Art. 4 (Derogations during a State of Emergency), *UN Doc. CCPR/C/21/Rev.1/Add.11*, 31 August 2001.

Monterrey Consensus, Report of the International Conference on Financing for Development, *UN Doc. A/CONF.198/11*, adopted on 22 March 2002.

Johannesburg Declaration on Sustainable Development, Annex to the Report of the World Summit on Sustainable Development, *UN Doc. A/CONF.199/20*, 26 August–4 September 2002.

ILA New Delhi Declaration of Principles of International Law Relating to Sustainable Development, adopted on 2 April 2002, *UN Doc. A/57/329* of 31 August 2002.

Final Report of the Special Rapporteur of the Commission on Human Rights, Mrs. Erica Daes, on Indigenous Peoples' Permanent Sovereignty over Natural Resources, *UN Doc. E/CN.4/Sub.2/2004/30* of 13 July 2004 and its addendum, *UN Doc. E/CN.4/Sub.2/2004/30/Add.1* of 12 July 2004.

Report of the High-Level Panel on Threats, Challenges and Change, *A More Secure World: Our Shared Responsibility*, United Nations: New York (2004).

Secretariat, "The Effect of Armed Conflict on Treaties: An Examination of Practice and Doctrine", Memorandum by the Secretariat, prepared for the Fifty-seventh session of the International Law Commission, UN General Assembly Document *A/CN.4/550* of 1 February 2005.

International Law Commission, Conclusions of the Work of the Study Group on the Fragmentation of International Law: Difficulties Arising from the Diversification and Expansion of International Law, *Yearbook of the International Law Commission*, 2006, vol. II, Part Two.

Secretary-General, Report Pursuant to Paragraph 8 of Resolution 1698 (2006) Concerning the Democratic Republic of the Congo, *UN Doc. S/2007/68* of 8 February 2007.

Report on the "Protect, Respect and Remedy Framework for Business and Human Rights" by John Ruggie, the Special Representative of the Secretary-General on the Issue of Human Rights and Transnational Corporations and Other Business Enterprises, *UN Doc. A/HRC/8/5*, 7 April 2008.

UNEP, Protecting the Environment during Armed Conflict: An Inventory and Analysis of International Law (2009).

UNEP, From Conflict to Peacebuilding: The Role of Natural Resources and the Environment (2009).

Committee on Economic, Social and Cultural Rights, Guidelines for the Treaty-Specific Documents to be Submitted by States Parties under Articles 16 and 17 of the International Covenant on Economic, Social and Cultural Rights, *UN Doc. E/C.12/2008/2* of 24 March 2009.

Committee on Economic, Social and Cultural Rights, General Comment 20 on Non-discrimination in Economic, Social and Cultural Rights (art. 2, para. 2, of the International Covenant on Economic, Social and Cultural Rights), *UN Doc. E/C.12/GC/20* of 2 July 2009.

Office of the High Commissioner for Human Rights, Report of the Mapping Exercise Documenting the Most Serious Violations of Human Rights and International Humanitarian Law Committed within the Territory of the Democratic Republic of the Congo between March 1993 and June 2003 (2010).

UNEP, Sierra Leone: Environment, Conflict and Peacebuilding Assessment, Technical Report (2010).

Human Rights Committee, Guidelines for the Treaty-Specific Document to be Submitted by States Parties under Article 40 of the International Covenant on Civil and Political Rights, *UN Doc. CCPR/C/2009/1*, 22 November 2010.

International Law Commission, Draft Articles on the Responsibility of International Organizations, *Yearbook of the International Law Commission*, Vol. II, Part Two (2011).

International Law Commission, Draft Articles on the Effects of Armed Conflict to Treaties, *UN Doc. A/CN.4/L.777*, 11 May 2011.

Report on the Guiding Principles on Business and Human Rights: Implementing the United Nations "Protect, Respect and Remedy" Framework, *UN Doc. A/HRC/17/31*, 21 March 2011.

Committee on Economic, Social and Cultural Rights, Statement on the Importance and Relevance of the Right to Development, Adopted on the Occasion of the Twenty-Fifth Anniversary of the Declaration on the Right to Development, *UN Doc. E/C.12/2011/2*, 12 July 2011.

United Nations Office of the High Commissioner for Human Rights, *Joint Statement of Chairpersons of the UN Treaty Bodies*, 1 July 2011.

UNEP, "Greening the Blue Helmets: Environment, Natural Resources and UN Peacekeeping Operations" (2012).

Report of the Secretary-General, "Intergenerational Solidarity and the Needs of Future Generations", *UN Doc. A/68/322*, 15 August 2013.

INDEX

Books in the series

International Law and Governance of Natural Resources in Conflict and Post-Conflict Situations
Daniëlla Dam-de Jong

Proof of Causation in Tort Law
Sandy Steel

Taking Economic, Social and Cultural Rights Seriously in International Criminal Law
Evelyne Schmid

Climate Change Litigation: Regulatory Pathways to Cleaner Energy?
Jacqueline Peel and Hari Osofsky

Mestizo International Law: A Global Intellectual History 1842–1933
Arnulf Becker Lorca

Sugar and the Making of International Trade Law
Michael Fakhri

Strategically Created Treaty Conflicts and the Politics of International Law
Surabhi Ranganathan

Investment Treaty Arbitration as Public International Law: Procedural Aspects and Implications
Eric De Brabandere

The New Entrants Problem in International Fisheries Law
Andrew Serdy

Substantive Protection under Investment Treaties: A Legal and Economic Analysis
Jonathan Bonnitcha

Popular Governance of Post-Conflict Reconstruction: The Role of International Law
Matthew Saul

Evolution of International Environmental Regimes: The Case of Climate Change
Simone Schiele

Judges, Law and War: The Judicial Development of International Humanitarian Law
Shane Darcy

Religious Offence and Human Rights: The Implications of Defamation of Religions
Lorenz Langer

Forum Shopping in International Adjudication: The Role of Preliminary Objections
Luiz Eduardo Ribeiro Salles

International Law and the Arctic
Michael Byers

Cooperation in the Law of Transboundary Water Resources
Christina Leb

Underwater Cultural Heritage and International Law
Sarah Dromgoole

State Responsibility: The General Part
James Crawford

The Origins of International Investment Law
Kate Miles

The Crime of Aggression under the Rome Statute of the International Criminal Court
Carrie McDougall

Crimes against Peace and International Law
Kirsten Sellars

The Non-Legal in International Law
Fleur Johns

Armed Conflict and Displacement: The Protection of Refugees and Displaced Persons under International Humanitarian Law
Mélanie Jacques

Foreign Investment and the Environment in International Law
Jorge Viñuales

The Human Rights Treaty Obligations of Peacekeepers
Kjetil Larsen

Cyberwarfare and the Laws of War
Heather Harrison Dinniss

The Right to Reparation in International Law for Victims of Armed Conflict
Christine Evans

Global Public Interest in International Investment Law
Andreas Kulick

State Immunity in International Law
Xiaodong Yang

Reparations and Victim Support in the International Criminal Court
Conor McCarthy

Reducing Genocide to Law: Definition, Meaning, and the Ultimate Crime
Payam Akhavan

Decolonizing International Law: Development, Economic Growth and the Politics of Universality
Sundhya Pahuja

Complicity and the Law of State Responsibility
Helmut Philipp Aust

State Control over Private Military and Security Companies in Armed Conflict
Hannah Tonkin

'Fair and Equitable Treatment' in International Investment Law
Roland Kläger

The UN and Human Rights: Who Guards the Guardians?
Guglielmo Verdirame

Sovereign Defaults before International Courts and Tribunals
Michael Waibel

Making the Law of the Sea: A Study in the Development of International Law
James Harrison

Science and the Precautionary Principle in International Courts and Tribunals: Expert Evidence, Burden of Proof and Finality
Caroline E. Foster

Transition from Illegal Regimes in International Law
Yaël Ronen

Access to Asylum: International Refugee Law and the Globalisation of Migration Control
Thomas Gammeltoft-Hansen

Trading Fish, Saving Fish: The Interaction between Regimes in International Law
Margaret Young

The Individual in the International Legal System: Continuity and Change in International Law
Kate Parlett

The Participation of States in International Organisations: The Role of Human Rights and Democracy
Alison Duxbury

'Armed Attack' and Article 51 of the UN Charter: Evolutions in Customary Law and Practice
Tom Ruys

Science and Risk Regulation in International Law
Jacqueline Peel

Theatre of the Rule of Law: Transnational Legal Intervention in Theory and Practice
Stephen Humphreys

The Public International Law Theory of Hans Kelsen: Believing in Universal Law
Jochen von Bernstorff

Vicarious Liability in Tort: A Comparative Perspective
Paula Giliker

Legal Personality in International Law
Roland Portmann

Legitimacy and Legality in International Law: An Interactional Account
Jutta Brunnée and Stephen J. Toope

The Concept of Non-International Armed Conflict in International Humanitarian Law
Anthony Cullen

The Challenge of Child Labour in International Law
Franziska Humbert

Shipping Interdiction and the Law of the Sea
Douglas Guilfoyle

International Courts and Environmental Protection
Tim Stephens

Legal Principles in WTO Disputes
Andrew D. Mitchell

War Crimes in Internal Armed Conflicts
Eve La Haye

Humanitarian Occupation
Gregory H. Fox

The International Law of Environmental Impact Assessment: Process, Substance and Integration
Neil Craik

The Law and Practice of International Territorial Administration: Versailles to Iraq and Beyond
Carsten Stahn

Cultural Products and the World Trade Organization
Tania Voon

United Nations Sanctions and the Rule of Law
Jeremy Farrall

National Law in WTO Law: Effectiveness and Good Governance in the World Trading System
Sharif Bhuiyan

The Threat of Force in International Law
Nikolas Stürchler

Indigenous Rights and United Nations Standards
Alexandra Xanthaki

International Refugee Law and Socio-Economic Rights
Michelle Foster

The Protection of Cultural Property in Armed Conflict
Roger O'Keefe

Interpretation and Revision of International Boundary Decisions
Kaiyan Homi Kaikobad

Multinationals and Corporate Social Responsibility: Limitations and Opportunities in International Law
Jennifer A. Zerk

Judiciaries within Europe: A Comparative Review
John Bell

Law in Times of Crisis: Emergency Powers in Theory and Practice
Oren Gross and Fionnuala Ní Aoláin

Vessel-Source Marine Pollution: The Law and Politics of International Regulation
Alan Tan

Enforcing Obligations Erga Omnes in International Law
Christian J. Tams

Non-Governmental Organisations in International Law
Anna-Karin Lindblom

Democracy, Minorities and International Law
Steven Wheatley

Prosecuting International Crimes: Selectivity and the International Law Regime
Robert Cryer

Compensation for Personal Injury in English, German and Italian Law: A Comparative Outline
Basil Markesinis, Michael Coester, Guido Alpa and Augustus Ullstein

Dispute Settlement in the UN Convention on the Law of the Sea
Natalie Klein

The International Protection of Internally Displaced Persons
Catherine Phuong

Imperialism, Sovereignty and the Making of International Law
Antony Anghie

Necessity, Proportionality and the Use of Force by States
Judith Gardam

International Legal Argument in the Permanent Court of International Justice: The Rise of the International Judiciary
Ole Spiermann

Great Powers and Outlaw States: Unequal Sovereigns in the International Legal Order
Gerry Simpson

Local Remedies in International Law
C. F. Amerasinghe

Reading Humanitarian Intervention: Human Rights and the Use of Force in International Law
Anne Orford

Conflict of Norms in Public International Law: How WTO Law Relates to Other Rules of International Law
Joost Pauwelyn

Transboundary Damage in International Law
Hanqin Xue

European Criminal Procedures
Edited by Mireille Delmas-Marty and John Spencer

The Accountability of Armed Opposition Groups in International Law
Liesbeth Zegveld

Sharing Transboundary Resources: International Law and Optimal Resource Use
Eyal Benvenisti

International Human Rights and Humanitarian Law
René Provost

Remedies Against International Organisations
Karel Wellens

Diversity and Self-Determination in International Law
Karen Knop

The Law of Internal Armed Conflict
Lindsay Moir

International Commercial Arbitration and African States: Practice, Participation and Institutional Development
Amazu A. Asouzu

The Enforceability of Promises in European Contract Law
James Gordley

International Law in Antiquity
David J. Bederman

Money Laundering: A New International Law Enforcement Model
Guy Stessens

Good Faith in European Contract Law
Reinhard Zimmermann and Simon Whittaker

On Civil Procedure
J. A. Jolowicz

Trusts: A Comparative Study
Maurizio Lupoi

The Right to Property in Commonwealth Constitutions
Tom Allen

International Organizations Before National Courts
August Reinisch

The Changing International Law of High Seas Fisheries
Francisco Orrego Vicuña

Trade and the Environment: A Comparative Study of EC and US Law
Damien Geradin

Unjust Enrichment: A Study of Private Law and Public Values
Hanoch Dagan

Religious Liberty and International Law in Europe
Malcolm D. Evans

Ethics and Authority in International Law
Alfred P. Rubin

Sovereignty Over Natural Resources: Balancing Rights and Duties
Nico Schrijver

The Polar Regions and the Development of International Law
Donald R. Rothwell

Fragmentation and the International Relations of Micro-States: Self-determination and Statehood
Jorri Duursma

Principles of the Institutional Law of International Organizations
C. F. Amerasinghe

Lightning Source UK Ltd.
Milton Keynes UK
UKHW021226260420
362095UK00010B/331

9 781107 093836